T0189882

Lecture Notes in Computer Science 2615

Edited by G. Goos, J. Hartmanis, and J. van Leeuwen

Springer
Berlin
Heidelberg
New York
Barcelona
Hong Kong
London
Milan
Paris
Tokyo

Noëlle Carbonell
Constantine Stephanidis (Eds.)

Universal Access

Theoretical Perspectives, Practice, and Experience

7th ERCIM International Workshop on User Interfaces for All
Paris, France, October 24-25, 2002
Revised Papers

Springer

Series Editors

Gerhard Goos, Karlsruhe University, Germany
Juris Hartmanis, Cornell University, NY, USA
Jan van Leeuwen, Utrecht University, The Netherlands

Volume Editors

Noëlle Carbonell
Université Henri Poincare, Nancy 1
LORIA, UMR CNRS & INRIA
Campus Scientifique, BP 239, 54506 Vandoeuvre-les-Nancy Cedex, France
E-mail: Noelle.Carbonell@loria.fr

Constantine Stephanidis
Institute of Computer Science
Foundation for Research and Technology - Hellas
Science & Technology Park of Crete, Heraklion, Crete, 71110 Greece
E-mail: cs@ics.forth.gr

Cataloging-in-Publication Data applied for

A catalog record for this book is available from the Library of Congress.

Bibliographic information published by Die Deutsche Bibliothek
Die Deutsche Bibliothek lists this publication in the Deutsche Nationalbibliografie;
detailed bibliographic data is available in the Internet at <http://dnb.ddb.de>.

CR Subject Classification (1998): H.5.2, H.5, H.4, H.3, C.2, K.4.2, K.4, K.3

ISSN 0302-9743
ISBN 3-540-00855-1 Springer-Verlag Berlin Heidelberg New York

Springer-Verlag Berlin Heidelberg New York
a member of BertelsmannSpringer Science+Business Media GmbH

http://www.springer.de

© Springer-Verlag Berlin Heidelberg 2003
Printed in Germany

Typesetting: Camera-ready by author, data conversion by PTP-Berlin, Stefan Sossna e. K.
Printed on acid-free paper   SPIN: 10872904   06/3142   5 4 3 2 1 0

EDITORIAL

The 7th ERCIM Workshop "User Interfaces for All" took place in Paris (Chantilly), France, on 24–25 October 2002, building upon the results of the six previous workshops held in Heraklion, Crete, Greece, 30–31 October 1995; Prague, Czech Republic, 7–8 November 1996; Obernai, France, 3–4 November 1997; Stockholm, Sweden, 19–21 October 1998; Dagstuhl, Germany, 28 November–1 December 1999; and Florence, Italy, 25–26 October 2000.

The vision of User Interfaces for All advocates the proactive realization of the "design for all" principle in the field of Human-Computer Interaction (HCI), and involves the development of user interfaces to interactive applications and telematic services, which provide universal access and usability to potentially all users.

In the tradition of its predecessors, the 7th ERCIM Workshop "User Interfaces for All" aimed to consolidate recent work and to stimulate further discussion on the state of the art in User Interfaces for All and its increasing range of applications in the emerging Information Society.

The emphasis of the 2002 event was on "Universal Access." The requirement for Universal Access stems from the growing impact of the fusion of the emerging technologies and from the different dimensions of diversity that are intrinsic to the Information Society. These dimensions become evident when considering the broad range of user characteristics, the changing nature of human activities, the variety of contexts of use, the increasing availability and diversification of information, knowledge sources and services, the proliferation of technological platforms, etc.

In this context, Universal Access refers to the accessibility, usability and, ultimately, acceptability of Information Society technologies by anyone, anywhere, anytime, thus enabling equitable access and the active participation of potentially all citizens in existing and emerging computer-mediated human activities. The user population includes people with different cultural, educational, training and employment backgrounds, novice and experienced computer users, the very young and the elderly, and people with different types of disabilities in various interaction contexts and scenarios of use. As people experience technology through their contact with the user interface of interactive products, applications and services, the field of HCI has a critical and catalytic role to play towards a universally accessible, usable and acceptable Information Society.

Efforts towards universal access to Information Society technologies have met wide appreciation by an increasing proportion of the international research community, leading to various European and international research and policy initiatives, and to the establishment of forums for the diffusion and exchange of ideas and research results. These initiatives contribute to appropriating the benefits of the increasing international momentum and interest in the topics of universal design and universal access. Among them, the ERCIM working group on "User Interfaces for All" plays a catalytic role in bringing closer researchers and teams working in the different ERCIM organizations (but also organizations beyond ERCIM or the European boundaries), and sharing common interests and aspirations to contribute towards making the emerging Information Society equally accessible to all.

The 7th ERCIM Workshop "User Interfaces for All" attracted the strongest ever interest worldwide, with submissions covering a wide range of topics that include novel interaction paradigms and contexts of use, universal access to multimedia applications, software design and architecture for User Interfaces for All, design issues in User Interfaces for All, new modalities and dialogue styles, accessibility issues in novel interaction paradigms, design and usability in mobile computing, privacy issues in Universal Access and assessment and standards. The workshop featured two keynote speeches: "The Kiss of the Spiderbot" by Dr. Steven Pemberton (CWI, The Netherlands) and "Universal Access and Privacy: Making AVANTI Legal" by Prof. Alfred Kobsa (University of California, Irvine, USA).

The present volume was organized into 6 thematic parts.

The first two parts focus on research aiming at increasing the accessibility of current software applications for users with disabilities. Contributions in the first part address usability issues dealing with experimental, methodological, and application-oriented approaches. In the second part, design approaches, tools, and an assessment methodology are proposed for implementing universal access.

The third part is centered on providing easy access for the general public to major emerging computer applications in the Information Society. The application domains addressed by papers in this part are e-government, digital and interactive TV, and collaborative or sociable virtual environments. The issue of privacy, which was the topic of the invited talk by Prof. Alfred Kobsa, is also addressed in a paper in this part.

In the fourth and fifth parts, new interaction media, modalities, forms of multimodality, and dialogue styles which may contribute to increased computer accessibility are considered from the software and usability points of view. A number of papers in the fourth part focus on the design and implementation of new interaction modalities, whereas other papers address software and the usability aspects of anthropomorphic HCI, and especially issues relating to the introduction of human avatars. The first three papers in the fifth part illustrate how alternative media and modalities can be used to improve computer accessibility, whereas the last paper draws on the results of recent scientific and technical advances in this area to facilitate the interaction of ill-sighted people with the real world.

Finally, in the sixth part, research on mobile human-computer interaction, another facet of universal access, is presented. In particular, one paper in this part hints at the fruitful relationships that could be developed between research on providing computer access for all and work on enabling computer access in all contexts by illustrating how mobile computing may benefit from research on augmentative alternative communication for users suffering from amyotrophic lateral sclerosis. Other contributions address design issues, usability assessment, and standardization.

We would like to thank all the contributors and participants who made this workshop a very successful international event. In particular, we wish to thank the Scientific Programme Committee and the external reviewers for their dedicated efforts to ascertain the scientific quality of the Workshop, as well as the invited speakers Dr. Steven Pemberton and Prof. Alfred Kobsa.

December 2002   Noëlle Carbonell, Constantine Stephanidis

7th ERCIM Workshop "User Interfaces for All"

Paris (Chantilly), France, 24–25 October 2002

Special Theme: "Universal Access"

Programme Chair & Local Organizer
Noëlle Carbonell

Workshop Chair
Constantine Stephanidis

Programme Committee

- Dr. Demosthenes Akoumianakis, ICS-FORTH, Greece
- Prof. Elizabeth Andre, DFKI, Germany
- Prof. David Benyon, Napier University, UK
- Dr. Markus Bylund, SICS, Sweden
- Prof. Noelle Carbonell, LORIA, France
- Dr. Pier Luigi Emiliani, CNR-IROE, Italy
- Dr. Giorgio Faconti, CNR-CNUCE, Italy
- Prof. Michael Fairhurst, University of Kent, UK
- Mr. Seppo Haataja, NOKIA Mobile Phones, Finland
- Dr. Ilias Iakovidis, European Commission, Belgium
- Prof. Julie Jacko, Georgia Institute of Technology, USA
- Dr. Eija Kaasinen, VTT, Finland
- Dr. Sri H. Kurniawan, UMIST, UK
- Prof. Mark Maybury, The MITRE Corporation, USA
- Dr. Michael Pieper, FhG-FIT, Germany
- Dr. Anthony Savidis, ICS-FORTH, Greece
- Prof. Andrew Sears, UMBC, USA
- Dr. Dominique Scapin, INRIA, France
- Prof. Cristian Stary, University of Linz, Austria
- Prof. Constantine Stephanidis, ICS-FORTH, Greece
- Prof. Jean Vanderdonckt, Université Catholique de Louvain, Belgium
- Prof. Michael Wilson, RAL, UK
- Dr. Juergen Ziegler, FhG-IAO, Germany

External Reviewers

- Prof. Julio Abascal, Euskal Herriko University, Spain
- Dr. Gérôme Canals, LORIA, France
- Dr. Simeon Keates, University of Cambridge, UK
- Dr. Pat Langdon, University of Cambridge, UK
- Dr. Fabio Paterno, CNR-CNUCE, Italy
- Dr. Yannick Toussaint, LORIA, France
- Prof. Gerhard Weber, Kiel University, Germany
- Dr. Harald Weber, ITA, Kaiserslautern, Germany

Sponsors

- European Research Consortium for Informatics and Mathematics
  (ERCIM - http://www.ercim.org/)
- Institute of Computer Science, Foundation for Research and Technology -
  Hellas
  (ICS-FORTH - http://www.ics.forth.gr/)
- Institut National de Recherche en Informatique et en Automatique
  (INRIA - http://www.inria.fr/)
- Laboratoire Lorrain de Recherché en Informatique et Ses Applications
  (LORIA - http://www.loria.fr/)
- Réseau Grand-Est (ACI 'Cognitique,' MENRT)

Table of Contents

Part V: Novel Interaction Paradigms – Accessibility Issues

Part I: User Interfaces for All -
Accessibility Issues

Effects of Multimodal Feedback on the Performance of Older Adults with Normal and Impaired Vision

Julie A. Jacko[1], Ingrid U. Scott[2], François Sainfort[1], Kevin P. Moloney[1],
Thitima Kongnakorn[1], Brynley S. Zorich[1], and V. Kathlene Emery[1]

[1] School of Industrial and Systems Engineering, Georgia Institute of Technology,
765 Ferst Drive,
Atlanta, GA 30332-0205, USA
{jacko,sainfort,kmoloney,kongnako,bzorich,
vkemery}@isye.gatech.edu
[2] Bascom Palmer Eye Institute; Department of Ophthalmology; University of Miami School
of Medicine, 900 NW 17th Street, Miami, FL 33136, USA
iscott@bpei.med.miami.edu

Abstract. The augmentation of computer technologies with multimodal interfaces has great potential for improving interaction with these technologies via the use of different sensory feedback. This may be of particular importance for individuals from divergent user populations, who have varying interaction needs and abilities. This study examines the effects of a multimodal interface, utilizing auditory, haptic, and visual feedback, on the performance of elderly users with varying levels of visual abilities. Older adults who possess normal vision (n=29) and those who have been diagnosed with age-related macular degeneration (AMD) (n=30), with different levels of visual acuity, were involved in the study. Participants were asked to complete a series of 'drag-and-drop' tasks under varying forms of feedback. User performance was assessed with the measure of final target highlight time. The findings suggest that the addition of other feedback modalities, to the traditionally used visual feedback form, can enhance the performance of users, particularly those with visual impairments.

1 Introduction

The development and application of multimodal interfaces provide a means to facilitate the interaction between human users and the technologies that they use. These interfaces, which augment users' perceptual processes through the use of different sensory information, show potential to enhance a user's interaction with information technologies [1, 2, 3]. Research has been conducted on both the use of multimodal feedback [4, 5] and the use of multimodal input [6, 7, 8]. However, a distinction needs to be made between the natures of these applications of multimodality. The former focuses on augmenting the output of the system (often referred to as feedback) with a minimal need for specialized devices and large alterations, which is consistent with the goals of universal design, while the latter often requires the use of specialized hardware and software to enhance interaction.

N. Carbonell, C. Stephanidis (Eds.): User Interfaces for All, LNCS 2615, pp. 3–22, 2003.

Despite the research conducted on both the use of multimodal feedback and the interaction of users from divergent populations, there have been few studies that investigate the union of these efforts. Consequently, this study seeks to examine how multimodal feedback, which has been shown to have positive effects on performance in various computer tasks, affects the performance of visually impaired users. More specifically, this study investigates how multimodal feedback affects the performance of older adults with normal vision, and older adults with visual impairment resulting from AMD. Those participants with AMD possessed varying levels of visual acuity, from nearly normal vision to near blindness. Users with AMD are of particular interest because this condition is one of the leading causes of visual impairment and blindness in the aging population.

A multimodal interface, which utilized auditory, haptic, and visual feedback, was used to examine the performance of participants on a series of 'drag-and-drop' tasks. This task was selected on the basis that it is highly representative of direct manipulation operations required in the use of graphical user interfaces. This study aimed to examine the effects of multimodal feedback on the task performance and interaction of older users, who have been diagnosed with AMD, and possess different levels of visual acuity.

2 Background

2.1 Addressing the Needs of Universal Access

Interest in Universal Access stems from a desire to meet the interaction needs of divergent user populations in the Information Society. Universal Access has been characterized as the ability or right of all individuals, possessing varying levels of abilities, skills, preferences, and needs, to obtain equitable access and have effective interaction with information technologies [9, 10, 11]. In other words, it involves designing standard environments and products that are usable by people with as wide a range of abilities (or constraints) as is possible [12].

A critical component of achieving this goal rests with the use of empirical research and field-testing, which integrates actual, representative users from these diverse user groups. User profiling, or understanding the specific characteristics and interaction needs of a particular user or group of users with unique needs and abilities, is necessary to truly understand the different interaction requirements of disparate user populations. This understanding of diverse users' needs will help to increase the quality of the interaction with, and the accessibility to, information technologies, while preventing a group's alienation from the information society [13].

It is important to note that the desired end-result of research in Universal Access is the ability to apply the principles and knowledge gained from diverse user populations to drive actual design of information technologies. The principle of universal access and design is to design products for the broadest possible user group, while not incorporating the need for adaptation by the user or specialized designs [10, 14]. This means that technologies designed to adhere to the principles of universal access should be accessible through easily imposed modifications, 'right out of the box' [15]. This said, universal access can be better achieved through a more direct, fundamental understanding of the variance of diverse users' needs that can be applied, resulting in flexible, manageable technologies rather than specifically designed, manufactured solutions that only meet the specific needs of a limited slice of the user population.

2.2 Individuals with Visual Impairments

The American Foundation for the Blind estimates that 10 million people in the United States are blind or visually impaired. Of the 1.3 million Americans that reported legal blindness, 80% of this legally blind population retains some residual vision [16]. Individuals in the United States over age 65, who experience visual impairments or blindness, number approximately 5.5 million. The 1999 Census Bureau's Survey of Income and Program Participation offers some insight into the rate of computer usage in the low vision population. As cited by Gerber [17], 53% of individuals with just general acuity loss report having access to the Internet, compared to access of only 28% of individuals with visual impairment extending beyond just general acuity loss.

While much research has been performed that investigates the human-computer interaction needs of completely blind users, focusing on the development of tools and devices to aid interaction, much less research has been done to investigate users with less severe visual impairments [18, 19, 20]. It is estimated that there are almost three times as many individuals with low vision than completely blind individuals [21]. Thus, given the shear number of individuals with low vision, there is a clear need to investigate the nature of their interaction with information technologies.

Individuals that retain residual vision, especially the aging population, are typically not willing to fully yield to these impairments, and would rather use visual capabilities they retain to the best of their ability [22, 23, 24]. This further suggests that a need exists to design and develop technologies that incorporate accessibility and usability features for low vision users, rather than simply relying on screen magnifiers and other additional assistive devices [13]. However, the level of visual impairment for this broad group of visually impaired individuals, and the relative effects that this impairment has on an individual's interaction with technologies, is quite diverse.

Comparisons of clinical diagnoses, severity of visual impairment, and the presence of other non-visual impairments, may all play a key role in understanding the nature of interaction with information technology for these individuals [25, 26, 27]. These studies have shown the utility of further investigating the nature of the interaction needs and requirements of low vision users compared with normally sighted users, as well as investigating the differences in abilities and interaction needs of users with varying levels of visual impairments.

2.3 Age-Related Macular Degeneration (AMD)

AMD is a medical condition that leads to severe visual impairment in the aging population [28, 29]. AMD is one of the leading causes of severe visual impairment for individuals 65 years and older, affecting nearly two million Americans [26, 28, 30].

As the name suggests, AMD is a progressive disease, in which the macula, or central portion of the retina, degenerates over time. While AMD progressively destroys general visual acuity, it does not always result in total loss of sight. AMD primarily affects the foveal area of the retina, which strongly affects central vision while often leaving peripheral vision intact [26, 30]. This results in a wide range of residual visual capabilities within those individuals who have AMD.

Despite this loss of visual acuity, individuals with AMD tend to rely on their residual vision to function within their environment [24]. A loss of central vision, which strongly affects high-resolution vision, has a very strong impact on an individual's ability to do focus-intensive activities, such as reading, driving, or using a computer.

As people with low vision, including those individuals with AMD, will remain an active part of society, they will need to have access to and be able to interact with information technologies [26, 31]. Moreover, given the ever-increasing size of the AMD population, it is necessary to understand how this clinical pathology affects the nature of the interaction that these users experience when using information technologies. Given the shear numbers of the rapidly growing AMD and low vision populations, it is critical to understand how information technologies, including GUIs and input/output modalities, should be altered and adapted to provide enhanced accessibility and usability for these users.

2.4   The Graphical User Interface (GUI) Environment

Today's computers take advantage of the huge advances made in the development of technology and computational power. Most computers used by the majority of general consumers will utilize a graphical user interface (GUI), which relies heavily on the use of graphical symbols and icons as visual elements of the screen. These screen elements serve as the representation of low-level computer functionality that users can manipulate through higher-level actions without having to use a complex syntax or direct programming language [32]. It is through the GUI that users can control complex computing functionality through the common actions of touching screens, typing buttons, manipulating icons and objects, and moving the mouse cursor [26, 27].

This translation of the complex functionality of the computing system into the relatively simple control 'language' of the users is often referred to as direct manipulation (DM). Eason, Johnson, and Fairclough [33] define direct manipulation as a "visual interface, which emphasizes eye-hand coordination skills as a prime requisite for successful and efficient interaction" (p. 116). As discussed, the typical GUI relies heavily on visual feedback to the user, which clearly places a user with visual impairments at a disadvantage [26]. Some initial research has been done to investigate the interaction needs of low vision users and how GUIs can be changed to make the visual aspect of this interaction more accommodating for these users [27, 34].

In addition, the direct manipulation paradigm employed in these GUIs also requires the use of a pointing device, such as a mouse [35]. There are two critical components of the interaction when using a pointing device, such as a mouse, to manipulate icons and other visual screen elements: selection and position [36]. That is to say, selection requires users to select an item from a set and positioning requires users to specify a point in one-, two-, or three-dimensional space. The aptly named 'drag-and-drop' task is a common representation of these components of interaction, which requires users to both select and position visual screen elements. The 'drag-and-drop' task has become one of the most commonplace user actions when interacting with information technologies today. The 'drag-and-drop' task is commonly characterized by the selection of an object (commonly an icon, such as a 'file') and positioning it (the 'drag') on top of another object (another icon, such as a 'folder') so as to insert this object into or on top of the second object (the 'drop').

These tasks require the successful integration of visual and motor functioning by the user. It is clear that users with AMD are often at a distinct disadvantage when forced to interact with these design paradigms [37]. Users with AMD are not able to properly capitalize on the visual nature of the GUIs, as their central vision has often deteriorated with the onset of the disease. It should also be noted that AMD is an age-related disease that can develop in individuals as early as age 45, and is most prevalent in those 65 years and older [28, 31, 38]. It is important to note that the increasing age of these individuals also corresponds to deterioration in manual dexterity [39, 40]. It is well documented that increasing age results in the deterioration of motor control and coordination (e.g., [41, 42, 43]), which means that many of the individuals diagnosed with AMD will also suffer from decreased motor control. This poses an even greater challenge for people with AMD in the use of computing technologies, as their abilities to use peripheral devices for selection and positioning tasks, like those required in a GUI environment, are greatly hindered.

2.5 The Use of Multimodality

Some research concerning technologies that utilize multimodal input has been conducted, mostly focusing on the use of assistive devices that utilize voice and gesture inputs [6, 7, 8, 44]. The use of multimodality with respect to input devices should be distinguished from the implementation of multimodal output, or as we refer to it in this paper, multimodal feedback. There has been limited research concerning the use of multimodal feedback, when investigating human-computer interaction. Much of the research on the use of different feedback modalities has focused on the use of auditory [1, 2, 4] and haptic [5, 45, 46] feedback in unimodal and bimodal conditions.

The focus of this study is to examine the effects of multimodal feedback on user performance. Traditionally, auditory, haptic, and visual feedback forms have been used extensively in HCI research, due to their relevance and applicability of use in current GUIs. Given the visual nature of the GUI, visual feedback is most often provided to users by their systems. The most common forms of auditory feedback used in multimodal research include the auditory icon and earcon [47, 48, 49, 50]. Much of the haptic feedback explored includes the use of kinesthetic feedback, or mouse vibration and movement, to provide users with tactile information [51, 52, 53].

For the purposes of this study, much of the relevant literature is comprised of studies that have examined the effectiveness of supplementing visual feedback with other forms. Brewster [2] found that sonically enhanced feedback on drag-and-drop tasks produced better user task performance compared with the basic visually enhanced version of the task. Brewster and Crease [50] investigated the use of auditory feedback in combating menu usability problems. Belz and Robinson [47] found that the addition of auditory icons to visual displays improved the collision avoidance of commercial motor vehicle operators. Researchers have also investigated the performance value of supplementing visual feedback with haptic feedback for several tasks, including selecting menu items using scroll bars [45, 46].

A review of the multimodal literature is provided by Vitense, Jacko, and Emery [3], and illustrates that additional research is needed that specifically examines multimodal (uni-, bi-, and trimodal) feedback, especially involving persons who are older adults and possess either normal or impaired vision. Furthermore, in their study [3] thirty-two young (ages ranged from 21-36 years) participants with normal vision were asked to complete a task consisting of a series of 'drag-and-drops' while the type of feedback was manipulated. Each participant was exposed to three unimodal feedback conditions, three bimodal feedback conditions, and one trimodal feedback condition that utilized auditory, visual, and haptic feedback alone, and in combination. The results showed that haptic and visual feedback were more beneficial, when used alone as well as in combination with each other, as compared to other unimodal, bimodal, and trimodal conditions. In addition, it was shown that the temporal nature of auditory feedback, alone and in combination, hindered performance.

As previously mentioned, multimodal feedback, as opposed to most multimodal input, provides researcher and developers with an approach consistent with the tenets of universal design. Multimodal feedback has been shown to provide performance enhancement in some tasks, when used to supplement visual feedback. This study will further investigate the effects of multimodal feedback in a common direct manipulation task, involving people who are older adults and possess either normal or impaired vision.

2.6 Current Study Objectives

The research presented in this paper represents selected components of a large empirical study, investigating the effects of multimodal feedback on the performance of people who are older adults and whose vision is impaired due to AMD (n=30), and older adults who possess normal visual capabilities (n=29), while performing 'drag-and-drop' tasks, representative of those performed in the use of graphical user interfaces. The direct manipulation task reported in this paper is the dragging and dropping of a file icon to a target folder icon. The sample of participants with AMD is further stratified into groups based on visual acuity, as measured with ETDRS visual acuity assessment. Auditory, haptic, and visual feedback forms, presented in unimodal, bimodal, and trimodal conditions, were used to investigate the relative effects of feedback on user task performance, as measured by final target highlight time (FTHT).

3   Methodology

3.1   Participants

Fifty-nine volunteers participated in this study. Participants ranged in age from 54 to 91 years (M = 76.0 years), including 36 females and 23 males. As compensation for participation in this study, participants were provided with comprehensive visual examinations free-of-charge and were paid $50. Licensed technicians and ophthalmologists of the Bascom Palmer Eye Institute performed visual examinations. All participants were identified and recruited with assistance from the Bascom Palmer Eye Institute. Participants were selected on the basis of general inclusion criteria including: 1) presence or absence of AMD, 2) visual acuity, 3) right-handedness, and 4) age.

In addition to the ocular diagnosis, information was also gathered from the participants concerning medical comorbidities, general mental and physical health (SF-12™ Health Survey), visual functioning (NEI VFQ-25), computer experience, and personal perceptions of the utility of their current eyesight. In order to assess the level of right-handed manual dexterity, participants were also asked to perform the Purdue Pegboard test of manual dexterity [54].

Prior to the computer task, participants completed the SF-12™ Health Survey, which yields general physical and mental health composite scores [55]. Overall, participants reported an average physical health composite score of 50.4 and an average mental health composite score of 55.0. The values for both scores are slightly better than the average scores for the general U.S. population age 55+, which range from 38.7 to 46.6 for the physical health composite score and from 50.1 to 52.1 for the mental health composite score [56].

Previous computer experience was also assessed via a background questionnaire, prior to the computer task. Thirty-three of the fifty-nine participants had used a computer within the last year prior to the present study. Of these individuals, an average comfort score of 3.6 was reported (on a 1 to 5 scale, with 4 representing 'comfortable' and 3 representing 'neither comfortable nor uncomfortable'), which indicated that these individuals were somewhat comfortable using computers. Twenty-nine of the participants were familiar with computer use, as indicated by varying frequency of use within the month previous to this study (m = 16.8 times). Twenty-five participants indicated that they had not previously used a computer, or had not used a computer within the last year. Of these individuals, eight reported that they had not used a computer within the last year (or not at all) due to their current eye condition.

Participants also completed the Purdue Pegboard test of manual dexterity prior to the computer task. Overall, participants produced an average score of 10.6 pins, using their right hands. This level of right hand dexterity score corresponds to the 40th-50th percentiles of performance based on the norms of men and women with low vision, developed by Tobin and Greenhalgh [57]. This corresponds to below the 5th percentile of performance for male and female industrial job applicants reported by Tiffin and Asher [54]. The samples from the Tobin and Greenhalgh study [57] and the Tiffin and Asher study reported a mean age less than the sample used in this study. As such, the scores reported in this study illustrate the decline in manual dexterity experienced by the participants in this study, due to age and visual impairment.

Refer to Table 1 for a summary of the demographic information and characteristics, as discussed above, of the overall participant sample.

As previously mentioned, participants were provided with a complete visual examination as part of their compensation for their participation in this study. This examination included tests of: 1) Visual acuity – the individual's ability to resolve fine detail [58]; 2) Contrast Sensitivity – the individual's ability to detect pattern stimuli at low to moderate contrast levels [27]; and 3) Color Perception – the individual's ability to discern and identify color. Visual acuity was assessed by using the ETDRS exam (normal acuity is reported as 20/20). A Pelli-Robson chart was used to assess contrast sensitivity, where a normal score is 48 and is based on the total number of characters correctly identified at a range of contrast levels [58]. The Farnsworth Dichotomous Test for Color Blindness was employed in this study [59, 60] to evaluate color perception. These particular ocular assessments were made in order to obtain a comprehensive profile of the participants' vision. Participants performed the computer task under conditions of best-corrected vision, employing the use of corrective frames when necessary (as determined by the clinical ocular examination).

Table 1. Summary of Overall Sample Demographics and Characteristics. Age represents the average number of years for the overall sample. Gender represents the frequency counts of males and females. Handedness denotes the dominant hand of participants. SF-12™ refers to the overall mean composite scores, with the physical health component score (PCS) and the mental health component score (MCS). Computer experience includes both comfort, referring the the mean reported comfort level of participants (with 3 is neither comfortable, nor uncomfortable and 4 is comfortable), and use, referring to the mean number of times participants used a computer, within the previous month. Manual dexterity refers to the overall mean number of pins placed in the board during the Purdue Pegabord trials.

N	Age	Gender		Handedness	SF-12		Computer Experience		Manual
		Male	Female		PCS	MCS	Comfort	Use	Dexterity
59	76.0	23	36	Right	50.4	55.0	3.6	16.8	10.6

Based on personal medical history and the eye examination, patients were initially stratified based on the presence or absence of age-related macular degeneration (AMD). Participants diagnosed with AMD were then further stratified based on best-corrected visual acuity. Refer to Table 2 for a summary of the participant visual characteristics, based on the groupings. It should be noted that participants in the control group were diagnosed as having no ocular disease.

Table 2. Summary of Group Profiles. Age represents the mean number of years for each participant group. Gender represents the frequency counts of males (M) and females (F) within each group. Visual acuity represents the range of Snellen scores (normal acuity = 20/20) for participants of each group. AMD refers to the absence or presence of this condition in individuals within each group. Contrast sensitivity represents the average Pelli-Robson scores (normal score is 48) for the right and left eyes. Color perception, as judged by the Farnworth D-15 color test, is depicted with the number of test failures within each group and color problems referring to the nature of each failure, with 1 = protan (red deficiency), 2 = deutan (green deficiency, 3 = tritan (blue deficiency), and 4 = general color confusion. Frequency of each color problem type in brackets (#).

Group	n	Age	Gender	Visual Acuity	AMD	Contrast Sensitivity		Color Perception	
						Right	Left	Failures	Problems
Control	29	73.83	M = 11, F = 18	20/20 – 20/40	Absent	34.1	35.0	0	N/A
Group 1	12	76.83	M = 4, F = 8	20/20 – 20/50	Present	28.8	31.2	1	3 (1)
Group 2	8	81.63	M = 5, F = 3	20/60 – 20/100	Present	25.3	25.9	4	1 (1), 3 (2), 4 (1)
Group 3	10	78.70	M = 3, F = 7	≥ 20/100	Present	19.5	25.0	8	2 (2), 3 (5), 4 (1)

3.2 Apparatus and Experimental Task Environment

The computer system used in this study was an IBM®-compatible computer with a Pentium III processor and 384 MB of SDRAM. Participants were seated approximately 24 inches from a 20-inch viewable Trinitron flat screen display. Screen resolution was set at 1152 X 864 pixels, with a 32-bit color setting. Keyboard use was not required of the participants to complete the task. To perform the drag-and-drop task, participants used a Logitech WingMan® Force Feedback Mouse. This input device provides feedback in the form of a mechanical vibration of the mouse unit, which is sensed by the individual's kinesthetic system (also known as haptic feedback).

The Multimodal AHV 2.0 software, developed using the Visual Basic programming language, was a custom product developed for this project. This software facilitated the task environment in which participants performed the 'drag-and-drop' tasks. This program consisted of a drag-and-drop task, in which users selected a file icon and dragged it into a folder target. For this study, familiar Microsoft® Word icon bitmaps were used for the mouse cursor, file icon, and target folder screen elements. Figure 1 represents an example screen shot from this program, illustrating the interface that users interacted with when performing the task. The file icon and target folder size was 36.8 mm (diagonal distance), based on findings from Jacko et al. [27, 61].

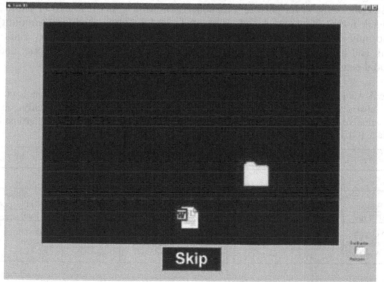

Fig. 1. Sample Screenshot. This picture represents a typical screen shot of the task. Each feedback condition contained 15 replications, in which the location of the target folder was randomly dispersed across the screen. Participants were asked to selection the file icon (position the cursor and click and hold the mouse button), drag it over to the target folder (reposition the cursor and file icon by moving the mouse while continuing to depress the button), and finally drop (release the mouse button) the file icon into the target folder. The 'skip' button was present to allow the participant to skip the trial if the target folder was not visible in their visual field or if they had positioned the file icon outside of the visible area or behind the target folder, or any instance in which the file icon was no longer accessible.

Three types of signals were provided to participants as forms of feedback, signaling the correct placement of the file icon in the folder target. An auditory icon that imitated the sound of something being pulled/sucked into something was used as the auditory feedback in the task. The volume level was adjusted for each participant to a level that was easily detectable. The visual feedback employed was a purple coloration that highlighted the file icon when the file icon was placed directly over the target folder. The haptic feedback used was a mechanical vibration in the Logitech WingMan® mouse. Haptic feedback was generated upon correct alignment of the file icon with the target folder.

The experimental task used in this study was a simplified version of the 'drag-and-drop' task employed in previous studies [2, 3]. A Microsoft Word® file icon was located in the bottom center of the task space, while a Microsoft® Windows target folder icon was randomly located in one of 15 discrete locations (A – O) in the task space. The order of the presentation of these 15 locations of the target folder icon was randomized across conditions and participants. The order of presentation of the feedback conditions was also randomized across participants.

Participants were instructed to select and retrieve the file icon with their cursor by moving it over the file icon and depressing the left mouse button. Once the file icon was 'grabbed', participants had to 'drag' it over to position it on top the target folder and, upon receiving the feedback, 'drop' this file icon into the target folder by releasing the mouse button. Participants were asked to complete 15 repetitions of the task in each of the seven different feedback conditions. As illustrated in Table 3, these feedback forms were combined as seven feedback forms, including: auditory only, haptic only, and visual only unimodal conditions; auditory and haptic, auditory and visual, and haptic and visual bimodal conditions; and an auditory, haptic, and visual trimodal condition.

Table 3. Auditory, Haptic, and Visual Feedback Conditions. The auditory absent, haptic absent, visual absent feedback condition was not employed, as the visual feedback only condition is representative of the minimum feedback commonly employed in today's graphical user interface (GUI) environments.

Auditory							
Present				Absent			
Haptic				Haptic			
Present		Absent		Present		Absent	
Visual		Visual		Visual		Visual	
Present	Absent	Present	Absent	Present	Absent	Present	Absent
AHV (tri)	AH (bi)	AV (bi)	A (uni)	HV (bi)	H (uni)	V (uni)	N/A
15 discrete locations (A – O)	15 discrete locations (A – O)	15 discrete locations (A – O)	15 discrete locations (A – O)	15 discrete locations (A – O)	15 discrete locations (A – O)	15 discrete locations (A – O)	N/A

3.3 Procedure

Participants were given an explanation of the procedure of the research study, their role in the study, and were asked to sign a consent form. Participants were then provided with the clinical eye exam. This was done to ensure that the experimenters had knowledge of the participant's visual status during the time of their actual participation. Corrective eyewear, to ensure best-corrected vision, was employed during the computer task when necessary.

Following completion of the questionnaires, which were all interviewer-administered, each participant performed the Purdue Pegboard test of manual dexterity. This employed the use of the Purdue Pegboard with the standard protocol developed by Tiffin and Asher in 1948 [54], which has been used extensively with this apparatus [62, 63]. The standard right-hand dexterity was performed three times by each participant, resulting in an average right-hand score of the three trials, each lasting 30 seconds.

Following this test, the participants were briefed on all of the equipment and the software used in the study and were then given training on how to use the equipment to perform the task. During this training period, participants were trained on how to perform the task and given practice. The meaning and nature of the feedback forms were also explained at this time. Explanations and practice with the computer hardware (e.g. the use of the mouse) varied with each participant's previous computer experience. Participants were trained until they indicated comfort and knowledge with the use of the input device. Finally, participants performed the series of 'drag-and-drop' tasks.

Following the computer-based task, participants were asked to complete an exit survey, also interviewer-administered, that was specific to their feelings and perceptions about their experiences with the program and the study. Participants then received a final eye examination, including examination of the retina, and were provided with the monetary compensation. New eyewear prescriptions were also given when appropriate.

3.4 Experimental Design

This study employed a 7 x 4 x 15 factorial design, with seven feedback modality conditions (as seen in Table 3), four groups of participants, stratified by visual acuity, and 15 locations of the target folder on the screen. The order of feedback conditions assigned to participants was randomized with a 7 x 7 counter-balanced latin square design. Each participant was randomly assigned a feedback condition order. Each feedback modality had 15 repetitions within the condition, in which the location of the target folder was evenly distributed across the screen. All participants received the same 15 target folder locations. However, the order of the presentation of these locations was randomized with a 15 x 15 counterbalanced latin square design and randomly assigned to the feedback conditions.

In this paper, the dependent variable used to assess participant task performance was final target highlight time (FTHT). FTHT represents the length of time, measured in milliseconds, that the participants received feedback information from the computer during the final attempt that the participant successfully placed the file icon into the target folder. This performance measure was similar to the time measure 'target highlight time' used in the studies by Brewster [2] and Vitense, Jacko, and Emery [3]. Target highlight time is believed to be a more specific measure of task performance for 'drag-and-drop' tasks involving multimodal feedback, because it focuses on the portion of the task that is most influenced by the user's response to encountering the feedback [2, 46]. FTHT was calculated for each of the 15 repetitions within each of the seven feedback conditions for each participant.

4 Results

Analyses of variance (ANOVA) were used to examine the presence of significant differences in task performance, as measured by FTHT. If significant differences were revealed by the ANOVA, then post hoc tests (Tukey's honestly significant difference (HSD) test) were also performed to further illuminate any differences. The following analyses were executed: 1) tests for significant differences in performance between visual acuity groups for each feedback condition; and 2) tests for significant differences in performance within each visual acuity group between feedback conditions.

The results of the tests together with summary statistics for FTHT in each feedback condition in each visual acuity group are summarized in Tables 4 and 5. The data shown in Tables 4 and 5 are also represented in Figures 2 and 3. Figure 2 illustrates FTHT for each feedback condition, by participant group. Figure 3 shows FTHT for each participant group, by feedback condition.

Table 4. Tests for significant difference in performance between visual acuity groups for each feedback condition. Each row that is associated with a significant result is colored gray.

Group Feedback Condition	Control Mean (S.D.)	Group 1 Mean (S.D.)	Group 2 Mean (S.D.)	Group 3 Mean (S.D.)	Tests of Sig. Diff. Between Groups	Post-Hoc Tests
A	659.01 (331.06)	959.06 (558.27)	1285.38 (730.83)	601.43 (332.50)	F = 5.161 p = 0.003	2 > Control (p = 0.005) 2 > 3 (p = 0.012)
H	808.65 (464.67)	993.86 (548.62)	1285.03 (725.22)	880.48 (460.15)	F = 1.570 p = 0.207	
V	923.72 (533.21)	1109.98 (356.14)	1452.27 (891.24)	1560.37 (561.67)	F = 3.803 p = 0.015	3 > Control (p = 0.023)
AH	585.24 (297.39)	859.62 (524.20)	908.71 (676.91)	729.63 (361.89)	F = 1.882 p = 0.114	
AV	678.02 (409.68)	990.87 (739.66)	774.19 (398.99)	656.38 (406.63)	F = 1.283 p = 0.289	
HV	705.31 (379.23)	1171.61 (749.31)	1556.94 (842.24)	842.96 (394.48)	F = 5.665 p = 0.002	2 > Control (p = 0.003) 2 > 3 (p = 0.047)
AHV	629.77 (293.10)	886.72 (590.90)	1044.47 (628.65)	469.08 (211.05)	F = 3.967 p = 0.012	2 > 3 (p = 0.025)

The results from Table 4 and Figure 2 show that visual acuity group had a significant effect on FTHT for the following feedback conditions:

- Auditory (F = 5.161; p = 0.003)
- Visual (F = 3.803; p = 0.015)
- Haptic and Visual (F = 5.665; p = 0.002)
- Auditory, Haptic & Visual (F = 3.967; p = 0.012)

Auditory. In the unimodal auditory condition, Group 3 demonstrated the shortest FTHT, followed by the Control Group. Group 2 had the slowest FTHT. The post hoc tests revealed that Group 2 performance was significantly different from both Group 3 and the Control group (p = 0.012 and p = 0.005, respectively).

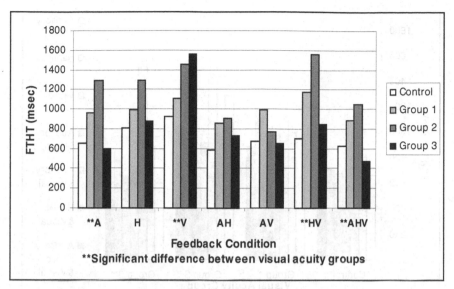

Fig. 2. FTHT for each feedback condition, arranged by normal visual acuity group (Control) to worst visual acuity group (Group 3). Order of groups is the same for each feedback condition: Control, shown in white; Group 1, shown in light gray; Group 2, shown in dark gray; and Group 3, shown in black.

Visual. In the unimodal visual condition, FTHT was slowest for those with the most impaired vision (Group 3), and was fastest for those with normal vision (control group). The relationship between performance and visual acuity appeared to be a step-wise function, with declining visual acuity associated with slower FTHTs. Group 3 demonstrated significantly slower FTHT compared with the Control group ($p = 0.023$).

Haptic and Visual. In the bimodal haptic and visual condition, the Control group exhibited the shortest FTHT followed by Group 3. Group 2 had the longest FTHT. The post hoc tests revealed that Group 2 produced significantly slower FTHT than both Group 3 and the Control group ($p = 0.047$ and $p = 0.003$, respectively).

Auditory, Haptic, and Visual. In the trimodal auditory, haptic, and visual condition, Group 3 demonstrated the fastest FTHT, followed by control group. Test of significant difference revealed that Group 3 produced a significantly shorter FTHT than Group 2 ($p = 0.025$).

Table 5. Tests for significant differences in performance within each visual acuity group between feedback conditions. Each column associated with a significant result is colored gray.

Group	Control	Group 1	Group 2	Group 3
Tests of Sig. Diff. Between Feedback Conditions	F = 2.441 p = 0.027	F = 0.429 p = 0.858	F = 1.169 p = 0.340	F = 7.339 p < 0.001
Post-Hoc Tests	V > AH (p = 0.026)			V > A (p < 0.0001) V > H (p = 0.008) V > AH (p = 0.001) V > AV (p < 0.0001) V > HV (p = 0.004) V > AHV (p < 0.0001)

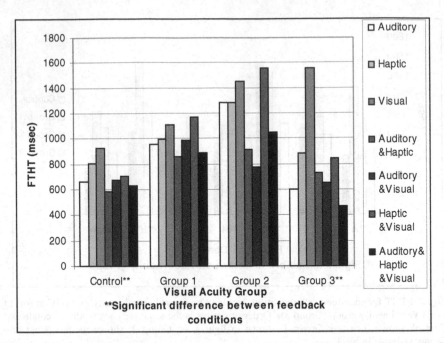

Fig. 3. FTHT for each participant group, by feedback condition. The order of the feedback conditions is the same for each visual acuity group: Auditory (A), shown in white; Haptic (H), shown in light gray; Visual (V), shown in dark gray; Auditory & Haptic (AH), shown in red; Auditory & Visual (AV), shown in blue; Haptic & Visual (HV), shown in green; and Auditory & Haptic & Visual (AHV), shown in black.

The results from Table 5 and Figure 3 show that feedback condition had a significant effect on FTHT for the following visual acuity groups:
- Control group (F = 2.441; p = 0.027)
- Group 3 (F = 7.339; p = 0.000)

Control Group. Individuals in the Control group generated significantly higher FTHT in the unimodal visual condition compared with the bimodal auditory and haptic condition (p = 0.026).
Group 3. Individuals in Group 3 generated significantly higher FTHT in the unimodal visual condition compared with all other feedback conditions (p < 0.01).

5   Conclusions and Discussion

The experimental task used for this study was indicative of a direct manipulation task, commonly used in current GUI environments. The purpose of the feedback in such environments is to serve as a cue to give indication to the user of the current status of the system, as a result of his or her actions. In this study, feedback was used as a cue to inform users that the file icon was correctly positioned for the successful completion of the drag-and-drop task. Given this understanding of the nature of feedback, final target highlight time (FTHT) is a particularly useful measure of how user performance was affected by the feedback provided. FTHT provides a measure of how quickly the meaning of the feedback is conveyed to the users [3].

From Table 5 and Figure 3, it is clear, as one would have expected, that the unimodal visual feedback condition led to the worst performance for Group 3. As shown in Figure 2, performance declined linearly with loss of visual acuity. This result is intuitive and reflects the distinct disadvantage encountered by individuals with visual impairments while using visually based interfaces. Figure 3 also reveals that visual unimodal feedback leads to significantly worse levels of performance than other feedback modalities for both Group 3 and Control Group and no significantly better levels than other modalities for both Group 1 and Group 2. Hence, other or additional feedback modalities have the potential to either improve or maintain performance for all groups.

This is a very important result, as it provides support for the use of additional feedback forms, or multimodal feedback, to support user interaction. It is important to note that the addition of other feedback forms did not significantly hinder performance in any instances. This result provides no support for the theory that multiple forms of feedback may hinder performance by overloading the sensory and perceptual systems of the user. As a result, multimodal feedback does not hinder the performance of normal users, while it does show promise as an aid for both users with normal vision and for those who have compromised vision. Figure 3 displays the relative impact of different feedback modalities on performance for individuals in specific groups and reveals interesting results.

First and foremost, the task performance, as measured by FTHT, for Group 3 was significantly better for all other feedback conditions, when compared with the unimodal visual feedback condition. In particular, the performance of Group 3 users was significantly better with both the auditory and haptic unimodal feedback conditions, compared with the unimodal visual condition, while auditory/visual bimodal and haptic/visual bimodal conditions were not different from auditory unimodal and haptic unimodal respectively. This suggests that the addition of visual feedback does not marginally improve performance for Group 3 users in performing the tasks studied. Since, however, visual feedback is commonly used in GUI environments, there is little or virtually no additional cost associated with continued use of visual feedback form in information technologies. In fact, the trimodal feedback condition appeared to produce the largest performance improvement for this group. Thus, the addition of other non-visual feedback modalities to visual feedback will significantly improve the performance of Group 3 individuals, with greatest benefits gained from trimodal feedback.

Second, significant improvement in performance over the unimodal visual feedback condition was achieved in the Control Group with the auditory/haptic bimodal feedback condition. It is also interesting to note that the level of performance reached by Control subjects with the auditory/haptic bimodal feedback condition is almost identical to the level of performance reached by Control subjects with the trimodal condition. However, no significant difference was detected between the trimodal condition and unimodal visual feedback condition for Control subjects.

Third, no significant differences in performance were detected between feedback conditions for Group 1 or Group 2. In Group 1, all feedback conditions seem to lead to nearly identical levels of performance, all very close to the level of performance reached with the unimodal visual feedback condition. In Group 2, however, while

Figure 3 seems to reveal potential gains in performance from auditory/haptic bimodal feedback, auditory/visual bimodal feedback, or trimodal feedback, none of these gains are significant.   Further studies, using additional participants, fitting the visual profiles of Group 1 and Group 2 may help to better define, for these groups, some of the differences in performance between feedback conditions. Nonetheless, it remains clear that Group 3 benefited a great deal more from the use of non-visual and multimodal forms of feedback, as compared to Groups 1 and 2.

This pattern, along with the clearly enhanced performance resulting from any non-visual feedback observed in Group 3, suggests a potential transition by which AMD patients rely on visual sensory channels despite declining visual capability loss until they learn to rely on non-visual sensory channels as losses in visual capabilities reach a certain threshold.   Thus, Group 3 subjects may have learned to adapt to their condition and rely on other sensory channels to compensate for their loss in visual capabilities.   As a result, Group 3 subjects benefit from non-visual feedback modalities whereas Group 2 subjects do not. It also appears, from Table 4 and Figure 2 that, compared to other Groups, Group 2 subjects reached significantly worse levels of performance for several feedback conditions: auditory unimodal, haptic/visual bimodal, and auditory/haptic/visual trimodal.

In conclusion, this study reveals clear benefits from multimodal feedback consistent with universal design principles (no group loses in performance and some groups significantly gain in performance) but also reveals heightened challenges encountered by individuals with declining visual capabilities not yet having developed the ability to compensate such losses with other non-visual sensory channels when using information technologies.   This suggests that information technology developers and HCI researchers should certainly consider the use of multimodal feedback when attempting to increase the accessibility and usability of systems for individuals with visual impairments. Future analyses and studies should be conducted to further examine the potential benefits of multimodal feedback on the performance of older adults and low vision users.

Overall, the important findings of this study can be summarized to include the following insights:

- Non-visual feedback and additional feedback (in addition to visual) have the potential to either maintain or improve task performance.
- The effectiveness of visual feedback is degraded in the presence of AMD and this becomes more pronounced as losses in visual acuity become more severe.
- The effectiveness of non-visual feedback and multimodal feedback generally is more apparent as visual acuity loss becomes more severe (e.g., Group 3).
- The results from Groups 1 and 2 indicate that additional participants with these visual profiles will aid in determining a threshold of visual acuity at which visual feedback is no longer helpful and non-visual feedback or multimodal feedback forms become more effective.

The results of this study provide insight into and support for the use of multimodal forms of feedback to augment the interaction of visually impaired users. While it may be expected that multimodal feedback will aid those with visual or sensory problems, this study provides a much needed, empirical investigation aimed at some of the interaction issues of this particular user group. By exploring the differences of individuals with a particular ocular condition, in this case AMD, as well as with varying levels of visual acuity, this study was able to highlight some discrepancies in the helpfulness of different forms of multimodal feedback. It was found that individuals with different visual profiles may be aided to different extents and by different feedback forms.

Further studies should be conducted that continue the examination of the issues addressed in this study. Different interaction tasks could be explored to examine if the effects of multimodal feedback extend to other common tasks, such as text editing or the use of menu hierarchies. The effectiveness of multimodal feedback in aiding performance of users with other ocular diseases should also be examined. These visual conditions should include some of the other more common forms of ocular disease, including: cataract, glaucoma, diabetic retinopathy, and retinitis pigmentosa.

Acknowledgments. This research was made possible through funding awarded to Julie A. Jacko by the Intel Corporation and the National Science Foundation (BES-9896304). The invaluable contributions of Dr. Dagmar Lemus are gratefully acknowledged, as is the support of Reva Hurtes and the Mary and Edward Norton Library of Ophthalmology at BPEI, for so generously providing the space within which this experimentation was conducted.

References

1. Brewster, S. A., Raty, V-P., & Kortekangas, A. (1996). Enhancing scanning input with non-speech sounds. Proceedings for the Second Annual International ACM/SIGCAPH Conference on Assistive Technologies (ASSETS '96), Vancouver, Canada: 10–14.
2. Brewster, S. A. (1998a). Sonically-enhanced drag and drop. Proceedings of the International Conference on Auditory Display (ICAD'98), Glasgow, UK: 1–7.
3. Vitense, H. S., Jacko, J. A., and Emery, V. K. Multimodal feedback: An assessment of performance and mental workload. To appear in Ergonomics, in press.
4. Brewster, S. A., Wright, P. C., & Edwards, A. D. N. (1994). The design and evaluation of an auditory-enhanced scrollbar. Proceedings of the 1994 ACM Conference on Human Factors in Computing Systems (CHI'94), Boston, MA: 173–179.
5. Keates, S., Clarkson, P. J., & Robinson, P. (2001). Cognitive considerations in the design of multimodal input systems. In C. Stephanidis (Ed.), Universal Access in HCI: Towards an Information Society for All (pp. 353–357). New York: Lawrence Erlbaum Associates.
6. Bolt, R. A. (1980). 'Put-that-there': Voice and gesture at the graphics interface. Computer Graphics, 14(3): 262–270.
7. Cohen, P. R., Dalrymple, M., Moran, D. B., Pereira, F. C., & Sullivan, J. W. (1989). Synergistic use of direct manipulation and natural language. Proceedings of the 1989 ACM Conference on Human Factors in Computing Systems (CHI'89), Austin, TX: 227–233.
8. Oviatt, S., Cohen, P., Suhm, B., Bers, J., Wu, L., Holzman, T., Winograd, T., Vergo, J., Duncan, L., Landay, J., & Ferro, D. (2002). Designing the user interface for multimodal speech and gesture applications: State-of-the-art systems and research directions from 2000 and beyond. Human-Computer Interaction in the New Millennium (in press). New York: ACM Press.
9. Stephanidis, C., Salvendy, G., Akoumianakis, D., Bevan, N., Brewer, J., Emiliani, P. L., Galetsas, A., Haataja, S., Iakovidis, I., Jacko, J., Jenkins, P., Karshmer, A., Korn, P., Marcus, A., Murphy, H., Stary, C., Vanderheiden, G., Weber, G., and Ziegler, J. (1998). Towards an information society for all: an international R&D agenda. International Journal of Human-Computer Interaction, 10(2): 107–134.

10. Stephanidis, C., Salvendy, G., Akoumianakis, D., Arnold, A., Bevan, N., Dardailler, D., Emiliani, P. L., Iakovidis, I., Jenkins, P., Karshmer, A., Korn, P., Marcus, A., Murphy, H., Oppermann, C., Stary, C., Tamura, H., Tscheligi, M., Ueda, H., Weber, G., & Ziegler, J. (1999). Toward an information society for all: HCI challenges and R&D recommendations. International Journal of Human-Computer Interaction, 11(1): 1–28.
11. Jacko, J. A., & Vitense, H. S. (2001). A review and reappraisal of information technologies within a conceptual framework for individuals with disabilities. Universal Access in the Information Society (UAIS), 1: 56–76.
12. Vanderheiden, G. (2003). Designing Interfaces for Diverse Audiences in J. A. Jacko and A. Sears (Eds.), Human-Computer Interaction Handbook. Mahwah: Lawrence Erlbaum & Associates, in-press.
13. Akoumianakis D., & Stephanidis, C. (1999). Propagating experience based accessibility guidelines to user interface development. Ergonomics, 42(10): 1283–1310.
14. Akoumianakis, D., & Stephanidis, C. (1997). Impediments to Designing and Developing for Accessibility, Accommodation and High Quality Interaction, Proceedings of the 3rd ERCIM Workshop on 'User Interfaces for All.' Obernai, France, November 3-4. Retrieved June 24, 2002 from http://ui4all.ics.forth.gr/UI4ALL-97/akoumianakis.pdf.
15. Trace Center (1998, January 13). Accessible Design of Consumer Products. Retrieved June 24, 2002 from http://trace.wisc.edu/docs/consumer_product_ guidelines/consumer.pcs/ intro.htm.
16. American Foundation for the Blind (2002). Statistics and sources for professionals. [On-line] Available at http://www.afb.org/info_document_view.asp?documentid = 1367, Accessed on June 12, 2002.
17. Gerber, E. (2001). Who's surfing? Internet access and computer use by visually impaired youth and adults. Journal of Visual Impairment & Blindness, 95 (3): 176–181.
18. Mynatt, E. D. (1997). Transforming graphical interfaces into auditory interfaces for blind users. Human-Computer Interaction, 12: 7–45.
19. Edwards, W. K., Mynatt, E. D., & Stockton, K. (1995). Access to graphical interfaces by blind users. Interactions, 2(1): 54–67.
20. Martial, O., & Dufresne, A. (1993). Audicon: Easy access to graphical user interfaces for blind people – designing for and with people. Proceedings of HCR'93, 19B, Orlando, FL: 808–813.
21. Newell, A. F, & McGregor, P. (1997). Human-computer interfaces for people with disabilities. In M. G. Helander, T. K. Landauer, & P. V. Prabhu (Eds.), Handbook of human-computer interaction (pp. 813–824). Amsterdam, The Netherlands: Elsevier.
22. Ahn, S. J., & Legge, D. K. (1995). Psychophysics of reading-XII: Predictors of magnifier-aided reading speed in low vision. Vision Research, 35: 1935–1938.
23. Den Brinker, B. P. L. M., & Beek, P. J. (1996). Reading with magnifiers. Ergonomics, 39: 1231–1248.
24. Jacko, J. A., & Sears, A. (1998). Designing interfaces for an overlooked user group: Considering the visual profiles of partially sighted users. Proceedings of ASSETS '98, The Third International ACM Conference on Assistive Technologies, Marina Del Rey, CA, April 15-17, 1998: 75–77. New York: ACM.
25. Jacko, J. A., Barreto, A. B., Scott, I. U., Chu, J. Y. M., Bautsch, H. S., Marmet, G. J., & Rosa, R. H. (2000a). Using eye-tracking to investigate graphical elements for normally sighted and low vision users. ACM Eye Tracking Research & Applications Symposium 2000, Palm Beach Gardens, FL, November 6-7, 2000: 112.
26. Jacko, J. A., Barreto, A. B., Marmet, G. J., Chu, J. Y. M., Bautsch, H. S., Scott, I. U., & Rosa, R. H., Jr. (2000b). Low vision: The role of visual acuity in the efficiency of cursor movement. Proceedings of ASSETS 2000, The Fourth International ACM Conference on Assistive Technologies, Arlington, VA, November 13–15, 2000: 1–8. New York: ACM.
27. Jacko, J. A., Rosa, R. H., Jr., Scott, I. U., & Dixon, M. A. (2000c). Visual impairment: The use of visual profiles in evaluations of icon use in computer-based tasks. International Journal of Human-Computer Interaction, 12(1): 151–164.

28. Varmus, H. (1997). Age-Related Macular Degeneration: Status of Research. Technical Report. National Eye Institute.
29. Backman, H., & Williams, R. (2002). Living with Age-Related Macular Degeneration. Journal of Visual Impairment & Blindness, 96(5): 345–348.
30. Sun, H., & Nathans, J. (2001). The Challenge of Macular Degeneration. Scientific American, 285(4): 68–75.
31. Quillen, D.A. (1999). Common Causes of Vision Loss in Elderly Patients. American Family Physician, 60(1): 99–108.
32. Shneiderman, B. (1998). Designing the user interface: Strategies for effective human-computer interaction. Reading, MA: Addison-Wesley.
33. Eason, K. D., Johnson, C., & Fairclough, S. (1991). The interaction of sensory modalities in the man-machine interface. In J. A. J. Roufs (Ed.), Vision and dysfunction: The man-machine interface. Boca Raton, FL: CRC.
34. Gunderson, J. (1994). Americans with Disabilities Act (ADA): Human computer interaction and people with disabilities. Proceedings of the CHI'94 Conference on Human Factors in Computing Systems (pp. 381–382). New York: ACM.
35. Kline, R.L., & Glinert, E.P. (1995). Improving GUI accessibility for people with low vision. Proceedings of the CHI'95 Conference on Human Factors in Computing Systems (pp. 474–481). New York: ACM.
36. Foley, J. D., Wallace, V. L., & Chan, P. (1984). The human factors of computer graphics interaction techniques. IEEE Computer Graphics and Applications, 89(8): 13–48.
37. Farrell, F. E. (1991). Fitting physical screen parameters to the human eye. In J. A. J. Roufs (Ed.), Vision and visual dysfunction: The man-machine interface. Boca Raton, FL: CRC.
38. The Lighthouse Inc. (1995). The Lighthouse National Survey on Vision Loss: The Experience, Attitudes and Knowledge of Middle-Aged and Older Americans. New York: The Lighthouse Inc.
39. Cooke, J. D., Brown, S. H., & Cunningham, D. A. (1989). Kinematics of arm movements in elderly humans. Neurobiology of Aging, 10: 159–165.
40. Darling, W. G., Cooke, J. D., & Brown, S. H. (1989). Control of simple arm movements in elderly humans. Neurobiology of Aging, 10: 149–157.
41. Verrillo, R. T., & Verrillo, V. (1985). Sensory and perceptual performance. In N. Charness (Ed.), Aging and human performance (pp. 1-46). New York: Wiley.
42. Smith, M. W., Sharit, J., & Czaja, S. J. (1999). Aging, Motor Control, and the Performance of Computer Mouse Tasks. Human Factors, 41(3): 389–396.
43. Serrien, D. J., & Teasdale, N. (1998). Age-Related Differences in the Integration of Sensory Information During the Execution of a Bimanual Coordination Task. Journal of Motor Behavior, 28(4): 337–347.
44. Oviatt, S., DeAngeli, A., & Kuhn, K. (1997). Integration and synchronization of input modes during multimodal human-computer interaction. Proceedings of the 2000 ACM Symposium on User Interface Software and Technology (UIST'00), San Diego, CA: 21–29.
45. McGee, M. R. (1999). A haptically enhanced scrollbar: force feedback as a means of reducing the problems associated with scrolling. Proceedings for the First PHANToM Users Research Symposium (PURS'99), Heidelberg, Germany: 17–20.
46. Oakley, I., Brewster, S. A., & Gray, P. D. (2001). Solving multi-target haptic problems in menu interaction. Proceedings of the 2001 ACM Conference on Human Factors in Computing Systems (CHI'01), Seattle, WA: 357–358.
47. Belz, S. M., & Robinson, G. M. (1999). A new class of auditory warning signals for complex systems: Auditory Icons. Human Factors , 41(4): 608–618.
48. Blattner, M., Sumikawa, D., & Greenberg, R. (1989). Earcons and icons: Their structure and common design principles. Human-Computer Interaction, 4(1): 11–44.
49. Brewster, S. A. (1998b). Using non-speech sounds to provide navigation cues. ACM Transactions on Computer-Human Interaction, 5(2): 224–259.

50. Brewster, S. A., & Crease, M. G. (1999). Correcting menu usability problems with sound. Behavior and Information Technology, 18(3): 165–177.
51. Akamatsu, M., & Mackenzie, S. I. (1996). Movement characteristics using a mouse with tactile and force feedback. International Journal of Human-Computer Studies, 45: 483–493.
52. Campbell, C. S., Zhai, S., May, K. W., & Maglio, P. P. (1999). What you feel must be what you see: Adding tactile feedback to the trackpoint. In M. A. Sasse and C. Johnson (Eds.), Human-Computer Interaction, Proceedings of INTERACT '99 (pp. 383–390). Amsterdam, The Netherlands: IOS Press.
53. Nelson, R. J., McCandlish, C. A., & Douglas, V. D. (1990). Reaction times for hand movements made in response to visual versus vibratory cues. Somatosensory and Motor Research, 7(3): 337–352.
54. Tiffin, J., & Asher, E. J. (1948). The Purdue Pegboard: Norms and Studies of Reliability and Validity. Journal of Applied Psychology, 32: 234–247.
55. Ware, J. E., Kosinski, M., & Keller, S. D. (1995). SF-12: How to Score the SF-12 Physical and Mental Health Summary Scales (2nd Ed.). Boston, MA: The Health Institute, New England Medical Center.
56. Lundberg, L., Johannesson, M., Isacson, D., & Borgquist, L. (1999). The relationship between health-state utilities and the SF-12 in a general population. Medical Decision Making, 19(2): 128–140.
57. Tobin, M. J., & Greenhalgh, R. (1987). Normative data for assessing the manual dexterity of visually handicapped adults in vocational rehabilitation. Journal of Occupational Psychology, 60: 73–80.
58. Kline, D.W., & Schieber, F. (1985). Vision and Aging. In J. E. Birren & W. Schaie (Eds.), Handbook of the psychology of aging (pp. 296–331). New York: Van Nostrand Reinhold.
59. Farnsworth, D. (1947). The Farnsworth Dichotomous Test for Color Blindness: Manual. New York: The Psychological Corporation.
60. Kraut, J. A., & McCabe, C. P. (1994). The problem of low vision. In D. M. Albert, F. A. Kakobiec, & N. L. Robinson (Eds.), Principles and practices of ophthalmology (pp. 3664–3683). Philadelphia: Saunders.
61. Jacko, J. A., Barreto, A. B., Scott, I. U., Chu, J. Y. M., Vitense, H. S., Conway, F. T., & Fain, W. B. (2002). Macular Degeneration and visual icon use: Deriving guidelines for improved access. Universal Access in the Information Society, 1(3): 197–206.
62. Costa, L. D., Vaughan, H. G., Jr., Levita, E., & Farber, N. (1963). Purdue pegboard as a predictor of the presence and laterality of cerebral lesions. Journal of Consulting Psychology, 27: 133–137.
63. Leslie, S. C., Davidson, R. J., & Batey, R. B. (1985). Purdue pegboard performance of disabled and normal readers: Unimanual versus bimanual differences. Brain and Language, 24: 359–369.

Age Related Differences and the Depth vs. Breadth Tradeoff in Hierarchical Online Information Systems

Panayiotis Zaphiris[1], Sri Hastuti Kurniawan[2], and R. Darin Ellis[3]

[1]The Centre for HCI Design, City University
London, EC1V 0HB, U.K.
zaphiri@soi.city.ac.uk
[2]Department of Computation, UMIST
Manchester, U.K.
s.kurniawan@co.umist.ac.uk
[3]Institute of Gerontology, Wayne State University
Detroit, MI 48202, USA

Abstract. We report the results of a study investigating the age related differences as they relate to the depth versus breadth tradeoff in hierarchical online information systems. Different stimulus of various depth and breadth combinations and expandable or non-expandable structure were used. Participants from two age groups (aged 36 years old and younger or 57 years old and older) took part in this study. Overall, shallow hierarchies were preferred to deep hierarchies. Seniors were slower but did not make more errors than their younger counterparts when browsing the different treatments.

1 Introduction

1.1 Defining Information Architecture

Information architecture has been defined as the "process of structuring and organizing information so that it is easier for users to find and for owners to maintain" [1] and as "a structure or map of information which allows others to find their personal paths to knowledge" [2] or as "simply a set of aids that match user needs with information resources" [3].

Although reports [4] stated that roughly two thirds of users browsing the World Wide Web (WWW) are looking for specific information and that people do not come to the web for an "experience" but rather for the information [5], the impact of a web site's information architecture on the ability of a user to navigate is very often overlooked by many web site designers.

How information is categorized, labeled and presented and how navigation and access are facilitated determines not only whether users will and can find what they need, but also affect user satisfaction and do influence return visits [6].

How well the information architecture of a site is designed also effects users' sense of orientation (knowing where they are in the hierarchy). The problem of disorientation in hypertext generally results in a measurable decline in user performance [7]. The disoriented user is usually unable to gain an overview of the

N. Carbonell, C. Stephanidis (Eds.): User Interfaces for All, LNCS 2615, pp. 23–42, 2003.

material, encounters problems in deciding if needed information is available, and has problems in deciding where to look for information and how to get there [8, 9]. Furthermore, disorientation can lead users to repeatedly open the same few nodes [10] and can increase the time users take to locate information, due to following less than optimal routes through the hypertext [11].

In general, most people need to know some basic information in order to orient themselves. This is true whether they are navigating a building or a web site. These basic navigation needs include answers to the following questions [12]:

- Where am I?
- Where can I go?
- How can I get back to where I once was?

Hierarchical structuring is one of the best ways to present information, especially to help non-knowledgeable users in navigating [11]. Two variations of the standard hierarchical structure is the expandable and non-expandable hierarchies or expandable indexes and sequential menus as they are respectively mentioned in Zaphiris, Shneiderman and Norman [13].

One advantage of using expandable hierarchies is that they preserve the full context of the choice within the hierarchy. While the user browses through the hierarchical structure, the tree is fully displayed. Thus, at any point, the user has access to the whole set of major and same level categories.

Non-expandable hierarchies, on the other hand, do not display the full hierarchical context as they drop down to deeper levels in the hierarchy. Only elements in the selected category are displayed as options for browsing. This is of particular importance on the WWW when the number of root levels alternatives is large and the depth of the hierarchy is greater than two. Examples of expandable and non-expandable hierarchies are depicted in Fig. 1 and Fig. 2.

1.2 Depth versus Breadth in Menu Selection

Menu panels usually consist of a list of options. These options may consist of words or icons. The word or icon conveys some information about the consequences of selecting that option. Sometimes the options are elaborated with verbal descriptors.

When one of the options is selected and executed, a system action occurs that usually results in a visual change on the system display. The total set of options is usually distributed over many different menu panels/frames. Web indexes are organized in a similar structure. Links (very often 2-3 words, sometimes elaborated with verbal descriptors) are arranged in various levels of homepages. These links convey information about the page (with information or further sub-categories) that will be displayed if that specific link is selected.

The topic of menu selection and especially the depth versus breadth tradeoff (Examples of deep and shallow web hierarchies are shown in Fig. 3 and Fig. 4.) has been extensively examined, both empirically and analytically. The navigation problem (i.e., getting lost or using an inefficient pathway to the goal) becomes more and more treacherous as the depth of the hierarchy increases. Research has shown [14] that error rates increased from 4.0% to 34.0% as depth increased from a single level to six levels.

It has been shown experimentally [15, 16] that hierarchical menu design experiments can be replicated to experiments on hierarchies of lists of web links. Hierarchical decomposition of the user's selection of action is often necessary to facilitate fast and accurate completion of search tasks, especially when there is insufficient screen space to display all possible courses of action to the user.

The challenge, therefore, is to enable the user to select the desired course of action using a clear, well-defined sequence of steps to complete a given task [17].

1.3 Empirical Results

Depth versus breadth in hierarchical menu structures has been the topic of much empirical research. The trade-off between menu depth (levels in a hierarchical menu structure) and breadth (number of menu selections present on a given menu in the hierarchy) is stated by some researchers as the most important aspect that must be considered in the design of hierarchical menu systems [18]. Questions such as "how long does it take to find a specific piece of information?" and "how many errors occur during the information search?" have been the main focus of previous empirical experimental research on the topic of menu selection.

Miller [19] found that short-term memory is a limitation of the increased depth of the hierarchy. His experiment examined four structures (64^1, 8^2, 4^3, and 2^6) with a fixed number of target items (64). The 64 items were carefully chosen so that "they form valid semantic hierarchies" in each of the 4 menu structures. As depth increased, so did response time to select the desired item.

Snowberry, Parkinson and Sisson [14] replicated Miller's study by examining the same structures, but this time included an initial screening session during which subjects took memory span and visual scanning tests. They stated that determination of whether short-term memory and visual scanning act as limiting factors in menu selection is also important for consideration of 'special' groups, such as older users, whose short-term memory capacity and processing speed are reduced relative to young adults. They found that instead of memory span, visual scanning was predictive of performance, especially in the deepest hierarchies. Their experiment compared performances on both randomized and categorized 64 item displays to performances on structures of increasing depth and decreasing breadth. They used a between-subject design with four different experimental conditions (menu structures - 64^1, 2^6, 4^3 and 8^2).

Their results provide a nice replication of Miller's results showing that search time for randomly arranged items for the four experimental groups produced a U-shaped function, with a minimum at the configuration of two levels with eight choices. With category organization held constant across conditions, search time improved as depth decreased and breadth increased. Accuracy was found to improve as breadth increased (and depth decreased) regardless of display format in the broadest display. They state three possible kinds of 'forgetting' which might have led to lower accuracy for deeper menus:

1. Participants might have forgotten the target word.
2. Participants might have performed less accurately in deep menus because they forgot the pathway to the target.

3.   Rather than associating a target with a path of options, participants might have based selections of options purely on the association formed between the items displayed and the target; forgetting the association would have led to inaccurate performance.

Fig. 1. Expandable hierarchical structure

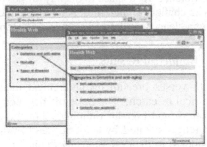

Fig. 2. Non-expandable hierarchical structure

Fig. 3. Broad hierarchical web index

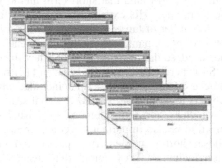

Fig. 4. Deep hierarchical web index

Kiger [20] extended Miller's research by designing an experiment that provided users with five modes of varying menu designs of 64 end nodes.

- 8^2: 8 items on each of 2 levels.
- 4^3: 4 items on each of 3 levels.
- 2^6: 2 items on each of 6 levels.
- $4^1 + 16^1$: A 4 item menu followed by a 16 item menu
- $16^1 + 4^1$: A 16 item menu followed by a 4 item menu

Kiger's experiment [20] showed that the time and number of errors increased with the depth of the menu structure. The 4x16 structure had the fastest response times and the fewest errors. The participants ranked the menus with least depth (the 8^2 structure) as the most favorable.

Parkinson et al. [21] built on Snowberry, Parkinson and Sisson's [14] research by examining different organization styles of menus. Three factors were varied in the categorized menus they used: alphabetical versus categorical ordering of words within categories; spacing versus no additional spacing between category groups; and category organization arranged by column or by row. Organization (row or column) and spacing exerted powerful effects on search time. Menus in which categories were arranged by column were searched faster than menus organized by row. Menus in which additional spacing was provided between groups were searched faster than menus with no spacing. For categorized menus, no advantage was found for alphabetical as opposed to categorical ordering of words within category. These results are in disagreement with previous research by Mc Donald et al. [22] who found that categorical menu organization is superior to pure alphabetical or random organization.

Similar results were also found in an experiment by Nygren [23] where scanning of a horizontal listing of items was found to be slower than scanning a vertical listing of items. Findings further indicated that scanning a single long vertical list was faster than scanning multiple shorter vertical lists. They also found that estimated scanning rate was dependent on subject's age. Searching for a target item was significantly faster if the target item was given a unique feature, compared with if no unique feature was used. The color, shade, space, slant and size features were equally effective compared with a control condition (without features).

Wallace et al. [17] confirmed that broader, shallower trees (4x3 versus 2x6) produced superior performance, and showed that, when users were stressed, they made 96 percent more errors and took 16 percent more time to browse to the target. The stressor was simply an instruction to work quickly ("It is imperative that you finish the task just as quickly as possible"). The control group received mild instructions to avoid rushing ("Take your time; there is no rush").

Norman and Chin [24] fixed the number of levels at four, with 256 target items, and varied the shape of the tree structures. They recommend greater breadth at the root and at the leaves, and added a further encouragement to minimize the total number of menu frames needed so as to increase familiarity.

An experiment by Jacko and Salvendy [18] tested six structures (2^2, 2^3, 2^6, 8^2, 8^3, and 8^6) for search time, error rates, and subjective preference. They demonstrated that as depth of a computerized, hierarchical menu increased, perceived complexity of the menu increased significantly. Campbell [25] identified multiple paths, multiple outcomes, conflicting interdependence among paths, and uncertain linkages as four characteristics of a complex task. Jacko and Salvendy [18] built on this framework to suggest that these four characteristics are present as depth increases, and the presence of these four characteristics is responsible for the increase in complexity.

Studies have also shown [26] that apart from the inherent complexity of a hierarchical structure, the depth versus breadth tradeoff is also influenced by cases where the user can restrict the scope of search either because of experience or because the options are organized into categories.

As mentioned earlier, the similarity between menu panels and hierarchical lists of web links has recently been studies (through a series of replication of previous web panel experiments) by researchers.

Zaphiris [16] replicated Kiger's [20] structures but this time on the WWW using hyperlinks. Overall, his results were in agreement with those of Kiger [20]. He found that of the structures tested (8^2, 4^3, 2^6 and 16x4, 4x16), the 8^2 structure was the fastest to search.

Larson and Czerwinski [15] carried out an experiment using 512 bottom level nodes arranged in three different structures (8x8x8, 32x16, 16x32). Subjects on average completed search tasks faster in the 16x32 hierarchy, second fastest in the 32x16 hierarchy, and slowest in the 8x8x8 hierarchy. Also, on average, subjects tended to be lost least often in the 16x32 hierarchy. The authors calculated "lostness" through an analysis of the number of unique and total links visited in comparison to the "optimal" path. Similar results to the above two web related studies have been found in a recent study by Zaphiris, et al. [13] when investigating the difference between sequential and expandable hierarchies of links.

In a study by Mead, et al. [27], age-related differences and training on WWW navigation strategies were examined. They found that novice users were more likely to "get lost" in a hierarchical structure than were more experienced searchers. In an experiment they conducted, where they asked their participants to complete nine search tasks on the WWW, they showed that seniors were significantly less likely to complete all tasks than were younger adults. However, seniors were as likely to complete the five tasks with short optimal path length (two moves or fewer) as younger adults. Seniors on the other hand, were significantly less likely to complete the tasks with long optimal path length (3 moves or more) than were younger adults. Error results showed seniors may experience considerable difficulty finding information on the WWW when path length is long. Finally seniors were reported to adopt less efficient search strategies and had more problems remembering which pages they had visited (and what was on those pages) than did younger adults.

1.4 Seniors and the Web

Administration on Aging [28] projected that by the year 2030 people aged 65 years and above will represent 20% of US population.

Recent data shows that among the 21.8 million U.S. households where the householder was 65 or older, 5.3 million households (24.3%) had a computer, slightly less than half the figure for the general population (51.6%). Internet access was present in 3.9 million (17.7%) of the elderly households, whereas for the general population this was 41.5%. On an individual basis, 9.3 million (28.4%) of the older persons had home computer access and 4.2 million (12.8%) used the Internet at home, which is 34% of the figure for the general population [28]. One of the main reasons senior citizens report for using a computer is to look for health information [29, 30].

This increase in computer and web usage by senior citizens is expected to follow a similar patter in other countries too. Various market research showed that the younger generation is getting more and more dependent on the internet/web in performing daily activities (entertainment, shopping, studying). Hence, in 20-30 years, we will be more likely to experience a more dramatic increase in web usage by seniors, making the study of aging issues effecting web usage a necessity, especially since some findings suggested that older adults have some disadvantages in fully utilizing the Internet as an information source. That is, older people have more trouble finding information in a Web site than younger people [27, 31].

One way to alleviate age-related barriers in using the Internet is by involving seniors in the design process.   Zaphiris and Kurniawan [32] proposed the term "senior-centered design" to refer to any design methodology that involves older users in the process of designing products that are targeted towards the aging population.

2   Research Methodology

2.1 Stimulus Material

Two sets of locally hosted (to eliminate delays due to network congestions) web sites, each containing 64 pages of health and medical-related information for older adults, were designed and presented to participants using a standard web browser. The test stimuli were taken from Health:Aging and Health:Senior Health directories of dmoz (http://www.dmoz.org). These sites were supposedly categorized by experts in the relevant areas. There were two groups of information used for test stimuli. There were two tested modes of hierarchical information structures: expandable and non-expandable as depicted in Fig. 1 and Fig. 2. There were 12 experimental conditions (two sets of hierarchies, with 2 structures and 3 depth conditions per structure) used as stimuli. For each hierarchical structure and each information group, there were 3 conditions with varying depth/breadth as listed in Table 1.

Table 1. Depth/Breadth combinations used in the stimuli

Depth	2	3	6
Breadth	8	4	2

2.2 Participants

Participants in the general browsing experiment consisted of 24 older Internet users (aged 57 years old and older) and 24 younger users (aged 36 years old and younger), who lived independently in the community (non-institutionalized) with no visual or cognitive impairment or functional illiteracy or any other deficit that would preclude them from successfully completing the protocol.

Participants were recruited from senior centers, senior church groups, community organizations, and the Wayne State University campus. The sample consisted of a variety of ethnic groups, gender, and education levels.

Participants were initially screened through brief conversation with the experimenter to assess their computer and Internet usage. By asking several Web-related questions, individuals with no prior experience with the WWW or who had not used a computer before were screened-out.

Individuals reporting a medical condition that would directly interfere with performance (e.g. severe carpal tunnel syndrome) were also excluded from the study. Participants' demographics data are listed in Table 2.

Table 2. Demographic data of participants of the general browsing experiment

Socio-demographic data		Young	Old
Age		26.8(5.18)*	67.5(6.5)*
Education		16.8(2.57)*	14.6(3.13)*
Gender	Male	18	10
	Female	6	14
Ethnicity	Asian/Pacific Islander	11	0
	African/African American	4	12
	Caucasian/Middle Eastern	9	12

* mean(standard deviation)

2.3 Apparatus

Pentium II-class personal computers operating with Windows 98, SVGA monitors (1280x1024 resolution, .22mm dot pitch @ 85 Hz) were used throughout this experiment. User behavior was recorded using server logs capable of recording time and page clicks. To verify that the server's log recorded the correct time and duration, Lotus Screen Cam® software was used to observe the first few participants.

2.4 Procedure

2.4.1 Pre-experiment Questionnaire
The participants were first asked to read and sign a consent form. The consent form outlined briefly the purpose of the experiment and listed all the participants rights. After signing the consent form, the participants were asked to fill a socio-demographic questionnaire that asked for their age, ethnicity and education level.

Following that, participants were asked to fill two questionnaires. In the first one their general computer and internet knowledge was assessed using a modified questionnaire from the user demographics section of the WWW User Survey of GVU Center of the Georgia Institute of Technology (http://www.gvu.gatech.edu/). In the second questionnaire the participants' domain (health information) pre-experiment knowledge was assessed.

Previous studies suggested that domain knowledge might contribute to the success of information search. Therefore, a bivariate correlation between domain knowledge and search effectiveness was calculated. The result showed that there was no significant correlation between domain knowledge and search effectiveness.

2.4.2 Browsing Practice
Before performing the main browsing tasks, participants were asked to browse dmoz (http://dmoz.org/) and to look for information about three non-health related topics (a recipe, a football team and a music band). The purpose of this task was two-fold: first, to provide a practice browsing session for the participants and second, to observe whether participants had sufficient browsing experience. Since this was a practice task no data was recorded.

2.4.3 Main Browsing Tasks and Post-browsing Questionnaires

The browsing task consisted of 72 information search tasks (6 tasks on each of the 3 depth treatments for two different hierarchical sets of pages) on health-related topics. The number of tasks was chosen in order to provide enough power to model the browsing behavior of the participants. The experiment was designed to allow breaks at the end of every task to minimize fatigue and boredom and maintain user's interest in the browsing process [33]. In line with previous studies [13, 17] the tasks were not time-limited to enable participants to find the answer without being under time stress.

Participants were given booklets of item cards containing various health-related topics which served as targets and were asked to browse the specific hierarchy of online information presented to them and to write down the unique portion of the URL when they reached the target pages. The order of presentation was counterbalanced across participants and hierarchical structures.

After finishing the browsing tasks with each hierarchical structure, participants were asked to fill a bipolar post-browsing questionnaire on user satisfaction, orientation and the system's ease-of-use.

3 Results and Analysis

3.1 Subjective Ratings

In the main browsing experiment participants were asked to rate the expandable and non-expandable hierarchical structures in two ways: by ranking their ease of use and by rating in five bipolar scales each of the hierarchical structures in terms of case of navigation, sense of orientation and users' satisfaction. Participants were also asked to rate their preferences in terms of the depth of the hierarchies.

3.2 Ease of Navigation

Participants were asked to rate how easy it was to navigate when browsing on a particular hierarchical structure, from 1 (very difficult) to 5 (very easy). The means and standard deviations for each age group and hierarchical structure are displayed in Table 3.

An Analysis of Variance (ANOVA) was performed on these ratings using the General Linear Model (GLM) of SPSS using a 2x3x2 (age x depth x structure) design. The results show a significant Depth main effect ($F(2,44) = 46.03$, $p<0.001$), a significant Structure*Age group effect ($F(1,45) = 5.44$, $p<0.025$) and a significant Depth*Structure*Age group effect ($F(2,44) = 3.76$, $p<0.032$). On the other hand, no significant between subject Age effect ($F(1,45) = 3.91$, $p>0.15$) was found, nor any significant Structure main effect ($F(1,45) = 2.05$, $p>0.15$) or Depth*Age group ($F(2,44) = 0.37$, $p>0.69$) or Depth*Structure ($F(2,44) = 5.44$, $p>0.44$) effects were found. Fig. 5 - Fig. 8 show the above analysis in graphical form.

Table 3. Means and standard deviations of ease of navigation

		N	Young mean (s.d.)	Old mean (s.d.)
Non-expandable	Depth2	48	4.58 (0.78)	4.21 (0.72)
	Depth 3	48	3.67 (1.13)	3.88 (0.80)
	Depth 6	48	3.04 (1.20)	3.33 (1.13)
	Overall	144	3.80 (1.22)	3.80 (0.96)
Expandable	Depth 2	48	4.63 (0.71)	4.33 (0.56)
	Depth 3	48	4.17 (1.09)	3.54 (1.02)
	Depth 6	48	3.91 (0.95)	3.21 (1.10)
	Overall	144	4.20 (0.96)	3.70 (1.03)

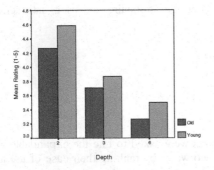

Fig. 5. Mean rating for ease of navigation by depth for the two age groups

Fig. 6. Mean rating for ease of navigation for the two structures

3.3 Sense of Orientation

In this part of the experiment, participants were asked to rate their sense of orientation (in the sense of knowing where they are in the hierarchy) while browsing a certain structure, from 1 (very disoriented) to 5 (very oriented). The means and standard deviations for each age group and structure are displayed in Table 4.

An ANOVA was performed on these ratings using the General Linear Model (GLM) of SPSS using a 2x3x2 (age x depth x structure) design. The results show a significant Depth main effect ($F(2,44) = 35.76$, $p<0.001$), a significant Structure*Age group effect ($F(1,45) = 4.50$, $p<0.04$) and a significant Depth*Structure*Age group effect ($F(2,44) = 4.57$, $p<0.02$) and a significant between-subject Age effect ($F(1,45) = 4.77$, $p<0.035$) was found. On the other hand, no significant Structure main effect ($F(1,45) = 1.40$, $p>0.24$) or Depth*Age group ($F(2,44) = 0.075$, $p>0.92$) or Depth*Structure ($F(2,44) = 2.66$, $p>0.08$) effects were found. Fig. 9 - Fig. 12 show in graphical form the above analysis.

Table 4. Sense of orientation

		N	Young Mean (s.d.)	Old mean (s.d.)
Non-expandable	Depth2	48	4.71 (0.69)	4.29 (0.69)
	Depth 3	48	3.92 (1.06)	3.96 (0.86)
	Depth 6	48	3.29 (1.12)	3.21 (1.22)
	Overall	144	4.00 (1.13)	3.80 (1.04)
Expandable	Depth 2	48	4.63 (0.65)	4.33 (0.56)
	Depth 3	48	4.25 (1.07)	3.46 (1.06)
	Depth 6	48	4.17 (0.89)	3.33 (1.55)
	Overall	144	4.40 (0.90)	3.70 (1.20)

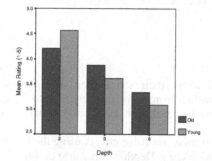

Fig. 7. Mean rating of ease of use for the non-expandable structure

Fig. 8. Mean rating for ease of use for expandable structure

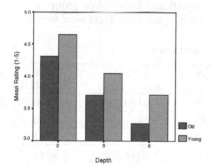

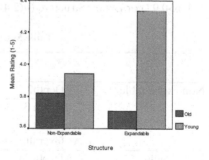

Fig. 9. Mean rating for sense of orientation by depth

Fig. 10. Mean rating for sense of orientation for the two structures

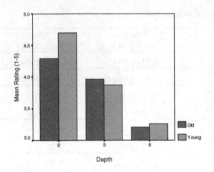
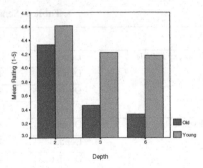

Fig. 11. Mean rating of sense of orientation for the non-expandable structure

Fig. 12. Mean rating for sense of orientation for expandable structure

3.4 Satisfaction

In this measure, participants were asked about their satisfaction when using a particular structure to browse for the information, from 1 (very unsatisfied) to 5 (very satisfied). The means, standard deviations for each age group and structure are displayed in Table 5.

An Analysis of Variance (ANOVA) was performed on these ratings using the General Linear Model (GLM) of SPSS using a 2x3x2 (Age x Depth x Structure) design. The results show a significant Depth main effect ($F(2,44) = 31.86$, $p<0.001$), a significant Structure main effect ($F(1,45) = 7.44$, $p<0.01$), a significant Structure*Age group effect ($F(1,45) = 12.05$, $p<0.001$) and a significant Depth*Structure*Age group effect ($F(2,44) = 3.34$, $p<0.05$) but no significant between subject Age main effect ($F(1,45) = 2.49$, $p>0.334$) was found. Similarly no significant Depth*Age group ($F(2,44) = 0.083$, $p>0.92$) or Depth*Structure ($F(2,44) = 0.87$, $p>0.42$) effects were found.

Table 5. User satisfaction

		N	Young mean (s.d.)	Old mean (s.d.)
Non-expandable	Depth2	48	4.50 (0.88)	4.25 (0.79)
	Depth 3	48	3.79 (1.14)	3.96 (0.91)
	Depth 6	48	3.00 (1.29)	3.37 (1.10)
	Overall	144	3.80 (1.26)	3.90 (1.00)
Expandable	Depth 2	48	4.54 (0.88)	4.37 (0.65)
	Depth 3	48	4.46 (0.72)	3.75 (1.03)
	Depth 6	48	3.96 (0.98)	3.25 (1.19)
	Overall	144	4.30 (0.89)	3.80 (1.07)

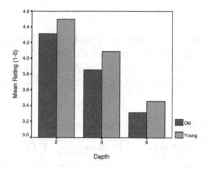

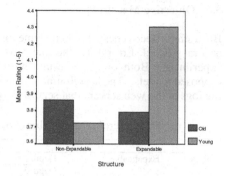

Fig. 13. Mean rating for satisfaction by depth for the two age groups

Fig. 14. Mean rating for satisfaction for the two structures

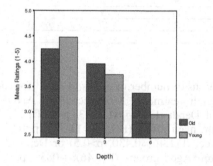

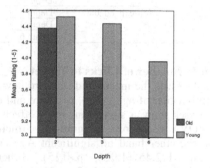

Fig. 15. Mean rating for satisfaction for the non-expandable structure

Fig. 16. Mean rating for satisfaction for expandable structure

3.5 Ranking in Ease of Use

As a measure of overall usability of the different treatments used in this experiment, participants were asked to rank those structures in terms of their ease-of-use. Sixteen younger and 14 older users ranked non-expandable structure as more difficult to use. Participants were also asked to rank their preferences in terms of depth. Both seniors and young participants preferred shallow to deep hierarchies as shown in Table 6.

3.6 Objective Measures

Browsing effectiveness (Search Time or time to complete a task) and browsing accuracy (Click Errors) are the main two objective measures of the main browsing experiment. Both of these results will be used later on to validate the different proposed models. The search time and number of clicks to target were obtained from the logs of the web servers that served the pages.

Table 6. Preference (number of participants per cell) in terms of depth

			1st Choice	2nd Choice	3rd Choice
Young	Expandable	Depth 2	15	3	3
		Depth 3	3	14	4
		Depth 6	3	4	14
	Non-expandable	Depth 2	19	3	2
		Depth 3	2	19	3
		Depth 6	3	2	19
Old	Expandable	Depth 2	11	6	6
		Depth 3	3	15	5
		Depth 6	9	2	12
	Non-expandable	Depth 2	12	3	7
		Depth 3	2	17	3
		Depth 6	8	2	12

3.6.1 Number of Clicks to Target

Table 7 lists the means and standard deviations of number of clicks to target for each combination of age group, structure and depth treatment. As expected, the ANOVA analyses show a significant main effect of Depth ($F(2,45)=137.53$, $p<0.001$). The ANOVA also shows a significant Structure main effect ($F(1,46)=11.387$, $p<0.003$). On the other hand no significant Age effect ($F(1,46)=0.430$, $p>0.5$) or Depth*Age group ($F(2,45)=1.926$, $p>0.15$), Structure*Age group ($F(1,46)=1.083$, $p>0.3$), Depth*Structure ($F(2,45)=2.258$, $p>0.11$) or Depth*Structure*Age group ($F(2,45)=0.936$, $p>0.4$) effects were found.

Table 7. Mean number of clicks to target for each treatment

Age Group	Depth	Structure	Mean (s.d.)
Young	6	Non-Expandable	11.93 (1.13)
		Expandable	9.23 (0.65)
	3	Non-Expandable	5.26 (0.39)
		Expandable	4.45 (0.18)
	2	Non-Expandable	2.74 (0.22)
		Expandable	2.45 (0.13)
Old	6	Non-Expandable	10.64 (1.13)
		Expandable	9.66 (0.65)
	3	Non-Expandable	4.60 (0.39)
		Expandable	4.04 (0.18)
	2	Non-Expandable	2.85 (0.22)
		Expandable	2.40 (0.13)

3.6.2 Search Effectiveness

Search effectiveness is described as the total time needed to arrive at the correct target. Table 8 lists the means (in seconds) and standard deviations of each age-group, structure and age group combination.

Table 8. Search Effectiveness (Time in seconds)

Age Group	Depth	Structure	Mean (s.d.)
Young	6	Non-Expandable	35.19 (3.86)
		Expandable	33.90 (3.56)
	3	Non-Expandable	23.91 (2.24)
		Expandable	23.37 (2.18)
	2	Non-Expandable	15.82 (1.80)
		Expandable	18.93 (1.79)
Old	6	Non-Expandable	45.93 (3.86)
		Expandable	55.55 (3.56)
	3	Non-Expandable	30.25 (2.24)
		Expandable	33.50 (2.18)
	2	Non-Expandable	26.12 (1.80)
		Expandable	24.18 (1.79)

The ANOVA analysis shows significant Age main between-subjects effect ($F(1,46)=13.689$, $p<0.002$), significant Depth main effect ($F(2,45)=77.280$, $p<0.001$), significant Depth*Age group ($F(2,45)=3.2$, $p<0.05$) and significant Depth*Structure*Age group effect ($F(2,45)=7.518$, $p<0.003$). On the other hand no significant Structure main effect ($F(1,46)=2.759$, $p>0.1$), Structure*Age group ($F(1,46)=1.77$, $p>0.195$) and Depth*Structure ($F(2,45)=0.96$, $p>0.39$) effects were found.

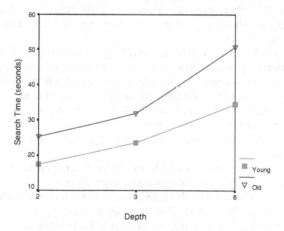

Fig. 17. Search time versus Depth for the two age groups

4   Discussions

4.1 Subjective Measures

Three measures of subjective ratings were collected in this study: ease of navigation, sense of orientation and satisfaction. The followings are the resulting observations:
   When asked to rate the ease of navigating of the different treatments the following results were obtained:
1. There was a significant Depth main effect (shallow hierarchies were rated as easier to navigate than deeper hierarchies).
2. There was a significant Structure*Age group effect (older participants found non-expandable hierarchies easier to navigate whereas younger participants found expandable hierarchies easier to navigate).
3. There was a significant Depth*Structure*Age effect (younger participants rated the depth 2 expandable hierarchy as the easiest to navigate and depth 6 non-expandable as the hardest to navigate, whereas the older participants found the depth 2 non-expandable hierarchy as the easiest to navigate and the depth 6 expandable as the hardest to navigate).
4. No significant Structure main effect or Age between subject effect was found.
   When the participants were asked to rate their sense of orientation (knowing where they are in the hierarchy) while browsing the different treatments the following results were obtained:
1. There was a significant between-subjects Age effect. Older participants rated their sense of orientation while performing the experiment lower than their younger counterparts.
2. There was a significant Depth main effect. Participants reported higher ratings for sense of orientation for shallow hierarchies.
3. There was a significant Structure*Age group effect. Younger participants stated that they had a better sense of orientation with expandable hierarchies whereas older participants showed a preference to non-expandable structures when it comes to sense of orientation.
4. There was a significant Depth*Structure*Age group effect. Younger participants rated the hierarchy with depth 2 of the non-expandable structure as the best in terms of sense of orientation, the older participants on the other hand rated the depth 2 structure of the expandable hierarchy as best. But both younger and older participants rated the hierarchy with depth 6 of the non-expandable structure lowest in terms of sense of orientation.
5. No significant Structure main effect, Depth*Age effect and Depth*Structure effect was reported.
   When the participants were asked to rate their general satisfaction while browsing the different treatments the following results were obtained:
1. There was a significant Depth main effect. Participants reported higher general satisfaction ratings for shallow than deep hierarchies.
2. There was a significant Structure main effect. Participants reported higher general satisfaction ratings for expandable than non-expandable structures.

3. There was a significant Structure*Age group effect. Younger participants showed a preference to expandable structures whereas older participants showed a preference to non-expandable structures when it comes to general satisfaction.
4. There was a significant Depth*Structure*Age group effect. Both young and old participants rated as best in terms of satisfaction the depth 2 expandable structure. The young group rated the depth 6 non-expandable structure as the worse in terms of satisfaction, whereas the older group rated the depth 6 expandable structure as the worse in satisfaction.
5. There was no significant Depth*Age group, or Depth*Structure effect.

Finally, as a measure of overall usability of the different treatments participants were asked to rank the different hierarchies in terms of their ease of use. The results are very interesting. Both young and old participants chose the hierarchies with depth 2 as their first preferences, the hierarchies with depth 3 as their second choice, and rated the hierarchies with depth 6 as the most difficult to use.

An important observation, is that older participants in general rated all treatments much lower than their younger counterparts. For example, although there is a Structure*Age group effect for overall satisfaction (older participants preferred non-expandable hierarchies but younger participants showed a preference to expandable hierarchies) it should be noted that the rating older participants gave to both expandable and non-expandable arrangements were lower that the respective rating given to these hierarchies by the younger participants. This observation, indicates that there are further dimensions (apart from the structuring of the information) that need to be taken into consideration when presenting information online for senior citizens.

4.2 Objective Measures

Objective measures consist of two items: search effectiveness (total browsing time to arrive at the correct target) and the search efficiency (actual number of clicks needed to reach the target).

4.2.1 Number of Clicks to Target
When analyzing the data relating to the number of clicks to reach the target, obtained from the server logs, the following results were obtained:
1. There was a significant main effect of Depth. As expected, users browsing deeper hierarchies needed more steps to reach the target than did users browsing shallow hierarchies.
2. There was a significant Structure main effect. Users browsing non-expandable hierarchies took on average significantly more steps to reach the target than users browsing expandable hierarchies did.
3. No significant Age main effect, Depth*Age group, Structure*Age group, Depth*Structure or Depth*Structure*Age group effects were found.

The last result suggest that, in contrary to findings from previous studies [27], in this particular task environment older adults did not make more errors than their younger counterparts and that any age-related differences in search time are not dependent on any differences in the number of clicks to target between the two age groups.

4.2.2 Search Effectiveness

Search effectiveness was the main investigation of the study. The GLM ANOVA analysis of search effectiveness showed that:

1. There was a significant Age main effect. Seniors on average took more time to reach the target in the browsing tasks.
2. There was a significant Depth main effect. Participants on average took longer to browse deep than shallow hierarchies.
3. There was a significant Depth*Age group effect. Older participants were slower in all depth hierarchies, and disproportionately effected by increasing depth.
4. There was a significant Depth*Structure*Age group effect. Younger participants browsed the depth 2 non-expandable hierarchy the fastest and the depth 6 non-expandable hierarchy the slowest. On the other hand the older participants browsed the depth 2 expandable hierarchy the fastest and the depth 6 expandable hierarchy the slowest.
5. There was no significant Structure main effect, Structure*Age group effect and Depth*Structure effect.

The aforementioned results suggest that information designers should take into consideration the fact that older users take longer time compared to younger users to find the answers they were looking for in hierarchical information structures. This result shows the importance of information architecture in optimizing the user experience online.

The results also show that, in contrary to findings from previous studies (e.g. [13]), users do not perform significantly better in the expandable hierarchy. Unlike the Zaphiris, Shneiderman and Norman [13] experiment; all the stimuli in the experiment described in this paper could fit into a single screen when fully expanded (in the case of the expandable hierarchies). This avoided the trouble of scrolling which the Zaphiris, Shneiderman and Norman's [13] study found to be the main reason of the difference in search effectiveness between expandable and non-expandable hierarchies.

5 Conclusions

The focus of this study was hierarchical online information structures. Previous studies have shown that investigating such structures and the depth versus breadth tradeoff in browsing hierarchical structures can provide valuable information to designers and researchers to better design online information. Information architecture (the art/science of optimally designing/arranging information online) is a crucial element in this task.

The results show that there was a significant Depth main effect with participants taking longer to reach the target in deep than shallow hierarchies. Also there was a significant Depth*Age group effect, with older participant being slower in all depth treatments. Furthermore, Shallow hierarchies were preferred to deeper hierarchies for ease of navigation, sense of orientation, and overall satisfaction.

Finally, a significant Structure effect was reported for general satisfaction with expandable hierarchies rated higher than non-expandable structures and a significant Structure*Age group effect reported for ease of navigation, sense of orientation, and general satisfaction ratings.   Older participants preferred the non-expandable hierarchies, whereas their younger counterparts preferred the expandable hierarchies.

Overall, seniors were slower and did make more mistakes than their younger counterparts when browsing the different treatments.

5.1 Suggestions to Researchers and Practitioners

There are several lessons learned from this study that are fruitful contributions to the area of human-computer interaction, especially for older information users.   First of all, as reported in the above analysis, there are age-related differences both in terms of preference and in terms of performance when it comes to browsing hierarchical online information structures.   This result should be taken seriously by web designers, especially when designing online information that targets senior citizens.   Where possible, shallow hierarchies should be preferred to deeper hierarchies and when targeting seniors, non-expandable hierarchies should be preferred.

5.2 Limitations

First (and most importantly) the current study was concentrated on homogeneous structures.   Future research could focus on strengthening these results by running similar studies for more complex (non-homogeneous) structures.   Secondly, this study was limited in that it was tested under the special case of text-only websites.   Web sites usually contain banner ads, pictures and icons.   The effect of such visual elements was not investigated in this study.   Finally, there is obviously a necessity for accurate mathematical models that could be used with confidence in predicting the complexity and thus the number of clicks to target when browsing hierarchical structures.

References

1.   Rosenfeld, L., *Special Report: Design Usability – Seven Pitfalls to Avoid in Information Architecture.* 2000.
2.   Wurman, R.S., *Information Architects.* 1996, Zurich: Graphics Prss.
3.   Davenport, T.H., *Information Ecology: Mastering the Information and Knowledge Environment.* 1997, New York: Oxford University Press.
4.   Korman, R., *Helping users find their way by marking your site 'smelly'.* 1998, webreview.com.
5.   Nielsen, J., *User interface directions for the web.* Communications of the ACM, 1999. **42**(1): p. 65–72.
6.   Gullikson, S., et al., *The impact of information architecture on academic web site usability.* The Electronic Library, 1999. **17**(5): p. 293–304.
7.   Elm, W. and D. Woods. *Getting lost: A case study in interface design.* in *The Human Factors Society 29th Annual Meeting.* 1985.
8.   Kim, H. and S.C. Hirtle, *Spatial metaphors and disorientation in hypertext browsing.* Behaviour and Information Technology, 1995(14): p. 239–250.

9.   Edwards, D. and L. Hardman, 'Lost in Hyperspace': Cognitive mapping and navigation in a hypertext environment, in Hypertext: Theory into Practice, R. McAleese, Editor. 1989, Intellect: Oxford. p. 90–105.
10.   Simpson, A. and C. McKnight, Navigation in hypertext: structural cues and mental maps, in Hypertext: State of the Art, G. C., Editor. 1990, Intellect: Oxford. p. 73–83.
11.   McDonald, S. and R.J. Stevenson, Disorientation in hypertext: The effects of three text structures on navigation performance. Applied Ergonomics, 1996(27): p. 61–68.
12.   Fleming, J., Web Navigation: Designing the User Experience. 1998, Sebastopol: O'Reilly.
13.   Zaphiris, P., B. Shneiderman, and K. Norman, Expandable versus sequential menus. Behaviour and Information Technology, In Press.
14.   Snowberry, K., S.R. Parkinson, and N. Sisson, Computer Display Menus. Ergonomics, 1983. 26(7): p. 699–712.
15.   Larson, K. and M. Czerwinski. Page Design: Implications of Memory, Structure and Scent for Information Retrieval. in CHI '98 Human Factors in Computing Systems. 1998: ACM Press.
16.   Zaphiris, P. Depth vs Breadth in the Arrangement of Web Links. in Human Factors Society, Fourty-Fourth Annual Meeting. 2000. San Diego.
17.   Wallace, D., N. Anderson, and B. Shneiderman. Time Stress Effects on Two Menu Selection Systems. in Human Factors Society, Thirty-First Annual Meeting. 1987.
18.   Jacko, J. and G. Salvendy, Hierarchical Menu Design: Breadth, Depth, and Task Complexity. Perceptual and Motor Skills, 1996(82): p. 1187–1201.
19.   Miller, D.P. The Depth/Breadth Tradeoff in Hierarchical Computer Menus. in Human Factors Society. 1981.
20.   Kiger, J.I., The Depth/Breadth Tradeoff in the Design of Menu-Driven Interfaces. International Journal of Man-Machine Studies, 1984(20): p. 201–213.
21.   Parkinson, S.R., N. Sisson, and K. Snowberry, Organization of broad computer menu displays. International Journal of Man-Machine Studies, 1985. 23: p. 689–697.
22.   McDonald, J., J. Stone, and L. Liebelt. Searching for items in menus: The effect of organization and type of target. in Human Factors Society, 31st Annual Meeting. 1983.
23.   Nygren, E., "Between the clicks" Skilled Users Scanning of Pages. 1996.
24.   Norman, K. and J. Chin, The effect of tree structures on search in a hierarchical menu selection system. Behaviour and Information Technology, 1988. 7: p. 51–65.
25.   Campbell, D.J., Task Complexity: a review and analysis. Academy of Management Review, 1988(13): p. 40–52.
26.   Paap, K.R. and R.J. Roske-Hofstrand, The Optimal Number of Menu Options per Panel. Human Factors, 1986. 28.
27.   Mead, S., et al. Effects of Age and Training on World Wide Web Navigation Strategies. in Human Factors Society, Forty-First Annual Meeting. 1997.
28.   Administration on Aging, A Profile of Older Americans: 2001. 2002.
29.   White, H., et al., Surfing the net in Later Life: A Review of the Literature and Pilot Study of Computer Use and Quality of Life. The Journal of Applied Gerontology, 1999. 18: p. 358–378.
30.   Cochrane, J.D., Healthcare @ the Speed of Thought. Integrated Healthcare Reports, 1999: p. 16–17.
31.   Zaphiris, P. and R.D. Ellis. Mathematical Modeling of Age Differences in Hierarchical Information Systems. in ACM Conference on Universal Usability. 2000. Arlington.
32.   Zaphiris, P. and S.H. Kurniawan. Using Card Sorting Technique to Define the Best Web Hierarchy for Seniors. in CHI 2001 Conference on Human Factors in Computing Systems. 2001. Seattle.
33.   Hirashima, T., et al. Context-Sensitive Filtering for Browsing in Hypertext. in International Conference on Intelligent User Interfaces. 1998. New York: ACM Press.

Criteria for Usability of Accessible Web Sites

Barbara Leporini[1,2] and Fabio Paternò[1]

[1] ISTI - C.N.R.- Pisa, Italy
[2] Department of Computer Science, University of Pisa, Italy
barbara.leporini@guest.cnuce.cnr.it,
fabio.paterno@cnuce.cnr.it

Abstract. The application of appropriate web site design and evaluation methods help to ensure more usable and accessible web sites. While in the literature guidelines and evaluation methods for accessibility and usability are given and discussed separately, we aim to identify the relationships between these two concepts, in particular considering usability criteria for accessible web sites. In this work, we propose a set of usability criteria for accessible web sites in order to improve the navigability for special users, i.e. the vision impaired. The identification of the 16 criteria suggested herein was performed through empirical feedback, in which simple hypotheses were formulated, then tested. Subsequently, a systematic method was developed on the basis of the tests, resulting in a classification of the criteria according to usability aspects. The proposed criteria have been applied to an existing public administration web site.

1 Introduction

In recent years the use of web sites has been widening, and the number of users who access them is increasing more and more. For this reason it is important that the information be easily reachable by all, including people with disabilities. The difficulties in providing such universal access are matters that can be addressed through application of the principles of usability and accessibility. A web site is accessible if it can be used by everyone, with special care to people with disabilities. Usability is a multidimensional concept, since it can refer to several aspects and the importance of each aspect depends on the application domain. We can note that accessibility and usability are closely related, but while accessibility is aimed at making the website open to a much wider user population, usability is aimed at making the target population of the website more efficient and satisfied. Usually usability and accessibility issues are dealt separately. We want to identify their relationships: in particular we want to address the meaning of usability when accessible web sites for disabled users are considered. Often, when we refer to people with special needs, we tend to consider only accessibility issues, and to ignore those regarding usability. Technical accessibility is a pre-condition for usability. However, even if a site is theoretically accessible because it completely complies with the technical accessibility standards, it can still be very hard to use for people with disabilities, so that they could not succeed to reach their goals. In our work we consider, in particular, accessibility usability issues for people who are blind or who

N. Carbonell, C. Stephanidis (Eds.): User Interfaces for All, LNCS 2615, pp. 43–55, 2003.

have vision impairment. So, we have to consider the context in which these users work, i.e., browsers, particular devices (voice synthesizer or display Braille), particular programs (screen readers, screen magnifier) and so on. When interacting with a screen reader, how the information is located in the page code is very important because it is interpreted differently from when users read the page from the screen. Therefore, during the phase of criteria identification, some blind and vision impaired people were involved to test some selected examples.

In the paper, we first discuss the previous work in the area to better position our contribution. Next, we introduce our proposed criteria to improve usability of accessibility aspects, organizing them according to the standard usability definition. Then, we provide some examples resulting from the application of the criteria. Lastly, we provide some concluding remarks and indications for further work.

2   Related Work

Usability and accessibility are two concepts that can apply not only to web sites, but in general to all interactive systems. In literature several evaluation techniques have been proposed, some of which have been widely used. A review of evaluation methods with automatic support is available in [1], where a classification is proposed. In order to obtain a more usable and accessible web site, the developer has to follow well defined criteria and guidelines. Several usability guidelines have been proposed. Most accessibility issues are taken into account especially by W3C (World Wide Web Consortium) in the project Web Accessibility Initiative (WAI) [8]. They pointed out a number of recommendations and guidelines to promote web accessibility: "Web Content Accessibility Guidelines 1.0" (WAI 1999). The guidelines are intended for all Web content developers (page authors and site designers) and for developers of authoring tools. Such guidelines focus mainly on web accessibility aspects for people with disabilities, but, in our opinion, they do not consider much usability in this context. Hence, we intend to investigate those aspects which act on the organization and rendering of information in the page. Practically, we would like to extend the accessibility guidelines, aiming also to improve and facilitate the task performance. WebSAT (Web Static Analyzer) is a tool that verifies, referring to several guidelines, the HTML code of web pages, in order to point out potential usability problems [5]. This tool carries out a usability evaluation, but does not provide any suggestion to the developer. In the field of accessibility evaluation based on criteria and guidelines, there are some tools, such as Bobby [2] [3] and LIFT [4]. Although such tools find out accessibility problems, they show several drawbacks, such as rather long reports whose understanding is not easy for developers not experienced, no automatic support for the repair of the problems identified, identification of a limited number of potential aspect of non-accessibility, etc. This kind of tools find out accessibility problems, regardless of usability aspects for persons with some disability. In fact, although LIFT does partially support usability evaluation, we must state that such aspects are not sufficient to outline usability for special users (e.g., consistency of text and background colours, but not specifically for vision impaired people).

There are various international projects involving accessibility and usability of user interfaces for people with special needs. Stephanidis' group has long been working on user interfaces for all, by finding methods and tools allowing the development of unified user interfaces [6] [7]. Although guidelines and tools have been taken into account, they are mainly related to accessibility issues. In our approach, we want to consider not only accessibility, but also usability for accessible web sites, in the context of common web browsers.

3 Proposed Usability Criteria for Accessible Web Sites

In this section we discuss the proposed criteria to improve usability of accessibility in web sites. We suppose that a web site is already accessible (i.e., it complies with accessibility guidelines), and we describe those aspects of web pages that have an effect on navigability by users with special needs, i.e. blind or vision impairment users. We propose a set of criteria that can be used to support both design and evaluation. We have focused on web page code, taking into account HTML/XHTML language, JavaScript and Style Sheets (CSS). Accessibility guidelines advise not using Javascript because some browsers may not support them. Even though we share such principles, we aim to provide possible suggestions which also involve Javascripts. We would like to improve usability even when developers still intend to use scripts. This is important especially when the site already exists and it has to be modified in order to fix potential usability problems. Our goal is to create a semi-automatic environment supporting the designer rather than a completely automatic solution that would be too restrictive. In fact, developers may often decide not to repair web sites because of the effort required, which depends on the number of changes necessary, and sometimes requires a general reorganization of the web site.

In defining the proposed criteria, we aimed to identify the main aspects that can cause usability problems in accessible web sites. Then, for each criterion we provide more technical solutions to reach that goal, taking in account developers' choices in building the web site (e.g., frames or javascripts, ...). So, we refer to these aspects in terms of the associated criteria and to technical solution in terms of checkpoints.

3.1 How the Criteria Are Organized

We consider the aspects which can be potential usability problems, and checkpoints associated to those criteria. We have one first more general set of criteria, and a second one made up of checkpoints which are more detailed and precise. This organization differs from that of W3C accessibility guidelines which are arranged in 3 layers: guideline statements (i.e., general principles of accessibility); checkpoint list (i.e., how the guideline applies in typical content development scenarios); and a techniques section (i.e., implementations and examples for the checkpoints). Our approach aims to provide developers and evaluators with a more compact version of criteria in order to simplify their use.

Moreover, similarly to three priority levels assigned to checkpoints based on impacts on accessibility, we group our proposed criteria according to usability definition. More precisely, first of all we classify the proposed criteria depending on effectiveness, efficiency and satisfaction principles; secondly we catalogue them depending on the type of impact on the user interface.

Classifying criteria according to usability definition (ISO 9241) means that we identify those that are most important to reach the users' goals (effectiveness), those that allow reaching them more quickly (efficiency), and those that best satisfy users (satisfaction). Taking into account the type of users considered (i.e., users with special needs), we identify three levels of importance. We consider effectiveness criteria more important than those based on efficiency and satisfaction, because failure to satisfy such criteria could lead to users' not being able to accomplish their tasks. Thus, we consider more important effectiveness (level 1), then efficiency (level 2), and finally satisfaction (level 3).

The other parameter used to classify the criteria is the user interface aspect involved. A user interface is composed of two main components: the presentation, indicating how the user interface provides information to the user, and the dialogue, describing how the actions that users and system perform can be sequenced. According to this, we label with "a" the presentation criteria, and with "b" those of dialog.

3.2 The Proposed Accessibility Usability Criteria

In our work we determined 16 criteria to improve accessible web site usability for users who read web pages by a screen reader. As mentioned above, the criteria have been grouped in three sub-sets: effectiveness (5 criteria), efficiency (9 criteria) and satisfaction (3 criteria). For each criterion several checkpoints are proposed in order to indicate how it can be applied. To identify the criteria our study followed various phases:

- *Empirical phase*. First of all we have taken into account those aspects (see below) that can be potential navigational problems for special users who use a screen reader or magnifier. Then, according to those aspects, we have analysed HTML specifications and javascripts, to determine possible solutions.
- *Simulation phase*. We have built examples considered valid for our purpose, and we have tested them by a screen reader, i.e. by user context simulation. More precisely, since our hypothesis on possible criteria as solution to the problems mentioned, some simple application examples has been built and then tested by a certain number of blind users (including one of the authors).
- *Systematic phase*. Lastly, the chosen criteria have been classified by a systematic way, according to usability definition, UI components and page elements involved.

The main aspects we found, which can be potential navigational problems by using a screen reader or magnifier, are the following:

- *Lack of context* – reading through the screen reader or a magnifier the user can loose the overall context of the current page and can read only small portions of texts. For example, skipping from link to link by tab key, a blind user reads on the display braille or hears from synthesizer the link text, but not what is written before and after (e.g. ".pdf", "more details", etc.). A similar effect occurs when using a magnifier: in a certain moment, only a small portion of enlarged text can be visualized on the screen.
- *Information overloading* – The portions of the page that are static (links, frames with banners, etc.), overload the reading through a screen reader, because the user

has to read every thing almost every time, thus slowing down the navigation. For instance, let consider the case in which the user wishes to send a sms message; after having filled in the form and sent it, he wants to read the success or failure response. Often that output message is visualized in some position in the page, among other content which, probably, is the same as in the page before sending it. So the user could spend a lot of time to find it because he has to read the information before the message, even if is still the same of the previous page. An appropriate frame and link number, a specific content marking, a more organized hierarchical structure of pages, can be possible solutions to this issue.

- *Excessive sequentiality in reading the information* – the command for navigating and reading can constrain the user to follow sequentially the content of a page. Thus, it is important to introduce mechanisms to ease the identification of precise parts in the page. An example is the result page generated by a search engine. Usually, in the top of such pages, there are several links, advertisements, the search fields and buttons, and so on, and then the search results begin. Furthermore, if the web pages contains more information blocks (e.g., paragraphs, short news, review lists, etc.), in order to read a specific block, the user has to read also the previous ones. A careful partitioning or structuring of the content could allow special users to find more quickly the desired information.

As result of this process 16 criteria have been identified grouped in three sub-sets.

To identify each criterion we use the format I.J.L where: I denotes the criterion kind, that is 1 for effectiveness, 2 for efficiency, or 3 for satisfaction; J is a progressive number to enumerate the criteria; L can be *a* (presentation) or *b* (dialogue) to indicate the aspect type to which the criterion acts. Moreover, the checkpoint associated to a certain criterion is identified by adding a forth index, thus obtaining expressions such as I.J.L.K, where the first part indicates the criterion to which the checkpoint is referred, and K numbers checkpoints for a same criterion.

Table 1. List of criteria classed according to the objects they affect

Objects	Criteria
Links	1.2.a, 2.1.b, 2.4.b, 2.5.b, 2.7.b, 2.8.b, 2.9.b, 3.1.b, 3.3.a
Frames	1.1.b, 1.4.b, 2.1.b, 2.2.b, 2.3.a, 2.8.b
Forms, buttons and fields	1.5.a, 2.4.b, 2.5.b, 2.6.a, 3.3.a
Pages	1.1.b, 1.3.a, 2.3.a, 2.8.b, 2.9.b, 3.1.a, 3.2.b
Sites	1.1.b, 1.3.a, 1.5.b, 2.7.b, 2.8.b, 3.1.b
Java scripts	1.4.b, 3.1.b, 3.3.a

3.2.1 Effectiveness Criteria

We consider a criterion belonging to the effectiveness sub-set if it is important to reach the user goal. This means that if it is not adopted then users could not be able to accomplish their tasks because they would encounter difficulties to identify important information.

1.1.b.   Logical partition of information.
   Use of markers or frames or headings to group texts, links, forms, etc. according to a logical division; e.g. frames "index", "search", "search results", etc.

1.2.a.   Proper link text.

Singling out of texts that would barely be used in links. E.g., "click here", "download", "file.zip". We must warn the designer that such texts can make the site of scarce usability, because they are not very clear or they are too "poor".

1.3.a.   Loading of proper style sheets.

Browsers can load specific sheets for different items using a particular tag (@media types). E.g., for braille display, braille printer, speech synthesiser, etc. This enables the definition of a style sheet for each requirement, thus improving the layout of web pages.

1.4.b.   Messages and dynamic data management.

A remarkable difficulty that special user meet is represented by yielding of confirmation or error messages about accomplished operations, or by information extracted from a database and showed not properly, such as in the middle of the page, among a lot of other information and links. This actually forces users to spend some time and execute some commands of the screen reader before reaching and reading these messages, not to mention that they could even fail at all.

1.5.a.   Terminological Consistency and layout.

Button features have a very important impact over the user: it is important that all the pages of the whole web site do not use different labels for buttons performing the same function (e.g. OK/Yes, quit/exit, next/forward), and that all pages have the same layout (e.g., dimension, form and colour). These two aspects have an important meaning both for users of screen readers with speech synthesiser or braille display, and for visually impaired users, who mainly rely upon dimension/colour references.

3.2.2 Efficiency Criteria

An efficiency criterion is a rule which allows users to find the desired information more quickly. We consider this rule less important then effectiveness, because if such criterion is not satisfied, users can still perform their task, although it may take more time.

2.1.b.   Number of links and frames.

It is important that a page does not contain too many links and frames, this makes difficult for the user to skim through all them.

2.2.b.   Proper name of the frames.

All frames should have a name and that the name should be a proper one. E.g., frames with names such as "top frame", "mid frame", "Left frame", are not helpful for the user. On the other hand, names such as "index", "search", "content", can make easier for the users to reach their goal, because of the possibility of skipping frames reduces the amount of information to read.

2.3.a.   Location of the navigation bar.

The so-called navigation links (i.e. the links appearing on each page and enabling users to reach the main parts of the site) represent a source of delay and inefficiency for the screen reader user. Since such links appear on each page (and often even twice), the user who is forced to read the contents in an almost sequential way (by means of a speech synthesiser or a braille display) is every time compelled to skim them, without being able to interpret the contents of the current page. Helping in a more logical and organized development of this aspect can increase navigation efficiency for these users. We need therefore to select criteria making navigation easier for people using a speech synthesiser (e.g., by graphic and/or text references or frames), and, on the other hand, for visually impaired people (e.g., by different colours and dimensions).

2.4.b.   Importance levels of elements.

It is possible to assign different importance levels to buttons, fields and links, so that, one reaches at first the most important, and later the less important, regardless of their location on the page. This helps the user to find quickly the needed buttons and links. E.g., in the case of filling in a form, it would be useful to reach, by tab, first the compulsory fields and later on the optional ones.

2.5.b.   Assignment of hot keys.

It is advisable to assign hot keys to the most important buttons, links and fields, so that the user is able to reach them quickly through a simple key combination. We classify this aspect among the "efficiency" criteria because it enables reaching an object more quickly, but we could also consider it within the "satisfaction" group, mainly for those users accustomed to using a lot of key combinations.

2.6.a.   Proper formatting of forms.

In forms dealing with several groups of data, we must properly lay out group titles and fields to achieve greater clearness, e.g., simply by using the return tag in the proper place.

2.7.b.   "Last update" section.

In sites dealing with frequent updating of information and/or new resources to download, we can help the user to find more rapidly the new elements by providing a specific section listing the new elements by date, sparing the user the trouble of going all over the site.

2.8.b.   Indexing of contents.

In pages containing information of different kind (paragraphs, news, etc), we can help the user to find information more efficiently by indexing and pointing out the different blocks, so sparing the need of a page skimming.

2.9.b.   Navigation links.

In order to reach more easily some location of the page (or of the site) we can insert local navigation links, referring to bookmarks in the ambit of the page (e.g., go to content, go to top, etc.).

3.2.3 Satisfaction Criteria

Satisfaction criteria help to produce a web site being more pleasant to navigate during the page visit or the site exploration.

3.1.b.   Addition of a short sound.

Associating a short sound to different elements and in different multimedia environment, can make the user more "satisfied". E.g., associating each page with a short sound indicating when the loading of the page is completed, so sparing him the need of repetitive control of the state bar. Associating different sounds to different links makes easier to identify the link type during the skimming.

3.2.a.   Colour of text and background.
This aspect can make easier the navigation of visually impaired people who, with a particular type of contrast, may feel less tired by navigation. It is therefore advised to avoid colour combinations giving a poor contrast.

3.3.a.   Magnifying at passing by mouse.
The use of this feature can help people with a good visual residue to better focus the pointed object.

3.3 Criteria and Checkpoints

As mentioned above, for each criterion more checkpoints are proposed in order to indicate how it can be applied and to facilitate developer's task. A checkpoint is a specific fragment of code. While for a certain criterion only one checkpoint may exist, for another there could be several. More precisely, the criterion application can differ from web site implementation (e.g., usage of frames or not). By reason of space, we can not report all checkpoints for every criteria. In the table below two examples of criteria-checkpoints association are showed.

Table 2. Examples of checkpoints associated to criteria

Criteria	Check points	Code
$C_{1,1,b}$ Logical grouping of information	$C_{1,1,b,1}$ Marking blocks	`<a title=""> </a>`
	$C_{1,1,b,2}$ Grouping by headings	`<h1> ... </h1>` `<h2> ... </h2>`
	$C_{1,1,b,3}$ Grouping by frames	`<frame name="" title=""`
$C_{2,1,a}$ Navigation bar identification	$C_{2,1,a,1}$ Marking the begin and the end	`<a title="navigation begin"> </a>` `<a title="navigation end"> </a>`

	$C_{2,1,a,2}$ Using iframe tag	`<IFRAME title="navlink"`
		`name="navlink" src="navlink.htm"`
		`width="" height=""`
		`frameborder="1"> </iframe>`

	$C_{2,1,a,3}$ Using frame	`<FRAME name="navlink"` `src="navlink.htm" scrolling="no">`

In the example showed in the table we have indicated criteria and check points by using full notation $C_{i,j,l}$. As mentioned in 3.2, to identify every criterion we use the notation like I.J.L (where I denotes the criterion kind, J is a progressive number to enumerate the criteria and L can be *a* or *b)*, and checkpoints associated to a certain criterion are marked with I.J.L.K (where K denotes checkpoint numbers for a same criterion).

4 Some Examples

In this section we want to show some examples of usability issues in accessible web sites detected when users interact through the screen reader Jaws. The examples shown in this section are taken from the web site of the Florence City Council. This web site provides information and services to citizens. We considered "The services" section, paying particular attention to the social security department. Moreover, this is the first empirical test in order to assess how developers deal with usability when developing accessible web sites and how the criteria are suitable to apply to an existing web site. For each example we show how the page is visualized on the screen, how that page is read by the screen reader before and after our suggested changes, and the code fragments involved. In the table showing how the web page is interpreted by the screen reader, the italic text with [1] indicates changes, while the italic text with [2] refers to the parts that are read by the synthesizer, but not visualized in the web page.

4.1 Significant Text: Names of Frames

An important issue of usability for special users who read the web pages by a screen reader is the text associated to links and name attribute of frames. The reason is that while exploring a page by a synthesizer or display braille, the user could not have a general view of the content. Therefore, if the name of frames or the text of links are significant, users can better orient themselves.

For instance, often the names of frames are like SX, DX, CENTRAL, MAIN, etc., and so they are not much meaningful. This is particularly important when users read by a screen reader. For a better usability the name of a frame is important for an easier understanding about both the page structure and the frame content. Usually this is not important, because the names of frames are not shown in the page visualized in the browser and so developers do not pay attention to them.

If we consider the web page in Fig.1 where services offered to people by city Council of Florence are listed. The structure of that page is composed of several frames which are not entirely visible.

In that page information and links to skip to other sections, are logically grouped in more nested frames. The picture shows how the page content is rendered on the screen. A screen reader reads that content in different way. In order to try to understand how the synthesizer or display braille considers the page, we provide a fragment of the web page text read by the synthesizer (see Fig. 2). As we can observe, the screen reader identifies clearly begin and end of every frame, thus the use of appropriate names is important.

As we can see in the figure, the screen reader distinguishes the frames of the page, and also their beginning and ending. Therefore it is useful to have significant names. Note that "main" frame is not very important, because it is actually used to contain the others.

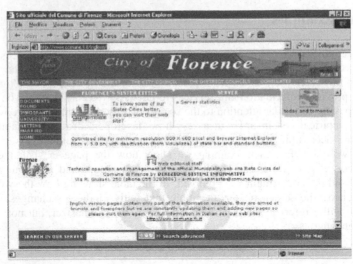

Fig. 1. Page of web site of Florence's Council where services offered to citizens are listed (http://www.comune.fi.it/inglese/)

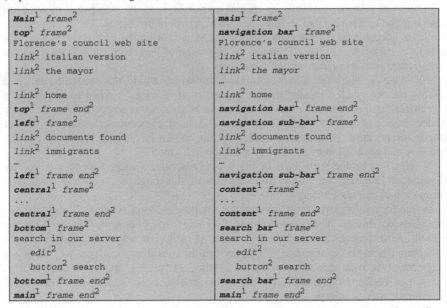

Fig. 2. Fragment of web page content read by the screen reader: The left part shows the reading of the page before changes, and the right part after the changes

The user can read the content of the page in sequential way, or skipping directly to a certain frame. In fact, some screen readers (like Jaws), have special commands to list available frames, and to activate one of them. The user can choose one frame access it. For instance, selecting "search bar", the user accesses the search frame so that he is able to find the search field more quickly.

In order to show the code related to names of frames, we consider the fragment of the web page taken into account. The code of the page associated to "main" frame and to others is in the Fig. 3. In particular, we consider the FRAME tags: first of all, the presence of both NAME and TITLE attributes , then their content.

```
<html>…<frameset cols="*,750,*">
<frame name="main"¹ src="main3ing1.htm" title="main"¹
frameborder="0"> <noframes>…</noframes> </frameset> </html>
<html>…<frameset rows="84,*">
<frame name="navigation bar" title="navigation bar"¹
frameborder="0" scrolling="NO" noresize src="top5ing.htm">
<frameset rows="*,29" > <frame name="content" title="content"¹
src="home3ing.htm" scrolling="yes" frameborder="0">

    <frame name="search bar" title="search bar"¹ scrolling="NO"
noresize src="bottom2ing.htm"
frameborder="0"><noframes>…</noframes> </frameset> </frameset>
</html>
```

Fig. 3. Code of web page at http://www.comune.fi.it/inglese/ (top), and at http://www.comune.fi.it/inglese/main3ing1.htm (bottom)

In order to evaluate the frame name we could use a dictionary in which the evaluator can store unsuitable terms, such as SX, DX, CENTRAL, MAIN, etc.. Using an external dictionary we can have two advantages: first, the evaluator can add new terms customizing the evaluation, second, there may exist different dictionaries for different languages.

4.2 Significant Text: Link Content

A similar problem occurs with links: links like "CLICK HERE", ".PDF", or "GO TO PARAGRAPH" are not very useful. Often the link text is referred to context so that if we consider links separately, we might not be able to understand the related content.

A user who cannot see the screen, many times uses the Tab key to search in the page the link wanted without reading the whole content. Another way to select a specific link is to use a particular command of the screen reader to open the link list. In both cases, the user reads only the text of the links, so a significant content is important.

In Fig. 4 an instance of this issue is showed. In the pictures there are the list of links associated to each topic belonging to an online guide organized in more paragraphs. There is one graphical link before every paragraph item. Since the links are images, the use of ALT is necessary. In the original version all links have the same text: 'go to paragraph'. In the fixed version, the ALT attributes contain also the name of paragraph (e.g., 'go to paragraph presentazione').

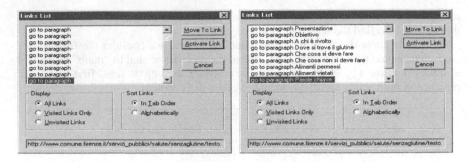

Fig. 4. List of links (produced by a specific screen reader command) available at
http://www.comune.firenze.it/servizi_pubblici/salute/senzaglutine/.
On the left the original version, on the right the fixed version.

In order to improve the usability of links, we can suggest some solutions. First, for graphical links, we have to apply the alt attribute, putting a significant description which has to refer to the meaning of the link rather than describing the image in itself. Second, for textual links we can change the entire text, or we can use ALT or TITLE attributes. This second alternative may be used if developers do not want to modify the writings visualized on the screen. In fact, the text associated to alt or title is read by the screen reader, and it is visualized in the status bar by passing mouse over links.

Reading the web page by a screen reader, the original links are like '$link^2$ *go to paragraph*[1]', while those modified are like '$link^2$ *go to paragraph presentazione*[1]'. So, in the original page there are too many links with similar text, such as 'go to paragraph'. In presence of many links of this kind, if users skip from link to link by using the tab key or by a special command of the screen reader which gives a link list, they read similar texts without knowing the context to which they refer. Therefore, in order to know which is the appropriate link to choose the correct guide chapter, a user has to explore the page reading line by line.

In order to solve this problem, we should modify the text of the links by adding the name of the chapter to which the link points (e.g., presentazione, obiettivi, etc.) to 'go to paragraph'. This effect can be obtained changing the link text, or using the ALT and TITLE attributes. This second possibility, among other things, allows two rendering: one visual and one for the screen reader. In our example, the links are graphics, therefore we have to modify the alt and title attribute text: on the screen the links are still graphics, while the screen reader reads the text 'go to paragraph presentazione', etc.. So, for each link the evaluation has to check if the text is non-recommended. Similar to frames, we suppose there exist external dictionaries in which non-recommended terms are listed. The evaluation criterion extracts text of links - including ALT and TITLE value - and checks they do not belong to that terms.

5 Conclusions and Future Works

In recent years there has been an increasing interest in accessibility and usability issues, because it is more and more important that the information be easy reachable from all. In this paper we have combined both concepts, and in particular we have considered usability for accessible web sites. Therefore we proposed criteria in order to improve user navigability, from potential usability problems encountered reading the web pages using special devices. We have identified 16 usability criteria for accessible web sites which we partitioned in three sub-set in according to usability aspects: effectiveness, efficiency and satisfaction. Proposed criteria can be used both in the design and the evaluation phase. Some examples that show how criteria can be applied and how they can be used to improve a site have been discussed. Since evaluating and repairing web sites by using the proposed criteria requires several efforts and a lot of time, a tool supporting this activity can be a valid help for evaluators and developers. Thus, we have started the implementation of a tool supporting the criteria introduced in the paper.

```
... <A target=content
href="http://www.comune.firenze.it/.../testo.htm#presentazione"> <IMG height=19
alt="go to paragraph Presentazione"¹ src="sommario_file/spunta2.gif" width=20
border=0></A> Presentazione <BR> <A target=content
href="http://www.comune.firenze.it/.../testo.htm#obiettivo"> <IMG
height=19 alt="go to paragraph Obiettivo"¹ src="sommario_file/spunta2.gif"
width=20 border=0></A> Obiettivo <br>
...
```

Fig. 5. HTML code of online guide web page; the piece of code corresponding to contents evaluated and already changed is in italic bolded

References

[1] Ivory M. Y. and Hearst M. A. (2001). "The state of the art in automating usability evaluation of user interfaces". ACM Computing Surveys, 33(4), pp. 470–516, December 2001.

[2] Rowan M., Gregor P., Sloan D. and Booth P. (2000). "Evaluating Web Resources for Disability Access". Fourth Annual ACM Conference on Assistive Technologies (ASSETS00), pp. 80–84, ACM, 2000.

[3] CAST: Center for Applied Special Technology. Bobby accessibility evaluation tool for web sites. http://www.cast.org/bobby

[4] UsableNet. LIFT, accessibility evaluation tool. http://www.usablenet.com/lift

[5] Nist Web Metrics: http://zing.ncsl.nist.gov/WebTools/tech.html

[6] Stephanidis, C., Akoumianakis, D., Sfyrakis, M., & Paramythis, A. (1998). Universal accessibility in HCI: Process-oriented design guidelines and tool requirements. In C. Stephanidis & A. Waern (Eds.), Proceedings of the 4th ERCIM Workshop on "User Interfaces for All", Stockholm, Sweden, 19–21 October (15 pages).

[7] Grammenos, D., Akoumianakis, D., & Stephanidis, C. (2000). Integrated Support for Working with Guidelines: The Sherlock Guideline Management System. International Journal of Interacting with Computers, special issue on "Tools for Working with Guidelines", 12 (3), 281–311.

[8] WAI Accessibility Guidelines, Web Accessibility Initiative, World Wide Web Consortium, 1999. Accessible at http:// www. w3. org/ wai

Making Accessibility Guidelines Usable

Alexis Donnelly[1] and Mark Magennis[2]

[1] Department of Computer Science, Trinity College Dublin,
Alexis.Donnelly@cs.tcd.ie
[2] National Council for the Blind of Ireland
mark.magennis@ncbi.ie

Abstract. Accessibility guidelines are aimed at all those with a role and responsibility in the procurement and development of IT products and services. However, many important members of this diverse audience find these guidelines difficult to use. The result is products with in-built accessibility barriers. This paper describes the structure and presentation of a new set of Irish national IT accessibility guidelines. Drawing lessons from past failures, it describes how this structure was developed. The development involved extensive consultation with prospective users of the guidelines, in an inclusive user-centred process. Preliminary feedback at this early stage indicates that the new structure is effective, even in the absence of legislation. The account underlines the importance of usability in creating useful resources of this type.

1   Introduction and Background

The need for IT-based products and services to be made accessible for people with disabilities is firmly stated in European Union and Irish Government policy [1] [2]. In February 2000, the Programme for Prosperity and Fairness, a national agreement between government and other social partners, called for the National Disability Authority (NDA) to develop a national set of IT-related accessibility guidelines to be used by government departments in implementing their commitments [3]. The guidelines would provide a focus for future development and would be referenced by future legislation. This paper concerns the development of these guidelines.

Simply providing guidelines does not guarantee that they will be followed. In the Irish case, a previous attempt to impose accessibility standards in publication guidelines for public sector websites [4] had resulted in a poor compliance rate. There are a number of reasons why guidelines are not followed. These include perceived conflicts with other guidelines and standards; difficulty in understanding or interpreting the guidelines; lack of knowledge about how compliance can be achieved; or simply lack of motivation. In short, guidelines are often not in a form that is most usable for the audience. Indeed, the most recognised set of accessibility guidelines, the Web Content Accessibility Guidelines (WCAG) 1.0 from the Web Accessibility Initiative (WAI), has been criticised for being difficult for much of its potential audience to understand [5], [6]. Consequently, the requirements document for the next version of the WCAG includes the provision for understanding by a wider, less technical audience [7].

N. Carbonell, C. Stephanidis (Eds.): User Interfaces for All, LNCS 2615, pp. 56–67, 2003.
© Springer-Verlag Berlin Heidelberg 2003

Mindful of the reasons for past failures and backed by new policy developments, the NDA took the step of commissioning a commercial user-centred design consultancy, Frontend Usability Engineering Ltd., to develop a usable set of Irish national IT accessibility guidelines. The resulting design of the guidelines is intended to tackle many of the problems that prevent guidelines being adopted. This has been achieved, chiefly, by following an inclusive user-centred development process. This paper describes that process and the resulting content and structure.

2   The Development Process

An inclusive user-centred development process was followed by the principle guideline authors, supported by an advisory group of accessibility experts[1]. This comprised the following stages:

- An initial scoping and resource identification phase
- Interviews with IT end users having various impairments
- An audience analysis and interviews with prospective users of the
- The development of an appropriate structure for the guidelines
- Audience review and user testing of the structure
- The development of content
- Reviews of the content by external domain experts

2.1   Scoping and Resource Identification

The first task was to decide which technologies the Irish IT guidelines should cover, draw up a plan of consultation and undertake a literature search to collect and study existing guidelines and sources of information. A scoping workshop identified some important stakeholders in the development process for public sector IT products, established audience and end user groups and drew up a preliminary plan for further work. The target list of technologies included websites and online applications; public access terminals and information displays; card-based access technologies; personal computer hardware; personal computer operating systems and software; broadcasting and multimedia services; digital interactive television; telecommunications devices and telephone-based services; mobile devices and emerging applications.

2.2   End User Interviews

Fifteen end users, having various impairments, were interviewed using an informal semi-structured questionnaire to enquire about their experiences with the different

---

[1] See http://accessit.nda.ie/about_these_guidelines.html for details of authors and members of the advisory group.

types of technologies. Interviews with end users having various impairments were used to identify the practical barriers encountered by these groups using current and future IT products and services. This was the first involvement of end user groups and they continued to be involved throughout the development process. The main aim of gathering this information was to humanise the guidelines by including real-life descriptions and anecdotes, explaining some of the practical problems that impaired end users have and why these occur. This immediately puts a designer into the user's position, giving them insight and understanding about what they are trying to achieve. This make it clear how following the guidelines will help support the goal of social inclusion, which promotes "buy-in" and results in better design.

2.3 Audience Analysis and Interviews

The end users of the technologies are not themselves the audience of the guidelines. The guidelines are intended for use by designers, developers and procurers. It was essential to know the audience, their background and their needs, because difficulty in understanding guidelines is a major problem which the design of these guidelines was intended to overcome. In practice, accessibility guidelines are often written solely for a technical audience. However, there are other important, but less technically oriented, actors in the IT procurement and development process.

The audience analysis began with a review of the typical development process for relevant public sector IT products and services, aiming to identify the major roles involved. This process review identified three major audience groups: Developers, Procurers and Testers/Evaluators. Interviews were carried out with representatives of each of these groups, in order to identify their likely backgrounds, expectations, specific needs and the contexts in which they would use accessibility guidelines.

Seven public sector procurers (mostly middle ranking civil servants with some technical knowledge) were interviewed. They indicated a positive attitude to including accessibility requirements into a Request For Tenders (RFT). Their principal requirements would be assistance in drafting the RFT and then in assessing compliance with the agreed contract. The guidelines would have to be closely aligned with relevant policy and legislation.

Four tender writers and five IT project managers (typically senior project or account managers in a development company) were interviewed. They also indicated a positive attitude to the provision of usable guidelines since this would provide a "more level playing pitch" against which their bid could be assessed. Their main concerns were to quickly gain an accurate overview of accessibility problems and the implications of compliance to avoid them. Clear, plain English explanations would be extremely useful and the complete set of guidelines should be available in a print formatted version.

Seven developers (typically programmers or engineers) were interviewed, These also indicated a positive attitude to guidelines. However, they stressed that guidelines should be practical. Detailed technical guidance should be available with illustrative examples including the reasoning behind them. Particular solutions should not necessarily be imposed, since these would rarely fit their specific development context, but the functional requirements demanded of a solution should be clear.

These interviews revealed that the main delivery channels of relevance for the public sector in the foreseeable future were websites, information kiosks, telecommunications and desktop application software. Other technologies, such as digital interactive television or mobile devices were thought to be of little relevance.

One of the main findings was that people wanted information that was tailored to their role and the task that they were doing. For example, procurers and project managers didn't want to be bogged down in detailed technical information aimed at programmers, but wanted practical answers to questions like "How do I specify accessibility requirements in an RFT?" or "How do I assess a proposed design that has not yet been built as a working prototype?". It emerged that the role of the procurement manager in the public body and the project manager in the developer organisation are often very similar and there is a need to communicate based on a common understanding. Both therefore require the same information. In general, people wanted interpretation and direction, rather than just rules. As for testing and quality assurance, although it was felt to be very important, there was rarely anyone assigned to it as a specific role and it was generally done in an ongoing fashion, throughout the process, rather than as a discrete stage. This had important implications for the kind of information that was given.

The results of these interviews were used to inform and guide the later design and development of the guidelines. Like the end users, audience representatives continued to be involved throughout the development process.

2.4 Development and Testing of the Structure

Based on the findings of the audience analysis and the project aims agreed at the scoping phase, an initial structure for the guidelines was developed. After a number of internal iterations, a draft website was created. This implemented the initial structure but only included a small amount of representative content, the remaining content being substituted by placeholder descriptions of the intended information. This was sufficient to evaluate in a stakeholder workshop and a set of user tests.

The draft structure was presented at a one day workshop of some twenty individuals, consisting of prospective users, end users, domain experts and other public sector stakeholders. This workshop was used to gauge initial reaction to the approach taken, obtain feedback on some early presentation ideas and explore possibilities for publicity and dissemination. The resulting discussions helped to refine many aspects of the design further.

Task based user tests were carried out with a representative sample group, comprising one public sector procurer, four IT project managers, one tender writer and four IT developers. There was a variable level of accessibility awareness within the group, mostly limited, but with two of the developers being regular users of the WCAG. Each user was given a number of typical scenarios in which they might need to use the guidelines. For example, developers were asked "You have been told that your company's Internet kiosk is inaccessible to people who are blind. Find out what extra development work will be involved in fixing this and meeting the NDA guidelines". These scenarios formed a context in which the users accessed the guidelines in a naturalistic way. All sessions were observed and follow up interviews were used to gauge reactions and opinions.

The findings of the user tests resulted in major changes to the structure of the guidelines as well as improvements to the intended content.

2.5 Development and Review of the Content

Once the structure had been fixed, work began on writing the bulk of the content. This relied heavily on the sources which had been identified in the initial scoping phase, but pulled in much information gleaned along the way from end users, developers and other stakeholders. Content was drafted by a number of authors, then edited by a single author, to achieve the goals of simplicity and consistency.

Lastly, the final draft content was reviewed by a panel of invited external domain experts, to ensure technical accuracy. Each expert concentrated on a single technology area, reviewing each guideline and all the supporting information. On the basis of these reviews, the content was updated prior to publication.

3   Description of the Content

Having agreed a set of four technology channels to produce accessibility guidelines for, and having defined the background and needs of the different audience types, it was possible to decide what information was required and determine an appropriate style and format. It was clear from the literature study, audience analysis and user tests that the following types of information were required:

- Introductory information about accessibility, from the end user's point of view
- An outline of relevant legislation and policy, with references
- Information about how to go about designing for accessibility
- Guidance on how to use the guidelines, broken down by role and focussed on specific tasks
- An easy-to-use printable checklist for each set of guidelines
- A simple, detailed definition and explanation of each guideline, to ensure correct interpretation and understanding
- A rationale for each guideline, to provide motivation
- Guidance on how to achieve compliance, with examples where appropriate
- Guidance on how to test for compliance, at any stage of development

The initial intention was not to create new guidelines, but to refer to existing authoritative guidelines and standards, adding explanation and help where appropriate as aids to understanding for the different audience types. This approach was intended to avoid exacerbating the known problem of conflicting guidelines and to avoid doing unnecessary work by creating guidelines where perfectly good ones existed already.

However, with the exception of the Web, in which a single de facto standard set of guidelines, the WCAG, existed and were referenced by both EU and Irish Government policy, it was not possible to identify single, authoritative sources which stood out above all the rest. That is not to say authoritative and useful guidelines do not exist for these other technologies. Indeed, many organisations such as Trace (http://trace.wisc.edu), IBM (http://www-3.ibm.com/able), Stakes (http://www.stakes.fi) and Tiresias (http://www.tiresias.org) have produced excellent guidelines and resources. There are also many relevant standards produced by organisations such as ISO, ANSI, ETSI and CEN. However, none of these are as comprehensive and widely adopted as the WCAG, so it was difficult to choose any particular instances as the ones that should be adopted within Ireland.

Another factor was the need for consistency and similarity across the different technology channels. The audience analysis had revealed that IT products and services often include technologies of more than one type. For example, many information kiosks use HTML for their user interfaces, so their design should follow the guidelines for both public access terminals and Websites. Similarly, a public telephone is a combination of a telecommunications device and a public access terminal. For this reason, it was felt that adopting four totally different sets of guidelines, each written from a different perspective and presented in a different way, would confuse the audience and seriously reduce usability. Instead, it was decided that, with the exception of the WCAG, completely new guidelines should be written, using a common, consistent style and format. Indeed, in the case of the WCAG it was decided that, even though they should be adopted with their meaning unchanged, they would be recast to fit the new style and format as closely as possible.

4   Description of the Structure

Initial ideas about an appropriate structure were influenced by Vanderheiden's work on priority setting for universal design [8]. Vanderheiden proposed a set of basic components of universal usability:

- Perceivability of presented information
- Operability
- Navigability of information and controls
- Understability of content

Vanderheiden also outlined the following four dimensions that can be taken into account when prioritising the application of universal design principles:

- *Severity of impact*: The number of people who will be negatively impacted by non-compliance and how severely.
- *Independence vs. co-dependence*: The extent to which users can be expected to have help available to them.
- *Impact on efficiency or urgency of use*: Whether functions are reversible or need to be carried out quickly.
- *Ease of implementation*: Referred to as a "pseudo dimension" since it can often work against universal usability.

Although Vanderheiden described these dimensions as ways to prioritise design principles, they can equally well be used as ways of organising the kind of information that was to go into the guidelines. Indeed, some of these dimensions had emerged in the audience analysis. For example, some interviewees had stated that they would prefer information to be organised in usage-based sections – operating controls, perceiving output, understanding content, etc. – similar to Vanderheiden's basic components. At least one developer held the view that the guidelines themselves should be organised according to ease of implementation (which Vanderheiden warned against).

When considering which organisational structures to use, it was noted that other accessibility guidelines use many different structures for different types and levels of information. Indeed, a given body of information can often be accessed through multiple structures. For example, the WCAG 1.0 consists of 66 technique-oriented checkpoints, such as "Provide redundant text links for each active region of a server-side image map" [9]. These are organised using two orthogonal classifications. On the home page, the checkpoints are organised under 14 guidelines – goal oriented categories, such as "Provide equivalent alternatives to auditory and visual content". In the checklist, the checkpoints are organised under 3 priority levels, relating to severity of impact. A given guideline may include checkpoints of any priority level. Both organisations serve different purposes. For example, the checklist is the preferred access point for many developers, since the priority breakdown is closer to their own priorities than the guideline categorisation.

An analysis of six existing sets of accessibility guidelines, including the WCAG 1.0, revealed the following organisational structures used for the guidelines and supporting information:

- Severity of impact
- Technology types and subtypes
- Information types (rules, techniques, examples, resources, etc.)
- End user activities (perceiving, operating, etc.)
- End user impairment types
- Accessibility principles (e.g. device independence)
- Audience roles and subroles
- Relevant statutory requirements impacted
- Industry sectors
- Project phases
- Organisational maturity

Seven of these are used in the final structure of the Irish IT Accessibility guidelines. Some as primary ways of structuring the site, others simply for presenting the text within a particular section. The audience analysis had revealed that users' primary considerations were the technology they were dealing with and the purpose for which they needed information (determined by their role). Therefore, in the first draft, the information was broken down at the top level by both technology and role. The home page provided a link into each technology section (Web, Telecoms, etc.) and a link into each role (Procurer, Developer, etc.). The intention of this was to cater equally for both role-focussed and technology-focused users. Each role or technology section provided links to items of information (introduction, checklist, etc.). The user could choose to narrow the focus further by selecting a role (if they were in a technology section) or a technology (if they were in a role section). A data base-driven design was used to generate virtual pages based on the choices made. For example, a person choosing *Procurer* on the home page, then *Web* and *Introduction* on the Procurer page, would be given an introduction to web accessibility tailored to the procurer role, with navigation links to further information which would be similarly tailored.

User tests revealed that this choice and customisation of information was not successful. Although the role- and task-based information was generally welcomed, users found it difficult to build a mental model of the site organisation due to the overly-complex design, and therefore had difficulty navigating. This, and many other issues, were tackled in the final version, the home page of which is shown in figure 1.

Home | Web | Telecoms | Public Access Terminals | Application Software |
A General Accessibility Process

Guidelines for accessible products and services, including:

- Descriptions of high level accessibility goals and the difficulties faced by users
- Prioritised guidelines for each technology
- Motivation and justification for each guideline
- Guidance on design techniques and testing methods

Guidelines are available for the following technologies:

Web	Telecoms
Websites, Online Applications, Online Forms.	Fixed line phones, mobile phones, IVR Systems.
Public Access Terminals	Application Software
ATMs, Information kiosks, Ticket vending machines, Information displays, Card readers.	Windows, Macintosh, Unix, Linux, Java

What is Accessibility?
Who is affected and how. The benefits of accessibility for users and service providers.

A general process for creating accessible products and services
An inclusive design process that can be applied to any technology. Explains who does what.

Legislation and Policy
Irish legislation and government policy relating to IT accessibility.

Fig. 1. Home page of Irish IT accessibility guidelines

The home page briefly describes the content of the site, then provides links to each technology section (but no role-based links). Following this are links to general information on accessibility (what it is and how to achieve it); guidance on how to follow an inclusive, user-centred design process so that a new product or service will be as accessible as possible; and relevant legislation and policy.

On each technology page, a short introductory paragraph defining what is covered is followed by a link to the guidelines themselves. This provides a sufficiently quick route to the guidelines for experienced users. Figure 2 illustrates this design for the case of telecoms. Also provided are links to a general introduction to accessibility of that technology (organised by end-user impairment) and a summary testing checklist (one of the most common requests received in the audience analysis).

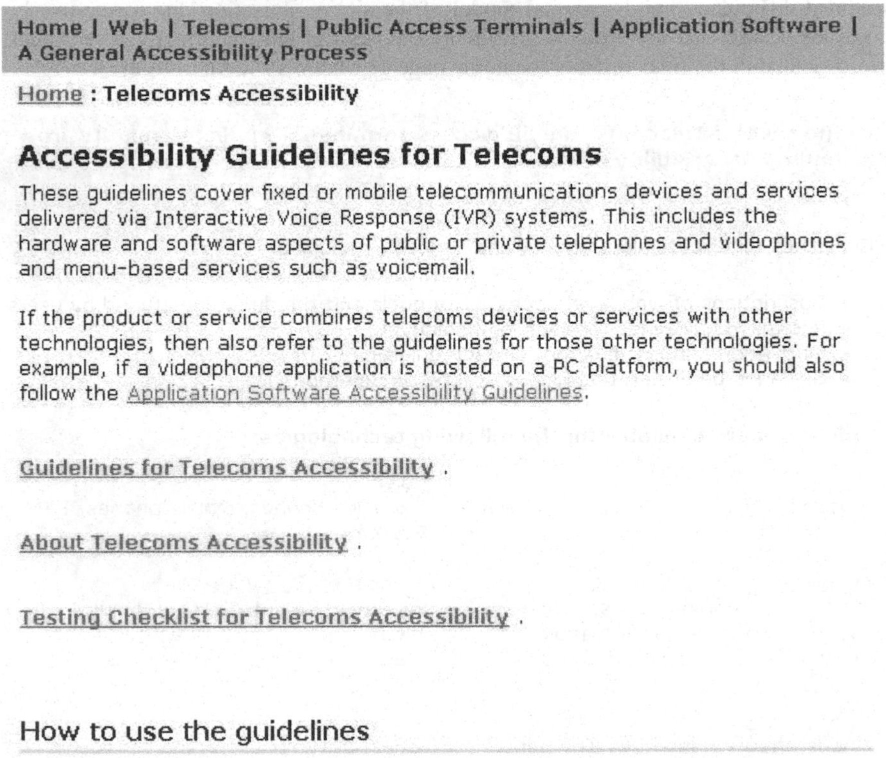

Home | Web | Telecoms | Public Access Terminals | Application Software | A General Accessibility Process

Home : Telecoms Accessibility

Accessibility Guidelines for Telecoms

These guidelines cover fixed or mobile telecommunications devices and services delivered via Interactive Voice Response (IVR) systems. This includes the hardware and software aspects of public or private telephones and videophones and menu-based services such as voicemail.

If the product or service combines telecoms devices or services with other technologies, then also refer to the guidelines for those other technologies. For example, if a videophone application is hosted on a PC platform, you should also follow the Application Software Accessibility Guidelines.

Guidelines for Telecoms Accessibility .

About Telecoms Accessibility .

Testing Checklist for Telecoms Accessibility .

How to use the guidelines

Fig. 2. Introductory page of telecoms accessibility guidelines – top half

---

The next section of the technology page provides information on how to use the guidelines (see Figure 3). This is presented in a way that caters for a broad range of users, from those who are just learning about accessibility to those in specific roles who have specific tasks to carry out. New users with a less technical background are offered a general introduction to accessibility of I.T. products, written in a non technology-specific manner. Users who have some knowledge of accessibility but not for this technology are guided to the 'About' section for that technology.

Following this are links to the role- and task-specific information which was successful in the user tests but which had to be moved in order to simplify the site design. Although the tabular structure and its content is identical for each technology channel, the information it links to is specifically tailored for each technology.

The guidelines themselves are presented as a list, broken down by priority, as seen in the successful WCAG checklist. Unlike the WCAG, however, this list does not contain the full text of each guideline (a 'guideline' in the Irish guidelines equates to a 'checkpoint' in WCAG), but a shortened title. This makes the list much easier to scan and easier to use when printed out in the form of a checklist.

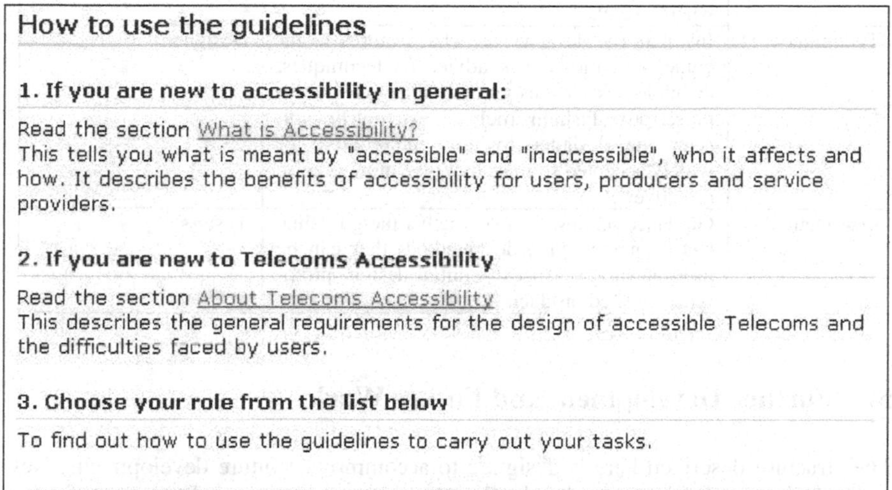

How to use the guidelines

1. If you are new to accessibility in general:

Read the section What is Accessibility?
This tells you what is meant by "accessible" and "inaccessible", who it affects and how. It describes the benefits of accessibility for users, producers and service providers.

2. If you are new to Telecoms Accessibility

Read the section About Telecoms Accessibility
This describes the general requirements for the design of accessible Telecoms and the difficulties faced by users.

3. Choose your role from the list below

To find out how to use the guidelines to carry out your tasks.

Planning and Procurement	Design and Development	Testing, Assessment and Quality Assurance
Tasks:	Tasks:	Tasks:
Assess a design concept or prototype	Plan a design project	User test a design or prototype
Assess a current offering for accessibility	Interpret accessibility requirements	Assess a design concept or prototype
Scope accessibility requirements	Choose design and implementation techniques	Assess a current offering for accessibility
Write a design brief or a Request For Tenders (RFT)		Scope accessibility requirements

Home | Web | Telecoms | Public Access Terminals | Application Software | A General Accessibility Process

Fig. 3. Role-specific information for the telecoms accessibility guidelines

Each guideline has a link to the full text plus the various elements of supporting information. These elements and their purposes are listed in table 1.

Table 1. Common structure for the presentation of each guideline

Element	Content	Intended User(s)
Statement	User-centred requirement or goal that the product or service should meet, stated as a concise directive ("Do this").	All users
Explanation	Defines and expands on words or phrases in the statement.	All users
Rationale	Explains why this requirement is important. Describes the consequences of not meeting it. Backs this up with examples and anecdotes where useful.	New users
Techniques	Instructs the designer on what features to include or avoid. Gives advice on techniques, technologies or design solutions in a non-prescriptive fashion. Includes external links to refer the designer to any authoritative or widely accepted sources that give more precise directives.	Designers
Test methods	Guidance on how to test whether the guideline has been met. Provides methods that can be used at various stages – initial design, prototype, finished product.	Testers

5   Further Development and Future Work

The structure described here is designed to accommodate future developments. New technologies can be accommodated using the common structures. Evolution of existing information is facilitated by the clear functional breakdown of elements. Future plans include expanding and improving the content of the guidelines by provision of:

- More links to external resources
- Additional resources, such as CAD objects defining user anthropometrics
- New guidelines for emerging technologies, such as interactive TV
- FAQs
- Rewritten and/or reprioritised guidelines in response to feedback from users, and others (the web section will need to be updated when WCAG 2 becomes a recommendation).

A major task in the future will be to encourage the growth of a community of users around the guidelines, to share expertise and techniques, provide feedback on how the guidelines might be improved and expanded and raise awareness of accessibility as a vital part of the development process. This can be done through the provision of an enhanced online support and feedback mechanism linking into discussions and FAQs. The availability of expert help is important. Eventually, it is hoped that new national legislation will reference these guidelines giving added urgency to extending access – see [10] for an eloquent anecdote on the effect of well-enforced legislation.

This paper has described a structure developed for usable accessibility guidelines that arose from extensive consultation with prospective users of the guidelines. Preliminary feedback indicates that the structure is effective in communicating the appropriate information to the appropriate users. Even at this early stage, the guidelines are being specified in RFTs for the re-design of government information services.

It is anticipated that the extensive consultation process described here will have created a more usable set of guidelines. Furthermore, the consultation process has served to promote "buy-in" by stakeholders in an environment with relatively weak legal compunction. The consultation process has also served to publicise the guidelines themselves. The requirements identified in the work reported here have much in common with those set out for the next version of WCAG, in particular to be more understandable to less technical users.

References

1. Council of the European Union, Commission of the European Communities: eEurope 2002: An Information Society for All, Action Plan. June 2000.
    http://europa.eu.int/information_society/eeurope/action_plan/pdf/actionplan_en.pdf
2. Information Society Commission: Information Society Ireland: Third Report. December 2000. http://www.isc.ie/thirdreport.html
3. Irish Government, Department of an Taoiseach: Programme for Prosperity and Fairness. February 2000. http://www.taoiseach.gov.ie/upload/publications/310.pdf
4. Irish Government, Department of an Taoiseach: Web Publication: Recommended Guidelines for Public Sector Organisations. November 1999.
    http://www.irlgov.ie/taoiseach/publication/webpg/guidelines.htm
5. Colwell, C., Petrie, H.: Evaluation of Guidelines for Designing Accessible Web Content. IFIP TC.13 INTERACT'99 Workshop: Making Designers Aware of Existing Guidelines for Accessibility. (31 August 1999).
    http://www.info.fundp.ac.be/IFIP13-3/INT99workshop-accessibility.htm#9
6. Colwell, C., Petrie, H.: Evaluation of Guidelines for Designing Accessible Web Content. In: Buhler, C., Knops, H. (eds.): Assistive Technology on the Threshold of the New Millennium. (AAATE 99). Amsterdam: IOS Press, 1999.
7. Vanderheiden, G., Chisholm, W.: Requirements for WCAG 2.0. W3C Working Draft dated 26 April 2002. http://www.w3.org/TR/wcag2-req/
8. Vanderheiden, G.: Fundamental Principles and Priority Setting for Universal Usability. http://trace.wisc.edu/docs/fundamental_princ_and_priority_acmcuu2000/
9. Chisholm, W., Vanderheiden, G., Jacobs, I.: Web Content Accessibility Guidelines 1.0. W3C Recommendation 5-May-1999, see http://www.w3.org/TR/WCAG10/
10. Vanderheiden, G.: Addition to the Record: House Judiciary Committee Oversight Hearing on "The Applicability of the Americans with Disabilities Act (ADA) to Private Internet Sites". 9 February, 2000.
    http://trace.wisc.edu/docs/ada_internet_hearing/#economic_motivation

Adaptive Navigation of Visually Impaired Users in a Virtual Environment on the World Wide Web

Vladislav Nemec, Zdenek Mikovec, and Pavel Slavik

Czech Technical University in Prague, Dept. of Computer Science and Engineering,
Karlovo namesti 13, 121 35 Prague 2, Czech Republic
nemecv@cs.felk.cvut.cz, xmikovec@fel.cvut.cz,
slavik@cslab.felk.cvut.cz

Abstract. The increasing amount of new technologies (including multimedia, internet and virtual reality) allows us to use new approaches in design and implementation of applications of various kinds. Specific requirements emerge in the case of users with specific needs. One such example might be the use of 3D information in the web environment (and navigation in such an environment) by visually impaired users. Our solution provides *semantic* and *functional* description of the scene objects and inter-object relations in addition to "standard" *geometric scene description*. This approach permits the user to query for various information in the virtual environment (e.g. searching for a path to a specific object, searching for an object with specific properties and particularly filtering scene information). The system should allow the visually impaired user to virtually walk through the scene and query for information about the objects in a scene. In such a way they are able to obtain information that has been available to users without visual impairments. The user interface itself provides the feedback in accordance with the user's group's specific requirements – the feedback is implemented as a human readable text that can be simply accessed using one of the common *accessibility tools* (screen reader, Braille display etc.). The embedded module capable of providing speech output has also been implemented.

1 Introduction

The opportunities for communication and information acquisition by people with disabilities are likely to be significantly expanded in the Internet environment. In the case of visually impaired people it is possible to gain access to the textual information provided through the WWW because of the availability of technologies that enlarge text or convert the information to audible or tactile media.

The problem arises for the "visual based" multimedia data (pictures, photographs, movies etc.) or very complex data structures (maps, 3D models, scenes etc.). Providing the access to these types of data using only existing "classical" technologies and methods is in general very complicated and usually not very user friendly for the given class of users.

As the share of 3D information on the web steadily increases (especially the VRML based applications) it is necessary to develop new methods that will provide an easy access to this type of information to visually impaired users. We have focused on the problem of providing a complex description of the 3D scene. The "complexity"

N. Carbonell, C. Stephanidis (Eds.): User Interfaces for All, LNCS 2615, pp. 68–79, 2003.

of the description is based on the fact that besides the description of geometric and topologic properties of objects also additional non-geometric information (*functional* or *semantic* description) is provided. The spectrum of applications of such a system is very wide e.g. it can serve as a means for training of navigation in a real environment.

All currently existing solutions to the problem of visually impaired people accessing the 3D model of real environment are based either on providing haptic access to the geometry of the scene using some force feedback device (e.g. Phantom [1]), or on *sonification* of the 2D view to the scene from some point [2]. Access to the additional information cannot be easily provided using these methods.

In a certain sense, our solution to this problem is the extension of the solution to the problem of communication of visually impaired users with 2D information by means of a semantic description of pictures [3]. The geometric description of a scene is more closely connected to a semantic description. The description itself is more complex – it describes miscellaneous object properties (object name, material etc.) including visual ones (colour etc.) and relations between objects (object A is positioned on object B; object X is situated in room Y etc.). The system also contains a special scene browser, which is capable of allowing the user to virtually walk through the scene and provides the feedback in a form relevant to the users' specific requirements. All feedback from the system is generated in a textual form that is readable for visually impaired users by using special tools (e.g. screen reader, Braille display).

The solution of the problem can be divided into several sub-problems: creation of the subsystem providing access to the scene description, implementation of the browser allowing user to virtually `walk through` the scene, designing the user interface for these two modules and implementation of the module providing speech output.

2 Scene Description Creation

Our solution does not only convert the 3D information to the 2D horizontal projection of scene but we use the complex geometrical description of the scene with additional semantic/functional information. The additional information can be very complex and comprehensive (see Fig. 1) - even for small scenes containing only a few objects. The hierarchical structure of objects can be described using VRML [4] or X3D [5] format. This is very convenient because the author of the scene can use some of the existing 3D authoring tools for creation of the geometrical representation of the scene.

As a suitable format for implementing additional semantic information, we can use the MPEG-7 [6]; the ISO/IEC standard for description of multimedia content. The retrieving of additional information from the scene requires human assistance.

The representation of the environment divided into the two parts (files) mentioned above (*geometric* and *functional* description) complicates the further manipulation of the scene. Therefore we will use our internal format combining both geometrical and semantic description. This internal format will be based on XML (as the flexible format allowing us to create a hierarchical structure implementing the complex scene description, in addition we can take advantage of the XSLT [7] – a powerful tool for structure transformations.

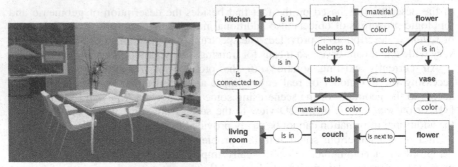

Fig. 1. The example of the 3D scene and its functional description

The transformation from one format to another can be divided into two parts: structure transformation and content transformation. The structure transformation converts data structures of different formats into our internal data structure (as shown in Fig. 2). The content transformation is used for the design of the querying process. XSL allows us to define both parts of transformation.

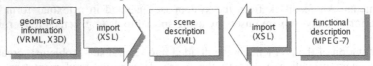

Fig. 2. Transformation of structural and functional description to the internal format

3   Querying for Information

Orientation with a large amount of information can be rather complicated for users who cannot see (they are not able to remember all objects, relations, attributes etc.). A good example might be the virtual walkthrough in a scene – the user must keep in mind his current position, the possible colliding with objects around him, various attributes of these objects etc.

A solution to this problem is the creation of a system that would allow information selection or filtering to an acceptable extent.

3.1   Query Specification

When designing the querying system, we must deal with two problems. The first problem is to enable complex queries and at the same time reduce the extent of user interaction (the amount of information that must be entered by user) when defining the query. The second problem is the presentation of the search results. Both of these problems are solved in our approach using XSL transformations.

The query specification can be done in two ways. The first possibility is to choose from a list of predefined queries. The second possibility is to define the custom query statement that can be saved and later used as predefined requests.

All transformations of the scene description data are done using XSL style sheets – this transformation process is called XSL pipeline. The second part of the pipeline (from scene description in internal format to the query result) is shown in Fig. 3. The scene description in internal format is enriched by an information inference algorithm according to the user's requests. This algorithm creates new attributes, which are not explicitly given in the scene description, by inferring them from existing attributes following certain rules [3]. Then the description is filtered – the filtering set-up can be based both on the user's querying and on internal requests coming from the browser module (e.g. when finding path to some object).

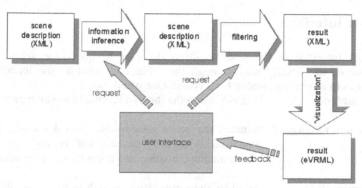

Fig. 3. The *XSL pipeline*

Fig. 4 shows the example schema of the apartment we will use for demonstration of the filtering process and the result of this process. For example we can define a query: "find the path from the kitchen (mark 1 in Fig. 4) to the workroom (2 in Fig. 4)". The scene is filtered in such a way that all rooms not included in this sequence are filtered out.

The result is shown in Fig. 4.

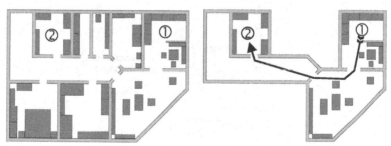

Fig. 4. Schema of the path finding and scene filtering process

3.2 Result Presentation and Feedback

The result of a request can be of two types. The first type is a message, such as the number of objects selected, relations among objects or value of an attribute (e.g. color = red). This type of result is presented in textual form to the user.

The second type of result is the filtered 3D scene itself (e.g. apartment scheme, which has been reduced to the query "Which rooms contain objects with a specific description?" All rooms that do not contain at least one specified object are filtered out). This type of result (reduced XML document) is transformed (using XSL sheet) to suitable output format and presented to the user. This transformation is used for generating the scene in eVRML ("extended VRML") format (described in the next part of this paper). The generated scene file is then "passed" to the browser part of the user interface.

4   User Interface

The user interface of the system allows the user to query the scene for some information, to virtually walk-through the scene and provides the feedback to all operations in a form acceptable for a visually impaired user.

The user interface can be divided into the three independent modular parts:

Description manager - handles the scene description, provides query and filter functionality used by the user and browser module when manipulating the scene and provides the appropriate output

Browser module - provides the virtual walkthrough in the scene allowing the user to "inspect" the scene, collide with objects etc.

Speech output module - is a stand alone text-to-speech system integrated with the previous two parts

Fig. 5 shows the structure of the user interface, communication between user and user interface and mutual communication between modules.

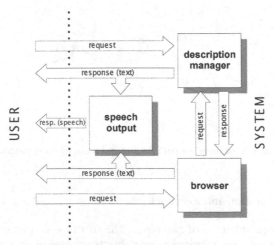

Fig. 5. Modular structure of the user interface

4.1 Description Manager

The user interface is usually composed of *components* (frames, buttons, labels etc.). Basically we can divide these components into two groups: *decorative* (providing only better organization of interface, look-and-feel etc. - e.g. split-panes) and *functional* (providing some input or output - e.g. buttons).

We focus on the functional components only, which are useful for visually impaired users. The functional components can be divided into four groups:
1. **single action components** - allow the user to perform a single action - e.g. button
2. **textual input/output components** - allow the user to enter the text or provide the textual output - e.g. text field
3. **single status components** - contain simple status information - e.g. check box
4. **multi status components** - contain status information - the status value can be selected from the set of predefined values - e.g. combo box, group of radio buttons
5. **containers** - can contain arbitrary number of other components; the container also defines the particular area of the user interface - e.g. panel, frame

Feedback. We have to implement appropriate feedback for these component types. There are two types of operations that should generate feedback:
1. component gets the focus – for the *containers* this is the only defined operation
2. the component action is performed or the state of the component is changed (including the textual input/output components[1])

Get Focus Operation. The feedback that is provided by this operation has a simple structure:
`<component identification>` + `<optional value part` depending on the type of the component>
The *identification* of the component has the following structure:
`<component type>` + `<component name>`

We cannot assume that the user is an expert with the graphical user interface design. That is why we will distinguish only among component groups mentioned above, not among various types of the component in the same group. Table 1 shows the component types reported for each component group.

Table 1. Component types reported for given component group

component group	reported type
single action components	action
textual input/output components - editable	text
textual input/output components – non-editable (output only)	read only text
single status components	switch
multi status components	selection
Containers	area

The *value part* has the following structure:
`<keyword "value">` + `<component value>`

---

[1] We will not "propagate" the change of the state for each character entered - the change of the state will be "mapped" only to some special keys (enter etc.).

The optional *value* part is, by default, provided only for components handling some status information (single status and multi status components). The content of the textual input/output component can be "huge" - that is why the value of this component is provided only "on demand".

Status Changed Operation. Because the state of the component cannot be changed without assigning the focus to it, we will not provide identification of the component in the feedback information.

First we will list the two exceptions in the *status changed* operation feedback generation:

1. *containers* – this operation is not implemented for this component group – the feedback is not generated
2. *single action components* – these components do not handle any status information – the action *mapped* to the single action component is performed when the *status changed* operation is realized – the *"action performed"* string is used as feedback

The "standard" structure of feedback information provided for all other components is: `<keyword "changed">` + `<new component value>`

In this case the *value* information is by default provided for all components including textual input/output ones. These "textual components" in conjunction with the speech output module (described later in this paper) allow us to design a graphical user interface that is fully *accessible*.

4.2 Browser

The browser module allows the user to virtually walk through the scene, to inspect the scene (e.g. "Which objects are in front of me?") and ask for additional information by formulating queries using the description manager module (these two modules are very tightly connected). The design concept of the user interface of this module depends on the conception of the avatar's (which represents the user in the virtual environment) movement in the scene.

Avatar's Movement. We have to determine the basic properties of the avatar's movement in the scene: whether the movement will be *discrete* (short steps of fixed length) or *continuous*, the speed and the method of changing the avatar's direction.

The avatar's movement must be implemented as *discrete*, because the continuous movement would generate too much feedback information. The question is how big should the *step* and the *rotation angle* (the angle between two adjacent directions) be? It is necessary to determine the capabilities of the visually impaired people to estimate the distances and angles in 3D space. For example it is meaningless to "report" the current avatar's direction to the user in tenths of a degree when for example the user is not able to estimate a smaller angle than fifteen degrees. We have performed several experiments and tests to determine the capabilities of visually impaired people to estimate various distances and angles in space.

Distance Estimation Capability Test. Depending on the results of these tests we have defined the set of the distances from which the user can select the length of the step.

The test method was simple – the person being tested is given various distances (from the set of 10cm, 20cm, 30cm, 50cm, 75cm, 1m, 2m, 3m and 5m) and was told to advance this distance in the current direction. The distances were then measured and the inclination was analysed. Based on results of these tests the predefined step lengths were set at 20cm, 50cm, 0.75cm, 1m and 2m.

Angle Estimation Capability Test. The main goal of this test is to determine the capability of visually impaired people to estimate angles in space. We also need to find out the level of "imagination" of the users – we need to know whether the user is able to imagine something "behind" the some type of angular value. It seems better to assign some label to each direction instead of using the numerical angular value.

In compliance with the "real world correspondence" rule the labels should be associated with some item from the real world. We will call it *direction associations*.

We have selected three possible *direction associations*:
1. **coarse compass** – a compass rosette distinguishing among eight directions (N, NE, E, SE, S, SW, W, NW)
2. **clock face** – a clock face distinguishing among twelve directions
3. **detailed compass** – a compass rosette distinguishing among sixteen directions

The testing method is quite simple. The person being tested stands in the center of the *direction marking*. He is given the various directions and is asked to turn in these directions. Table 2 shows the summary of the test results.

Because we also need to test the "imagination" of the users (as mentioned before) we use three different *interpretations* of the *circle dividing*:
• "compass" or "clock face" direction
• angular value (in degrees)
• number of *rotation steps* from the current direction to the new one

Table 2. The rotation angle estimation test results

association	rotation step	decision level	average inclination
coarse compass	45%	22.5%	40.88%
clock face	22.5%	15%	20.04%
detailed compass	22.5%	11.25%	30.85%

The results of the tests showed that both *compass associations* are unusable - the average *inclination* of the estimated angle is too close to the *decision level* (deviation of more than 50% would cause wrong recognition of the direction). This is partly induced by the fact that the users are confusing the east and west directions.

The results for the *clock face association* were more satisfactory - the average deviation is only about 20%. The users are also more "comfortable" with this way of direction marking. We will use this *direction association* for designing the avatar's movement and control concept.

Interface. We will combine two control methods in the browser module's user interface: "textual components" described in section 4.1 along with the "mouse gestures" (we define a *mouse gesture* as the continuous movement of the mouse that is subconsciously accomplished once it is started).

The user interface consists of three components:

1. **configuration component** – allows the user to set up some properties of the browser (e.g. speech output, collisions with the obstacles)
2. **navigation component** –allows the user to control the avatar's movement and perform some "inspection" operations (will be described hereafter)
3. **textual component** – allows textual input/output communication (e.g. providing textual feedback from the browser)

Mouse Gestures. To define the set of possible *mouse gestures* we have performed another preliminary test trying to determine the capabilities of the visually impaired users to precisely control the movement of the mouse pointer in various directions. To compare the abilities of the users we have used two user groups: normal sight and visually impaired (see Table 3).

Table 3. Results of the mouse control capabilities test

	inclination			
	average	maximal	orthogonal	non-orthogonal
normal sight	4.78%	11%	1.5%	6.42%
visually impaired	13.72%	36%	6.42%	20.5%
average	**11.42%**	**43%**	**5.14%**	**14.58%**

We have also examined the inclination for the *orthogonal* (e.g. 12, 3 o'clock) and *non-orthogonal* directions. The results show that the users are able to control the mouse in horizontal and vertical directions very precisely. The experiment also demonstrated that the control of movement in other directions is very inaccurate - the average *inclination* is 13.72°. This value is very close to the *decision level* (15° for this *direction association*), which makes the control method based on more than four directions "unusable".

We can suppose that the user uses the two-button mouse (or that there is some mechanism to *emulate* the second button) and the keyboard. To design *mouse gestures* we can use four possible mouse operations:

1. **click (c)**– pressing and releasing of the given mouse button
2. **drag (d)**– pressing the mouse button, moving the mouse in given direction, releasing the mouse button
3. **click with modifier (cm)** – pressing the *modifier*[2] key, click, releasing the *modifier* key
4. **drag with modifier (dm)** – pressing the *modifier* key, dragging, releasing the modifier key

Along with the four possible dragging directions and two mouse buttons we now have twenty different gestures.

---

[2] A key that only has a meaning when combined with another key – it changes the meaning of that key; for example control, shift.

We have determined the *performance time* (using the modified GOMS method [11]) for each gesture and defined the priority of individual operations that will be assigned to these gestures.

Scene Inspection. The avatar is able to query the *scene database* using the *description manager* module and is also able to *inspect* the scene in a "geometric way" - e.g. asking questions like "What objects are in front of me?".

The inspection operations are (along with the movement control operations) bound to the mouse gestures. The following *inspection* operations are defined:

- inspection of the avatar's current view direction
- inspection of the "pie wedge" (four adjacent directions) in front of, to the left, to the right and behind the avatar

The feedback from this operation contains the names of the objects found – the user is then able to query the scene database for other information/object's properties.

Avatar Movement Control. The user can control the avatar's movement by performing mouse gestures in the navigation area. The navigation "operations" that the user can perform are step forward, step backward, step to the left and step to the right, rotation to an arbitrary direction, rotation 90° to the left / right and turning back.

Rotation to an arbitrary direction is not simply mapped to the one gesture. The *direction indicator* is changing its value while the user is dragging the mouse without releasing the mouse button. The avatar turns to the direction indicated by *direction indicator* when the mouse button is released.

Feedback. The browser, as well as the description manager module, provides the text-based feedback. We have created the *feedback dictionary* used when generating the feedback. Terms in the dictionary are selected to meet the following requirements:

- the term must not be technical, expert etc.
- the term should (as much as possible) correspond with the "real world"
- the term should be as short as possible not to overload the output

In the following example we will demonstrate the user's communication with the browser. We have the scene shown in Fig. 4. The avatar stands in the middle of the bedroom and is trying to get to the bathroom. The user is using only the browser module's features (without querying the scene database). The particular steps performed by the user are listed using `mono-spaced` font in the format <performed operation> # <generated feedback>:

1. get information about avatar's current position, view direction and speed
`overall information # position 4.0 10.0 direction 1 speed 0.75`
2. try to find the door leading to the hallway
`inspect the front pie wedge # wardrobe door found direction 11 distance 1.8, bedroom door found direction 12 distance 2.2` (note: the list of the found objects has been shortened)
3. rotate in the direction 12
`decrease direction indicator # twelve`
`rotate to given direction # rotated to twelve`

4. the user makes three steps to get to the hallway
`step forward # step` (three times)
5. the user is trying to find the door leading to the bathroom
`inspect the front pie wedge # workroom door found direction 12`
`distance 1.2, wall between workroom and hallway` (shortened)
6. `inspect the right pie wedge # <snip> bathroom door found`
`direction 3 distance 9.6` (shortened)

eVRML. For our purposes we need to extend the standard VRML format so we can add the *link* to the non-geometrical description to the individual objects in the scene. We have insisted on the validity of the extension - the extension cannot affect the given scene geometry or topology when the scene containing additional information is displayed using a common browser.

This limitation is very strict – we cannot add a new element (the standard parser would report an error) – the additional info can be only added as a comment or embedded to some existing element or element's attribute.

The `anchor` element was chosen. It contains the string `description` attribute – the usage of the attribute value depends on implementation of the browser. We can set the additional information as the value of this attribute. Since these elements allow the grouping of the objects as the children of the element, we can assign this additional information to all elements in the sub-tree of the `anchor` element.

The original function of the `anchor` element ("teleportation" of the avatar) is not affected – if the `URL` attribute's value is set and is not equal to the empty string, the avatar is "teleported" to the new scene/location and the `description` attribute is ignored. In the other case the value of the attribute is used as the additional information.

4.3 Speech Output

This module does not have the graphical user interface. The system provides output in the form of human readable text. The speech output module (if enabled) automatically converts all text in the output area to fluent speech. The module is implemented using Java Speech API [13] and the FreeTTS [14] library. The module is capable of "reading" text of an arbitrary length. At this time English is the only language that is supported.

5 Conclusion

We have built an experimental system allowing visually impaired users to virtually walk through a 3D scene and query for information about the objects in the scene.

Our approach is based on the complex scene description defined in XML. This allows efficient querying (due to the description of semantic relations among objects). The increasing complexity of queries calls for new flexible and dynamic querying methods. The transformation pipeline was designed to handle this problem. There are three types of transformations:

1. transformation into internal format for better querying
2. transformation for "new information inference" and querying
3. transformation for query result presentation and export to other data formats

XSL was used for transformation definition. XSL sheets allow users to define more complex queries and reduce the user interaction (using pre-defined XSL sheets). The "accessible" browser of the 3D scenes was also implemented. The browser provides the functionality comparable to a common VRML browser (e.g. Cortona). The system was tested on several 3D scenes with very good results and thus showed the applicability of the approach chosen. In our future work we will focus on a greater variety of 3D scenes and their accessibility for visually impaired users.

The research was funded from the following grant: GACR 201/02/1553.

References

[1] SensAble Technologies. *SensAble Technologies – Haptic Research.*
     http://www.sensable.com/haptics/products/phantom.html (June 2002)
[2] MEIJER, Peter B.L. *The vOICe: Accessible VRML for the Blind.*
     http://www.seeingwithsound.com/winvrml.htm (June 2002)
[3] MIKOVEC, Zdenek; SLAVIK Pavel. *Tool for Pictorial Data Transformations.* In: Intelligent Multimedia, Computing and Communications, Technologies and Applications of the Future. New York : John Wiley & Sons, 2001, p. 10-19. ISBN 0-471-20435-8
[4] Web3D Consortium. *VRML Specification.*
     http://www.web3d.org/technicalinfo/specifications/vrml97/ (June 2002)
[5] Web3D Consortium. *X3D Specification.* (February 2002)
     http://www.web3d.org/TaskGroups/x3d/specification-2002february/index.html
     (June 2002)
[6] ISO/IEC JTC1/SC29/WG11. *MPEG-7 Standard.* (December 2001)
     http://mpeg.telecomitalialab.com/standards/mpeg-7/mpeg-7.htm (June 2002)
[7] W3C. *Extensible Stylesheet Language (XSL) W3C Recommendation.* (October 15, 2001)
     http://www.w3.org/TR/xsl/ (June 2002)
[8] FAGIN Ronald. *Fuzzy Queries in Multimedia Database Systems.* ACM Press, 1998. ISBN 0-89791-996-3
[9] NEMEC, Vladislav. *User Interface for Blind.* MSc. thesis , Czech Technical University.
     http://www.cgg.cvut.cz/~sloup/Diplomky/2002/VladislavNemec/ (June 2002)
[10] NEMEC, Vladislav; SPORKA Adam J. *The Blind's Dog Project – User Interface Approach Evaluation and Testing Specification.* (September 18, 2001)
     http://enorasi.avista.cz/bdn_testing.pdf (June 2002)
[11] RASKIN, Jeff. *The Humane Interface.* Addison-Wesley, 2000. ISBN 0-201-37937-6
[12] CARD, Stuart K.; MORAN, Thomas P.; NEWELL, Allen. *The Psychology of Human-Computer Interaction.* NJ: Lawrence Erlbaum Association, 1983. ISBN 0-898-59859-1
[13] Sun Microsystems Inc. *Java Speech API Specification.* http://java.sun.com/products/java-media/speech/forDevelopers/jsapi-doc.pdf (June 2002)
[14] Speech Integration Group, Sun Microsystems Laboratories. *Free TTS 1.1 – A speech synthesizer written entirely in the Java (TM) programming language.* (January 2002)
     http://freetts.sourceforge.net/docs/ (June 2002)

Fax Registration of Information about Disaster Victims

Tsuyoshi Ebina, Fumiko Matsumoto, and Hiroyuki Ohno

Emergency Communications Section,
Communications Research Laboratory,
4-2-1, Nukuikita-machi, Tokyo, 184-8795, Japan
{ebi, fumi}@crl.go.jp, hohno@ohnolab.org
http://www.crl.go.jp/jt/a114/index-e.html

Abstract. We are developing a survival-information registration system called IAA system. The IAA system allows disaster victims to register their survival information (kind of injuries, damage to property, etc.) through the Internet. However, elderly people were hard to register survival information because they were poor at using keyboard. We developed interactive fax user interface, which allows a user to check and correct the handwritten information using paper user interface. Experimental result showed that elderly people could register their survival information without help.

1 Introduction

We are developing a survival-information registration system called IAA (meaning gI am Alive h)[1]. The IAA system allows disaster victims to register their survival information (kind of injuries, damage to property, etc.) through the Internet. Figure 1 shows an outline of the IAA system. This system uses a Web-based IAA user interface via a keyboard and a mouse.

However, not all the disaster victims can use a keyboard and mouse. For example, many elderly people and children cannot use a keyboard and mouse. Before starting to develop a system, we tested three IAA user interfaces on five different kinds of user groups: children, elderly people, hearing-impaired, visually impaired, and normal adults[2]. The test results showed that the elderly group and the children found it hard to register survival information. These two groups commented that fax registration is the best among the three kinds of IAA user interfaces; however, fax registration faces two problems.

One problem is a lack of interaction in fax registration. That is, because fax communication is one way, subjects cannot check, modify, and confirm their survival information. The second problem is the need of volunteer help. Because handwritten characters on a fax sheet are translated into character code by optical character recognition (OCR) technology, the recognized characters may be miss-recognized. Thus, the obtained character codes must be confirmed by on-line Internet volunteers. However, if an insufficient number of volunteers are on-line, the character-check procedure will not work.

N. Carbonell, C. Stephanidis (Eds.): User Interfaces for All, LNCS 2615, pp. 80–87, 2003.

In response to these problems, we developed an interactive-fax user interface for use in disaster situations. This interface enables victims to write, confirm, and modify their own information on a fax sheet without the need for help from Internet volunteers.

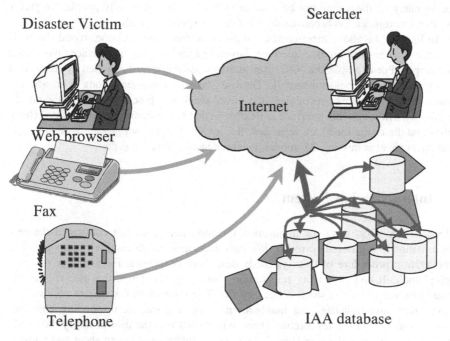

Fig. 1. An image outline of the IAA system

2 Related Work

Traditional emergency communication systems are not designed for non-expert users. For example, emergency radio communication systems are designed for use by local-government staff, not for use by victims. However, survival information registration and search systems have recently been developed. Survival information includes the survivor fs name, injuries, date of birth, and so on.

For example, the saigai dengon dial system provided by NTT East allows victims to register their spoken messages via a telephone interface. This registration method is quite simple because victims are able to register their information by simply using a telephone-number key. However, this interface is limited in that the survival information registration and its retrievals are based on a telephone-number. For example, people who do not know an acquaintance fs telephone number cannot search for victim information about that person.

Another user interface used for a survival-information registration system is via a web page on the Internet. For example, the gI am OK h system enables a user to register and search for a certain victim on the Internet. The same interface is also used for the IAA system. However, a web interface is not suitable for elderly people because many of them may not be familiar with a keyboard; elderly people are prefer written communication because they have much experience with writing.

In light of the above-mentioned circumstances, we designed paper-based survival-information-registration user interface. Several paper-based user interfaces have been developed. For example, the XAX user interface using paper, developed by Johnson et al., processes paper documents[3]. The user faxes a document along with a cover sheet. The XAX server recognizes the cover sheet and processes the document accordingly. Although this interface is flexible in that the document and program (check boxes on the cover sheet) are separated, the XAX server cannot process a document if the cover sheet is missing. Moreover, it cannot handle iterative tasks.

3   Interactive Fax System

Because fax is one-way communication medium, people cannot confirm if the sent information is registered correctly. We thus developed an interactive fax system. The registration procedure of this system is described as follows. First, a user makes a telephone call and gets a fax registration sheet (Fig. 2). Then, the user fills in the blanks on the sheet and sends it back by fax. The interactive fax system receives the faxed data and translates the handwritten characters into corresponding character codes. The system creates a return sheet, which confirms the user to notify the result, and sends it back to the user (Fig. 3). The user confirms the return sheet and corrects the data if the information is incorrect. Then, if recognition errors were found, the system corrects the mistaken characters and sends the same return? sheet back to the user again. For example, if the year of birth was 1975 but OCR recognized the year as 1915, the user should write "7" under the number "1" (Fig. 4). This procedure is continued until no recognition errors are found on the returned sheet. If no errors are found on the returned sheet, the user does not send the sheet back. If the fax server receives no response within a couple of minutes, the server sends the fax information to the IAA server. The user tears the user ID part from the returned sheet keeps it. The ID sheet is then retained in order to update the registered information.

Figure 5 shows an image of the first prototype system. When people send a fax registration sheet to the interactive fax system, an fax server receives the fax data and sends it onto a pop server by a electric mail attached form. The interactive fax server gets the fax information from the pop server and analyzes the format. If the format matches that of the registration form, the server translates all handwritten characters into character code. Then the server creates the return sheet and sends it back to the user. If the format matches that of the returned sheet, the fax server simply translates the updated handwritten characters into character code and re-creates the return sheet, which it then sends back to the user.

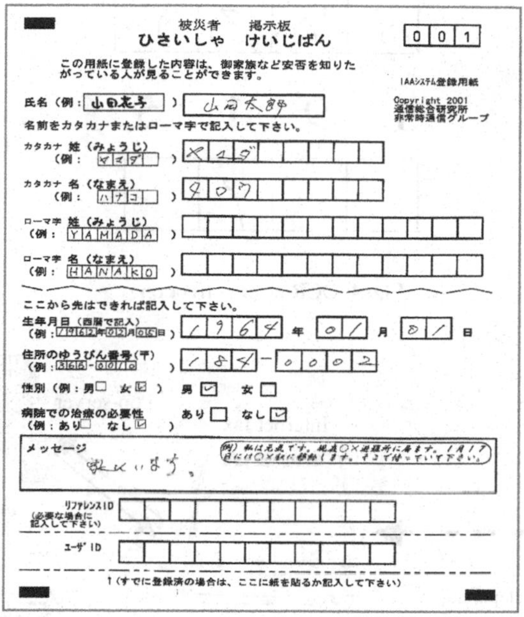

Fig. 2. Fax registration form

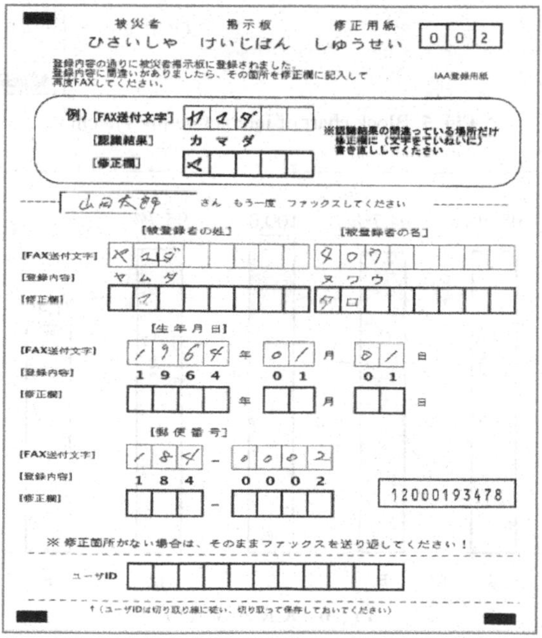

Fig. 3. Returned check sheet

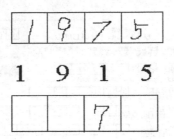

Fig. 4. OCR error correction

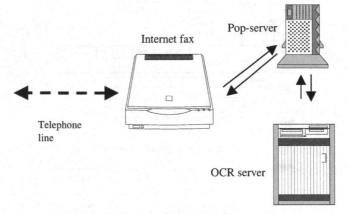

Fig. 5. Block chart of interactive fax system

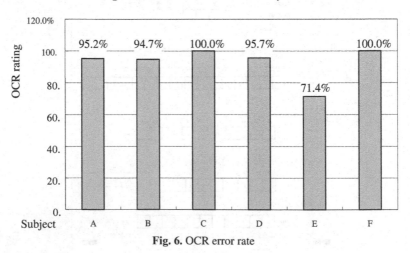

Fig. 6. OCR error rate

A user test was conducted to determine if elderly people could register their survival information by using the interactive fax system. Six elderly people, all over 65 years old and with poor keyboard typing skills, participated in the experiment. They are referred to as A, B, C, D, E, and F, respectively. At first, the purpose and the registration procedure of this experiment were explained to the subjects. No pre-tests were conducted before the experiment. Namely, the subjects were asked to send, receive, and modify the data on a sheet without any practice.

4 Experiments and Results

A user test was conducted to determine if elderly people could register their survival information by using the interactive fax system. Six elderly people, all over 65 years old and with poor keyboard typing skills, participated in the experiment. They are referred to as A, B, C, D, E, and F, respectively. At first, the purpose and the registration procedure of this experiment were explained to the subjects. No pre-tests were conducted before the experiment. Namely, the subjects were asked to send, receive, and modify the data on a sheet without any practice.

No Optical Mark Recognition (OMR) error was found in the experiment. Figure 6 shows the OCR-recognition error ratings; namely, 71 percent and 100 percent. The OCR recognition rating regarding subject D is low (six recognition errors), but the ratings regarding the other subjects are high (only one or two errors). These errors were successfully corrected by the subjects.

The number of fax-sending iterations is shown in Fig. 7. It is clear that the subjects can complete the fax registration task within two iterations. This means that even if the OCR error rating is high, the number of fax-sheet-return iterations does not increase.

The time taken to complete the iteration procedure was also analyzed. Figure 8 shows that the return-sheet waiting time was between 48 percent and 83 percent of the total time. This waiting time was due to the fact that data transfer between the fax machine and the interactive fax server consumed time. This is because the mail pop server polling interval was set to one minute, and the subject was forced to wait until the data was transferred. By changing the protocol from pop protocol into Simple Mail Transfer Protocol, this part of the total time consumed will be reduced.

5 Discussion

The experimental results showed that elderly people could register their survival information using interactive fax user interface. The time spent in this experiment was long, but total operation time will be reduced by changing a data transfer protocol. If the time is shorter, interactive fax user interface will acceptable for emergency situations. From the universal access point of view, this interface is accessible because from child to elderly can write characters without experiments.

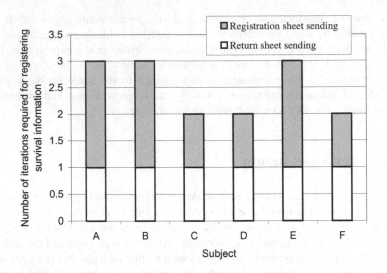

Fig. 7. Number of iterations required for registering survival information

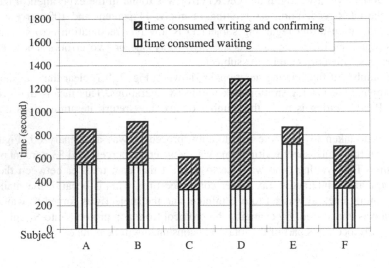

Fig. 8. Time consumed for conducting a task

Advantage of fax user interface is discussed. The advantage of the developed registration method is that people are able to register survival information without having to buy special devices. A home fax machine can be used as a user interface for a survival-information registration system. All people have to do is to fill in the registration form and update the returned sheet.

From the viewpoint of an emergency situation, designing an information-registration interface must meet two requirements: universal accessibility and quick registration. A Web interface enables quick registration but people not experienced in typing cannot use it easily. Voice-recognition technology may helpful to such people, but even if this technology is implemented, they have to start the computer, start the web browser, and find the right URL before using the voice-recognition function.

6 Functional Extension

The current prototype system does not have a function to update registered data. A user has to re-register all of their survival information every time the information is updated. To overcome this problem, we added two functions to system in order to reduce the victims writing load and the number of information-registration tasks.

First, we added a user ID. This allows users to add new information by simply filling in their reference ID. For example, if their health status has changed (injured but cured later), they write this information and their previously registered ID; they do not have to write unchanged information again.

Second, we added a reference ID, which allows a user to replace unchanged information into the same part of previously registered information. For example, if a user wants to register their family information at one time, they first register the family name and postal code. The ID is written on a returned sheet. They then write their personal information on the sheet with their reference ID.

7 Conclusion

A paper-based user interface for registering and searching for victim information was developed. this system uses an interactive fax interface so that it is more accessible to disaster victims such as elderly people who are unfamiliar with computers. It was experimentally shown that elderly people could register information about themselves by using our prototype system with this interface. In the near future, it is planned to reduce the response time of the system.

References

1. Tada N. et al., gIAA System {"I Am Alive"}: The Experiences of the Internet Disaster Drills, h Proceedings of INET2000, (2000)
2. T.Ebina, "An analysis of Safety Information Registration Interface on the IAA System", Proceedings of ICME2001, (2001)
3. W. Johnson, H. Jellinek, L. Klotz Jr, R. Rao and Stuart Card, "Bringing the paper and electronic worlds: The paper user interface," Proceedings of CHI93, (1993), pp.507–512

Part II: User Interfaces for All - Design and Assessment

Designing User Interfaces for a Variety of Users: Possible Contributions from Model-Based Development Schemes

Chris Stary

University of Linz, Department of Business Information Systems
Communications Engineering, Freistädter Straße 315, 4040 Linz / Austria
`Christian.Stary@jku.at`

Abstract. As User Interfaces for All penetrate software applications, multi-dimensional design concepts become increasingly important. Both, for structured and user-oriented interface development, model-based approaches have turned out to be beneficial. However, most of these approaches remain vague with respect to the explicit representation of information about users and different modalities of interaction, as well as the structural and dynamic interfacing of user models to context and interaction models. However, these interfaces are required to provide different access possibilities for a functional core, and to allow switching between different modalities of interaction when serving a variety of users. In this paper we structure the requirements and evaluate existing model-based representation schemes against the structured set of requirements. The results reveal that model-based representation schemes should be enhanced through dedicated relationships and interface-management capabilities to mutually tune the models representing users, tasks, application-domain data, interaction styles and interactive devices.

1 Introduction

As information technology becomes increasingly pervasive in the information society, not only our environment is augmented with computational features leading to ubiquitous applications, but also applications are run through various interactive devices and interaction styles, in order to be continuously present (e.g., Abowd et al., 2000). Pervasiveness of interactive technologies also means that increasingly different people are getting in contact with software. Hence, besides the omnipresence of interactive devices and software, the diversity of users has to be taken into account in the course of interactive-software design.

Design for All targets towards an understanding of attitudes, capabilities, skills, values, experiences, and needs of a broadest possible user community of interactive applications. It reflects attempts to accommodate the broadest possible range of human abilities, requirements and preferences in the development of technical artifacts (Stephanidis, 2001). As such, design support for User Interfaces for All should target

N. Carbonell, C. Stephanidis (Eds.): User Interfaces for All, LNCS 2615, pp. 91–105, 2003.

towards accurate representations of contexts of use, at least in terms of diverse user populations as well as of various interaction styles and interactive devices.

The principles of model-based user interface development (see, e.g., Szekely, 1996; Puerta, 1997) have been touted to have the potential to improve the methodological basis for task-based and user-centered interface design (see, e.g., Stary, 2000). Hence, it has to be investigated in how far this vision can become true. In particular, answers to some of the questions shown in Figure 1 should be provided. In this paper we check whether and how model-based representation schemes are able to cope with a diverse population of interactive-technology users. Original and recent model-based frameworks are evaluated with respect to the representation of user characteristics and interaction features across different modalities in relation to user tasks. In section 2, categorization schemes are revisited and a set of characteristics is introduced that should be captured from and for users. In section 3 we try to match these requirements with model-based frameworks. The paper concludes with a summary and interpretation of results in section 4.

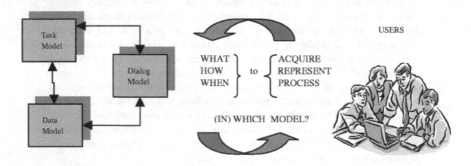

Fig. 1. Problem Description

2   A Structured Set of Requirements

Differences between users when interacting with interactive applications exist either with regard to gender, mental effort to be spent for task accomplishment, or functional roles of users, e.g., BIT (2000); Chen (2000), based on underlying physiological, psychological, and sociological individual differences (Benyon et al., 2001). Traditionally, developers categorize users according to different roles, skills, and human capabilities. For instance, Cotterman et al. (1989) introduced a scheme that captures (i) the organizational role users might play within an organization with respect to information technology (developer, provider, manager), (ii) their functional role with respect to business processes, in particular with respect to the production and the consumption of information, and (iii) the required level of skill and expertise, through assigning values between 0 and 1. In addition, from the field of user modeling, capturing user characteristics requires an implicit acquisition of assumptions with respect to (i) (the process of) interaction, (ii) the application domain, (iii) problem solving procedures of users (e.g., Woywod, 1997). Consequently, a user model contains all properties about individual users, in order to adapt a computer system to this user's way to handle tasks. The adaptation is oriented towards the experiences, the behavior in the course of interaction, the goals and further needs of users. Hence, besides adaptation to the individual user, user modeling targets towards the acquisition and representation of relevant information about users (McTear, 2000). Shneiderman (2000) assumes this information has also to bridge the 'gap between what users know and what they need to know' for successful interaction (p. 90).

Table 1. Inputs from Different Communities

Community Type of Characteristics	Design for All	Empirical Studies	Software Engineering	User Modeling
Individual	Human abilities: skills, capabilities, experiences; Human values, Attitudes, Preferences	Personal characteristics: gender, mental effort for task accomplishment	Profiles based on physiological, psychological and sociological differences	Problem solving behavior of users along goals, Behavior in interaction, (Media) Competence, Task motivation, Values
Organizational	User requirements and needs	Functional roles in organizations	Role descriptions with respect to IT, business process, skills, experience	Application domain knowledge

Table 1 wraps up the fundamental inputs from the various disciplines. It reflects the basic terminology and scope along individual and non-individual characteristics of users.

The advent of AI (Artificial Intelligence) techniques for user modeling has led to a shift from more or less implicit specifications of user properties in traditional software-engineering methods towards explicit representations and symbolic processing of user characteristics. Besides static representations user-modeling components of software systems might keep data that can be updated dynamically (e.g., Pohl et al., 1999). As a consequence, changes in the functionality or in interfacing users, e.g., through switching between interaction devices, might be supported through representation schemes and corresponding processing. Representation schemes are also required to specify and communicate design specifications. Processing is required for prototyping, and becomes increasingly important when providing applications with multiple interaction styles and mobile interaction devices. A typical example for such settings is the access to public information systems via mobile devices (WAP (Wireless Application Protocol)-based cell phones, palmtops, PDAs (Personal Digital Assistants), tablet PCs, hand-held devices etc.) as well as stationary user-interface software, such as kiosk browsers at public places (airports, cine-plexes, malls, railway stations etc.). In these cases, the same data (content) and major functions for navigation, search, and content manipulation become available through various presentation facilities and interaction features. This kind of openness while preserving functional consistency does not only require the provision of different codalities of information and corresponding forms of presentation, such as text and audio streams, but also different handling of navigation and manipulation (e.g., Arehart et al., 2000).

Rich (1989) proposed user stereotypes containing similar patterns of actions with respect to the same prescribed task specification. Stereotypes are described through: User experience with respect to that task, system experience, task motivation, and experience with handling interactive devices. Syntactic task knowledge refers to the allocation of the task and to the position of the task in a business process. This type of knowledge corresponds partially to application-domain knowledge as listed in Table 1. Semantic task knowledge refers to objects of the application domain, as well as actions required for task accomplishment. This type of knowledge represents the other part of application-domain knowledge as mentioned in Table 1. System experience addresses the level of skills a user has, in order to use technological means, such as text-processing systems, for the accomplishment of tasks. Task motivation concerns the attitude of a user towards a certain task. Experience with state-of-the-art devices for human-computer interaction indicates the level of media competence. These elements have been considered to be individual characteristics of users, and thus, have been added to the other inputs from the user-modeling community – see the upper part of Table 1. These stereotypes might change over time, which brings along two dimensions for representations:

Static User Modeling. Users of interactive applications can be categorized according to (i) their individual skills, experiences, and preferences in the context of their work tasks, the application domain data, the (interactive) technology; and (ii) their organizational setting in terms of their functional role(s).

Dynamic User Modeling. As users as well as work settings change over time, user-modeling components have to support (i) changing individual skills and preferences, either with respect to interaction styles and devices or task accomplishment; (ii) changing work settings, i.e. changing assignments of work tasks, problem domain data, and interactive technology.

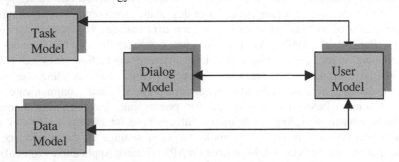

Fig. 2. Conceptual Relationship of User Models

Figure 2 structures the above mentioned requirements in terms of models. A User Model has to be related to an interaction or device model (in the figure termed Dialog Model). This relationship of individuals to interactive technology has primarily to reflect what type of interactive devices is available to a user, and can actually be used by him/her (at a certain level of skills). A User Model has also to be related to a Task Model, in particular, reflecting which work tasks are assigned to a user and how this user accomplishes these work tasks. Finally, a User Model has to be related to a Data Model, since interactive applications provide mechanisms for data manipulation. The relationship corresponds to the view on the data to be manipulated. Since that view depends on the tasks to be accomplished interactively, additional relationships between the models have to be considered. It has to be specified which data are required for which task, namely through explicitly relating the Data Model with the Task Model. For instance, booking a flight requires flight and schedule data. It also has to be specified, how the task-relevant data are presented at the user interface and manipulated interactively, e.g., how flight data can be viewed and confirmed. This requires explicit relationships between the Data Model and the Dialog Model. Finally, the presentation of tasks at the user interface has to be specified, e.g., how a flight agent might proceed from flight selection to booking a flight for a customer. This requires explicit relationships between the Task and the Dialog Model.

3 Model-Based Representation Schemes

After completing the list of requirements in section 2, existing model-based representation and processing schemes for interface development can be reviewed. Most of the schemes are based on object-oriented specification languages or design notations, such as UML, and/or object-oriented prototyping technology. Most of them contain a Data Model as the starting point for specification. One of the first approaches, suggested by de Baar et al. (1992), consists of two models: The Data Model and the Graphical User Interface (GUI) Model. The latter corresponds to a Dialog Model, however, restricted to a single modality for interaction. The Data Model consists of an object class hierarchy in which each object has an associated set of attributes and methods. The attributes and methods of an object are either internal or external. Internal attributes and methods are meant for use within the application and are not shown in the user interface. External attributes and methods are presented in the user interface as standard interaction objects such as buttons, settings, or sliders or as data manipulated directly by the user. The GUI Model determines through which GUI element the data represented by the Data Model are to be displayed. It can only be designed after the Data Model has been completed. This is a very common strategy, cf. UIDE (Sukaviriya et al., 1993) or GENIUS (Jansen et al., 1993). The external attributes and methods of the Data Model must be mapped onto a set of controls in the target GUI, at least at the declarative layer. A user-specific view on either GUI elements or application data is not provided in a straightforward way. Support of different types of users with different GUIs or problem-domain data requires the re-assignment of data-model elements to GUI elements.

In contrast to those approaches, GENIUS is view-oriented: Functions of two different types can be associated to view definitions: Data-manipulation functions and navigation functions. Navigation functions call other views. They define the dialog structure and are used to create appropriate controls, such as menu items or push-buttons. Two levels of dialog control are distinguished. The "coarse grain dialog" defines the sequencing of views (mapped to application windows) and the call of functions as the result of user input. The "fine grain dialog" defines state changes on the level of single user-interface objects. This includes the alteration of text values and changes in the sensitivity of menu items. Based on these definitions, dialog-Petri nets are used to specify the behavior of an application. Although this approach does not provide an explicit user model, the view concept can be used to identify a user-centered perspective on the navigation and data manipulation of an application.

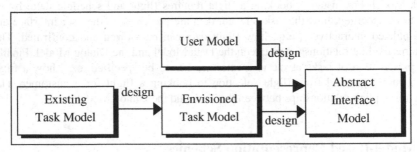

Fig. 3. ADEPT Frame of Reference

The ADEPT framework (Wilson et al., 1996) for prototyping-oriented development of interactive systems is a task- and model-based approach. It consists of a Task, User, and an Abstract Interface Model (Figure 3). The Existing Task Model contains the information of the tasks before development. The Envisioned Task Model is a model of the anticipated nature of work which would come about as a result of designing an interactive computer system. The User Model captures all user-relevant information: user group(s), preferences, special needs etc. The Abstract Interface Model contains all the artifacts that are necessary to (re)present the Envisioned Task Model and the User Model through Graphical User Interfaces (GUIs). This way user characteristics directly influence the prototype generation (based on the specifications).

The MOBI-D (Model-Based Interface Designer) development environment (Puerta, 1997; Eisenstein et al., 2000) is based on conceptual models of user-tasks, users, the domain, and presentations. A User-Task Model describes the tasks to be accomplished by the user of an application through the application's user interface as well as information regarding subtask ordering. The Domain Model defines the data that a user can view, access, and manipulate through a user interface, as well as their inter-relationships with respect to the various domain objects. The User Model defines the different types of users through their attributes and roles. The Presentation Model contains the visual, haptic, and auditory elements that a user interface offers to its users, whereas the Dialog Model defines the way in which those elements interact with users. The authors have recognized the mapping problem between the different models by recognizing that each user may be involved in 'all tasks in a user-task model, or just in a subset of these tasks'. In making explicit this mapping task of the designer the approach, in principle, enables open architectures for functional cores as well as for switching between modalities for interaction in the course of adaptation.

The Teallach MB-UIDE (daSilva et al., 2000) also strives for the generation of executable user interfaces from declarative models, namely a Task, Domain (data) Model and Presentation Models, providing an open architecture and programming interfaces. In Teallach the relationships between the models can be set and edited by designers explicitly. In addition, behavior models can be constructed. The Teallach concept has been successfully enhanced through user modeling in the TADEUS (Task Analysis/Design/End-User Systems) (Stary, 2000). It is a model-based approach that supports the explicit understanding of users and their organization of work. It is based on various models: Task-Domain Model (including a model of the organization and its workflows), Problem-Domain Data Model, User-Domain Model and Interaction-Domain Model. As indicated in Figure 4, these models have to be related to each other statically and dynamically through declarative and procedural specification, respectively.

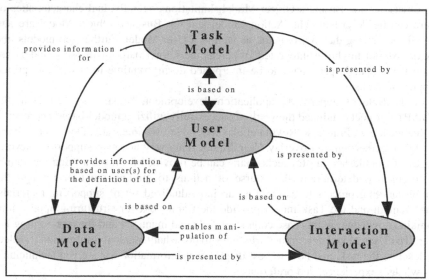

Fig. 4. TADEUS Frame of Reference

The Task Model comprises the decomposition of work tasks according to the organization of work. The User Model details the individual perception of tasks, data structures, interaction devices and modalities. It captures personal experiences, preferences, access modalities to tasks and data, as well as the individual organization of work tasks. The Data Model provides the declarative and procedural information about the functionality of the system and has to be derived from the Task Model. The Interaction Model captures all devices and styles that are required by the users in the course of interaction. In relation to the Task and the Data Model all presentation issues concerning tasks, functions, and data structures have to be specified in the Interaction Model. This way, it captures the Presentation and Dialog Model of other approaches, such as MOBI-D or Teallach.

In order to be able to represent tasks and user profiles designers have to detail business processes and the flow of work of the enterprise. This information includes primary information about users, such as work roles, individual skills and levels of experience. Since the User Model is related to all other design models the approach enhances the capabilities of approaches similar to ADEPT. It is possible to develop user-specific views not only for the Dialog Model, but also for the Task and Data Model. The adaptation is given similar to ADEPT, namely through influencing the prototype generation.

Other approaches to model-based design in the field of Human-Computer Interaction integrate ADEPT- and TADEUS-like approaches. They do not only focus on the mutual integration of Task and Dialog Models, but also on the status of organizational development, and as such on user characteristics. For instance, Forbrig (1999) assumes that the integration of adapted (sub)models allows the development of more flexible software systems. In an adapted Action Model, additional restrictions on the objects of the Business-Object Model, limitations or individual characteristics of users can be described. The Action Model and the Business-Object Model are sub models describing the environment, as well as a User Model. Further sub models like a Goal Model might be integrated. Whereas the kernel parts of the sub models are static the adaptable parts have to be interpreted during runtime to ensure an optimal support of the user.

In the field of hypermedia-application development, Brusilovsky (2002) in the ADAPTS project continued the work of successfully utilizing model-based approaches in this area, e.g., Francicso-Revilla et al. (2000). He uses integrated Domain and Task Models together with an overlay User Model. This way adaptive support on several stages of troubleshooting for technicians can be provided from identifying the source of troubles to determining the course of actions to guiding the user through the troubleshooting process to assembling an individualized set of supporting materials. The Domain and the Task model provide the framework for structuring application-domain knowledge (in this case content of technical manuals) and for representing the user. The User Model determines what task to do, what technical information to select to describe the task, and how to best display that information for a given technician's knowledge, experience, and preferences.

Tasks are usually indexed as a one-to-one relationship with a set of problem-domain elements with a specific concept or topic. The specific content that is accessed from the set (to support each step in the task) depends on the User Model. In addition, a one-to-many indexing scheme is used with content elements. This way, a technician may receive several links as optional navigation paths. Roles are used to identify the context within which a certain concept (component, system, task) appears. These roles are categorized in various ways so that the adaptation engine can make decisions on how and where the content is displayed in the interface.

The User Model is the source for personalizing the data and navigation. A user's experience 'value' is calculated from various evidences of user behavior collected by the system at various levels. Experience with data or a task is judged on various aspects. Each aspect is weighted according to its importance in determining overall user performance. The User Model independently accumulates several aspects (roles) of the experience and knowledge of each technician for each component or task. Whatever is done that is performance-relevant is immediately reflected in the User Model, since each user action is annotated with performance information.

Following the objectives of the paper, the review of model-based approaches has to be performed according to

(i)   to their capability to capture knowledge about users, in particular which perspective they address, either the individual or the organization of work

(ii)   the type of specification that is provided for representation, either declarative, procedural or both

(iii) the relation(s) of user models to the organizational context as well as to interaction facilities

(iv)   to their capability to support different styles of interaction and/or interactive devices, thus, enabling different contexts of use or users.

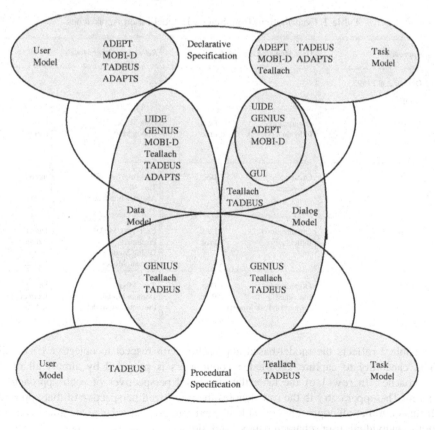

Fig. 5. Positioning of Selected Model-Based Approaches

Figure 5 gives a structured overview including the aforementioned approaches along two categories. The first category is the set of models, comprising the main types of models, namely the Task, Data, Dialog, and User Model. The positioning of the four types of models in the figure reflects the origin of model-based development. It started out with data- and GUI modeling – both consequently located in the center of the figure – and has been extended with task and user modeling. The second category of knowledge concerns the type of specification used for representation. We distinguish declarative specifications from procedural ones. At the intersections of these two categories, it can be visualized which approach contains structure and behavior specifications for which type of model.

As can be seen from the entries in Figure 5, most of the approaches follow the traditional lines of model-based development and comprise a Dialog and Data Model. Most of the Dialog Models have been developed for GUI-based applications. The majority of approaches also supports task and/or user modeling, however, preferably at the declarative layer of specification. Only few approaches support behavior specification, unfortunately only one user-specific procedures.

Table 2. Contributions from Selected Model-based Approaches

Approach	*User Modeling Approach*		*Relation to Other Models*	
DeBaar et al., 1992 UIDE	---		---	
GENIUS	Organization Individual (views)	Dec. Proc.	Data Model Dialog Model	Indirect Indirect
ADEPT	Organization Individual	Dec.	(Existing, Envi-sioned) Task M. Abstract Interface Model	Indirect Direct
MOBI-D	Organization Individual	Dec. Proc.	User-Task Model Presentation Mod. Dialog Model Domain Model	Direct Indirect Indirect Indirect
Teallach	Organization Individual (as part of Task Model)	Dec. Proc.	Task Model Domain Model Presentation Model	Direct Indirect Indirect

Table 2 reflects the model-based approaches with respect to objective (i) to (iii). The capability to capture knowledge about users is provided by almost all of the approaches. In row 1 of the table the supported perspectives of each approach are given. The upper entry in the row denotes the prioritized perspective of that approach. It turns out that all approaches capable to represent user knowledge are able to capture both, individual user characteristics, and organizational user knowledge, such as functional roles according to the organization of work.

Table 2. (cd.). Contributions from Selected Model-based Approaches

Approach	User Modeling Approach		Relation to Other Models	
TADEUS	Organization Individual	Dec. Proc.	Task Model Data Model Interaction Model	Direct Direct Direct
Forbrig, 1999	Organization Individual	Dec. Proc.	Business Object Model Action Model	Direct Direct
ADAPTS	Organization Individual	Dec.	Task Model Domain Model	Direct Direct

Objective (ii) asks for the type of specification that is provided for representation, either declarative, procedural or both. Each of the user-modeling approaches enables a declarative specification of user characteristics, some of them also a procedural one. Declarative specifications often represent the dialog control over presentation and functional issues. Objective (iii) concerns the relation(s) of user models to the organizational context as well as to interaction facilities and interactive devices. It turns out that the majority of user-modeling components are only related to a single model directly. Most of the approaches have merely indirect relationships to Dialog, Data and/or Task Models. From the data shown in Table 2 no general guidelines can be derived on how to relate User Models to other models. Rather, each model might influence user modeling, either through problem-domain elements (tasks or data), such as reflecting task perspectives on users, or through presentation elements (interaction styles, devices), e.g., mapping stereotypical interaction behavior on user profiles.

Table 3 shows the results for analyzing the capability of model-based approaches to support different styles of interaction, thus, enabling different devices or modalities of interaction for different contexts of use or users. In table 3, row 1, an indicator for the capability to assign different interaction styles or devices to software functions is addressed, namely, the question, in how far do the respective model-based approach allow to decouple functional core elements of applications from presentation, navigation, and interactive-manipulation facilities. This decoupling might be able to the full extent, in case the models concerning the functionality of an application and concerning the user interaction might exist separately. It might be partially enabled through separating at least some parts of the model elements, but permanently linking presentation, navigation or manipulation elements to core functions of an application. In row 2, the capability to assign various user interfaces to different core functions is discussed. Although the original introduction of the analyzed approaches might not have aimed at switching between interaction modalities or interactive devices, for the field of User Interface for All it is of interest, whether the approach could contribute to such flexible assignment activities. The entries also show whether such an implementation of the respective approach already exists. Finally, in row 3 the results of analyzing a further issue of switching between modalities and interactive devices is addressed. It has been questioned whether the model-based approaches allow to reflect dynamically occurring changes, either in terms of user behavior or the (organizational) setting a user is part of. The options for answering this issue range from manual generation of user interfaces (after changing the specification) to automated adaptation – the latter in case the interactive software system recognizes changes in behavior or setting characteristics without intervention of developers (see also section 2 on static and dynamic user modeling).

Table 3. Contributions to User-Interfaces-for-All-Developments from Selected Model-based Approaches

Approach	Decoupling UI from Functional Core	Flexible Assignment of Devices and Modalities	Reflection of Dynamic Changes
DeBaar et al., 1992 UIDE	Partially	Possible – not impl.	Manual generation
GENIUS	Partially	Possible – not impl.	Manual generation
ADEPT	Fully	Possible – not impl.	Manual generation
MOBI-D	Fully	Possible – not impl.	Manual generation
Teallach	Partially	Possible – not impl.	Manual generation
TADEUS	Fully	Possible – not impl.	Dyn. adaptation
Forbrig, 1999	Partially	Possible – not impl.	Dyn. adaptation
ADAPTS	Partially	Possible – not impl.	Dyn. adaptation

The results given in Table 3 show that not all approaches are capable to decouple functional core elements of applications from facilities for presentation, navigation, and interactive manipulation fully. The reason for that lies partially in the fact that some of the approaches do not cover fully either facilities for interaction (due to the lack of explicit presentation models) or the functionality of an application (since the do not go beyond domain-data modeling). However, their principal capability to enable the assignment of various user interfaces to different core functions is not affected by the results of the first item. Each of the investigated approaches provides means, such as generic representations, for switching between interaction modalities or interactive devices. Interestingly, there have not been published explicit results on that issue. This indicates that model-based design tools are not commonly used for the development of User Interfaces for All.

The final item that has been investigated addresses the capability of approaches to process user or context characteristics in a way that dynamically occurring changes can be captured dynamically, e.g., through adapting the user model to another level of skill during runtime. The results show that only some of the recent approaches allow the dynamic adaptation of user or context representations. In all the other cases developers have to change the specification and re-start the generation of user interfaces manually.

4 Conclusion

With information technology increasingly pervading information society interactive applications have to provide various interactive devices and interaction styles, in order to support a diverse user population. Taking that into account in the course of interactive-software development *pro-actively* is one of the core objectives in the Design-for-All concept. Thus, development schemes have to represent a variety of contexts of use and users, both, with respect to work tasks, and interaction facilities. Model-based user-interface development schemes might contribute through representing and processing several content elements stemming from usability engineering, see, e.g., Adler et al. (1992):

- User characteristics,
- the organization of the environment (tasks and problem domain data), e.g., specified as a set of goals in a specified context of use
- technical features (functions and user interface elements), *and*
- their intertwining.

Investigating traditional and recent model-based approaches reveals that most of them still follow the traditional lines of representation, combining a Data and Dialog Model. The latter focuses on GUI-based interaction. However, the majority of approaches enables task and/or user modeling, at least at a declarative layer of specification. The capability to represent knowledge about users is given by almost all of the approaches, both, in terms of individual user characteristics as well as organizational user knowledge, such as functional roles according to the organization of work.

User Models, in general, are related either to the organizational context or to interaction facilities directly. No general guidelines can be derived on how to relate User Models to other models – the approaches are too diversified to that respect. Some of the investigated approaches require tight coupling of functional core elements with facilities for presentation, navigation, and interactive manipulation. They either lack explicit Dialog or Data Models. However, they enable the assignment of various user interfaces to different core functions of applications. This way, they provide principal means to support switching between interaction modalities or interactive devices. Apparently, this feature has not been applied extensively. It can be expected that this potential will be used for future application developments.

The capability of model-based approaches to process user or context characteristics in a way that dynamically occurring changes can be captured dynamically has not been an explicit requirement for model-based approaches so far. Based on recent results also stemming from other fields, future developments will focus on adapting models to recognized changes in the environment of an application without intervention of developers. Overall, the study shows that model-based approaches are promising candidates for the comprehensive, but still structured development of User Interfaces for All. They require some innovation with respect to dynamic adaptation, in order to meet the objectives of universally-accessible technology development fully.

References

1. Abowd, G.D.; Mynatt, E.D.: Charting Past, Present, and Future Research in Ubiquitous Computing, ACM TO-CHI, Vol. 7, No. 1, pp. 29–58, March 2000.
2. Adler, P.S.; Winograd, T. (eds.): Usability: Turning Technologies into Tools, Oxford University Press, Oxford, New York, 1992.
3. Arehart, C. et al.: Professional WAP, WroxPress, 2000.
4. Benyon, D.; Crerar, A.; Wilkinson, S.: Individual Differences and Inclusive Design, in: Stephanidis, pp. 21–46, 2001.
5. Brusilovsky, P.: Domain, Task, and User Models for an Adaptive Hypermedia Performance Support System, Proc. IUI'02, ACM, pp. 23–30, 2002.
6. BIT: Behaviour and Information Technology: Special Issue on Individual Issues in the Use of Computers, Vol. 19, No. 4, pp. 283–313, July-August 2000.
7. Chen, Ch.: Individual Differences in a Spatial-Semantic Virtual Environment, J. American Society for Information Science, Vol. 51, No. 6, pp. 529–542, 2000.
8. Cotterman, W.W.; Kumar, K.: User Cube: A Taxonomy of End Users, Communications of the ACM, Vol. 32, No. 11, pp. 1313–1320, 1989.
9. da Silva, P.P.; Griffiths, T.; Paton, N.W.: Generating User Interface Code in a Model-Based User Interface Development Environment, Proc. AVI'00, ACM, pp. 155–160, 2000.
10. deBaar, D.J.M.; Foley, J.; Mullet, K.E. Coupling Application Design and User Interface Design, Proc. CHI'92, ACM, pp. 259–266, 1992.
11. Eisenstein, , J.; Puerta, A.R.: Adaptation in Automated User-Interface Design, Proc. IUI'00, ACM, pp. 74–81, 2000.
12. Forbrig, P.: Task- and object-oriented Development of Interactive Systems – How Many Models are Necessary?, Proc. DSVIS'99, Braga, 1999.
13. Francisco-Revilla, L.; Shipman III, F.M.: Adaptive Medical Information Delivery: Combining User, Task, and Situation Models, Proc. IUI'00, ACM, pp. 94–97, 2000.
14. Janssen, Ch., Weisbecker, A., Ziegler, J. Generating User Interfaces from Data Models and Dialogue Net Specifications, Proc. INTERCHI'93, ACM/IFIP, pp. 418–423, 1993.
15. McTear, M.F.: Intelligent Interface Technology: From Theory to Reality, Interacting with Computers, Vol. 12, pp. 323–336, 2000.
16. Pohl, W.; Nick, A.: Machine Learning and Knowledge Representation in the LabUr Approach to User Modeling, Proc. 7th Int. Conf. on User Modeling, Springer, Vienna, pp. 179–188, 1999.

17. Puerta, A.R.: A Model-Based Interface Development Environment, IEEE Software, Vol. 14, No. 4, pp. 40–47, 1997.
18. Rich, E.: Stereotype and User Modeling, in: User Models in Dialog Systems, eds: Kobsa, A.; Wahlster, W., Springer, Berlin, pp. 35–51, 1988.
19. Shneiderman, B.: Universal Usability. Pushing Human-Computer Interaction Research to Empower Every Citizen, Communications of the ACM, Vol. 43, No. 5, pp. 85–91, May 2000.
20. Stary, Ch.: TADEUS: Seamless Development of Task-Based and User-Oriented Interfaces, IEEE Transactions on Systems, Man, and Cybernetics, Vol. 30, pp. 509–525, 2000.
21. Stephanidis, C. (ed.) : User Interfaces for All. Concepts, Methods, and Tools, Lawrence Erlbaum, Mahwah, NJ, 2001.
22. Sukaviriya, P.N.; Foley, J.D.; Griffith, T.: A Second Generation User Interface Design Environment, Proc. INTERCHI'93, ACM/IFIP, pp.375–382, 1993.
23. Szekely, P.: Retrospective and Challenges for Model-Based Interface Development, Proc. DSV-IS'96, pp. 1–27, Springer, Vienna, 1996.
24. Wilson, St.; Johnson, P.: Bridging the Generation Gap: From Work Tasks to User Interface Design, Proc. CADUI'96, pp. 77–94, 1996.
25. Woywod, A.: Verfeinerung von Expertisesystemen durch Benutzermodellierung, Peter Lang, Frankfurt, 1997.

Implementing Inclusive Design: The Discrepancy between Theory and Practice

Hua Dong[1], Simeon Keates[1], P. John Clarkson[1], and Julia Cassim[2]

[1] Engineering Design Centre, Department of Engineering, University of Cambridge,
Trumpington Street, Cambridge CB2 1PZ, UK
{hd233, lsk12, pjc10}@eng.cam.ac.uk
http://www-edc.eng.cam.ac.uk
[2] The Helen Hamlyn Research Centre, Royal College of Art, Kensington Gore,
London SW7 2EU, UK
j.cassim@rca.ac.uk http://www.hhrc.rca.ac.uk

Abstract. The theory of inclusive design tends to require user involvement and iterative assessment throughout the whole design process. However, in an industrial context, companies are restricted by design constraints such as time and cost. Through investigating eight projects focusing on inclusive design, the authors highlight discrepancies between theoretical models and industry practice and analyse the underlying reasons. Related issues such as bottom-up design approaches and estimates of design exclusion are also discussed. It is concluded that a change of attitudes towards people with disabilities by people commissioning, as well as performing, design and the provision of design support tools are necessary to bring inclusive design theory and practice closer together.

1 Introduction

The building of the information society brings a question of inclusion/exclusion. Does new technology and production development promise better social inclusion? In recent years there has been a shift in attitude away from treating typically socially excluded groups, for example disabled and older people, as special cases requiring special design solutions, and towards integrating them into the mainstream of everyday life. It is commonly accepted that such integration can be best achieved through a more inclusive design approach.

The intent of inclusive design is to improve quality of life for as many people as possible by making products/systems, communications, built environments and services more usable and accessible. It goes beyond user-centred design in that it caters for a wider population rather than *ad hoc* user groups. Inclusive design should benefit people of all ages and abilities [3]. Consequently, there is a need for design practitioners, commissioners, and service providers to better understand user characteristics and capabilities.

The emerging theory of inclusive design, influenced by user-centred design, tends to emphasise *end-user involvement* in the design process and *iterative assessment*

N. Carbonell, C. Stephanidis (Eds.): User Interfaces for All, LNCS 2615, pp. 106–117, 2003.

starting from the very beginning, and continuing throughout, the whole design process [12]. However, both end-user involvement and iterative assessment are time-consuming and consequently, expensive. As the design process is typically constrained by both time and budget, it may not be practical to implement them. There appears to be a clear discrepancy between theory and practice.

With trend-setting design companies, such as IDEO, pioneering industrial inclusive design, and the concept of inclusive design being gradually introduced to a wider range of industries, more and more UK design consultancies have begun to learn about inclusive design and to practise it for particular projects [1], [2], [5]. The intensive investigation into the design practices of eight design consultancies discussed in the paper reveals a number of significant discrepancies between inclusive design theory and industrially-viable practice. For example, aside from the time and cost issues associated with user involvement in the design process, many of the companies inter-viewed also questioned the value of such involvement and the feasibility of iterative design assessment in real-life situations.

This paper will present and analyse such discrepancies between inclusive design theory and practice. It comprises three major parts: firstly, a method for practising inclusive design is introduced, together with a method for a descriptive study of the practice; secondly, several findings resulting from the investigation on the practice are presented; and thirdly, a number of theoretical models are compared with practical models. This paper concludes with a clarification of the problem, an exploration of possible solutions and an introduction of support tools developed by the Cambridge Engineering Design Centre.

2 Methodology

In encouraging industry to practice inclusive design, the Helen Hamlyn Research Centre (HHRC) at the Royal College of Art has teamed up with the Design Business Association (DBA) to stage two events[1] - DBA Design Challenge 2000, "care for our future selves;" and DBA Design Challenge 2001, "innovation through inclusive de-sign." A number of interested design companies participated in the challenges. Their experiences were investigated through interviews by two researchers from the Cam-bridge Engineering Design Centre, and one from HHRC. The two institutes are team members of the EPSRC funded "i~design" research project.

2.1 DBA Design Challenges

As most of the designers participating in the DBA Design Challenges knew little about inclusive design, the HHRC provided resource packs of related publications, web-sites and expert contact information to all participants. Forums of "critical" users were also organised for each consultancy. The forums were a mix of users with congenital and

---

[1] A further one is planned for December 2002.

acquired disabilities and consisted of (volunteer) wheelchair users, users with arthritis, one-arm users, partially sighted and blind users, those with degenerative conditions such as MS, and/or cognitive disabilities [5]. The design consultancies were given a 6 - 8 week period for developing their concepts. All of the consultancies consulted the user forums at least once in the early stages of the challenges. Table 1 shows the profiles of the eight design consultancies interviewed and their DBA projects.

Table 1. Profile of design consultancies

Design consultancy	Specialist area	DBA Challenge project
Consultancy A	Product, transport and structural packaging design	**"Milkman"** (packaging design)
Consultancy B	Product, environment and transport design	**"Sensory web"** (interface & product design)
Consultancy C	Multiple-disciplinary design & brand strategy consultancy	**"Broadband internet site"** (web-site design)
Consultancy D	Product design excellence	**"Kettlesense"** (product design)
Consultancy E	Retail, leisure and workplace design	**"Mobospace"** (architectural/interior design)
Consultancy F	(A large) integrated design firm	**"Inspiration park"** (environmental design)
Consultancy G	Independent brand consultancy	**"Re: mind"** (graphic & product design)
Consultancy H	Packaging and brand design	Products & packaging for the bathroom

Among the above projects, *Inspiration park*, *Kettlesense*, *Milkman* and *Broadband internet site* have been praised widely or even resulted in new business opportunities.

2.2 Interviews

The interviews were conducted between March to May, 2002 [5], and aimed to:
1. find out about the consultancies' perspectives of inclusive design;
2. gain an understanding of how design companies implement inclusive design; and
3. understand what they have learned from the challenges and the impact on their future working practice.

All interviews took place at the design consultancies. The interviews were structured around a pre-prepared set of questions closely related to the above objectives, but performed in an open-ended manner. On average the interviews lasted 90-120 minutes and typically involved 1-4 designers/project managers [5]. All the interviews were tape-recorded.

3 Findings

The interviews provided an insight into industrial /commercial perspectives of inclusive design and the challenge of implementing inclusive design in industrial and commercial contexts.

3.1 Perspectives on *Inclusive Design* and *User Involvement*

Most of the design consultancies interviewed had no relevant experience before the DBA Challenges, but they began to gain an understanding of the concept through practice. Inclusive design is considered to be rooted in social consciousness, and concerned with a wider range of people's requirements. A number of design consultancies asserted that inclusive design should be in *"everybody's interest."* [5] However, it appears that some consultancies still tend to associate inclusive design with designing for disabled people.

The involvement of disabled users was a new experience to all of the design consultancies. Designers considered the experience very useful and valuable. Their opinions were reflected by their comments:
- *"Talking to people is very important. It offers a fast understanding of the users."*
- *"Disabled people are expert users as they always look beyond the product features to detect potential problems. They select their products thoroughly."*
- *"Designers can get inspiration from users about how to make everyday things more accessible and interesting."*
- *"Users can change designers' wrong perceptions and help designers work in a more organic way."*
- *"Even some common sense from the users is valuable to designers, as designers seldom think in that way, or they tend to ignore it."*

3.2 Design Processes

Although design processes may differ slightly from one design consultancy to another, they all typically follow the same generic procedure:

→ get brief from the client (the company commissioning the design);
    → interpret the brief;
        → agree with the client on the finalised brief;

→ develop concepts (often through brainstorming);
    → present several concepts to the client and select the solution;
   → develop, refine and implement the design.

In this typical (and almost always short) design process, the consultancies perceive that there is little room for user involvement. The clients generally commission external research companies to run focus groups independently of the design consultancies. Sometimes the designers may audit such focus group meetings, but they are most typically only observers of the process. Consequently, it can be said that there is no direct contact between the designers and the users. Indeed, of the eight design consultancies interviewed, five stated that the DBA Challenge project was their first chance to talk to real end-users, whether disabled or not.

It was also interesting to note that the consultancies' current design processes typically do not include explicit design assessment, although some of the design consultancies occasionally carry out informal assessment in which designers play the role of consumers. Designers tend to rely a lot on their own experience and the information they can get immediately, for example, through consultation with their colleagues, family members or friends. Sometimes the designers find products available on the market and test them in order to detect potential problems. Sometimes they perform simulation testing, for example, wearing layers of gloves to hamper dexterity when testing prototypes. Most of the design consultancies have shown an interest in in-house simulation assessment.

3.3 Design Approaches

Since each design consultancy had been provided with a user forum consisting of disabled users only, all projects started, more or less, with a "design for disabled people" mindset. The approaches adopted by *Inspiration park*, *Milkman*, the *Broadband internet site* and *Kettlesense* focused on the mainstream market, aiming to design for people with and without disabilities. The other four projects, however, seemed to focus on the disabled users' special needs, although some solutions may happen to be beneficial for people without disabilities.

A typical design approach for the DBA Design Challenge project can be seen clearly from the development of the *Kettlesense* concept. The design team started by targeting on "*something mundane.*" They found kettles were intended for everyday use, but still presented difficulties for users, especially older and disabled people. The design team studied a range of kettles on the market and identified a number of good features and bad features. They then consulted the user forums. Through interaction with four disabled users (one with arthritis, one blind, one partially-sighted and a stroke patient with the use of one hand), the designers not only confirmed their initial assumptions, but were also informed about latent problems they would not otherwise have predicted. For example, the users said they would not spend more than £50 for even a "perfect" kettle. This prompted the design team to think of using simple boiling systems. Key priorities were listed based on the users' comments, namely:

- safety (heat of unit/boiling water);
- filling (spout size/location, water level, lid removal and replacement);
- pouring (seeing cup/tipping; weight, secure grip/low strength);
- lifting (weight, accurate water level);
- base (stability/cable management); and
- stigmatism (not for "the disabled").

Fig. 1. A "no-pour" kettle

The solution *Kettlesense* (Fig. 1), is a 1-litre aesthetically pleasing, lightweight, "no-pour" kettle with a cool wall, audio alert, auto-retractable cable, and a tactile water level indicator. In addition, the new design adopted the existing technology of a simple coffee-maker system for boiling water, which costs less than £15.

The solution is appealing and danger-free, even for children.

4 Discussions

The results of the interviews were compared with related models and established theories. Notable discrepancies were found and are presented in this section.

4.1 Questioning the Lack of User Contact

It was pointed out by Zeisel [10] in 1984, and shown in Fig. 2, that there are "gaps" between users and designers, as well as between users and clients.

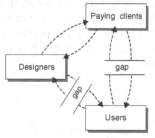

Fig. 2. Zeisel's user-needs gap model

It has also been said that users are generally more remote from designers than from clients. Whilst the designers may be able to interact with a motivated client, there is rarely any formal access to users at all [10]. This was certainly the case for the eight design consultancies interviewed.

The user forums proved helpful in enabling designers with little experience of inclusive design to fulfill the role of "design for inclusion." This seems to have confirmed the rule-of-thumb for any user-friendly design, i.e. getting users involved is always helpful. However, despite all the positive opinions about user involvement, real-life project circumstances reveal completely different attitudes. The majority of the consultancies interviewed do not usually involve users as directly as they did for the Design Challenges [5]. When asked about the feasibility of involving users in their future practice, most of them showed reservations. There are several reasons for this:

-   User involvement is not a part of their current design processes and it is thought to be *"time consuming," "complicated"* and *"difficult to organise."* Designers also cited lack of contact with users beyond conventional market research data.
-   The user research undertaken depends on what the clients would like to pay for. It is not a decision made by the design consultancies.
-   The results from focus groups can be contradictory and are not always useful and reliable. It is difficult to find informative user representatives. Moreover, the organiser or dominant participants can easily manipulate the focus group. This adversely affects how the designers perceive the overall usefulness of interaction with users.
-   The designers worry that they may inadvertently offend disabled users when attempting to work with them, because the designers have little or no experience interacting with disabled users. (NB: This was their reaction prior to meeting the users, and disappeared after contact with the user forums)

All in all, because of the general constraints of time and budget, and also the inherent complexity of the task, user involvement is not likely to be integrated into the design consultancies' current design processes for the foreseeable future. In addition, the designers do not think they are in the right place to run user-consulting sessions, because their expertise is not in that area and they are afraid of influencing focus groups by their particular opinions. If they have to get information from real users, all the design consultancies said they would like to refer to specialist research institutes. This may indicate a possible way forward: some design consultancies may become specialised in running "special" user groups and providing information for a more inclusive solution. Their expertise may fall into the first part of James Pirkl's *"new market equation,"* as shown in Fig. 3 [11].

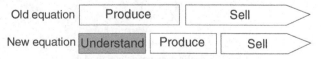

Fig. 3. A new market equation

4.2 Facilitating Design Assessment

There are a number of design theories in which evaluation/assessment is considered an integral part of the design process, such as shown in Fig. 4, the generic design phases [13]

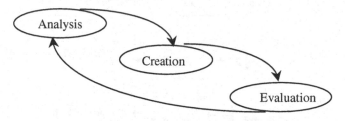

Fig. 4. Generic design phases

It is also suggested that when designing any new product, a three-stage development strategy should be adopted [8]:

Stage 1 - define the problem;
Stage 2 - develop a solution;
Stage 3 - evaluate the solution.

Markus and Maver [10] produced rather more elaborate maps of the design process, such as shown in Fig. 5, which are focused on architectural design, but are also applicable to product design:

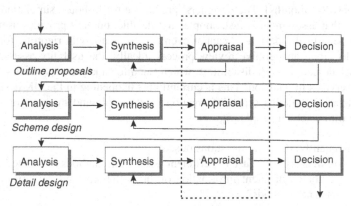

Fig. 5. Markus & Maver's map of the design process

The recent research on inclusive design at Cambridge Engineering Design Centre proposed a design review process that also addresses the importance of design assessment, shown in Fig. 6 [9].

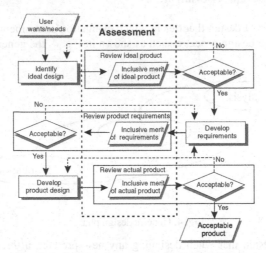

Fig. 6. A design review process for inclusive design

However, as mentioned in section 3.2, the current design processes do not facilitate such iterative design appraisal/assessment procedures. For the eight design consultancies, assessment is often carried out in an informal manner. The question of why design assessment is regarded as so important in theoretical research while almost always ignored by practising design consultancies needs further investigation. However, the need to make quick launches to market might account for the lack of practical design assessment. Current design, especially product design, often has extremely strict time limits (for example, a product project from brief to final solution on average takes only 2-3 months). The designers' preference for in-house simulation is probably because that assessment is fast, simple, and flexible, but still provides useful information. Normally the designers cannot even carry out a single rigorous formal assessment, let alone an iterative review process. Ideally, the usability assessment should also include people with disabilities, which can inform key issues relating to the product or services in question. This is currently not happening in the UK design industry. The literature contains scant information on the tools and methods of user/product testing with disabled people [6].

Consequently, there are questions raised:
- Are there simple, fast and efficient assessment methods available?
- Are there sufficient information on the reliability and validity of the testing tools and methods?

These questions are addressed in Section 5.

4.3 Bottom-Up and Top-Down Approaches

Two basic approaches to inclusive design have been found in the DBA Design Challenges (see Sect. 3.3), which can be abstracted as bottom-up approach and top-down approach (Fig. 7).

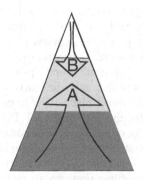

Fig. 7. The bottom-up approach and top-down approach

The triangle in Fig. 7 symbolises a user pyramid with three colors: dark gray, pale gray and white, representing fully able users, users with slightly restricted capabilities, and users with severely restricted capabilities, respectively. Arrow A symbolises the "bottom-up" approach, which extends the usability of products from large numbers of able-bodied people (the "mainstream") to include people with disabilities. Arrow B symbolises the "top-down" approach, which meets the specialised requirements of people with more severe disabilities and extends to appeal to a larger number of users with less severe impairments.

Considering the aim of inclusive design, to make products accessible to the widest population, the bottom-up approach is preferable. However, in the field of product design, "*special aids and equipment for disabled people are devised top-down rather than bottom–up*" [6] and "*the special needs of disabled people are not, however, by any means always best accommodated by targeting them specifically*" [7]. The top-down approach may risk denying the access need of people with mild or moderate disabilities. For example, it is very possible for designers to take into account blind users by putting Braille on lift buttons, without considering improving the contrast and size of the letters or providing tactile signage. The Braille solution, however, will only be of benefit to 3%[2] of the total vision-impaired population at most, as the majority of them need not, or cannot, read Braille. The bottom-up approach has the potential to cater for more users, but cannot reach the top of the user pyramid. As demonstrated by the DBA practices, both approaches are possible for inclusive design. As long as designers keep the widest population's requirements in mind and try to accommodate the maximum number of people, the adoption of either approach is potentially suitable.

---

[2] According to the 1986-7 estimation of the Royal National Institute for the Blind, about 3 per cent of registered blind or partially-sighted people in the UK can actually read Braille.

4.4 Playing the Numbers Game

Although inclusive design was promoted as a business case promising a larger market, the interviews found, however, that designers themselves were not particularly interested in the numbers *per se*. Rather, they considered numbers would be a strong argument to be presented to their clients. They can use estimates of exclusion numbers to persuade their clients to adopt a more inclusive solution. Clients will be more interested in the number of people excluded, as the numbers represent potential customers, and customers represent money. A more inclusive product may also win them a previously unavailable extra market share. Consequently, methods for estimating the number of new customers that might result from a particular design decision would be helpful. It has been recognised that sales to individuals without disabilities would presumably increase if products were made easier to use. However, little data is available to support this except for the case of the BT Big Button telephone, which was designed initially for older users and those with partial sight, but became a popular mainstream product. Notably absent are any concrete numbers indicating the relationship between specific features and the additional numbers of potential new customers without disabilities or less disabling impairments (for example: poor sight alleviated by lens) that those features would attract [14].

5   Conclusions

As the interviews demonstrated, progress has already been made in raising awareness of inclusive design. Some design companies' attempts to associate inclusive design with *designing for disabled people* might result from the inherent restriction of the DBA project, namely: the "disability care"– skewed design briefs and the interaction with user forums consisting exclusively of people with moderate or severe disabilities.

Although the DBA Design Challenge project is not a precise reflection of a typical design project in that it is a short-term collaborative project free from the many typical constraints of a real design commission, it still provides a platform for gaining an insight into implementing inclusive design in an industrial (commercial) context. In particular, the investigation of the discrepancies between established design theories and current design practices has highlighted a couple of critical issues relating to the implementation of inclusive design. Although the social attitudes to people with disabilities are of most importance in embracing the concept of inclusive design, the investigation indicates that the trigger of a more inclusive approach will also depend on the provision of supportive methods and tools to designers.

Currently, a number of research tools are being generated at Cambridge Engineering Design Centre and HHRC, which promise to provide such support. The tools are intended for designers, design managers, and marketing executives to use. They include:

- the market share estimation based on the Cambridge population model – the Inclusive Design Cube [8];
- the mapping model of product features and user capabilities;

- ycapability database with consideration of multiple capability losses [4];
- yfast product assessment tool;
- on-line inclusive design resources.

The usefulness of the above tools depends on the thorough understanding of the range of users' capabilities and industry practices. The reliability and validity of the tools/methods, however, need to be tested with potential users, which consequently requires working closely with designers and end-users.

Acknowledgements. The authors wish to thank Roger Coleman of the HHRC for facilitating the interviews, and Carlos Cardoso for his assistance with the interviews.

References

1. Cassim, J.: Innovate. Issue 1 (spring), HHRC, Royal College of Art. London (2001)
2. Cassim, J.: Innovate. Issue 2 (autumn), HHRC, Royal College of Art. London (2001)
3. Centre for Universal Design: What is Universal Design. At:
    http://www.design.ncsu.edu/cud/univ_design/ud.htm (1998)
4. Clarkson, P. J., Keates, S., Quantifying Design Exclusion. In: Keates, S., Langdon, P., Clarkson, P. J., Robinson, P. (eds.): Universal Access and Assistive Technology. Spinger-Verlag, London (2002) 23–32
5. Dong, H., Cardoso, C., Cassim, J., Keates, S., Clarkson, P. J.: Inclusive Design: Reflections on Design Practice. Technical report of Cambridge Engineering Department, CUED/C-EDC/TR118-June 2002
6. Goldsmith, S., Designing for the Disabled: The New Paradigm. Architectural press, Oxford (1997)
7. Goldsmith, S., The Bottom-up Methodology of Universal Design. In: Preiser Wolfgang, F., E., Ostroff, E., (eds.): Universal Design Handbook. McGraw-Hill, New York (2001)
8. Keates, S., Clarkson, P. J., Countering Design Exclusion. In: Keates, S., Langdon, P., Clarkson, P. J., Robinson, P. (eds.): Universal Access and Assistive Technology. Spinger-Verlag, London (2002) 33–42
9. Law, C., M., Barnicle, K., Vanderheiden, G. C.: Usability Testing of People with Disabilities: Where Do You Begin. At:
    http://www.adptnev.org/21century/proceedings3php#5E2 (2000)
10. Lawson, R.: How Designers Think: The Design Process Demystified (3rd edn.) Architectural Press, Oxford (1997)
11. Pirkl, J. J.: Transgenerational Design: Products for an Aging Population. Van Nostrand Reinhold, New York (1994)
12. Säde, S.: Towards User-Centred Design: Method Development Project in a Product Design Consultancy. The Design Journal. Vol. 4, Issue 3. Hobbs the Printers, Totton (2001) 20–32
13. Stanton, N.: Key Topics in Consumer Products. In: Stanton, N. (ed.) Human Factors in Consumer Products. Taylor & Francis, Padstow (1998)
14. Vanderheiden G., Vanderheiden K., and Tobias, J., Universal Design Motivators and Facilitators. At: http://www.adpatenev.org/21century/proceedings4.php#6F1

Scenario-Based Argumentation for Universal Access

Demosthenes Akoumianakis[1] and Constantine Stephanidis[1,2]

[1]Institute of Computer Science, Foundation for Research and Technology-Hellas
Science & Technology Park of Crete
Heraklion, Crete, GR-71110, GREECE
Tel: +30-810-391741 - Fax: +30-810-391740
{ demosthe, cs }@ics.forth.gr
[2]Department of Computer Science, University of Crete

Abstract. We present two analytical techniques, namely *scenario screening* and *growth scenarios*, for engineering universal access into interactive applications and services. The techniques are intended to bridge across design reflection and envisioning of new practices through use cases. They foster an exploratory approach to design, progressively leading to an understanding of the global execution context of tasks, thus towards universal access. In this paper, we elaborate on the rationale and basic concepts behind scenario screening and growth scenarios, and discuss their application in a small case study in the domain of Health Telematics.

1 Introduction and Background

The IS4ALL project[1] is a *thematic network* that seeks to advance the principles and practice of universal access in the field of Health Telematics. The specific objectives of the project can be summarized as follows:

- To consolidate existing knowledge on Universal Access in the context of IST, which is currently dispersed across different international sites and actors, into a comprehensive code of design practice (e.g., enumeration of methods, process guidelines, etc).
- To translate the consolidated wisdom to concrete recommendations for emerging technologies (e.g., emerging desktop and mobile platforms) in Health Telematics.
- To demonstrate the validity and applicability of the recommendations in the context of concrete scenarios drawn from an experimental regional Health Telematics network.
- To promote the Universal Access principles and practice in Health Telematics through a mix of outreach activities, which include seminars, and participation in major international conferences, concertation meetings, and project clustering events.

The primary focus of IS4ALL is on the impact of advanced desktop and mobile interaction technologies on emerging Health Telematics products and services. The

---

[1] "Information Society for All", IST-1999-14101, http://is4all.ics.forth.gr

N. Carbonell, C. Stephanidis (Eds.): User Interfaces for All, LNCS 2615, pp. 118–128, 2003.
© Springer-Verlag Berlin Heidelberg 2003

domain of Health Telematics has been selected on the grounds of being a critical service sector, catering for the population at large, and at the same time involving a variety of diverse target user groups (e.g., doctors, nurses, administrators, patients). These characteristics render it a complex domain, due to the inherent diversity, and an ideal "testbed" for exemplifying the principles of Universal Access and assessing both the challenges and the opportunities in the context of the emerging Information Society.

This paper sets out to briefly elaborate one of the technical objectives of the project, namely the compilation of the IS4ALL method base, which will provide the means through which universal access principles can be put into practice in the domain of Heath Telematics. In doing so, the paper is divided into two sections. The following section briefly outlines the project's methodology, which links with scenario-based design approaches and in particular requirements engineering through scenarios. In the latter part, the paper presents how methods and techniques for universal access are being consolidated and provides an illustrative example.

2 Methodology

To attain the above stated objectives, IS4ALL has defined a technical approach, which links with *scenario-based* perspectives on systems development [1,2] and in particular the cluster of techniques for *requirements engineering through scenarios* [4]. Scenarios in the context of IS4ALL are perceived as narrative descriptions of computer-mediated human activities in a Health Telematics environment. The social setting of a Health Telematics environment may be bound to a clinic within the hospital, a ward within a clinic or even to an end-user's residential environment. The scope of such scenarios is intended to be narrow and focused on a very specific issue.

As an example, a possible scenario could consider patient's access to the electronic healthcare record from home, or while on the move, using a portable or network attachable device. Such reference scenarios are typically extracted by reference to technical developments planned in the course of a particular project (either industrial or EC-funded), a national initiative or alternatively, they may depict post-project activities relevant for exploitation and take-up. Nevertheless, irrespective of their source, IS4ALL scenarios serve a dual role, namely as a *resource* for subsequent design deliberations and/or as a reference point for *validating* specific universal access methods and techniques.

2.1 Scenario Development

IS4ALL's approach to scenario-based design entails a process of extracting and developing scenarios for two primary purposes: firstly, to obtain a detailed insight into the universal access requirements relevant to Health Telematics, and secondly, to demonstrate the validity and applicability of the envisioned universal access code of practice. To this effect, scenarios are being formulated around an agreed common theme, namely *electronic patient records* and applications or services built around them. Scenario formulation is an *iterative* process.

Initially, narrative descriptions of designated tasks, as carried out by actual users, are developed, and subsequently peer reviewed by health professionals or end-user communities. This peer review acts as validity check to ensure that the scenarios are relevant and realistic accounts of computer-mediated human activities. In the course of this iterative phase, any system mock-ups, prototypes or other artefacts, which reveal aspects of the scenario's real execution context are taken into account.

2.2 Scenario Screening

Once an initial formulation is compiled and agreed upon, scenarios are articulated in such a way so as to unfold various perspectives relevant to universal access. Two primary scenario articulation mechanisms are supported, namely *scenario screening* and *growth scenarios*. Both mechanisms serve the purpose of extrapolating (some of) the universal access design considerations relevant to a particular scenario. In other words, by screening initial scenarios and compiling growth scenarios, one can gain a thorough understanding of the global execution context of the tasks designated in the original formulation of the scenario.

Scenario screening assumes the availability of artefacts for review and discussion. It entails a structured process whereby implicit or explicit assumptions embedded in an artefact and related to the intended users, the platform used to implement the artefact and the context of use, are identified and documented. Typically, scenario screening is a group activity, which is initiated and guided by an analyst. Participants may include representatives of end user communities, project managers, developers, etc. Thus, screening is best organised as a collaborative activity in which participants converge to obtain a common understanding of what is at stake, by identifying implicit or explicit assumptions in the reference scenario.

2.3 Growth Scenarios

In a subsequent phase, these assumptions are relaxed to facilitate envisioning and generation of new artefacts through compiling growth scenarios. Growth scenarios are slightly different in the sense that they are instruments for envisioning rather than reflection. Growth scenarios are formulated as a result of argumentation based on the identified assumptions in the reference scenario. Argumentation is facilitated by addressing critical design issues or questions, such as "what if … the task was to be used by another user?", "what if … the task was to be carried out through an alternative device?" etc. Through such argumentation, the group reaches consensus on the new relevant task execution contexts which in turn, is documented as growth scenarios comprising narrative descriptions of envisioned activities and corresponding artefacts in the form of mock ups or low fidelity prototypes.

3 An Example Case Study

To illustrate the use of scenario screening and the compilation of growth scenarios, we will make use of a case study. We assume that following a patient's visit to his/her General Practitioner, the doctor compiles a prescription for several pharmaceuticals items. The prescription can be processed on-line using the doctor's desktop terminal, which can access the on-line pharmacy store. In this context, one of the tasks to be performed entails the on-line pharmacy store's request for specifying payment details in order to process the transaction. The dialogue used is depicted in Figure 1.

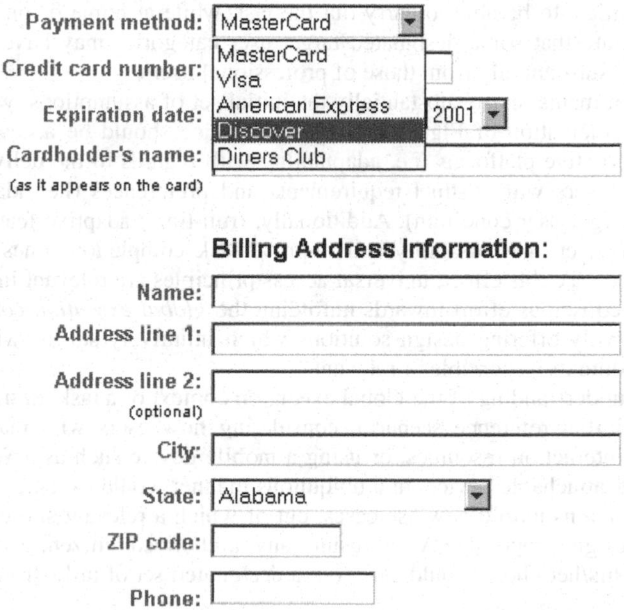

Fig. 1. A tentative artifact for specifying method of payment and billing address; it is assumed that the user has already compiled the order for pharmaceuticals and that this order is pending clearance once the payment details and the billing information are specified

As shown, in order to complete the task, the user will have to fill-in a form-like Graphical User Interface, providing information such as type of card, card number, expiration date, user's name as printed on the card, billing address information, etc. Such a scenario designates a particular execution context for the task, which implicitly assumes, at least the following:

- the target user is a professional with access to a personal computer, and in possession of all necessary human capabilities to operate the designated dialogue
- the underlying technology platform offers the needed resources, in terms of software libraries, input / output devices, etc to realize the graphical dialogue
- the task is to be executed from a residential or business context of use.

Accordingly, the dialogue of Figure 1 has been designed to suit the specific execution context described above.

3.1 Universal Access Challenges

Let us now assume that the on-line pharmacy store wishes to expand the scope of the service in such a way so that professionals can compile prescriptions on the move and upon visiting patients at home. In such a case, the same functionality should be made available via a PDA or a mobile device. Moreover, it is deemed appropriate that the service should be also available over the WWW to meet the growing demands of end users. An added element for consideration is that for the on-line pharmacy store, the re-engineering of the service implies more than mere flexibility of the way in which the application is delivered. Specifically, they would like end users, including people with disabilities, to be able to carry out the task while at home or on the move and they appreciate that some designated target user categories may have requirements, which differ substantially from those of professional users.

These requirements revise substantially the initial set of assumptions, which gave rise to the implementation of Figure 1. The new service should be accessible not only through alternative platforms (i.e. adaptability with regards to the delivery medium), but also by users with distinct requirements and preferences (i.e. adaptability with regards to target user condition). Additionally, (run-time) adaptive features may also be required to enhance usability and improve task completion times under certain circumstances. To this effect, universal access principles are relevant in so far as they postulate a conscious effort towards unfolding the *global execution context* of a task and respectively offering design solutions which intuitively suit as wide a range of execution contexts as possible or relevant.

To gain an understanding of the global execution context of a task, designers typically revisit the initial reference scenario, considering how users who may not possess designated interaction resources, or using a mobile device such as a WAP phone, or any network attachable device, in a ubiquitous manner, could execute the task. These scenario revisions unfold new use cases, out of which a relevant subset may become concrete design proposals. As a result, any authorized citizen, using an access terminal of his/her choice could carry out a designated set of tasks from anywhere, at any time.

Towards, such a vision IS4ALL is developing both macro- and micro-level instruments [5] to help designers gain an understanding of the global execution context of tasks and to structure design in such a way so as to empower access to applications and services by authorized users, anytime, anywhere. At macro-level, the project is working on general process-oriented guidelines and methods, which bring universal access considerations to the forefront in early stages of a product's lifecycle. At the micro-level, IS4ALL seeks to provide validated techniques, which can be applied to address specific challenges (i.e. artefact reengineering, understanding the global execution context, user profiling, platform integration, etc).

In what follows, we describe how two micro-level analytical techniques, namely scenario screening and growth scenarios can be used to facilitate, on the one hand identification of the scope of universal access relative to a particular task and on the other hand a structured process whereby a tentative artefact is revised, extended and reformulated to suit new execution contexts.

Figure 2 describes the concept and interrelationship between the two scenario articulation mechanisms.

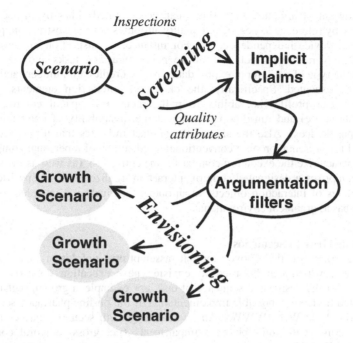

Fig. 2. Scenario screening and growth scenarios. Inspections and quality attributes are indicative techniques for screening. The shaded parts depict envisioned use practices.

3.2 Scenario Articulation Mechanisms

Scenario Screening

Scenario screening seeks to identify and formulate implicit claims embedded in an artefact into suitable argumentation filters. Argumentation filters may take several forms, such as heuristics, structured questions or narratives. Examples of the latter are depicted in Table 1.

Table 1. Examples of screening or argumentation filters

Code	Description
Af-1:	How can the task be carried out with an alternative pointing device (e.g. a stylus of a palmtop computer)?
Af-2:	How can the task be performed in a public kiosk?
Af-3:	How can users with gross-temporal control perform the task?
Af-4:	What artifact is appropriate to facilitate switch-based interaction?

A relevant set of argumentation filters can be compiled either by inspection of an artefact or by reference to designated quality attributes such as abstraction, portability, scalability, device independence, etc. For instance, by inspection of the artefact of Figure 1, several implicit claims can be made regarding tasks and sub-tasks (i.e. indicate the type of card, input expire data, specify credit card number) and how they are to be executed. Specifically, the choice of interaction elements, suggest a particular user profile (i.e. ability to pull targets, fine spatial control, eye-hand coordination, etc) and run-time environment (i.e. availability of conventional input and output devices). Also the size of the artefact indicates that it was intentionally designed for presentation on a conventional sized screen of a personal computer. The above characterize the execution context for the entire task (as well as the sub-tasks), which comprises a designated style of interaction, realized using a specific platform (i.e. libraries of interaction objects, input/output terminal) and intended for users of desktop-based graphical environments.

Compiling Growth Scenarios

Relaxing some of the above implicit assumptions unfolds a space of design alternatives, which can be used to envision new execution contexts or *growth scenarios* for the designated sequence of task. For example, a growth scenario can be formulated to depict a possible implementation of the on-line pharmacy services over the World Wide Web (WWW). An alternative growth scenario may consider how users at home with mild physical impairments (i.e. gross temporal control) can operate the WWW services of the on-line pharmacy. In general, growth scenarios are tightly linked with the screening process and each growth scenario should refer to one or more of the argumentation filters designated in the screening phase.

It should be noted that for some of the growth scenarios or the "envisioned" execution contexts (i.e. WWW), the basic design principles and design rationale leading to the artefact of Figure 1 could be equally valid, but for others there may be a need for radical changes in the look and feel of the artefact. For example, if the task were to be carried out using a WAP phone, then the WAP embodiment of the artefact, as well as the interaction techniques to be used would probably differ substantially from the corresponding desktop embodiment. Alternatively, if the target user group is not homogeneous, which is likely to be the case, then perhaps additional changes would be required in case that the user is a medical doctor, an elderly or a disabled person. Some of these changes may reflect variations in the interactive manifestation of the artefact; others may force adaptation in the content being presented, or both.

Growth scenarios may be developed either bottom up or top-down. Bottom up entails consideration of subtasks and subsequent generalization to the level of the task. Top-down on the other hand implies a revised description at the task level, which will designate how subtasks are to be carried out. Having said this, it is really indifferent which approach is followed provided that consistency is preserved through out the refinement process. For purposes of illustration, we propose to rework our reference scenario in a top-down fashion, starting with relaxing the assumptions about the target platform and the user's profile. Our guiding argumentation filters will be *Af-1* and *Af-2* from Exhibit 1. Figures 3, 4 and 5 depict examples of growth scenarios and corresponding revised artefacts.

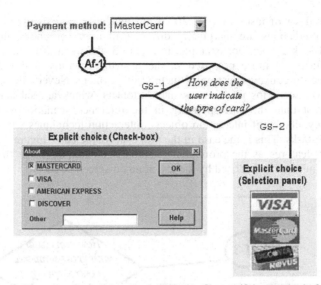

Fig. 3. Example of possible growth scenarios for specifying method of payment

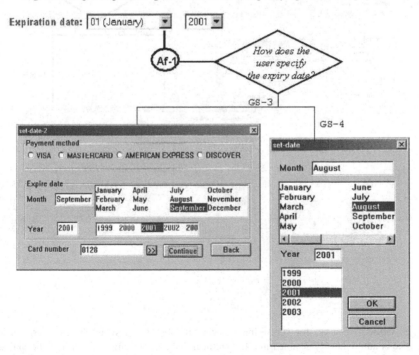

Fig. 4. Growth scenario for designating 'expire date'

As shown through these examples, the main issue involved in screening and compiling growth scenarios is the enumeration of design alternatives so as to convey how a designated set of tasks can be carried out under different regimes. In some cases, design alternatives are marginally different in terms of underlying design philosophy and look & feel. For example, in Figure 3, the main difference between the initial artefact and those proposed in the growth scenarios is the choice of interaction object to convey selection of method of payment. Nevertheless, in other cases, the growth scenarios may involve new artefacts, which are substantially or radically different than the corresponding in the reference scenario, in terms of navigation policy, choice of interaction objects, interaction techniques and sequence of tasks and sub-tasks. This is the case in the proposals depicted in Figure 4 and 5, in which scanning features as the prominent interaction technique, while the task of editing the card number is mediated by the use of an on-screen keyboard.

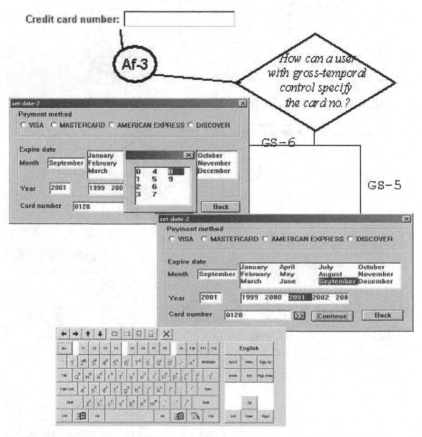

Fig. 5. Growth scenario for specifying the card number via a switch-based interface. The dialogue is automatically scanned in a hierarchical fashion (starting at the top of the dialogue and moving into subgroups such as logical group "payment method" logical group "expiry date", etc). When focus is on the "card number" text field the virtual (on-screen) keyboard is automatically displayed.

4 Discussion & Concluding Remarks

The paper has described two analytical design-oriented techniques, which are being developed and refined in the context of the IS4ALL project. Both these techniques seek to facilitate an understanding of the global execution context of a designated set of tasks, and thereby contribute towards a design code for practicing universal access. We have used these techniques to guide design work in a few reference cases, and from these early experiences, several conclusions can be drawn. First of all, the techniques raise several demands upon the analyst. Some of these relate to preparatory steps, such as finding the appropriate peers to become engaged in screening and growth scenario compilation, while others relate to the conduct of the screening phase. Specifically, it turns out that the choice of argumentation filters is non-trivial and may undermine the outcomes of the entire re-design activity.

As a general guideline, designers should seek to work on argumentation filters which cover as many as relevant of the three aspects which determine the execution context of a designated set of tasks, namely the target users, the platform and the context of use. One way to approach the task is to start with relevant non-functional quality attributes and incrementally derive a set of argumentation filters. For example, a non-functional quality attribute is *"scalability"* to another platform, which may lead to argumentation filters regarding the delivery medium of an application or a service. Another approach is to formulate argumentation filters by consulting assessment manuals or human performance criteria. Examples of such argumentation filters are the following:

- "How is the task performed by a user who possesses alternative reliable control acts, such as movement of one / both hands, directed eye-gaze, head movement, movement of lower limbs, vocalizations, etc?"
- "How is the task performed by a user who cannot push and pull targets, or cannot isolate finger movement, or cannot initiate movement on demand, or does not have fine spatial control"

In a similar fashion, one can devise argumentation filters on the basis of terminal- or platform-specific issues. Representative examples include: locating and accessing the terminal, card systems, keypads, typefaces and legibility, touch-screens, screens and instructions, external features, labels and instructions, operating instructions, etc.

Acknowledgements. The work reported in this paper has been carried out in the framework of the European Commission funded Thematic Network (Working Group) "Information Society for All" - IS4ALL (IST-1999-14101) http://is4all.ics.forth.gr/.
The IS4ALL Consortium comprises one co-ordinating partner, the Institute of Computer Science, Foundation for Research and Technology – Hellas (ICS-FORTH), and the following member organisations: Microsoft Healthcare Users Group Europe (MS-HUGe), European Health Telematics Association (EHTEL), Consiglio Nazionale delle Ricerche – Institute for Applied Physics "Nello Carrara" (CNR-IFAC), Fraunhofer-Gesellschaft zur Foerderung der angewandten Forschung e.V. - Institut für Angewandte Informationstechnik (FhG-FIT), Institut National de Recherche en Informatique et Automatique - Laboratoire lorrain de recherche en

informatique et ses applications (INRIA) and Fraunhofer-Gesellschaft zur Foerderung der angewandten Forschung e.V. - Institut fur Arbeitswirtschaft und Organisation (FhG-IAO). Several other co-operating organisations participate as subcontractors.

References

1. Carroll, J. (Ed.) (1995). Scenario-Based Design: Envisioning Work and Technology in System Development. New York: Wiley.
2. Carroll, J. (2001). Making Use: Scenario-Based Design Human-Computer Interactions. Cambridge: MIT Press.
3. Akoumianakis, D. Savidis, A., Stephanidis, C (2000): Encapsulating intelligent interactive behaviour in unified user interface artifacts, Interacting with Computers, 12, 383–408.
4. Jarke, M., Tung Bui, X., Carroll, J. (1998): Scenario Management: An interdisciplinary approach, Requirements Engineering Journal, 3(34) , pp. 155–173, 1998.
5. Olson, J. S. & Moran, T. P. (1996) Mapping the method muddle: Guidance in using methods for user interface design. In M. Rudisill, C. Lewis, P. B. Polson, & T. D. Mackay (eds.) Human-Computer Interface Design: Success stories, emerging methods and real-world context. San Francisco: Morgan Kaufmann Publishers.

Computer Environments for Improving
End-User Accessibility

M.F. Costabile[1*], D. Fogli[2*], G. Fresta[3], P. Mussio[2*], and A. Piccinno[1*]

[1]Dipartimento di Informatica, Università di Bari, Bari, Italy
{costabile, piccinno}@di.uniba.it
[2] Dipartimento di Elettronica per l'Automazione, Università di Brescia, Brescia, Italy
{fogli, mussio}@ing.unibs.it
[3] ISTI "A. Faedo", CNR, Pisa, Italy
giuseppe.fresta@cnuce.cnr.it
[*]Pictorial Computing Laboratory, Università "La Sapienza", Roma, Italy

Abstract. In several computer applications, end-users are experts in a specific domain, not necessarily experts in computer science, who use computer environments to perform their daily tasks. In this paper we present a methodology for designing interactive systems based on the development of multimedia and multimodal environments for supporting the activities of such domain-expert users. We call these environments *Software Shaping Workshops*: they aim at easing the way people program and interact with computers, thus allowing domain-expert users to develop software applications without the burden of using a traditional programming language, but using high level visual languages tailored to their needs. It is shown how this design methodology is easily applicable through the software tool BANCO.

1 Introduction

One of the main objectives of Human-Computer Interaction (HCI) is the development of computer systems, which provide accessibility and high quality of interaction to their end-users. In accordance with [1], we recognize that most end-users are experts in a specific domain, not necessarily experts in computer science, who use computer environments to perform their daily tasks. End-users are responsible for the activities accomplished through the system and for the produced results. They are the stakeholders in the system development process [2]. Our work primarily addresses the needs of such *domain-expert* users.

As defined in [3], *universal access* implies accessibility, usability, and acceptability of Information Society Technologies by anyone, anywhere, anytime, thus enabling equitable access and active participation of potentially all citizens in existing and emerging computer-mediated human activities. Our view of *universal design* does not imply that a single user interface is suitable for all end-users (or simply *users* in the rest of the paper). Instead, as designers we put effort in proposing solutions adaptable to the needs of different user populations. Great care must be devoted to the study of the user population that is the target of the system to be developed, so that computer environments best suited to their users can be created. However, as highlighted in [4], hurdles arise in designing interactive systems because of user diversity within a same population. User diversity depends non not only on

N. Carbonell, C. Stephanidis (Eds.): User Interfaces for All, LNCS 2615, pp. 129–140, 2003.
© Springer-Verlag Berlin Heidelberg 2003

user skill, culture, knowledge, but also on specific abilities (physical and/or cognitive), tasks and context of activity. It is also well known that "using the system changes the users, and as they change they will use the system in new ways" [5]. These new uses of the system make the environment evolve, and force to adapt the system to the evolved user and environment. This phenomenon is called co-evolution of system, environment and users [6].

The problem of managing user culture and co-evolutive diversity is growing in importance because the WWW technologies allow users of different cultures to share data and knowledge, and to collaborate in real time to perform common tasks. In this paper we refine a collaborative design methodology that faces the challenges posed by user diversity [4]. The aim is to design multimedia and multimodal environments that support the activities of domain expert users, with the objective of easing the way these users program and interact with computers. The design methodology is *collaborative* in that, by recognizing that users are experts in their domain of activity, it requires that representatives of the users collaborate to the development of the system as *domain experts,* in a team with HCI experts and software experts. Moreover, domain experts are in charge of driving the co-evolution of the system.

The developed environments appear to their users as workshops, providing them with the tools, organized on a bench, that are necessary to accomplish their specific activities. Users work in analogy to artisans, who carry out their work using their real or virtual tools, as it occurs in blacksmith or joiner workshops. For this reason, the computer environments developed with this methodology are called *Software Shaping Workshops* (SSWs).

SSWs allow users to develop software applications without the burden of using a traditional programming language, but using high level visual languages tailored to users' needs in a programming by example style [7]. User tailoring is achieved by exploiting the decoupling between pictorial and computational representations of concepts [8]. Moreover, users get the feeling of simply manipulating the objects of interest in a way similar to what they might do in the real world. Indeed, they are creating an electronic document through which they can perform some computation, without writing any textual program code.

The design of SSWs proved easily applicable through the software tool BANCO, which permits the decoupling between pictorial and computational representations [9]. The rest of this paper has the following organization. Sect. 2 presents our proposal of Software Shaping Workshops. In Sect. 3, pictorial and computational representations are formally defined. Sect. 4 describes an application to a medical domain. Sect. 5 briefly illustrates the BANCO software tool. Finally, Sect. 6 concludes the paper.

2   Software Shaping Workshops

In our work, we primarily address the needs of communities of experts in scientific and technological disciplines. These communities are characterized by different technical methods, languages, goals, tasks, ways of thinking, and documentation styles [10]. The members of a community communicate among them through documents, expressed in some notations, which represent (materialize) abstract or concrete concepts, prescriptions, and results of activities. These notations emerge from the practical experience in an activity domain and are focused on their users' communicational and reasoning needs, because, as Petre and Green observe, "every notation highlights some kind of information at the expense of obscuring other kinds" [11]. Often, dialects arise in a community, because the notation is applied in different practical situations and environments. For example, technical mechanical drawings are organized according to standard rules which are different in Europe and in USA [12]. Explicative annotation are written in different national languages. Often the whole document (drawing and text) is organized according to guidelines developed in each single company. The correct and complete understanding of a technical drawing depends on the recognition of the original standard as well as on the understanding of the national (and also company developed) dialects.

Recognizing users as *domain experts* means recognizing the importance of their notations and dialects as reasoning and communication tools. The *SSW methodology* is aimed at generating virtual environments, the workshops, in which the user interact using a computerized dialect of their traditional languages and virtual tools which recall the real tools with which users are familiar. Recognizing the *diversity of users* calls for the ability to represent a meaning of a concept with different materialization, e.g. text or images or sound, and to associate to a same materialization a different meaning according, for example, to the context of interaction. For instance, a same radiography is interpreted in different ways by a radiologist and a pneumologist, as we will see in the sequel. The two physicians are however collaborating to get a diagnosis. For this, they use a same set of data (of a patient), which is however represented according to their specific skills. This is a common case: often experts work in a team to perform a common task. The team might be composed by members of different sub-communities, each sub-community with different expertise. Members of a sub-community should need an appropriate computer environment, suitable to them. Hence, the SSW approach provides each sub-community with a personalized workshop, called *application workshop*. Using an application workshop, experts of a sub-community can work out data from a common knowledge base and produce new knowledge, which can be added to the common knowledge base. All the data available for the community are accessible by each expert using the specialist notation of its sub-community.

An activity of particular interest is the design, implementation, and co-evolution of a set of application workshops. In this case, the design team is composed by various experts, who participate to the design using workshops tailored to them. These workshops are called *system workshops* and are characterized by the fact that they are used to generate or update other workshops. In other words, using a system workshop, experts of a certain discipline define notations and tools, which are added to the common knowledge base and exploited in the generated workshops. This approach leads to a workshop hierarchy that tries to bridge the communicational gap between domain experts and other experts, since all cooperate in developing computer systems customized to the needs of the users communities without requiring them to become skilled programmers [13].

The system workshop at the top of the hierarchy is the one used by the software engineers to lead the team in developing the other workshops. This workshop is called *B-SwEngineer* in Fig. 1. Each system workshop is exploited to incrementally translate concepts and tools expressed in computer oriented languages into tools expressed in notations that resemble the traditional user notations and therefore understandable and manageable by users. More precisely, at each level of the hierarchy but the bottom level, experts use a system workshop to create a child workshop tailored to a more specialized user.

The hierarchy organization depends on the working organization of the user community to which the hierarchy is dedicated: each hierarchy is therefore organized into a number of levels. The top level (software engineering level) and the bottom level (application level) are always present in a hierarchy. The number of intermediate levels is variable according to the different working organization of the user community to which the hierarchy is dedicated.

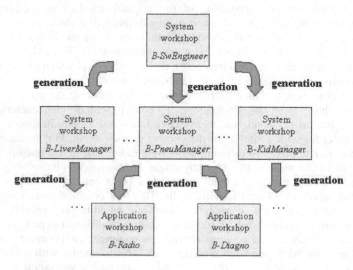

Fig. 1. Hierarchy of Software Shaping Workshops

To make clear the concepts about the SSW hierarchy, we refer to a prototype under study, designed to support different communities of physicians, namely radiologist and pneumologist, in the analysis of chest radiographies and in the generation of the diagnosis. Radiologists and pneumologists represent two sub-communities of the physicians community: they share patient-related data archives, some models for their interpretation, some notations for their presentation, but they have also to perform different tasks, documented through different sub-notations and tools. Therefore, their notations can be considered two (visual) dialects of the physicians' general notation.

The SSW hierarchy for this prototype is presented in Fig. 1: at the top there is the already mentioned *B-SwEngineer* workshop; at an intermediate level there are a number of system workshops (*B-LiverManager, B-PneuManager* and *B-KidManager*) representing the environments used by senior physicians specialist in certain fields. We call them *manager* since they are responsible of each specialty. They perform some activities in these workshops and also generate the application workshops for other physicians. In the example in Fig. 1, a senior specialist in pneumology generated *B-Radio* and *B-Diagno*, two application workshops devoted to radiologist and pneumologist communities respectively. They are two communities of physicians involved in the study of pulmonary disease. The rationale for this will be illustrated in the next section.

The hierarchy should be designed so that, in each workshop, users find all and only the tools required to perform their specific tasks, according to their culture, skill, and experience. During task execution, at each stage of the work, users organize their working bench by selecting from a repository and making available on the working area the tools required at that work stage. In this way, users should more easily orient their navigation in the virtual space to achieve their goals and avoid loosing themselves in the virtual space. However, in our experience, not every working situation can be foreseen in advance. Therefore, in each workshop, it must be possible for the user to perform local adaptation.

3 Pictorial vs. Computational Representations

In our approach, we capitalize on the theory of visual sentences developed by the Pictorial Computer Laboratory and on the model of WIMP interaction it entails [8, 14]. From this theory, we derive the formal tools to manage the decoupling of the pictorial and computational representations of a concept, which is a basic requirement of the SSW methodology. In the PCL model, user and system interact by materializing and interpreting a sequence of messages at successive instants of time. Users interpret the messages by applying human cognitive criteria, while the system applies criteria embedded in the underlying program. In WIMP interaction, the messages exchanged between the user and the system are pictorially represented on the computer screen as images, formed by texts, pictures, icons, etc. Users understand the meaning of such messages because they recognize some subsets of pixels on the screen as functional or perceptual units that we call *characteristic structures* (css), or *structure* for short. The system, on its side, captures every gesture of the user, and interprets it with respect to the image i, that is currently on the screen, using a description d of it. d is defined as a set of attributed symbols, each describing the meaning of a cs in i.

The relation between css in the image and attributed symbols in the computational representation describing the meaning of the css is specified by two functions. Let CS_i be the set of characteristic structures in the image i. An *interpretation function int*: CS_i → d associates css with attributed symbols. A *materialization function mat*: d → CS_i associates attributed symbols with css. A *visual sentence* (vs) is defined as a triple $<i,d,<int,mat>>$. A *visual language* (VL) is a set of vss.

Given a visual sentence $vs = <i,d,<int,mat>>$, a *characteristic pattern* (cp) is a triple $cp = <s,u,<intcs, matcs>>$, where $s \in CS_i$, $u \in d$, $s=matcs(u)$ and $u=intcs(s)$. A cp specifies the state of a computational process that generates and maintains active a virtual entity. Such a virtual entity is graphically represented in the bitmap by s, u is the attributed symbol completing the description of the generating process, i.e. it contains the executable code of the program and the current values of its variables and the pair $<intcs, matcs>$ specifies the link between the bitmap and components of u. A vs is characterized by the set of its cps.

4 Software Shaping Workshops for a Medical Domain

Let us describe in more details the prototype to support different communities of physicians, i.e., radiologist and pneumologist, in the analysis of chest radiographies and in the generation of the diagnosis. The SSW life cycle follows a star approach [15], starting by the analysis of the users of the application workshops. The design process proceeds by developing incremental workshop prototypes at various levels in the hierarchy, going bottom-up as well as top-down.

In the case study, user analysis started by examining how the radiologists classify, interpret, and annotate chest radiographies, and how the pneumologists use the interpreted images, provide their diagnoses and record them using an annotation tool.

On the basis of this analysis, the team of experts involved in the design felt the need of developing two separate but consistent application workshops. The first one, *B-Radio*, supports the radiologists in their image interpretation activity and is equipped with tools for interactive image processing and data annotation, and for archiving the interpreted images and annotations in the shared knowledge base. The second one, *B-Diagno*, supports the pneumologists in their diagnosis activity and is equipped with tools for the retrieval of data and images, for their annotation, and for formulating diagnoses. Moreover, the team of experts observed that not all situations can be foreseen in advance and that sometimes *B-Radio* and *B-Diagno* must be together and consistently adapted to new different tasks and situation. This adaptation requires the knowledge of both dialects and activities, of the tasks to be executed and of the working organization, and the awareness of the use of diagnostic documents outside the organization. Only senior pneumologists have such a global skill and knowledge, and can assume this responsibility. Therefore, the team decided that a senior pneumologist should act as a manager of the whole activity and be responsible of recognizing the tasks to be performed, identifying the dialect notations of interest, and consequently defining the system of consistent application workshops. The senior pneumologist achieves these goals using a workshop, called *B-PneuManager*, where s/he finds usable tools for implementing and adapting both *B-Radio* and *B-Diagno* (see Fig. 1).

Working with the various SSW, users perform visual programming activities without writing code as in traditional programming. The created visual programs reflect the physician's model of the activity rather than the algorithmic structure of the computation. Data and tools are analogous to those used in the traditional medical documentation. They are even enriched because they are supported by a computer, which can perform several computation activities, such as relieving users from clerical work and enabling them to perform new calculations and simulations.

It is worth noticing that different workshops, such as *B-Radio* and *B-Diagno*, associate to a same characteristic structure (**cs**) a different computational representation. In this way, the representation of the meaning of the **cs** is adapted to the different culture of the two communities of users. The rules of this transformation are established in *B-PneuManager* by the senior pneumologist.

Fig. 2 and Fig. 3 illustrate how the radiologist annotates and classifies a radiography of a patient with the support of *B-Radio*. The SSWs are implemented with the BANCO prototype, which is described in the next section. Due to space limitations, only Fig. 2 shows the complete web page, while the remaining figures show snapshots representing a part of the web page. Snapshot shows a part of a working area, which may contain various images. Each image is characterized by a handle, which is the rectangular **cs** on its top and permits its selection (the dark rectangle at the top left of img1 in Fig. 2). More images may be stacked one of top of the other. In this case, more handles will be visible, each referring to an image. In Fig. 3a, two images are superimposed, as indicated by two handles. The raster radiography of Fig. 2 underlies a transparent vector image on which the radiologist traces the structures of her/his interest.

Each image is framed by: on the top, a tool menu; under the menu, a button for governing the transparency of the background, followed by a context-dependent caption automatically produced by the system. In Fig. 2, this caption indicates that the figure is a chest radiography of a patient called Rossi. In Fig. 3a, the caption indicates that the radiologist Dr. Galeone is making an annotation. At the bottom of the frame, a further caption identifies the image (e.g., img1). Under the image, there is a button to modify the transparency of the image. Each snapshot shows the data related to the image on the top of the stack, i.e. the one that is in Fig. 3a.

Let us consider Fig. 2. If the radiologist selects from the menu on the top of the window the tenth button from left (whose icon is a close curve), the system reacts by presenting the user a cursor, the cross in Fig. 3a, indicating the possibility of tracing curves on the image. The radiologist then surrounds a set of pixels s/he classifies as a pleural effusion. Snapshot 3b, shows the situation after the radiologist has closed the curve around the area of interest and has selected the eighth button ('a') in the top menu, firing the annotation activity. The radiologist is associating to the contoured area the annotation shown in the left window, which consists of a classification of the area (the type 'Pleural effusion') and some comments ('Potential pneumonia'). The system captures the input events generated by the radiologist, records them, and associates the framed area to some programs. Moreover, it adds to the framed area an icon of a pencil to signal that an annotation exists. This icon is a new button, which, when clicked, fires computational activities specific to the type assigned by the radiologist to the framed area.

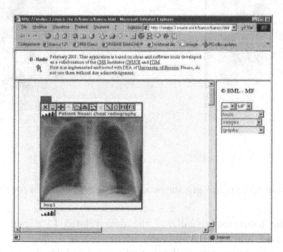

Fig. 2. Web page with *B-Radio* workshop in BANCO. The radiologist is analyzing chest radio-graphy

By the annotation activity, the radiologist defines those sets of pixels s/he recognizes as significant css, and associates them with a classification and a description (type). Once a **cs** is classified by the user, *B-Radio* creates an active widget, represented in our formal model (see Sect. 3) as a **cp** of type defined in the annotation and with a program defining its behavior. Each new **cp** is added to the set of **cps** known to the system and becomes available to the users. In our example, a new **cp** of type 'Pleural effusion' has been created.

Fig. 4 shows the interaction of the radiologist with this new widget, still in the *B-Radio* workshop. In Fig. 4a, the radiologist selects the **cp** of type 'Pleural effusion'. This selection results into the opening of the 'Potential pneumonia' menu, presenting the radiologist the possibility of executing three different computational activities to gain insight into the case at hand. For example, the selection in Fig. 4b of the 'Density evaluation' button fires a computation whose results are shown in Fig. 4c.

At the end of these activities, two different types of tools are available for the users. Tools of the first type are those associated to system predefined **cps** (system **cps**). Tools of the second type are associated to **cps** defined by the users (user-defined **cps**). Notice that the rules by which a user-defined **cp** is created are established by the senior pneumologist in *B-PneuManager*. More precisely, the senior pneumologist established that to a **cs** classified as 'pleural effusion' two activities should be associated: 'density evaluation' (after having determined the density through a TAC) and 'link to NMR'. S/he also decided that the density evaluation results could be presented to the user as a graph, as a table or as a voice message, as shown in Fig. 4b.

Moreover, using the Software Shaping Workshops, the behavior associated to a **cs** can be adapted to the necessities of different communities of end-users. For example, in defining *B-Diagno*, the senior pneumologist prescribes that buttons of type 'pleural

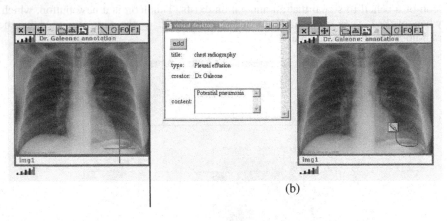

(b)

Fig. 3. Using *B-Radio*, the radiologist surrounds (a) and annotates (b) a zone of potential pleural effusion

effusion' be the tools for visualizing the data related to a patient with potential pneumonia and to allow the annotation of the reached diagnosis. This change of meaning of the **cs** representing the pencil associated to the 'pleural effusion' is performed by *B-Diagno* at start-up time. Indeed, on its starting, *B-Diagno* applies a set of rules which were established by the senior pneumologist when defining *B-Radio* with the use of *B-PneuManager*. These rules state which data and which method of visualization and annotation are to be associated to each button.

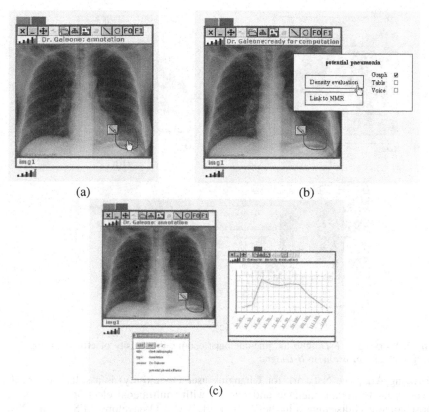

(a)   (b)

(c)

Fig. 4. In *B-Radio* the radiologist obtains the density evaluation of the potential pleural effusion using the button 'density evaluation'

Therefore, when the pneumologist selects the pleural effusion widget (the circled area in Fig. 5a), *B-Diagno* interprets this selection as a query and displays a multi-link to different activities. If in Fig. 5b the pneumologist selects 'radiological interpretation' as further activity to perform, s/he obtains data related with the density of the pleural effusion and the tools to provide her/his diagnosis, as shown in Fig. 5c.

5 Implementing the Software Shaping Workshop Hierarchy

The SSW methodology requires the ability to decouple the pictorial representation of data from their computational representation, so that the system is able to represent data according to the user needs. This feature is obtainable through XML technology, which allows computational representations to be transformed into their pictorial representations by suitable programs, the Style Sheet Transformers (SST). The workshops in the SSW hierarchy are implemented as BANCO documents. BANCO

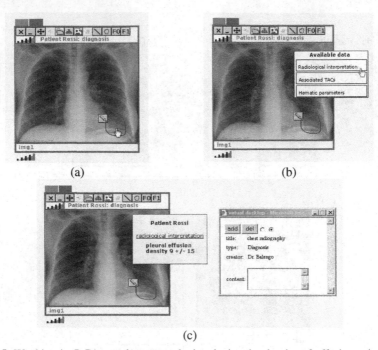

(a)   (b)

(c)

Fig. 5. Working in *B-Diagno* the pneumologist obtains the density of effusion using the widget 'pleural effusion' in *B-Diagno*

(Browsing Adaptive Network for Changing user Operativity) is a software tool that allows users to create, manage and interact with multimodal electronic documents, whose content is distributed in the Web [4, 9]. BANCO develops on SVG (the XML specification for vector graphics [16]) to best manage graphical WIMP interfaces.

The core of BANCO is the mark-up language BML that permits the distributed creation and management of operable electronic documents shareable on the Web. A BANCO document, whose name has always the structure B-xxx, is a BML document in which users find a bench (notice that BANCO in Italian means bench) and a set of tools through which users can collect data from the Web and organize them into new BML documents, which become available on the Web .

A B-xxx includes a style sheet defining its own transformers. At present, an SST consists of a kernel of scripting programs (about 50 KB) implementing rules which describe how to customize documents and materialize data fragments into B-xxx. In other words, thanks to such rules, data from whichever source on the web are materialized on the client so that the css appearing on the screen, as well as the interaction modalities, are tailored to users.

Any B-xxx organizes its data as BML documents. In particular, B-xxx products can be organized as a new BANCO document, B-yyy, i.e., a BANCO document can be steered by its users to self-transform into a new BANCO document. This self-transformation property is used to generate a SSW hierarchy. For example, the hierarchy of Fig.1 is generated starting by the collaboration of software experts with senior pneumologists to steer the self-transformation of B-SwEngineer into B-

PneuManager. Senior pneumologists in turn steer B-PneuManager to self-transform into B-Radio and B-Diagno. Note that the steering activity is complex, implying usability evaluation, and it is performed following a star lifecycle [15]. The results of the evaluation may require that senior pneumologists go back to the collaboration with software experts to refine B-PneuManager. On the whole, SSW hierarchy is generated from B-SwEngineer by an evolutive process determined by the activities of the experts of the design team.

6 Conclusion

This paper presents a methodology for developing computer environments, the Software Shaping Workshops, aimed at supporting end-user activities. Novel features of our approach are: 1) the methodology is collaborative in that end-users, as domain experts, assume a responsibility in the design; 2) system design becomes an evolutive process determined by the activities performed in the various workshops of the SSW hierarchy by the experts of the design team; 3) the SSWs are able to associate different pictorial representations to a same computational representation, and vice versa, thus permitting end-user tailoring; 4) end-users, including the system developers who are end-users of the system workshops, can perform their tasks interacting with the environments through interaction visual languages, which resemble their traditional documentation notations and tools.

We are experimenting this methodology in various domains. An application to a medical domain has been here illustrated while the application to the environmental science domain is reported in [13].

References

1. Brancheau, J.C., Brown, C.V.: The Management of End-User Computing: Status and Directions. ACM Computing Surveys 25(4) (1993)
2. Redmiles, D.F.: Supporting the End Users' Views. Proc. AVI '02, Acm Press, N.Y., (2002) 34–42
3. Stephanidis, C. et al.: Toward an Information Society for All: HCI Challenges and R&D Recommendations. Intern. Journal of Human-Computer Interaction 11(1) (1999) 1–28
4. Carrara, P., Fogli, D., Fresta, G., Mussio, P.: Toward overcoming culture, skill and situation hurdles in human-computer interaction. To appear on Journal Universal Access in Information Society (2002)
5. Nielsen, J.: Usability Engineering. Academic Press (1993)
6. Bourguin, G., Derycke, A., Tarby, J.C.: Beyond the Interface: Co-evolution inside Interactive Systems – A Proposal Founded on Activity Theory, Proc. IHM-HCI 2001.
7. Lieberman H. (Guest Editor): Programming by Example. Special Section on CACM 43(3) (2000) 72–74
8. Bottoni, P., Costabile, M.F., Levialdi, S., Mussio, P.: Defining Visual Languages for Interactive Computing. IEEE Trans. SMC, Part A, 27 (6), November 1997
9. Carrara, P., Fresta, G., Mussio, P.: SVG: More than a Markup Language for Vector Graphics. Proc. of "The Web in Public Administration" (EuroWeb2001), Pisa, 245–257
10. Varela, F. J.: Principles of Biological Autonomy. GSR Amsterdam, North Holland (1979)

11. Green, T.R.G, Petre, M.: Usability Analysis of Visual Programming Environments. Journal of Visual Language and Computing 7(2) (1996) 131–174
12. ISO Standard: ISO 5456 Technical Drawing Projection Methods
13. Carrara, F., Fogli, D., Fresta, G., Mussio, P.: Co-operative Design of Visual Interactive Systems. Accepted for presentation at the Worskhop on Visual Computing in the 2002 Int. Conf. on Distributed Multimedia Systems (DMS'2002), San Francisco (CA), USA, September 2002.
14. Bottoni, P., Costabile, M.F., Levialdi, S., Mussio, P.: From User Notations to Accessible Interfaces through Visual Languages. In: Stephanidis, C. (ed.): Universal Access In HCI: Toward an Information Society for All, Vol. 3. Lawrence Erlbaum Associates, Mahawah, New Jersey, London (2001) 252–256
15. Hix, D., Hartson, H. R., Developing User Interfaces: Ensuring Usability through Product & Process, John Wiley (1993)
16. W3C: Scalable Vector Graphics (SVG), [Online] 2001 <http: //www.w3c.org/Graphics/SVG/>

USERfit Tool. A Tool to Facilitate Design for All

Julio Abascal, Myriam Arrue, Nestor Garay, and Jorge Tomás

Laboratory of Human-Computer Interaction for Special Needs
Euskal Herriko Unibertsitatea. Informatika Fakultatea.
Manuel Lardizabal 1, 20018. Donostia-San Sebastián. Spain
{julio,myriam,nestor,jorge}@si.ehu.es

Abstract. USERfit is a well-established methodology focused on the generation of usability specifications, specifically created for the Assistive Technology field that proved to be very suitable for the Design for All paradigm. This methodology uses paper-based forms to store and propagate the design related information. For this reason, some issues, such us the inclusion and elimination of new users or contexts of use or the need to propagate the results between forms, make the specification process tedious. This paper presents an application called *USERfit Tool* developed in order to facilitate the use of the USERfit design environment. In addition, *USERfit Tool* allows for the reuse of previously developed material and the sharing of design information among remote groups of designers, maintaining coherence and compatibility.

1 Tools for Design for All

Design for All, also known as Universal Design, is a well-known design philosophy that supports taking all type of users into consideration from the starting point of the design process. Its objective is to avoid designs that exclude a number of the possible users due to their physical or cognitive characteristics.

This philosophy, firmly supported by people working for users with disabilities, is quickly spreading among other sectors of the industry. Diverse web sites[1], conferences[2] and books[3] have very much contributed to this diffusion. Nevertheless, it must be acknowledged that it is still a long way from being adopted by mainstream industry. There are many reasons for this situation; however, one of the most important is the lack of methodologies and tools that help the designer through the whole process.

This paper presents a tool, based on the previously developed USERfit environment, intended to help designers produce usability specifications orientated to the Design for All.

---

[1] E.g. the one of TRACE Centre: http://www.trace.wisc.edu/world/gen-ud.html

[2] 1st and 2nd International Conference on Universal Access in Human - Computer Interaction. http://uahci.ics.forth.gr/

[3] For example, "User Interfaces for All: Concepts, Methods, and Tools" edited by C. Stephanidis [10].

N. Carbonell, C. Stephanidis (Eds.): User Interfaces for All, LNCS 2615, pp. 141–152, 2003.
© Springer-Verlag Berlin Heidelberg 2003

2 The USERfit Methodology

USERfit is a design methodology with a particular orientation towards usability and accessibility. It could be defined as an aid environment for the design that has been developed within the area of Assistive Technology. This methodology materializes a philosophy of design that can be described as *user centred* (as the starting point involves user requirements, instead of technological availability), *system orientated* (as it considers that all technology operates in an environment) and *iterative design promoter* (as it allows for the modification of requirements in later design phases and to repeatedly validate the new requirements) [7]. However, we cannot forget that its main goal is the capture and specification of user requirements.

Although the original intention of this methodology is mainly devoted to the design of interfaces for people with disabilities[4], its approach is not limited to users with specific physical, sensorial or cognitive characteristics. Therefore, this methodology is valid for any type of users and situations. In this way, it is highly suitable in order to produce specifications of products and services that are going to be used by all. In fact, the application of this methodology is extremely useful to train designers in the Design for All philosophy as it helps in the analysis of the needs of all the implied users taking into account the needs of all the stakeholders to perform specific tasks in particular environments.

USERfit emphasizes in detecting and applying particular characteristics of the user group to whom the product is orientated, avoiding generalizations and presuppositions. For this reason, this is a clear and easy-to-use methodology, and it has the advantage of directing the designer's mind to the diversity of the users, avoiding considering the users as a standard and homogeneous group. Therefore, USERfit can also be useful in the education of the usability-orientated design, as it allows for the analysis of features the user has that are hidden in other contexts. In fact, some authors, such as Newell and Gregor [4] or Nielsen [5], think that a special ability, to confront general problems in usability, is generated when designing for people with disabilities. For this reason *USERfit Tool* is being used to teach Design for All in graduate courses [1].

In the following sections, some of the characteristics of USERfit and the developed *USERfit Tool*, created to facilitate the design through the USERfit methodology, are shown. Additionally, its ability to include Design for All features is revised in order to show how to produce design products or services designed for all using this tool.

3 Structure of the USERfit Methodology

There are many methodologies that try to help the design team in collecting and processing all the necessary information in order to produce user-orientated specifications. In most cases, they consist of some type of document where relevant aspects of the interaction (characteristics of the user, task, work environment, team,

---

[4] It was developed within the USER (Tide-1062) European project that was performed by HUSAT Research Institute (UK), Sintef Unimed Rehab (N) and COO.S.S. Marchebscrl (I).

methods of work, attitudes, etc.) are compiled. After that, this information is used as a support to extract design specifications[5].

USERfit is one of these design environments, composed by a set of nine protocols, called "summarising tools". Each one includes several forms covering the following areas: user analysis, activity analysis, product analysis, context, product environment, matrix of product attributes, summary of requirements, summary of usability design and evaluation. The main characteristics of the nine protocols are summarized in Table 1.

The purpose of these protocols is to allow the design team to collect, evaluate and develop information in order to construct a specification of the product. The interest of this methodology is that it makes the designers face the questions that are to be considered to obtain usable products. Therefore, this methodology could be considered as a framework that allow one to reunite and compare design material and produce specifications of usability and accessibility rather than a design methodology.

Table 1. Elements of the USERfit methodology[6]

USERfit	Objectives
Environmental context	Provides a high level summary of the product, covering such issues as the initial justification for it: who its users are likely to be, who will purchase it, etc.
Product environment	Summarizes what is known about the support environment for the product (including likely training, documentation, installation, maintenance and user support).
User analysis	Identifies the range of people who should be considered in the development of the product, and describes their attributes in detail.
Activity analysis	Identifies and describes the range of activities that people will engage in when using the product and the implications that these will have for product design.
Product analysis	Summarizes the functional aspects of the product as they are understood and lists these as operational features.
Product attribute matrix	Summarizes the match between emerging functional specifications and product attributes inferred from user and activity analysis.
Requirements summary	Summarizes the design features identified through user and activity analysis and their degree of match to user requirements.
Design summary	Summarizes, in more detail, the functional specification for the product and its operational details.
Usability evaluation	Summarizes plans for evaluation along with objectives, methods to be used and evaluation criteria. Also documents the degree of match between evaluation criteria and the results of the evaluation activities.

If we consider the design phase life cycle composed of four different parts: definition of the problem, functional specification, development and evaluation,

---

[5] For example, some tools of this type are: UCD [9]; EuCase99 [http://www.foruse.com/Tools.htm]; EZSort [3] and [http://www-3.ibm.com/ibm/easy/eou_ext.nsf/publish/649]. There are also multiple tools for usability orientated design of web pages: WebSAT, Lift Online and Lift Onsite, Max, NetRaker Suite [2].

[6] More information about USERfit methodology can be obtained in [7].

USERfit can help in all of the parts except in the development phase. In addition, it does not offer a concrete method for the evaluation phase but it does help in the selection of the most adequate method for the product or service that is being developed. One of its advantages is that the designer team can select its preferred method, (according to its availabilities, experiences and preferences) from among the documented ones. It is possible, for instance, to adopt one of the methods proposed by Nielsen & Mack [6] or Rubin [8].

4   From USERfit to *USERfit Tool*

The nine protocols of USERfit methodology allow for the analysis of all the aspects related to the user, the task and the environment. In order to perform this task, the following process should be followed. The designer team analyses the different types of potential users, their role in relation to the product or service, the design implications, etc., using the User Analysis 1 (UA1) form. A User Analysis 2 (UA2) form, where the functional implications and the product characteristics are specified based on the user attributes, is created for each type of user. The User Analysis 3 (UA3) form allows for the joining of the mentioned user requirements, desired characteristics, possible conflicts among diverse necessities and their development priorities.

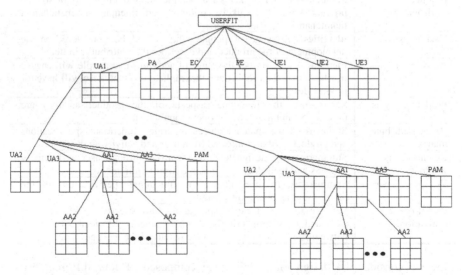

Fig. 1. Propagation of the information through the structure of the forms of USERfit

In the same way, the analysis of the activities, which will be possibly performed by the product, is realized in Activity Analysis 1 (AA1) forms. Possible scenarios of use along with their characteristics are enumerated in these forms. Each one of these scenarios is individually analysed in Activity Analysis 2 (AA2) form, where functional implications of the activities and the product characteristics are included.

Form Activity Analysis 3 (AA3) allows for the combination of the product characteristics, possible conflicts and their priorities.

The manner of work with the rest of the protocols is similar. Therefore, the number of documents that must be handled rapidly expands according to the increase of the user categories, the contexts of use, etc., as can be seen in Figure 1. On the other hand, due to the iterative nature of the design process, it could be necessary to create or delete categories, contexts, functionalities, etc. throughout the design process. Therefore, it is clear that the main problem of this methodology is the management of the information, fundamentally due to the use of forms on paper for which it was initially conceived.

USERfit Tool was created in order to take advantage of USERfit methodology and avoid the need to handle a large number of forms. Its structure accurately reproduces the protocols defined for USERfit. In addition, some extra features, which will be detailed later on, have been added.

5   *USERfit Tool* Development

The *USERfit Tool* has been developed by the *University of the Basque Country* and the *Fraunhofer Institute for Applied Information Technology* within the frame of the IRIS[7] European project, with the intention of facilitating the application of the USERfit methodology. It has been developed in Java, which makes it almost completely independent of the platform (JDK 1.2 or later is required). The data handled by the application are in XML format. Part of the structure of the XML files can be seen in Figures 2 and 3. This structure combines, on the one hand, all the data (characteristics, attributes, scenes, etc.) related to each implied actor (user, family, maintenance staff, etc.) and, on the other hand, all the data referring to the service or product that is being designed.

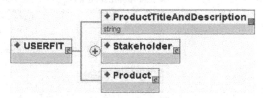

Fig. 2. First level of the data structure of USERfit

When a new project is started, the tool allows for the creation of the *basic* forms, such as UA1. New *attached* forms, UA2 in this case, are automatically created when new users are added to the original UA1 form. This means that when the user adds or deletes a row, to introduce or eliminate data within each form, the consequences of this action are propagated to all the forms related to the modified one. As a result,

---

[7] IRIS: *Incorporating Requirements of People with Special Needs or Impairments to Internet-based Systems and Services.* Ist-2000-26211. Partners: European Dynamics (GR), University of the Aegean (GR), Fraunhofer for Institute Applied Information Technology (D), Information Society disAbilities Challenge (B), The University of the Basque Country (E). [http://www.iris-design4all.org/]

adequate fields are created within. For example, when a row containing a specific type of user is removed from the UA1 form, the UA2 and UA3 forms related to this type of user will disappear. Analogously, when a new user is introduced, new UA2 and UA3 forms are created for this user.

The generation of new forms and the propagation of the generated information between forms are based on internal events that are triggered when the user activates certain elements of the application. Thus, this mechanism starts the creation (or destruction) of the necessary forms and the data compiled in one level of the USERfit environment are transmitted to the following levels, where they will be reused.

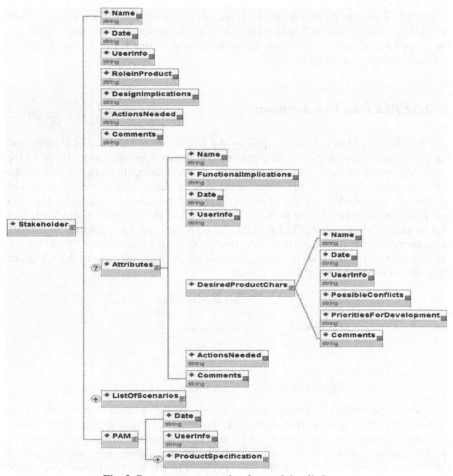

Fig. 3. Data structure associated to each implied actor

In order to facilitate the reusability of the available information, the *USERfit Tool* allows one to have several open files simultaneously, add implied users from other files, print the generated forms, load an example and consulting online basic help.

6 Development and Architecture of the *USERfit Tool* Application

The *USERfit Tool* consists basically of Java code that uses a processor of style sheets in XML and a XML analyser to implement the functionality of the USERfit environment. This application follows the typical structure of any Java application developed around a XML analyser. It has two interfaces, one with the user and another with XML input documents.

Turbo XML 2.1 for XML elements, which permits graphical visualization of the XML structure/schema and Jbuilder for the Java application, were used in the development of the *USERfit Tool* application. Figure 4 shows the modules that compose the application.

Data introduced by the user through the graphical interface of the tool are saved in a XML format file. In order to carry out the conversion from the internal structure to XML format, the system uses the Xerces package. The SUN's JHelp package is used by the system when the user chooses the print option. This package is responsible for showing the respective HTML pages of the forms that the user wants to print and it prints then them. Before printing the data, the system uses the Xerces package to transform it to XML format and then performs the transformation from XML structure to the HTML page using the Xalan package. This package uses XSLT files to transform the XML structure.

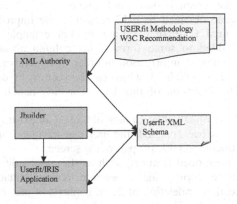

Fig. 4. Development of the *USERfit Tool* application

The Jhelp package is also used to visualize the Help and the examples of the application.

The structure of the application is shown in Figure 5. This structure is composed of the user interface, the body of the application with the following libraries: Xalan[8], Xerces[9] (Apache) and Help (Sun) and XML data storage.

---

[8] Xalan is a XSLT transformer to turn the XML documents into HTML, text or any other type of XML documents. It implements the W3C recommendations for the XSL and the XML

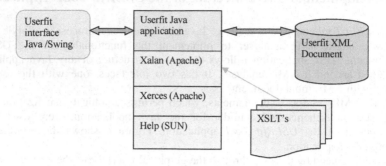

Fig. 5. Architecture of the application

7   Features of the *USERfit Tool* Application

The use of the tool is very simple for people who know the USERfit environment, as it maintains the same structure as the original paper forms. For example, the UA1 form, as displayed on the screen, is shown in Figure 6.

Due to the experience obtained in IRIS project, some improvements have been introduced to the original USERfit environment. For example, a new column of comments has been added to some forms. This column allows the designer to introduce any type of relevant information in order to remember decisions taken in previous phases. A basic online help, which can be seen in Figure 7, has also been added to the tool. The inclusion of this feature avoids handling the voluminous manual of USERfit.

The application allows one to create a new file, open an existing one or consult an example. Once a file has been opened, the user can navigate through the different forms using the tree structure on the left part of the screen.

In addition to the mentioned features, such as the automatic propagation of the information to adequate forms, the generation and elimination of associated documents and the creation or deletion of users, contexts of use, etc., this tool allows for the reusing of information. Therefore, the information created in previous designs (analysis of users or contexts, product characteristics and environments, etc.) can be reused. This feature will allow for the saving of time and effort in later designs.

Furthermore, *USERfit Tool* can be helpful when the design team is distributed in different remote points, as it allows for the generating of homogenous and compatible specifications. *USERfit Tool* allows also for the sharing the information generated by each group. Therefore, the material related to a design is stored in files that can be

---

Path Language (Xpath) transformations. It can be used from the command line, in an applet or servlet, or as a module in other program.

[9] Xerces allows the XML analysis and generation. There are analysers for Java and C++ that fulfil the W3C XML and DOM (level 1 and 2) standards as well as SAX (version 2) standard. The analysers are highly modular and configurable.

sent in electronic manner among all the design team members. Concretely, *USERfit Tool* has been used to generate the functional specifications of the *Domosilla*[10] and *Heterorred*[11] projects. Each member of the consortium has generated specifications for diverse contexts and all the specifications have then been easily incorporated in a unique document. The successive versions of this document have circulated among the members of the consortium, until consensus has been achieved.

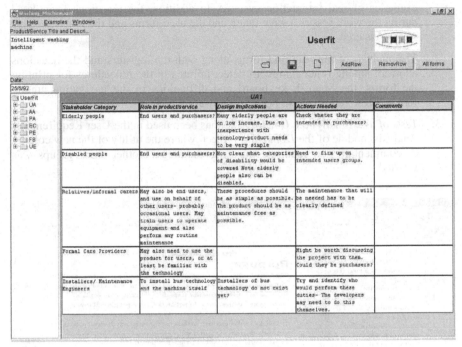

Fig. 6. The UA1 Form

8 Usability of the *USERfit Tool*

USERfit Tool itself has been developed following a usability orientated design process, based on the analysis of the possible users' characteristics, the tasks and the context. The usability of the generated prototypes has been analysed in the following contexts.

---

[10] *Domosilla* "Study, evaluation and design of an interconnection system between local network for wheelchairs (DXBus) control and domotic network (EHS)". TIC2000-0087-P4. Partners: University of Seville, Bioingeniería Aragonesa and The University of the Basque Country.

[11] *Heterorred* "Study and development of a heterogeneous personal area network for interoperability and access to wireless services and communications" [No. TIC2001-1868-C03]. Partners: University of Seville, Universities of Saragosse and the Basque Country.

1. *Evaluation by experts.* The tool has been used by two usability experts who have simulated the process of the specifications design of an Accessible Web Site authoring tool. Procedures for form storing, recovering and printing have been improved as a result of these analyses.

2. *Heuristic evaluation.* The tool has been used by a group of ten doctorate students who were asked to generate the usability specifications of two examples of real interaction systems. In addition, the questions formulated during the work sessions were taken and the used forms and the required times were registered.

   The analysis of the resulting forms along with the registers and the questions allowed, among other things, to detect failures in the procedures for printing the forms, the Spanish keyboard and difficulties in the navigation among forms. These failures have been properly corrected.

3. *Tests of use.* Finally, the *USERfit Tool* has been used in the User Requirements Analysis module of the *Domosilla* project, where the utility of the new column of commentaries to facilitate the understanding of other work groups was verified.

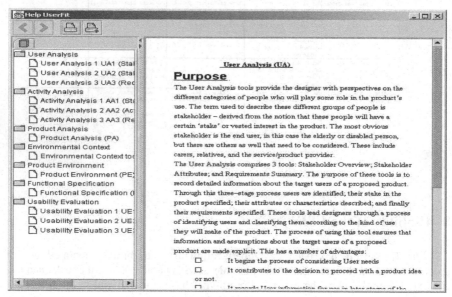

Fig. 7. Online help

From these tests, it can be concluded that the tool adjusts to the necessities and ways in which the types of users work producing specifications of usability in a design context.

9 Conclusion

The use of the USERfit methodology for the generation of functional specifications can become boring as it requires working with pencil and paper and handling many forms. The added effort that the management of the multiple forms generated in the design process of a medium-sized project involves can make this environment tedious. To avoid this problem, a tool that automates the most monotonous parts of the design process has been developed. Furthermore, in order to facilitate the use of the USERfit methodology, the *USERfit Tool* has demonstrated its usefulness to reuse parts of previous specifications and to share the design between remote groups, with homogenous results. The performed usability analysis of the tool, allows for the assurance that the tool adjusts to the necessities and ways of work of the potential users.

The Laboratory of Human-Computer Interaction for Special Needs is currently studying some enhancements for *USERfit Tool*. One, is the creation of a CSCW environment to support interactive remote development of specifications. The other, is the development of a particular tool to generate the user interface code for specific application domains (for instance, user interfaces for mobile devices).

The IRIS partnership, which has developed the USERfit Tool, has requested the opportune permission of the CEC DG XIII, which holds the rights of USERfit, in order to make the USERfit Tool available to all those that wish to use it.

Acknowledgement. The work presented in this paper has been partially financed by the European Commission within the IST-2000-26211 IRIS project (*Incorporating the Requirements of People with Special Needs or Impairments to Internet-based Systems and Services*) developed by European Dynamics (GR), Fraunhofer for Institute Applied Information Technology (D); the University of the Aegean (GR); the University of the Basque Country-Euskal Herrriko Unibertsitatea (E) and the IsdAC International Association (Information Society disAbilities Challenge) (B). The authors would like to specially thank Carlos Velasco, from Fraunhofer for Institute Applied Information Technology, for his very valuable contribution.

References

1. Abascal J., Nicolle C.: The Application of USERfit Methodology to Teach Usability Guidelines. In J. Vanderdonckt & C. Farenc (eds.): Tools for working with guidelines. Springer Verlag, London (2001) 209–216
2. Chak A.: Usability Tools: A Useful Start. New Architect (Web Techniques). [http://www.webtechniquescom/archives/2000/08/stratrevu/] (2000)
3. Dong J., Martin S., Waldo P.: A user Input and Analysis Tool for Information Architecture [http://www-3.ibm.com/ibm/easy/eou_ext.nsf/Publish/410/$File/EZSortPaper. pdf]
4. Newell A. F., Gregor P.: Human Computer Interfaces for People with Disabilities. In: Helander M. et al. (eds.): Handbook of Human-Computer Interaction. North Holland/Elsevier Science, Amsterdam (1997) 813–824.
5. Nielsen J.: Usability Engineering. Morgan Kaufmann, San Francisco (1993)

6.   Nielsen J., Mack R. (eds.): Usability Inspection Methods. Wiley, New York (1994)
7.   Poulson D., Ashby M., Richardson, S. (eds.): USERfit, a practical handbook on user centred design for Assistive Technology. ECSC-EC-EAEC, Brussels-Luxembourg (1996). Also in: http://www.stakes.fi/include/1-0.htm
8.   Rubin J.: Handbook of Usability Testing. Wiley, New York (1994)
9.   Scanlon J., Percival L.: UCD for different project types. [http://www-106.ibm.com/developerworks/library/us-ucd/index.html?n-us-372]
10.   Stephanidis C. (ed.): User Interfaces for All: Concepts, Methods, and Tools. Lawrence Erlbaum Associates, London (2001)

Universal Access to Assistive Technology through Client-Centred Cognitive Assessment

Patrick Langdon[1], Ray Adams[2], and P. John Clarkson[1]

[1] University of Cambridge, Dept. of Engineering
Trumpington Street, Cambridge. CB2 1PZ UK
{pml24, pjc10}@eng.cam.ac.uk
http://www-edc.eng.cam.ac.uk
[2] Middlesex University, School of Computing Science,
Trent Park, Bramley Road, London N14 4YZ
r.g.adams@middlesex.ac.uk

Abstract. As a basis for user needs and system design assessments in assistive technology (AT), we have developed a new conceptual framework and battery of tests and research paradigms, on a continuing improvement basis. The framework consists of three levels, to provide; overall guidance, specific models for understanding data and task analysis. Following earlier work [1], we report three case studies, considering attentional problems and user-specific needs, to validate our core test elements and conceptual framework. Our systematic method generated specific benefits for our users and pointed out the need for cognitive software in assistive technology.

1 Introduction

Initial work on assistive technology for people with disabilities tended to be polarised into either those starting with the technology or those starting with the client group. With the development of advanced information technology, there is now the third option of an interactive approach, iterating repeatedly between the demands of both. Such an approach requires a conceptual model which guides both the interpretation of results and the conduct of research into design issues and user needs. Our earlier work, developed such a conceptual model in the form of a simplistic framework. At one level, it guides the practical evaluation of user needs and system design options. At a second level, it provides a conceptual framework within which to subsume detailed models with which to understand specific results [1].

We have also developed a simple, hypothesis-based process for the assessment of client needs, and assistive system design. The work reported here tests our process model through the use of individual case studies conducted at the Papworth Trust and Cambridge University. Rather than test the needs of a defined group of users against a simple assistive system, we are concerned with the capability for identification of the detailed needs of specific individuals and the provision of the appropriate interface components in the AT interface.

N. Carbonell, C. Stephanidis (Eds.): User Interfaces for All, LNCS 2615, pp. 153–164, 2003.

1.1 Aims of Assessment

The approach described is aimed at organizations who carry out assessments as part of a program of progression, or match adaptive technology and products to populations on the basis of individual profiles. The principal aims of the techniques will be to provide an assessment that yields information to enable the individual to improve their employability; independence of living and levels of education or training. The main goals of the approach are to develop a client-based method of assessment, with specific reference to general cognitive factors, that will enable the identification of the detailed needs of specific individuals and the provision of the appropriate interface components and content in the AT interface.

1.2 Intended Users of the Assessment Method

The intended users of the assessment method will be carers and assessment practitioners in post-clinical rehabilitation organisations or in assessment contexts such as educational centres. The AT therapeutic component is aimed at end-users who are assessment clients. The aim is to provide an implementation in a form that may be used by both experienced clinicians and also by therapists of various levels of training and experience. The software and assessment materials are intended to be usable after only a short training period covering the psychological background of the simplistic framework and the specific tests, as well as the systematic method and its operational requirements.

1.3 The Assessment Context

Improved post-clinical assessment of people with acquired physical disabilities is necessary for a number of reasons. There are over 6.6 million people with disabilities in Great Britain. Disabled people are twice as likely as non-disabled people to have no qualifications. They are only half as likely as non-disabled people to be in employment. There is an increasing need for better assessments of cognitive and psychomotor factors which are important for an individual's progression. Assessment centre practices are often out of date using outmoded methods based upon limited psychometric models. These approaches often do not address cognitive deficits such as those involving memory, concentration, spatial or attentional problems. In addition, the resulting assessment is rarely linked adequately to computer based therapy or training in assistive technology using information and communication technology (ICT) computer-based methods.

1.4 A Systematic Model for Assessment

There is therefore a need to develop a simplistic model or framework upon which to base research into systematic methods and tools. Such a model is important for the following reasons. First, when conducting a vocational assessment of an individual, the aim is to enable that individual to make significant progress while minimising subjective bias. Second, the selection of the most suitable methods is also aided by a consideration of the assessment process itself and how it may be optimised.

Hypothesis Testing. One approach to achievement of a good quality assessment is to view it as a process of hypothesis development and testing. Pre-morbid information plus evidence from any other source can thus be seen as a potential basis for hypothesis formation and allows the assessor to take such evidence into account. In practice, the selection of methods with which to evaluate practitioners' hypotheses has often been arbitrary, reflecting their availability and the experience of the assessor. We propose an assessment approach broadly based on a hypothetico-deductive method, using standard tests and preliminary information about the client to set up hypotheses which are then sequentially tested using a suite of special tests drawn from the cognitive psychology literature. By differential elimination of hypotheses, a profile of the clients capabilities is derived that is linked to prescriptions for training and vocational guidance through the cognitive theory and psychological evidence behind the model.

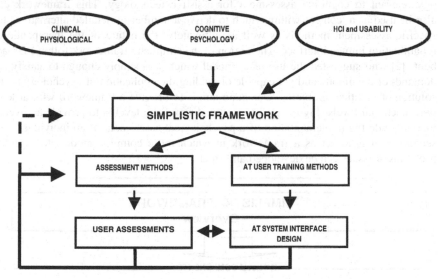

Fig. 1. The research strategy for the assessment method

1.5 The Research Strategy for Assessment and AT

The simplistic model acts as the framework of the assessment method. It draws its structure from well tested theories in mainstream cognitive psychology (Figures 1, 2). The capability of the model for indicating specific tests and the direction of hypothesis testing is because it is drawn from relevant findings in clinical psychology and the more robust experimental psychological evidence associated with cognitive psychological theory. The simplistic framework and the cognitive simplistic model associated with it should not be considered to be fixed. Instead, it is assumed that both models may be modified in the course of development of the assessment approach [6]. Hence, the assessment strategy is developed at four levels: (1) Cognitive simplistic model; (2) Psychological evidence from case studies and experiments; (3) Assistive technology methods and interface; (4) Neuro-physiological correlates such as specific aphasias, word deafness associated with left hemisphere damage [3], or an inability to recognise individual voices whilst understanding what they say (phonagnosia), [4] which is more likely to reflect right hemisphere damage [5].

2 The Simplistic Framework

The purpose of a simplistic model in this context is to act as a framework of psychology relevant to cognitive assessment for assistive technology. This framework can also be used as a context within which to derive a number of detailed alternatives for specific assessment methods as well as, ultimately, the nature of the therapeutic or rehabilitation human interface. The notion of the simplistic framework follows Broadbent [2] who suggested the use of a model which was simply enough to satisfy the demands of parsimony and yet capable of guiding the application of psychology to the solution of practical problems. Our main aim is to provide a framework with at least two functional levels (Figure 2). The first and simplistic level is to provide an overall map to guide the implementation of a psychological assessment of an individual. The second level is to act as a framework in which more complex models for specific problems or issues can be developed and sited.

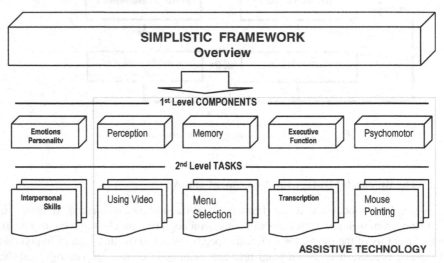

Fig. 2. Unpacking the simplistic model as a framework for practical application

2.1 Psychological Background

Cognitive psychology can provide a rich variety of architectures for working models. For example, simplistic architectures like Broadbent's Maltese Cross [2] capture an overview of cognition but do not attempt to be complete, whereas more complex models like the Interacting Cognitive Subsystems approach [7] that consists of an information processing, parallel approach that attempts to be totally complete and to address the complexity of realistic cognition. In addition, there are neural networks [8] which aim to mimic the human brain and provide a computer instantiation; production systems such as Anderson's ACT* [9] which reflect both cognitive psychology and computer simulations of cognitive processes. There are also approaches such as Marr's computational model and broader framework [10] that derive from research into Artificial Intelligence, exploiting neurophysiology, engineering, and computer science. Whilst any of these could be used to model the assessment of cognitive skills, we adopt a parsimonious approach based on Broadbent's [2] simplistic model. The aim of this work is to develop a simplistic framework based on our model, which provides a first approximation for a full model of cognition.

2.2 The Cognitive Model Structure

The overall structure adopted in shown in Figure 3. It consists of a set of four processing zones that are linked by a central processing system., each with its own memory facilities.

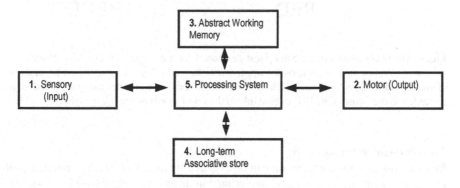

Fig. 3. The cognitive structure of the simplistic framework

One of the roles of this central system is to transfer or copy memory traces from one area to another. The processing system also acts as a selection filter. This initial formulation [2] leaves out any indication of input and outputs to the system, implying some form of selection or filtering before the sensory memory store. The model allows for memories to be present in one or more stores, either partially or fully.

3   The Development of Cognitive Assessment Methods

It is important that we can use our simplistic model to guide the implementation of an assessment in practice. Consider the individual who has problems of selective attention. Unpacking the overall model to focus upon a sub-model of attention, we are then be able to explore this area with a more complex model as a basis for understanding. In the case of attention, the sub-model then points to suitable methods of assessment that will now be outlined.

3.1   Example: Assessment of Attentional Capability

Individuals must be highly selective in their responses to potential information overload but without missing vital new information or sources. The research literature identifies several important dimensions of selective attention that are relevant. For example, there is an important distinction between active, goal driven, attention and passive, externally driven, attention [11]. Active attention requires more resources than does passive attention, even though the former is more typical of the tasks that individuals face. Similarly, divided attention (responding to more than one type of item) is more taxing than focused attention (responding to one type of item only).

RED   BLUE GREEN **BLACK RED**

BLUE   **RED** BLACK GREEN **BLUE**

Fig. 4. The two versions of the Stroop test developed for assessment. In matching Name > Ink the client matches the red name on the upper left to the red coloured word 'BLACK' in the set of words on the upper right. In matching Ink > Name the client matches the green word on the lower left to the word 'GREEN' in blue ink in the set of words on the lower right

The Assessment Stroop Test
Mechanisms of selective attention can be explored by means of the Stroop test, a well-known task in which colour names are printed in different colour inks (Figure 4), [12], [13]. Individuals find naming the ink colours of such items to be more difficult (and slower) than the reading the ink colours of neutral items like rows of XXX's. Such problems of attention can be due to either difficulties in attending to the correct aspects of the display or difficulties in selecting the correct responses. On this basis, we have developed an assessment version of the Stroop test based on that of Hartley & Adams, [13] that allows us to distinguish between input and output problems of attention. This result, in turn, enables the recommendation of appropriate Assistive Technology and user training solutions.

3.2   Case Study Example 1: The Stroop Test as a Discriminating Method

The discriminatory power of the modified Stroop task is well illustrated by the comparative case study between Client A and Client B:

Client A is an individual who was involved in a road traffic accident, with resulting frontal lobe damage. His overall aptitude was evaluated by means of Ravens Standard Progressive Matrices (RSPM),[14]. He also completed a task to assess his pre-morbid IQ. A reduction of ten or more IQ points obtained would only be expected in the normal population in ten percent of cases. His perceptual speed and accuracy were good. He carried out the Stroop task as a measure of his higher cognitive processes. It was observed that he required significantly more time to learn each version of the task, but when he had learned each task he performed them relatively well. This suggested that he faced problems with executive processes. This individual did not show attention deficits but he did present problems of acquisition of a cognitive, attentional task as if his executive attention skills were impaired but low level attention processes were not. A comparison was made of his behavior post head injury with his underlying personality. His perceived personality was assessed with the Myers-Briggs Type Indicator, (MBTI) and a 16 Personality Factor Inventory (16PF), [15], and there were indications that his underlying personality and his post injury behavior were sometimes contradictory. His frontal lobe injuries seem to be related to his passive approach to tasks; his executive function problems; his competent memory and basic attentional processes; lack of drive and observed social inhibition. He reported a poor memory, yet performed well on a simple memory function task but displayed poor meta-memory.

Client B   is schizophrenic, with his condition controlled by medication. When working under direct supervision, he starts well but when left to work alone, his performance declines significantly. He was first given a measure of his overall aptitude (RSPM) [14] which produced a low score with reference to the general population. The Cognitive Failings Questionnaire (CFQ) [2] explores the frequency of everyday mistakes. It requires the individual to report on the perceived frequency of their errors. He produced a score of 34 /100 indicating that he is unaware of his mistakes.

These findings suggest serious problems with cognitive skills, a hypothesis which was tested by use of the Stroop test. This individual seemed to experience no problems in learning and organising the tasks. However, he displayed difficulties carrying out the task and appeared to experience significant negative transfer from one task to another. Since it was not clear if this was due to the difficulty or the order of the tasks, the tasks were given again, after a rest day, in the reverse order. Whatever the order, he experienced negative transfer from the first to the second task. This hypothesis was tested and confirmed by a test of his memory showing that he cannot cope well with similar tasks with competing demands.

3.3   Client-Centred AT Training Recommendation

Client A would not be expected to require help with basic processes of attention and memory, However, his inability to self-organise and to track his own actions suggested the need for an IT organising, planning or prompting system. He also needs social skills training to understand the perspectives of others.

Client B again shows lack of insight into his problems and unawareness of his performance limitations. The tests suggested that he cannot cope well with conflicting task demand. The Stroop task suggested that he cannot learn well under error making conditions. This suggests that benefit would result from an error-free learning regime where the cue stimuli and responses are simultaneously present. Specific stringent learning requirements would best be implemented on a computer.

3.4 The Assessment Strategy

A similar strategy as that used with the Stroop test can be adopted for other memory, perception, and reasoning capabilities. Our test battery is currently derived from two sources, (a) framework based, where tests are supported and explained by our conceptual framework or a sub-model of it and by utilisation of experimental psychological methods from research literature, or (b) by inheritance i.e. they were currently available and proved useful. These methods were supported by a range of clinical and psychometric tests, including IQ measures, specific aptitudes including social skills, literacy and numeracy, dyslexia tests and personality inventories. These were used to establish hypotheses to be clarified by the specific cognitive tests. Some tests are relevant to specific zones of the framework and they are indicated in the following table.

Table 1. The Assessment Tests

TEST NAME	MEASURES	ZONES
Stroop test	Input, output and central attentional processes.	1,2,5
	Task learning [13].	3, 4
Structured interview	Expectations and insight (executive functions).	5
	Background information.	4
Meta-memory	Accurate articulation of memory issues / usage.	5
CFQ	Meta cognition and insight into common errors.	5
	(Cognitive Failings Questionnaire).	
Digit Span	Memory i.e. input, output and working memory.	1,2,3
	Modality.	1
Sentence Memory.	Memory structures and output processes.	3.4.5
	(Cued recall or recognition) [16].	
Cued recall.	Storage processes in memory [16].	1,3,4
	(word pairs or fragments).	
Cued recognition.	Retrieval processes in memory.	3,5
	(word pairs or fragments).	
Visual Search.	Serial and parallel input processes [17].	1
Mental Rotation.	Manipulate of visual spatial information [18].	1,5

3.5   Case Study Example 2: The Use of the Systematic Method

We propose an assessment approach broadly based on a hypothetico-deductive method using standard tests and preliminary information about the client to set up hypotheses which are then sequentially tested using a suite of tests drawn from the cognitive psychology literature. Firstly, an initial assessment is made with reference to the client's history. This takes the form of a structured interview, the outcome of which is intended to be a series of hypotheses as to the individuals underlying capability that can be tested using specific tests from the Assessment Method.

Initial Assessment

Client C sustained a head injury as a result of a road traffic accident twelve months previously. The resulting closed head injury involved the left frontal lobe and left parietal lobe, producing right hemiparesis and mild left hemiparesis. His health was good, as was his concentration and memory. His responses were all consistent with the view that he lacked full insight into his cognitive problems, significantly underestimating them. He had difficulty organising his own timetable and actions without significant prompting and guidance. He was asked to complete an un-paced personality questionnaire (16PF) which normally takes approximately 45 minutes to complete but took over two and a half hours. This suggested evidence of slowed information processing skills. His overall aptitude was evaluated by means of Ravens Standard Progressive Matrices (RSPM) and Ravens Coloured Progressive Matrices (RCPM). The NART (National Adult Reading Test) which uses knowledge of irregular words to estimate pre-morbid IQ indicated a significant differential. Further analysis revealed low numeracy and literacy using the Foundation Skills Assessment (FSA).

The preliminary assessment therefore suggested that Client C was deficient in concentration and attention, with possible memory problems This suggested problems impaired executive function rather than input-output disorders.

Cognitive Tests

His existing memory performance was examined, using the Digit Span task from the Assessment Method. This consisted of a simple free recall task for short digit sequences presented in auditory, visual and combined visual-auditory modes. Client C managed 100 % recall in all three tasks for every sequence, so further evaluation of his memory was not seen as a priority.

His performance on the modified Stroop task. was very slow, completing approximately 25% of the typical number of items. He was only able to complete four versions of the task in the time available. His performance actually declined from the practice session to the main session. In two cases, this decline was big enough to be statistically significant on a t-test for proportions ($p < 0.001$). This implied a difficulty with his ability to organise the demands of the tasks, even though he had been given opportunity to learn them, suggesting a problem with executive functioning, thought to be associated predominantly with the frontal lobes. This conclusion was supported by the fact that his performance declined significantly across the different versions of the task. An interview or a discussion would not have provided an accurate picture of his strengths or weaknesses as he significantly underestimated the magnitude his problems.

3.6 Conclusions of Case-Study Development of the Assessment Method

Using a selection of case-studies we have shown, firstly, how an individual test assessment method can be validated in use. Secondly, we have shown how a systematic approach to assessment can enable an assessor to converge from general testing methods to tests of specific cognitive capabilities eliminating hypotheses and finally generating conclusions and prescriptions for computer-based assistive training. The example Stroop test method has proved to be capable of discrimination of attentional disorders, especially in conjunction with memory tests such as digit span and cued recall. We have also demonstrated the use of quantitative inferential statistics as a diagnostic tool. We cannot claim to have generalised our methods through testing on a normalised population but we are not trying to match our users to a standard test result. Instead, we seek to identify a capability profile that enables an assessor to accurately conceptualise an individual users problems and identify abilities that would benefit from training.

AT Design and Rehabilitative Training

The concise conclusions resulting form the assessment method are well suited to the provision of computer-based Assistive Technology as well as rehabilitative training regimes. For example, Client A would benefit from planning or organisational assistant tools and computer-based social skills training. Client B would be best trained under an error-free learning regime best implemented using computer training aids in conjunction with further testing using the assessment methods. He needs an alerting system which causes him to re-attend on his duties on a regular and frequent basis. Client C would benefit from an interactive memory aid and in view of his poor level of awareness, training based around learning meta-memory strategies. He needs both executive support and training and task specific cognitive support, benefiting from planning or organisational assistant tools and computer-based social skills training.

4 Evaluation of Method and Software

There are a number of levels of evaluation of the assessment method and of the assistive technology software that implements it. Firstly, candidate assessment tests drawn from experimental psychology using the simplistic framework as a guide will be evaluated in clinical use, as presented in this paper. The principle criteria for inclusion in the assessment suite is (1) empirical proof of capability for discrimination of specific cognitive impairments using (2) a clear operational relationship between the test and the cognitive model (Fig 3). Secondly, the specific user training therapeutic methods implemented in the software will be empirically assessed for the degree of improvement they give rise to both at an individual and at a group level. Feedback in the form of amendments to the method and the software implementation will be used to modify both the simplistic framework and the AT software design in an iterative manner, following standard usability approach, as indicated in Figure 1.

Evaluation in Practice

An important objective will be to test the program and evaluate its overall effectiveness in the context of existing practical assessment and progression programs. Initially, the enhanced approach will be assessed in the context of day-to-day Rehabilitation, assessment activities and the detailed feedback from practitioners used to modify and improve both the theoretical basis and the practical application. In a longitudinal study, evaluation will be managed using the newly developed approach alongside existing services and measuring the relative success of the two systems by measuring their effect on a number of previously defined success criteria such as employment rates and assessed improvement. The outcomes of the use of the method will be assessed using systematic empirical methodology, such as blind studies where the method will be used before or after existing assessment techniques in counterbalanced trials by trained practitioners who are unaware of the trials' purpose. The dependant variables will include measured performance in independent living skills, success in gaining employment and measures of usability.

5 Conclusions

We have outlined the cognitive components necessary for a simplistic model to be used to support the assessment of individual assistive technology needs and rehabilitation. Specifically, we have demonstrated and validated a number of concepts that have guided the successful implementation of the assessment method for a number of example cases studies showing how they may provide insights into capabilities as well as practical recommendations for progression and assistive technology.

The approach developed was based on the large investment in time and resources necessary for client-centred assessment as contrasted with a normative approach to assessment that assumes high levels of insight and awareness on the part of the practitioners and tested individuals. The method demonstrated points the way to better ways to carry out assessments for assistive technology for disabled people as well as defining the contents of such assessments. We have shown how prescriptions for design of assessment and therapeutic AT interfaces are generated by the method. This research is embedded in the Inclusive context of assessment and holds the potential to provide assessment for computer users. Practitioners and therapists will gain more usable methods and this will enable a better quality of interaction between carers and their clients.

References

1. Adams, R., Langdon, P., and Clarkson, P.J., (2002), A systematic basis for developing cognitive assessment methods for assistive technology. C6. pp 53–62. In Keates, S., Langdon, P., Clarkson, P.J., and Robinson, P. (Eds.) Universal Access and Assistive Technology. Springer.
2. Broadbent, D. E. (1984) The Maltese cross: a new simplistic model or memory. Behavioral and Brain Sciences 7, 55–94.
3. Franklin, S., Howard, D., & Patterson, K. (1994). Abstract word meaning deafness. Cognitive neuropsychology, 11, 1–34.
4. Van Lancker, D., Cummings, J. L., Kreiman, J. & Dobkin, B. H. (1988). Phonagnosia: A dissociation between familiar and unfamiliar voices. Cortex, 24, 1–15.
5. Baddeley, A. D. (1990). Human memory: Theory and Practice. Hove, U.K. Lawrence Erlbaum Associate
6. Shallice, T. (1991). From neuropsychology to mental structure. Behavioral and Brain Sciences, 14, 429–439.
7. Barnard, P.J., May, J., Duke, D. and Duce, D. (2000). Systems interactions and macrotheory. Transactions on Computer Human interface, 7, 222–262.
8. Rumelhart, D. E. and McClelland, J. L. (1986). On learning the past tenses of English verbs. In Parallel distributed processing. Volume 1. (McClelland, J. L. and Rumelhart, D. E. Eds.). Cambridge Mass : MIT Press.
9. Anderson, J. R. (1983). The architecture of cognition. Cambridge M. A. : Harvard University Press.
10. Marr, D. (1982). Vision : A computational investigation into the human representation and processing of visual information. New York : Freeman.
11. Handy, T. C., Hopfinger, J. B. and Mangan, G. R. (2001). Functional neuroimaging of attention. In Cabeza, R. and Kingstone, A. (Eds.) Handbook of Functional Neuroimaging of Cognition. Cambridge, MA. MIT Press.
12. Stroop, J. R. (1935). Studies of interference in serial verbal interactions. Journal of Experimental Psychology, 18, 643–662.
13. Hartley, L. R. and Adams, R. G. (1974). Effect of noise on the stroop test. Journal of Experimental Psychology, 102, 62–66.
14. Raven, J. (2000). The Raven's progressive matrices; Change and stability over culture and time. Cognitive Psychology, 41, 32 47.
15. Lord, W. (1994).a review of item content in the fifth edition of the 16PF. London: ASE.
16. Adams, R. G. and Berry, C. (1981). Cued recall of sentences. Quarterly Journal of Experimental Psychology, 33A, 295–307.
17. Treisman, A. M. & Gelade, G. (1980). A feature integration of attention. Cognitive Psychology, 12, 97–136.
18. Shepherd, R. N. (1978). The mental image, American Psychologist, 33 125–137.

Applying a Holistic Approach to Develop User-Friendly, Customer-Oriented E-government Portal Interfaces

Maria A. Wimmer and Ute Holler

Institute of Applied Computer Science, Division: Business, Administration and Society,
University of Linz, Austria
{mw, holler}@ifs.uni-linz.ac.at

Abstract. e-Government is an important field of application for providing electronic public services to a wide range of users. Especially in the public sector, the customers are very heterogeneous with different expertise and know-how on using electronic media such as the Internet. Moreover, the public sector is characterised by providing a wide range of different kinds of public services varying for the distinct user groups. Developing appropriate, user-friendly portal interfaces for virtual administrations, which offer a broad range of public services to the distinct user groups, requires a careful investigation of the user needs and service requirements. In this contribution, we provide a first examination of usability and easy-to-use requirements in relation to target user groups and process models for electronic public service delivery. We define an overall interface architecture and discuss the required front-office functionality for a user-friendly and intuitive e-Government portal serving distinct target groups.

1 Introduction

In general, electronic Government (e-Government, virtual public administration) covers the development, implementation and application of IT to government and governance. In a more narrow sense, it is concerned with the provision of electronic public services to a wide range of user groups. Thereby, the user groups can be categorised into citizens, employees of businesses and public servants. More concrete, the first two reflect the customers of public administration from an external perspective. They are of main interest in this contribution. Yet, in digging deeper into the argument, distinctions even within the three general clusters have to be made.

Since the different groups of customers of public administration have different expertise and know-how on using electronic media such as the Internet, portal interfaces for virtual administrations have to meet the distinct user needs accordingly. As a starting point in navigating through the different offers of public administrations, however, no specific knowledge on how to surf through the online services must be required. Here, usability criteria become important. However, up to

N. Carbonell, C. Stephanidis (Eds.): User Interfaces for All, LNCS 2615, pp. 167–178, 2003.

now, not much attention has been paid to usable interfaces and universal access[1] when developing e-Government portals.

Despite of different customer groups, user interaction in public administration is always impacted by the underlying objectives of a public service: the characteristics of e-Government processes have a strong influence on the design of the user interface. Hence it follows that for the wide range of public services for distinct user groups specific usability criteria have to be considered. As a consequence of this interdependency between user groups and kinds of public services, a holistic approach integrating different views based on processes and target groups is required to develop adequate user interfaces.

When offering public services via virtual administration portals, a shift in designing governmental work has to take place. Since customers will serve themselves through the virtual portal, a service-oriented presentation (instead of a task-oriented one) of the offers is needed. Some requirements emerging from this claim are that

- the user needs not to be aware of the functional fragmentation of public administrations for consuming a specific service,
- the structure of public service offers and navigation through the portal must lead the users to the searched public services with only a few mouse clicks,
- the information on public services must be intuitive and in the everyday speech of the user,
- the user is at any time aware of the steps already completed and still to be performed and
- the system provides help and support for each step to be performed when interacting with the virtual public administration.

In order to elicit the different user requirements for distinct target groups, careful analysis of the user needs in respect to the public services is of utmost importance. In this contribution, we first discuss the general frame and preconditions for e-Government interfaces towards the customers of public administration. In section 3, we investigate the process perspective of e-Government services. Section 4 provides insight into different stakeholders and user groups of e-Government portals. We then define an overall interface architecture of a virtual public administration portal and the required front-office functionality (sections 5 and 6). In section 7, we briefly summarise overall usability criteria thereby relating them to the respective application domain of virtual public administrations. Finally, we provide a first draft of requirements specification for user-friendly portal interfaces for a one-stop Government platform.

---

[1] Though we claim that public administrations have to provide universal access to everybody, we do not discuss specific accessibility requirements for people with special needs in this contribution (this topic would fill an own paper contribution). Instead, we focus on usability and accessibility of virtual administration portals for ordinary e-Government users, which are strongly neglected in current e-Government developments.

2 Frame and Preconditions for E-government Interfaces towards the Customers of Public Administrations

e-Government portals reflect the entry point of external customers (i.e. citizens and employees of businesses) to electronic public services and information thereof. In order to design such e-Government portals, several preconditions and general requirements have to be met. The holistic development framework as discussed in [13] represents a guideline to investigate distinct requirements for e-Government portals. It combines three different dimensions (see Figure 1):

1. Abstraction layers: from strategic considerations towards concrete IT solutions
2. Progress of public services: electronic public service delivery has to be provided with different phases of progress (information - interaction - service delivery / transaction - aftercare)
3. Different views: e-Government is a socio-technical system and so, distinct issues have to be investigated and related to each other (processes; users; data, information and knowledge; technology; security; laws; organisation; social and political aspects).

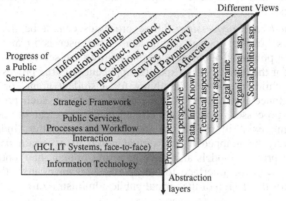

Fig. 1. Holistic development framework

Based on this holistic development framework, we henceforth focus on the requirement clusters most relevant for the design of a portal interface towards the citizens and businesses: different types of processes, access for distinct user groups, the general architecture of the portal interface, the functionality to be provided at the portal and front-office layer of a virtual administration and usability criteria to provide electronic public services through the virtual administration portal.

3 Access to Different Types of Processes

Up to now, e-Government discussions often suffered from the negligence of deliberating the process perspective. Yet, with the visions of e-Government, where the citizens and businesses should take over a more active role - e.g. self-service through the virtual portal, data entry done by the customer, etc. -   the process perspective becomes of utmost importance. More concrete, this means that traditional processes need to be re-thought and adapted for electronic service provision where the customer performs several tasks as well.

Apart from that, e-Government is a domain with different types of processes for public services. In literature, four principal kinds have been identified in governmental action (e.g. [6], [7], [8], [REF12]):

1. *Routine processes and well structured standard processes:* For these processes, the operating sequence is known in advance. They are well structured and can be automated easily (e.g. the process of "applying for a passport renewal" or of "applying for a new passport"). However, when designing such types of processes for the electronic service delivery via the virtual portal, one has to be mindful in respect to the final product, because not all routine processes can be fully mapped to the electronic service delivery. As the examples indicate, at a certain point, a direct interaction and appearance of the applicant might still be required, e.g. in order to personally sign and pick up the passport in front of an authorised public servant. Other public services like the "certificate of residence" or the "declaration of change of place of residence" might be fully treated electronically in all phases of the process.

2. *Individualised case processing:* These processes cannot be treated like routine ones, because of the special circumstances the user is in and because of the discretionary power of public servants that allows the servant to individually treat such cases for the benefit of the specific applicant (e.g. the processes "enrolling an under-aged child in school", "applying for a student grant" or "applying for a family assistance payment"). In many cases, however, such processes may turn into routine processes, i.e. when all circumstances are clear and no objections and disagreements exist in regards to the final official letter. Individualised case processes may be mapped to the virtual portal to a certain degree. At certain points, such process models also have to permit human intervention and decision tasks (here, even the interface for the public servant treating the case becomes significant for the design of the virtual public administration).

3. *Negotiation processes:* Like individualised case processing, these processes are semi-structured. In addition to the individual case treatment, however, many parties involved and the complex investigations of the circumstances and disagreements of the different interests of the involved parties are characteristic. These oppositions have to be negotiated in detail and agreed upon among the relevant stakeholders involved. Examples of such types of public services are e.g. the processes of "applying for a building permission" or the "application of a foreigner for a working permit". Such processes can only be performed electronically to a certain extent and they rather reflect ad hoc decisions.

4. *Weakly structured processes:* This type of process includes democratic deliberation and the field of policy-making. Electronic service provision is probably not the right expression here to deliver content to the customers. Instead, here, discussion facilities, opinion polling and information sharing are the most important electronic support mechanisms.

These types of processes require distinct process models to be implemented at the virtual front-office. In a sophisticated e-Government solution, all four types of processes have to be supported.

Since e-Government processes strongly involve the customer, the sole investigation of process perspective will not suffice. Processes have always to be related to the target user groups and, hence, an investigation in the target customers of a respective public service is necessary.

4   Identification of Target Users

According to Freeman [1] "a stakeholder in an organisation is (by its definition) any group or individual who can affect or is affected by the achievement of the organisation's objective". As already pointed out before, e-Government processes have many stakeholders, which, on an overall level, can be divided into four user groups:

- Citizens
- Businesses
- Public authorities
- Intermediaries for citizen or business

Yet, problems with making current e-Government developments success show, that one uniform portal for a category is not the cream of the crop. Instead, each of the groups has to be further broken down into occasional users (having to perform the process once a year or less), frequent users (several times a year) and power users (several times a day) such as intermediaries like tax advisors, notaries, car dealers, architects. This distinction strongly relates to the public service to be performed. It even provides a hint towards so-called "killer"-applications to be implemented first in order to exploit the benefits and minimise the costs on both sides (customer and public administrations).

Especially in regards to citizens as customers of virtual public administrations, alternate target groups (e.g. families, students, employees, unemployed, parents, pensioners, etc. as specific target groups of the citizen cluster) for specific processes have to be addressed. Further, the virtual portal interfaces have to reflect these two interrelations. In this respect, the so-called life-event metaphor represents a good and useful concept. For example, the Austrian portal "@mtshelfer online"[2] [14] bases on the life-event concept for structuring public services for citizens according to birth, family concerns, education, marriage, employment, taxes, death, etc. Within the concept of such a life-event, the respective pubic services can be reached by the citizen in an intuitive way with a few simple mouse-clicks.

Not only provides this life-event metaphor a structuring concept to offer public services in an intuitive and understandable way from the citizen's point of view. It further allows to bundle public services for a certain life situation in logical sequence.

---

[2] http://www.help.gv.at/

In this way, the portal can provide a meaningful guidance in the obligations and duties the citizen has to perform in such a situation. E.g. when moving home, one not only has to care about the declaration of change of place of residence to the municipality, but also to update the address in the driver's licence, to update the car admittance, to change the address at the tax office, the electricity and energy provider, etc. A user-friendly and customer-focused virtual portal should intuitively provide all these information and guidance in the service completion to a citizen.

5   Interface Architecture of a Virtual Administration

There exist already many discussions on how to present information via web interfaces to the user in an user-friendly and intuitive way. Garzotto et al [2] have developed a reference framework for hypermedia applications basically dividing content, structure and navigation. This Hypermedia Design Model (HDM) represents a valuable concept for e-Government interfaces, which we adopt for our approach. It suggests to investigate the following five layers:

- *Content:* This layer includes all the information which is displayed by a web application such as information or data and instructions regarding an e-Government process. It further contains information about e.g. the forms, procedures and descriptions about legal background.

- *Structure:* The content of a hypermedia application is organised by the structure. As already mentioned above, for virtual administrations, the concept of structuring public services according to life episodes and business situations and to bundle related public services appropriately has become quite popular in recent time.

- *Presentation:* The presentation layer describes the visualisation of content and structure to the user. It includes the individual granules of information and dynamic features such as navigation. Here, the process flow and content for a specific public service are integrated and visualised to the user through the interface.

- *Dynamics:* How users interact with individual parts of information (e.g. control the active media till playing) and how they move among them are treated in the dynamics layer. This layer is crucial for the phases of interaction and transaction within a public service, which is object to the fifth layer of the HDM. It takes e.g. care of first proofs of data entries in online forms and supports the interaction in transactional web dialogs.

- *Interaction:* The dynamic functions of the application are used by operating the presentation elements. e-Government processes require the workflow and a series of interfaces to back-office systems and databases. This interaction between a customer at the portal layer and the authorities in charge of delivering a specific public service has to be implemented adequately without hampering legal grounding (e.g. data protection, access rights) and in order to be able to fully exploit the potential of virtual public administrations.

The concept of the HDM and the interrelations of the five layers are demonstrated in Figure 2 as an interface architecture for virtual public administrations. The right side of the figure shows the requirements categories per user group that detail the functionality at each of the HDM layers as introduced in the last part of the paper.

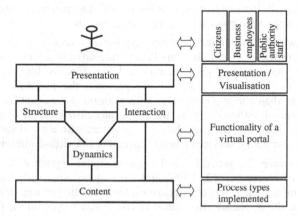

Fig. 2. HDM concept adopted to define requirements for user-friendly virtual public administration portals

6 Portal (Front-Office) Functionality

Future virtual administrations have to go far beyond simple information provision. To run a sophisticated portal for virtual administrations to enable electronic service delivery, the following front-office and portal functionality has to be provided:

- *Forms service*: In order to invoke a public service in a traditional way, an applicant has generally to fill in and hand in a form, where the requested data and documents have to be provided. Online forms basically have the same functionality, except that they can facilitate and guide the applicant in completing the data and that, with modern communication means and networked public administrations, the user can be supported in pre-filling fields. In this way, the task of data-entry in the virtual public administration is shifted to the customer at the front-office side, while the public administration, with the appropriate standardised interfaces to back-office systems, can directly integrate the data into the electronic workflow and database systems. Despite of this feature, a good layout design of forms guides the user step-by-step in the provision of the right data and document resources. Also, the proof of correctness and completeness of the filled-in data and accompanying documents can be partially assigned to the system.

- *Routing service:* In the one-stop concept, the offers and information towards the customer are provided according to life-events and public services. The customer does not need to know the respective public authority at the back-office side in charge of the service completion and delivery. So, a routing mechanism is required that directs the application of the customer from the portal to the authority in charge of the public service the customer has applied for.

– *Information service:* It contains all information on the online request, the portal functionality and the description of the e-Government online offer. It includes details on the offered services such as the needed documents, the process structure, legal grounding of the process, fees, preconditions, etc.

– *Authentification:* Since public service applications require a clear, unique and trusted identification of the applicant, identification and authentification mechanisms like login, digital identity and functionality for intermediaries are necessary. The login for intermediaries provides the possibility that s/he can manage more than one application for citizens or business clients in parallel. Apart from the general authentification, the login may also be used to personalise the portal for the user. E.g. the user should be provided with a list of currently invoked applications for public services when logging into the virtual administration portal.

– *Digital signature:* In general, the European digital signature directive of 1999 (99/93/EC of December 13, 1999) and the national approvals thereof officially equate digital and hand-written signatures. Since public services mostly require the signature of the applicant, the portal interface has to provide a functionality to digitally sign applications and documents.[3]

– *Payment service:* Electronic public services are, in most cases, associated with fees. In a sophisticated virtual administration, an online payment functionality for directly carrying out the payment has to be integrated with the electronic service performance.

– *Encryption, security and authenticity of data:* e-Government processes deal with rather sensible and personal data and documents, which are transmitted via an insecure Internet. Security and encryption mechanisms have to be provided between the client at the customer side, the portal and the back-office to secure data and documents and to ensure that these are not manipulated, wiretapped and object to fraud.

– *Process workflow on the portal layer:* The front-office needs to properly support the tasks to be performed by the customer. A process workflow at the front-office has to guide this interaction and task performance of the customer within a running public service from the invocation of the service until it's completion.

– *Interfaces to the back-office:* Despite of the workflow at the front-office, appropriate standardised interfaces are required to ensure interoperability and direct integration to the back-office.

---

[3] However, in order to promote the electronic service delivery, the Austrian "Allgemeines Verfassungsgesetz" (general laws on public administration concerns) has been modified in the "Verwaltungsverfahrensnovelle 2001" in a way that, in some cases of electronic intake of applications, no signature is required any more. Instead, the trusted identity is proven and this suffices for treating an application.

7 Usability Criteria

In order to develop user-friendly and easy-to-use portal interfaces for the distinct user groups of virtual administrations, the above mentioned aspects on processes, user groups, interface architecture and front-office functionality also need to be balanced with usability criteria. The following usability criteria from Jacob Nielsen [10] (also reflected in the ISO standards 9241 [4] and 13407 [5]) as well as the "quality in use" criteria of the ISO/IEC 9126 [3] have to be integrated into the design of online public services:

- *Learnability:* The system should be easy to learn so that the user can rapidly start getting some work done. Especially the functionality of the form service have to ensure an easy settlement of online transactions within services of virtual public administrations.

- *Efficiency:* The system should be efficient to use, so that once the user has learned the system, a high level of productivity is possible. If the user needs help with an online request, the portal logic has to provide proper help topics for the used service including references to related services.

- *Memorability:* The system should be easy to remember, so that the casual user is able to return to the system after some period of not having used it, without having to learn everything all over again (which is a very important feature for citizens as non-frequent users of virtual administration portals). Further, if a service procedure is available for the user, it should stay this way. The design of the service flow should be well considered (cf. section 6).

- *Errors:* The system should have a low error rate, so that users make few errors during the use of the system (cf. forms service functionality), and so that if they do make errors they can easily recover from them. Further, catastrophic errors must not occur. In particular, portals of virtual administrations should guarantee a safe handling of online services.

- *Satisfaction:* The system should be pleasant to use, so that users are subjectively satisfied when using it. This criterion might not directly apply at first hand. It has to be interpreted in relation to the purpose and benefit behind using the virtual administration portal. In most cases, a customer of public administration is obliged to carry out the invocation of a public service, even if s/he does not really want to. Here, the criterion of satisfaction has to be measured as to which extent the virtual way of performance is more efficient and effective than the traditional way. Hence, if the virtual portal interface is pleasant to use and delivers the requested results quickly and efficiently, the user will be satisfied. In the early phases of virtual administration portals, satisfaction can also be supported with well-structured "hot testing" functionality.

- *Functionality:* Each service should be designed in a clear way that the users can easily find out, what it is good for and how it works. At best, it is represented in a way that a user knows intuitively how to use it, but there should be help topics available if needed. Especially for non-expert user groups of e-Government portals, the interface must give the user the feeling that it is easy to use and that the system operates intuitively. Hence, an important requirement is that the requested functionality and process flow at the portal layer are visualised appropriately and intuitively.

– *Reliability:* The user should be able to rely on the way the system works and to count on its timelines. Therefore, the system should be predictable. In other words, the user not should be surprised by the way the system reacts and it should react within a short time. The user should also be informed that something is going on and what is going on at any time.

Designing user-friendly, intuitive virtual administration portals for distinct target user groups requires a strong integration of above mentioned aspects. In the following section, we provide a guideline and some examples of requirements for one-stop government portals.

8   Sketching Some Requirements for Virtual Administration Portals

The integration of the different aspects discussed above reflect an important design criterion for user-friendly portal interfaces for online public services targeting distinct user groups. Table 1 shows a non-exhaustive list of such integrated requirements for user-friendly e-Government portals. The matrix integrates and structures requirements that have been partially elaborated within the eGOV project[4], an EC co-funded project, where an integrated platform for online one-stop Government is developed. Further work in this direction has been performed by the working group on "best practices" of the Austrian Forum e-Government[5] (cf. [11] and [9]). The current requirements matrix is structured according to the general user groups and categories investigated above.

The requirements matrix for user-friendly e-Government portals as presented in Table 1 reflects a draft version of work in progress. We are aware of further research and empirical work to be performed to provide a sophisticated guideline for requirements specification for user-friendly e-Government portals, especially, because the aspects of usability requirements in electronic public service provision targeted for specific user groups has not been investigated properly, yet. However, the investigation on specific aspects performed so far as well as the attempt to interrelate and integrate these aspects is a starting point for future work to be done in order to properly address usability features for virtual public administration portals serving distinct user groups.

---

[4] http://www.egov-project.org/
[5] http://egov.ocg.at/

Table 1. List of requirements for user-friendly e-Government interfaces towards the citizens and businesses

		User Groups		
		Citizens	**Businesses**	**Intermediaries**
Requirements regarding	**Presentation/Visualisation**	Simple and intuitive representation of the information and process flow; Preview of web forms before submitting; Compact representation of the data after service submission for printing; Customising of the online representation; Interactive, intelligent online help in interacting with the portal to perform a public service;		
		Appropriate presentation of a service performed for distinct user groups of citizens & for the special target process; Alternative representation for handicapped people;	Appropriate presentation of a service performed for distinct user groups of business employees & for the special target process;	Appropriate presentation of a service performed for the special target process; grouping mechanism for different clients;

		User Groups		
		Citizens	**Businesses**	**Intermediaries**
Requirements regarding	**Functionality**	Forms service including indication points to required and optional fields and well-structured online forms, which will not be bigger than a screen; Routing service; Authentification & personalisation; Payment service including the option of differential paying modes; Encryption, security and authenticity of data; Email confirmation after submission; Testing of the services without consequences; Anonymous logins for e.g. complaints; Information about which files are kept by the authority; Downloadable forms have also to be enabled as direct upload for electronic submissions; Electronic submission of (scanned) plans or documents; During the whole task of filling in an online form, the user has to be informed about the steps already performed and the ones still to be done (e.g. page 2 of 4); Downloadable notice for further electronic processing by the user; Supporting the service flow at the portal side; Integration with the back-office systems; Status report of services and personal data; Online Service Delivery; Definition and using of logical sequences for services;		
			Enterprise Application Integration (EAI);	EAI; Supporting multi-client access;
	Processes	Online implementation of information, interaction & contracting, service performance, payment, service delivery and aftercare for: - Routine processes; - Individualised case processing; - Negotiation processes; - Weakly structured processes;		

References

1. Freeman, R.E., Strategic management: a stakeholder approach, Boston: Pitman, 1984.
2. Garzotto, F., Mainetti, L., Paolini, P., Hypermedia design, Analysis, and Evaluation Issues, Communication of the ACM, Vol. 38, August 1995, pp. 74–86.
3. ISO/IEC 9126, Software product evaluation – Quality character and guidelines for their use, 1991.
4. ISO 9241, Ergonomic Requirements for Office Work with Visual Display Terminals (VDTs), 1998.
5. ISO/DIS 13407, Human-centred design processes for interactive systems. International Standards Organisation, 1999.
6. Lenk, K., Klee-Kruse, G., Multifunktionale Serviceläden, Ein Modellkonzept für die öffentliche Verwaltung im Internet-Zeitalter, Edition Sigma Rainer Bohn Verlag, Berlin, 2000.
7. Lenk, K., Traunmüller, R., Öffentliche Verwaltung und Informationstechnik: Perspektiven einer radikalen Neugestaltung der öffentichen Verwaltung mit Informationstechnik, Schriftenreihe Verwaltungsinformatik Bd. 20, im R. v. Decker's Verlag, Heidelberg, 1999.
8. Lenk, K., Traunmüller, R., Wimmer, M., The Significance of Law and Knowledge for Electronic Government, in: Grönlund (ed.), "Electronic Government – Design, Applications and Management", Idea Group Publishing, 2001, pp. 61–77
9. Lindlbauer, O., Makolm, J., Skerlan-Schuhböck, T., Bericht der Arbeitsgruppe Best Pracitice, in: M. Wimmer (Hrsg.), "Impulse für e-Government: Internationale Entwicklungen, Organisation, Recht, Technik, Best Practice", Österreichische Computer Gesellschaft, Wien, 2002, pp. 171–180.
10. Nielsen, J., Usability Engineering, Morgan Kaufmann, Academic Press, San Diego, CA, 1993.
11. Makolm, J., Best Practice in eGovernment, in: Proceedings of 1st International Conference on Electronic Government (EGOV) in conjunction with DEXA 2002, Aix-en-Provence, 2-6 September 2002, Springer, Heidelberg, pp. 377–381
12. Wimmer, M., Traunmüller, R., und Lenk, K., Prozesse der öffentlichen Verwaltung: Besonderheiten in der Gestaltung von e-Government, Im Tagungsband zur gemeinsamen Arbeitskonferenz GI/VOI/BITKOM/OCG/TeleTrusT "Elektronische Geschäftsprozesse", Klagenfurt, 24-25 September 2001, pp. 436-445.
13. Wimmer, M., Integrated service modeling for online one-stop Government. EM – Electronic Markets, special issue on e-Government, 12(3):2002, pp. 149–156.
14. Winter, A., 'www.help.gov.at – Die österreichische Verwaltung im Internet', in: H. Reinermann (Hrsg.), "Regieren und Verwalten im Informationszeitalter, Unterwegs zur virtuellen Verwaltung", R.v. Decker Heidelberg, 2000, pp. 170–185.

Digital Television for All: User Preferences and Designers' Views on What Would Suit the User

Leena Eronen

Telecommunications Software and Multimedia Laboratory,
Helsinki University of Technology, P.O.Box 5400,
FI-02015 HUT, Finland
leronen@niksula.hut.fi

Abstract. This paper presents results from a user study and a set of design sessions conducted in a broadcasting company. During the design sessions, the designers created new concepts of interactive television programs for given TV viewers. The creative work was based on user profiles collected in the preceding user study. The aim of research was to include the future users into the product development in the early stages of new product design. Both TV viewers and designers created innovations of future interactive applications and the results are discussed.

1 Introduction

Design activities have been called as 'a process of communication among various audiences' [3]. Interactive television programs and services for digital television are an example of novel products that must meet the needs of a broad range of audiences. For example, re-design of many consumer products is based on modifications made to the latest product versions to meet the new user needs. Sometimes a fresh marketing campaign will do. Concept design of new and novel products on the other hand faces many challenges. Modifications made to previous product versions are not enough for the television audience, as TV viewers want to get surprised by new television programs, not the old ones.

Interactive television programs and applications have been a subject of research in a number of studies. There are results from prototyping personalized TV news [9], usability testing Electronic Program Guide prototypes [6] and designing on-screen displays and remote controls [8]. There are also results from an ethnographic study of set-top-box use [10], a study resulting in a set of user groups for digital television [4] and a user study resulting in new concepts of interactive television programs made by TV viewers [5]. The next subsection deals with issues concerning user research and user centered concept design for digital television.

N. Carbonell, C. Stephanidis (Eds.): User Interfaces for All, LNCS 2615, pp. 179–186, 2003.

1.1 Methods

The study presented here consists of a user study and a set of design sessions held in a broadcasting company. It is a continuation of a study resulting in a set of user groups for digital television [4]. The aim of research was to include the future users into the product development in the early stages of new product design. The new products are interactive television programs and applications for digital television. The user study took place in study participants' home environment. Five women and five men in the age range of 16-78 years received an envelope with questionnaires, separate questions, two diaries and a disposable camera. The approach has been adapted from a research called 'Cultural Probes' and other, more traditional ethnographic methods [7, 1, 10]. The study participants also designed innovations of future interactive applications for themselves. A subsequent one-hour interview with the researcher revealed more of the study participants' needs for specific types of information and their thoughts of the television in the future. The interview materials were analyzed to find important examples and user experiences [11]. The approach was not an ethnographic user study as it was the user study participants who collected the data instead of researchers. The approach enabled the study participants themselves to gather the results in their home environment, explain them and give their interpretations as why events happened. An ethnographic study made by an observer would not reveal enough of the user's motives to watch television.

A series of five design sessions followed in the public service broadcasting company YLE (Finnish Broadcasting Company). YLE's share of total TV viewing in the Finnish-language television network was 43% during year 2001. Each session included a researcher and two participants from YLE: concept designers, producers, television editors and audience researchers. Altogether ten participants from YLE took part in the sessions which took 60-90 minutes each. The session participants explored the user profile, discussed about their findings and then designed new concepts of interactive television programs. A lively discussion provoked the session participants to imitate the program hosts, television announcers and the studio audience. The new program concepts were therefore created with the help of storytelling and role playing [3, 2]. The aim of each session was to concentrate specifically on one TV viewer at a time instead of groups of people familiar from the audience research. At the end of a session, the user's innovations were presented to session participants as a feedback. They could now compare their new concepts to user's innovations. This was a way to provide an instant feedback to designers.

2 Results

Results from the user study and the five design sessions are presented here next. In the user study the emphasis was put on finding user preferences and expectations instead of particular user needs. Digital television is a novel product and it is not possible to perform research on user needs concerning a product or service the user has never used before. For new concepts of interactive television programs and services, it was

| User profile: Bethy, 78 years, Retired |
| Family: - |
| (Two adult sons not living with her) |
| Pets: - |
| Entertainment equipment at home: TV, Radio |
| Bethy prefers to watch: Comedy, Current affairs, Documentaries, Domestic movies, Entertainment, Music (rock, pop, dance), Nature, News, Politics, Quiz, Weather |

"In your opinion, what is best about television?" *"News and documentaries and a few commercials."*
"In your opinion, what is worst about television?" *"Violence and sex."*
"Which video tapes are most important to you? *"There is no VCR."*
"Do you read Program Guides?" *"I don't read much movie reviews. I do read the interviews and short funny stories."*

Fig. 1. Bethy on her leisure time

anticipated that the user interaction can take place in four different ways. There is the interaction with the remote control and the set-top-box, an SMS sent from a mobile phone, a phone call or a postcard sent to the TV show.

2.1 User Study

User study results are responses to questionnaires, diaries, photographs, users' innovations and notes from the interviews [5]. The study participants also made scenarios about what their television will look like in year 2006, five years ahead of the present moment. The study results were collected in user profiles. Each profile is 8-18 pages long. One of the user profiles is presented here next. For the purposes of this paper, it was shortened to fit half a page. All names appearing in this and the next subsection were changed to protect privacy. Fig. 1 presents Bethy in her living room. The photograph is an example of the photograps the study participants were asked to take that present their daily life and the objects and incidents at home. The newspaper on the table contains television program listings. Bethy said: *"Yes, there are enough interesting programs on TV. ..For me, it's more important to read the books. I always have something to do if there is nothing on TV that interests me."*

Five study participants' innovations of future interactive television programs and applications are presented in Table 1. 75 innovations altogether were made by ten study participants. As is seen in Table 1, the user preferences and innovations of

Table 1. User preferences for future interactive television programs and applications

Name, Age (years), Profession	Users' concepts
1. Henri, 16, High school student	• Internet chat on TV via set-top-box or a mobile phone • Email and SMS on TV while watching the TV • Load books and magazines on TV • Wallet on TV you can fill in through a bank Web pages • TV games • Interactive role playing game, new episode every week • TV reminds him of important events • Demonstration and information sharing of his hobby (judo) • Information on travel destinations and cities • Holiday reservation requests on TV
2. Patrick, 27, Product manager	• Email and Web on TV • SMS and video snapshots to friends • DVD and video storage capability • Board games like 'Trivial Pursuit' on TV, PC games on TV • Family photo album on TV • Quick online quiz that doesn't disturb watching the TV show • 'Home Shop' with a catalog on the screen. A video connection to the salesperson in case he wants to ask a question • Links to shops, banks and civil service departments • Program Guide of his favourite TV shows. Preceding and up-coming episodes • TV recommends his favourite TV program types
3. Alicia, 34, Children's nurse	• 'F1 Quiz'. TV viewers get points for guessing on who will make the next pit stop or who will drop out. TV viewers have a table of their score • More camera angles from the pit during F1 racing • News on F1 racing and criminal investigation • Video connection to friends and family • Email on TV • Program Guide of her favourite TV shows • Bus and train timetables • Calendar for the family and the Todo list
4. Bruce, 46, Chief coastguard	• On-demand cookbook for both children and adults. Recipies in chosen breadth with pictures, video and text • On-demand private study English language course • Do-it-yourself directory on renovations at home • Information and video on travel destinations • Holiday reservation requests on TV • Travellers' stories from their holidays • Sharing of experiences with other parents whose children play football. Information on children's football camps
5. Bethy, 78, Retired	• Interactive 'Wheel Of Fortune' program • All-day TV channel for retired people that presents Church services, programs on current affairs, gymnastic exercises and stories on recovery from diseases

future services are quite personal. If we try to find some common concept for these five TV viewers it must be Email on TV. Other favourite concepts were SMS on TV, TV games, video connection on TV, Electronic Program Guides (EPGs), information on travel destinations and Quiz on the ongoing TV show.

2.2 Design Sessions

There were five design sessions in the public service broadcasting company YLE. A set of user profiles was selected, namely those presented in Table 1. The aim of each session was to concentrate specifically on one TV viewer at a time instead of groups of people familiar from the audience research. The session participants designed new concepts of interactive television programs for this particular TV viewer. As a feedback, they were given the TV viewer's own innovations at the end of the session. Altogether 29 new concepts were designed. Table 2 represents designers' views on which interactive concepts would suit these users. Most of the new concepts really are new and do not yet exist on Finnish television. Some concepts like hosted TV chats, 'Entertainment Program For Teenagers' and 'Local Events' programs already have some examples to draw influence from.

2.3 Analysis of Results

The user study resulted in 75 innovations altogether which were made by ten user study participants. In this paper, innovations made by five TV viewers were presented. The innovations were based on personal preferences. The most popular concept was Email on TV. Other favourite concepts were SMS on TV, TV games, video connection on TV, Electronic Program Guides (EPGs), information on travel destinations and Quiz on the ongoing TV show. TV viewers' concepts can be considered as new or novel and they do not yet exist on Finnish television except for some interactive SMS based TV games and an EPG in the set-top-box. It is likely that in the future we well see many SMS based TV games and Quizzes on the ongoing TV show, as the mobile phone density is very high in Finland and people use them with pleasure.

The five design sessions in the broadcasting company resulted in altogether 29 interactive concepts. The concepts differ significantly from each other from session to session and no common concepts were found. There are however two types of user interaction that were in designers' favour. First, designers innovated concepts of TV shows that rely on the TV viewer to send his or her opinion or story to the show. For example 'Criminal Investigation' program for Alicia, 'Our Family Life' for Bruce and 'Recent History' for Bethy are concepts that rely on the TV viewer to send solutions, stories and recollections to the show. The other type of interaction asks for TV viewers' participation already during the show. For example 'Science Program For Teenagers' for Henri, 'Chat For Formula 1 Fanatics' for Alicia, 'Wheel Of Fortune' for Alicia and Bethy and 'Sing Along' for Bethy are based on user interaction during the show, not before or after the show.

Table 2. Designers' views on what would suit the user

Session	Designers' views
1. Henri	• 'Science Program For Teenagers'. Themes of the program vary from the new technology to how Darude makes computer music. People of different ages and backgrounds do the program. Henri can send his opinion on the 'Question Of The Week' to the show with an SMS • 'Entertainment Program For Teenagers'. Young celebrities like singers and musicians appear in the program. There are funny mishaps during the show, nothing too profound. User interaction with an SMS
2. Patrick	• 'Personalized News'. A program of rapid pace covering only prespecified subjects Patrick has chosen for himself • TV games for both Patrick and his daughter • Interactive features on movies. Patrick sees background information on his favourite movie, for example interviews with the actors, the special effects and the shooting of the movie • 'Interactive Action' series. Patrick answers questions or solves small problems and collects points • 'Interactive Nature' series. Patrick sees background information on the creatures. He can also take snapshots of both domestic and wild animals and send them to the show
3. Alicia	• 'Chat For Formula 1 Fanatics' program. Alicia can chat with other Formula 1 experts about the race. It is a hosted chat in Finnish for her convenience and she can watch the race at the same time in the background • 'Criminal Investigation' program. Based on both historical material and dramatized scenes. First some clue is given to the case and then the TV viewers are asked to send their solution to the mystery, an art robbery, etc. The show can also include cases from her neighbourhood • 'Wheel Of Fortune' program. Alicia can write her guess while watching the program and win instantly. The winner gets her name on TV • 'Who Wants To Be A Millionaire' for fast answers from the TV viewers
4. Bruce	• 'Our Family Life'. The program tells about what it is like to live in a one-family house as a type of living. Themes vary from the maintenance of the house to kitchen work, gardening and parenting. There are also examples of 'How To Get Along With Your Neighbour'. Bruce can make a call and dictate his own story on the 24-hour phone line. The next week he sees his story dramatized on TV. All TV viewers can now call the show and give their suggestions as how to best solve the situation
5. Bethy	• 'How To Utilize The New Technology' program. Short and humoristic in style, much like a commercial • 'Local Events' program. Bethy sees what's happening in her home town • 'Wheel Of Fortune' for Bethy to type in her guesses. Very quiet in pace • 'Recent History' program addressing issues from politics to pop music, to fashion and daily life. The program proceeds one year at a time. Bethy can send her interesting recollection to the show. The program is a way to transfer the cultural heritage, to maintain the memory of a generation • 'Sing Along' program. TV viewers choose by voting both the next artist and the song this artist will perform. Bethy can sing along with the show • 'Cuisine Program For Home Chefs'. Traditional Finnish food made easy. Bethy can send recipes from her childhood to the show

Most of designers' concepts are new and do not yet exist on Finnish television. Some concepts like the hosted TV chat for Alicia, 'Entertainment Program For Teenagers' for Henri and 'Local Events' program for Bethy do have some examples to draw influence from. Of the new concepts of two types of user interaction, it is most likely that the concepts of instant user interaction will succeed. Watching the television is considered a pleasant leisure time activity that does not involve too much concentrated brainwork. Interaction before or after the show would need quite a lot of user motivation.

When we compare the user preferences to designers' views on what would suit the particular TV viewer, we see that designers' concepts suit Henri and Patrick quite well. For Alicia, who is a home centered, the designers could have created a program on family issues. For Bruce, who is both information and entertainment oriented, the designers could have created a program on travelling. He was also interested in on-demand applications about cooking, English language studies and home renovation. As on-demand applications were not considered TV programs, designers didn't create any of these. For Bethy, the designers could have created programs on Church services or health and fitness programs for retired people. As many of these preferences are quite personal, it is not easy to say if the new concepts will appeal to a broad range of TV viewers.

2.4 Analysis of Methods

The five design sessions in the broadcasting company were started with reading a given user profile. It was found during the sessions that sometimes the session participants considered the TV viewer as older or younger than the group of people they considered 'their audience'. It could increase the session participants' motivation and commitment to the design session if they could choose their favourite user profile beforehand. Also, the reading of the profile shouldn't take more than 10 minutes as the idea is to use the material to provoke lively discussions and not to 'study' the material in great detail.

The other design methods used were storytelling and role playing. When the two session participants found an interesting user comment, they started to imitate fictitious program hosts, television announcers or members from the studio audience. This was a fast method to visualize their new ideas. The session participants considered the results from an interview with the TV viewer and the user's innovations especially useful as these contained data of user's tastes and preferences and stories of his daily life. This material was quite easy to exploit in storytelling and role playing during the design session.

As the user study method is a time-consuming exercise including data collecting and data analysis, it is recommended to start early. The user profiles are then reusable for any future design sessions.

3 Conclusion

This paper presented results from a user study and a set of design sessions conducted in a broadcasting company. The user study put emphasis on finding user preferences and expectations instead of particular user needs. The design sessions concentrated specifically on one TV viewer at a time. The use of individual user profiles was a new idea in this broadcasting company as today they use the results from the audience research as a basis for their design work. Innovations of future interactive applications were created by both TV viewers and designers. Future research has two goals arising from the needs of product development. First, we want to know which concepts are likely to suit a large audience and second, we want to make scenarios of selected new concepts to get feedback from TV viewers.

References

1. Blomberg, J., Giacomi, J., Mosher, A., Swenton-Wall, P.: Ethnographic Field Methods and Their Relation to Design. In: Schuler, D., Namioka, A. (eds.): Participatory Design: Principles and Practices. Lawrence Erlbaum Associates, Hillsdale, NJ, USA (1993) 123–155
2. Buchenau, M., Suri, J. F.: Experience Prototyping. In: Conference proceedings on Designing interactive systems DIS '00: processes, practices, methods, and techniques. ACM Press, New York, NY, USA (2000) 424–433
3. Erickson, T.: Notes on Design Practice: Stories and Prototypes as Catalysts for Communication. In: Carroll, J. M. (ed.): Scenario-Based Design: Envisioning Work and Technology in System Development. Wiley, New York, NY (1995) 37–58
4. Eronen, L.: Combining Quantitative and Qualitative Data in User Research on Digital Television. In: Proceedings of the 1st Panhellenic Conference with International Participation on Human-Computer Interaction PC HCI 2001. Typorama Publications, Patras, Greece (2001) 51–56
5. Eronen, L.: Design of Future Television. In: Proceedings of the HF2002 Human Factors Conference, a joint Conference of the Ergonomics Society of Australia (ESA) and the Australian CHISIG. Melbourne, Australia (November 2002) 8 pages
6. Eronen, L., Vuorimaa, P.: User Interfaces for Digital Television: a Navigator Case Study. In: Proceedings of the Working Conference on Advanced Visual Interfaces AVI 2000. ACM Press, New York, NY, USA (2000) 276–279
7. Gaver, B., Dunne, T., Pacenti, E.: Design: Cultural Probes. Interactions, Vol. 6, No. 1. (1999) 21–29
8. Logan, R. J.: Behavioral and Emotional Usability: Thomson Consumer Electronics. In: Wiklund, M. E. (ed.): Usability in Practice: How Companies Develop User-Friendly Products. AP Professional, Boston, MA, USA (1994) 59–82
9. Merialdo, B., Lee, K. T., Luparello, D., Roudaire, J.: Automatic Construction of Personalized TV News Programs. In: Conference proceedings of the seventh ACM international conference on Multimedia. ACM Press, New York, NY, USA (1999) 323–331
10. O'Brien, J., Rodden, T., Rouncefield, M. and Hughes, J.: At Home with the Technology: An Ethnographic Study of a Set-Top-Box Trial. ACM Transactions on Computer-Human Interaction 6, 3 (September 1999), 282–308
11. Rubin, H. J., Rubin, I. S.: Qualitative Interviewing: The Art of Hearing Data. Sage Publications, Inc., Thousand Oaks, CA, USA (1995)

A Metaphor for Personalized Television Programming

Konstantinos Chorianopoulos and Diomidis Spinellis

eLTRUN, Athens University of Economics & Business
47A Evelpidon Str & Lefkados 33
GR-11362 Athens, Greece
{chk,dds}@aueb.gr
http://www.eltrun.aueb.gr/

Abstract. Traditional human-computer interaction settings involve a task-oriented approach where the human interacts with an application to accomplish a particular goal. The emergence of media-rich computer-mediated leisure applications requires a fresh view of the current paradigms and a careful examination of how this change of perspective affects their relevance. This paper proposes a metaphor for accessing personalized television programming and suggests an approach for integrating the metaphor into the design of a television user interface. The proposed metaphor is tested in the design of a personalized advertising service. The results of the empirical research are discussed and the suitability of the metaphor for other television programs is examined.

1 Personalized Television Programming and Metaphors for All

Long before consumers could access digital TV applications, researchers predicted a shift in the way television programs were going to be produced, transmitted and consumed. Nicholas Negroponte (1995) said that: 'TV benefits most from thinking of it in terms of bits. Once in the machine, there is no need to view them in the order they were sent', implying that some kind of logic —either user choice or from some other source— could be applied on the television content. Then he went on to forecast with accuracy the ability to time-shift broadcast transmissions: 'All of a sudden television becomes a random access medium, more like a book or newspaper, browsable and changeable, no longer dependent on the time or day, or time required for delivery'. This change of television use patterns requires a new user interface paradigm. The accessibility of a novel information system for a wide group of users can be ensured using a familiar metaphor. 'Metaphors for All' have been studied before in the case of the emerging mobile commerce services (Karvonen 2000).

For the purpose of this work,[1] digital television is defined as a device, which features Digital Video Broadcasting (DVB) reception, persistent local storage (Hard Disk

---

[1] Parts of this work were supported by the IMEDIA (IST-1999-11038) and CONTESSA (IST-2000-28567) projects, partially funded by the European Commission under the Information Society Technology program.

N. Carbonell, C. Stephanidis (Eds.): User Interfaces for All, LNCS 2615, pp. 187–194, 2003.

Drive-HDD) and data processing abilities. This research focuses on the broadcast mentality of delivering broadband information to masses of people. It also examines future scenarios of satellite transmission, instead of today's popular optical media and Internet unicast distribution mechanisms. The broadcasting mentality enforces an unequal relation between the producer and the consumer, one that may seem arbitrary in today's Internet world. On the contrary, there is strong evidence that the broadcast relation, established and enforced by mass communication, is often the most economically efficient compromise between the needs of the producer and the needs of the consumer. The broadcasting mentality for the delivery of personalized multimedia information has been also replicated and proposed as a more accessible method for using the Web (Kapyla et al. 1998), although its adaptation for the Internet environment was in the end not commercially successful.

Our research is based on the realization that the currently dominant metaphor for the personal computer —i.e. the desktop metaphor— is not appropriate for television, because it is adapted to fundamentally different user and task sets. Therefore, there is a need to design a user interface for digital television that considers the user as a television viewer. In summary, the rationale behind the necessity for reexamining the traditional set of human-interface paradigms is an evolving complex set of features, such as digital broadcasts coupled with rich metadata, digital recording of programs and random access playback, local processing logic, dynamic presentation of content and services, and, most crucially, a different context of use.

The rest of this paper is organized as follows: Section 2 introduces the metaphor for personalized television programming, describes the rationale behind its choice and makes an analogy with the development of the desktop metaphor. Section 3 provides an overview of related scientific disciplines for the purpose of identifying forces that affect the design of applications for digital television. Section 4 presents the problem of personalization for television advertisements, offers a user interface solution based on the proposed metaphor and analyses the results from empirical testing. Section 5 discusses the fitness of the proposed metaphor to other types of personalized television programming.

2   The Virtual Channel Metaphor

Strong evidence of the importance of a metaphor as a basis for human-computer interaction is provided by O'Brien et al. (1999), in an ethnographic study of a digital set-top box trial, in which they point out the need for a 'working model' of the technology being employed by users in home activities. They discuss the need for a conceptual model for digital set-top box usage, because household members appeared confused about the location of their data and how the system worked. Therefore, there is a need to develop a metaphor for digital set-top box storage and presentation of programming that moves away from the desktop-web couple and the notion of information retrieval and active search. Digital broadcasting transmission and persistent local storage should be used to augment television as a medium of entertainment and passive discovery. We therefore propose the following metaphor and describe our motivation.

Metaphor. The digital set-top box can be imagined as a virtual television channel provider, where audiovisuals, applications and data are produced from a combination of local storage and real time broadcast transmissions.

Motivation. The organization of television programs into a small number of personalized virtual channels simplifies the choice from a vast array of available broadcasts and stored programs. The presentation of television programs from virtual channels gives more control to the television viewer, who becomes an important factor in the televised content. The virtual channel metaphor suggests only a minimal shift from the current television metaphor of use, while, at the same time, it focuses the research on the design of a user interface for managing virtual television channels.

By making an analogy to the development approach used for the personal computer human interface, it is possible to identify and focus on a small set of attainable actions that have to be performed towards the direction of a human interface for the digital television. XEROX Star's designers, Johnson et al. (1989), distinguish among four levels of system architecture: 1) Machine and network, 2) Window and file manager, 3) User interface, 4) Document editor. Smith et al. (1982) offer a design methodology and a number of principles. Both of these reference works describe in detail how the desktop metaphor and guided user interface was developed to model, complement and augment office work —i.e. use of documents, mails, memos, network files and printers. Apart from being further evidence to the inappropriateness of the personal computer paradigm for the digital television, the above works emphasize the need to have a conceptual model of use —conveyed through a metaphor— and a number of representative activities after which the user interface will be modeled.

The proposed metaphor has been initially employed into a personalized advertising service. In addition to the virtual channel metaphor, the design of personalized advertising is based on an explicit analysis of the forces that affect the use of digital television applications. Design forces' analysis addresses the issues that are generic in the user interfaces for all types of digital television applications.

3 Forces That Affect the Design of Digital Television Applications

The field of HCI has been benefited by a multidisciplinary approach to design problems (Ballay 1994). Besides proven methodologies and multiple design iterations, successful user interfaces demand a diverse array of design specialties. For the case of digital television, an exploratory literature review has revealed three important disciplines of design: 1) Broadcasting and consumer electronics engineering, 2) ethnographic study of media consumption at home and 3) Interactive and multimedia content creation. Researchers from the respective fields have addressed the design case of multimedia services in the home, but there is currently no aggregate effort towards the direction of a holistic design for digital television applications. Following a survey of diverse scientific perspectives into the field of digital television applications, the most useful findings from each discipline have been collected and analyzed.

The next paragraphs are representative of the approach that has been followed for the analysis of the related scientific disciplines. Each paragraph presents an instance of the role of a discipline to the design of digital television applications and a respective design force. This formal method of analysis, as suggested by Alexander (1964), provides a well-defined environment of relationships and dependencies.

Broadcasting and Consumer Electronics Engineering

The broadcasting model of computing encompasses a radical shift in the mentality of application development process and tools. Milenkovic (1997) highlights the differences with the client-server mentality, describes the carousel concept and explains why the characteristics of the networking infrastructure are an important factor in the type of feasibly deployed applications. Engineers should also justify the use of digital local storage (Whittingham 2000), which currently makes inroads on a multitude of consumer electronics products (Bell 2002). Persistent local storage takes viewer control one big step further —from simple channel selection with the remote— by offering the opportunity for non-linear local programming and content selection.

Design Force. The design should integrate seamlessly and reflect appropriately both the broadcasting computing model and local storage functionality.

Dependency. Both types of programming, stored and broadcast, should be available, without sacrificing easy access to either type of content. Each type should complement instead of competing with the other.

Ethnographic Study of Media Consumption in the Home

The role of ethnographic research in the home, regarding the use of digital television applications, is instrumental. There has been an important technology-driven shift in the household's media consumption patterns every decade or so —in the 80's there was the PC (Vitalari et al. 1985) and in the 90's there was the Internet (Kraut et al. 1996). It is likely, that the first decade of the new millennium will see the introduction of a new range of home entertainment appliances. This trend is already apparent and has been studied with ethnographic methods in the case of the digital set-top box. O'Brien et al. (1999) identified that the 'concentration of functionality' sometimes works against the solitary use of information technology.

Design Force. Different designs are needed for family viewing in the living room and single users in their bedrooms.

Dependency. The system should be designed to handle either group or solitary use and to provide means of adapting to different situations if both are desirable.

Interactive and Multimedia Content Production

When contemplating the impact of technical change on the media industry, there is a common pitfall to avoid. It goes under the view that new technologies and media will completely substitute the old ones, rather than coexist —for example that television and radio would mean the end of newspapers, or that the PC will bring the paperless office. Henry Jenkins (2001), the director of the program in 'Comparative Media Studies' at MIT, opposes the popular view that interactive television will support only the needs of the channel surfers by making an analogy: 'With the rise of printing, intensive reading was theoretically displaced by extensive reading: readers read more books and spent less time on each. But intensive reading never totally vanished.'

Design Force. Design should support both interactive and passive users.

Dependency. Interactivity can be feasibly deployed over digital television, although current television patterns of use are passive.

4 Case Study: The Design of Personalized Television Advertising

Personalized television advertising—although it does not contain an extensive user interface—offers a number of advantages as a test-bed for applying the proposed metaphor. Advertising is, together with subscriptions, the main financial lever behind commercial television. Market success for digital television depends on the evolution and adaptation of advertising models to the new environment. Additionally, the advertising break has a fixed duration, small hard-disk storage requirements and is relatively simpler to integrate with real-time broadcasts. A personalized television advertising prototype was designed using the design forces' analysis (Table 1), within the IMEDIA (Intelligent Mediation Environment for Digital Interactive Advertising) project.

Table 1. The previously identified design forces are explicitly addressed in the design of the personalized adverting system

Design Force	Dependency and Resolution Strategy
Real Time Vs Time Shift	Television programming is transmitted as usual, although the advertising break is dynamically created for each set-top box. The overall experience is seamless for the viewer.
Group Vs Individual	Each set-top box holds general household demographics and optionally individual demographics and preferences.
Interactive Vs Passive	Some advertisement spots may have additional interactive content. The viewer is notified and has the option to 'bookmark' an advertisement for later browsing of interactive content.

The IMEDIA system offered a prototype implementation for enhancing advertisement effectiveness for the digital television environment. According to the advertising research literature, advertisement effectiveness is improved through better targeting of viewers. Targeting is based on accurate consumer data such as demographics, psychographics and buying behavior. The need of marketers for accurate data collides with the consumers' concern for privacy intrusion. Protection of consumer privacy is recognized and a solution for the benefit of both advertisers and viewers has been suggested (Lekakos and Giaglis 2002). Personalized prerecorded advertising does not distort the predominant passive television consumption patterns, because from the user's point of view the experience remains the same with optional personalization and interactivity.

From testing with users, it was found that a number of basic human factors principles hold true for the television user interface. For example, 'visibility of system
status' (Norman 1990) becomes very important when system output is identical among
different situations —personalized advertising looks just like normal advertising, although it may be targeted to either the individual or the household level. On the other
hand, user testing revealed that a task bar was considered irrelevant to the television
experience. The solution given consisted of two parts: 1) 'Push' the current status of
the system, each time there is a new session, by using icons on the screen, 2) 'pull' the
status with a special hardwired key, instead of having to navigate through menus. In
general, the findings from user testing in the case of personalized advertising suggested directions for the design of both digital television applications and devices
(Lekakos et al. 2001).

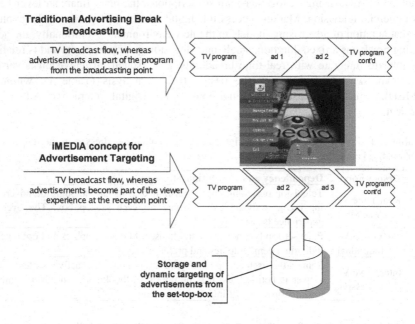

Fig. 1. A personalized advertising break that is based on the virtual channel metaphor

From the part of the television viewer, personalized advertising is a gentle introduction to the virtual channel metaphor through a push paradigm that is closer to the
established patterns of television use. From the part of the television program provider, personalized advertising is a showcase of a radical shift in the mentality of
broadcasting a linear program towards making television viewing a dynamic and personalized experience. As depicted in figure 1, the advertising break is created dynamically from a pool of advertisement spots that have been downloaded from a hidden
broadcast channel and stored on the hard disk of the set-top box. The exact spots to be

included on a given advertising break are selected by the classification and targeting sub-system, which is based on media planning industry's standard procedures, as described in detail in Lekakos and Giaglis (2002).

5 Applying the Metaphor

A limitation of the virtual channel metaphor in the case of personalized advertising is that it addresses only the problem of organization and presentation of content within a single television airtime segment —the advertising break— while it misses the case of organizing television channels as a whole. Nevertheless, the above case offered the opportunity to successfully test the technical feasibility of dynamic synthesis of stored and broadcasted content for the production of a seamless, yet personalized television experience. The viewer remains passive in terms of involvement with the digital television system, while the overall experience is improved, which represents a strong case against the popular trend to make television totally interactive. The case of personalized television advertising has also demonstrated the validity of the virtual channel metaphor and suggests that further evidence is needed from other important classes of digital television programming, like the personalized television program guide (Smyth and Cotter 2000) and personalized television news (Mcrialdo et al. 1999), and transcoding applications.

The proposed metaphor may be refined and enhanced, as it is being applied and tested with the above types of television programming. By making an analogy with the desktop metaphor, it is evident that there are multiple commercial implementations of the same basic human interface principles for interacting with personal computers — Windows, Mac and Unix variants to name the most popular. In this fashion, the virtual channel metaphor may be implemented to support diverse commercial policy objectives. It may also be complemented with other metaphors and use paradigms, in order to support easy access to digital television applications that offer multiple cameras, such as sports and game shows.

Following the test of personalized advertising, empirical research will continue with prototyping and user testing of an enhanced television program guide that is based on the proposed metaphor of personalized television programming. The empirical research will also be complemented with a desk-research of interactive and personalized television news. Television news have been implemented and published extensively in the past —'News of the Future' from the MIT MEDIA lab (Gruhl and Bender 2000) and related activities in the area of 'Multimedia Indexing' offer resources for understanding the important case of television news.

Overall, the virtual channel metaphor has proved to be an invaluable tool for thinking about personalized television programming. Television producers should start to think of their programming in terms of discrete modules—audiovisual, executable code, data—and in terms of their dynamic synthesis personalized for the digital television user in the form of virtual channels.

References

1. Alexander, C. *Notes on the Synthesis of Form*. Harvard University Press, 1964.
2. Ballay, J. M. Designing workscape: an interdisciplinary experience. In *Conference proceedings on Human factors in computing systems : "Celebrating interdependence"*, pages 10–15. ACM Press, 1994.
3. Bell, G. and J. Gemmell. A Call for the Home Media Network. *Communications of the ACM*, 45(7):71–75, July 2002.
4. Gruhl, D. and W. Bender. A new structure for news editing. *IBM Systems Journal*, 39(3/4):569–588, 2000.
5. Jenkins, H. Tv tomorrow. *MIT Technology Review*, May 2001.
6. Johnson, J., T. L. Roberts, W. Verplank, D. C. Smith, C. H. Irby,   M. Beard, and K. Mackey. The Xerox Star: a retrospective. *Computer*, 22(9):11–26, 28–29, Sept. 1989.
7. Kapyla, T., I. Niemi, and A. Lehtola. Towards an accessible web by applying PUSH technology. In *Proceedings of the 4th ERCIM Workshop on 'User Interfaces for All'*, number 15 in Position Papers: Information Filtering and Presentation, page 15. ERCIM, 1998.
8. Karvonen, K. Experimenting with metaphors for all: A user interface for a mobile   electronic payment device. In *Proceedings of the 6th ERCIM Workshop on 'User Interfaces for All'*, number 16 in Short Papers, page 6. ERCIM, 2000.
9. Kraut, R., T. Mukhopadhyay, J. Szczypula, S. Kiesler, and W. Scherlis. Communication and information alternative uses of the Internet in households. In *Proceedings of the Conference on Human Factors in Computing Systems (CHI-98) : Making the Impossible Possible*, pages 368–375, New York, Apr. 18–23 1998. ACM Press.
10. Lekakos, G., K. Chorianopoulos, and D. Spinellis. Information systems in the living room: A case study of personalized   interactive TV design. In *Proceedings of the 9th European Conference on Information Systems*, Bled, Slovenia, June 2001.
11. Lekakos, G. and G. Giaglis. Delivering personalized advertisements in digital television: A methodology and empirical evaluation. In *Proceedings of the AH'2002 Workshop on Personalization in Future TV*, may 2002.
12. Merialdo, B., K. T. Lee, D. Luparello, and J. Roudaire. Automatic construction of personalized tv news programs. In *Proceedings of the seventh ACM international conference on Multimedia (Part 1)*, pages 323–331. ACM Press, 1999.
13. Milenkovic, M. Delivering interactive services via a digital TV infrastructure. *IEEE MultiMedia*, 5(4):34–43, Oct.-Dec. 1998.
14. Negroponte, N. *Being digital*. London: Hodder Stoughton, 1995.
15. O'Brien, J., T. Rodden, M. Rouncefield, and J. Hughes. At home with the technology: an ethnographic study of a set-top-box trial. *ACM Transactions on Computer-Human Interaction (TOCHI)*, 6(3):282– 308, 1999.
16. Smith, D. C. S., C. Irby, R. Kimball, B. Verplank, and E. Harlem. Designing the Star user interface. *Byte Magazine*, 7(4):242–282, Apr. 1982.
17. Smyth B. and P. Cotter. A personalized television listings service. *Communications of the ACM*, 43(8):107–111, 2000.
18. Vitalari, N. P., A. Venkatesh, and K. Gronhaug. Computing in the home: shifts in the time allocation patterns of households. *Communications of the ACM*, 28(5):512–522, May 1985.
19. Whittingham. Digital local storage. Technical report, Durlacher, May 2001.

Universal Access to Multimodal ITV Content: Challenges and Prospects

Soha Maad

Fraunhofer
Institute for Media Communication (IMK)
Germany
Soha.Maad@imk.fhg.de

Abstract. Research in the area of universal access has gained a wide interest in the past 7 years [1]. This is attributed to the versatility of the subject and its prospect in a wide range of applications for pervasive[1] computing technology. This paper considers the prospects and challenges of providing universal access to a multimodal interactive television (ITV) content. First, the paper overviews the evolution of the ITV technology: the market, the distinctive features, and the developmental needs and requirements. Second, the paper discusses the relevance of the concept of universal access and its portability to an ITV platform. Third, the paper considers the ITV presentation of financial news and tickers by a virtual human avatar as a case study of an innovative prototype for Business Television (BTV) that reveals the prospects and challenges of universal access to a domain specific ITV content. The case study proposes a new paradigm for authoring universally accessible multimodal ITV content and draws a future research agenda in this respect.

1 Introduction

The growth of the digital TV market varies across Europe and USA depending on several factors: [2], [3]

The growing number of digital TV platforms. These platforms are specified in term of operating system, set top box technology, broadcasting technology, and content delivery technology (hardware and software). The Multimedia Home Platform (MHP) is one of the many available platforms. [4]

The services offered. These are mainly services that differentiate digital from analogue TVs. They include traditional and new styles of TV programs, and value added features such as e-commerce, e-mail, chat, etc.. Various digital TV services are offered on demand in a subscription package that specifies the technical connectivity features as well as the permissible access to various TV channels and to value-added services.

The national demand. This demand is assessed by the rate of digital TV households.

---

[1] The use of computing technology in various devices.

N. Carbonell, C. Stephanidis (Eds.): User Interfaces for All, LNCS 2615, pp. 195–208, 2003.

The national acceptance. This is translated in issuing supporting legislation for the penetration and uses of the digital TV.

The organisation of the market. The digital TV market may follow a utility model (the cable operator sells access to the consumers to TV channel operators) or a Pay-TV model (The cable-operator acts as a service provider or packager, selecting channels for a banded package and marketing it to its subscribers).

The adopted set-top box technology. The first generation of set-top box software technology relied on HTML-based technology (based on the Advanced Television Enhancement Forum ATVEF specification). Emerging technologies such as OpenTV, PowerTV, and JAVA TV technologies promise greater interactivity for the next generation set-top boxes [5], [6].

A rising concern in the digital TV market is the role of interactive television (ITV) in boosting the growth of this market and constituting a new industry. The entire delivery chain of ITV involves: (1) systems operators, set-top box technology providers, broadcasters, and content providers.

The ITV makes it possible to use the data bandwidth in providing services unrelated to video data, such as stocks and news tickers, e-mail, chat, games, etc.. These value-added services give broadcasters and content providers the potential to differentiate their products and to attract a wider range of viewers.

Authoring content for ITV (including ITV programs and value-added features such as e-commerce, interactive financial news, e-mail, web and channel surfing, as well as other feature that render the TV more interesting and more responsive to the user needs) should now rely on new development paradigms that adapt to universally accessible multimodal style of applications. A multimodal ITV content[2] necessitates a rich multi-media support and cross platform portability.

This paper assesses the prospects of universal access to a multimodal ITV content. It addresses key issues for authoring universally accessible multimodal ITV content. The case study of ITV presentation of financial news by a virtual human avatar is considered. This case study delivers an innovative prototype for business television (BTV). The human avatar (animated 3D humanoid) is supposed to interact with ITV viewers having diverse financial background and various financial interests and learning and analysis needs. This interaction takes the form of voice replies, facial expressions, and hand gestures to edutain (educate and entertain) the ITV viewer. The objective of the case study is to support the analysis in tackling the addressed key issues for authoring universally accessible multimodal ITV content, and to suggest new paradigms for universal accessibility within the framework of a future research agenda involving novel software system development (SSD) practices. This agenda benefits from research in the area of Empirical Modelling technology[3] that aims at establishing a software system development culture that emphasizes a central user role in the Software System Development (SSD) activity and a growing software boundaries and requirements.

---

[2] In the context of this paper, a multimodal content is defined as "a content with growing boundaries and that is adaptable to different model of uses and access and tailored to various needs and operations".

[3] http://www.dcs.warwick.ac.uk/modelling/

2 The Prospects and Challenges of Universal Access to ITV Content

So far, the concept of universal access was supported, among others, by research in the area of User Interface for All (UI4ALL). This research is described in [1] as *"being rooted in the concept of Design for All in HCI, and aiming at efficiently and effectively addressing the numerous and diverse accessibility problems in human interaction with software applications and telematic services. The underlying principles is to ensure accessibility at design time and to meet the individual requirements of the user population at large, including disabled and elderly people"*. The key concept of UI4ALL was supported practically by devising the unified user interface development methodology [7] and by constructing the user interface development platform [8].

It is plausible to claim that the prospect of authoring universally accessible multimodal ITV content is strongly linked to the success of the practical implementation of the concept of universal access, and the development of a suitable corresponding versatile platform, while taking into consideration the following key issues:

Media deployment and the development of novel mediums of interaction
Developing various means of user interaction (beyond voice and remote control mediums of interaction) for an ITV platform would serve a wider ITV audience including the disabled viewer (physically handicapped) and ensure a greater universal access to the ITV mutimodal content. However, this is strongly linked to the technical advances in media deployment across various platforms, media interoperability, and the development of the corresponding supporting standards.

Openness of interaction
Authoring ITV content with non-preconceived modes of interaction is essential to serve a wider audience need and edutain[4] the viewer in a less constrained and dictated way. In this respect various levels of interaction can be identified: the constrained, the semi-constrained, and the open-ended levels of interaction. The success of ITV relies, among other factors, on providing an open-ended interaction with the user (ITV viewer). Open ended interaction designates interaction evolving with users' needs and requirements, involving various medium of interaction, and relying on well-established paradigms for user-developer collaboration in the corresponding Software System Development activity [9]. So far practically, this interaction has been constrained by pre-conceived features and options for interaction that reduced the aimed interactivity of the ITV.

Open-ended interaction is associated with the intelligent ITV reply to the user (ITV viewer) interaction. With the aim of developing truly interactive and universally accessible TV content, it is of particular importance to serve the ITV viewers needs on demand intelligently. This is strongly dependent on the paradigm of interaction, the quality of the information repository at the back-end of the interactive interface,

---

[4] A term coined by Sepideh Chakaveh at Fraunhofer – IMK to designate an education and entertainment role for the ITV.

and the intelligent routine to access this repository. The structure and design of the meta-data about this repository is of critical relevance to enable the open-ended interaction and facilitate the intelligent accessibility to the multimodal content.

Open-ended interaction suggests user-developer collaboration[5] in authoring the universally accessed multimodal ITV content.

Developing and sharing interfaces for a multimodal content

The information horizon[6] [11] of the ITV viewer traces some boundaries on the interface design and the development of the multimodal ITV content. This information horizon is wide ranging and may pose great challenges to traditional paradigms for interface development. Authoring universally accessed multimodal content is a challenging task given the specific context dependent characteristics of various applications (e.g. the characteristics of finance content vs. manufacturing content). Providing universally accessed interfaces for a multimodal content is strongly dependent on a proper authoring of this multimodal content and on the design of the appropriate means for its universal access. The ITV platform can be conceived as a vast repository of multimodal content that is intelligently accessed by a wider community of ITV viewers.

Sharing interfaces by various ITV viewers (with the aim of forming a collaborative network of ITV viewers) is a step ahead in promoting ITV uses and providing added value over enhanced and HTML based digital TV. This necessitates the deployment of state of the art research and practices in developing virtual environments for collaboration and providing shared ITV views. Beynon (et al 2000) [12] proposed new principles for virtual collaboration to meet the complex and dynamically evolving requirements of virtual collaboration in all its form (e-business, e-learning, and e-projects). These requirements include customisation, the integration of the electronic and human activity, adaptation, and the resolution of the fundamental mismatch between the roles that humans and electronic devices play in communication and interaction.

Integrating a multimodal content and providing a universal access to this content across different platforms

The most important criteria in the integration practice is the plethora of ways in which data of the multimodal content is accessed and processed. This can be interpreted as a need for better models of data and agency [13]. The focus is no longer on abstract data alone, but on the state-changing activities that surround that data, to include the protocols and interfaces of all the agents that operate upon it. In this respect, an *agent* can refer to a computer program or procedure, a human agent, or an electronic device

---

[5] Research in the area of software system development reveals the importance of user – developer – designer collaboration at every stage in software system development [10].

[6] D. H. Sonnenwald (1999) discusses human information behaviour with reference to three basic concepts: the context (the general setting within which an individual's interactions take place), the situation (a particular setting for an interaction within a context) and the social network (defined by characteristic patterns and resonances of interaction between individuals within a context). The *information horizon* is defined by the variety of information resources upon which an individual within a social network can draw.

that mediates between the internal representation and the external world. With this interpretation, agency is manifest at many levels of abstraction, in low-level data exchange, in interactions, and in the viewers' horizon. In general, the problems of integration cannot be resolved without taking account of the multiple views imposed upon data through different types of agency.

The case study considered in the following section addresses the issues of media deployment and the development of novel mediums of interaction and universal access. It frames the requirements for open-ended interaction with a domain specific ITV content, and motivates a research agenda that tackles the issues of developing and sharing interfaces for a multimodal ITV content as well as integrating diverse multimodal contents.

3 Case Study: ITV Presentation of Financial News

This section describes research in progress on the development of a platform for ITV presentation of financial news by a virtual human avatar to create an innovative prototype for BTV. First, an overview of the TV production-delivery chain[7] for the specific content of financial news presentation by a human TV presenter is provided. Second, the ITV production-delivery chain for the specific content of financial news presentation by a virtual human avatar (humanoid) is depicted. Third, the various development stages of the case study under consideration are described. The case study considered serves three purposes:

First, it explores the prospect of using virtual human avatars to enhance the universal accessibility to a multimodal ITV content. This benefits from drawing a comparison between the traditional ITV production scenario that involve human TV presenters and the ITV production scenario where the human TV presenter is replaced by a virtual human avatar (humanoid) to support universal access.

Second, it presents the challenges facing ITV technology in implementing the concept of universal access to a multimodal content. These challenges are revealed by considering domain specific characteristics of a particular ITV content (e.g. financial news presentation ITV content).

Third, it helps in drawing a future research agenda for authoring universally accessible multimodal ITV content.

3.1 The TV Production-Delivery Chain: The Case of Human TV Presenter

It is interesting to draw a comparison between the traditional way of presenting financial news on analogue TV and on the digital interactive TV.

On analogue TV, daily financial news presentation by a human TV presenter is limited to showing the passive pre-recorded video presentation of international stock exchanges indicators and of breakthrough activities of local and international stock

---

[7] The chain from producing the media content of a TV program to broadcasting it on a particular TV channel and receiving it by the TV viewer system.

exchanges. The analogue TV production-delivery chain in this case is depicted in the following figure.

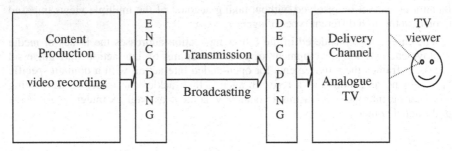

Fig. 1. TV production – delivery chain: the case of traditional TV production involving human TV presenter

Media digitization has changed the whole TV production-delivery chain. Digital broadcast applications and interactive internet services are converging to interactive multimedia services for a broad audience [14].

On digital interactive TV (ITV), more enhancement and value added features are aimed for financial news presentation. This motivates the consideration of several templates for financial news, tickers, and statistical indicators to develop interactive financial programs with various edutainment objectives for various categories of ITV viewers. Enhanced and value added features may include: e-trading features, edutaining the ITV viewer on financial trading practices in various stock exchanges, supporting the analysis of the expert financial viewer, etc.. The ITV production – delivery chain for the presentation of financial news by a human TV presenter differs from the analogue TV production- delivery chain. This difference stems from the resorting to more advanced digital recording techniques in a virtual studio[8] and the use of diverse authoring packages to insert virtual media objects in the virtual studio scene. Figure 2 describes this chain. In this case, the human TV presenter standing in the virtual studio scene presents financial news that were developed by some authoring packages. The financial news templates developed by the authoring package are inserted as media elements in the virtual studio scene. The digital video recording takes place once the virtual studio scene is properly set up and the human TV presenter starts performing by presenting the pre-published financial news. Interactivity is introduced at a later stage by manipulating the frames of the digital video recording to allow various play-out of and clickable interactivity with the pre-recorded financial news presentation. The recorded video and the associated interactivity are encoded using some encoding tools[9], transmitted, then decoded and delivered to the viewer through an ITV delivery channel.

---

[8] For more information about production in a virtual studio visit the web page of the Fraunhofer Institute For Media Communication (IMK) at http://www.imk.fhg.de

[9] Such as MPEG encoding tools.

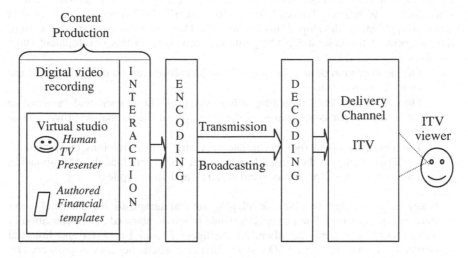

Fig. 2. TV production – delivery chain: the case of traditional TV production involving human TV presenter

3.2 The ITV Production-Delivery Chain: The Case of Virtual TV Presenter

The ITV production – delivery chain in the case of virtual TV presenter differs from the one involving a human TV presenter in five respects:

1. The virtual studio production involves a virtual human avatar authored with a particular authoring package.
2. Interactivity is embedded during the virtual studio production stage.
3. There is no need for digital recording unless a web cam of a stock exchange operation is necessary.
4. The encoding, transmission, decoding, and delivery, takes into consideration universal accessibility to the ITV content produced.
5. Real time production (content authoring) may be possible or even mandatory.

3.3 The Development Stages of the Case Study

Java technology is mainly used in the development of the case study for the convenience of portability across an ITV platform and an internet platform. Five development stages are adopted in the case study (see Fig. 3):

Stage 1. This stage involves developing a scripting language to describe an animated virtual human avatar (3D humanoid) enriched with facial expressions, voice replies, and hand gestures. A 3D audio display viewer is needed to translate this scripting language into an appropriate 3D visualised human avatar and to facilitate the play-out of the corresponding animation (facial expression, hand gestures, and voice reply) on demand. Different tools may be used to achieve this objective, such as Cartoon2D[10], Web Face Toolkit[11], the M3D viewer[12], MPEG tools[13], or a custom tailored application developed using Java3D. The latter is used in the current development of the case study. On going research work in this development stage involves:

- The identification of an appropriate 3D object abstraction of the geometry of the virtual human avatar.
- The use of 3D visual recording utilities (such as 3D scanners and cameras) to obtain the proper co-ordinates of the geometry of the animated virtual human avatar.
- The identification of the appropriate geometric transformations to manipulate the 3D geometry of the virtual human avatar and to produce the corresponding animation (facial expressions, hand gestures, and voice replies).

Stage 2. This stage involves developing several templates for financial news content and presentation. Such templates would provide enhanced 3D visualisation of financial tickers and facilitate advanced intelligent financial analysis and financial information retrieval. Enhanced 3D visualisation of financial tickers was pioneered by New York Stock Exchange that developed the first large-scale virtual reality environment for navigating the stock exchange trading floor and the Advanced Trading Floor Operations Center in a 3D virtual scene[14]. Maad (et al, 2001) [15] addressed the use of Virtual Reality (VR) technology in building virtual environments for financial trading and in providing the appropriate 3D interface. Tackling the challenge of capturing the complex trading environment in a VR model was tackled by proposing new principles for the development of environments for virtual trading to deliver VR using a new approach to computer-based modeling. These principles served in modelling interaction in a trading environment while combining real-world knowledge with real-time interpretation of abstract numerical data and indicators and in opening up VR technology to embrace complex social environments.

Various design and structures can be adopted for each of the financial templates corresponding to an interactive financial program. In the current development of the case study a simple template for the presentation of 3D financial tickers is considered. The role of the virtual human TV presenter is to serve the financial news intelligently in reply to the ITV viewers demand.

---

[10] CharToon is the name of a system to animate 2D CharToon faces, it aims at building models that can be animated and used to re-produce facial expression reflecting emotions and mouth movements. Further information about the project is found at:
www.cwi.nl/projects/FASE/CharToon/

[11] http://www.winteractive.fr/

[12] The M3D viewer is a tool developed at Fraunhofer-IMK with a motivating objective of providing online training in engineering production. It consists of: 1) an M3D scripting language which is an XML based language to describe learning content (machines and their behavior); and 2) An M3D java viewer to visualise the M3D specification. 3D enhanced visualization is provided through the viewer.

[13] http://www.comelec.enst.fr/~dufourd/mpeg-4/

[14] http://www.nyse.com/floor/floor.html

Stage 3. This stage involves establishing a bi-directional communication medium between the virtual human avatar (TV presenter) and the financial news templates. The virtual human avatar is conceived as a mediator between the ITV viewer and the financial content, thus providing the mean for universal access to this content. The role of this avatar is to respond to the ITV viewer's demands by providing the requested financial content synchronized with the human avatar's voice reply, and hand and facial gestures. The virtual human avatar has two responsibilities: (1) to serve the ITV viewer intelligently by channeling the ITV viewer's demand to the appropriate ITV content; and (2) to edutain the ITV viewer through voice replies, hand gestures, and facial expressions. These two roles for the virtual human avatar implies an embedded intelligence in this avatar that helps in providing intelligent universal access to the ITV content for presentation.

Stage 4. This stage involves establishing an interactive communication medium between the animated virtual human avatar and the ITV viewer. Initially, the ITV viewer is supposed to be a casual viewer with minimal or no financial knowledge background. More financially educated ITV viewers are considered at a later stage. In establishing this medium of interaction three levels of interaction are considered: i. the constrained; ii. the semi-constrained; and iii. the open-ended.

- The constrained medium of interaction reduces the interaction between the ITV viewer and the virtual human TV presenter to preconceived modes of interaction that follows a menu driven style of interaction with audio and visual multimedia enhancement. In this case, the embedded intelligence of the virtual human avatar is restrained to the reply to specific queries from the ITV viewer and to the serving of pre-published ITV financial content that fulfils the viewer demand. All voice replies as well as the facial expressions and hand gestures of the virtual human avatar are fully preconceived.

- The semi-constrained medium of interaction relies on conventional artificial intelligence techniques for retrieving and serving the ITV financial content on demand. The boundary of the financial content and the boundary of the intelligent interaction are pre-defined in this case. Spontaneous responses of the virtual human avatar to a wider space of ITV viewers' interaction are aspired, however, the ITV financial content might still be restrained to pre-published financial templates.

- The open-ended medium of interaction suggests a universal access to on-the-fly and on-demand authored ITV financial content. As such the virtual human avatar gives the ITV viewer an indirect mean for the universal access to the ITV financial content. This universal access may extend to the level of authoring the financial content. This necessitates novel software system development practices that take into consideration the needs and requirements for the universal access to the multimodal financial content by the ITV viewer in a non-preconceived way. It also gives the ITV viewer the potential to intervene in authoring the multimodal content to suit his/her edutainment needs.

Studying various categories of ITV viewers is also essential to establish various modes of interactions with various categories of viewers.

Current development of the case study is limited to the constrained medium of interaction, with a longer-term objective to evolve towards less constrained and more open and intelligent mediums of interaction and universal access.

Stage 5. This stage involves checking the compliance of the used technology with prevailing standards for ITV technology.

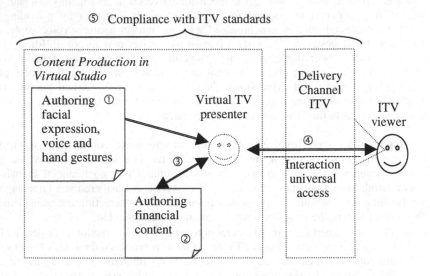

Fig. 3. Different stages in the development of the case study

4 Universal Accessibility to a Multimodal ITV Content: Practical and Theoretical Perspectives

This section addresses the issues raised in section 2 with reference to the previously introduced case study and its motivating objectives.

4.1 Novel Mediums of Interaction and Universal Access: The Role of Virtual Avatars

This paper claims a central role for virtual human avatars in providing universal accessibility to a domain specific content. By taking off the role of the human TV presenter, the virtual human avatar helps in bypassing the rigidity in interaction introduced when resorting to digital video recording and subsequent added pre-conceived interactivity. Supporting this claim at a practical level is beyond the scope of this paper and the currently achieved technical development. The paper supports this claim at a theoretical level by providing evidences of enhanced interactivity and promised universal access when comparing the proposed paradigm for universal access through virtual human avatars with the traditional ones involving human TV presenters and interactivity with pre-recorded video.

In fact the description of the ITV production-delivery chain in the two cases (the first case involving a human TV presenter, and the second case involving a virtual TV presenter) that was overviewed in the previous section reveals a noticeable improvement in the paradigm of accessibility and the style of content authoring in the second case involving virtual human avatars.

Several metrics can be adopted in assessing the added value of the use of virtual human avatars to enhance universal accessibility to and interactivity with a multimodal ITV content. These include:

- The measure of the extent of cost reduction in the ITV production – delivery chain. It may be the case that the use of virtual human avatars reduces the overhead cost of resources used in the virtual studio production.
- The assessment of the reduction in the number of stages of the ITV production delivery chain. Resorting to virtual TV presenters suggests a reduction and greater efficiency in the various stages of the ITV production – delivery channel. This would involve the elimination of the encoding and decoding stages and the adoption of embedded interactivity in the virtual studio production.
- The assessment of the popularity for ITV viewers of virtual human characters as compared to real characters.
- Results of surveys circulated to ITV viewers assessing the extent to which the aimed open-ended interactivity and universal accessibility is achieved by introducing virtual human avatars.
- The number of additional new paradigms of interaction and universal accessibility that are inspired by the use of virtual human avatars and that goes beyond the clickable interactivity for accessing a pre-published content.

4.2 Interface Development for Universally Accessible Multimodal ITV Content: Perspectives on Domain Specific Needs

Domain specific needs impose different paradigms for authoring content and providing universal accessibility to this content through specific interfaces and advanced interaction mediums. Generalizing domain specific needs and identifying general characteristics and paradigms of accessibility to multimodal content still pose major challenges to the SSD activity. This motivates a broad research agenda in the area of software system development (SSD). This agenda aims at investigating SSD practices that considers the extent to which the universal access to ITV multimodal content should be detached from this content. Two cultures might arises: the first culture would aim at abstracting the universal access and detaching it from its multimodal content; the second culture would aim at establishing an indivisible relationship between the universal interface (medium of interaction) and its corresponding multimodal content. The latter culture invokes the re-thinking of the software system development activity in a wider context to account for the pervasive emergence of technology and novel uses of computing theories and practices. Putting a great emphasis on the role, categories, and capabilities of ITV viewer suggests user (ITV viewer) - developer collaboration at all stages of the software system development activity associated with the ITV production-delivery chain. In the second SSD culture, the boundaries of the universal access would be growing with rising requirements and the diversity of the multimodal content.

Developing an appropriate technology to implement the two above described SSD cultures is a challenging task that can be first approached by developing tools for authoring a multimodal ITV content. These tools should be designed with universal access in mind. It might be the case, in the long term, that the development of universally accessible multimodal ITV content would converge to providing means for users (ITV viewers) to author the multimodal content.

Basic concepts and principles should be adopted in either SSD culture. Developing key concepts and principles to implement the second culture may benefit from advances in research in the area of Empirical Modelling. Empirical Modelling is a suite of key concepts, tools, techniques, and notations that aims at achieving a greater integration of the human and computational activity by adopting novel software system development practices. Model building in EM is a situated activity in which the roles of the modeller, the artefact, and the situation are inseparably linked, and leads to the construction of computer-based artefacts that stand in a special relation to the modeller's understanding and to the situation to which they refer.

4.3 Future Research Agenda

The motivating objectives of the case study helps in drawing a future research agenda addressing the following main issues:

  i.   The study of the role of virtual human avatars in enhancing universal accessibility to a mutimodal ITV content and in suggesting paradigms for universal access to a multimodal ITV content;

 ii.   The re-thinking of the software system development activity to accommodate new paradigms for universal access to a multimodal ITV content. This would aim at reconstructing the software system development activity in a wider context, for a wider audience, and for various emerging pervasive technologies, while taking into consideration the evolving and growing needs of ITV viewers for edutainment, a growing boundary for an integrated ITV content that can accommodate various contexts and various template for a specific content, the user's (ITV viewer) involvement in authoring the multimodal ITV content, the reuse of various interaction features with various contents, the universal access to a multimodal content by various categories of ITV viewers with varying backgrounds and edutainment needs, and the generalization of the SSD practices across various ITV platforms.

iii.   The development of metrics for assessing the enhanced universal accessibility to a multimodal ITV content through the use of virtual human avatars.

 iv.   The re-thinking of the ITV production-delivery chain to accommodate new paradigms for universal access.

  v.   The development of novel paradigms for artificial intelligence that can cope with open-ended interaction with an ITV viewer querying a multimodal content for edutainment purposes.

 vi.   The study of various categories of ITV viewers and the appropriate medium to serve their needs for universal access to a multimodal ITV content. This would involve the classification of the ITV viewers in pre-defined categories based on the initial interaction of the virtual human TV presenter with these ITV viewers.

5 Conclusion

This paper traced the evolution of ITV and discussed the challenges and prospects of universal access to multimodal ITV content with reference to the case study of financial news ITV presentation by an animated virtual human avatar. The case study motivates a future research agenda that considers the prospect of the role of virtual human avatars in suggesting new paradigms for universal accessibility, novel software system development practices, and the re-thinking of the ITV production – delivery chain to adapt to the needs and requirements for authoring universally accessible multimodal ITV content.

Acknowledgement. The author is indebted to many members of the Fraunhofer-Interactive Media Communication (IMK) group for relevant ideas, in particular to Sepideh Chakaveh for valuable discussions and comments and for proposing the project of virtual TV presenter. The author would like to thank Detlef Skaley and Patricia Lainé for developing the M3D viewer that was quite inspiring for the technical development of the case study considered in this paper. The author is also thankful to Stephan Werning, Olaf Geuer and Hüttemann Kai for sharing their experience in the virtual studio production for ITV content. Finally a great thanks is directed to ERCIM (The European Research consortium for Informatics and mathematics) for sponsoring the author's postdoctoral fellowship at Fraunhofer - IMK.

References

1. Stephandis, C., From User interfaces for all to an information society for all: Recent achievements and future challenges, Proceedings of the 6th ERCIM Workshop "User Interfaces for All", October 2000, Italy
2. Meyer L., Fontaine, G., Development of Digital Television in the European Union, Reference report/1999, IDATE Institut de l'audiovisuel et des telecommunications en Europe, June 2000
3. Peters, J.J., A history of television, European Broadcasting Union, 2000.
4. Evain, J.P., The Multimedia Home Platform – An overview, EBU Technical Department, 2002
5. JavaTM Technologies, Consumer and Embedded technologies: Digital Interactive TV, java.sun.com, 2002
6. Sun Microsystems, JavaTM Technologies for Interactive Television, Technical white paper, 2001
7. Stephanidis, C., Savidis, A., and Akoumianakis, D., Tutorial on "Unified Interface Development: Tools for Constructing Accessible and Usable User Interfaces". Tutorial no. 13 in the 17th International Conference on Human Computer Interaction (HCI International'97), San Fransico, USA, 24–29 August. [Online] Available: http://www.ics.forth.gr/proj/at_hci/html/tutorials.htm
8. Akoumianakis, D., Stephanidis, C., USE-IT : A Tool for Lexical Design Assistance. In C. Stephanidis (ed.) User Interfaces for All – Concepts, Methods and Tools. Mahwah, NJ: Lawrence Erlbaum Associates (2001)

9. Beynon, W.M., Rungrattanaubol, J., Sun, P. H., Wright, A. E. M., Explanatory Models for Open-ended Human-Computer Interaction, Research report CSRR-346, Warwick Univ., 1998
10. Maad, S., An Empirical Modelling Approach to Software System Development in Finance: Applications and Prospects, PhD thesis, Department of Computer Science, University of Warwick, 2002
11. Sonnenwald, D. H., Evolving Perspectives of Human Information Behavior: Contexts, Situations, Social Networks and Information Horizons, In Proceeding of Information Seeking in Context'98, 1999, London.
12. Beynon, W. M., Maad, S., Integrated Environments for Virtual Collaboration: an Empirical Modelling Perspective, In Proc. The Fifth World Conference On Integrated Design & Process Technology, Incorporating IEEE International Conference on Systems Integration, Texas, USA, 2000.
13. Beynon, W. M., Maad, S., Empirical Modelling of Real Life Financial Systems: The need for Integration of Enabling Tools and Technologies, In Proc. The Fourth World Conference On Integrated Design & Process Technology, Incorporating IEEE International Conference on Systems Integration, Texas, USA, 1999.
14. http://www.imk.fraunhofer.de
15. Maad, S., Beynon, W. M., Garbaya, S., Realising Virtual Trading: What Price Virtual Reality?, Usability Evaluation and Interface Design: Cognitive Engineering, Intelligent Agents and Virtual Reality, M.J. Smith, G. Salvendy, D. Harris, R.J. Koubek (editors), Lawrence Erlbaum Associates, Mahwah, N.J., pp. 1007–1011, ISBN 0-8058-3607-1, Volume 1

Multimodal Dialogue Systems: A Case Study for Interactive TV

Aseel Ibrahim[1,2] and Pontus Johansson[2]

[1] Nokia Home Communications,
Universitetsvägen 14, S-583 30 Linköping, Sweden

[2] Department of Information and Computer Science
Linköping University
S-581 83 Linköping, Sweden
{asebe, ponjo}@ida.liu.se

Abstract. Many studies have already shown the advantages of building multimodal systems. In this case study we have shown the advantages of combining natural language and a graphical interface in the interactive TV domain. In this paper we describe a multimodal dialogue TV program guide system that is a research prototype built for the case study by adding speech interaction to an already existing TV program guide. Study results indicate positive attitudes towards providing two input modes — spoken natural language input and direct manipulation by means of remote control.

1 Introduction

Many studies have been conducted in order to investigate the advantages of spoken language systems. Studies have reported 20-40% efficiency increase using speech systems compared with other interface technologies, such as keyboard input [1,2]. Rosenfeld et al. [3] divides the advantages of speech into three categories. First, speech is an ambient medium rather than an attentional one, which refers to the possibility to interact with the system while doing something else. Second, speech requires modest physical resources. Third, speech is descriptive rather than referential and is powerful to describe objects so it can successfully be combined with other modalities. Combining speech with other modalities is a strategy that has been used when developing multimodal systems where the strength of one modality is used to overcome the weakness of another [4].

Multimodal and dialogue systems have been developed in various domains where speech has been combined with other modalities, for example gestures. Building multimodal dialogue systems for the television (TV) domain, which differs from the computer domain, has not been explored. The new concept of digital and interactive TV provides a huge range of TV channels, programs, games, and other services. Thus, the problem with a TV program guide with graphical interface manipulated by means of remote control is that the search for a desired program requires many steps. More efficient program guide systems can be provided by combining the flexibility of

N. Carbonell, C. Stephanidis (Eds.): User Interfaces for All, LNCS 2615, pp. 209–218, 2003.

natural language and graphical presentation by integrating speech and graphical interfaces. However, in an earlier study, speech command input has been recommended as a complement to remote control input [5].

This paper presents a case study where multimodal dialogue system for a program guide was developed for interactive TV. The purpose of the case study is to uncover design knowledge for multimodal dialogue systems in the interactive TV domain that has not been explored so far.

2   The Multimodal Program Guide System

The program guide used in the study is a dialogue system research prototype with a natural language interface combined with visual representation that is provided for a digital TV set top box [6].

2.1   User Interface Design

The user input is provided by means of spoken or written natural language and the system output is provided by means of visual representation. The purpose of this combination is to take advantage of the strengths of visual representation and the natural language flexibility of expression. The system provides access to a database containing TV program information about titles, categories, channels, starting times, dates, credits (such as actors, directors, presenters), as well as a brief program synopsis (see Figure 1).

The system provides three types of output: tables of TV programs, text to cater for sub-dialogue clarifications, and text to provide miscellaneous information (such as detailed description of programs).

The natural language interface provides functionality that handles the added flexibility of searching for TV programs using a natural dialogue with a mixed-initiative strategy [7]. The following is an excerpt of an interaction with the system (U = user, S = system):

```
U:    Are there any movies on tonight?
S:    There are 35 movies on tonight. Would you like to
      see all of them?
U:    No, only the ones on channel Cinema between 9 pm
      and 8 am.
S:    [Presents information of the movies at the
      required channel and time]
```

The prototype interface is built by developing an existing menu-based program guide which is direct manipulated by means of remote control. The menu-based program guide provides the same type of domain information as the dialogue system prototype.

TV programme list
(or other response)

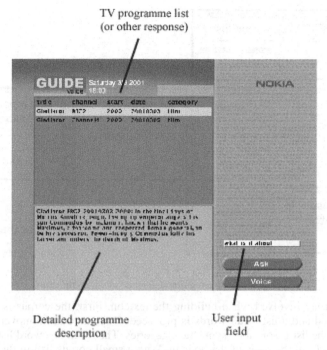

Detailed programme
description

User input
field

Fig. 1. Graphical user interface for the multimodal dialogue TV program guide system.

2.2 System Architecture

The TV program dialogue system is a modularized dialogue system [8,9], with the two main modules being the dialogue manager (DM), and the domain knowledge manager (DKM). The DM is the central controller of the system. The system handles user task requests, system requests, and communication management. The capabilities of the DM include a dialogue history, sub-dialogue control and clarification questions. The DKM is responsible for handling reasoning about the domain, such as TV programs, movie information, and temporal reasoning.

Other modules include an interpretation manager and a response generator. The system architecture is shown in Figure 2. The remainder of this section describes the components and the system's capabilities.

Interpretation Manager. The interpretation manager is a robust chart parser, which produces a feature structure representing the user utterance as one or many objects, whose properties the system and user reason about. The feature structure also consists of markers that handle distinctions between task requests (e.g. database queries), system requests (e.g. questions about the system's capabilities), and dialogue management (e.g. greetings and farewells). The parser uses lexicons and context-free grammars, and is capable of shallow parsing (i.e. it can skip words in a user utterance that are not included in the lexicon but still produce a parse tree).

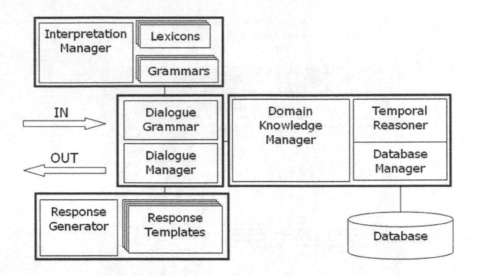

Fig. 2. The TV program guide dialogue system architecture.

Two steps are involved when building the lexicon. First, the corpus is automatically tokenized and a list of all words is produced. Duplicates are removed from the list. Second, the list is sorted by syntactic categories. The result is a word list with 120 words, which form the basis of the lexicon. With a small corpus like in this case, the lexicon can be manually completed with synonyms and related vocabulary. For example, all weekdays were added, even though only "Monday" and "Friday" actually occurred in the original list. Tokenization also includes the identification of lexical units, and abbreviations, which was done manually in this case. Some words are ambiguous, and need to be considered in the generation of lexicon and grammar (such as the verb and the noun "show"). The created lexicon serves as a generic, static resource for the TV program domain, independently of what actual instances of titles, and channels etc. are included in the database. To accommodate the actual instances, a second lexicon is created automatically from the database content. It is necessary to include all program titles, channels, actors, presenters, directors, and categories in the lexicon if the system is to understand a user's question that deals with explicit channels or titles etc. This second lexicon is more dynamic to its nature, since it is constantly updated as new TV shows are added to the tableaus in the database. The advantage of keeping two lexicons is that the dynamic lexicon can be exchanged on for example a daily or weekly basis, without interfering with the static lexicon. A third lexicon is needed for temporal expressions, and is used by the temporal grammar discussed below. All lexicons are loaded at system start.

Two grammars are used in this system. The first one is a domain-specific grammar modeling phrases encountered in the TV program domain. This grammar uses the static and the dynamic lexicon. The second grammar is a generic, but language-specific, grammar for temporal expressions, and uses the temporal lexicon. Both grammars are loaded, and produce one feature structure for each user utterance. A typical user utterance in the TV domain consists of at least one phrase "belonging to" the domain-specific grammar and one phrase consisting of temporal information, thus "belonging to" the temporal grammar. Consider the following example:

```
U:    What movies are on BBC1 tomorrow night after
      five?
```

Here, the domain-specific grammar handles the first part of the utterance, identifying that the user is naming a category (movies) and a specific channel (BBC1). The temporal grammar handles the last part of the utterance, identifying the necessary deictic (tomorrow), and relation (after), etc. When such an utterance is parsed, the structures from the two grammars are unified into one feature structure. This structure is then used by the DM.

Dialogue Management. The DM incrementally builds a dialogue tree as the interaction in a session progresses. The dialogue tree encapsulates the notions of a dialogue history (i.e. a record of what has been said during the user-system interaction), and focus management (i.e. what topic is currently discussed). The dialogue tree consists of a three-level structure, where the top level is structured into discourse segments. A segment is called an initiative-response node, which is further divided into dialogue moves [10]. Focus handling is represented horizontally in the dialogue tree, whereas sub-dialogues are built vertically by utilizing a dialogue grammar. The dialogue history allows for anaphora resolution, such as in the following example:

```
U1:    Who is starring in the James Bond movie?
S1:    [Presents actor information for chosen James
       Bond film.]
U2:    And who directed it?
S2:    [Presents director information for the same
       film.]
```

In this case, the dialogue tree keeps record of that the current focus is the "James Bond movie" found in the earlier result set. Hence, the information in utterance U2 is assumed to involve the property "director" of the "James Bond" movie object.

Certain phrases contain markers for focal shift. The markers are identified at utterance level rather than discourse level. For example, after a series of questions about a certain movie, the user might want to know something about news broadcast. The system then has to abandon the search criteria that are connected to the discussed movie (e.g. actor and director properties). However, certain search criteria might still be valid for the new focus (e.g. temporal information, etc.). When the dialogue manager encounters a marker that signals a new focus, a new discourse segment is created in the dialogue tree and the old is abandoned.

Sub-dialogue is catered for by vertically adding nodes in the dialogue tree. This happens for example when a user request results in too many hits (such as: "show all movies"), or no hits. The system then keeps the focus from previous queries, and takes the initiative. In the case of too many hits, the system keeps the category focus (i.e. "movies"), but asks the user for a specific day or channel. The system can also use sub-dialogue to correct misconceptions. For example, if the user asks for actors in a show that does not have this property (e.g. news shows) the system informs the user that news do not have actors. The system then continues to ask if the user wants to view news shows, or if s/he wants to name a show that actually has actors (such as a movie). The DM gets such domain knowledge from the DKM.

Domain Knowledge Management. The DKM is responsible for reasoning about aspects connected to the domain. In this case, the DKM possesses knowledge about relations between entities in the world of TV shows. It also contains temporal reasoning capabilities via its temporal reasoner (TR). The TR holds temporal knowledge and a set of heuristics for interpreting the often vague user notions of time (e.g. "tonight", "tomorrow afternoon" etc.), and convert them to date instances which can be compared to the starting times and dates in the database. The TR operates on the part of the feature structure produced by the temporal grammar and lexicon. This information is needed when constructing queries dealing with starting times for various TV shows.

After interpreting the meaning of the temporal information in the feature structure the DKM utilizes a database manager to formulate a valid database query based on the feature structure. The database manager is responsible for executing the query and collecting the result set. For exceptional results (i.e. empty or too large result sets) the DKM informs the DM, which initiates a clarification sub-dialogue (see above).

Response Management. The response manager is responsible for generating the system response. Typically, an answer consists of the collected result set from the database. The result is presented on-screen in the graphical user interface. In the case of sub-dialogue, the response manager can generate simple natural language responses. This is done by using canned templates, which are customized depending on the situation.

3   Method

A qualitative method based on observations and interviews was used in the study. The purpose of the study was explorative to collect information about the users' experiences of the interaction with the system by using and testing it. The study was conducted in a home environment that represents a normal living room environment at Nokia Home Communications in Sweden. Five users with prior experiences on the menu-based program guide participated in the study where task scenarios were used. The aim of the scenarios, that correspond to real life situations, was to find TV programs (e.g. a particular movie), general information about the program (e.g. general description of the movie), and specific information (e.g. the director or the main actor of the movie). Each user was given seven task scenarios.

The users were observed while they tested the system and the observations were documented by the test leader. After the test, a follow-up interview was undertaken with each user. The purpose of the interviews was to yield qualitative assessments of (a) system satisfaction and (b) experiences of the user interface. The interviews were documented by the test leader.

4 Results

The documentation from the observations and interviews were transcribed and analyzed by organizing the material in categories. Five design issues appeared from the categories: freedom of interaction mode, the concentration of the information load, the unclear data quantity as well as type, the increased system efficiency, and the lack of the mixed initiative.

4.1 User Interaction

The spoken input was acceptable by the users but they preferred multimodal input where direct manipulation and speech input could be used unaccompanied as well as combined. The direct manipulation would be conducted by means of remote control. The users mentioned three situations where they would like to use the remote control:

1. When they are not allowed to make noise (e.g. the rest of the family is sleeping).
2. When the mouth is busy (e.g. talking with someone else).
3. When they do not know how to express a query.

4.2 Information Load

The users considered the information load was being carried by the system rather than by themselves, which was regarded as a positive result. The users could find what they were searching for even when their knowledge about the desired object was limited. The users did not need to exactly know what they were looking for as long as they had some relevant knowledge. For example:

```
U:   Anything with Ford tonight?
S:   [Displays a list with all TV program includes the
     word "Ford"]
     Title              Channel  Start   Category
     ------------------------------------------------
     Air Force One      Sky      19:00   Film
     The Devil's Own    Movie    22:00   Film
     The Ford           BBC      16:00   Documentary
```

4.3 Data Quantity and Type

The users expressed that they initially regarded the system as being less knowledgeable than it in fact was. As the system understood and answered their questions the users learn that they system had access to more data. They still, however, were unclear about the extent of the systems capabilities. The users considered the system to be have a sufficient database but they expressed uncertainty about the type and amount of data available to them. For example, the users did not know whether they could search for categories (such as action movies) or not.

Because of this combination (not knowing about how much data the system supplied and which kind of data it supplied) the users in the beginning felt that the system could not provide them with the desired information. Thus, the users were surprised when it did as the interaction progressed.

4.4 Efficiency

The system was considered as more effective than the menu-based program guide because of two reasons. The first one is related to the user's input where natural language flexibility contributed to the efficiency since the amount of information given in a query was not limited. Moreover, the system used the dialogue history, which enabled the users to continue working iteratively with a certain topic. For example:

```
U:   Are there any movies on tonight?
S:   [The system shows the list below]
     Title              Channel     Start
     --------------------------------
     Batman             TV1         18:00
     Friends            TV5         18:00
     From Hell          Sky movie   19:00
     In the beginning   TV4         20:00
     Pretty woman       Movie       22:00

U:   Only the ones after 8 o'clock please
S:   [The system show the list below]
     Title              Channel     Start
     --------------------------------
     In the beginning   TV4         20:00
     Pretty woman       Movie       22:00

U:   What is Pretty Woman about?
S:   [The system shows a description about the film]
```

The second reason is related to the system output. The system delivered search results that matched the query and therefore the users received only relevant and significant information and the superfluous information was not included.

4.5 Mixed Initiative

The system was considered as passive and the users preferred a system with more initiative in a way that the user would receive alternative choices and suggestions when the query did not give any results. For example:

```
U:   Will Friends be shown at 6 o'clock.
S:   No
```

The system should instead reply:

```
S:   No, Friends is shown everyday at 5:30. "Spin City"
is shown at 6:00.
```

5 Discussion

The results of the case study gave indications to a lack in the interface design. The users felt that the system provided less data than it, in fact, did. They were also unaware of the type of data available to them. The grounds for these two issues can be based on a lack on the graphical interface since the type and amount of data in the database was not viewed graphically and the users gradually understood that the system's knowledge was not as limited as they had initially assumed. Our suggestion is to provide this information graphically, e.g. by having an informative field where all types of data are listed. This can also increase the system efficiency since the users' knowledge about the system is increased and that will affect the queries.

Another way to increase system efficiency is to increase the system initiative. Providing a system with more initiative supplies the user with more information. However, this can be both useful and problematic. On the one hand, the user receives information that can be a source of inspiration. On the other, the information can be irrelevant and therefore confuse rather than contribute. The case study shows that this is a real risk, since the users considered the system as efficient because it delivered relevant information and was not superfluous. One way to overcome this problem is to adapt the system to the users' behavior either by learning user behavior or by having users provide the knowledge directly. Moreover, Ibrahim and Johansson [11] mentioned a lack of feedback and dialogue. Building a system with more mixed initiative can make the system more co-operative and therefore the feedback and dialogue feeling can be increased.

Moreover, in this study the users preferred availability of two communication modalities (speech input and direct manipulation by means of remote control) alone as well as combined. Cohen [4] claims that two or more communication modalities should not only be available but also integrated together. This claim supports our proposal to integrate the modalities. Providing a combination requires a re-design of the user interface in a way that support input from two integrated modalities. The integration raises new design problems that should be considered carefully.

6 Future Work

Iteration of design and evaluation is necessary in order to collect more design knowledge. There are various aspects based on the case study that should be investigated further. First, integrating the remote control manipulation with speech input should be built and evaluated. Second, the impact of a system with user modeling capabilities should be investigated. Third, we need also to investigate whether the system is considered as more intelligent and efficient if it provides more initiative in the dialogue.

7 Conclusions

Combining the advantages of graphical, spoken, and direct manipulated interface could ease the use of a system. However, this combination demands a thorough design of the multimodal interface in order to make use of the modalities. Yankelovich et al. [12] claims that building speech-only systems should be done from scratch and our case study suggests that this holds for this sort of multimodal system as well.

This case study gives indication to positive attitudes towards multimodal interaction with interactive TV where two communication modes (spoken natural language input and direct manipulation by means of remote control) are provided together with visual representation.

Acknowledgements. This work is a result from a project on multimodal interaction for information services supported by Santa Anna IT Research/SITI and VINNOVA [13].

References

1. Martin, G.L.: The utility of speech input in user-computer interfaces. International Journal of Man-Machine Studies 30 (1989). pp. 355–375.
2. Visick, D., Johnson, P., Long, J.: The use of simple speech recognizers in industrial applications. In: Proceedings of Interact´84. (1984).
3. Rosenfeld, K., Olsen, D., Rudnicky, A.: Universal speech interfaces. In: Interactions, VIII (6). (2001). pp. 34–44.
4. Cohen, P.R.: The role of natural language in a multimodal interface. In: ACM UIST'92 Symp. on User Interface Software & Technology. (1992). pp. 143–149.
5. Ibrahim, A., Lundberg, J., Johansson, J.: Speech enhanced remote control for media terminal. In: Proceedings of Eurospeech '01. Volume 4., Aalborg, Denmark (2001). pp. 2685–2688.
6. Johansson, P.: Iterative development of an information-providing dialogue system. Master's thesis, Linkoping University (2001).
7. Walker, M.A., Whittaker, S.: Mixed initiative in dialogue: An investigation into discourse segmentation. In: Proc. 28th Annual Meeting of the ACL. (1990). pp. 70–79.
8. Allen, J.F., Ferguson, G., Stent, A.: An architecture for more realistic conversational systems. In: Intelligent User Interfaces. (2001). pp. 1–8.
9. Flycht-Eriksson, A., Jonsson, A.: Dialogue and domain knowledge management in dialogue systems. In Dybkjaer, L., Hasida, K., Traum, D., eds.: Proceedings of the First SIGdialWorkshop on Discourse and Dialogue. Association for Computational Linguistics, Somerset, New Jersey (2000). pp. 121–130.
10. Jonsson, A.: A model for habitable and efficient dialogue management for natural language interaction. Natural Language Engineering 3 (1997). pp. 103–122.
11. Ibrahim, A., Johansson, P.: Multimodal dialogue systems for interactive TV. In: Proceedings of ICMI'02. (2002).
12. Yankelovich, N., Levow, G.A., Marx, M.: Designing speech acts: Issues in speech user interfaces. In Katz, I.R., Mack, R., Marks, L., Rosson, M.B., Nielsen, J., eds.: Proceedings of the Conference on Human Factors in Computing Systems (CHI'95), New York, NY, USA, ACM Press (1995). pp. 369–376.
13. Multimodal interaction for information services [www]. Available at http://www.ida.liu.se/~nlplab/mifis/ (2002-09-24).

Toward Cultural Representation and Identification for All in Community-Based Virtual Environments

Elaine M. Raybourn

Sandia National Laboratories, P.O. Box 5800, MS 1188
Albuquerque, New Mexico USA, 87185
emraybo@sandia.gov

Abstract. The paper describes research undertaken to provide the empirical basis for engendering group or community identification in future iterations of an adaptive community-based collaborative virtual environment (CVE) designed to facilitate communication where there are mutual concerns or interests among virtual communities within or across organizations. The system taken as an example in this paper consists of a WWW-based collaborative virtual environment comprised of intelligent software agents that support explicit information sharing, chance meetings, and real time informal communication. Results from ethnography, questionnaires, and Persona design inform future directions that include cultural cues in intelligent community-based systems in order to enhance information sharing and real time communication among strangers toward more equitable cultural representation for all. It is argued that users' experiences are enhanced in community-based virtual environments through supporting intercultural communication and designing opportunities for equitable representation of and identification with individual, group, and organizational cultures.

1 Introduction

Lessons learned from face-to-face communication tell us that the quality of successful collaborations depends largely on sharing cultural and contextual information [1]. Culture [is] those deep, common, unstated experiences which members of a given culture share, which they communicate without knowing, and which form the backdrop against which all other events are judged [2]. Sharing cultural and contextual information minimizes uncertainty in interpersonal relationships. In much the same way, collaborating organizations, individuals, or communities of practice share cultural information to reduce uncertainty and strengthen notions of common ground. Cultural information often shared across and within members of organizations includes assumptions, values, goals, meanings, and histories that are shared, negotiated, and co-created by the members [3]. However, sharing cultural and contextual information with members of our own multi-national organizations is becoming increasingly more complex as many employees participate in virtual teams (within an organization) or are fully engaged in distance collaborations with others.

Studies of workplace practices indicate that the ways people actually work often differ fundamentally from the ways organizations describe that work in manuals,

N. Carbonell, C. Stephanidis (Eds.): User Interfaces for All, LNCS 2615, pp. 219–238, 2003.

organizational charts, and job descriptions. Informal communication and social relationships around work that develop in an organizational community influence workplace practices, or the ways that real work gets done [4]. Frequently we find members of organizations that also belong to communities of practice. The term "community of practice" [3] describes the informal groups where much knowledge sharing and learning takes place over a period of time. Communities of practice develop when there is 1) mutual engagement—the community creation and negotiation of actions or meanings, 2) a joint enterprise—a communal response to demands placed on the community, and 3) shared resources, or repertoire—the routines in which work gets done, that contribute to understanding the ways in which work is accomplished within a community. Communities of practice develop in community-based virtual environments when these attributes are evident.

Additionally, as communication media make it easier for each of us to interact with members of different cultures and contexts, intercultural communication becomes more commonplace in our daily work. Intercultural communication is the exchange of information and the co-creation of meaning between individuals or among groups (teams, organizations, etc.) that perceive themselves to be different [5]. We can no longer assume that most of our interactions will be primarily with those whom we perceive to be similar to us. A long-term research interest at British Telecom (BTexact Technologies) has been the issue of getting people who are distributed across the globe to meet, and develop relationships with others through their habitual use of communication technologies. Consequently, a significant BTexact effort explores the role of communications technologies in the workplace. Communications technology has become increasingly salient in the workplace as our organizations move toward teleworking, virtual teams, and global collaborations.

Nevertheless, existing community-based virtual environments that support collaborative working have at least one thing in common. Most, if not all, omit the presence of cultural or organizational cues as an integral component of the virtual communication space. However, it has been demonstrated that designing subtle cultural and contextual cues into a text-based collaborative virtual environment such as a multi-user dimension, object-oriented (MOO) is an effective way to encourage collaboration and awareness of intercultural communication including the negotiation of power, and exploration of identity [6]. The future success of collaborative work in community-based virtual environments requires not only understanding the socio-cultural dynamics that manifest in online communication and communities of practice, but also considering how the design of these environments can support intercultural communication with cultural or organizational contextual cues that are aimed at engendering affiliation and identification in the virtual environment.

In this paper I describe an experimental British Telecom (BTexact Technologies), adaptive community-based system for which I conducted research in order to better facilitate communication where there are mutual concerns or interests among individuals, teams, or groups within or across organizations. The system, called Forum, consists of Jasper II and Contact Space, a WWW-based knowledge-sharing environment comprised of intelligent software agents that support explicit information sharing, chance meetings, and real time informal communication. Jasper II agents adaptively learn their user's interests by observing users' behaviors, while Contact Space agents dynamically move avatars to designated locations in a collaborative virtual environment in order to support real time informal communication. The functions of the Jasper II and Contact Space agents are discussed separately in this paper, even though they work together to create an intelligent, real time, information-sharing environment.

In order to meet the future needs of intelligent community-based systems, I propose incorporating cultural cues in the virtual environment. At some level, fostering shared culture is essential to collaboration [7]. Additionally, researchers have recently noted that cultural sensitivity is paramount in designing interaction systems [8], [5]. In answer to this call, data collected from ethnography, questionnaires, and Persona development provide the basis for designing cultural and organizational cues into the community-based system in order to engender identification among the members of the community of practice. Using Wenger's [3] framework that characterizes the three essential attributes (mutual engagement, joint enterprise, and shared resources) of communities of practice as a guide, I conclude that cultural cues in intelligent community-based systems support information sharing and real time, spontaneous communication, and enhance users' experiences by facilitating intercultural communication among individuals as well as provide an cultural context for strangers, or newcomers, to better identify with their community of practice.

2   Information Sharing and Informal Communication in an Adaptive Community-Based Virtual Environment

The following section describes the Forum, a BTexact Technologies desktop system that facilitates both asynchronous and real-time, informal communication and information sharing through the Contact Space and the Jasper II document-sharing environment. A similar description of the system described in this section is also available in [9].

The Forum is a WWW-based 3D virtual world that supports informal communication via user avatars that are powered by Jasper II agents [10]. In order to best describe the mechanism by which informal communication is supported in the Forum, we must begin with a description of the Jasper II agents that comprise (1) the document-sharing environment, and explain how the agents provide (2) the communication supports for the Contact Space.

2.1   Jasper II Supports for Sharing and Retrieving Information

Jasper II software agents hold details of the interests of their users in the form of user profiles [10]. Jasper II summarizes and extracts key words from WWW pages and other sources of information (i.e., personal notes, intranet pages, applications) and then shares this information with users in a virtual community of practice whose profiles indicate similar interests. No collaborative filtering is utilized; Jasper II agents classify the text into groups of significant phrases, and a user's profile consists of a list of words and phrases that the agents recognize.

Jasper II agents are used to store, retrieve, summarize and inform other agents about information considered in some sense valuable by a Jasper II user. Each Jasper II user has a personal agent that holds her/his profile based on a set of key phrases which models her/his information needs and interests. Thus, Jasper II agents modify a user's profile based on their usage of the system, seeking to refine the profile to better model the user's interests.

In order for a user to share information with the community of practice, a 'share' request is sent to Jasper II via a menu option on the individual's WWW browser. Jasper II extracts the important details from these documents, including the summary and keywords, as well as the document title, its URL, and the date and time of access. Users may annotate, and specify one of a predefined set of interest groups to which to post the information being stored.

This information captured by the Jasper agents is maintained locally and serves several purposes. Firstly, the summary provides the user with an abridgement of the document without the need to retrieve the remote pages unless greater detail is desired at the time. The ProSum text summarizer extracts key theme sentences from the document based on the frequency of words and phrases within a document, using a technique based on lexical cohesion analysis [11].

Secondly, the content of the HTML page is analyzed and matched against every user's profile in the community of practice. If the profile and document match strongly enough, Jasper II emails the user, informing her/him of the page that has been shared, by whom, and any annotation added by the sharer. The profiles stored within Jasper II are used as a basis for the user's static profile, within the Contact Space: each user profile contains a list of words and phrases, which have been identified as useful to that particular user. In addition to that list, each person can be subscribed to a number of interest groups within the community of practice. The Contact Space agent will infer a profile for each interest group, based upon the summation of all the subscriptions and profiles.

Thirdly, the posted information is also matched against the sharer's own profile. If one's profile does not match the information being shared, the agent will suggest phrases that the user may elect to add to her/his profile. Additionally, a feedback mechanism is provided whereby a user can indicate interest or disinterest in the information by clicking on a button (indicated by ☺ or ☹ as shown in Figure 1). Thus Jasper agents adaptively learn their user's interests by observing their user's behavior. A typical Jasper home page is shown in Figure 1.

Jasper II agents provide a repository tool for managing information and sharing resources that contribute to the development of the shared repertoire of a community of practice. Not only do the participants of the community of practice post information that they find valuable to getting their work done, but users may decide to annotate, or comment on the perceived value of the information they post. In this manner, Jasper II aids the community to co-create their repertoire by providing the place where users can manage information in an historical context (i.e., who posted what, when, why, and with what effect). The meaning, or knowledge, in this case, is co-constructed by the users and resides within each of them. Jasper II agents facilitate user's expressing their information with other users in order to create knowledge. Therefore a discussion of knowledge co-creation is outside the scope of this paper, as knowledge is a complex internalization that rests among the members of the community of practice.

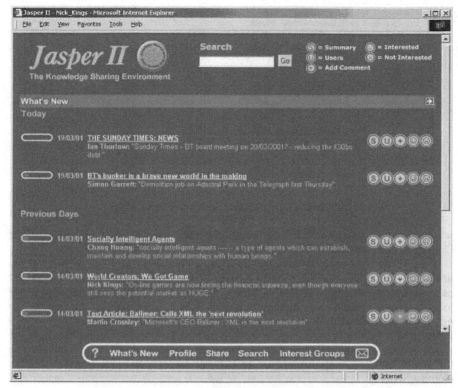

Fig. 1. Jasper II Homepage.

2.2 Jasper II Supports for Informal Communication in the Contact Space

The Contact Space was explicitly designed to support one's work by providing an opportunity to interact informally online with colleagues who may help one do one's work. That is, the Contact Space offers users' avatars the ability to "hang out" online while fostering chance encounters with others in one's community of practice who share common interests.

An individual's initial placement in the Contact Space is based upon the complete set of profiles stored within Jasper II. That is, each user has a notional home area, which is calculated by the similarity between a user's profile and the derived profile for each group within the community of practice in which common interests are shared. As a day progresses, the focus of a user's work, which is reflected in the different documents and applications that are being used on a computer, is monitored by the Contact Space agent. The Contact Space agent uses information sent continuously from an individual's computer to determine each individual's current activity. The agent maintains a list of the most recent words associated with each person's activities, which is then used to form a dynamic profile. The words are derived from the application titles and the contents of the web pages that have been read. By performing similarity calculations on these word lists, the agent determines

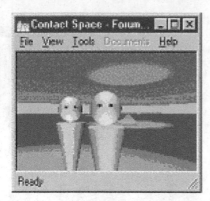

Fig. 2 a and b. The Contact Space: Interactive Pyramids and Avatars.

which person is most similar to another, and then suggests that the users of the Contact Space be placed in close proximity.

Thus, the contact space monitors users activity and moves their avatars to locations in the shared world where other users' similar activity is also represented. If no other users inhabit the shared world at the time, then the agent will move the user to the location in the space that reflects the topic of their current work at the desktop. In other words, a specific location, or action layer, symbolically represents the user's job-related activities or tasks. Users are also able to navigate themselves through the space by highlighting their location of choice in a drop-down menu and clicking on the selection. Users may also choose to navigate to other individuals inhabiting the Contact Space.

Additionally, the Contact Space is interactive, in that users may manipulate objects in the environment, such as the pyramid visible in the background of the first image, as shown in Figure 2a. If one were to click on a pyramid in the "Adaptive User Interfaces" area, it would link to the Jasper II summary page for that topic (See Figure 1). Early designs for Jasper II and the Contact Space concentrated on deriving the algorithms that infer the dynamic interests of users, support collaborative information sharing, and facilitate real time informal communication.

When one or more users have similar long-term interests, the Contact Space agent will move an avatar and orient the avatars facing each other. This movement facilitates spontaneous informal communication [12] in that users may choose to enter a chat environment via a text chat pop-up window, or upgrade their communication to a space that offers a more formal, graphically enhanced audio and data conferencing setting. When a user is away from her/his desk, the avatar in the Contact Space goes into "sleepy" mode, as shown in Figure 2b, where the avatar's head has sunk its shoulders.

3   Cross-Cultural User Study Rationale and Methods

A number of user trials informed the various iterations of the Forum design over the years [12], [13]. Although the Forum was generally perceived positively by users who knew each other from a face-to-face setting, neither the Jasper II repository nor the Contact Space seemed to successfully encourage interactions among strangers, or persons who did not know each other very well. The Jasper II repository was static and did not provide a feature for synchronous communication. The Contact Space provided a more dynamic environment with text chat capability. However, while the technical opportunity for synchronous communication resulting from agent-generated online chance meetings certainly existed in the Contact Space, users still reported feeling uncomfortable about initiating a chat session with someone they did not know well. Thus, newcomers, or strangers to the Forum, could feel marginalized, as they do not yet identify with a group of regular inhabitants of the Forum. In seeking new ways to encourage communication among strangers in the organization's community of practice, a cross-cultural user study of the forum was proposed, in which the research question, "How can we motivate users to identify more strongly with their community of practice, and take the first steps towards opening a chat with others whom they may share common interests with, but do not know well enough to feel comfortable communicating with in a virtual environment?" It was believed that a cross-cultural user study of the Forum would more quickly identify the strengths and weaknesses of the current system. We believed that enhancing the Forum such that members of a community of practice could familiarize themselves with the group's informal work culture—the routines in which work gets done, would engender trust among new users and therefore foster greater identification with others. The following sections describe the cross-cultural, multi-method user study undertaken by the author when she was employed as a research fellow at BTexact Technologies. The research study was completed in approximately 6 months and employed diverse methodologies including informal interviews, ethnography, questionnaires, and a persona design methodology.

I conducted informal onsite interviews at both BTexact and Sandia National Laboratories, and logged into the Forum from New Mexico as a participant/observer for approximately four months. The purpose of investigating as a participant/observer was to familiarize myself with the technology, and experience what it felt like to be a remote user that did not benefit from co-location. Familiarity with the difficulties associated with incorporating usage of a collaborative virtual environment in one's daily life served to inform subsequent design recommendation discussed in this paper. Additionally, as a member of the Sandia National Laboratories Advanced Concepts Group at the time this research was conducted, I could see first hand how members of my group might also use such a tool. Questionnaires were then later developed and administered with each group, and finally the redesign suggestions were developed through the use of creating a hypothetical user, or persona.

Personas are hypothetical archetypes often used to identify the needs of a single user in a scenario, and therefore focus one's design goals [14]. Instead of referring to an unidentified "user" in a scenario, a specific persona (complete with a name, occupation, age, etc.) is constructed to guide the design process. Part of the challenge of this research was the opportunity to make sense of the respondent's cultural values orientation and later provide design recommendations for engendering an adaptive community-based environment in which group identification and cultural representation among participants of the virtual community of practice is enhanced. Therefore, it was important to present research findings to the reader in a personalized story, or ground our research findings within a cultural context that is the design scenario in which we explore how the persona would use our redesigned system. We constructed our persona, Adam, (whom the reader will meet later) as a composite, or aggregation of the cross-cultural values revealed by each organization participating in the questionnaire study. In focusing our redesign to meet the requirements of our hypothetical user, our design was more universal and might have wider appeal and accessibility. We also believed the approach of designing for a persona to be better than listing system features in a table.

3.1   The Questionnaire Research Study Background

In this section I describe a cross-organizational questionnaire research study conducted at BTexact Technologies and Sandia National Laboratories. A questionnaire was developed in collaboration with researchers from BTexact and distributed to the group members of both organizations in order to gather insights on how their experiences might inform a potential redesign of the Forum environment to incorporate individual, team, and organizational cultural cues aimed at strengthening an individual's identification with a community of practice, especially if s/he were a newcomer to the virtual community. The questionnaire was designed to bring out the respondents' perspectives on their work habits, organizational practices, communication media choices, and cultural work norms. The findings would then later be compared in order to discover the values that of each group that facilitated group identification. Questionnaire methodology was chosen after a 'quick and dirty' ethnographic evaluation of each organization revealed that the respondents' schedules coupled with the relatively short amount of time (six weeks vs. one year) spent by the research fellow at BTexact precluded conducting extensive interviews. Nevertheless, some informal interviews were conducted at both sites after the results of the questionnaire had been compiled. These interviews served to validate the researcher's interpretation of the findings.

The researcher was sensitive to the fact that many people do not explicitly share information about their cultural background or organization for a variety of reasons; including diverse orientations toward privacy and public vs. private information. The questionnaire was carefully designed not to force the respondent into divulging sensitive information about themselves or others. Instead, the following questions guided the questionnaire design: How can we design an intelligent community-based environment that facilitates communication interactions that engender feelings of trust, or curiosity, and are associated with desiring to learn more about the people you work with? What design improvements might strengthen an individual's identification with others in the community of practice?

Twenty-one respondents participated in the research including 12 respondents from the BTexact group and 10 respondents from Sandia National Laboratories' Advanced Concepts Group (ACG). The BTexact group respondents represented computer science researchers (including designers and social scientists) as well as system developers, while the Advanced Concepts Group respondents represented engineers and scientists with backgrounds in physics, mathematics, chemistry, engineering, and political science. Several user trials had previously been conducted with respondents from BTexact, and we wanted to learn more about the work practice similarities and differences between a telecommunications company and a science and technology-based organization such as a national lab in order to gain a fresh perspective on the ways the system was used then, and ways it would need to be redesigned in order to meet future cross-cultural challenges.

3.1.1 The Advanced Concepts Group

The Advanced Concepts Group (ACG) is a Sandia National Laboratories multidisciplinary think tank of 16 scientists that was formed in August 1998, in Albuquerque, New Mexico. The think tank was charged with investigating potential technical contributions Sandia National Laboratories might make to address long-range global challenges. Each member of the ACG may have participated on one to three teams, although most did not. At the time of this research two members of the ACG were located in California, and interacted with the larger group via weekly videoconferencing and often daily with team members via audio conferences augmented by Microsoft NetMeeting sessions. Organizationally as well as culturally, the ACG is very different from the rest of Sandia National Laboratories. The ACG physical office space was designed to promote face-to-face collaboration. Offices are small, and usually shared by two people. Informal interactions are encouraged in the collaborative area that is equipped with electronic white boards, a plasma display, and videoconferencing capability. Much of the group's 'business' was conducted via informal communication channels. Each time a member is away on travel, s/he had to re-orient her/himself with the group's activity. This update is usually done informally, and members found that they frequently had to give 'briefings' or keep their colleagues abreast of changes. One group member said, "Work doesn't get done if you are not physically here." The members of the ACG report directly to Sandia National Laboratories Vice President and Principal Scientist. Additionally, each member of the ACG has a two-year tenure with the group. At the conclusion of a member's participation with the group, s/he leaves the ACG to either joins an existing Sandia National Laboratories line organization or spin off to start-up a new laboratory line organization. Further, the ACG is in the 'big idea' business and responsible for 'selling' future directions of science and technology to internal and external customers. In many ways, the ACG functions as a high-performance team for the laboratory. Although they were all familiar with using computers, only three had experience with NetMeeting, and none had ever used another collaborative virtual environment.

3.1.2 The Developers and Researchers

The BTexact Technologies software developers and researchers comprised a team working on a closely related group of projects. The two main activities were the Meeting Space, which supports remote, collaborative work in the context of a formal business meeting [14] and the Contact Space, which supports team awareness and chance encounters among a dispersed work group. Some of the team members also focused on developing a collaborative virtual environment that is appropriate for a home environment, and a collaborative European project, whose purpose is to build on their research experience so far. Members of the team included mostly software engineers but other disciplines are also represented, such as social scientists and artists/designers. At the time of this research, the BTexact researchers who participated in the study were all based with the Internet and eBusiness part of

BTexact, however, as far as line management was concerned, the respondents belonged to teams based in three different areas of that organization. Many members of the team had worked together on other projects in the past and knew each other fairly well although they may not have all be co-located. Individuals were mostly based in two locations on the Ground Floor and the Third floor of the Main Laboratory Block of BTexact at Adastral Park, but some members of the team were based in other parts of the same building or worked remotely. The team held fortnightly progress meetings, which were sometimes held in the same physical location, or at other times within the formal Meeting Space. Other ad hoc meetings were held as necessary, often face to face, so, overall, the team interacted frequently but not on a daily basis. They were all very familiar and at ease using computers and virtual environments.

4 Patterns of Organizational Practices Informing the Usage of the Adaptive Community-Based Virtual Environment

The two groups of respondents represented very different organizational cultures as described above. Differences are evident in the questionnaire responses especially in terms of 'buying into' the organization's vision or mission, the mean age of the respondent (BTexact respondents were an average of approximately 10 - 15 years younger), and communication media usage (Sandia scientists preferring synchronous communication media such as video conferencing). At least one member of BTexact was a remote worker, while two members of the Sandia ACG were co-located in California but participated in distance collaboration with the larger group of ACG members located in Albuquerque, New Mexico.

4.1 Advanced Concepts Group Questionnaire Responses

ACG members' responses tended to reflect a propensity toward valuing ideas, working with others as opposed to working on one's own, and a strong sense of mission. For example when asked the question, ' At the end of a working day, how would you describe a good day?' Some ACG responses included 'when new ideas are invented and explored, when I can see a new idea documented, when I can see a specific outcome or product, when I get good results, and when I get something accomplished.' When asked the question 'What positive qualities do you get out of communicating with your fellow team members?' the responses ranged from 'we generate new ideas out of pieces from each member, formulating ideas, and testing ideas, having new ideas, and getting unstuck to it's more fun.' And when asked what they found most fulfilling about their jobs, several ACG members responded that most fulfilling was 'working on real problems that a nation cares about, the chance to develop important things, and inventing and exploring.' Additionally the ACG responses reflected a desire for communication in face-to-face settings. Even when ACG members engage in distance collaboration, they prefer synchronous communication tools (video conferencing, and desktop video conferencing) to virtual synchronous or asynchronous collaboration tools (i.e., NetMeeting and email).

4.2 BTexact Questionnaire Responses

The BTexact respondents indicated valuing making progress, working with other talented individuals, getting feedback while appreciating time away from others to work on one's own, and working in an environment that is intellectually stimulating. Responses to the question, 'At the end of a working day, how would you describe a good day?' included 'progress in the right direction, learned something new, tangible progress on tasks, and engaged in creative conversation.' When asked the question 'What positive qualities do you get out of communicating with your fellow team members?' responses included 'motivation and enthusiasm, sense of belonging and intellectual support, working with exciting people, access to information, and feedback and fresh perspectives.' When asked what was most fulfilling about their jobs, the respondents offered 'it's an opportunity to explore new ideas, chance to go wherever intellectually stimulating, talking with others, and freedom to direct research.' Finally, BTexact respondents were familiar and comfortable with virtuality. For example, although both the ACG and BTexact respondents' preferred communicating in a face-to-face environment, BTexact respondents also indicated a fairly strong preference for email and asynchronous collaboration.

4.3 Persona Illustration of the Design Challenge

The interviews and questionnaire responses served to provide a context for developing a persona scenario for redesigning the Forum to address the research questions: "How can we motivate users to identify more strongly with their community of practice, and take the first steps towards opening a chat with others whom they may share common interests with, but do not know well enough to feel comfortable communicating with in a virtual environment?" It was determined from interviews, participant/observation, and analyzing the emergent patterns in both sets of responses that if both groups were to use the space redesigned to answer the question above, their usage would each be quite different. For example, the work practices of the BTexact respondents support the use of a computer-mediated communication environment as a viable tool for remote collaboration. Most of the team members reacted positively to email and asynchronous communication. Ethnography revealed that most were at their desks when not engaged in meetings. Co-located team members used the Contact Space and often augmented their online communication with interpersonal communication in the face-to-face setting. On the other hand, Sandia National Laboratories ACG members were rarely at their desks at any given time. A propensity to work collaboratively in face-to-face groups inhibited the amount of time that a team member would work alone. Additionally, ACG members were encouraged by management to work away from their desks in a collaborative workspace located in the outer office and therefore very infrequently used synchronous computer-mediated communication.

Organizational cultures differed between the two sets of respondents as well. For example, the ACG formed teams around available human resources that could inform a problem that needed to be solved, and interacted primarily with each other's ideas instead of interacting on more personal levels. BTexact, on the other hand, formed teams around similar interests, interpersonal communication, and creativity. The resources an individual brought to bear were considered to be part of the entire offering an individual could make, not the primary reason for collaboration. Identifying these different approaches and underlying values were instrumental to formulating subsequent design recommendations for enhancing usage of a virtual environment, and group identification among the members of the community of practice. Interaction patterns and communication preferences emerged from categorically analyzing the open-response data of the questionnaires, conducting interviews at both worksites, and participant/observation in the Jasper II and Contact Space environments. The following persona reflects the aggregation of the methods used and the important themes that emerged from our user study participants. The persona provides the focus for developing system redesign recommendations. Since the research was primarily conducted to improve the group identification of a newcomer, or stranger to a community, a persona named Adam was developed to represent a newly hired remote, mobile worker at BTexct.

4.3.1 Adam: A Newly Hired Mobile Worker
In this scenario, a newly hired remote worker named Adam has just joined BTexact. Adam is Welsh, speaks several languages, and lives and works from London, while the rest of the Internet and eBusiness team is co-located at BTexact Adastral Park, in Martlesham Heath. Adam is a 26-year-old software developer and has been with BTexact for a month or so. He is comfortable with computer-mediated environments, but has never been in the Forum before. He has not met any of his teammates face-to-face yet, but he often participates in weekly team meetings via telephone. Whenever he joins the meeting by phone, he has to disconnect his computer from the network. Therefore, for the duration of the meeting, Adam is unable to participate in a collaborative virtual environment, or receive email. In addition, there are times when he is not at his computer. Adam's role demands that he travel several times a month, attend offsite meetings, and interact daily with clients in London. He carries a pager, laptop, and a mobile phone. He is still trying to get used to the fact that when he is away from his email or unable to participate in audio conferences, he tends to miss a lot of what happens in the office.

4.3.2 Discussion of the Design Challenge
As a newcomer, Adam will have needs that might not be as obvious to his teammates, who are co-located and have been employed in the organization for some time. For example, organizational myths and stories, and both formal and informal norms or practices are co-created and disseminated over time among employees [4]. Individuals who are co-located have the luxury of gathering data on organizational practices day after day, and are privy to the implicit information that a remote worker would not readily have access to. It's hard enough for Adam to join the new organization, without the added stress of not being able to adequately understand the informal norms, or 'how we do things here' at BTexact. Adam will undoubtedly need the additional team support, or the social infrastructure, that is available to workers who are co-located. Additionally, team calendars, meeting schedules, and team news might not only be beneficial, but also necessary to Adam's acculturation process. Finally, Adam favors computer-mediated synchronous or asynchronous environments since switching media (from computer to phone) is not an efficient use of his time or energy. While Adam is traveling, he may need document sharing capability, or ways

to disseminate organizational stories, client decisions, ideas, and action items to others. That is, when Adam is mobile, he may not use the Contact Space all day or to it's full potential, but instead may primarily use the virtual space as a repository, or shared workspace. Additionally, a more lightweight, text-based version of the adaptive community-based virtual environment may be necessary to access from his mobile phone. Adam will need to inhabit a space in which the informal norms of his team organizational culture are communicated through the artifacts discussed in previous sections (text chat, Jasper II repository, avatar movement) left in the Contact Space.

5 System Redesign Recommendations for Engendering Cultural Identification and Representation

The next few sections briefly outline conceptual design ideas, or themes, that emerged from gathering all of the data collected in order to develop the persona, Adam. Clearly, each section proposes a broad research topic in which one could write a separate paper. The goal in presenting these themes is to provide the reader with examples of system implementation ideas within the context of the characteristics of community of practice development.

Trends towards flexible working and globalization have led to interest in supporting local, regional, and geographically dispersed communities of practice using Internet technology. The challenge for organizations and community-based virtual environments is to 1) support mobile virtual communities of practice, 2) make them more effective by encouraging mutual engagement, joint enterprises, and a shared repertoire, and 3) incorporating a level of cultural sensitivity into the design of the system such that users' individual identities can be expressed, while simultaneously supporting community development. I describe below design recommendations aimed to meet the challenge I have set forth for community-based environments. The design recommendations are proposed within the context of the persona developed for our situation, Adam, and the guidance of the three characteristics of community development described by Wenger [3].

5.1 Engendering Cultural Identification and Representation by Mutual Engagement

Mutual engagement of participants is essential to the development of a community of practice. Mutual engagement refers to participants' co-creation and negotiation of actions or meanings. Mutual engagement is facilitated by communication, whether occurring in the face-to-face context, or virtually [3]. Just as meeting with one's peers physically around the workplace water cooler facilitates sharing stories on how to get things done at work, mutual engagement is also facilitated through mediated communication environments such as the telephone, email, collaborative virtual environments (CVE), and community-based systems. Storytelling, social signposts, and silently lurking are actions whose meaning is negotiated by members of the virtual community.

5.1.1 Supporting Organizational Storytelling

A virtual environment that provides Adam with the social infrastructure he needs to feel part of the organization offers the opportunity to share and receive information (visual and text) in the form of storytelling, or sharing organizational culture myths. Examples might include postings of team awards, team happenings, and stories of the social activities of the team and organization at large. A newcomer like Adam may want to know *how* things are done in the organization, *who* the opinion leaders and influential members of the community are, who he has most in common with, *what* will happen next that shouldn't be missed, and *when* it will happen.

Designers can also foster feelings of belonging by using inclusive language throughout the space. A sense of community may be created by using language that psychologically shortens the distance between the inhabitants of the virtual space—such as 'us' and 'we', versus 'them' and 'I' [15].

5.1.2 Social Signposts Provided by Teammates

Most users who inhabit virtual worlds like to leave their mark on the shared space whether it is through building artifacts (objects) or becoming influential members of the community [16]. Allowing each person to contribute to development or design of the space creates more community. Therefore, we could allow Adam's teammates to create web pages, or objects to be manipulated by others in the shared space. In other words, we could provide Adam and his teammates the opportunity to express their individual or team identities through visual and textual cues in the virtual environment.

A graffiti board, or bulletin board, arouses curiosity and participation among the community by arousing curiosity among teammates—whether it is curiosity about other members of the community, or the shared space itself. We could use principles from computer game design to motivate teammates to become contributing members of the virtual community [17], [18]. That is, we create more motivating environments by designing for user fun, curiosity, and fantasy exploration. We could create a place where Adam can enter on his own and learn about others, his team, and his organization *especially* when other persons do not populate the environment. One of the reasons why text-based collaborative virtual environments are so successful is because a user can enter the environment by her/himself and not get bored. Users often enter 'quiet' spaces in MOOs to build objects, read community news, post information, see what others have posted or built, or just traverse the space. Additionally, newcomers, or strangers like Adam may enter the environment when it is unpopulated to familiarize themselves with the cultural cues in the environment.

5.1.3 The Presence of Silence in Collaborative Virtual Environments

Opportunities for 'invited lurking' or listening to conversation threads without having to participate in the conversation may allow users to learn by "watching or copying" [12]. Additionally, merely inhabiting a virtual environment may foster a sense of belonging, and initiating conversation is sometimes not necessary. For instance, would the virtual environment be experienced differently if Adam had the ability to 'hear' conversations taking place in his vicinity without having to actually initiate a chat? This provides the sensation of being part of a vibrant community, or an open plan office setting.

Additionally, designers could consider giving more 'silent' members of the team a mechanism to express themselves anonymously in the virtual setting. In certain cases anonymity can create more equitable communication (especially for newcomers) by reducing the appearance of hierarchy and power in a collaborative virtual environment and fostering more peer-based communication events [16].

5.2 Engendering Cultural Identification and Representation by Joint Enterprises

Joint enterprises among the participants of a community of practice refer to the conditions, resources, and demands placed on a community—and the subsequent negotiated communal response [3]. A community's enterprise is never fully determined by organizational mandates, or prescription of behavior. Instead, a joint enterprise develops through the practice that eventually evolves into the community's response. Therefore, a community-based system that attempts to *prescribe* group social behavior will likely fail. Although designers and developers cannot prescribe or control social interactions, planning the social aspects of the virtual community-based system early and incorporating good usability in design encourages communities to evolve [19] as participants form a new culture through the negotiation of their social interactions in the virtual space [5]. Virtual tours, albeit with agents or avatars, supporting mobile colleagues, and allowing more personal information to be accessed by the system, are examples of engendering identification and representation by joint enterprises.

5.2.1 Virtual Tours That Provide Cultural Cues for New Employees
Imagine it's your first day on the job and that a colleague is showing you around your new workplace. What are the artifacts present in colleagues' offices and on bulletin boards that give you clues about the organizational culture? How might you go about showing Adam his new workplace and providing the same opportunity to experience organizational artifacts in the workplace?

A virtual tour of BText Adastral Park, and the building in which the team works helps Adam visualize where his teammates reside and provide an awareness function during their online conversations [13]. Jasper II agents could greet new employees upon logging into the Contact Space for the first time and provide a personal tour of the organization and the important details Adam will need to know about maneuvering in his new workplace as a remote worker.

A virtual tour of the physical space, the team members, and perhaps a FAQ on the formal and informal organizational cultural norms will help Adam feel more like part of the team, and thus identify more strongly with the community. In other words, the group members and their activities could also be showcased in addition to a virtual tour of the space. A team gallery of interests might be an informal mechanism for obtaining meta-level information on the team culture and individual identities.

5.2.2 A Virtual Environment Supporting Mobile Workers

Extending the Forum's capability to include wireless telephony is a good idea for a mobile worker like Adam who would prefer to use one device such as a WAP or 3G enabled phone, or PDA to access all of his information while he is away from his desk. In this case, textual cultural cues could be incorporated given the constraints on the size and functionality of the display if necessary.

5.2.3 System Social Navigation

Avatar movement may be based on common cultural attributes, or common social interests, in addition to movement throughout the space based on keywords and common work products. Jasper II agents could connect users of common social interests (generated from social profile), and provide reasons for the movement in the space (i.e., Adam is doing a search on rock climbing, and so the Jasper II agent moves his avatar to another avatar in the Contact Space with the accompanying text, 'Nick rock climbed in Germany last summer').

5.3 Engendering Cultural Identification and Representation by Shared Repertoire

The shared resources, or shared repertoire, belonging to a community of practice are characterized by the routines in which work gets done, informal and formal communication, tools, stories, symbols, actions, or concepts that have become an integral part of the community's practice during its existence [3]. A challenge for community-based systems is facilitating participants' co-creation of meaning in an historical context that promotes negotiation. When members of the community of practice engage in sharing pertinent information about oneself within the work context, and allowing conversations to be persistent [20], they are accessing shared resources that enable them to learn 'how work is done here.'

5.3.1 Interactive Team Member Profiles

Adam may decide that he wants to learn more about his teammates so that next time he runs into them in the Contact Space, he has an entry point next time he strikes up a conversation with them. Adam could click on an avatar in the Contact Space to get user profile information in Jasper II, or a link to its owner's web page. A mouse over which enables audio files of the individual's voice and information in the individual's profile or preferred work habits may also be appropriate. An interactive profile allows readers to post comments to individual's profiles in order to serve as a basis for an asynchronous conversation of a more social nature.

Social information about the team (hobbies, families, etc.) may be made available in the Contact Space via interactive objects. For example, the interactive Jasper II pyramids may also serve as portals to an alternate 'contact space' that is more social in nature—providing the opportunity to take virtual coffee breaks with remote collaborators.

5.3.2   Organizational Memory

Adam could have access to conversation logs that inform subsequent conversations. In other words, Adam may often find himself in a situation in which he is expected to represent the thinking of others on his team with clients. Being privy to salient conversations becomes key. Providing news flashes of decisions being made in Adam's absence would be very helpful. Designers might want to consider 'broadcasting' news within the Contact Space--so all can 'hear.' It would be helpful to keep the entire team abreast of decisions that affect the group as a whole. This is particularly important for team members like Adam who frequently travel.

6   Redesign Scenario: Adam's First Day on the Job in the Redesigned Adaptive Community-Based Virtual Environment

It is Adam's first day on the job, and the Forum has been redesigned to incorporate organizational culture cues to enhance Adam's experience as a Btexact remote worker. As his computer (connected to the network) starts up, He sees the self-view of his avatar and the Contact Space. The system welcomes him and asks him if he would like to virtually tour his organization, and meet his teammates. Adam is excited to get started, so he takes the tour. On his virtual tour he is led around the virtual representation of the open plan office in which some of his co-located colleagues work. The rest of his colleagues are on a different floor. He is able to interact with objects on his tour. He can click on the bulletin board and get the latest news, and interact with the avatar profiles. As Adam interacts with Regan's avatar, she is alerted that Adam is reading her profile. Knowing he is new to the team, Regan decides to open a synchronous chat with Adam. During their chat, Adam learns that the team is will be responsible for a new project. He decides to learn more about it by going to the team gallery of projects, etc. Later he finds that some of his teammates have left him messages, since they knew he would be logging on. The messages direct him to peruse the chat log for a conversation that took place in the Contact Space earlier that day. He believes the communication log is important enough to send to another colleague at Sandia National Laboratories, so he saves the log and inserts it into his email. This way, he doesn't have to waste time on the phone repeating what he knows to a third party. A few more messages later, Adam learns that Sara needs his comments on a proposal. She has left the proposal for him in Jasper II. He retrieves it and provides comments. Finally, at the end of the day, Adam logs off. When Adam starts up his computer after one week The Jasper II agents ask him if he would like to make changes to his avatar's profile, create interactive objects, or post comments to the team bulletin board.

7   Conclusions

The data collected from this study provided the basis for discovering that incorporating cultural and organizational cues into the intelligent community-based system could foster stranger affiliation and identification with the community of practice. These cultural cues are presented to the reader in terms of a conceptual design scenario (Persona) based on the research findings.

Initially, it was believed that system support of chance encounters online would be enough to facilitate informal communication and information sharing among strangers in an organization. However, it is now believed that it takes more than system functionality to motivate human communication in the virtual setting. Strangers who have difficulty opening a conversation—could benefit from a third party that serves to "introduce" them. Our ongoing research has shown that a redesign of the Forum to include user or agent-generated cultural cues, or interactive social cues could motivate informal communication among strangers in the community of practice [19], [9].

Recall that culture includes the assumptions, values, goals, meanings, and histories shared, co-created, and negotiated by the members of the community of practice. Intercultural communication is the exchange of this information between individuals or among groups (teams, organizations, etc.) that perceive themselves to be different. It is imperative to design adaptive community-based virtual environments that foster intercultural communication in order to develop a shared understanding for 'how we do things here,' and 'how we behave here' in order to address the issue of taking steps toward cultural identification and representation for all. As the systems we design bring diverse members of communities of practice together and facilitate their real time communication and knowledge sharing, designers could be attuned to creating environments that support users' intrinsic motivation for participation and interdependency [5].

I have described how Jasper II and Contact Space facilitate the sharing of information among the members of virtual communities of practice and addresses the characteristics essential to the development of a community of practice. I discussed how the system fosters the sharing of information by encouraging people to interact in real time where there are mutual concerns or interests, and further presented how the data collected from user studies informed a design scenario for incorporating cultural signposts into the adaptive community-based virtual environment in order to offer enhanced support for intercultural communication among remote or mobile workers.

In presenting the findings from the questionnaires, the subsequent examples, persona development, and design scenario, "Adam's first day on the job" I intended to show how system enhancements can be made from a perspective that advocates cultural sensitivity in system development. Mudur [8, p. 304] indicated, "Cultural sensitivity must be built in during the initial design stages itself...Sensitivity to the requirements of individual cultures is of utmost importance."

Representing culture in intelligent community-based systems cannot be prescribed (there is no recipe, or standard format), nor should any *one* cultural perspective be forced on a community. Nevertheless, "interactive digital technology is a covert carrier of cultural values" [8, p. 304]. Therefore, as designers, it behooves us to guide a community's culture to emerge from the user's co-creation of narratives and the subsequent communication events transpiring in the virtual space. In other words, users should own the cultural co-creation process. Our community-based systems can assist them. The quality and nature of the users' interactions determine the direction and rate with which a third culture emerges. A 'third culture' is what is created from an intercultural interaction when persons from different cultures communicate equitably and with respect for the other such that the emergent culture reflects appropriate input from each interlocutor. A third culture is the co-creation of meaning in which all interlocutors are participants as well as co-owners. In effect, together users co-create a "third culture" that is neither one nor the other, but a combination of the two, or three, and so on. The successful future design of intelligent community-based system requires considering how the design of these environments support intercultural communication and a greater awareness of cultural orientations in the organizational context.

Acknowledgements. I thank the respondents and collaborators at BT, especially Nick Kings, and John Davies, and those at Sandia National Laboratories who supported this research. *The research reported here was carried out while British Telecommunications employed the author as a research fellow at their Adastral Park R&D facility in Ipswich, UK. Sandia is a multiprogram laboratory operated by Sandia Corporation, a Lockheed Martin Company, for the United States Department of Energy under Contract DE-AC04-94AL85000.

References

1. Rogers, E. M., Diffussion of Innovations, The Free Press, New York, (1995)
2. Hall, E. The Hidden Dimension, Doubleday, New York, (1966)
3. Wenger, E. Communities of practice: Learning, meaning, and identity. Cambridge University Press, (1998)
4. Orr, J. E. Talking about machines: An ethnography of a modern job. Cornell University Press, (1996)
5. Raybourn, E.M. Designing an Emergent Culture of Negotiation in Collaborative Virtual Communities: The DomeCityMOO Simulation. In Collaborative Virtual Environments, E. Churchill, D. Snowden, & A. Munro, (Eds), Springer, 247–64, (2001)
6. Raybourn, E. An intercultural computer-based simulation supporting participant exploration of identity and power in a text-based networked virtual reality: DomeCityMOO. PhD dissertation, University of New Mexico, Albuquerque, (1998)
7. Leevers, D. Collaboration and shared virtual environments—from metaphor to reality. In Frontiers of human-centered computing, online communities and virtual environments. R. Earnshaw, R. Guedj, A. van Dam, & J. Vince (Eds.), Springer, 278–98, (2001)
8. Mudur, S. On the need for cultural representation in interactive systems. In Frontiers of human-centered computing, online communities and virtual environments. R. Earnshaw, R. Guedj, A. van Dam, & J. Vince (Eds.), 299–310, Springer, (2001)
9. Raybourn, E. M., Kings, N. J., & Davies, J. Adding Cultural Signposts In Adaptive Community-Based Environments. *Interacting With Computers: the Interdisciplinary Journal of Human-Computer Interaction*, Special Issue on Intelligent Community-based Systems, Elsevier Science Ireland Ltd, (in press 2002)
10. Davies, J. Intranet community development: Communities of practice at BT. *Virtual Business 4*, 8, 15–18, (2000)
11. Davies, N.J. & Weeks, R. ProSum: Profile-based text summarization, First Automatic Text Summarization Conference (SUMMAC-1), Virginia, USA, (2000)
12. Jeffrey, P., and McGrath, A. Sharing serendipity in the workplace. *Proceedings of CVE 2000* San Francisco, CA, September, ACM Press, 173–179, (2000)

13. McGrath, A., & Prinz, W. All that is solid melts into software. In Collaborative Virtual Environments, E. Churchill, D. Snowden, & A. Munro, (Eds), Springer, 99–114, (2001)
14. Cooper, A. *The inmates are running the asylum.* SAMS, Indianapolis, Indiana, (1999)
15. Wiener, M. & Mehrabian, A. Language within language: Immediacy, a channel in verbal communication. Appleton-Century-Crofts, (1968)
16. Raybourn, E., The quest for power, popularity, and privilege: Identity construction in a text-based multi-user virtual reality. Unpublished Paper presented at the Western Communication Association, Denver, CO, (1997a)
17. Malone, T. What makes things fun to learn? A study of intrinsically motivating computer games. Unpublished doctoral dissertation, Stanford, CA: Stanford University, (1980)
18. Preece, J. Online Communities: Usability, Sociability, Theory and Methods. In Frontiers of human-centered computing, online communities and virtual environments. R. Earnshaw, R. Guedj, A. van Dam, & J. Vince (Eds.), Springer, 263–77, (2001)
19. Raybourn, E. Computer game design: New directions for intercultural simulation game designers. In developments in business simulation and experiential learning, 24, pp. 144–5, (1997b)
20. Erickson, T., Smith, D., Kellogg, W., Laff, M., Richards, J., & Bradner, E. "Socially Translucent Systems: Social Proxies, Persistent Conversation, and the Design of "Babble." In Human Factors in Computing Systems: The Proceedings of CHI, ACM Press, (1999)

Sociable Information Environments[1]

Michael Pieper[1] and Renate Anderweit

Fraunhofer Institute for Applied Information Technology (FhG-FIT)
Schloss Birlinghoven,
D-53754 Sankt Augustin
{michael.pieper, renate.anderweit}@fit.fraunhofer.de

[1] at present:
Institute of Computer Science, Foundation for Research and Technology-Hellas
Science & Technology Park of Crete
Heraklion, Crete, GR-71110, GREECE
Tel: +30-810-391741 - Fax: +30-810-391740
pieper@ics.forth.gr

Abstract. This paper aims at stimulating further discussion about future work in the realm of „Intelligent Environments of Use" (EoUs). Under concern are Sociable Information Environments. Up to now user interface design has been discussed with regard to standardization or even personalization. User interfaces which push towards sociability will have a new quality which implies a seamless symbiosis between humans, EoUs and the real world. Some examples of "visualizing presence in social cyberspaces" show the importance of sociable user interface to reflect group performance and cohesion. Sociological reasoning to define a conceptual model for sociable interface design is grounded on two sociological concepts; "situated life" and "supply and demand concatenation". The concept of supply and demand concatenation" has to be operationalized by ontologies to be derived from the circumstances of "situated life" in different societal subsystems.

1 Introduction: Sociable User Interfaces

The new concept of "Intelligent Environments of Use" (EoUs) to be designed as community-centred, sharable, expandable, co-operative and collaborative spaces of responsive media requires to rethink current user interface design. Under concern are no longer standardized or even personalized user interfaces based either on pretendedly common design assumptions about the average user or on interface adaptations to individualistic preferences, which in its negative impact on the designer's as well as on the user's side may promote and petrify self-conforming idiosyncratic views about the architecture of our entrances to information society, but user interfaces which push towards ...

---

[1] This paper aims at stimulating further discussion about future work within a proposed Network of Excellence (NoE) about "Intelligent Environments of Use" (EoU). A corresponding proposal was recently submitted to the European Commission by ERCIM-WG UI4ALL as an Expression of Interest (EoI) for FP6.

N. Carbonell, C. Stephanidis (Eds.): User Interfaces for All, LNCS 2615, pp. 239–248, 2003.
© Springer-Verlag Berlin Heidelberg 2003

- sociability by taking into account how cognitive behaviour is socially bound, influenced, motivated, shaped and manifested in distributed computational EoUs and
- seamless symbiosis between humans, EoUs and the real world

To distinct these user interfaces from interface personalization - which by no means shall be substituted but rather completed by a new quality of user interfaces - we suggest to designate this new quality of user interfaces "sociable user interface". Or as Jenny PREECE recently put it "Achieving the goal of universally usable online communities and community networks poses two challenges. The first is we must focus on developing technologies accessible to a wide range of users on a variety of devices. The second is to ensure the software also supports sociability, that is, effective social interaction online" [13, 14].

2   Community-Centred EoUs and the Real World

In the physical world social relationships are extensively structured by the semantics of symbolic cues. „Humans are remarkably skilled at using subtle cues about the presence and activities of others to govern their interactions" [4]. We have since long referred to this circumstances by the term symbolic interactionism [11, 12], taking into account previous work of G. H. MEAD [9] and E. GOFFMAN [5, 6]. More recent sociological reasoning about this issue is offered by W. H. WHYTE [19] and ethnomethodologists like C. HEATH and P. LUFF [7].

Cues about the presence and activities of others can adequately be understood only if one is able to re-establish for oneself their spatial and historic meaning as complete as possible. "Cues are differentially propagated through space – something which, as social creatures, we understand and make use of in governing our interactions. Thus we know that those across the room may see we are talking, but will be unable to hear what we say; and we adjust our interactions to take advantage of this" [3]. On the other hand "a key finding of collective action studies shows that mutual understanding of other participants' histories is critical to a cooperative outcome" [15].

Social Psychology refers to this so to say emphatical ability to slip into the shoes of the other by the term "role taking". It is the role-taking ability, which is restricted and difficult to achieve in online environments, because symbolic interaction obviously requires a certain kind of reciprocal intimacy, otherwise symbolic cues like gestures, loudness, nervousness or relaxation cannot be perceived adequately within their semantic context. This context is first of all determined by space and time (or history) - but not exclusively. It is also closely related to the so called immediacy of the medium being used for interaction. The most immediate interaction is of course supported by face-to-face communication. Computer-supported social interaction is on first sight less immediate. Immediacy however could be improved, "if participants in social cyberspaces could easily access histories of each other and the spaces they interact within" [15, 2].

Whereas sociologists for long regarded enhanced immediacy and accordingly social immersion, i.e. the awareness of being an integral part of a comprehensive social context, an important factor for the success and the subjective satisfaction of end users participating in online communities or telecooperation systems, the development of adequate tools to assure this kind of social immersion is lagging behind. Up to now „interfaces like email and news browsers that provide access to social cyberspaces such as discussion boards, email lists and chat rooms present limited, if any, information about the social context of the interactions they host" [15]. Abstract sociological reasoning so far seemed not to be extremely suitable to serve the pragmatic needs of conceptual modelling for sociable interface design. However, since lately sociological concepts about building social capital, i.e. "the capacity of individuals to accrue benefits by dint of their personal relationships and memberships in particular social networks and structures" [17] became more explicitly focussed on their socio-psychological implications of space and time, this has influenced some extraordinary attempts of sociable interface design and implementation trying to support symbolic interaction by mediating the semantics of social cues.

2.1 Visualizing Presence in Social Cyberspaces

One impressive approach to visualize presence in social cyberspaces is based on a so called social proxy, which provides minimalist visualization of people and their activities within a system called Babble. Over the last four years Babble has been designed, deployed, and studied at IBM T. J. Watson Research Centre [2].

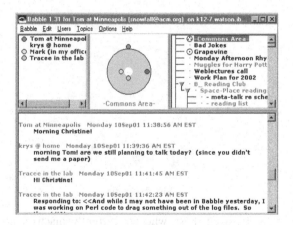

Fig. 1. The Babble user interface.[2]

Figure 1 shows a screenshot of the Babble user interface. What is important is the visualization in the upper middle pane of the window. This is the social proxy, and its purpose is to provide cues about the presence and activity of those in the current conversation. The way it works is that people in the conversation are shown within the circle; people logged on but in 'other 'rooms' (shown in the list to the right) are

---

[2] Fig.1, 2 and 3 are taken from *J. Donath: A Semantic Approach to Visualizing Online Conversations*, Communications of the ACM, April 2002/Vol. 45, No. 4.

positioned outside the circle; and, most importantly, when people are "active" in the conversation, meaning that they either 'talk' (type) or 'listen' (click and scroll), their dots move to the inner periphery of the circle, and then gradually drift back out to the edge over the course of about 20 minutes.

Reportedly Babble users regard the social proxy engaging and informative. "They speak of seeing who is 'in the room', noticing a crowd 'gathering' or 'dispersing', and seeing that people are 'paying attention' to what they say (when other dots move into the centre of the proxy after they post)." It has to be noted however that „many of the things users report 'seeing' are inferences. For example, the social proxy does not show that people are 'paying attention', only that someone has clicked or typed" [4].

The Sociable Media Group at the MIT Media Lab has been exploring other ways of visualizing online social interaction. One of these sociable user interfaces is Coterie, a conversation-centric visualization for an Internet Relay Chat (IRC) [16]. In typical use of standard IRC one can normally request a list of those participants who are actively messaging.

Fig. 2. Coterie.

In Coterie all users, even those who are currently inactive, are represented by coloured ovals. When a user posts a message, the corresponding oval "hops" and "bounces" above the crowd. The colours of ovals of users who are having a conversation become brighter and they are brought together into the centre area of the display. Users who don't interact ("lurkers") exist in the background. Thus Coterie also depicts the cohesiveness of the group and makes apparent who are the initiators of new discussions. User interface reflections of social cohesion have at least conceptually already been placed in the centre of the discussion about design recommendations for sociable user interfaces [12] Coterie is one of those quite recent examples for sociable user interfaces which for the first time also in its technological implementation takes into account that "strong conversational cohesion is a sign of cooperation, showing that the members of the group share similar interests and are motivated to sustain a common discussion, rather than individually attempting to redirect the topic" [1].

Another example for a sociable user interface to reflect group performance and cohesion is PeopleGarden which has also been developed, experimentally explored and deployed at the MIT Media Lab. "PeopleGarden uses a flower and garden metaphor to visualize participation on a message board [20]. Participants are each represented by a flower. The longer they have been involved, the higher the stem; the more they have posted, the more petals. Initial postings are shown in red, replies in blue. One can easily get a sense of an individuals role as an active participant, long-time lurker, and so on" [1]. For instance in the following figure (see figure 3) the left picture depicts a group with one dominating voice with a large number of replies in blue. The right picture reflects a more democratic group with a large number of initial posts in magenta.

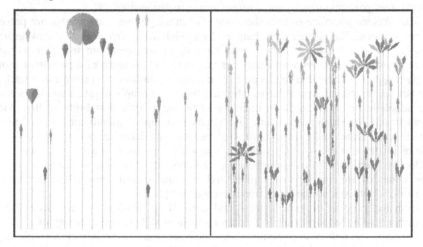

Fig. 3. PeopleGarden

2.2 Tracking History in Social Cyberspaces

Large social cyberspaces like e.g. the Usenet in which no authority controls its borders or content are predestined for an anarchic social organization. Information overload prevails in its detrimental consequences for the search of useful information and meaningful social interaction. As has repeatedly been pointed out [12], large online communities thus fundamentally challenge the question "of how a group of individuals can organize and govern themselves to obtain collective benefits (or social capital, see above) in situations where the temptations to free-ride and to break commitments are substantial" [10]. However "a key finding of collective action studies shows that mutual awareness of other participant's histories and relationships is critical to a cooperative outcome (...) Thus, it would make many of the social processes that bind collective projects together more effective if participants in social cyberspaces could easily create and access histories of one another and the spaces they interact within" [2, 15].

Current interfaces to large social cyberspaces like news browsers, e-mail lists, bulletin boards and chat rooms present limited, if any, information about the histories of the interactions they host. Mostly they present information about the messages themselves (e.g. postings date, subject matter, lines of text etc.), thereby forcing the users to pay more attention to the structure of the medium than to the qualities of the participants who would more naturally draw the user's focus. For that reason the Netscan project at Microsoft Research tries to add sociability based on so called social accounting metrics to these kind of interfaces. "Social accounting metrics are measures of the social dimensions of online spaces, like the size of newsgroups in terms of messages and participants along with the histories of the participating authors in each, such as how long they have been active in the group, in what other newsgroups they participate, to what threads of conversation they contribute, and which other participants they most often engage in discussion" [8].

The Netscan interface reports the number of messages and authors that are present in newsgroups. "These measures help to distinguish active from inactive newsgroups and broadcast newsgroups (which may have many messages but few authors) and more diverse newsgroups with many contributors. The presence of a persistent group of participants is indicated in a report of 'returnees', authors who have come back to the newsgroup on a frequent basis. They are the newsgroup's regulars and the size of the population of regulars is an indicator of the maturity and stability of the space. Newsgroups in which few people are retained month to month may have limited value, while those with large groups of people who have several month or more tenure in the newsgroup may indicate a more active group with a potential for a collective memory and the emergence of acknowledged leaders or authorities. (...) The count of the number of replies and repliers is also reported to distinguish conversational from nonconversational groups" [15].

If in the process of generating social accounting metrics we are successful in identifying so called signature indicators to distinguish between a variety of different newsgroups or online communities this may help us to construct sociable user interfaces that enhance the discovery of interesting discussions and improve users' awareness of the dynamics of online communities. "Successful social processes rely upon a group's awareness of the various levels o f contribution that members provide to group projects, the size of the group, and its relationship to other groups. Introducing such information into social cyberspaces may help orient participants and support self regulation and boundary maintenance activity that could improve content quality and user satisfaction" [18].

3   From Personalized to Sociable Information Environments

In the light of the above the development of intelligent environments of use (EoU) to facilitate community activities (which) may range from business and work tasks to a broad range of social encounters requires an extension – not a revision – of the basic programmatic orientation of the ERCIM WG UI4ALL. This programmatic HCI orientation, which for years worked satisfactorily for user interface design, is based on the Unified User Interface concept (U^2I) which most generally combines user modelling technologies and user profiling with adaptation features for purposes of user interface personalization in the run-time environment of information systems separated from application software and operating platforms.

Table 1. Netscan subject-selected newsgroups by number of unique authors for the period January 1, 2001 through July 31, 2001

Newsgroup	Authors	Repliers	Initiators	Returning authors	Posts	Replies
alt.comp.periphs.mainboard.asus	14856	10211	7654	2634	74290	57236
comp.sys.palmtops.pilot	8093	5391	3655	1788	44965	34991
microsoft.public.windowsme.general	8086	4916	5401	881	56895	45649
rec.woodworking	6347	4492	3324	1863	64544	54066
comp.dcom.sys.cisco	5282	2912	2867	998	23114	15810
rec.food.cooking	4905	3755	1969	1147	72710	65759
microsoft.public.xml	3917	1939	1993	402	11384	6595
rec.models.rockets	2083	1665	1112	758	45055	39487
rec.arts.sf.fandom	1602	1138	332	521	83501	79846
alt.binaries.sounds.mp3.d	1596	1075	468	238	11313	8611
rec.windsurfing	1497	1015	768	432	13013	10823
comp.software.testing	1491	334	360	202	4082	1028
microsoft.public.outlook.mac	1404	593	610	9	2892	1506
rec.equestrian	1327	959	562	437	24087	21373
comp.sys.mac.programmer.help	1178	719	565	319	6382	4705
alt.sports.baseball.sea-mariners	1029	780	414	233	17341	14868
alt.aldus.pagemaker	483	232	165	67	1183	753
seattle.eats	481	375	172	146	2050	1713
sci.agriculture.beekeeping	458	293	230	146	2543	1902
microsoft.public.vb.vbce	436	228	193	55	1287	665
microsoft.public.certification.networking	370	184	120	28	688	379
alt.support.ex-cult	315	221	53	62	1307	1000
microsoft.public.platformsdk.mslayerforunicode	54	36	26	0	336	271

Required is some kind of lateral or dialectical thinking about the U2I concept encountering – so to say – the other page of the medail. It is suggested that U2I-based lateral thinking aiming at establishing further improved conceptual models for sociable user interfaces takes two sociological concepts into account; the concept of "situated life" (terminus technicus in German language: "Lebenslagen-Konzept") and the concept of "supply and demand concatenation". In the following these concepts will briefly be circumscribed by taking into account (i) their added-value for interface design and (ii) their interconnectedness and relationship to the current U2I paradigm.

3.1 The Concept of "Situated Life" (Lebenslagen-Konzept)

The concept of "situated life" is based on the assumption that communities or the society as a whole is substructured into certain societal subsystems which create the prerequisites of the survival of a society as a living system. Thus societal subsystems shape the living circumstances (another circumscription of "situated life") of citizens or community members. Three subsystems and corresponding prerequisites can be distinguished:

- the economical subsystem, to cater for consumption and production
- the cultural subsytem to cater for the maintenance of value patterns
- the social subsystem to cater for the integration of citizens or community members

If one of the above mentioned societal subsystems becomes dysfunctional in creating these prerequisites the society or community in question tends to dissolve.

Societal subsystems use certain resources to ensure the prerequisites for the survival of certain communities or the society as a whole. In the economic subsystem work or employment is the resource for the production sector. For economic consumption availability of services and goods is an indispensable resource condition. Group dynamic opinion-formation by discursive interaction is the resource for the maintenance of value patterns in the cultural subsystem., whereas group-dynamic enfolding of empathy (the ability of so-to-say "slipping into the shoes of the ‚other'") is the resource precondition for the integration of community members in the social subsystem [12].

The central assumption at this point is, that in Information Society (IS), Information Society Technologies (IST) mediate these resources by EoUs. CSCW applications or teleworking environments can for instance be regarded as mediating resources for economic production, and further EoUs to mediate resources to ensure community survival in the other societal subsystems are already in place (see above) or can be conceptualised on the background of this paradigm.

3.2 The Concept of "Supply and Demand Concatenation"

The "supply and demand" concept rounds off the paradigmatic background for deriving conceptual models for sociable information environments. The EoU-mediated resources to ensure society or community survival requisites can be regarded as the supply side in sociable information environments. The demand side can be derived from user profiles being part of the already mentioned and well established Unified User Interface concept (U2I).

User profiles are always interest profiles and the demands to be derived from interests simply refer to the fact that personal interests are always achievement or goal-oriented in the meaning of interest implementation. Thus, to be distinguished from regular EoUs, intelligent EoUs can conceptually be regarded as being based on a reasonable and meaningful "supply and demand concatenation" (i.e. the highest possible supply/demand compatibility) in the different societal subsystems.

Technologically supply and demand concatenation has to be based on ontologies. Ontologies establish a joint terminology between members of a community of interest. To acquire an ontology means to make something explicit that is usually just implicit. Concerning our concept of supply and demand concatenation ontologies can thus be regarded as being another representation of the above mentioned signature indicators to be derived from social accounting metrics. Needless to say that these ontologies or signature indicators are of course differently shaped by the different prerequisites of the distinguished societal subsystems (see above).

The term "concatenation" implies even more that we have also to deal with ontology interoperability. The distributed development of ontologies, i.e. one for the demand side and another for supply, needs not only tools for synchronizing but finally for mapping these different ontologies.   Mapping finally allows for computing signature indicators in terms of correlation or proximity measures giving an indication of the responsiveness of social online encounters, thus reaching beyond the nonetheless impressing current examples of accessing EoUs by sociable user interfaces.

4 Conclusion

Only under the conceptual and technological conditions of ontology based supply and demand concatenation EoUs can be regarded as being intelligent in that they are responsive to individual demands (operationalised terms of user/interest-profiles) by a directed supply of resources to be derived from the circumstances of situated life in different contexts, which can be specified with regard to different societal subsystems.

References

1.   Donath, J.: A Semantic Approach to Visualizing Online Conversations, in: Communications of the ACM, April 2002, Vol. 45, (2002), pp. 45
2.   Erickson, Th., Smith D.N., Kellogg, W.A., Laff, M., Richards, J. T. and Bradner, E.: Socially translucent systems. Social Proxies, Persistent Conversation, and the design of Babble in: Proceedings of CHI 99: Human Factors in Computing Systems. ACM Press, New York, (1999) pp. 72
3.   Erickson, Th. and Kellogg, W.A.: Social Translucence: An approach to designing systems that mesh with social processes, in: Transactions of Computer–Human Interaction, 7, 1. ACM Press, New York, N.Y., (2001) pp. 59–83
4.   Erickson, Th., Halverson, Ch., Kellogg, W.A., Laff, M. and Wolf, T.: Social Translucence. Designing Social Infrastructure that make Collective Activity Visible, in: Communications of the ACM, April 2002, Vol. 45, (2002) pp. 40
5.   Goffman, E.: Behavior in Public Places: Notes on the Social Organization of Gatherings. The Free Press, New York, NY (1963)
6.   Goffman, E.: The Presentation of Self in Everyday Life. Garden City, NY (1969)
7.   Heath, C. and LUFF, P.: Technology in Action. Cambridge University Press, Cambridge, MA (2000)
8.   Hill, W. and Hollan, J.: History enriched data objects: Prototypes and Policy Issues, in: Information Society 10 (2001)
9.   Mead, G.H.: Mind, Self and Society from the perspective of a behavioris. Chicago: University of Chicago Press (1934)
10.   Ostrom, E.: Governing the Commons: The Evolution of Institutions for Collective Action. Cambridge University Press, New York (1990)
11.   Pieper, M.: 'Calling the Blind' is 'Watched by the Deaf'– Directions for Multimodal CSCW-Adaptations to Receptive Disabilities, in: Proceedings of the 1st ERCIM-Workshop 'User Interfaces for ALL', Heraklion, Greece, FORTH – Institute of Computer Science (1995)

12. Pieper, M.: Sociological Issues in HCI Design, in: Stephanidis, C. (ed.), User Interfaces for All – Concepts, Methods, Tools, chapter 11, pp. 203–221, Mahwah (NJ), London, Lawrence Erlbaum Associates (2001)
13. Preece, J.: Online Communities: Designing Usability, Supporting Sociability. John Wiley, Chichester, U.K. (2000)
14. Preece, J.: Supporting Community and Building Social Capital, in: Communications of the ACM, April 2002, Vol. 45, (2002) pp. 36
15. Smith, M.: Tools for Navgating large Social Cyberspaces, in: Communications of the ACM, April 2002, Vol. 45, (2002) pp. 51
16. Spiegel, D.S.: Coterie: A Visualization of the Conversational Dynamics within IRC, Massachusetts Institute of Technology (School of Architecture and Planning), Cambridge, MA (2001)
17. Warschauer, M.: Social Capital and Access. University of California, Irvine (Dept. of Education and Dept. of Computer Science), (2002) unpubl. man.
18. Whittaker, S., Terveen L., Hill, W. and Cherny, L.: The Dynamics of Mass Interaction, in: Proceedings of CSCW '98, ACM Press, New York (1998)
19. Whyte, W.H.: City: Return to the Center, Doubleday, New York (NY) (1988)
20. Xiong, R. and Donath J. (1999): PeopleGarden: Creating Data Portraits for Users, in: Proceedings of UIST (1999)

Part III: Towards an Information Society for All

Using Biometrics as an Enabling Technology in Balancing Universality and Selectivity for Management of Information Access

M.C. Fairhurst, R.M. Guest, F. Deravi, and J. George

Department of Electronics, University of Kent, Canterbury, Kent, CT2 7NT, UK.
{mcf, rmg, fd4, jg31}@ukc.ac.uk

Abstract. The key concept of Universal Access in the Information Society has important and far-reaching implications for the design of a wide range of systems and data sources. This paper sets out to examine two fundamentally conflicting aspects of the broad principle of universality in design, pointing to the opposite requirement that, in many applications, access to a system or set of data must be limited to an identifiable population of "authorised" users. However, the idea of universality then applies at a lower level, since the mechanisms used to impose these limitations should themselves not be dependent on the physical attributes or expertise of individuals, but rather related to their identity and designated level of authorisation. This leads to an interesting situation where the concept of universality must be implemented at different levels and, equally, must be balanced against the competing claims of the constraints imposed by authorisation-determined selectivity. This paper argues that technology based on biometric processing – the exploitation of measurements relating to individual physiological or behavioural attributes – provides a key platform on which an access management structure can be realised. Experimental results based on various biometric modalities are used to support and illustrate the ideas proposed.

1 Introduction

The theme of universal access is of increasing importance in an age where technology penetrates almost every aspect of daily life for increasing numbers of citizens. There are many, often inter-related, reasons for this. For example, we recognise that different individuals have different skills and aptitudes for technology-based interaction, that some individuals have special needs for daily living and are all too easily excluded from activities which others can take for granted, that more and more data is being made available for general use, and that increasing numbers of people are responding to the benefits of technology to expand horizons and enhance possibilities for engaging in social interactions in a meaningful way. Interestingly, however, looking at the other side of the coin, an issue which is often overlooked is that the increasing availability of information and data itself imposes a greater necessity for ensuring that access to data sources is controlled or constrained, at least in the sense that not all information can or should be made available to everyone, and

N. Carbonell, C. Stephanidis (Eds.): User Interfaces for All, LNCS 2615, pp. 249–259, 2003.

that some data sources should, of necessity, be restricted in terms of their accessibility. For these reasons very important questions of security, privacy, reliability and trust assume a paramount importance. It is apparent that attention to these areas has not developed at the same pace as that associated with the provision and desirability of facilitating access to systems and data on a universal basis, yet in an increasingly complex society such issues will assume an ever-increasing importance.

In this paper we will consider exactly these issues and, in doing so, we will attempt to broaden our perspective on the way in which universal access can be seen as raising both sociological and technological questions representing two, sometimes competing, aspects of a single issue. We would argue that the enormously important area of universal access can only develop its full potential if both aspects are properly addressed and if the twin concerns of accessibility and constraint are equally recognised. Our discussion will, in fact, itself address two aspects of the accessibility issue. First, we will argue that imposing bounds on access to data or systems is, for almost all prospective users, generally an important and unavoidable issue, and we will review ways of regulating access through establishing identity and authority in potential users. As our second major point we will then focus on a key question which arises from this and which is absolutely central to the theme of User Interfaces for All. This is the question of how to ensure that the techniques and methods proposed can adapt and be tailored to meet the widely varying requirements of all users, irrespective of particular physical, behavioural or other limitations which they may experience. Thus, in a sense, we will be identifying the importance of regarding the Universal Access paradigm as something which must operate at different strata within user populations or systems.

In fact, the paper is fundamentally concerned with the use of biometric measurements as a means of establishing or verifying individual identity. This is increasingly regarded as a prerequisite for regulating access to systems or data in a meaningful way, and is an area of technology which is gaining an increasing penetration into practical systems. At the same time, little attention has hitherto been given to the relation between biometric-based access regulation and the theme of Universal Access as it is currently understood, and we will address a number of relevant and important issues arising in this regard.

2   Biometrics and Identity Authentication

Biometric measurements – the measurement of attributes of an individual which help to identify that person uniquely [1] – can be categorised as either *physiological* or *behavioural*. The first type, examples of which include iris patterns [2], fingerprints [3] etc, relate to inherent physiological characteristics of an individual, while the second type, such as handwritten signatures [4], keystroke dynamics [5], gait patterns [6], etc, arise from activities carried out by that individual, either those which occur spontaneously or, in some cases, those which are specifically learned. Some examples of common biometric modalities of current interest are:

- Facial features
- Voice characteristics

- Fingerprints
- Handwritten signature
- Iris patterns
- Hand shape
- Hand vein patterns
- Keystroke dynamics
- Odour
- Ear shape
- Gait patterns
- Retinal blood vessel patterns

This list shows an extensive range of possible biometric modalities, illustrative rather than exhaustive, since others could also be envisaged, and it is clear that many options can be considered to support identity checking with a range of different individuals, different environments and different application domains. Although the handwritten signature [7,8,9] has perhaps the longest history in this respect, many other biometric modalities which exploit technology developed primarily for other purposes (for example, face or voice recognition) have gained popularity in recent years.

Although for most biometrics widespread practical exploitation is a comparatively recent phenomenon and, indeed, practical biometric implementation is an area which is still moving towards maturity, research interest in biometrics has a long history, and experience has clearly shown that different biometric modalities are suited in different degrees to different applications (see, for example, [10]). Similarly, an important factor in choosing an appropriate biometric for a given task is the degree of acceptability which it is accorded within the prospective user community. Although biometric authentication can also engender scepticism or outright negative reactions (for example, sometimes poor reliability, concerns about privacy and civil liberties, and so on), there is general agreement, however, that in many applications biometrics offer advantages over other approaches to identity checking. For example, a "sign-on" facility to a computer system can circumvent problems of the ease with which passwords can be intercepted, deliberately shared or forgotten. A fingerprint system might increase security in physical access control compared with, say, visual inspection of badges which is often error-prone or carelessly executed. In other situations such as on-line monitoring, face recognition can prove an effective and non-intrusive means of continually monitoring user identity beyond initial system registration, and many other examples could also be discussed.

This issue of matching biometric modality to a particular application or scenario becomes especially important when the broader concepts of universality are considered, since particular individual needs, limitations and preferences then become of primary concern. For example, hand tremor will impose restrictions on the efficacy of handwriting-oriented behavioural biometrics or, in some cases, will preclude the use of this possibility, and similar arguments apply in other situations. Indeed, similar arguments also apply to questions about the suitability or usability of certain devices in relation to individual characteristics, as well as simple matters of choice and preference.

Hence, the potentially enormous benefits of biometric-based identity checking must be balanced against the difficulty of making a universal and application-led decision about choice of biometric modality or of devising a control structure which allows flexibility in matching specific modality to user abilities, requirements and preferences. It is this latter issue which impinges especially and directly on the theme of Universal Access, and which provides the focus for this paper.

3   Experimental Framework

In order to illustrate the arguments to be developed later in this paper we will draw on a range of experimental results deriving from a large-scale exercise which we have recently undertaken to acquire biometric data in order to support a more effective evaluation of biometric-based identity authentication. In this experimental study, part of an on-going project designated IAMBIC (Intelligent Agents for Multi-modal Biometric Identification and Control [11]), data collection trials have been undertaken which have gathered biometric data from a range of commercially available biometric devices. Although device-specific (the individual devices are not explicitly identified here) the results provide clear insights into the relative characteristics of the different modalities which the devices adopted embody. The data collection protocol itself is designed to focus on the well established scenario testing regime and conforms to the recognised guidelines of good practice laid down for biometric testing [12].

The data collection trial is based around a group of 221 volunteers recruited from a cross-section of the general public, each of whom receive a small payment for participation, and each formally giving fully informed consent to their participation. Each volunteer takes part in two separate data collection sessions, the first involving enrolment on each of the devices under test, when up to three attempts at enrolment are permitted, together with a post-enrolment verification check. A second session is undertaken at least one month later, at which a second verification process is carried out using the enrolment templates generated at the first session. Each volunteer undertakes three verification attempts at this session, and this allows re-try scenarios in addition to the one-shot case to be evaluated. Although in the data acquisition process basic precautions are taken to avoid unnecessary and disruptive environmental disturbances (for example, voice sample collection takes place away from noisy public areas) no formal optimisation of acquisition conditions is undertaken in this study.

The distribution of ages for the group of volunteer subjects and between male/female participants is shown in Table 1.

The data acquired in these trials are stored for analysis and linked to basic personal and demographic information provided by the participants. The database thus constructed forms the basis of the experimental results reported in the following sections.

Table 1. Age/sex distribution of subjects

Age range	Female	Male
18-24	49	42
25-34	17	29
35-44	9	18
45-54	12	11
55-64	7	15
65 +	5	7

4 Biometric Control of Data Sources

We have argued that the corollary of a strategy which encourages "Universal Access" is to ensure that there is a balance between facilitating ease of access to specific information for those, whatever their individual characteristics, needs and abilities, who are entitled to such access, while providing assurance that access is not permitted to those without such an entitlement.

We must first examine, therefore, some issues concerning biometric access control which relate to general performance characteristics and functionality. We have already noted that many different biometric modalities can exist, and it is self-evident that for a particular user-group, different modalities have different properties and, especially, that the effectiveness of use for different modalities in differing situations is also likely to vary. More fundamental than this, however, is the observation that the measurement acquired can itself inherently vary considerably for any individual.

This can be illustrated as follows. Let us consider a biometric modality based on, for example, the use of a fingerprint to generate the requisite biometric measurement. The performance characteristics of this modality may be investigated by considering a wide variety of factors. For example, problems may be experienced by some users at the enrolment stage itself, perhaps because of unfamiliarity with the acquisition infrastructure, or difficulty in generating a fingerprint image of sufficient quality for accurate processing, and so on. Even after enrolment, the passage of time may give rise to a situation where, while having successfully enrolled and verified at an initial session, re-testing at a later date results in a verification failure (for example, because of damage to the finger in the intervening period, or a fundamental change in the way in which the finger is subsequently presented to the capture device). Even more serious would be a situation where, following a successful enrolment, the verification process fails on all attempts to verify a subject's identity.

Table 2 shows an analysis of our test data for the fingerprint modality based on each of these scenarios. The inherent difficulty of selecting an appropriate biometric modality is further illustrated if this is compared with Table 3, which shows equivalent data for biometric data derived from the voice modality. Here we see how different modalities show very different patterns of effectiveness in use. Over the population tested it is clear that satisfactory enrolment is significantly easier with the fingerprint modality compared with the voice modality. On the other hand, where successful enrolment is achieved, the voice modality is significantly more stable during the verification process.

Table 2. Performance characteristics for fingerprint modality

Error	Failure rate (%)
Failure to enrol	2.7
Failure to verify at second visit	14.4
Enrol but fail to verify	4.2

Table 3. Performance characteristics for voice modality

Error	Failure rate (%)
Failure to enrol	10
Failure to verify at second visit	1.5
Enrol but fail to verify	0

Although these results should be interpreted with some caution, because no analysis of impostor testing has yet been carried out, it is apparent that a principal observation here is that no single biometric modality or device is likely to provide a universal solution for every potential user in every proposed application scenario.

This leads directly and conveniently to the next and most pertinent part of the discussion, which concerns the nature of choice and strategies for exploiting biometric control in a way which meshes satisfactorily and supportively with the central principles of the universal access philosophy.

5 Choice and Selectivity in Biometric Control – The Universal Access Question

The principle of universal access seeks to ensure that variations in individual abilities and circumstances do not inhibit participation in activities to which they otherwise have a right of access. We can now see how this principle might apply in situations where biometric control is being exercised, for we should not deny access to information to which an individual is entitled simply because a particular modality is unsuitable for that individual or because inherent unreliability degrades performance to such an extent that the system ceases to be viable.

Thus, the first observation which can be made in this context is to draw attention to the need for an assessment of potential users of a system in relation to the biometric modalities which are suitable for the pool of users for which a system is intended. An appropriate choice of biometric modality and/or device should be made in the light of this assessment.

There is, however, a much wider issue here. This concerns the fact that, as we have already seen, in any application where a large user population is implied, or where the characteristics of the individual members of the population might be expected to be particularly variable, it becomes increasingly unlikely that a single biometric can be identified which can meet the needs of all potential system users, and this points to the need for further consideration of the problem and a more powerful strategy for implementation.

One particularly promising approach to the problem is to adopt a methodology based on the use of multiple biometric modalities – in other words, accumulating evidence of identity from more than one biometric source [11,13,14,15]. While, at one end of the spectrum, this can lead in many cases to an increase in the security and reliability afforded by an overall system (in the sense that requiring a user to satisfy identity checking in more than one modality is likely to improve the confidence in the resulting identification decision), at the other end of the spectrum it is clear that a system designed around the availability of identification evidence from more than one biometric source can also offer exactly the degree of selectivity and personalised matching for which we have been arguing. It is the latter option which is of primary interest here, however, but two specific issues are of great importance if the potential power of multiple modality processing is to be successfully adopted as a means of furthering progress towards the goal of universal access. These relate to the questions of selection flexibility on the one hand, to harmonise user characteristics and modality constraints, and on the other to compensate for individual characteristics and needs. We will consider these in turn.

5.1 Selection Flexibility to Harmonise User Characteristics and Modality Constraints

We first note that the availability of more than one modality immediately increases the potential for successful operation of a biometrics-controlled information access scheme. This can be illustrated effectively through further analysis of the data obtained from the experimental trials described earlier.

For example, we first consider the improved performance which accrues simply as a result of the availability of more than one modality, and where a weakness in one modality can be compensated by strength in another. Returning to an example where we consider a fingerprint modality and a voice modality biometric, Table 4 shows the Failure to Enrol rate and the Verification Failure rate when a combination of the two modalities is adopted. In the first case a Failure to Enrol is defined as a failure to complete a satisfactory enrolment process on both of the available devices, while Verification Failure refers to the situation where successful verification based on at least one of the modalities in the chosen combination has not been achieved.

Clearly, a significant improvement in performance is evident in the multiple modality scenario. In fact in other combinations considered (for example, combining , say, fingerprint data and facial characteristics or voice and face features) it can be shown that it is possible to reduce these error rates to zero with appropriate choice of the modalities to be combined.

Table 4. Performance characteristics for dual modality scenario

Error	Failure rate (%)
Failure to enrol	0.9
Verification failure	0.5

5.2 Selection Flexibility to Compensate for Individual Characteristics and Needs

Of course, in the present context, the most important aspect of exploiting flexibility through modality integration is to allow the option of alternative biometric sources to compensate for specific characteristics and needs of individual system users which might render certain modalities ineffective.

For example, an individual with poor limb control would be likely to find a significant degree of difficulty in manipulating a device which extracts a fingerprint image, but a biometric based on, say, face recognition, could be much easier to work with. A speech-impaired individual, on the other hand, may experience considerable difficulty with a voice-based biometric, but may be able to interact perfectly adequately with a system where a fingerprint modality is made available.

Thus, inherent flexibility at the level of modality selection now becomes realisable purely from the provision of a structure which embodies a capability for multimodality in biometric sources. Embedding intelligence within the processing structure which both embraces knowledge of user requirements and access rights and which also possesses a capability for matching individual characteristics to selection of available biometric sources provides a very effective strategy for progress towards *universality* in systems which exploit biometric control of information access.

6 Implementation Issues

In both the scenarios outlined above, a potentially serious drawback of introducing the concept of multimodality to improve either reliability or flexibility is the increasing complexity of the biometric data generated, the implications for the processing of that data, the diverse factors relating to personal choice, degree of security required and individual permissions profiles which become live issues in such a system, and, indeed, the form of the algorithm whereby evidence of different biometric sources is combined for an overall decision. Thus, the issue of the *management* of the complexity of a multiple modality biometric identity checking system becomes, in itself, a design problem which must be addressed.

This is an area which will not be specifically addressed here in detail, though it is the subject of related work which has been reported elsewhere [16]. In brief, however, a processing structure based on an implementation which adopts intelligent agent technology [17, 18] as the focus for managing complexity in the system has been shown to offer a very flexible and robust framework for the implementation of an overall system design. The benefits of such an approach are related particularly to the negotiating power of the agents and the ease with which their interactions can support processing through which individual needs can be reconciled with the inherent features of different modalities and levels of permitted access. Further work in this area is expected to be very fruitful in providing practical support to the more general principles of concern in this paper, and is clearly likely to develop key components to underpin attempts to specify and realise in practice biometric-controlled universal access strategies.

7 Exploitation of Re-try Strategies and Learning Effects

Finally, it is useful to note some results which shed light on the related issue of multiple enrolment attempts, since it is usual to allow more than one such attempt in initiating the exploitation of a biometric-based system.

Table 5 shows the relationship between false rejection rates and the number of enrolment attempts allowed for the fingerprint modality, showing the positive effect of "training during use" associated with this type of activity. Similar information with respect to failure to enrol rates is recorded in Table 6.

It is of particular interest to see this type of analysis in the context of adopting biometric measures for use by individuals who may have special needs, where such an effect could be especially important, but the results also point to the need for the design of appropriate interfaces to promote ease of interaction. Indeed, adaptable HCI strategies could play a key role in future development of biometric-controlled data access.

Table 5. False rejection rate as a function of number of enrolment attempts (Fingerprint modality)

Attempt	False rejection (%)
1st enrolment attempt	11.2
2nd enrolment attempt	9.8
3rd enrolment attempt	2.8

Table 6. Failure to enrol as a function of number of enrolment attempts (Fingerprint modality)

Attempt	Failure to enrol (%)
1st enrolment attempt	28.5
2nd enrolment attempt	7.7
3rd enrolment attempt	2.7

8 Conclusion

Against a background of the established principles associated with the concept of universal access, we have argued that such a paradigm should be seen as multifaceted, balancing the imperative to facilitate information/system access for individuals with an entitlement to such access against the need to avoid unauthorised access to data or systems in situations where a structure of predefined privileges and restrictions are inherently required.

Our approach has been to develop ideas and strategies based on the adoption of biometric techniques for establishing individual identity, an area of increasing importance in today's society, and to define an approach which exploits the power of biometrics in a way best suited to the stringent requirements for robustness and flexibility which the universal access paradigm imposes when seen in this broader context. In particular, we have invoked the principle of integrating multiple biometric modalities as a means of dealing with the twin issues of reliability in performance and evolving a system structure which can accommodate widely varying needs and levels of user ability.

We have presented data based on an extensive data gathering exercise with a representative sample of members of the general public, and we have shown, through an initial analysis of the data obtained, how the ideas embraced by the approach proposed can, both in principle and in practice, be utilised to achieve the balance noted above.

Although the data reported is extracted using specific devices and based on a sample of volunteers without any known special needs other than requirements arising from natural variations in biometric characteristics, it is clear that the results presented provide a firm basis for developing a strategy which is generic in its applicability, and which can be seen as an important contribution to progress towards achieving universal access in practice. Although specific limitations arising from individual characteristics involving severe disabilities are naturally not included in the data reported here, the principles of how to deal with issues of variability and inconsistency apply even in these cases. The concept of Universal Access is far-reaching in its implications. This paper illustrates this point directly, and shows how an inclusive and wide-ranging view of universality will be increasingly important if it is to exploited to its full potential.

Acknowledgement. The authors wish to acknowledge the support of the UK Engineering and Physical Sciences Research Council and the Department of Trade and Industry for this work and, especially, the contribution of the industrial partners in the IAMBIC project, Neusciences and Cardionetics. The significant contribution to the collection and processing of the biometric data made by Mr. N. Mavity is also gratefully acknowledged.

References

1.   Parkes, J.R.: Personal identification – biometrics, In: D.T. Lindsay and W.L. Proce, (eds.): Information Security, North Holland (1991)
2.   Daugman, J.G.: High confidence visual recognition of persons by a test of statistical independence, IEEE Trans. Pattern Analysis and Machine Intelligence 15 (1993) 1148–1161
3.   Jain, A.K., Hong, L., Bolle, R.: On-line fingerprint verification, IEEE Trans. Pattern Analysis and Machine Intelligence 19 (1997) 302–313

4. Fairhurst, M.C.: Signature verification revisited: promoting practical exploitation of biometric technology,: Electron. Commun. Eng. J. **9** (1997) 273–280
5. Obaidat, M.S. and Sadoun, B.: Verification of computer users using keystroke dynamics, IEEE Trans. Systems, Man and Cybernetics **27** (1997) 261–269
6. Huang, P.S., Harris, C.J., Nixon, M.S.: Human gait recognition in canonical space using temporal templates, IEE Proc. Vision, Image and Signal Processing **146** (1999) 93–100
7. Plamondon, R. and Lorette, G.: Automatic signature verification and writer identification – the state of the art: Pattern Recognition **22** (1989) 107–131
8. Leclerc, F. and Plamondon, R.: Automatic signature verification – the state of the art 1989–1993, Int. J. Pattern Rec. Art. Intell. **8** (1994) 643–659
9. Allgrove, C and Fairhurst, M.C.: Majority voting for improved signature verification, Proc. IEE Colloquium on Visual Biometrics, London, (2000) 10.1–10.4
10. Jain, A., Bolle, R., Pankanti, S.(Eds.): Biometrics – personal identification in a networked society, Kluwer (1999)
11. Deravi, F., Fairhurst, M.C., Mavity, N.J., Guest, R.M.: Design of multimodal biometric systems for universal authentication and access control, Proc. WISA, Seoul (2001) 9–20
12. Best practices in testing and reporting performance of biometric devices, Biometrics Working Group/NPL (2000)
13. Chibelushi, C.C., Mason, J.S.D., Deravi, F.: Feature-level data fusion for bimodal person recognition, Proc. 6th IEE Int. Conf. Image Processing and its Applications (1997) 399–403
14. Su, Q. and Silsbee, P.L.: Robust audiovisual integration using semicontinuous Hidden Markov Models, Proc. 4th Int. Conf. Spoken Language Processing (1996) 42–45
15. Hong, L and Jain, A.: Integrating faces and fingerprints for personal identification, IEEE Trans. Pattern Analysis and Machine Intelligence **20** (1998) 1295–1306
16. Deravi, F., Fairhurst, M.C., Guest, R.M., Mavity, N.J., Canuto, A.: Intelligent agents for the management of complexity in multimodal biometrics, Int. J. UAIS (In press)
17. Wooldridge, M and Jennings, N.R.: Intelligent agents – theory and practice, The Knowledge Engineering Review **10** (1995) 115–152
18. Wooldridge, M.: Agent-based software engineering, IEEE Trans. Software Engineering **144** (1997) 26–37

Part IV: Novel Interaction Paradigms – New Modalities and Dialogue Styles

Ubiquitous Interaction – Using Surfaces in Everyday Environments as Pointing Devices

Albrecht Schmidt, Martin Strohbach, Kristof van Laerhoven,
and Hans-W. Gellersen

Computing Department,
Lancaster University
Lancaster, LA1 4YR, UK
{albrecht, strohbach, kristof, hwg}@comp.lancs.ac.uk
http://ubicomp.lancs.ac.uk

Abstract. To augment everyday environments as interface to computing may lead to more accessible and inclusive user interfaces, exploiting affordances existing in the physical world for interaction with digital functionality. A major challenge for such interfaces is to preserve accustomed uses while providing unobtrusive access to new services. In this paper we discuss augmentation of common surfaces such as tables as generic pointing device. The basic concept is to sense the load, the load changes and the patterns of change observed on a surface using embedded load sensors. We describe the interaction model used to derive pointing actions from basic sensor observations, and detail the technical augmentation of two ordinary tables that we used for our experiments. The technology effectively emulates a serial mouse, and our implementation and use experience prove that it is unobtrusive, robust, and both intuitively and reliably usable.

1 Introduction

To use our everyday environments as interface to computer-based services is an intriguing vision toward more accessible and inclusive user interfaces. The principal idea is to augment common structures and everyday artifacts as interaction devices that inherit design affordances from the physical world for interaction with the digital realm. The key motivation is to yield interfaces that are experienced as familiar, natural and fitting in our environments, to the extent that they become peripheral to everyday activity. The design challenge for such interfaces is therefore to preserve the original appearance, purpose and function of augmented structures and artifacts, and to exploit their affordances rather than break with accustomed use.

Weiser's vision of ubiquitous computing was an early suggestion of the world as interface to computing, referred to by him and his colleagues as embedded virtuality [18]. This has since been followed by many inspirational research contributions, exploring notions of augmented environments [19], tangible user interfaces [16] and ambient information display [17]. This research has yielded a wide range of illustrative examples demonstrating the combination of 'real world' affordances with access to the digital world. However these examples tend to be highly application specific, while there appears to be no notable work on more generic interfaces embedded in everyday environments.

N. Carbonell, C. Stephanidis (Eds.): User Interfaces for All, LNCS 2615, pp. 263–279, 2003.
© Springer-Verlag Berlin Heidelberg 2003

In a recent publication we have discussed augmentation of common surfaces in everyday environments such as table-tops, shelves and floor space with load sensors to render them responsive to activity occurring on them. We have demonstrated that surface-based load sensing is a very robust and versatile source of information that can be used as context for ubiquitous computing applications [21]. More specifically, we have shown that three basic types of context can be obtained from events on a load-sensitive surface. These are the measured overall force (corresponding to the weight of an object or to explicitly applied pressure), the position on the surface at which a change in force is observed (corresponding to where an object is placed or removed), and the type of interaction expressed in the signal waveforms (corresponding to how an object is placed). We have further shown that more elaborate context can be obtained by combining observations over time (tracking activity) or space (relating activity across multiple surfaces). The use of such context in computer applications effectively constitutes *implicit human-computer interaction* [22] as it is based on human activity but not created as explicit input to the application.

In this paper we extend our work on load-sensitive surfaces to demonstrate their use for *explicit human-computer interaction*. We do this by considering use of ordinary surfaces as generic pointing device. The guiding scenario is that we might simply use the surface of a coffee table in the living room as track pad to navigate the Web on the TV screen. The challenges are interesting: obviously we do not wish a coffee table to appear wired and instrumented, and more importantly we expect the placement of cups and other items not to be prohibited by the new function of the table.

Our contribution is organized as follows. In section 2 we analyze the challenges of implementing of a pointing device on a common surface. This is followed by an introduction of our technology concept in section 3, and of recorded sensor data in section 4, illustrating how our approach works. In section 5 we provide further detail on the implementation of two tables that we augmented as wireless trackpads, and in section 6 we briefly relate use experience. The final sections 7 and 8 reflect on related research, future work and our main conclusions.

2   Analysis of Everyday Surfaces as Interaction Device

In this section we first consider general challenges in augmenting common surfaces for pointing, and then consider the specific problems arising with the use of load-sensing as basic interface technology.

2.1   Challenges

The following four points are particularly critical for a successful implementation of a ubiquitous pointing device.

Preserving the Original Functionality of the Surface. When adding functionality to objects of everyday life it is important that the original functionality of the artefact is not sacrified. In the case of a table – augmenting the coffee table with a pointing functionality should not enforce a different way of using the table while it is used in its usual way. Even when it is used for pointing it should still be usable for its original purpose. In other words pointing should be still feasible when the table is occupied with objects.

Many Surfaces – one Pointing Device. It is obvious that an interface that is ubiquitous can not be bound to a specific place or artefact. In an ideal case, interaction is possible from everywhere without switching interfaces. In the case of surfaces the challenge is to realise a seamless transition from surface to surface when interacting. The anticipated implementation would allow the user to use any surface – that is convenient at this moment in time – to be used as a pointing device.

Unobtrusive Realisation. Building a ubiquitous interface should not make the table look like a computer. The appearance of artefacts is often one of their main properties. Especially in personal environments furniture and artefacts are an essential part of the interior of a home. Introducing the technology should no require a change in the appearance of a table or shelf. The interface should be a part of a invisible computer – because the interface is often what people perceive as their computer.

Robust and Reliable Implementation. When including sensing capabilities into surfaces it has to be done in a robust and reliable way. The different ways in which surfaces are being used have to be taken into account, e.g. it has to be anticipated that people may sit on a table. Especially when considering home environments reliability and zero maintenance becomes a crucial issue. When designing a solution one should be aware that calibration and maintenance are hindering the deployment of such technologies.

2.2 Load Sensing as Approach to Surface Augmentation

The basic idea of the approach is to interpret the shift in load distribution on the surface as pointing and clicking action. The change in the load distribution is induced by the user's interaction on the surface. Pressing a finger onto the surface and moving it will change the load distribution on the surface. The assumption is that this change can be measured and converted into a pointing action. The hypothesis is that by these means pointing – tracking a finger – anywhere on the surface can be converted into a relative change of a pointer. If during the pointing action there is an increase in pressure followed by a release in pressure at the same position this can be interpreted as a clicking action.

To measure the load distribution the surface has to be placed onto load cells that allow a precise acquisition of the weight on the surface and also how it is distributed. Having the load on each corner it becomes possible to calculate the centre of pressure on the surface and also the absolute weight on the surface. The centre of pressure moves when a users tracks the finger across, but it also moves when objects are placed onto the surface.

The further assumption is that detecting the manual interaction and converting these relative moves of the centre of pressure should allow the generation of relative moves of a pointer. The overall weight represents all the items on the surface (in some cases the weight of the surface itself) and also the manually applied pressure. By analysing the changes to the overall pressure in context of the interaction taking place it becomes possible to determine when there is a click operation performed.

These assumptions made here are tested with experiments gaining data sets as described in section 4.

2.3 Problems Arising with Load Sensing

To realise the idea of using load sensing technologies to add pointing capabilities to a surface further obstacles have to be overcome.

Changing Load on the Surface. The load on the surface is changing also without it being used as a pointing device. E.g. what is on a table changes over time, objects are moved, taken away, and put down. These events have to be discriminated from the user interaction that is made to interact with the computer. The algorithms have to take into account that the base load may change.

Recognising Start and End of User Interaction. The user interacts with the surface in two different ways – using the original functionality and using it as a pointing device. E.g. it is essential to recognize whether someone puts a cup of tea on the table or someone is pointing.

Distributed Sensing. Using more than one surface makes it necessary to have distributed sensing. Each surface is a load sensing platform, but the resulting interaction should be coherent as coming from one input device. Communication between the backend – e.g. the computer the pointer is attached to – and the various sensing devices is required.

Sampling Speed and High Resolution. To acquire the user interaction with high precision it is necessary to sample the load cells output very quickly and also with a high resolution of the analog-digital conversion. Most commerciality available solutions for scales and weighing technologies sample with high resolution but very slow just a few readings a second.

Noise due to interaction. Surfaces are connected to other parts of the environment, e.g. furniture is standing on the floor and shelves are mounted to the wall. Interacting in such an environment the user may introduce noise into the load sensing system by walking around or leaning against a wall. Because the acquisition is done with high precision walking up to the table may already change the load distribution on the table slightly.

3 Load Sensing to Detect Point and Click Interactions

In order to realise pointing and clicking on a surface based on load sensing technology it must be possible to calculate changes in position and other actions from the forces measured.

3.1 Acquisition of the 2D Position

The anticipated setup consists out of a flat surface (e.g. the top of a table) that is supported by four load cells, one in each corner. Load cells are sensors that measure the force that is applied; they are typically used in scales to indicate the weight. Here the obvious rule summing the forces from all 4 load cells are equal to the force created by the weight of the surface and the objects on to of the surface. Scales typically offer a mechanism to subtract a base weight (tare) so that only the object placed on the surface are considered. Applying manual pressure onto the surface, will increase the forces on the corresponding load cells.

Depending on the position of the surface where an object is placed or where pressure is applied the forces measured at the individual load cells are different. To find the point where the object is placed or pressure is applied it is necessary to map the load measured at each corner onto the 2d layout of the surface, see figure 1.

Assuming a static force F_x is applied at position x, y on a surface of the size x_{max} by y_{max} forces in each corner F_1, F_2, F_3, and F_4 can be measured. Using the following equation the position can be calculated:

$$F_x = F_1 + F_2 + F_3 + F_4 \qquad \text{(Equation 1)}$$

$$x = (F_2 + F_3)\frac{x_{max}}{F_x} \qquad \text{(Equation 2)}$$

$$y = (F_3 + F_4)\frac{y_{max}}{F_x} \qquad \text{(Equation 3)}$$

Summing up the forces of all load cells gives the total, see equation 1. Knowing the forces and the overall size of the surface (or more precise the corners where the surface touches the load cells), the centre of pressure can be calculated, see equations 2 and 3. When more than one object is placed in the surface or when pressure is applied at more than one point, the calculation results in a point in between.

As mentioned earlier usually the surface itself has a weight, too. For calculating the position of an object or a point of pressure this has to be taken into account, see equations4, 5 and 6. In an environment where objects are placed and removed from the surface this tare-weight is changing. By keeping track of changes that became stable, e.g. typically objects that have been placed on the surface, or objects that have been removed; it is possible to dynamically adjust the tare-weight. Knowing the pre-load it is still possible to find the position of objects or interaction. These pre-loads to the surface result in forces denoted as $F0_1$, $F0_2$, $F0_3$, and $F0_4$. The sum of the pre-load is $F0_x$. To calculate the position where pressure is applied in a setting where already load is on the surface equation 4, 5, and 6 can be used.

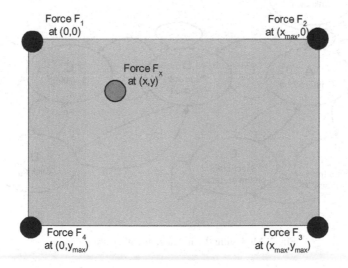

Fig. 1. Determining the 2D position using 4 Load sensors.

$$FO_x = FO_1 + FO_2 + FO_3 + FO_4 \qquad \text{(Equation 4)}$$

$$x = ((F_2 - FO_2) + (F_3 - FO_3))\frac{x_{\max}}{(F_x - FO_x)} \qquad \text{(Equation 5)}$$

$$y = ((F_3 - FO_3) + (F_4 - FO_4))\frac{y_{\max}}{(F_x - FO_x)} \qquad \text{(Equation 6)}$$

3.2 Interacting with Surfaces

To understand and model interaction with a surface we looked at the states that occur and events that can happen. The resulting state diagram, depicted in figure 2, becomes the foundation for the software that translates changes recorded by the load cells into mouse movements and events.

In the following, we characterize the states and also some of the transitions. The variable used to explain are the forces here as discrete values over time: $F_1(t)$, $F_2(t)$, $F_3(t)$, $F_4(t)$. Representing the load measured by each of the load cells on which the surface is resting at time t. The coordinates of the position of the centre of pressure at time t is denoted p(t) or as its components x(t) and y(t).

When starting up there is no knowledge available in what state the surface is, this is denoted by state X. In our model we have decided that this state can only be left via a transition to the state "no interaction". The transition from X to A occurs when the sums of absolute changes of the forces over the last n discrete time steps is close to zero (ε instead of 0 to overcome problems with noise), see Equation 7. This means that the only transition takes place when the forces on the surface do not change.

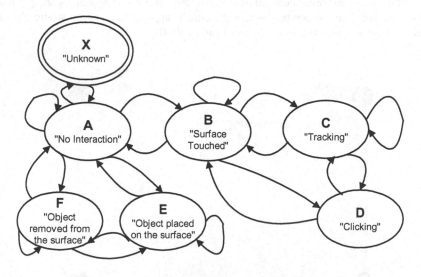

Fig. 2. Modelling the interaction with a surface.

$$\sum_{i=1..4} \sum_{j=(t-n)..(t-1)} |(F_i(t) - F_i(j))| < \varepsilon \qquad \text{(Equation 7)}$$

The system stays in state A as long as this condition is true. The value for ε may be slightly greater than for entering the state so minimal change in the load distribution on the surface are not overlooked. The state A is independent of the pre-load that is applied to the surface; as long as forces are static – e.g. from objects that have been placed onto the surface previously – they have no influence. When the system is in state A also the values for the pre-load $F0_y$ and $F0_x$ are set. The equation assumes noise-free data. However, to deal with noise instead of the raw values for $F_i(t)$ a filtered value can be used, see the next section. From state A transitions to B, E, F, and X are possible.

The state B is reached when the system recognizes that the user has put her finger onto the surface. The transition from A into B is characterized by a monotonous increase in the sum of load over all load cells over the transition time. This leads to the first derivative being greater or equal 0. Instead of calculating the first derivative the simple condition $F_x(t) < F_x(t+1)$ can be used to check whether or not this criteria is met. Furthermore, the sum of the forces has to be in a certain interval (D_{min}, D_{max}), see equation 8.

$$(F(t)_x - F0(t)_x > D_{min}) \wedge$$
$$(F(t)_x - F0(t)_x < D_{max}) \qquad \text{(Equation 8)}$$

The transition from B to A, e.g. when lifting the finger off the surface is similar, only the derivative is less or equal 0 in this case.

As long as the position is not changing over the last n readings and the force is in the interval used in equation 8, the system stays in this state. As there is manual interaction on the surface the forces are not quite stable and therefore a further condition can be stated: the square of sums of changes of the forces over the last n discrete time steps is greater than a threshold δ, see equations 9.

$$\sum_{j=(t-n)..(t-1)} |(F_x(t) - F_x(j))| > \delta$$
$$\sum_{j=(t-n)..(t-1)} |(p(t) - p(j))| < \varepsilon \qquad \text{(Equations 9)}$$

From state B transitions to C, D, and A are possible. When in the state tracking (C) it is assumed that the user is moving a finger on the surface resulting in a change of the measured centre of pressure (δ_p), see equation 10. Other features are similar to the state B. When the user stops moving, a transition to B occurs.

$$\sum_{j=(t-n)..(t-1)} |(p(t) - p(j))| > \delta_p \qquad \text{(Equation 10)}$$

While the surface is touched an increased pressure at the same point is resulting in a change to state D (clicking). This transition occur when the system is in state B or C. The state clicking is characterized by the fact that within a given time span (e.g. about a second) the overall load is first increased and then decreased. The position of the centre of gravity however stays roughly the same. The increase must be in a predefined interval stating a threshold which separates clicking from the changes that occur while tracking. It also should not exceed a maximum force.

The states E and F are specific to surfaces that are used to put things on temporally. The state "object placed on the surface" (E) is similar to touching the surface. However, after the object has been placed, the weight distribution is stable again. When this is recognized, a transition is made back to the state A and the initial load is updated with the new weight. Similarly when an object is removed from the surface (F), this will lead to a change in the weight distribution and possibly to a change of the centre of pressure. However, after the object is taken away the system will be stable again. In this case, the initial weight distribution will be updated with the new values for each of the load cells, too. In this way also multiple objects can be placed on the surface or taken away.

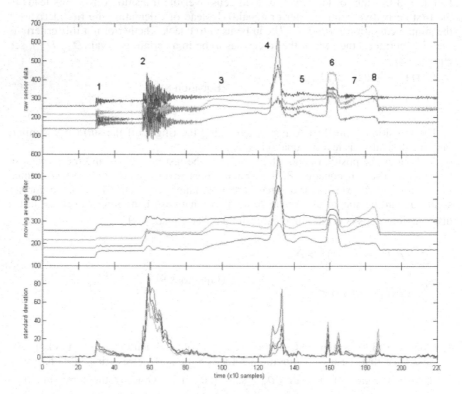

Fig. 3. Load sensing data during various events: (1) placing a cup onto the coffee table, (2) placing a book next to it, (3) putting the index in the middle of the table, pressing slightly, and moving to the right, (4) 'clicking', (5) going back to the left, (6) 'clicking', (7) going more to the left, and (8) 'clicking' and releasing. The top plot shows the raw sensor data, the middle and bottom plots the moving average and standard deviation over 10 samples respectively. Notice how moving the index over the surface is clearly visible, for example at (7), and the value of the standard deviation to pick out significant events.

When objects are placed on the surface or removed from the surface while a tracking action or a click action is performed (in state C or D) this becomes much harder to recognize. Initial data analyses shows, that it may be possible, but we excluded these case in our first implementation.

4 Analysis of Load Sensor Data

We build an experimental data acquisition setup, using 2 different types of load cells and two table tops (see the implementation section for details). Various data sets have been recorded and plotted to gain an understanding of the load data measured during typical interaction. We were particularly interested in events such as putting down objects, removing objects, moving the finger over the surface, and increasing pressure at a certain point while tracking.

The dataset presented here contains typical sensor data from the load cells that has been gathered to demonstrate the feasibility of the approach. Our particular interest was in investigating tracking and clicking on a populated surface as well as putting down different objects onto the surface. The dataset is from a small 80x80cm coffee table, on which two objects were placed, after which it was used to track the movement direction of the finger, plus the force that was used on it to identify a 'clicking' event.

Figure 3 shows the time series plot of the dataset, where the raw sensor data is plotted in time against its filtered moving average and standard deviation (See the figure caption for a concise description of the events). The interval over which these statistics were evaluated was experimentally verified at 10 samples.

We have also recorded data sets using considerably larger surfaces (such as a dining table, 135x75 cm approximately) and less sensitive load cells. Although there is a less distinguishable response for events in the standard deviation plot, peeks remain present, albeit with a significant difference between objects being placed onto the surface, and the user directly touching it.

The basic statistics based on averaging and standard deviation can effortlessly be implemented on small microprocessor. This approach proved to be sufficient in our first prototypes to let the user control a mouse cursor on a nearby computer screen. This can also be deduced from Figure 3, where standard deviation of the raw sensor signals gives distinct peaks whenever new pressure points are introduced, whether they are from an object that has been placed on the surface, or from explicit user interaction.

Although the moving average filter over 10 samples produced satisfactory results for our initial tracking purposes, we believe that using more elaborate tracking algorithms (such as a Kalman filter, see [20] for an excellent introduction) could enhance performance even more, with a negligible cost in implementation.

The dataset presented here and other datasets are available for download at the project website at [11].

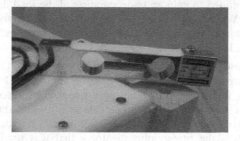

Fig. 4. Coffee table with build in load cells.

5 System Implementation

Based on the experience gained we implemented a distributed ubiquitous pointing system. It incorporates two tables that offer pointing capabilities and that are connected over a wireless link to a device that is attached to a PC emulating a serial mouse.

5.1 Tracking Tables

We converted two of the shelf tables into pointing devices by building load cells between the supporting structure and the table top. To explore the possibilities we used two different tables and different types of load cells.

The coffee table is equipped with load cells that measure a maximal load of 1kg each, so that the surface can reliably measure 4kg of load, see figure 5. A mechanical overload protecting is build into the table. If the table is in overload state (e.g. someone is sitting on the table) pointing is suspended.

For the dining table we used 4 load cells each capable of measuring load up to 50kg, resulting into an overall load of 200kg. Each load cell is robust against overload up to 100kg to ensure the system will not break under exceptionally high load. The

Fig. 5. Resting point and load cell mounted under the table top of a dinning table.

load cells are mounted to the table top and on the legs of the table frame there are planes where the load cells rest. See figure 4 and the accompanying video for details.

5.2   Data Acquisition and Communication

The load cells used on the small table are essentially a wheat stone bridge providing a maximal output signal of 20mV when the driving voltage is 5V. This output signal is amplified by a factor of 220, resulting in a output signal of 0 to 4.4V (different values apply for the larger table). The amplified output voltage of each of the load cells is then converted into a digital value using the AD converter in the MCU, sampling each at 250Hz. The four input values correspond to $F_1(t)$, $F_2(t)$, $F_3(t)$, and $F_4(t)$.

The microcontroller (PIC16F876) is initialized with the size of the table and calculates the position of the centre of pressure. If it is recognized that the table is in the "no interaction" state (A) the values for $F0_1$, $F0_2$, $F0_3$, and $F0_4$ are updated with the average over the last 16 readings. Whenever the state "tracking" (C) is recognized the relative change is calculated and is communicated. When the state "clicking" (D) is recognized by the software on the microcontroller this is also communicated as a button press event.

The communication is done wireless using a RF transceiver module (Radiometrix BIM2) that offers up to 64kbit/s. As the amount of data to communicate is very small and in order to get a better error performance, we run the protocol at 19200 bits/s. Events, either tracking or clicking, are communicated in one packet, which consists of a preamble, followed by a start-byte, the identifier of the objects (coffee table or dinning table), an identifier stating that it is a mouse event, and then the offset in x, the offset in y, and the click state. Finally two bytes of 16-bit CRC are attached to ensure that the transmitted data is correct. The unit only transmits data, no acknowledgement for packets are performed, using a lower transmission speed proved very reliable and also loosing a mouse movement or a button state is generally uncritical.

The block diagram of the system is depicted in figure 6 and a labelled photo is shown in figure 7. The full schematic and further information on the components are available from the project web page [11].

5.3 Mouse Emulation

The ubiquitous pointing device is attached to a PC via serial line. On the PC no extra software is needed. The protocol used is the Microsoft mouse protocol, consisting of three 7 bit words coding the button states and the relative movement since the last packet was sent. The same hardware as for data acquisition with different software is used as a base station receiving the pointing operations from the tables and converting them into the serial Microsoft mouse format. When no packets are received the units sends from time data that indicates zero movements to the PC. When receiving the packets from the RF-transceiver and converting them into a mouse data stream it is not differentiated from where the events have come from. For the PC it looks as a stream of mouse movements and events from a single mouse.

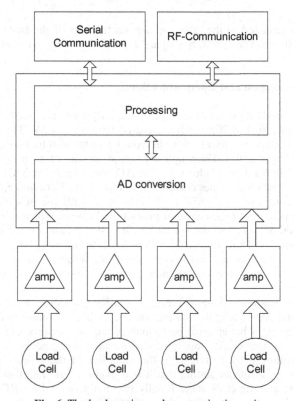

Fig. 6. The load sensing and communication unit.

Fig. 7. Microcontroller unit for load sensing, data acquisition, and wireless communication.

5.4 Access Control

In the implementation we omitted to enforce access control. When on two surfaces tracking and clicking actions are performed they are multiplexed into one stream of events. In longer time intervals that is very reasonable, e.g. using the coffee table to switch to another TV program and walking over to get some food and switching off the TV from the dining table. However, in competitive situations where more people are pointing at the same time the outcome is not meaningful. As the envisioned use cases are in spaces where people communicate with each other we decided to leave access control to be a social factor.

In case where a strict access/token control is required an implementation using locking mechanism are straight forward. Whenever tracking or pointing action from one device is received all other devices are locked out till the device communicates a "no interaction" state or a timeout has passed.

6 Use Experience

The described system has been fully implemented and installed in the Innovative Interactions Lab at Lancaster. This is an environment designed to flexibly recreate domestic settings with everyday furniture, facilitating research into augmented everyday environment. Part of this lab has been fully augmented with load sensing as described in an earlier publication [21].

Following the initial installation of the trackpad-enabled tables we first conducted trials to establish reliability and robustness of the technology under simulated real-world conditions. This involved use of the surfaces for controlling a web browser on an adjacent screen, in the presence of other interactions on the surface, such as placement and removal of books, use of coffee cups, and so on. The technology proved to be perfectly reliable in detecting the correct interaction state, ie. not mistaking object placement as click for example. Some of these test sessions have been video taped for closer inspection of sensor-level observation and signal analysis in relation to carried out interactions.

A second set of tests involved a larger number of users from other research groups at the Department. These users were all highly familiar with the use of the mouse as pointing device. The test was aimed to establish whether a regular user of mouse or trackpad devices would experience any difficulty in using our embedded technology. All of these users found our system intuitively usable, and were instantly able to control a mouse on a screen, and to apply this in conjunction with our web browsing scenario. An interesting observation though was that the surface quality influenced use experience. One of the tables had a nicely polished wood finish whereas the wood grain on the other could still be felt. Tracking on the first surface was much more pleasant than on the second. On the second surface we could also observe that people tried using objects that where on the table, such as a book or a lighter, instead of their finger for pointing. In some instances, we covered the rough surface with a glass plate halfway through the test, and feedback from users generally indicated that the smoother surface greatly improved usability.

As an installation in the Innovative Interactions Lab, the trackpad-enabled tables continue to be used spontaneously in particular with visitors. Spontaneous use without particular maintenance or preparation further supports our claim that the technology is robust, reliable, and intuitively usable.

7 Related Work

Interaction in non-desktop environments is a central research question addressed in many projects recently. In [9] a number of issues are addressed that arise from putting computing into everyday surroundings. Ethnographic research carried out in such environments, which differ significantly from work desktop environments, suggests that tables often are the centre of interaction [5].

Tables have been investigated as computing and CSCW platform in various projects. In most projects the focus is to integrate input and output media into the table and create a new interactive experience. An advanced system of this type of user interface is described in [6]. In our work we deliberately concentrated on using tables as input devices only while preserving their original properties and expression. The InteracTable [15] is a table that offers both input and output. A touch screen technology is used for the input, however, which makes the table rather an additional computing device than a table with additional capabilities, as objects can not be placed on the table surface.

A different approach to realize ubiquitous pointing is to provide the user with an additional device. An example of a generalized contextual remote control is presented in [2]. The FieldMouse is an approach to realizing ubiquitous interaction as well [14]. Its extension, using barcode tagging offers a general mechanism for interaction that is related to physical objects [12]. In contrast to our work the interface is a device that the user carries along rather than a direct interaction opportunity within the environment.

In [4], issues and techniques that are relevant in the process of designing touch sensitive input devices are presented. A comprehensive directory of input devices is also maintained at [3] by the same author.

Load cells and force sensing has been used in a number of projects where ground reaction forces were used as additional or alternative input. A tiled floor that can distinguish people was presented in [1], while a similar arrangement using a single floor tile is describe in [13]. Experiments in these publications show that ground reaction forces are different between people and can therefore be used to discriminate them. The tiled floor was also used as input device to a computing game [8]. For measuring the ground reaction force, especially in biometrics, commercial products such as the Kistler Plate [10] are available as well. Using load cells in our prototype we exploit the same phenomenon, however the forces introduced are intended to be from explicit manual interaction rather than from walking or jumping.

8 Discussion and Future Work

The implementation and use of the trackpad-enabled tables leads to some interesting observations and considerations for future work.

The implementation of the state transitions requires selection of threshold values. In general a trade-off between two approaches, defensive or optimistic, exists. In the defensive version actions and events are only performed when the recognition algorithm is absolute sure that the event was performed. This usually introduces some delay or the interaction is not performed at all. The optimistic approach performs actions and events even when the recognition algorithm is not quite sure if the event has really occurred.

The sensor pattern created when putting an object onto the surface, for instance, is often similar to the initial phase of the tracking. In a defensive approach the system waits till it can reliably discriminate the two actions and only performs tracking when it is sure that the action is tracking, as opposed to it being an object that has been put down. In an optimistic approach, the data is used from the very start to move the pointer and when it is recognized that it was an object pointing is suspended. Our experience showed that immediate reaction is a critical feature for novel users, and therefore our implementation leans towards an optimistic pointing behavior, risking displacement of the pointer when the system gets it wrong. For the clicking we implemented a defensive approach, as clicks tend to be unacceptable at the wrong location.

In casual settings we also realized that people often put their elbows onto the edges of the table, while no pointing takes place. This can easily be detected using position information, also providing a means to adjust to the orientation of the user that is sitting in front of the surface. This could also offer a solution to the table top orientation problem discussed in [7]. We assume as a rule that during pointing the elbows are not placed on the surface. The current implementation showed also that the captured data is most critical for determining the user interaction. The second hardware generation will therefore contain increased precision amplifiers and 24bit A/D converter to increase the quality of the sensor data.

In the wireless protocol from the surface to the base station, the additional information on which surface the interaction took place is communicated as well. This information is not being used at this point, as it has solely been connected as a serial mouse so far. However, it could prove interesting to use this as contextual information on where the pointing action was performed.

9 Conclusions

This paper proposes the use of load sensors on the corners of a surface as an affordable alternative to traditional pointing methods, using infrastructure that is present in every home and office environment.

Both experiments and prototype implementations indicate that it is feasible to add pointing capabilities to traditional tables without scarifying or interfering with the original properties and intended use. Initial experiences while running the prototypes in our living lab environment show a potential and suggested also further improvements.

Acknowledgements. This research was made possible with funding from the UK Engineering and Physical Sciences Research Council for the Equator IRC (EPSRC GR/N15986/01, http://www.equator.ac.uk/), and from the Commission of the European Union for the Smart-Its project (IST-2000-25428, http://www.smart-its.org/).

References

1. Addlesee, M.D., Jones, A., Livesey, F., and Samaria, F. ORL Active Floor. *IEEE Personal Communications*, Vol.4, No 5, Oct 1997, pp. 35–41.
2. Beigl, M.. Point & Click – Interaction in Smart Environments, *Proc. 1st Intl Symposium on Handheld and Ubiquitous Computing* (HUC99), Karlsruhe, Germany, October 1999, Lecture Notes in Computer Science No. 1707, Springer-Verlag, pp 311–314.
3. Buxton, B. A directory of sources for input technologies. 2002.
    http://www.billbuxton.com/InputSources.html
4. Buxton, W., Hill, R. and Rowley, P., *Issues and Techniques in Touch-Sensitive Tablet Input* in Proceedings of Siggraph '85 (July 22–26, San Francisco), ACM/Siggraph, 1985, pp. 215–224
5. Crabtree, A., Hemmings, T. and Rodden, T.. Pattern-based Support for Interactive Design in Domestic Settings. *Technical Report Equator-01-016*, University of Nottingham, The School of Computer Science and IT, December 2001.
    http://www.equator.ac.uk/papers/Authors/crabtree.html
6. Deitz, P. and Leigh, D. (2001). DiamondTouch: A Multi-User Touch Technology. *Proc. of UIST'01*, pp. 219–226.
7. Hancock, M.S. Mandryk, R. L. Scott, S. D, Inkpen, K. M. Determining User-Location at Interactive Tabletops. *Submitted to CHI 2002*
    http://www.sfu.ca/~mhancock/portfolio/tableaware.html
8. Headon, R. and Curwen R. Ubiquitous Game Control. In *UBICOMP Workshop on Designing Ubiquitous Computing Games*. Atlanta, 2001.

9. Kidd, Cory D., Robert J. Orr, Gregory D. Abowd, Christopher G. Atkeson, Irfan A. Essa, Blair MacIntyre, Elizabeth Mynatt, Thad E. Starner and Wendy Newstetter. The Aware Home: A Living Laboratory for Ubiquitous Computing Research. *In the Proceedings of the Second International Workshop on Cooperative Buildings – CoBuild'99*. Position paper, October 1999.
10. Kistler force plate. http://www.kistler.com/
11. Lancaster University, Embedded load sensing project http://www.comp.lancs.ac.uk/~albrecht/load/
12. Masui, T., Siio, I.. Real-World Graphical User Interfaces. *In Proceedings of the International Symposium on Handheld and Ubiquitous Computing* (HUC2000), pp.72–84, , 2000.9.25–27.
13. Orr, R. J. and Abowd G. D. The Smart Floor: A Mechanism for Natural User Identification and Tracking. *In Proceedings of CHI 2000 Human Factors in Computing Systems* (April 1–6, 2000, The Hague, Netherlands), ACM/SIGCHI.
14. Siio, I., Masui, T., Fukuchi, K. "Real-world Interaction using the FieldMouse" *CHI Letters, Vol.1, Issue 1* (Proceedings of the UIST'99), pp.113–119, ACM Press, Nov. 7–10,1999
15. Streitz, N.A., Geißler, J., Holmer, T., Konomi, S., Müller-Tomfelde, C., Reischl, W., Rexroth, P., Seitz, P., and Steinmetz, R. i-LAND: An interactive Landscape for Creativitiy and Innovation. *Proc. CHI '99*, Pittsburgh, PA, U.S.A., May 15–20, 1999. ACM Press, New York, pp. 120–127.
16. Ishii, H. and Ullmer, B., "Tangible Bits: Towards Seamless Interfaces between People, Bits and Atoms," Proceedings of Conference on Human Factors in Computing Systems (CHI '97), ACM, Atlanta, March 1997, pp. 234–241.
17. Elin Rønby Pedersen, Tomas Sokoler: AROMA: Abstract Representation of Presence Supporting Mutual Awareness. CHI 1997: 51–58
18. M. Weiser, "The Computer for the 21st Century," *Scientific American* 265, No. 3, 94–104 (September 1991).
19. Wellner P, Mackay W, Gold R (1993). Computer-Augmented Environments: Back to the Real World. Communications of the ACM, 36(7), pp. 24–26.
20. Welsch, G. and Bishop G. An introduction to the Kalman Filter. *TR 95–041*, Department of Computer Science, University of North Carolina at Chapel Hill. March, 2002.
21. A. Schmidt, M. Strohbach, K. Van Laerhoven, A. Friday and H.W. Gellersen. Context acquisition based on Load Sensing. Proc. Ubicomp 2002, Gothenburg, Sweden, Sept. 2002.
22. A. Schmidt. Implicit Human Computer Interaction Through Context. In *Personal Technologies* Volume 4(2&3), June 2000. pp 191–199.

3D-Audio News Presentation Modeling

Safia Djennane

Siemens Corporate Research, Inc.
755 College Road East, Princeton, New Jersey. 08540 USA.
sdjennane@scr.siemens.com

Abstract. With the emergence of the mobile Internet combined with wearable personal computing, we are now entering a new information era where PCs are self-adapting their resources to human bodies, minds and preferences, prevailing a more effective work environment. In this new world, working effectively is inextricably related to accessing reliable information sources when needed. Therefore, people eager to stay connected, consume daily information in a myriad of forms: news, weather, business, road/traffic reports, voicemails, emails, as well as information associated to their daily activities or interests. In this paper, we propose innovative UI information presentations based on three-dimensional (3D) audio modeling. In this framework, we illustrate how news, weather and business reports are extracted, spatialized and presented to end-users using 3D audio modality.

1 Introduction

Presenting information to mobile users on wearable computers is a challenging process as mobility and device wearability impose many UI constrains. Users should be able to move and perform daily activities independently from any computational unit. In Siemens Corporate Research (SCR), we are working on methods to present HTML documents using 3D audio technology [10], [11]. Our ultimate goal is to augment user's real world with useful spatialized audio information automatically generated by a computer. We believe that in the upcoming mobile, wearable, pervasive and ubiquitous computing technologies, these innovative UIs will be better suitable to the new computational world. In this paper, we present innovative UI information presentations based on 3D audio modeling. In section 2, we present some related projects addressing similar 3D-audio research work. Section 3 describes three models for audio news spatialization and presentations. Section 4 details the framework components, functionality and architecture. In section 5, we conclude and address future directions for this work.

2 Related Work

Sound has always been used to illustrate system functions [4] [7] [9], for debugging [8] [9], in audio-only or multimodal human-computer interfaces [2] [12] [14]. More recently, spatialized audio is becoming more appealing for new areas such as augmented reality, wearable, ubiquitous or pervasive computing [1] [3]. The *Aura project* [1] is an example of a visionary philosophy aiming to build a pervasive environment, where the decision maker can roam around and being able to keep

N. Carbonell, C. Stephanidis (Eds.): User Interfaces for All, LNCS 2615, pp. 280–286, 2003.
© Springer-Verlag Berlin Heidelberg 2003

contact with a main computer unit. This latter one takes charge of analyzing the changing environment and adapting the UI to the user's vicinity. *Audio aura* [16], in particular focuses on augmenting the real world with 3D auditory lightweight cues. The cues are personalized information (meeting, alert, email, news...etc) projected in the 3D space around the mobile user. Although, the philosophy is outstanding in terms of perspectives, the implementation of the idea is still at its early stages. *Nomadic Radio* (NR) is a radiobroadcast messaging and notification system for voicemail, news, calendar, weather and music on wearable computers [16] [17]. The system is based on spatial presentation of digital audio by defining a clock-type metaphor around the user head. The position of the sound source in the space reflects the time of the arrival of the message (voicemails, news etc). Although the clock metaphor is very appealing because it is very intuitive, this work is limited in the use of the 3D space and doesn't take into account the multiple human 3D audio possible perceptions. In [10], an audio-only browser is described to present HTML structured documents. The browser projects the document's content in a semi arc area in front of the listener, called *stage-arc*. The document's content is rendered using Text-To-Speech synthesis. In another paper, the authors detail a streaming method to deliver audio presentations to Personal Digital Assistant devices (PDAs) using 3D audio SMIL [13]. The streaming approach is interesting regarding to the limited resources constrains of the small devices. Nevertheless, streaming QoS is not highly efficient and relies on the server-client and/or protocol architecture. Additionally, this work's focus is to build a client-server architecture to support the streaming delivery method. Therefore, the work doesn't address the type/content of information to be delivered to the client side; nor how this information will be presented. Our paper extends this latter work to address these issues by:

- Proposing an initial study on information 3D audio modeling, taking into account the information type (news, weather, business etc.) and the human 3D audio perception capabilities,
- Enabling an automatic extraction, processing and delivery of the 3D audio augmented information content.
- Proposing a flexible UI where users can configure at their convenience, the type of 3D audio experience they would like to hear.

3 News, Weather & Business Information Modeling

In this paper, we selected the news as an example of information to be spatialized and presented. News is the most daily consulted information by the public as well as weather and business reports. The typical scenario in this case, is to provide a user with a 3D audio experience listening to news. The user wears an ear set (as shown in figures below), that is connected to a computational unit (cellular phone, PDA etc). This section describes audio models for presenting news, weather and business reports in 3D audio space above the user's head.

3.1 One Speaker Model

In this model, the listener is hearing to a moving speaker voice, announcing the news content over his/her head. The voice starts from the left to the right side following an arc trajectory (C.f. figure). This model can also be implemented using a single static speaker where the voice is coming from a fixed position on the space over user's head. This model is inspired by a one-man news show reading the news content. In the same time, the listener can also hear weather and business reports presented and repeated as the

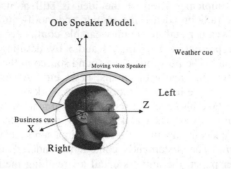

One Speaker Model.

news is rendered. The weather is reported by an audio message such as *"Current temperature is X degrees. Rainy."* coming from the back left side of the ear. The business report, on the other hand, is presented by another audio message such as *"Dow Jones is up by Y %. Nasdaq is down by Z% etc"*, coming from the right backside of the ear (C.f. figure). All three audio messages are rendered in parallel.

3.2 Two Speakers Model

In this model, we propose two speakers to announce the news: a male and a female voices. This model is obviously inspired by a TV news show model, where two journalists (a male and a female) are presenting news content. In the 3D audio presentation, the speakers' voices are positioned in fixed locations on opposite sides, over the listener's head and are taking turns. As the speakers are presenting the news, weather and business reports are announced

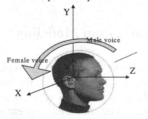

Two fixed-position speakers Model.

and repeated in parallel in the same pattern shown in the previous model (Cf section 3.1).

3.3 Headline-Oriented Model

In this model, we present news by headlines. The headline content is announced by a voice from a fixed location on the arc trajectory. In this model, we suggest that the main headline is recognized by it center position and the accessory news being on the edges of the trajectory arc. In this model, we use either a single or multiple voices to announce the news content. Selecting accentuated voices when dealing with foreign headlines is an suggested enhancement to this model. The model does also include weather and business reports presented from the backside of the head.

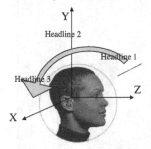

Three fixed-position headlines Model.

The three news models are clearly influenced by the particular nature of the information i.e. news, weather and business reports and how people are used to perceive the TV or radio news shows. The trajectory above the user's head has been selected after multiple testings for the best location to listen to a continous stream. This resulting trajectory pattern, i.e "the arc", heuristically fits well the news, weather and business reports information type. Obviously, other type of information would lead to other modeling patterns.

4 Framework Architecture

In order to provide a user with an up-to-date 3D audio experience listening to the daily news; we implemented this framework, so that the system extracts news content from pre-selected sources (URLs). The news content is refreshed periodically and updated presentations are rebuilt and delivered to the user. Once the news content is extracted, the audio presentations (or scenes) are described in 3D-SMIL documents. **SMIL** is a language for describing and presenting interactive synchronized multimedia distributed on the Web. SMIL 2.0 in its current version is unable to provide constructors to describe 3D-audio scenes. In order to support this description, SMIL has been extended to include additional elements for 3D audio scenes specifications (Cf. section 4.1). To deploy its functionality, the framework uses:

- An extraction module, which fetches the news content periodically,
- A 3D-SMIL language parser to validate the 3D-audio scene specifications,
- A 3D audio spatializer to construct and render the 3D audio scene.
- And the configuration module to set up user's preferences for the 3D audio model,

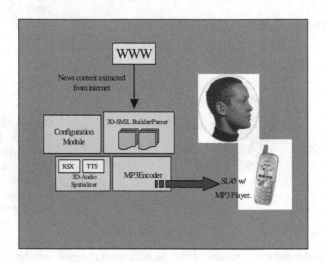

The 3D-SMIL documents describing the audio scenes are parsed and validated by the parser module and passed them on to the spatializer, which implements the 3D-Audio scenes creation and rendering. The audio spatializer uses the Intel 3D Realistic Sound Experience (RSX) toolkit [18] and a Text-To-Speech engine to produce and render the audio scenes. As the audio presentation is delivered to the end-user, we included a MP3 encoder to compress the audio streams, prior to their delivery to the end-user. In this example, the file is routed to a cellular phone integrating a MP3 Player, namely the Siemens SL45 cellular phone.

4.1 3D-SMIL Document Example

In the SMIL document below, we present an example of audio scene specification using 3D-audio SMIL description. In the body section of the document, four stationary audio sources are rendered in parallel *(<par>)* in independent locations. The exact location of the audio object is defined by the *<3Dregion>* element described in the layout section. Moving audio objects are described by trajectories declared by the *<Trajectory>* element, the audio object source follows the trajectory during the rendering and therefore provides the listener with spatial audio experience.

```
<?xml version="1.0" ?>
<Smil>
<trajectory id='traj1'>
<y expression="cos(x)^2+y^2" values="0..4"/>
<x values="-4..4"/>
<z values="0"/>
<head> <layout>
 <3DRegion id="BusinessPos" x ="-4.0" y="0.0" z="-4.0"/>
 <3DRegion id="WeatherPos" x="4.0" y="0.0"   z="-4.0"/>
 < 3DRegion id="NewsMovingPosition" trajectory="traj1"/>
 < 3DRegion id="NewsFixedPosition" x ="0.0" y="4.0" z="0.0"
</layout> </head>
<body>
<par>
<tts voice="Mary" path="NewsPosition"> The widow of murdered Wall Street Journal
reporter Daniel Pearl Tuesday sounded an "alarm for everybody" in Pakistan and across
the globe about international terror groups. This is "a vast and international network of
terrorists," not just a group of extremist Pakistanis, Mariane Pearl told CNN's Chris
Burns in an interview Tuesday. "Wherever there is misery they will find people." </tts>
<audio src="NiceWeather.Wav" path="WeatherPosition"/>
<audio src="CurTemp.Wav" path="WeatherPosition"/>
<audio src="MarketInfo.Wav" path="BusinessPosition"/>
</par>
</body>
</Smil>
```
Example1: 3D-SMIL specification

5 Conclusion

This work deals with using human 3D audio perception to build innovative UI
information presentations. The ultimate goal is to be able to augment user's real world
with useful summarized audio information automatically generated by a computer.
The nature of the information is obviously a critical factor for building such
presentations and even determinant to modeling the audio presentations. Our goal is
to be able to associate for each type of information the best 3D audio presentations
possible. In this paper, we presented an example of news information, which is
automatically extracted, spatialized and presented to the end user. News is the most
consulted daily information by the public and so are daily weather and business
reports. Our preliminary testing of the news modeling showed that users were excited
about the news 3D audio presentations. They were able to locate the audio sources,
movements as well as perceive the news content. However, these testing need to be
completed by a larger population and a real world environment to prove the feasibility
of the approach. Additionally, we would like to extend this work to a larger scale of
information types but also being able to provide advanced navigational tools in the 3D
audio space using for instance head or body gestures.

References

1. http://www-2.cs.cmu.edu/~aura/
2. Back J. Cohen, R. Gold, S. Harrison, S. Minneman., " Listen Reader: An electronically augmented paper-based book ", 2000.
3. L. Babarit, C. Low, "Talkspace: A tool for multi-user 3D audio communications," Proceedings of the Multimedia Conference. 1998.
4. W. Buxton, " Using our ears: An introduction to the use of non-speech audio cues." In extracting meaning from complex data: processing, display, interaction. E.J Farrel Editions, Vol. 1259. SPIE 1990.pp.124–127.
5. Bregman, A., Auditory Scene Analysis: The Perception and Organization of Sound. MIT Press, 1990.
6. J. Cohen, "Monitoring background activities" In Auditory Display: Sonification, Audification, and Auditory Interfaces. Edited by G. Kramer. Addison-Wesley, 1994.
7. C. DiGiano, R. Baecker " Program Auralizaion: Sound Enhancements to the Programming Environment." In Proceedings of the graphics Interface ''92. pp-44–52.
8. J. Francioni, L. Alright, J. Jackson "Debugging parallel Program using sound.", In the processing of ACM workshop on parallel and distributed debugging, Addison-Wesley, 1991.
9. W. Gaver, "Using and creating auditory icons" ICAD, 1992.
10. S. Goose, C. Möller, "A 3D Audio Only Interactive Web Browser: Using Spatialization to Convey Hypermedia Document Structure," Proceedings of the ACM International Conference on Multimedia, Orlando, USA, pages 363+371, October, 1999.
11. S. Goose, S. Kodlahalli, W. Pechter, R. Hjelsvold "Streaming Speech 3: A framework for generating On-demand and streaming compelling 3D Text-To-Speech and Audio Presentations to Wireless PDAs as specified Using Extensions to SMIL," Proceedings WWW Conference, Hawaii, USA, Mai 2002.
12. M. Krueger, D. Gilden "KnowWhere: An audio/Spatial Interface for blind people." 2000.
13. T.Kennedy, M. Slowinski, "SMIL adding multimedia to the web" SAMS editions, 2002.
14. E. Mynatt, W. Edwards, "The Mercator Environment: A Non-visual Interface to the X Window System," Technical Report GIT-GVU-92-05, February 1992.
15. E. Mynatt, M. Back, R.Want., R.Raer., "Designing audio aura," Proceedings of the ACM Conference on Human Factors in Computing Systems (CHI'98), New York, Pages 566–573.
16. N. Sawhney, C. Schmandt, "Design of Spatialized Audio in Nomadic Environments," International Conference on Auditory Display, Xerox PARC, Palo-Alto, November 5, 1997
17. N. Sawhney, C. Schmandt, "Nomadic Radio: Speech and Audio Interaction for Contextual Messaging in Nomadic Environments," ACM Transactions on Human Computer Interface (CHI'2000). Journal Paper, vol. 7 pages 353–385.
18. http://www.intel.com/RSX

Toward Optimization of Multimodal User Interfaces for Tactical Audio Applications

Zeljko Obrenovic[1], Dusan Starcevic[1], and Emil Jovanov[2]

[1] Faculty of Organizational Sciences
The University of Belgrade
Jove Ilica 154, 11000 Belgrade
+381 11 3950 894
{obren@computer.org; starcev@fon.bg.ac.yu}

[2] Electrical and Computer Engineering Dept.
The University of Alabama, 213 EB
Huntsville, AL 35899
(256) 824 5094
jovanov@ece.uah.edu

Abstract. Tactical audio uses audio feedback to facilitate the precise and accurate positioning of an object with respect to some other object. Existing solutions in pointing and trajectory based Human Computer Interface (HCI) tasks have primarily explored visual feedback, sometimes in rather limited conditions. In this paper we have examined different sonification paradigms for tactical audio to improve the accuracy of pursuit tracking. We have developed a multimodal simulation system as an open environment for evaluation of different sonification and visualization techniques in tactical audio applications. The environment is implemented as an audio-visual scene using the Java3D package. The paper presents the quantitative results of of three pursuit tracking applications using a combination of acoustic and visual guidance and different background conditions. Experiments with 19 participants have shown that acoustic presentation improves the quality of human-computer interaction and reduces the error during pursuit tracking tasks for up to 19%. Moreover, experiments have shown that benefits do not exist in all conditions, indicating the existence of perceptual boundaries of multimodal HCI for different scene complexity and target speeds. Significant benefits of audio modes exist for medium complexity of interaction. User's questionnaires indicate that users are not aware of quantitative benefits of applied sonification paradigms. We have shown that the most appealing paradigms are not the most effective ones, which necessitates a careful quantitative analysis of proposed multi-modal HCI paradigms.

1 Introduction

Sonification as acoustic data presentation can significantly improve the quality ofof human computer interaction particularly in the case of virtual/augmented reality systems. One of the most important advantages of sonification in augmented/virtual

N. Carbonell, C. Stephanidis (Eds.): User Interfaces for All, LNCS 2615, pp. 287–298, 2003.

reality systems using audio modes is that a computer generated sonic scene leaves the visual field unimpaired, unobstructed, and ready for investigation of the environment for surprises [1, 2].

However, the use of sound is not panacea and wider acceptance of sonification and tactical audio applications will primarily depend on quality of user interfaces and how quick users can effectively learn to use the environment. Exploration into perceptual features of a plethora of sonification paradigms requires a flexible environment that could be easily customized to suit user or applications needs [3].

In this paper we present our multimodal simulation and training system for tactical audio applications and the quantitative results of experimental evaluation of selected sonification techniques. We investigated different sonification paradigms in customized sonification environments for dynamic target tracking applications. Primary contribution of this paper is experimental evaluation of user interaction in dynamic trajectory-based environments using combination of acoustic and visual guidance. We have shown that acoustic presentation improves the quality of human-machine interaction and reduces the tracking error during guidance tasks.

Typical issues and survey of sonification and tactical audio applications are given in section two. Design and implementation of the environment are presented in section three. Organization of experiments is described in section four, while analysis of results of experiments is given in section five. Results and discussion of user performance is given in section six. Section seven concludes the paper.

2   Sonification and Multimodal Interaction

Sonification is the second most important presentation modality after visualization [4, 5]. Relationship between visualization and sonification is itself a complex design problem, due to the nature of the cognitive information processing. Efficiency of sonification, as acoustic presentation modality, depends on other presentation modalities [6].

Some characteristics of visual and acoustic perception, such as spatio-temporal resolution, are complementary. Therefore, sonification naturally extends visualization. The system that supports sonification must provide the ability to extract the relevant information features. Some useful guidelines about the use of sound and nonspeech audio cues can be found in [7, 8].

It has been shown that the use of sound, especially when coupled with other modalities of interaction, such as pointing and gesturing, improves multimodal interaction [7]. Well-designed multimodal systems integrate complementary modalities to yield a highly synergistic mix in which the strengths of each mode are used to overcome weaknesses in the other. Such systems can function more robustly than unimodal systems [9, 10].

Sonification could be used to facilitate insight into complex phenomena. We have applied sonification of brain electrical activity to improve the presentation of complex spatio-temporal patterns of brain electrical activity [11].

2.1 Tactical Audio

Tactical audio systems use audio feedback to facilitate the precise and accurate positioning of an object with respect to some another object [1, 2]. Tactical audio has valuable applications in the field of surgery. Just as musicians use aural feedback to position their hands, surgeons could position instruments according to a pre-planned trajectory, pre-placed tags or cues, or anatomical models. Although ultrasound and other imaging modalities attempt to alleviate this problem, the nature and configuration of the equipment requires the surgeon to take his/her eyes off the patient. The use of tactical audio feedback enables the surgeon to effect a precise placement by enhancing his/her comprehension of the three-dimensional position of a surgical instrument with respect to some predetermined desired position within the patient's body. This clearly benefits both patient and healthcare provider [2]. However, more research have to be done in order to develop more efficient tactical audio applications.

3   The Design of a Multimodal Simulation System

We have developed a multimodal simulation and training environment for experimental evaluation of different sonification paradigms for tactical audio. The environment allows recording of relevant parameters of user interaction during guidance tasks. The environment is developed in order to support quantitative evaluation of effectiveness of sonification methods and assess user's learning curve in a large population of users [3, 12]. In addition, our goal was to investigate suitability of standard PC software and hardware modules for efficient implementation of tactical audio applications.

3.1   The Architecture

The architecture of the multimodal test environment is shown on Figure 1. The environment consists of an interaction space and a control interface. Main interaction between the user and the environment occurs in the interaction space, where the user tracks animated target on a 2D polygon.

The interaction space consists of a multimodal integration module and of a path interpolator. Multimodal integration module does the multimodal presentation of data. We used one graphics mode in form of animated circle object. In experiments user simply tries to "cover" the center of the target using cursor. We also used two different sound modes: variable position sound object representing target position in 3D acoustic space [13, 14], and variable intensity sound object representing a distance from the target, e.g. the error in tracking of target object. The user could use any combination of these three modes.

Position interpolator calculates new target position on each timer tick using discrete set of coordinates to provide "smooth" trajectory in space/time.

In the control interface user can set various parameters including multimodal combination, speed, and file parameters. It also maintains generation of a path from a text file, and writes the results to a file. A path file is simple text file that contains trajectory of object as discrete set of X and Y coordinates. A result file is a XML file that contains samples of user cursor coordinates together with samples of object coordinates. The result file also contains a description of experimental conditions.

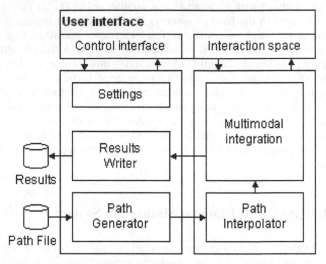

Fig. 1. The architecture of our environment.

Although the environment is used to estimate possible performance improvement using tactical audio support, it is designed flexible in order to allow easy plug-and-play addition of new graphical and acoustic modes.

The environment is based on commercially available technology, implemented using Java3D package [15] and standard Java components. This approach allows transparent execution of the environment on various platforms including stand-alone workstations, as well as distributed Web environment in the form of a Java applet. The Java3D package is primarily used for acoustic 3D effects. This package allows relatively easy real-time manipulation of sound objects .

The environment can be used in two modes: *training* and *experiment* mode. In the training mode a user can arbitrarily set multimodal combination, speed of the object, start and duration of a session. This mode is particularly suitable for user training before the experiment, and for pilot testing of new modes. *Experiment* mode is designated for predefined tests, where users are not allowed to change any of the parameters in the environment. All parameters are preset in a file. The experiment is defined as a sequence of tests. For each test we define speed of the target object, duration of interaction, length of pause between two tests, as well as presentation modes used in the test.

3.2 The Multimodal Presentation Environment

We have developed and tested three presentation variants of the environments in order to facilitate testing of interaction complexity:

- **E1 - Homogenous background**
  The simplest environment presents the circular object that moves over homogenous single-color background.

- **E2 - Static heterogeneous background**
  In this environment the object moves over static heterogeneous background, which effectively adds visual noise to graphical presentation. Static heterogeneous background was simulated with a static picture of the map (Figure 2).

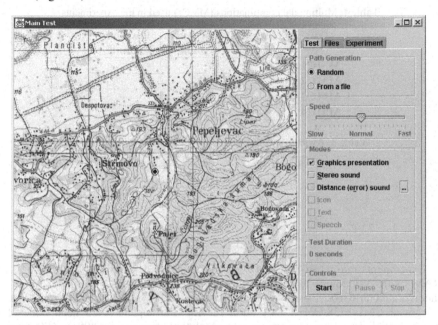

Fig. 2. The user interface of the environment with static heterogeneous background.

- **E3 - Moving background**
  In this variant of the environment the object is part of static heterogeneous background. The object does not move relative to the background. Instead, whole background, including the object, moves across the screen. For example, this way of interaction can be illustrated with aircraft simulation where you have to pursuit a static object on the ground while driving an aircraft.

4 Experiments

Target tracking experiment was conceived to assess user performance in two-dimensional pursuit tracking applications. We organized three experiments, each with one variant of the environment, as described in Chapter 3.2. Experimental setup, parameters, methods and procedures were the same for all tests.

292   Z. Obrenovic, D. Starcevic, and E. Jovanov

4.1 Method

The task of a user was to pursuit a moving object on the screen as close as possible. Target object was positioned according to a predefined trajectory taken from a file, and coordinates of both the target object and the cursor were written to the result file for off-line processing.

We created four multimodal combinations (MMCs) (see Table 1). Each of the multimodal combinations was tested with four object speeds (see Table 2).

Table 1. Multimodal combinations (MMCs) used in the experiments.

	Graphics mode	Distance sound	Positional sound
MMC1	+	-	-
MMC2	+	+	-
MMC3	+	-	+
MMC4	+	+	+

Table 2. Average speeds of the target object in the experiments.

Speed ID	Average speed (pixels per second)
1	50
2	100
3	200
4	300

Experiments ran on an 800 MHz Intel Pentium III desktop PC with 128 MB of RAM with Windows 2000 Professional operating system. Computer had S3 Incorporated Trio3D/2X graphics card, Samsung 15'' SyncMaster 550s monitor and integrated CMI 8738/C3DX PCI audio device. Participants used headphones for better spatial sound perception. Screen resolution was set to 800 x 600 pixels. Dimensions of the interaction space were 500 x 500 pixels. Mouse motion sensitivity was set to medium. Frame rate for the first two experiments was about 50 frames per second, and for experiment E3 it was about 30 frames per second.

4.2 Participants

Nineteen persons participated in experiments. Participants were unpaid volunteers from military academy. Age of the participants ranged from 19 to 30 years. All participants had normal or corrected-to-normal vision and normal hearing, and were right-handed. All of them were regularly use GUI and mouse. Participants were asked to fill a questionnaire that assessed their prior experience with computers and mouse use. Twelve participants completed all three experiments. Sequence of experiments for participants in the group was not the same. Six participants took part in only one experiment, while one participant took part in two experiments.

4.3 Experimental Procedure

All three experiments followed the same procedure. Initially, participants practiced interaction with the environment in the training mode. During this period all the speeds, as well as multimodal combinations covered in experiment were presented to the user.

Each experiment consisted of 16 tests (4 multimodal combination x 4 speeds). Each test lasted for 35 seconds. Total duration of one experiment for each participant was around 10 minutes. This relatively short duration of each test is chosen since longer sessions had resulted in strong finger and wrist fatigue of participants. The experiment started with lowest speed, where all combinations were tested. After that the speed was increased. Before new test at higher speed, participant was able to make a pause. We encouraged participants to rest before proceeding to the next level.

After experiment completion, participants were asked to rank multimodal combinations from one to four, where one represents the best combination.

5 Analysis

Positions of the target object and the cursor were collected directly by the scene generation software. The data were then prepared for statistical analysis by computing values of a tracking error for each trial, and average tracking error for each speed and multimodal combination.

We excluded trials of participants who reported "loss of control" during interaction due to the lack of attention or problems with handling a mouse. We excluded approximately 5% of all trials.

For each sample in all experiments we calculated error as Euclidean distance between user cursor and the target object. After that, we calculated mean error and standard deviation for each multimodal combination and speed. We also calculated benefit ξ of using multi modal HCI compared to pure graphics mode (MMC1) running at the same speed as:

$$\xi = 1 - \frac{error_{AUDIO}}{error_{MMC1}} \tag{1}$$

where $error_{MMC1}$ represents an average error for first multimodal combination (MMC1), and $error_{AUDIO}$ is average error for multimodal combinations with multi modal combinations (MMC2-MMC4) running at the same speed. We defined three relative errors, each for one multimodal combination with sound nodes. We calculated paired T-test between multimodal combinations (MMC2-MMC4) and pure graphics mode (MMC1) for the same target speed.

6 Results and Discussion

Figures 3, 4, and 5 illustrate dependencies among speed, multimodal combination and benefits of multimodal HCI for all three experiments. Values marked with '*' are statistically significant.

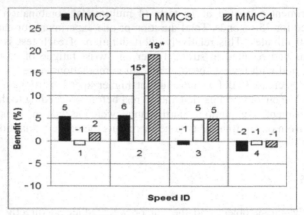

Fig. 3. Benefits of multimodal HCI in the first experiment (Homogenous background).

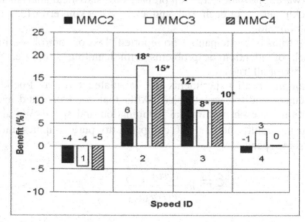

Fig. 4. Benefits of multi-modal HCI in the second experiment (Static heterogeneous background).

It could be seen that the spatial audio mode improved significantly pursuit precision for the second target speed , since benefits of MMC3 and MMC4 combinations were significant and positive for all three experiments. Benefits of MMC3 and MMC4 were in first experiment 15% and 19%, in second experiment 18% and 15%, and in third experiment 14% and 8%. Second experiment exhibited benefits for all audio modes for third speed although these benefits were smaller than in the case of the second target speed (12%, 8%, and 10%). Third experiment has shown significant benefit for distance mode (MMC2) in first speed (18%). For other tests benefits were smaller and not statistically significant.

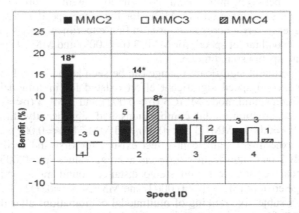

Fig. 5. Benefits of multi-modal HCI in the third experiment (Moving background).

Table 3 summarizes results of the analysis for all experiments. Results are grouped by speed and multimodal combination. Average errors in all three experiments are shown in first three columns, while benefits of using audio modes compared to pure graphical mode for the same speed are shown in last three columns.

Table 3. Average distance errors with standard deviations and benefits multi-modal combinations for all three experiments (E1, E2, E3). Values marked with '*' are statistically significant.

Speed	MMC	Average error in pixels (SD)			Benefit in %		
		E1	E2	E3	E1	E2	E3
1	1	7.40 (2.42)	7.18 (1.60)	7.69 (1.45)			
	2	7.03 (2.05)	7.45 (2.40)	6.55 (1.29)*	5.3	-3.7	17.5
	3	7.47 (2.04)	7.51 (1.68)	7.92 (2.14)	-0.9	-4.4	-2.8
	4	7.27 (3.36)	7.57 (1.92)	7.69 (1.58)	1.7	-5.2	0.1
2	1	12.81 (3.30)	13.74 (3.39)	12.37 (1.68)			
	2	12.14 (2.87)	12.99 (3.91)	11.79 (1.48)	5.6	5.8	4.9
	3	11.17 (2.22)*	11.68 (2.42)*	10.82 (1.73)*	14.7	17.6	14.3
	4	10.76 (1.75)*	11.96 (2.74)*	11.44 (2.00)*	19.1	14.8	8.2
3	1	21.21 (2.60)	24.20 (2.96)	23.19 (2.84)			
	2	21.38 (3.33)	21.57 (3.33)*	22.30 (3.71)	-0.8	12.2	4.0
	3	20.25 (3.49)	22.45 (4.04)*	22.31 (3.42)	4.7	7.8	3.9
	4	20.24 (3.50)	22.09 (4.10)*	22.84 (4.63)	4.8	9.5	1.5
4	1	33.45 (3.79)	36.75 (4.21)	40.18 (6.79)			
	2	34.20 (5.55)	37.24 (5.48)	38.96 (4.86)	-2.2	-1.3	3.1
	3	33.72 (3.79)	35.61 (3.86)	38.92 (6.27)	-0.8	3.2	3.2
	4	33.91 (4.78)	36.70 (5.30)	39.92 (8.86)	-1.4	0.1	0.6

Paired t-tests between multimodal combinations with audio modes (MMC2-MMC4) and pure graphics mode (MMC1) for the same speed revealed significant differences in average error across ten tests. In first experiment only significant effect existed for the second target speed, for MMC3 (p=0.009) and MMC4 (p=0.002). Both combinations use spatial sound mode.

In second experiment significant change can be seen at the second and third target speed. For the second speed significant effect existed for multimodal combination with stereo position sound mode MMC3 (p<=0.002) and MMC4 (p<=0.0009). At the third target speed all multimodal combinations had significantly different average errors, MMC2 (p<=0.001), MMC3 (p<=0.01), and MMC4 (p<=0.002).

In the third experiment significant effect existed for first and second speed. For first speed MMC2 had significantly different average values (p<=0.005). For second speed multimodal combination with stereo distance sound mode had significantly different average errors MMC3 (p<=0.0004) and MMC4 (p<=0.002).

Results of user's subjective ranking of multimodal combinations after the experiment are presented in Table 4:

Table 4. User's evaluation of multimodal combinations. Smaller grade represents better rank.

	Average grade	Rank
MMC1	2.73	3
MMC2	1.55	1
MMC3	3.00	4
MMC4	2.55	2

6.1 Discussion

Experiments have shown that audio modalities could significantly improve the quality of human-computer interaction. Users were more precise when they used multimodal combinations with acoustic modes, but benefits do not exist in all conditions. Experiments have shown that benefits exist only for one or two speeds, indicating perceptual boundaries for efficient use of audio modalities.

Results have shown that complexity of visual presentation, simulated with different backgrounds, also influences benefits of audio modalities, probably because of cognitive overload. This suggests extension of experiments to include other visualization paradigms, in order to find relationship between parameters of visual presentation and benefits of audio modalities.

It is worth noting that multimodal combination with stereo positioning sound (MMC3) had the most stable behavior in all experiments. Figure 6 illustrates dependency between speed and benefits of MMC3 for all experiments.

It is interesting to note that there exists a gap between user's grades and experimental results. Users ranked highest audio distance mode (MMC2), which alone showed statistically significant benefits only twice. On the other hand, user ranked as the worst the stereo position sound (MMC3) which alone showed statistically significant benefits four times. Analysis of users grades indicates that users are not aware of benefits of spatial audio mode.

Our goal was to investigate how much are standard PC software and hardware modules suitable for efficient implementation of tactical audio. For that reason, our experiments ran on relatively inexpensive equipment, using the Java3D packet in spite of some limitations for sounds effects.

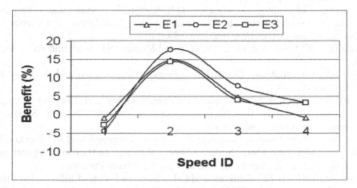

Fig. 6. Benefits of spatial stereo sound for all experiments and different target speed.

7 Conclusion

Tactical audio display, as a tactical aid to achieve precise positional control in pursuit tracking applications, exhibits a significant potential for improved user performance and better quality of human-computer interface. In this paper we have examined different sonification paradigms for tactical audio. Our experimental results indicate that audio can significantly improve the accuracy of pursuit tracking.

We have developed a multimodal simulation system as an open environment for testing of different sonification and visualization paradigms in tactical audio applications. Despite relatively poor audio quality of standard PC systems, the experiments in our environment have shown that acoustic modes improve human computer interaction. In addition, the experiments have shown that benefits are limited by user perception .

Experiments have also shown that users are not aware of quantitative benefits of applied audio modalities. Therefore, it is necessary to experimentally evaluate audio user interfaces , as we cannot rely on users' subjective estimation.

Future research will also include a larger number of experiments, analysis of users learning curves, and multimodal guidance of a truly portable, PDA based, guidance system.

Acknowledgments. The authors would like to acknowledge Dragan Gasevic and Miroslav Havram for their valuable help in the organization of the experiments.

References

1.   E. Jovanov, K. Wagner, V. Radivojevic, D. Starcevic, M. Quinn, D. Karron, "Tactical Audio and Acoustic Rendering in Biomedical Applications", IEEE Transactions on Information Technology in Biomedicine, Vol. 3, No. 2, June 1999, pp. 109–118.

2. Wegner K, Karron D, "Surgical Navigation Using Audio Feedback." In Morgan KS et al (eds): Medicine Meets Virtual Reality: Global Healthcare Grid. IOS Press, Ohmsha, Washington, D.C., pp 450–458, 1997.
3. E. Jovanov, Z. Obrenovic, D. Starcevic, D.B. Karron, "A Virtual Reality Training System for Tactical Audio Applications", SouthEastern Simulation Conference SESC'99, Huntsville, Alabama, Oct 1999, pp. 149–154.
4. Begault DR, 3D Sound for Virtual Reality and Multimedia, Academic Press, Inc., Boston, 1994.
5. Kramer, G., Ed., Auditory Display, Sonification, Audification and Auditory Interfaces, Addison Wesley, 1994.
6. Barnard PJ, May J, Eds, "Computers, Communication and Usability: Design Issues, research and methods for integrated services," North Holland Series in Tele-communication, Amsterdam, Elsevier, 1993.
7. Buxton, W. (1995). Speech, Language & Audition. Chapter 8 in R.M. Baecker, J. Grudin, W. Buxton and S. Greenberg, S. (Eds.) (1995). Readings in Human Computer Interaction: Toward the Year 2000, San Francisco, Morgan Kaufmann Publishers.
8. Deatherage, B. H. (1972). Auditory and Other Sensory Forms of Information Presentation. In H. P. Van Cott & R. G. Kinkade (Eds), Human Engineering Guide to Equipment Design (Revised Edition). Washington: U.S. Government Printing Office.
9. Meera M. Blattner, "Multimodal Integration", IEEE Multimedia, Winter 1996, pp. 14–24.
10. Sharon Oviatt, "Ten Myths of Multimodal Interaction", Comm. of the ACM, Vol. 42, No. 11, Nov 1999, pp. 74–81.
11. E. Jovanov, D. Starcevic, V. Radivojevic, A. Samardzic, V. Simeunovic, "Perceptualization of biomedical data", IEEE Engineering in Medicine and Biology Magazine, Vol. 18, No. 1, pp. 50–55, 1999.
12. Zeljko Obrenovic, Dusan Starcevic, Emil Jovanov, "Experimental Evaluation of Multimodal Human Computer Interface For Tactical Audio Applications", IEEE International Conference on Multimedia and Expo (ICME) 2002, August 26–29, 2002, Lausanne, Switzerland.
13. John G. Neuhoff, "Perceiving Acoustic Source Orientation in Three-Dimensional Space", Proceedings of the 2001 International Conference on Auditory Display, Espoo, Finland, July 29-August 1, 2001, pp. 231–234.
14. William L. Martens, "Psychophysical Calibration for Controlling the Range of a Virtual Sound Source: Multidimensional Complexity in Spatial Auditory Display", Proceedings of the 2001 International Conference on Auditory Display, Espoo, Finland, July 29-August 1, 2001, pp. 231–234.
15. H. Sowizral, K. Rushforth, M. Deering, The Java 3D API Specification, Second Edition, Addison-Wesley Pub Co, Januar 2000, ISBN: 0201710412.

A Computer Vision and Hearing Based User Interface for a Computer Game for Children

Perttu Hämäläinen[1] and Johanna Höysniemi[2]

[1] Helsinki University of Technology, Laboratory of Telecommunications Software and Multimedia, P.O.Box 5400, FIN-02015 HUT
perttu.hamalainen@hut.fi
[2] University of Tampere, Tampere Unit for Computer-Human Interaction,
Kanslerinrinne 1, FIN-33014 University of Tampere
johanna.hoysniemi@uiah.fi

Abstract. This paper describes the design of a perceptual user interface for controlling a flying cartoon-animated dragon in QuiQui's Giant Bounce, a physically and vocally interactive computer game for 4 to 9 years old children. The dragon mimics the user's movements and breathes fire when the user shouts. The game works on a PC computer equipped with practically any low-cost microphone and webcam. It is targeted for uncontrolled real-life environments such as homes and schools.

1 Introduction

Computer vision and hearing[1] technologies have been used in various human-computer interaction applications. However, there is little written about designing computer vision and hearing-based computer games and user interfaces for child users in uncontrolled real-life conditions, for example homes and daycare centers. The main difference to installations and exhibitions, such as the Kidsroom [17], are that the lighting and the position of the cameras cannot be assumed to be constant. The technically illiterate end users must also be able to setup the software. Ideally, initialization and adjusting of technical parameters should be as automatic as possible. The games developed by Intel and Mattel [4] come close to that, but they still have usability defects, like voice prompts that instruct the user to step aside so that the computer vision can be properly initialized.

Perceptual user interfaces are interesting when designing computer games, since they enable the user to naturally act out the role of the main character. The natural user interface can deepen the user's emotional commitment to the game and make the game more compelling and exciting. Properly designed perceptual user interfaces can also add physical exercise to the game. This is a benefit compared to traditional computer

---

[1] We use the term computer hearing for consistency with the term computer vision, emphasizing that it refers to an electronic sense, although terms like machine listening and computer audition are more common in the literature.

N. Carbonell, C. Stephanidis (Eds.): User Interfaces for All, LNCS 2615, pp. 299–318, 2003.
© Springer-Verlag Berlin Heidelberg 2003

games, the overuse of which may have negative effects on children's physical health
(see e.g. Subrahmanyam et al. [22]).

This paper describes the design of the first game task and user interface of QuiQui's
Giant Bounce, a computer game controlled with movement and voice and targeted at 4
to 9 year old children. The novelty of the approach is that the technology is designed
for children in their natural environment from the point of view of usability. The user
interface also combines immediate response to both motion and voice input to deepen
the illusion of being the main character of the game.

The user interface uses a webcam and a microphone to see and hear the user. The
main character and avatar QuiQui mimics the user's movements and lets out a fiery
breath when the user shouts, as shown in Figs. 1 and 2. The game is a work in progress
and it is designed to have several game tasks. Each task has its own way of moving;
for example swimming, flying or jumping. In the game task presented in this paper,
QuiQui has to fly through the clouds over a desert to make them rain.

The paper first discusses the technical requirements of the user interface from a usability point of view. Then a set of simplifying assumptions is defined, aiming at a
practical implementation that satisfies the requirements. Finally, the design and implementation of the user interface is presented together with the findings of the testing
with child users.

Fig. 1. QuiQui breathes fire when the user shouts

2   Background

Computer vision and hearing were chosen as the interaction technology for QuiQui
because we wanted to provide a natural and unencumbered user interface that would
also be robust and accessible in every home. We did not want to use any sensors attached to the user's body. Such sensors are easy to break and are also awkward if several children want to play the game together or by taking turns. Because of the variety
of webcams on the market, we did not want to optimize the game for a particular
hardware setup. Although this adds a number of unknown variables such as frame rate,
optical parameters and noise, game requires no purchasing of specific hardware. Thus,
it can be simply downloaded from the project's homepage, *http://www.kukakumma.net*.

Fig. 2. A typical setup of the game: The camera is mounted on the monitor and the user moves in front of the screen

Much work has been done in the field of perceptual user interfaces based on computer vision and hearing. Our work is closely related, for example, to the Perceptive Spaces and physically interactive story environments developed at MIT Media lab [23][17]. These projects include several applications where one or multiple human users are tracked and the sensory data is used to control a graphical representation of the user or the reactions of the other characters.

Considering game applications, QuiQui's peers can be divided into two categories based on the user's representation in the game. In the first category are games that use a "video avatar", that is, the video image of the user or a part of it is directly interacting with computer graphics, as shown in Fig. 3. The approach was experimented as early as 1984 in Myron Krueger's pioneering work Video Place [15] and it has been commercialized by Intel and Mattel [4], as well as by Vivid Group [24].

QuiQui's Giant Bounce is an example of the second category, that uses a computer-generated avatar in the same way as traditional computer games. The avatar mimics the user's movements. In general terms we are talking about human motion capture, which has been researched intensively, as seen for example in Moeslund's survey of more than 130 related papers [16]. However, the solutions presented in the literature are rarely applicable to computer games in home and school environments. One reason for this are the requirements of the users and the target environment, elaborated in the next chapter. Also, in consumer applications the methods used can never be fast enough because the more effective the algorithm, the wider range of computers can run the program.

Games often restrict the space of possible movements, which is fortunate from the point of view of technology. Exploiting the knowledge about possible movements may enable solutions that would not work in other contexts. Following this principle, several user interfaces for existing games were developed by Freeman et al. at Mitsubishi labs [7][8][9]. However, designing a user interface for an existing game is restricted compared to designing the game and user interface together. For example, in games in which the avatar jumps when the user presses a button, the height of the jump is usually constant. A perceptual user interface should allow the user to jump to different heights, which requires that more control data is extracted from the user's movements.

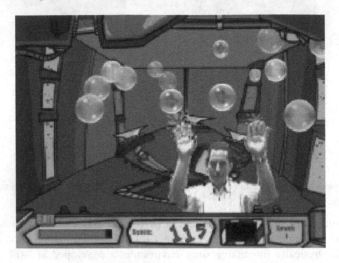

Fig. 3. An example of the "video avatar" games [4]

3 Requirements and Assumptions

In this paper we have mostly developed further the ideas presented by Freeman et al. [7][8][9]. Considering the target group and the environment of use, the challenge was to find a technical solution that does not sacrifice usability and approachability. For this we defined the following requirements:

1. Completely automatic operation without any learning stages, initialization or settings that need user participation. Our goal is that children can use the game without adult guidance.
2. The methods must adapt rapidly to changes in the environment, including lighting and camera position.
3. The methods must adapt to the differences in various camera models, including frame rates in the range 15...30 fps, noise, motion blur and color resolution.
4. The system responds with as low latency as possible.
5. The system must tolerate several visible humans, either one player and viewers or several users participating collaboratively.
6. The user must not have to wear any specific clothing or markers.
7. As low computational complexity as possible to enable maximal computational resources for the actual game application.

The requirements are based on the three requirements for human-centered perceptual user interfaces by Crowley et al. [3]: robustness and autonomy, low latency and privacy protection, the last of which is irrelevant here since it applies mainly to multi-user applications and the video footage of the user is not stored in QuiQui's Giant Bounce. As Crowley et al. put it, *"Usability determines the requirements for technological innovation."*

The requirements 1 and 2 rule out many of the existing computer vision systems, for example all the systems based on an assumption of a constant or almost constant background. This includes the technology behind Intel and Mattel's games [4], most of the MIT Media lab experiments mentioned and also the only webcam based game study we know of [19]. Assuming a constant background is lucrative for computer games, because a two-dimensional silhouette of the user can be obtained simply by subtracting every video frame from a sample of the background. Once a silhouette is obtained, simple shape recognition techniques can be applied to produce the control signals needed for a variety of games, as shown by Freeman et al. [7][8][9].

The requirements 1 and 2 are based on the fact that our target group is illiterate and technically incompetent, which makes it difficult for the software to instruct the user. Unexpected changes in the environment do happen when the system is used at homes and the users are children, as D'Hooge points out [4]. Our own usability tests also verify this. Intel and Mattel use voice prompts to guide the user for example to step away from the camera view for initialization [4], but we find that awkward.

The requirement 3 has severe implications on the computer vision methods. The low color resolution, noise, and unpredictable, often automatically controlled color settings such as white balance imply that color based skin and face detectors (see for example Bradski [2]), cannot be used reliably. Fitting curves to image contours (see for example Blake and Isard [1]) is unreliable because of noise and motion blur. The low frame rates decrease the accuracy of predictive methods. The motion of the user may have sudden changes and because of the frame rate, the user may suddenly be hundreds of pixels away from the predicted location. For example in a platform jumping game, the user may stay still, waiting for the right timing, and then suddenly bounce in any direction. An example of the amount of motion blur and changes between successive frames is shown in Fig. 4. The figure contains two frames of a jumping user recorded with a Logitech Quickcam Express webcam in daytime home conditions.

The requirement 4 rules out various gesture recognition methods that recognize movements after they have been completed. Low latency is important for the overall feeling of the game. For example, in a game played by jumping, latency can cause the virtual world to feel sticky, like the avatar was standing in a pool of thick mud.

The requirement 5 is based on our usability tests and the findings of Inkpen et al. [14] and Stewart et al. [21]. It appears that gaming is a social event for the children. It is hard to restrict the situation to one visible user since the others want to watch, standing or sitting beside the main player or for example crouching on the floor. In our tests, children also liked playing the flying game together with a friend, so collaborative operation should be supported when possible.

Fig. 4. Two successive frames captured by a webcam when the user is jumping

Requirement 6 further restricts the computer vision methods. It is defined to enable more convenient collaborative play and the delivery of the game in fully digital form as a simple downloadable software package.

Adding the requirement 7 to all the previous ones, one may wonder what is possible in practice. Fortunately, game applications allow many contextual simplifications. We use the following assumptions:

1. The background is temporally "piecewise" constant. If there are changes, they are either immediate or slow and gradual. This includes changes in lighting, sudden movements of the camera (if a child for example bumps into the table on which the camera is placed), and changes in the physical environment, like closing or opening of a door. According to our experience, it also includes automatic adjustments of exposure and gain done by the webcam drivers, since they usually happen slowly or in discrete steps.
2. The user's movements are restricted. The user faces the camera because the camera is mounted near the screen. Distance from the camera is limited because the user must be close enough to the screen to see the graphics and also because there is a limited amount of space available at people's homes. Because of the spatial constraints the user's legs do not necessarily fit into the camera view and we restrict the tracking to the upper body of a standing user, a convention also used by Intel and Mattel [4]. The movements are also often restricted to a set specific to the game context, a principle often exploited by Freeman et. al. [7][8][9].
3. If there are more than one people visible, the user is not severely occluded by others. This is natural since the user usually wants a clear line of sight to the computer and thus to the camera.
4. Responsiveness is more important than correct tracking of the user. It doesn't matter if the game can be "cheated" using movements other than intended, as long as controlling the avatar is most convenient using the intended movements so that the "right" way of moving is encouraged.

In our opinion, the assumption 4 is the key to designing practical computer vision and hearing methods for perceptually interactive games. In our tests with children, we have noted that the game experience is generally not degraded if the player can cheat the game. Many times it only challenges the child's creativity. For example when testing an early prototype of the flying game, a six year old girl started experimenting with different movements. In the interview after the testing she stated : "The best way to get up in the air is to first flap your hands and then you can jump up and down. " She was clearly satisfied about her finding. The negative side is that the feedback given by the game can be confusing when the user is learning to play the game.

4   Design and Testing of the User Interface

This paper presents the user interface of the first game task of QuiQui's Giant Bounce, a game of flying. The treatment is focused on the *human-avatar interface*, that is, the mapping of user's actions to avatar's actions and the technology behind this. The overall game design and the *avatar-virtual interface* are beyond the scope of this paper. By avatar-virtual interface we mean the interaction happening in the game world, the design of which is more close to user interface and usability design in general, including metaphors, logic, information design etc.

Fig. 5. Starting the flying game

In the context of computer games, the definition of usability is rather vague (see for example the discussion in ACM CHI-WEB archives [10]). The basic contradiction is that a good user interface tries to make things easier for the user, but a computer game needs to present a challenge to the user. Our view is that the human-avatar interface should be as intuitive and transparent as possible. It should let the user focus on the challenge presented by the avatar-virtual interface, to let the user think and act from the point of view of the avatar. It is a usability issue, if the user, as his or her real-world self, does not know how to move so that the avatar flies to a certain direction.

However, it is a more general game design problem to for example place the clouds in the sky so that the user, as the avatar, can find them in a certain time.

Note that the division into the human-avatar and avatar-virtual interfaces is not clear when considering game physics. Game physics are the general laws controlling the avatar's movement in the virtual world. The game physics largely define the over-all feeling of the user interface, described with adjectives like light, heavy, fast, slow etc. Variables such as gravity have an effect on how the avatar reacts to the user's movements. However, they also have an effect on how the avatar interacts with the game world. Properly designed game physics should increase the feeling of being in control of the game. On the other hand, in games like Liero [26], the game physics constitute the main challenge and enjoyment of the game. The physics are adjusted so that the game requires lightning fast reflexes and decisions when the avatar is flying through the air or swinging at the end of a rope.

In general, it seems that the human-avatar interface is designed to be as simple as possible, with the exception of games like Tomb Raider [27] or Die By The Sword [25]. Those games offer increased realism with a more complex and expressive inter-face that enables actions such as somersaults or separate control of the avatar's upper and lower bodies.

QuiQui's Giant Bounce uses simple sets of movements that vary according to the game task (sub-game). The user interface design is based on the game design and narrative. In the flying game presented in this paper, the basic setting we started with was that QuiQui has to help a yellow watering can to water the dry desert. This is done by flying through the clouds on the sky to make them rain. QuiQui holds a pair of big leaves in its hands so that they act like wings. The game starts with a metaphorical instruction spoken by the watering can "Flap your hands like a bird to fly up to the sky". A screenshot of this is shown in Fig. 5.

4.1 Methodology: Usability Testing with Functional Prototypes

For example Druin [5] and Hanna et al. [11] have written about collaborative design and usability testing with children. Druin et al. present a method called Cooperative Inquiry for incorporating children in the design process, for example through collabo-rative low-tech prototyping sessions. Hanna et al. give guidelines for adapting con-ventional usability testing methodology for children.

Since we were interested in aspects such as the intuitiveness of the user interface, we adopted an approach of iterative usability testing and interviews with users that are new to the game. Druin suggests a long-term relationship with a group of children [5], but in our case such approach would be more useful considering the overall design of the game or for example the story and character design.

The main testing method used was peer tutoring [12]. The test was started with the metaphorical instructions and with instructions to fly through all the clouds. After that the test subject tried to learn to fly and instructions were given only if they were not successful or seemed frustrated. After the test subject had played the game for a cou-ple of times, it was his or her turn to teach the next child to play. We used two approaches, where one child tutor instructed one child tutee and where two child tutors instructed one child tutee. We used the peer tutoring method because we wanted that children are able to teach other children how to use the game, which is important in social settings such as schools.

The tests were conducted at homes and at a preschool and school. The tests were videotaped to record the movements and gestures of the users. The tests were done using perceptually interactive prototypes, initially with more simplifications than in the final version. Although there has lately been some research on prototyping tools for perceptual user interfaces [18], they are more suitable for user interfaces where the user for example points at things. In skill-and-action games such as the flying game, the interaction is more fast-paced and prototyping is more difficult.

Two iterations of the user interface were produced based on tests with 12 and 16 children, respectively. The subjects were of ages 5 to 9. In addition to the second test, the final prototype has been tested informally with several users. Informal tests were also used between the two usability tests to try out various technical implementations of the second and final user interface. We have also had feedback from teachers and parents who have downloaded and installed the game.

4.2 Results

We evaluated the different iterations and technical implementations of the user interface based on how quickly the users were able to fly through all the clouds. Only the human-avatar interface was changed between the tests. Other aspects of the game, such as the locations of the clouds, were not modified. The results of the second test were that all the children were able to play the game and the average playing time dropped by 66% from the first test. All children learned to fly and could fly through all the clouds. The children also wanted to play the game several times, which indicates that they liked the game. In the informal tests it was also found out that the game is suitable for at least some 4-year-old children.

4.2.1 Interaction Model

In addition to the conclusive results the tests provided significant information during the design process. In the first test, the most frequent reaction to the metaphorical instructions was that the children waved their both hands to fly and bent their upper bodies sideways to control the direction of the flying, as shown in Fig. 2. In the first prototype our initial suggestion was that the user would use only one arm to fly sideways. This was changed to match the observations in order to make the user interface more intuitive.

A screenshot of the second and final prototype is in Fig. 6, showing the user flying to the left.

Fig. 6. The flying game in operation

4.2.2 Technical Design

From the point of view of technical design, the main point learned was that the variety and flexibility of children's movements are very difficult to anticipate, even if certain ways of moving were more frequent than others. This directed the computer vision methods towards analyzing holistic and rather vague image features such as image moments instead of precise tracking of the user. Examples of the various ways the children moved are shown in Fig. 7.

4.2.3 Spatial Design

We also encountered problems with the spatial design of the user interface. Because of the limited space available at schools and especially at homes, the camera cannot be placed so that the user is always visible. Instead, the user must be guided to stay within the field of view of the camera. This is problematic especially when an exact one-to-one mapping between the user and the avatar is not possible. For example when the avatar is flying in the air, there is no intuitive mapping for the user moving sideways. Because of this, there is a gap in the feedback of the user interface, and the user can accidentally step out of the camera view. This happened several times in the usability tests.

The problem was initially tackled with the small camera view window in the bottom left corner of the screen, as shown in Figs. 5 and 6. It helps in verifying that the user is positioned correctly, but it was found out that it was hard for the test users to monitor their position. It appears that the camera view is mainly helpful for adults in determining the correct placement of the camera. In general, the younger the users, the easier they forgot that they should stay near a certain optimal location.

Fig. 7. Test users learning to fly. Note that the figures at the bottom are blurred because of the rapid movements of the user

We did not want to abandon the concept of a flying avatar. Also, we did not want to set more technical constraints for the game, such as a specific camera model with a wide enough field of view. Our solution was to create an approximately one meter wide "magic square" on the floor using marker tape. Our tests show that this considerably helps the children to remember the spatial constraints. They seemed to understand it easily when we explained that "You must stand in the magic square so that the eye of the computer (the camera) can see you." This instruction was usually the first one given when the children explained each other how to play the game. Although adults might regard things like magic squares as cheap compromises or cheating, magic is a useful concept when designing children's technology. It is important and natural in children's fantasy and play. Another good example of using magic to overcome difficult design constraints is given by Druin [6].

The difficulties encountered were caused by the real world constraints, i.e. limited playspace and field of view of the camera, and the mismatch between the game and real world physics. The magic square is not necessarily the right solution for all games. For example, in a platform jumping game the game physics may match the physical world, but moving in the virtual space becomes a problem if the virtual space is larger than the real playing space. One solution is to map the location of the user to avatar velocity, that is, to map physical variables to derivatives of their virtual counterparts. An example of this is the SURVIVE system [23].

4.2.4 Cognitive Load and Feedback to the User

We also encountered problems that were apparently caused by the high cognitive load of the user interface. The main observation was that it is hard to get the user's attention when he or she is learning to fly. The user is also further away from the screen than in traditional computer games, so that the graphics must be scaled, making the avatar larger in relation to the size of the screen. This further complicates things as the user has less time to react when flying around. Although we tried to keep the visual appearance of the game as simple as possible, there was so much happening that the test users did not notice everything. For example, the user's did not always notice the raindrop symbols of the top right corner of the screen. New colored raindrops are added when QuiQui flies through a cloud.

We did not yet find any general solutions to provide feedback that inevitably catches the user's attention. It seems that rather extreme techniques might be needed, such as cinematographic close-ups of important events.

5 Technical Design and Implementation

This chapter describes and evaluates the technical design and implementation, including game physics, computer hearing and computer vision. The design is an example of a simple and practical technical solution that relies on the requirements and assumptions presented in chapter 3.

The general design principle is to use as low-level features of the image and sound data as possible, considering the game context. An example of a low-level image feature is the center of mass, in contrast to a high-level interpretation such as three-dimensional pose of the user.

The more decisions and interpretations are made, the more there are chances for errors. Since the environment of use and the actions of the child users are unpredictable, it is difficult to ensure that the assumptions behind the decisions and interpretations hold in every situation. A simple motion tracker that interprets various movements as flying is better than a sophisticated tracker that causes the avatar to fall down when it makes a false interpretation and moves the avatar's legs instead of its arms.

The main benefits of the approach are robustness and simplicity. The main drawback is the dependency on the game context, that is, the loss of generality. The computer vision methods used in a user interface for flying are not necessarily applicable to for example a user interface for platform jumping.

5.1 Computer Hearing

The computer hearing is the simplest part of the technology since we only need to detect whether the user is shouting or not. This can be done by simple thresholding. The first step is to compute the signal power in each 50ms window of audio samples delivered by the sound card's capture driver:

$$P(m) = \sum_{i=1}^{N} x(n)^2 ,\qquad (1)$$

where m is the window index, N is the window length in samples and $x(n)$ is the input signal. Since we are only interested in the signal power relative to the background noise power, we filter the power values using a first order IIR highpass filter derived from [13]

$$P_{hp}(m) = \frac{1}{1+\omega} P(m) - \frac{1}{1+\omega} P(m-1) + \frac{1-\omega}{1+\omega} P_{hp}(m-1) ,\qquad (2)$$

where ω is the cutoff frequency of the filter in the range $0...1$. With a constant level background noise $P_{hp}(m)$ is close to zero. When the user begins to shout, $P_{hp}(m)$ peaks and begins to decay exponentially. A threshold value T is used so that the avatar breathes fire as long as $P_{hp}(m) > T$.

The system detects all loud sounds as shouting, but it does not matter because falsely detected shouting has no negative consequences in the game. This is in agreement with the assumption 4 presented in chapter 3. The main benefit of the design is computational simplicity. Children also have fun experimenting with different sounds. For example in one test with three children, a boy found out that he could make QuiQui breath fire by clapping his hands. After that, the other children tried it out enthusiastically. According to our tests, especially young boys are excited about the voice interface.

Although the voice input mechanism is simple, it seems to increase the excitement of the game and supports the fantasy of being a dragon. Because of the direct mapping between shouting and breathing fire, the voice interface does alienate the user from the game. The interface allows the user to express himself or herself *as* the avatar, in contrast to voice interfaces that for example recognize commands spoken *to* the game.

5.2 Game Physics

The first step in the design of the motion analysis was to design game physics for the avatar. The physics determine the control signals computed from the user's movements. Our solution uses loosely interpreted Newtonian mechanics simulated with finite differences, that is, by replacing time derivatives of variables with differences between the variables at successive simulation steps. Note that when designing game physics, the real laws of physics are merely exemplary conceptual tools.

Our solution has two masses connected by a weightless rod as shown in Fig. 8. Instead of the center of mass the moments caused by the forces F and G are computed relative to the origin. The forces G denote gravity and F denotes the "thrust" force caused by the user's movements. The angle between the vector F and the rod equals the angle between the user's spine and the vertical axis. This allows the user to control the rotation of the avatar by bending sideways when flying. The mass at the lower end of the avatar is further away from the origin so that it causes the avatar to rotate back to upright position if the user is not moving.

Note that the avatar is not flexible like the user. The animation simply has three frames with hands held up, down and straight to left and right.

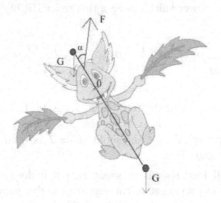

Fig. 8. Physics of the flying avatar

5.3 Computer Vision

To make the system robust to changes in the environment, the basic approach of the computer vision is differential motion analysis [20], based on intensity differences between consecutive video frames (temporal difference). The intensity differences are strongest at areas containing motion. Changes in lighting etc. cause only temporal disturbances in the system, opposite to for example the games by Intel and Mattel [4].

The drawback of using only the temporal difference data is that only the moving parts of the user can be detected. Fortunately, the analysis is simplified by the assumption that the movements of the user are limited to those relevant to the game context. Our system assumes that if the user is not simply standing still or walking around, he or she is trying to fly.

The system consists of the following processing stages, operating on 8-bit grayscale images:

1. Reduction of resolution to 120x96 pixels with spatial averaging (lowpass filtering) to reduce noise. The intensity of each output pixel is the average of an 8x8 pixel area of the input. The video is originally captured at 320x240 pixels or the closest resolution to that supported by the camera drivers.
2. Temporal differencing. Each output pixel is the absolute value of the difference of the corresponding input pixels of the last two input frames.

3. Thresholding. A threshold value is determined and pixel values below it are considered as noise and set to zero.

4. The image and the trajectory formed by its topmost nonzero pixels are analyzed to determine the output variables used to update the game physics.

Fig. 9 visualizes the operation, starting with the grayscale input image and ending with an image output by the third stage, augmented with visualization of the analysis of the fourth stage. The pose of the upper body is visualized as a straight line and the topmost nonzero pixels are plotted with maximum intensity. Note that the brightness of the images has been increased for better printing quality.

The threshold value of stage 3 is determined using histogram-based thresholding, various approaches of which are presented in [20]. It is assumed that the center of the background noise distribution is at the maximum of the histogram and that the distribution decreases monotonically at both sides of the maximum. The threshold is determined as the first local minimum of the histogram when searching from the maximum towards greater intensity values. According to our tests in various environments with a total of seven different camera models these assumptions seem to hold.

The first step in stage 4 is to detect whether the user is doing something or standing still. The criterion used is the amount of nonzero pixels. Analysis is continued only if the amount exceeds an experimentally determined value, currently the half of the image width.

The next step is to detect that the user is trying to fly instead of simply walking around. A parabola is fitted to the topmost pixels of the image in least-squares sense, as shown in Fig. 10. When the user is walking, the parabola usually fits well and its peak is located near the head of the user. The analysis is not continued if the quadratic coefficient of the parabola is negative enough and the peak of the parabola is horizontally near the center of the detected topmost pixels.

The analysis of the angle α and force F in Fig. 8 is based on image moments. Image moments are statistical characteristics that have been used for computer vision based game user interfaces by Freeman and Sengupta et al. [7][8][19]. An image moment of order $(p+q)$ is computed as the summation [20]

$$m_{pq} = \sum_{x=-\infty}^{\infty} \sum_{y=-\infty}^{\infty} x^p y^q i(x,y), \qquad (3)$$

where $i(x,y)$ is the pixel intensity at coordinates x and y.

For user interface purposes, moments up to second order can be computed from silhouette representations of the user to obtain estimates of the size, location and orientation of the silhouette [7][8]. Freeman et al. also suggest that they could be computed from the temporal difference [8]. However, in this case the orientation information obtained from the moments is ambiguous, depending on the parts of the user that are moving. The principal axis of the difference may appear to be in the direction of the user's hands as well as the user's body.

Fig. 9. The original input and the four processing states of the computer vision (from left to right and top to bottom)

Fig. 10. Detecting a user walking

Our solution for determining the pose of the upper body is to compute two spatially biased mass centers from the thresholded temporal difference. We use a left and right mass center, (x_{left}, y_{left}) and (x_{right}, y_{right}), marked with short vertical lines in the bottom right image in Fig. 9. The orientation of the user's shoulders is approximated with a line drawn through the centers, also shown in the figure.

The coordinates of the mass centers are computed from moments up to third order, by weighing the pixels differently depending on their position:

$$x_{right} = \frac{1}{k_{right}} \sum_{x=1}^{w} \sum_{y=1}^{h} x(x^2 + y)i(x, y),$$

$$y_{right} = \frac{1}{k_{right}} \sum_{x=1}^{w} \sum_{y=1}^{h} y(x^2 + y)i(x, y),$$

$$x_{left} = \frac{1}{k_{left}} \sum_{x=1}^{w} \sum_{y=1}^{h} x((w - x)^2 + y)i(x, y),$$

$$y_{left} = \frac{1}{k_{left}} \sum_{x=1}^{w} \sum_{y=1}^{h} y((w - x)^2 + y)i(x, y),$$

(4)

where h and w are the height and width of the image in pixels. The scaling factors k equal the sum of the weights,

$$k_{right} = \sum_{x=1}^{w} \sum_{y=1}^{h} (x^2 + y)i(x, y),$$

$$k_{left} = \sum_{x=1}^{w} \sum_{y=1}^{h} ((w - x)^2 + y)i(x, y).$$

(5)

Pixels closer to the left edge of the image are given more weight in the summation of the left mass center. The pixels closer to the top of the image are also given more weight in both mass centers to reduce the effect of the movement of the user's lower body. The y coordinates start from 1 at the bottom of the image, growing towards the top.

The position of the hands is practically impossible to detect accurately because of the motion blur. If the user's hands are moving fast enough, they can be perceived as an almost constant area of movement in the temporal difference. If flying is detected, the hand position information is changed by one animation frame according to the vertical movement of the mass center of the temporal difference. According to our tests this works sufficiently well.

Because of the ambiguity of the hand position information, the thrust force F in Fig. 8 cannot be computed from the angular velocity of the user's hands, although this would probably be the most intuitive interpretation. Instead, it is directly proportional to the amount of movement, measured as the amount of non-zero pixels. This is clearly a weakness, because it makes the system variant to changes in camera optics and the distance of the user. However, considering a single setup of the game, these properties vary only little. The user can adjust the overall sensitivity of the game in the main menu, which would be a useful feature even if the force could be determined more accurately. Because of the manual adjusting of the sensitivity, the requirement 1 presented in chapter 3 is only partially fulfilled. The game works with the default sensitivity, but in some cases it may feel too light or heavy.

The requirements 2, 3, 4 and 6 are met because of the use of temporal differencing and low-level image features. The system analyzes all movement, regardless of shape, color etc. The latency of the system is only one video frame.

Considering the requirement 5, the presence of other people than the user does not affect the game as long as they move less than the user so that the user dominates the analysis. However, the game is sensitive to other movement when the user wants to fall down and just stands still.

The system also supports collaborative play because the motion analysis based on image moments is vague enough to treat several users as one. However, this requires that the users are standing close enough to each other and flying in the same direction.

Considering the requirement 7, the computer vision is computationally efficient, leaving most of the processing power of current PC computers for the actual game. The implementation only caused an increase of 10% in the CPU load in our test system, compared to a bypassed situation, where a video stream was captured and converted to grayscale, but it was not fed through the processing stages described in this paper. The test system used was a 1GHz Pentium III Dell Inspiron 8100 laptop computer capturing video at 30fps using a Creative Video Blaster Webcam 5 camera.

To summarize, the computer vision solution is tested to work and enable an enjoyable game experience, although it is not perfect according to the requirements defined in chapter 3. The main drawback of the solution is that it is highly specific to the flying game.

6   Conclusions and Future Work

From the point of view of usability, we have defined a set of technical requirements for webcam and microphone based games for children in uncontrolled real-life environments like homes and daycare centers. We have also defined a set of simplifying assumptions to meet the requirements. An example game and user interface has then been designed and implemented based on the requirements, assumptions and testing with end users.

Iterative usability testing was carried out during the design. According to observations about the actions of the users, the user interface was redesigned to be more intuitive. The tests also showed that the child users act in a spontaneous and unpredictable way, which caused us to adapt a technically simplistic approach based on low-level image and audio features. The usability tests also pointed out general problems related to using camera based user interfaces in a space where the user may get out of the camera's view.

We are currently building more game and user interface prototypes and designing new computer vision algorithms, focusing on improving the collaborative aspects and robustness. The spatial design of perceptual user interfaces is also a topic that will be researched further.

The flying game described in this paper can be downloaded as an automatic installer package from the project's homepage *http://www.kukakumma.net*.

Acknowledgements. The work has been supported by YLE (Finland's national public service broadcasting company), Alfred Kordelin Foundation and University of Arts and Design Helsinki UIAH. The authors are currently receiving funding from the HeCSE and UCIT graduate schools of the Academy of Finland.

References

1. Blake, A., Isard, M., Active Contours The Application of Techniques from Graphics, Vision, Control Theory and Statistics to Visual Tracking of Shapes in Motion, Springer-Verlag London Limited, 1998
2. Bradski, G.R., Computer Vision Face Tracking For Use in a Perceptual User Interface, *Intel Technology Journal* Q2 '98. Available electronically at http://developer.intel.com
3. Crowley, J.L., Coutaz, J., Bérard, F., Things That See, *Communications of the ACM,* March 2000/Vol. 43, No. 3
4. D'Hooge, H., Game Design Principles for the Intel® Play™ Me2Cam∗ Virtual Game System, *Intel Technology Journal* Q4, 2001
5. Druin, A., Cooperative inquiry: Developing new technologies for children with children. In *Proceedings of CHI '99,* (1999) ACM/SIGCHI, N.Y., pp. 592–599
6. Druin, A., Children as our technology design partners: The surprising and the not-so-surprising, *Proceedings of International Workshop on Interaction Design and Children,* Aug. 28–29, 2002, Eindhoven, The Netherlands
7. Freeman, W.T., Tanaka, K., Ohta, J., Kyuma, K., Computer vision for computer games, *IEEE 2nd Intl. Conf. on Automatic Face and Gesture Recognition,* Killington, VT, October 1996
8. Freeman, W.T., Anderson, D., Beardsley, P., Dodge, C., Kage, H., Kyuma, K., Miyake, Y., Roth, M., Tanaka, K., Weissman, C., Yerazunis, W., Computer Vision for Interactive Computer Graphics, *IEEE Computer Graphics and Applications,* May-June, 1998, pp. 42–53
9. Freeman, W.T., Beardsley, P.A., Kage, H., Tanake, K., Kyuma, K., Weissman, C.D., Computer Vision for Computer Interaction, *SIGGRAPH Computer Graphics Newsletter – Applications of Computer Vision to Computer Graphics,* Vol.33 No. 4 November 1999, ACM SIGGRAPH.
10. Gerig, J., Summary: Usability issues in computer games, http://www.listserv.acm.org/archives/wa.cgi?A2=ind0205E&L=chi-web&D=0&m=10716&P=720, 4th September 2002
11. Hanna, L., Risden, K., Alexander, K., Guidelines for Usability Testing with Children, *Interactions,* Vol.4 No.5 1997 pp. 9–14
12. Höysniemi, J., Hämäläinen, P., Turkki, L., Using Peer Tutoring in Evaluating the Usability of a Physically Interactive Computer Game with Children, *Proceedings of International Workshop on Interaction Design and Children,* Aug. 28–29, 2002, Eindhoven, The Netherlands
13. Ifeachor, E.C., Jervis, B.W., Digital Signal Processing A Practical Approach, Addison-Wesley, 1993, p. 400
14. Inkpen, K., Ho-Ching, W., Kuederle, O., Scott, S., Shoemaker, G., "This is fun! We're all best friends and we're all playing.": Supporting children's synchronous collaboration. Proceedings of *Computer Supported Collaborative Learning (CSCL) '99.* December 1999. Stanford, CA.

15. Krueger, M., Gionfriddo, T., Hinrichsen, K., VIDEOPLACE - An Artificial Reality, *Proceedings of CHI 85*, (1985) ACM/SIGCHI, N.Y. pp. 35–40

16. Moeslund, Thomas B.Computer vision-based human motion capture – a survey. Aalborg: Aalborg University, Laboratory of Computer Vision and Media Technology, 1999. (LIA Report; LIA 99-02.-ISSN 0906-6233)

17. Pinhanez, C.S., Wilson, A.D., Davis, J.W., Bobick, A.F., Intille, S., Blumberg, B., Johnson, M.P., Physically Interactive Story Environments, *IBM Systems Journal*, Vol. 39, Nos 3–4, 2000

18. Sinha, A.K., Landay, J.A., Visually Prototyping Perceptual User Interfaces through Multimodal Storyboarding, in *Proceedings of Workshop on Perceptual User Interfaces*, Nov. 15–16, 2001, Orlando, Florida

19. Sengupta, K., Wong, H. and Kumar, P. Computer Vision Games Using A Cheap (<100$) Webcam, in proceedings of *6th International Conference on Control, Automation, Robotics and Vision (ICARCV 2000)*, 5–8 December 2000, Singapore.

20. Sonka, M., Hlavac, V., Boyle, R., Image Processing, Analysis and Machine Vision, 2nd edition, Brooks/Cole Publishing Company, 1999

21. Stewart, J., Bederson, B.B, and Druin, A. (1999). Single display groupware: A model for co-present collaboration. *Proceedings of CHI 99*.(1999) ACM/SIGCHI, N.Y., pp. 286–293.

22. Subrahmanyam, K., Kraut, R.E., Greenfield, P.M, Gross, E.F., (2000), The impact of home computer use on children activities and development, *Children and computer technology*, vol. 10, No. 2, Fall/winter 2000.

23. Wren, C.R., Spacarino, F., Azarbayejani, A., Darrel, T., Davis, J., Starner, Kotani, A.,Chao, C., Hlavac, M., Russel, K., Bobick, A., Pentland, A., Perceptive Spaces for Performance and Entertainment (Revised), *ATR Workshop on Virtual Environments*, April 1998, Kyoto, Japan.

24. http://www.vividgroup.com, 4th May 2002.

25. http://www.interplay.com/games/product.asp?GameID=114, 5th September 2002

26. http://www.lieroextreme.com, 5th September 2002

27. http://www.tombraider.com, 5th September 2002

Software Architecture for Multimodal User Input – FLUID

Tommi Ilmonen and Janne Kontkanen

Helsinki University of Technology
Telecommunications Software and Multimedia Laboratory
Konemiehentie 2, Espoo, Finland
{Tommi.Ilmonen,Janne.Kontkanen}@hut.fi

Abstract. Traditional ways to handle user input in software are uncomfortable when an application wishes to use novel input devices. This is especially the case in gesture based user interfaces. In this paper we describe these problems and as a solution we present an architecture and an implementation of a user input toolkit. We show that the higher level processing of user input such as gesture recognition requires a whole new kind of paradigm. The system we designed and implemented - FLexible User Input Design (FLUID) - is a lightweight library that can be used in different kinds of software. The potential application areas include all system where novel input devices are in use: virtual reality, entertainment systems and embedded systems.

1 Introduction

Input devices used by most of the computer software are a mouse and a keyboard. Still there are many applications and platforms in which using these standard devices is awkward or impossible. Currently, interest in alternative input methods is increasing, because lots of new kinds of devices that cannot use the conventional input methods are emerging into the market. These devices include information appliances such as mobile phones and hand-held computers as well as embedded systems. Embedded systems, such as those in modern washing machines, have been around for long, but their programming is still done on relatively low level without sophisticated toolkits for user interaction.

This paper introduces a new paradigm and a toolkit for managing input devices. This architecture is suitable for any application where novel input devices are in use. The system is scalable from embedded systems to ordinary computers. The design takes into account the needs of higher-level application development – support for input data processing (gesture detectors etc.) and ease of programming. While the system is generic in nature we have developed and used it primarily in virtual reality (VR) applications.

The novelty of our approach is in the new architecture to handle multimodal user input. While our approach shares common features with some previous systems, the overall structure is unique. Also it seems that the FLUID architecture is the first to emphasize the need to design the low-level input API and data processing layers at the same time. In addition to restructuring ideas from previous research our system introduces the concept of device-specific *history buffer*. This paper focuses on presenting

N. Carbonell, C. Stephanidis (Eds.): User Interfaces for All, LNCS 2615, pp. 319–338, 2003.

the architecture, but also introduces our implementation of the architecture and examples of how we have used it.

When designing the architecture we have taken into account the need to collect data from various devices and the need to further process the data. It also enables efficient sharing of input processors (gesture detectors etc.) between possibly very different applications. The architecture is composed of two layers: the input layer and the data processing layer (figure 1). The input layer handles the devices and maintains a buffer of history data for each device. The data processing layer is used to process the data – detect gestures, generate events and calculate features. The purpose of these layers is to offer a simple and universal method for application developers to access the devices and to refine the data.

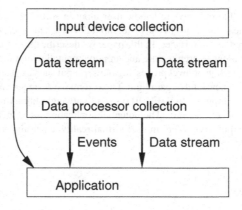

Fig. 1. Overview of the FLUID architecture.

The architecture we designed satisfies the following requirements:

- Manage arbitrary input devices for any kind of application
- Offer a good infrastructure for data processing
- Offer a way to share data processing elements (gesture detectors etc.) between applications
- Specify a simple architecture for these tasks

In the end we hope to make multi-modal input management easy for the application developer. In the ideal case a developer would select the desired input devices and data processing modules (gestures detectors, signal converters etc.), add the necessary callbacks to pass the event and signal information from the input toolkit to the application and then concentrate on the application development.

Our test-bed for these experiments is a virtual reality system. Since normal input devices – mouse and keyboard – function badly in VR applications we must employ novel devices and combine data from those. The FLUID project was started to enable faster and more cost-effective application development in VR environments. At the same time we wanted to create a system that is not VR-centric. Instead these new tools should be re-usable in other contexts – desktop computing, entertainment systems and even in embedded (or ubiquitous) systems.

This paper first describes the FLUID architecture and toolkit for collecting and refining input data. We then introduce a way in which it can be used in virtual reality software and give examples of applications that we have built with FLUID.

FLUID is an attempt to create a framework that fits to the needs of applications that need user input and that need to process that data. It's design supports any number of concurrent input devices and fulfills the needs of data processing algorithms. It is easy to extend – a programmer can add new device drivers, device types and data processing algorithms. FLUID offers a design framework that enables developers to avoid application-specific custom-solutions. Thus FLUID promotes software re-usability.

This work is heavily influenced by our earlier work on full-body gesture recognition and gesture-based user interfaces [1][2]. These earlier systems were not VR-driven, instead they were built for musical goals. As we have kept working with multimodal gesture-based interfaces it became clear that working with various kinds of non-conventional input devices is anything but straightforward. We think that it is necessary to try to attack this problem and try to make the application development for multimodal environments easier in this aspect. During our previous research we created highly customized pieces of software for collecting and processing the input data. Unfortunately it is difficult to reuse these components in any other application due to lack of well designed standard framework. We would like to avoid this situation in the future. FLUID project was started since we could not find toolkits or architectures that would offer the features that were needed. The FLUID toolkit will be released under an open-source license.

2 Multimodal Interaction

As long as people are forced to interact with computers using mice and keyboards important elements of human communication are lost. One cannot use gestures, speech or body motion with such clumsy devices. Instead we are forced to express ourselves with key-presses and mouse.

Our research is inspired by the needs for different interaction modalities. This need is caused by the fact that mouse and keyboard do not offer the best interaction method for all applications. Embedded applications (phones, PDAs) as well as immersive applications (virtual and augmented reality) cannot rely on the same interaction modalities as normal desktop computers.

We believe that the interaction style has direct impact on how people perceive technology. There is a difference between entering text by handwriting, typing and talking. Even tough people seldom use computers just for the sake of interacting with them the method of interaction needs to be considered carefully. For this reason we believe that it is necessary to offer alternative interaction modalities when appropriate.

Having alternative interaction methods is also a way to find new target groups for technology. For example children or illiterate people cannot use text-based communication with a computer. By enabling multimodal interaction we can make information technology more accessible for these people thus leading to more universal access of computers. Since FLUID can be used to enable different input strategies for a single application it is a useful tool for building applications with universal access in mind.

In this part we share view with Cohen who argues that voice/gesture -interaction can offer significant advantages over classical interaction modalities[3]. Cohen also gives examples of how a multimodal interface has been found to make applications more productive. Although Cohen is primarily concerned with immersive applications we feel that multimodal interaction is important in other environments as well.

An interesting view to human-computer interaction is given by Schoemaker et al. who have studied the levels of observation[4]. Their work classifies four levels of observation – physical/physiological, information theoretical, cognitive and intentional. Many user input toolkits work on the information theoretical level of this model – they are only concerned with raw input data or simple manipulation of the input data. For real applications the cognitive level is usually more important since this is where the data gets its meaning.

The word "multimodal" is widely used to describe interaction systems. Unfortunately it is a word with many meanings. Term multimodal can be used to describe a system with multiple communication devices (mice, keyboards, cameras). The term can also be used to mean communication that uses different modalities (writing, drawing, gesturing, talking). The first definition is device-centric while the second is more human-centric.

To be able to utilize different communication modalities computers must also have different input devices. This is where our research is targeted. In this paper we use term "multimodal input" to refer to systems with multiple novel input devices. Of course any multimodal application is likely to have multiple output devices as well.

2.1 Software for Multimodal Input

Multimodal software is difficult to create. There are several obstacles – novel input and output devices and the need for diverse special software (rendering, animation, audio processing). In our own work we have found that there are few if any toolkits that would make it easier to handle multimodal user input.

The first task for an application is to collect the input data. This is a difficult task when one considers all the possible goals that should be satisfied. The system should not consume excessive amount of resources, it should be portable, it should accommodate different versions of the same device class (devices from different manufacturers), it should be extendible and it must fulfill the needs of the data processing algorithms.

An application seldom uses the input data directly. Instead of using raw input data an application needs refined data – information about what the user is doing. To bridge this gap we utilize gesture detectors and feature extractors. These algorithms turn the low-level numeric signals into more descriptive form, often compressing a multichannel signal to just a few events. An algorithm can be very simple – for example it is easy to create ad-hoc algorithms to detect hand claps, provided that the user has tracker sensors attached to both hands. A more complex algorithm might be used to interpret sign language.

All the data processor algorithms have one thing in common; they need data that is precisely in specific form. Most time-based gesture analysis algorithms work best with constant-rate signals. That is, the input device generates samples at fixed intervals and the analysis algorithm is designed to work with such constant frequency signal. For example all digital filtering algorithms rely on constant sampling rate (see for example the algorithms in common DSP books[5]). The same is true for artificial neural networks that use the time-delay approach.

These considerations lead us to set the following requirements for the input layer:

- Data should be collected at constant sampling rate
- The system should know when a given sample was sampled
- It must be possible to utilize signals of different sampling rates
- The application must be allowed to access the input devices at arbitrary rate
- The user may instantiate several devices of the same type

The data processor layer in turn must have the following properties:

- Ability to turn input data into events – for example motion signal can be used to detect gestures
- Ability to transform signals to other kinds of signals – we might be only interested in the velocity of a sensor, or the mean velocity of a sensor
- Support re-use of data processors – we want to re-use the analysis tools in many applications

3   Related Interaction Research

In interactions research our topic is the design of input toolkits. While there are several competing toolkits for graphical 2D user interfaces (GUI) we have not been able to find general-purpose toolkits that would be designed to manage multiple novel input devices and support the input data processing.

The other trends in interactions research are not directly related to this work. For example Nigay's and others' work on the design spaces is directed towards the classification of different interaction modes and modalities[6]. The authors also propose an architecture for complex multimodal systems, but their architecture is more concerned with application logic and application interaction design. Thus it has little to say about how the user input is collected and processed. While our work is not directly connected to their's it is worth noting that these approaches are not conflicting.

Salber et al. have published a "The Context Toolkit" for sensing the presence of the user acting upon that information[7]. Their approach is to gather data from environmental sensors and create widgets and turn the information into events. The context toolkit has been used in another project by Mankoff where it was combined with speech recognition engine to collect and process ambiguous user input data[8]. FLUID differs from the context toolkit by being aimed at a wider audience – while the context toolkit is targeted at sensing the presence of the user FLUID is intended for any kind of work. The example applications described by Salber and Mankoff do not apparently stress low latency, high performance or quality of the input data or the easy programming interface that are the basic requirements of the FLUID architecture. The context toolkit could be implemented with FLUID by creating the desired device drivers and coding the processor objects that correspond to the widgets in the context toolkit. The ambiguity management described by Mankoff has no direct equivalence in FLUID although it seems it could be implemented on top of the generic FLUID framework.

The need to extract higher-level information from low-level data is shared between many kinds of applications. Often such applications separate the information retrieval (or gesture detection) to separate layer. This is the case with applications that use computer vision for user input and gesture-based interaction systems. For example Landay has used such approach in creating the SILK-library for handling 2D-sketches[9]. While this approach resembles the way FLUID is structured it does not implement some of the key features that a multimodal input system needs: inclusion of arbitrary input devices and accommodation of devices with different sampling rate.

4   Related Virtual Reality Research

In VR applications one is always confronted by non-conventional input hardware. As a result VR toolkits usually offer a way to access novel input devices. A practical example of such a system is the VR Juggler[10]. VR Juggler offers an abstraction for a few input device types – motion trackers, data gloves and analog inputs. It also includes a few utilities that can process the data further. VR Juggler includes simple finger gesture detector code and coordinate transformation code for the motion trackers. Also the older CAVELib[tm] toolkit can manage motion trackers[11].

There are also VR toolkits for input device management. OpenTracker is an example of such an approach [12]. It is a toolkit that is aimed at making motion tracker management and configuration easy and flexible. The VRPN (virtual reality peripheral network) system is another toolkit for managing input devices[13]. While OpenTracker is an effort at high-quality tracker management VRPN is a more general-purpose system – it can be easily extended to handle any kind of input devices. The VRPN shares many features with FLUID. The main difference is that FLUID includes an architecture for processing the input data.

Cohen has created a *QuickSet* -system for multimodal interaction with distributed immersive application[3]. QuickSet is directed towards commanding 2D and 3D environments and it supports gesture and voice interaction. It covers all areas of multimodal application development – input, application logic and output. It is created with distributed processing in mind. Our approach differs in that FLUID architecture is more simple, it is not targeted only at detecting commands and it is does not address the distribution of processing elements. FLUID is also intended to be a small component that can be added to any application – not an application framework that would require specific programming approach.

Bimber has published a multi-layered architecture for sketch-based interaction within virtual environments[14]. Although that work is directed at sketching applications the software architecture could probably be used for other purposes as well.

5   The Fluid Architecture

At present there is no common way to handle the novel input devices. If one builds a 2D GUI then there are several toolkits available. All of these toolkits include similar structure – a collection of graphical elements and user input via call-back functions. This contrasts the way one handles non-standard devices. Each application has its own special way of handling input devices and -data. For this reason we propose a new architecture for handling multi-modal user input.

The FLUID architecture contains 1) input layer, 2) data processor layer and 3) application (see figure 1). The application executes in its own main loop and refreshes the FLUID layers frequently. All the input devices are managed by a central object – the input device collection. The application may use one or more data processor collections to refine the input data into more usable form.

The main purpose of the input layer is to collect data from various devices and present it to the application and data processors with a simple, monolithic API. Although this process is simple there are still pitfalls that must be taken care of. If we think about multimodal interaction this layer corresponds to the device-oriented definition – it is responsible for handling multiple different devices.

The data processor layer refines the input data in a way that application can better utilize it. The purpose of this layer is to extract semantic information from the raw input data. If we follow Schoemaker's terminology then we can say that this layer tries to obtain cognitive information from the user input.

If necessary the processor layer can be used to hide the input devices from the application. This way the input devices can be changed with minimal changes to application structure. For example hand claps can be detected with different input devices – camera, microphone or motion tracker. If the application only wants know that the user clapped his hands together then it does not make difference how this information is obtained.

6   Input Layer

All the input devices share the same abstract base class. To create a device type one needs to inherit this base class and add the device-specific data structures to the new class. This new class is effectively an API for that device. The FLUID library contains definitions for a limited number of input device types, but users can add new device types without modifying the core library. In practice all device APIs should be defined in the base library. If they are not, then people may create different and conflicting APIs for the same device types. At any rate we feel that is it necessary to offer users the possibility to add device types of their own.

The type of the data that is stored into the buffers depends on the type of the device. Thus motion tracker samples are stored as an array of rotation matrices and location vectors, data glove samples are stored as an array of finger joint angles etc.. Each data element is timestamped with its measurement time. The time-stamping is necessary since the higher-level components may need to fuse signals of different sampling rates together (for example magnetic tracker at 68 Hz and data glove at 50 Hz). Without timestamping there would be no way to tell which samples coming from different sources took place simultaneously.

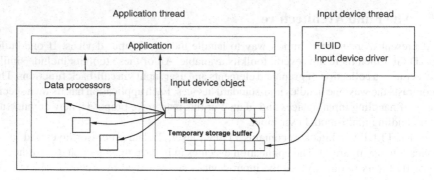

Fig. 2. The input thread, buffers, and data transfer paths

6.1 Threading and Buffering

The input layer contains objects that take care of all the input devices. Figure 2 outlines the way input devices work. Input objects are threaded – they collect data in the background and move the data to a temporary buffer. This means that each device object contains an internal thread that reads the input from the device's native API. The data is then moved to a history buffer when requested. This makes the data available for the application.

Double buffering is necessary since it is the only way to guarantee that every input sample becomes available to the application and data processors. If this was not done then the application would have to update the input devices at such a rate that no sample can escape. In practice this is a difficult requirement – the application main loop would have to check the devices at fixed sampling rate. With our approach the application simply needs to re-size the history buffer and temporary buffer to be large enough to contain the necessary amount of data. While the size of the history buffer determines how much history data is available for higher level analysis the temporary buffer sets the upper limit for the input layer update interval. In any case the history buffer needs to be at least as large as the temporary buffer.

As a result the application can run its main loop in variable frame rate and update the input layer only when necessary. Even tough the input layer is updated at random intervals it will read the input data at fixed rate and store the data in the internal buffers. This threading approach is similar to the approach used by VRPN[13].

We chose to store the data to buffers since this makes the history data directly accessible to the processor layer. Thus if a processor in the higher level needs to access the history data (as gesture detectors frequently do) then the data is available with no extra cost. A gesture detector may require several seconds of input data. It is natural to use the input data buffer to store this data so that the gesture detectors do not need to keep separate input history buffers. In the general case the input device object cannot know how much history is required by high level analysis. For this purpose the processor objects request the input device to enlarge its buffer to be large enough for the needs of the processor. This leads to minimal memory consumption as all data is buffered only once (in the input device object).

The buffering can also increase performance: If the samples were handed out one at a time (via call-back as in VRPN) then each new sample would have to be separately handled. This is not a problem with devices with low sampling rate, but if we consider audio input at 44.1 kHz then this approach takes lots of computational resources. In these cases the most efficient approach is to handle the data as a buffer of samples and process many samples whenever the application main loop executes.

The buffering approach is also useful when different kinds of data are used together. If there is one object receiving data from several sources it is usually best to update this object once all the source devices have been updated. Then the receiver can process all the new data at once. If we used call-back functions to deliver each new sample to the high-level processors then a processor might need to first wait until it gets all the necessary data from various sources via the call-backs, store the data internally and eventually process the data.

6.2 Device Management

Even tough the input layer is highly threaded, this is invisible to the application programmer; the history buffers are guaranteed to change only when they are explicitly updated. Thus the application programmer does not need to take threading issues into account.

The input device drivers are hidden from the application. This is necessary since they are used to abstract the exact device brand and model from the user. The drivers are designed to be very simple – they simply output one sample at a time.

The driver can be used in one computer, its data is sent over the network to the application running FLUID and received by the corresponding network driver. This distribution of device drivers over a network is necessary since VR installations often have several computers with one computer handling one physical input device. For example in our installation we have an SGI computer for graphics, but the data glove is connected to a Linux PC. The speech recognition software also runs on the Linux PC. The only way to cope with such complex hardware/software dependencies is to run the device-specific servers in the machines that can run them and transfer the data to the computer that is running the actual application (like VRPN).

6.3 Input Device Collection

The input devices are managed by a central input device collection -object. This is a singleton object that is globally accessible[15]. The device drivers are plug-ins that are loaded into the application as the input device layer is initialized. The user can configure the devices via a text file. Thus there is no need to recompile the application to get access to new devices or to change the devices.

When an application needs a particular device it requests the device from the input device collection. If the device is already initialized it is returned, but if not, the system tries to initialize it and then returns it. This allows applications the ease to ask for any device at any time. Since the input collection keeps track of devices the programmer does not need to worry about how to start or shut down the devices.

If the application needs to do complex operations on the input devices then this approach may not fit the needs. The most problematic part is a case where an application would like to reconfigure the input devices after they have been initialized. As this is a rare case we have not created very elaborate system for these cases. In these cases the application can how-ever stop the desired device, reconfigure it and restart the device.

7 Data Processor Layer

Typically applications cannot use the input data directly. Instead the input data needs to be refined to be useful. For this purpose FLUID has a data processor layer. The objects in the data processing layer transform the data into a form that is more usable for the application.

It is possible for the application to transfer parts of the application logic to the processor objects. Although we make clear distinction between input data processing and application it should be noted that these are not at all independent components. This separation is only intended to serve as borderline between reusable software components and application-specific code. A developer can freely use minimal data processor layer and keep the application monolithic. An extreme alternative is to put as many application components as possible to the data processor layer.

One reason why one might put application logic into the data processing layer is that it can be used as an abstraction layer between the input devices and and the application. For example an application might be able to operate with mouse or camera input. If the camera- and mouse-specific parts of the application can be isolated to the processor layer, then the application logic does not need to know how the input data was collected.

Another element further confuses the separation of input processing and application: Situation-specific tuning of the data processors. This means that the behaviour of the data processors may need to be adjusted to match the current program state. For example we might need to instruct some gesture detector that some of the potential gestures are not accepted when the application is in some state. This has already been the case in our previous research where the gesture detectors and semantic analyzers formed feedback-cycles[16]. With FLUID this is possible, but one must build the data processors to offer the necessary application-specific functionality.

7.1 Processor Collections

The data processing layer is a collection of data-processing objects. Each object performs some operation on either the input data or data coming from other processor objects. The processor objects fall into roughly two categories: gesture detectors and data converters. The gesture detectors serve the application by detecting gestures (or events) as they take place. Data converters do some operations on the input data, but do not try to detect explicit gestures. In some cases high-bandwidth signals can be compressed into simple events. In some others the processor objects simply change the representations of the data – for example from 3D location data to 3D acceleration data. Figure 3 shows how data might flow from the input devices to the application.

In the data processing layer we have adopted a design principle that algorithms are broken down into parts when possible. The advantages of this approach are that processor objects can rely on other objects to perform some routine calculations. This

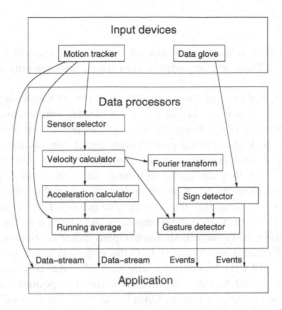

Fig. 3. An example of how data can flow from input devices to the application.

enables different processor algorithms to share parts, resulting in less coding work due to code re-use.

This approach can also result in better computing performance. The reason for this is that if two or more algorithms use the same feature that is extracted from input data, this feature can be calculated only once and the results are shared by all the algorithms utilizing it. For example in figure 3 there are several gesture detectors that need velocity information. With this approach the velocity can be computed only once and the data is then available to all interested objects. While this design promotes modularity it does not rule out big monolithic data processors.

Originally the data processing layer was split into four parts. The purpose of this split was to separate different parts of the signal processing to different layers with one layer following another. Later we realized that the layering was artificial and any layering would be totally application-specific. In practice one can design different layering structures with each layer performing some small operation on the data. For example Bimber's architecture contains eight layers[14]. Of these eight six correspond to the single data processing layer in FLUID. Such layering can be useful for separating tasks, but it also requires application programmers to be aware of all the layers and their interaction. Once we take into account the fact that modules that operate in lower level may need to be controlled by modules from higher level we end up with feedback-cycles that essentially break down the layering approach. For these reasons we selected a single monolithic data processing layer. The users can create arbitrary data processing networks within this layer. Since the FLUID data passing mechanisms are very flexible it is possible to create any kind of layering within data processing layer.

7.2 Data Flow

FLUID has a data-flow architecture that allows arbitrary data to be passed from one object to another. There are two ways to pass data: data streaming via IO-nodes and event passing.

Each processor object can have an arbitrary number of named output nodes. When other nodes need to access the data they typically need to perform two tasks. First they get access to the node that contains the data. At this phase they must also check that the node is of correct type. Typically a processor object stores pointers to its input data nodes and only performs this operation once during its life-time. Once the processor has access to the IO-node they can read data from it. Since the IO-node is of known type the processor object can access its data directly, with minimal overhead. This data-flow architecture causes minimal run-time performance penalty. The user can introduce new IO-node types by inheriting the virtual base class and adding the data structures for the new type. In practice this scheme is similar to OpenTracker's data-flow architecture[12]. The primary differences are that in FLUID the users can create new processors and IO-node types and FLUID does not (yet) support XML-based processor-graph creation. Additionally the FLUID data-flow architecture is based on polling – data is not pushed from processor to another. In fact the OpenTracker framework could be implemented on top of FLUID's input-device and data-flow components.

While the data-flow architecture is good for dealing with fixed-rate signals it is not ideal for passing events that take place seldom. For these situations we have augmented the system with message-passing interface. Each processor can send events to other processors. Events are delivered with push-approach. FLUID has definitions for the most common event types (integer- and floating point numbers and character strings) and users can introduce new event types when needed.

7.3 Processor Creation

The processor objects are recursively created as needed. For example the application might request for an object that detects hand claps. In this case the application passes a request-object to the processor collection[15](page 233). This request object first checks if the requested object type (with matching parameters etc.) already exists. If the object does not exist then the request-object tries to create one. This may lead to new requests since the gesture detector would need to know the acceleration of the hands. This causes a request for an acceleration object. As the acceleration calculator is created it needs a velocity calculator. The velocity calculator in turn needs a motion tracker which it requests from the input layer.

If the gesture detector programmer had been very clever there might even be a possibility that if there is no way to detect hand claps with motion trackers (they might be missing) then the request-object could try to create a clap detector that relies on microphone input or accelerometer input. At any case the request tries to create the processor object and all necessary objects recursively. If the process is successful then it returns an object that outputs events as user claps hands.

This infrastructure enables the application to ask for a particular data processor without knowing what is the exact method by which the data processing detector works (or even the needed input devices). This system also enables different algorithms to share common parts without knowing much else than the output node types of the relevant objects. While this infrastructure provides a way to share algorithms and algorithm parts between applications it is heavy if one only needs to create specific processor object. To accommodate these cases there is a possibility to directly add a data processing detector to the collection, bypassing the request approach.

The system includes dependency management that tries to optimize the call-order of the processors. Thus the system first calls the nodes that are closest to the input and once they are updated it goes on to the higher-level nodes.

There can be multiple data processor collections in one application. This makes it easy for an application to shut down one processor section if it is not needed. For example when application changes its state and user interaction type it might switch over to a totally different set of data processors.

7.4 Example

An example of how the nodes behave is in figure 3. The left side of the figure shows how a stream of data is transformed as it passes through the system. The motion tracker object has an output node called "location". This node contains a ring-buffer of motion samples. The sensor selector reads data from the motion tracker and stores data from one sensor to two output nodes (velocity and rotation). The velocity calculator reads data from this node, calculates the velocity of the tracker sensor and places the data to its own output node. The acceleration calculator is in fact identical to the velocity calculator. The only difference is that it takes its input from the output of velocity calculator. The running average calculator in turn uses the acceleration data it obtains from acceleration calculator and calculates the average acceleration over a period of time. The application in turn can use this as parameter according to the application logic.

In the right hand side there is a sign detector that relies detects different finger signs. As the sign changes the information is passed to the application in the form of an event.

In the center there is a network that combines data from two sources. The Fourier transform calculator performs Fourier separately on each three dimensions of the velocity vector. The gesture detector then uses information coming from the Fourier transformation, sign detector and velocity calculation to trigger an event as the user performs some gesture.

8   Implementation

Above we have outlined the FLUID architecture. This architecture could be implemented in nearly any language or platform. In this section we outline our proof-of-concept implementation. By proof-of-concept implementation we mean that the current FLUID toolkit does not have support for a wide range of input devices, device types or data processors. It has been used in pilot applications to test the architecture in practice.

We have implemented FLUID with C++. This choice was made since we already use C++ and it offers high performance, reasonable portability and support for object-oriented programming. At the moment the FLUID core libraries work on IRIX and Linux operating systems. The drivers in turn are rather platform-specific, so some of them work on IRIX, some on Linux and some on both. The FLUID library is very compact and it can be easily ported to any platform that offers support for ANSI C&C++ and POSIX threads. FLUID does not have any other external dependencies so porting it to different platforms should be fairly easy.

Any application can use the components of FLUID – it does not force the application into certain framework (internal main-loops etc.). As such it can be added to nearly any software with ease.

The input layer and processor layer are in separate libraries. It is therefore possible to use only the input layer in projects where the data processors are not needed.

FLUID library is internally multithreaded, but it hides the complexity of multi-threaded programming from application developer. However, the system is not thread safe in a sense that if the application developer utilizes the FLUID input API from multiple threads the results are undefined. It should be noted that this is a limitation of the current implementation and as there are only a couple of places where a conflict might occur, it should not require much effort to make the system fully thread safe.

The current version has an API and input drivers for mice, motion trackers, data gloves and speech recognition. The speech recognition system is based on the commercial software package ViaVoice by IBM[17]. The speech recognition API is independent of the ViaVoice package however.

There is also possibility to write data onto the disk and read it later (as with VRPN). This enables us to simulate and debug application behaviour without actually using the physical devices. This cuts down costs as one can test VR applications with realistic input data without using the expensive VR facilities. It also helps in debugging since we can use identical input data sequences between runs.

All of the device drivers have option for network-transparent operation – the physical device and the application can be in different computers. The device data is transmitted over a TCP/IP connection from the physical device to the application. This network operation is encapsulated within the FLUID device drivers so that application developers do not need to know about such details. This feature was necessary since some of the devices we use can only be attached to one kind of computer (Linux PC) while the application runs in other kind of machine (IRIX workstation). While network transparency has not been a primary goal for us it is a positive side-effect of our implementation strategy. This only applies to the input drivers, we have not tried to make FLUID processor collection a distributed system like QuickSet[3]. A programmer creating a new data processor can of course distribute the processors to multiple CPUs with multithreading or to multiple computers via network interface.

The FLUID device drivers are implemented as plugins that are loaded as the application starts. Thus there is no need to modify the core libraries to add new device drivers. This also guarantees that the device APIs do not depend on any particular device manufacturer's proprietary APIs or protocols.

An important detail we only realized when implementing the input layer is that the input threads must have a possibility run often enough. The problem is that a multitasking operating system may well give plenty of CPU-time to the main thread of the application, but fail to give enough CPU-time to the input threads. As a result the input data buffers do not get new data even tough there would be new data available. This problem occurs when the main thread of the application is very busy (many multimedia application – games and VR systems – do just this). The way to overcome this problem is by increasing the priorities of the input threads so that they can run as fast as they need to run. This also reduces the latency caused by threading.

We have also built a small library of data processors. This library offers a few gesture detectors (simple hand clap- and finger sign detectors) and some feature extractors (velocity and acceleration calculators and finger flexure calculator).

8.1 Performance Issues

The FLUID architecture has been designed with performance issues in mind. Depending on the application there are two alternate bottle-necks.

The first cause for overhead is the input layer. The threading and buffering of input data cause extra overhead for the application. In normal circumstances this is hardly a problem. As a benchmark we created a minimal application that reads data from motion tracker, mouse and two data gloves – all at 33 Hertz sampling rate. This application consumes less than 3 percent of the available CPU time on low-end hardware (SGI O2 with 195MHz R10k processor). This reflects the fact the the input driver threads do not have much to do. Most of the time they wait for new data to come. This figure does not tell the actual overhead of the input layer, but even if the load of 3 percent was caused solely by FLUID overhead this is seldom harmful for the application. A situation where such overhead might become significant is in the realm of ubiquitous computing. In these cases the host computer may have the computing power of an old 386 or 486 -processor. In any case the computer running FLUID must be powerful enough to run a multitasking operating system. Obviously many embedded systems do not fulfill this criterion.

The other potential bottle-neck is the data-processing layer. Even tough the data processors may do heavy computation this layer should not cause significant overhead. The data is passed from one processor object to another directly without any generalization mechanisms. In theory the only source of overhead compared to a dedicated solution should be the single virtual function call per data processor.

8.2 Latency

Some multimodal applications require minimal latency between input data measurement and the moment when the data is used. For example in immersive virtual reality systems it is necessary to update the projection with data that is as new as possible. Thus the toolkit should not induce extra latency in the data transfer path.

In the FLUID architecture the device driver threads are run at high "real-time" priority that guarantees that the drivers threads can always operate when new data becomes available from the physical data source (device/network). As a result the device threads can offer the data immediately to the application thread. In practice this approach minimizes the latency caused by FLUID to the short time that the operating systems spends when switching between threads.

9 Fluid and Other Toolkits

It is sometimes the case that the application is using another toolkit that depends on user input. This might impose a problem, since it is rare that input device APIs have support for accessing the input from multiple toolkits at the time. Typical case like this arises in VR systems since virtual reality toolkits must utilize some input devices to be successful. The most common reason for this is the projection calculations that are done to compensate user movements. As a consequence many toolkits (VR Juggler, DIVE) have integrated motion tracker support. While this makes life easy for the toolkit it poses a problem for a programmer who wishes to use FLUID – the tracker device is managed by the other toolkit with it's internal API. This makes it impossible for FLUID to connect to the device.

We have solved this problem with VR Juggler by creating new VR Juggler device drivers that actually run on top of FLUID input layer. In this way VR Juggler works perfectly while the actual data is coming from FLUID. One might also do the reverse – use VR Juggler native device drivers and transmit data from those over to FLUID. This latter alternative would have the problem that VR Juggler does not maintain history of samples in the low-level drivers. As a result the FLUID drivers would have to re-sample the VR Juggler input devices with some frequency hoping that no samples would be lost. This would certainly lead to loss of data quality.

With our current approach one has the benefits of both systems: VR Juggler's integrated projection management and FLUID's high quality input data and data processing libraries.

10 Building Applications with FLUID

The FLUID libraries has been designed to fit easily into many kinds of applications. To outline how one can use FLUID in a new application we give an example of how one can use FLUID in a multimodal application. Although this example is expressed in general terms it matches the AnimaLand application that we have build (explained in section 11).

A typical multimodal application collects input data from several devices and delivers output to the user via multiple media. The application has a main loop that is synchronized to one of the devices – for example the application may draw a new graphics frame each time the main loop is executed (common approach in games). In each loop iteration the application collects input data from the devices and uses application logic to control the output devices (graphics, sound, etc.). The loop iteration rate can vary as the application runs depending on how heavily the computer is loaded.

The threaded and buffered input device layer of FLUID fits this scheme well – the application can run at nearly any iteration rate and the input devices will not lose data. The application can use the gesture detector layer to extract information from the input data. The input data is turned into fixed-rate data streams or events that the application receives via call-backs functions (as in many GUI toolkits). The application builds one or more processor collections to match its needs. While one collection might fit to the needs of a particular application there are cases where the ability to remove parts of the processing is necessary. For example the application might require special processing when it enters a given state. In these situations the application can build new gesture detector collections on demand and erase them as they are no longer needed. Alternatively the application can create the detectors in the beginning and later on simply use the relevant processor collections.

There can be special output and input devices that need to be controlled separately from the application main loop. Often the reason for this separation is that there are strict latency limits that some input/output -operations must meet (force-feedback and audio systems being common examples). The processing for these special devices often happens in a separate high-priority thread. If the application needs such high-priority threads to process data at rate that differs fro the main loop rate these threads must have processor collections of their own. All the threads can how-ever access the same input devices as long as the application makes sure that the different application threads do not update the input devices while another thread is reading data from them.

11   Examples

We have used FLUID in three cases. These cases illustrate how building multimodal applications is easier with FLUID and how it can be used as a small component to intro-duce novel input devices to any application. The first two applications also demonstrate user interaction that is very different from the traditional computer usage. Such new interaction styles could potentially be used to enable more universal access to informa-tion technology and information networks. Compared to our previous experience with handling novel input devices [1][2] these new applications were easier to create.

In the AnimaLand project we built an application where user can control computer animated particle system in real-time[18]. The control mechanisms are gesture-based. For interaction we selected gestures that are easy to detect – hand claps and finger gestures. We also included some generic parameters to be used as control – average velocity of and the average joint angle ("fistiness") of user's left hand. Figure 4 shows the application in use. The processor layer with its gesture detectors simplified the application development significantly. Instead of building the data-processing blocks inside the application we coded the gesture detectors into the FLUID library. As a result the gesture detectors are usable in other applications as well. The application architecture became more modular since we could separate input processing from the animation engine. We could also take advantage of FLUID's ability to store the input data to a file. We used this feature for debugging and also as a way to store the control information for post-processing the animations later on.

In another project undergraduate students of our university created a virtual reality sculpting application "Antrum" (figure 5). The user can "draw" lines and surfaces in 3D space by moving hands. In this case the ability to collect data at constant sampling rate is very important. The application must collect motion data at constant rate even if the rendering process slows down significantly. In practice artists always create models that eventually choke the computer. With FLUID the application can refresh the graphics at any rate (be it 6 or 60 Hz) and we can still guarantee that all details of the user's motion will be stored at the specified sampling rate (be it 33 or 133 Hz). If one only got the

Fig. 4. The user is working in the AnimaLand environment.

motion samples as the application main loop executes once then we would lose data as the graphics frame rate goes down. Although Antrum does not use the FLUID processor layer the input layer is used since it offers a simple API to access the devices and handle the buffering issues.

Our third project was a desktop-application that needed to get input data from a cheap motion tracker. The application was a sound-processing engine Mustajuuri that is running the signal processing at very low latency – less than 10 milliseconds[19]. The motion tracker access was a cause for random latency – it took some time to read each new sample from the device. To move this cause of latency to another thread we used the FLUID input layer. As a result the sound-processing thread can execute at the required rate and the data from the motion tracker is made available to it when the data is read from the device. In this case FLUID was only a small component within a large pre-existing application. Since FLUID does not enforce any particular application framework it was easily integrated in this case.

12   Conclusions and Future Work

We have presented an architecture for user input data management and outlined our implementation of the architecture.

This architecture incorporates support for arbitrary input devices and arbitrary input processing networks. It is intended to make programming of multimodal applications easier.

We have created a toolkit to handle user input. The toolkit is fit for different applications, but it has been tested and proved only in VR applications so far. We have found

Fig. 5. Sculpting in virtual reality.

that FLUID makes application development easier. It offers a clear distinction between input data, input processing and application and offers a useful set of data processors.

The FLUID architecture has proven to be solid and thus there is no need for major adjustments. In future we expect that most of the work will be in adding new device drivers and device types (audio, video and MIDI input for example). We are also planning to test FLUID in a multimodal desktop application that relies on video and audio input.

References

1. Ilmonen, T., Jalkanen, J.: Accelerometer-based motion tracking for orchestra conductor following. In: Proceedings of the 6th Eurographics Workshop on Virtual Environments. (2000)
2. Ilmonen, T., Takala, T.: Conductor following with artificial neural networks. In: Proceedings of the International Computer Music Conference. (1999) 367–370 URL: http://www.tml.hut.fi/Research/DIVA/old/publications/1999/ilmonen_icmc99.ps.gz.
3. Cohen, P.R., McGee, D.R., Oviatt, S.L., Wu, L., Clow, J., King, R., Julier, S., Rosenblum, L.: Multimodal interactions for 2d and 3d environments. IEEE Computer Graphics and Applications (1999) 10–13
4. Schoemaker, L., Nijtmans, J., Camurri, A., Lavagetto, F., Morasso, P., ıt, C.B., Guiard-Marigny, T., Goff, B.L., Robert-Ribes, J., Adjoudani, A., Deféé, I., Münch, S., Hartung, K., Blauert, J.: A taxonomy of multimodal interaction in the human information processing system. Technical report, ESPRIT BRA, No. 8579 (1995)
5. Proakis, J.G., Manolakis, D.G.: Digital Signal Processing. Macmillan Publishing Company, New York (1992)

6. Laurence, N., Joëlle, C.: A design space for multimodal systems: Concurrent processing and data fusion. In: The proceedings of InterCHI '93, joint conference of ACM SIG-CHI and INTERACT. (1993) 172–178

7. Salber, D., Dey, A.K., Abowd, G.D.: The context toolkit: Aiding the development of context-enabled applications. In: Proceeding of the CHI 99 Conference on Human factors in Computing Systems, Pittsburgh, Pennsylvania, United States, ACM Press New York, NY, USA (1999) 434–441

8. Mankoff, J., Hudson, S.E., Abowd, G.D.: Providing integrated toolkit-level support for ambiguity in recognition-based interfaces. In: Proceedings of the CHI 2000 conference on Human factors in computing systems, The Hague, The Netherlands, ACM Press New York, NY, USA (2000) 368–375

9. Landay, J., Myers, B.: Sketching interfaces: Toward more human interface design. Computer **34** (2001) 56–64

10. Bierbaum, A., Just, C., Hartling, P., Meinert, K., Baker, A., Cruz-Neira, C.: Vr juggler: A virtual platform for virtual reality application development. In: The Proceedings of IEEE VR Conference 2001. (2001)

11. CAVELib: Cavelib user's manual. WWW-page (Cited 24.6.2001) http://www.vrco.com/CAVE_USER/.

12. Reitmayr, G., Schmalstieg, D.: An open sotfware architecture for virtual reality interaction. In: Proceedings of the ACM symposium on Virtual reality software and technology, ACM Press New York, NY, USA (2001) 47–54

13. Taylor, R.M., Hudson, T.C., Seeger, A., Weber, H., Juliano, J., Helser, A.T.: Vrpn: a device-independent, network-transparent vr peripheral system. In: Proceedings of the ACM symposium on Virtual reality software and technology, ACM Press New York, NY, USA (2001) 55–61

14. Bimber, O., Encarnação, L.M., Stork, A.: A multi-layered architecture for sketch-based interaction within virtual environments. Computers & Graphics **24** (2000) 851–867

15. Gamma, E., Helm, R., Johnson, R., Vlissides, J.: Design Patterns: elements of reusable software. Addison Wesley Longman Inc. (1994)

16. Ilmonen, T.: Tracking conductor of an orchestra using artificial neural networks. Master's thesis, Helsinki University of Technology, Telecommunications Software and Multimedia Laboratory (1999)

17. IBM: Ibm voice systems. WWW-page (Cited 24.6.2002) http://www-3.ibm.com/software/speech/.

18. Ilmonen, T.: Immersive 3d user interface for computer animation control. In: The Proceedings of the International Conference on Computer Vision and Graphics 2002, Zakopane, Poland (2002 (to be published))

19. Ilmonen, T.: Mustajuuri - an application and toolkit for interactive audio processing. In: Proceedings of the 7th International Conference on Auditory Displays. (2001) 284–285

Anthropomorphic vs. Non-anthropomorphic Software Interface Feedback for Online Systems Usage

Pietro Murano

University of Salford, Computer Science, School of Sciences, Gt. Manchester,
M5 4WT, UK
p.murano@salford.ac.uk

Abstract. This paper answers an important question concerning the effectiveness of anthropomorphic user interface feedback. The issue of effectiveness has been unresolved for some time, despite the efforts of various prominent computer scientists. By means of a carefully controlled tractable experiment, significant statistical evidence has been found to suggest that anthropomorphism at the user interface in the context of online systems usage is more effective than a non-anthropomorphic method of feedback. Furthermore, the results can be generalised to most software systems for online systems usage, thus potentially changing the way user interface feedback is designed, developed and thought about. This will lead to the improvement of user interfaces making them more usable, more effective and more accessible to all. Computer systems are being used more and more, where potentially every household and work environment will have a computer in the near future. Hence making systems accessible to all, including 'non-traditional' users is becoming increasingly more important. This research is making a contribution to this general aim.

1 Introduction

User interfaces using some element of anthropomorphism have attracted the attention of various computer scientists, where some have attempted to make conclusions on the effectiveness and user approval of such interfaces. Currently there is a dichotomy between computer scientists. Some are in favour of interfaces using some anthropomorphic element (e.g. Agarwal [1], Cole et al. [4], Dertouzos [5], Guttag [6], Koda and Maes [9], Maes [10] and Zue [17]) while others are against such interfaces (e.g. chapter by Shneiderman in [2] and [16]). However both sides do not provide concrete enough evidence to suggest that they are correct in their stance.

Certain individuals in favour of anthropomorphic interfaces (e.g. Koda and Maes in [8] and [9]) appear to begin with the premise that these are beneficial in nature, despite leaving the issue open concerning the appropriateness of using facial expressions at the user interface as expressed by Maes [10]. Others such as Microsoft [2] are favourable to anthropomorphic interface feedback as can be seen by the Persona Project which uses a parrot to help a user find and play music tracks. They indirectly justify their use of such an interface by using the work of Nass et al [14]. However the work by Nass does not prove that anthropomorphism is more effective.

N. Carbonell, C. Stephanidis (Eds.): User Interfaces for All, LNCS 2615, pp. 339–349, 2003.

The main sceptic concerning anthropomorphism is Ben Shneiderman [16]. He argues that anthropomorphism is ineffective and mainly disliked by users. He uses evidence from various sources, e.g. Brennan and Ohaeri [3] and Resnik and Lammers [15], to support his stance. However the quoted works did not particularly look at the issue of effectiveness and user approval of such interfaces. These were mainly concerned with user behaviour issues [15] and user interaction in a social sense [3]. Furthermore, the feedback tested by these individuals was solely textual in nature thus not necessarily being representative of other anthropomorphic types of feedback such as 'faces'. Also the experiments by Brennan/Ohaeri and Resnik/Lammers used between users elements in the experimental design, which involved users not trying all types of feedback. It would have been more reliable to have a within users design where subjects tried all types of feedback with appropriate tasks. This is because despite randomisation, a group of subjects assigned to a particular interface feedback could have a confounding disparity compared with the other group(s) of subjects.

Recently the dichotomy mentioned at the outset of this paper has begun to be resolved particularly in the interface feedback setting. The first set of results from the experiment by Murano [12], concerning user approval issues of anthropomorphic interface feedback, show with clear statistical results that in the context of online systems usage, specifically UNIX commands, subjects preferred the anthropomorphic feedback. This was compared against a non-anthropomorphic feedback. Given a choice of the anthropomorphic or non-anthropomorphic feedback, a high proportion of subjects (63.64%) said they would have chosen the anthropomorphic feedback. Furthermore, certain subjects felt more secure with the anthropomorphic feedback. Some subjects expressed that they felt they could trust the information being given to them in an anthropomorphic manner and that they liked it.

Hence the results presented below concern effectiveness issues of such feedbacks and combining the user approval results from [12], conclude this particular experiment. Based on significant statistical evidence (presented below), in the context of online systems usage, specifically using UNIX commands, the anthropomorphic interface feedback was more effective than the standard non-anthropomorphic feedback. This is very useful and interesting for the overall aim of improving access to computer systems and for helping novices use computer systems they are unfamiliar with.

2   Online Systems Usage Experiment – UNIX Commands

2.1   Hypotheses

Answers to the following questions were the aim of this part of the experiment.

- Is a direct mapping (using video of a human as the direct mapping, i.e. anthropomorphism) of human-oriented information to software interface feedback effective? (effectiveness in this case was defined as the user achieving the tasks, the user achieving the tasks in as few incorrect attempts as possible and the user faltering as few times as possible.)

- Is an indirect mapping (using guiding text as the indirect mapping, i.e. non-anthropomorphism) of human-oriented information to software interface feedback effective?
- What guideline(s) can software interface feedback designers receive?
- Furthermore, a null hypothesis (H_0) linked to the first two questions above was tested:
- There will be no difference between the 2 conditions (video and guiding text) - for effectiveness.

An alternative hypothesis (H_1) considered was:

- Video (anthropomorphic) feedback would be more effective than the text feedback (non-anthropomorphic).

Further, this experiment, where UNIX commands was the 'foundation', rested within the broader area or domain of software for online systems usage knowledge. The reason for this was to try if possible, to make a generalisation based on the results of this experiment, to cover the broader area of similar software.

2.2 Users

- All the users taking part in the study were adults.
- Males and females took part.
- All the subjects had differing personal backgrounds. This was taken to be individuals studying different courses, having varied birthplaces and having varied hobbies/work experience. This information was elicited by pre-experiment questions.
- Subjects were found through the university population.
- 55 users new to UNIX commands took part in the study.

2.3 Experimental Design

A within users design was used for this experiment. For the experiment the subjects tried a set of designed tasks. These were:
- Task 1 - The displaying of files in a current directory in long format.
- Task 2 - The displaying of the full path name of the current directory.
- Task 3 - Compressing a file showing the resulting percentage of file reduction.
- Task 4 - Deleting a given file.

Subjects used both types of feedback, i.e. the video and the guiding text condition. Two tasks would be given video as the attached feedback and the remaining two would receive the guiding text. The first two tasks were more simple (i.e. less key strokes and easier syntax) compared to the last two tasks which were deliberately made a little more complex (i.e. more key strokes and more difficult syntax). Furthermore these were typical UNIX tasks that a beginner could wish to do. This was realistic because these were the types of commands the author began with, while learning UNIX with a community of students. For randomisation purposes the feedback conditions were rotated, so that one type of feedback was not always linked to a particular task.

2.4 Variables

The independent variables were the types of feedback, i.e.:
- Guiding text.
- Video.

To measure feedback effectiveness the dependent variables concerned observing for each task if the subjects completed a task and if so how many attempts it took to complete. User hesitation if present was also recorded. If user hesitation was recorded, the number of times it occurred was noted. The dependent measures used were by observation.

2.5 Apparatus and Materials

The equipment used for the experiment was:
- A PC running Windows 95, 400 MHz and 128 Mb RAM.
- External speakers.
- IBM ViaVoice Executive Automatic Speech Recognition (ASR) engine [7] (including text-to-speech), trained with a male English accented profile. A full training was the reading of 496 English phrases, predefined in ViaVoice. An English female profile was also obtained for use with female subjects (in practice the author obtained several profiles for having a better chance with voice matching issues).
- Head mounted microphone supplied with the ViaVoice kit.

The prototype was engineered with C++ Builder 3 and the ViaVoice Software Development Kit (SDK), and it was made to 'look like' a UNIX environment.

Running the prototype would present to the user a screen with a single X-Window containing a 'classic' UNIX type shell prompt. At all times an 'end program' button would be available at the top left part of the screen.

Allowing the system's learning algorithm [11] to take effect, would mean the software agent [11] would infer that the current user was a beginner and therefore present a smaller window to the left of the main X-Window asking the user what they wanted to do. The smaller window always contained a 'close' button in case the user wished to not have any feedback. The user would then input via the microphone the appropriate request for obtaining the required information for accomplishing the given tasks (described in Experimental Design section).

Upon a successful ASR, the prototype would display in the smaller window, relevant interface feedback (this was randomised so that one command was not tied to one type of feedback).

If the guiding text (non-anthropomorphic) was presented, the appropriate command would be displayed in the smaller window. If the video (anthropomorphic) feedback was presented, a video clip of a person verbally uttering the appropriate command would be played in the smaller window.

2.6 Procedure

The procedure described below was carried out in the same way for all subjects using the same equipment, questions asked and methods of observation. Each subject was treated in the same manner. This was all in an effort to control any confounding variables.

The experiment took about 30 minutes to complete per volunteer. Subjects were given £3 in cash as a reward, which they signed for, for their participation.

Each subject was booked an appointment during the day. Upon arrival the subjects were given a brief overview of the purpose of the research and then were asked a set of pre-experiment questions concerning the subject's personal background (see section 2.2).

A verbal introduction to the system itself was given, to help the subject overcome any false notions about the system. This included aspects of how to use the ASR module, e.g. to speak clearly and 'normally' (ASR was used to increase the level of usability). Each person was given an indication of the type of feedback that was being tested. Subjects were also briefed on the system behaviour, e.g. the sequencing of the screens involved in the interaction. Furthermore the subjects were assured that the aims of the experiment were to test the software and hypotheses concerning the software, and not to test the person. Each participant was also given a brief explanation as to what UNIX is, and the concepts surrounding UNIX commands. Furthermore in this explanation subjects were told where they would be typing the commands (i.e. which window) and how a command was to be concluded (i.e. by pressing the return key). A description of what they would see was also given, for the reason that a UNIX interface does not look like a regular PC interface. Each subject was also asked if they understood what each task meant and if they indicated they did not know, these would be explained clearly, usually in terms of the equivalent MS Windows operations (as all subjects had used MS Windows but not UNIX commands).

When the subject felt they were ready to start the experiment, they were given the head mounted microphone to put on. Upon running the program the subject would input (via the microphone) the appropriate feedback request for the first task. Upon a successful ASR, the appropriate UNIX command would be issued to the user, where the user would read the text command or view the video (depending on what feedback was issued). The user would then try to input, via the keyboard, the UNIX command the system advised the subject to use. Assuming the subject entered the command in the correct manner, they could then proceed to try the remaining tasks. If they failed/made mistakes in entering the command, they had the option of calling the appropriate feedback help to view the advised command again. This would go on until they achieved the correct command.

The number of attempts a user had in achieving the appropriate command was recorded. Issues causing wrong attempts were to do with syntax. If the user faltered/hesitated in an obvious manner, this was recorded based on observation of the user. A typical example of a user faltering was the user developing a strong puzzled expression at the moment of seeing the feedback and then trying to use the information to complete a task. A further example was a user verbally saying something to the effect of puzzlement. If a user seemed to get 'stuck', they were encouraged to review carefully the feedback they had already seen. If appropriate, issues explained at the outset of the experiment (e.g. basic UNIX concepts) would be briefly reiterated. A few users had a lot of difficulty in achieving the tasks correctly. This was due to them not seeing the importance of reproducing the command exactly as they were given it even though they had been briefed to follow precisely the feedback given. It was the aim of the experiment for subjects to achieve the tasks on their own by using the feedback. Hence if too much prompting was given for achieving a task, it was deemed that the person had not succeeded in that particular task, while still recording the number of errors made.

Final results, e.g. the subject entered the correct commands upon having viewed the feedback etc. would be carefully recorded on an appropriate observation protocol sheet.

At all times during the experiment, the author observed the system behaviour and subject behaviour. For each task completed/not completed a score was assigned for use in the statistical analyses. The score for each task was based on a points system. For each task each subject (unknown to them) was started on 10 points. Each incorrect attempt resulted in the deduction of 1 point. Each hesitation observed, resulted in 0.5 points being deducted. If the task was completed, the score would remain as described. However if the task was not completed a further 1.5 points were deducted from the score. This scoring method was devised to represent fairly a subject's results, e.g. it was felt that each hesitation observed should carry less weight than an actual incorrect attempt, due to hesitation observation being potentially more subjective. Also each 'factor' described, was used to reach a single score because it was felt that they were closely linked together, e.g. an incomplete task could have been due to many hesitations. Confidence in the scoring system was also seen by plotting the scores on a normal distribution plot diagram, which showed the data to be approximately normally distributed.

2.7 Results

The data collected for the UNIX commands experiment was concerned with the effectiveness of the interface feedback (see [12]). The scores of all subjects were approximately normally distributed and were used in an F test and a t-test for the determination of feedback effectiveness.

For 55 subjects, combining the four tasks and comparing video over text, the t observed was 9.45, and the t critical (5 %) was 1.68. This is illustrated in Table 1 below:

Table 1. Comparison of Video vs. Text (t-test Over 4 Tasks)

Comparison of Video vs. Text (Over 4 Tasks)
t-Observed   9.45
t-Critical (5%)   1.68

For 55 subjects, combining the four tasks and comparing video over text, the F observed was 2.42, and the F critical (5 %) was 1.60. This is illustrated in Table 2 below:

Table 2. Comparison of Video vs. Text (F-test Over 4 Tasks)

Comparison of Video vs. Text (Over 4 Tasks)
F-Observed 2.42
F-Critical (5%)   1.60

For the 55 subjects in the combination of the 4 tasks comparing video over text, one subject's data showed an outlier in the normal distribution plot diagram for the video feedback. Hence the outlier was removed and the t-test and F test were conducted again for the remaining 54 subjects over the 4 tasks. The results were a new t observed of 10.21 with a t critical (5%) of 1.67. The new F observed was 5.68, while the F critical (5%) was 1.60. This is illustrated in Table 3 below:

Table 3. Comparison of Video vs. Text (t-test & F-test Over 4 Tasks With Outlier removed)

Comparison of Video vs. Text (Over 4 Tasks) Outlier Removed
t-Observed   10.21
t-Critical (5%) 1.67
F-Observed   5.68
F-Critical (5%) 1.60

For 55 subjects, combining tasks 1 and 2 and comparing video over text, the t observed was 4.14, and the t critical (5 %) was 1.68. This is illustrated in Table 4 below:

Table 4. Comparison of Video vs. Text (t-test Over Tasks 1 & 2)

Comparison of Video vs. Text (Tasks 1 & 2)
t-Observed   4.14
t-Critical (5%)   1.68

For 55 subjects, combining tasks 1 and 2 and comparing video over text, the F observed was 16.03, and the F critical (5 %) was 1.60. This is illustrated in Table 5 below:

Table 5. Comparison of Video vs. Text (F-test Over Tasks 1 & 2)

Comparison of Video vs. Text (Tasks 1 & 2)
F-Observed 16.03   F-Critical (5%) 1.60

For 55 subjects, combining tasks 3 and 4 and comparing video over text, the t observed was 5.67, and the t critical (5 %) was 1.68. This is illustrated in Table 6 below:

Table 6. Comparison of Video vs. Text (t-test Over Tasks 3 & 4)

Comparison of Video vs. Text (Tasks 3 & 4)
t-Observed   5.67   t-Critical (5%)   1.68

For 55 subjects, combining tasks 3 and 4 and comparing video over text, the F observed was 1.59, and the F critical (5 %) was 1.60. This is illustrated in Table 7 below:

Table 7. Comparison of Video vs. Text (F-test Over Tasks 3 & 4)

Comparison of Video vs. Text (Tasks 3 & 4)
F-Observed   1.59   F-Critical (5%)   1.60

Concerning the 55 subjects, for tasks 3 and 4 comparing video over text, one subject's data (same subject as for the combination of the 4 tasks above) showed an outlier in the normal distribution plot diagram for the video feedback. Hence the outlier was removed and the t-test and F test were conducted again for the remaining 54 subjects over tasks 3 and 4. The results were a new t observed of 7.27 while the t critical (5%) was 1.67. The new F observed was 4.21, while the F critical (5%) was 1.60. This is illustrated in Table 8 below:

Table 8. Comparison of Video vs. Text (t-test & F-test Tasks 3 & 4, With Outlier removed)

Comparison of Video vs. Text (Tasks 3 & 4) Outlier Removed	
t-Observed	7.27
t-Critical (5%)	1.67
F-Observed	4.21
F-Critical (5%)	1.60

2.8 Conclusions

The results were studied firstly by combining the four tasks together in order to get an overall reliable conclusion. However it was also of interest and importance to look at the combination of tasks 1 and 2 and tasks 3 and 4 as two separate groups, as tasks 1 and 2 were 'simpler' tasks compared to tasks 3 and 4 (simpler is defined by the author as being fewer keystrokes and easier syntax). It was important to try and find out if one type of feedback was more effective for 'simpler' tasks while perhaps not being as effective for more difficult tasks (or vice versa).

Concerning the results for the combination of the 4 tasks, the t-test shows a large significance in favour of the video feedback (anthropomorphic). The F test conducted confirms the large significance in favour of the video feedback. Hence in this context, the video (anthropomorphic) feedback is more effective than the text feedback (non-anthropomorphic), over a span of various tasks of various complexity. Furthermore the significance in this conclusion is strengthened if one removes the outlier described in the previous section. This is because the t test and F test becomes even more reliable when outliers are removed and because the significance figures are much larger.

Significance can also clearly be seen for the combination of tasks 1 and 2. The t-test and F test both show a large significance in favour of the video feedback (anthropomorphic). Clearly the video is specifically more effective over 'simpler' tasks.

There is also significance in favour of the effectiveness of the video feedback for the combination of the 'more difficult' tasks 3 and 4. The t-test shows a large significance in favour of video for effectiveness. The F test is just reaching the 95% confidence margin, but is so close that between this score and the t-test score significance can be taken from the F test as well. The reason the F test score does not greatly exceed the 95% confidence interval is because the outlier of before has been left in the figures. If the outlier is removed, then both the t-test and F test dramatically exceed the 95% confidence interval, allowing one to conclude that the video was more effective for the 'more difficult' tasks 3 and 4.

These results show that the video feedback (anthropomorphic) was significantly more effective compared to the text feedback (non-anthropomorphic). This conclusion applies to 'simpler' and 'more difficult' tasks either combined or separated.

Therefore from the results, the null hypothesis (H_0) raised at the beginning of the experiment, can be confidently rejected. There was clearly a difference for effectiveness. Hence, the second hypothesis (H_1) can be confidently accepted as it hypothesised that the video would be more effective. Confidently one can suggest that video feedback is more effective in a UNIX commands situation, particularly where beginners to the environment are concerned. This result for this particular software domain and particular context within this domain has been missing in the current 'world knowledge' and will therefore add to and hopefully modify the current thought about interface feedback design.

From the discussion, one can generalise concerning these results. In the software domain of online systems usage knowledge, a direct mapping of human-oriented information to software interface feedback, such as video, is highly desirable. The overall suggestion is that this type of feedback would be more effective and preferred by users [12]. Since all of the subjects for this experiment were complete beginners to UNIX commands, one should take this aspect into consideration. Due to this aspect being of importance it would be prudent to have such software with an alternative means of feedback. This is because once the basic syntax/format is learned in an environment such as UNIX commands, more experienced users are likely to not require the full explicit video feedback. A further aspect that could be considered is to have a more explicit video feedback for beginners and a less explicit video feedback for more experienced users, always with the option of perhaps having the text feedback available if wanted. Various other types of software within this domain (online systems usage) can be used as examples. Software such as word processors, painting packages, spreadsheet packages and interface navigation fall within this domain. The better systems of this type currently use 'tutorials' to help a user achieve systems usage knowledge by sometimes running a closed session showing the various buttons and menu options to be chosen to achieve a particular task. The idea is that then the user can remember or perhaps write down the steps to be followed. These though would be better served by the type of feedback (e.g. video) of this experiment, where a 'tutor' could 'walk' the person through the appropriate steps. This is used sometimes in teaching environments, where in the author's teaching experience, one or more beginners are 'walked' through the various steps for achieving a task, e.g. a mail merge in MS Word or creating combo boxes in MS Access. Clearly in this situation the beginner has the responsibility of practising the steps on their own in order to master them. With such a system online though, the beginner could call the appropriate feedback when required.

It is therefore recommended for designers of this type of software and interface feedback in this particular domain, to use a direct mapping of human-oriented information (anthropomorphism), such as video. It would also be prudent to include other types of feedback, perhaps similar to the current methods of using a closed session for illustration purposes. This would be with the idea of catering for the more experienced user who may not need to have a 'hand holding' feedback.

3 Concluding Remarks

As has been seen from the results and conclusions, the dichotomy concerning the effectiveness of anthropomorphism at the user interface has been resolved specifically for the domain of online systems usage. Hence the overall issue is on the way to being fully resolved by using the results presented in this paper and by using the results addressed by the overall research conducted by the author experimenting in other domains (e.g. [13] addresses the above issues in the context of English as a Foreign Language pronunciation). This has been made possible by designing carefully controlled tractable experiments which deal directly with the questions of effectiveness and user approval of such interface feedback.

Furthermore the results and conclusions add to the world knowledge of user interface feedback design/development, which had been deficient. This is always with the aim of enabling users to use computer systems more effectively with a higher level of satisfaction, where it has been seen that in the context discussed above the anthropomorphic user interface feedback was more effective than the standard non-anthropomorphic feedback.

Acknowledgements. The author would like to thank Computer Science at the University of Salford and all the willing volunteers who took part in the experiment.

References

1. Agarwal, A. Raw Computation. Scientific American. (1999), 281: 44–47.
2. Bradshaw, J. M. Software Agents, AAAI Press, MIT Press. 1997.
3. Brennan, S.E and Ohaeri, J.O. Effects of Message Style on Users' Attributions   Toward Agents. CHI '94 Human Factors in Computing System,. (1994).
4. Cole, R., D. W. Massaro, et al. New Tools for Interactive Speech and Language Training: Using Animated Conversational Agents in the Classrooms of Profoundly Deaf Children. Method and Tool Innovations for Speech Science   Education, London, (1999), Dept. of Phonetics and Linguistics, University College London.
5. Dertouzos, M. L. The Future of Computing. Scientific American. (1999), 281: 36– 39.
6. Guttag, J. V. Communications Chameleons. Scientific American. (1999), 281: 42,43.
7. IBM, IBM ViaVoice 98 User Guide, IBM, 1998.
8. Koda, T. and Maes, P. Agents With Faces: The Effect of Personification. Proceedings of the 5th IEEE International Workshop on Robot and Human Communication, (1996), *IEEE*.
9. Koda, T. and Maes, P. Agents With Faces: The Effects of Personification of Agents. Proceedings of HCI '96, London, (1996), British HCI Group.
10. Maes, P. Agents That Reduce Work and Information Overload. Communications of the ACM. (1994), 37(7): 31–40, 146.
11. Murano, P. A New Software Agent 'Learning' Algorithm. People in Control An International Conference on Human Interfaces in Control Rooms, Cockpits and Command Centres, UMIST, UK, (2001), IEE.
12. Murano, P. Mapping Human-Oriented Information to Software Agents For Online Systems Usage. People in Control An International Conference on Human Interfaces in Control Rooms, Cockpits and Command Centres, UMIST, UK, (2001), IEE.
13. Murano, P. Effectiveness of Mapping Human-Oriented Information to Feedback From a Software Interface. 24th International Conference Information Technology Interfaces, Cavtat, Croatia, (2002).
14. Nass, C., Steuer, J. et al. Computers are Social Actors. CHI '94 Human Factors in Computing Systems – 'Celebrating Interdependence', Boston, Massachusetts, USA, (1994), ACM.
15. Resnik, P.V. and Lammers, H.B. The Influence of Self-Esteem on Cognitive Responses to Machine-Like Versus Human-Like Computer Feedback. The Journal of Social Psychology. (1986), 6 : 761–769
16. Shneiderman, B. Designing the User Interface - Strategies for Effective Human Computer Interaction, Addison-Wesley, (1992).
17. Zue, V. Talking With Your Computer. Scientific American. (1999), 281: 40,41.

A Scalable Avatar for Conversational User Interfaces

Uwe Berner and Thomas Rieger

Technische Universität Darmstadt, Interactive Graphics Systems Group,
3D Graphics Computing, Fraunhoferstraße 5,
64283 Darmstadt, Germany
{uberner, rieger}@gris.informatik.tu-darmstadt.de
http://www.gris.informatik.tu-darmstadt.de

Abstract. Computers are becoming more and more ubiquitous, moving from the desktop into our everyday life. Today's challenge is to build a suitable visualization architecture for anthropomorphic conversational user interfaces which will run on different devices like laptops, PDAs and mobile phones. This new kind of interface will be adaptive to the current user, personal preferences, the history of the conversation, the device and the current context. Concrete implementations as a part of conversational interfaces are User-Interface Avatars, anthropomorphic representatives on the base of artificial 2D or 3D characters. The user can talk to an avatar on every device he is using. The avatar system is designed to exchange different graphical representations of the avatar easily. The existing system and ongoing work on optimization and renderers implementation are discussed.

1 Introduction

Computers are becoming more and more ubiquitous. You can see it, if you look around you: Laptops, PDAs, Smartphones and other gadgets like MP3-Player. They are moving from the desktop into our everyday life. This leads to the important question of how the user interfaces should look like for this new generation of computing.

An important field of activity at the Interactive Graphics Systems Group (GRIS) is Conversational User Interfaces where the primary goal is to give the computer a face to talk with. This includes natural dialog-centric communication patterns to interact with the computer. The user is migrating from the paradigm of direct manipulation to the usage of assistance functionality. The goal is the development of software architecture to shift complex tasks to human like assistants (avatars) which can be incorporated on different stationary and mobile devices like laptops, PDAs and mobile phones.

Everyday technology, such as office and home equipment, has become more and more powerful – and the corresponding interfaces more and more complex. Consequently, most people have problems to control the various systems and appliances and hardly anybody knows how to access all features of a device. Think for instance of a VCR and its programming features. One reason for this problem is that traditional interfaces, mostly based on the WIMP metaphor (windows, icons, menus, pointers),

N. Carbonell, C. Stephanidis (Eds.): User Interfaces for All, LNCS 2615, pp. 350–359, 2003.

are not sufficient to control all aspects of today's technology or are not able to display complex menu structures on small devices. For the question of designing the PDA of the future see [1]. One possible approach will be to provide an assistance function with a universal, easy to use, and efficient interface. In this context our vision is that the new human computer interaction paradigm "assistance" is going to replace the so far valid paradigm of the "computer as a tool" [2] and will be used on a wide variety of devices.

This new kind of interface includes the design and control of the conversation, not only to mediate the information, also to establish a relationship with the user. Furthermore the system is adaptive to the current user, personal preferences, the history of the conversation and the current context.

Conversational User Interfaces represent such an interface and provide complex dialogue structures. Conversational interfaces evolve beyond natural speech interaction, including nonverbal behavior such as facial expressions and gestures towards new kinds of face-to-face interactions. [3] [4]. A new approach is to use methods of story telling to create the conversation like in [5].

2 Overview

Concrete implementations at the Interactive Graphics Systems Group (GRIS) as part of conversational interfaces are User-Interface Agents/Avatars, anthropomorphic representatives on the base of artificial 2D or 3D characters. They represent a human-computer interaction with the explicit presence of emotional aspects contained in every communication using facial expressions, gestures, and poses. The overall human-machine dialogue is controlled by a preceding dialogue control, which manages all user-interface components and modalities. It also decides on given sentences to be generated by a speech synthesis software, and delivers them to the avatar platform.

Our goal is to make this conversational user avatar available for different use cases, different users and different devices. The user interface avatar should be adaptable to different performance conditions, environments and devices. To achieve this goal the graphical representation should be scalable depending on the graphic performance, the environment, the conversation modus and the available devices. At the same time the generation of the avatar animations and the interface to the dialogue controlling parts of the software system should be unchanged.

The steps to achieve this "User Interface for all" are:

1. Implement the Avatar-Platform
2. Separate the graphical representation (renderer)
3. Construct different renderers for different devices
4. Optimize the renderers
5. Construct an Adaptation Engine

So far we have done step one and two. Step three, four and five are work in progress. In Figure 1 the idea of the different renderers and the adaptation is illustrated.

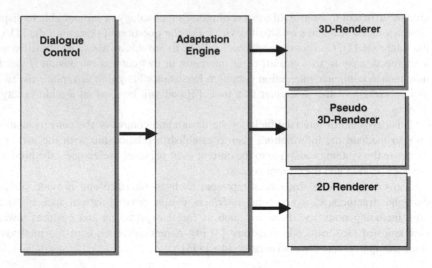

Fig. 1. Adaptation and Renderers

The graphical adjustments mentioned above are driven from the Adaptation Engine that controls the appearance of the avatar depending on the context. Thereby the emerging graphical bottlenecks are registered and different optimization methods are used to avoid a slow down of the output.

There should be three classes of renderers. 3D -Renderer uses real 3D systems and require the highest performance of the hardware. Pseudo 3D-Renderer uses images of 3D heads and produces a stream of pictures. 2D-Renderer uses points to illustrate an icon-like head (note that the 2D version should be used on small devices, for example, mobile phone displays). For different renderer output see Figure 2.

Fig. 2. Different renderer output

One important point is that all the animations generated by the Dialogue Control are independent from the renderers. This means you can easily exchange the graphical appearance without changing the generation of the dialogue i.e. the interface to the Dialogue Control. The selection of the different representations (3D / pseudo3D / 2D) takes place with a combination of user-, environment- and device-profiles. An adaptation of the speech output to different devices is not in the scope of this paper.

3 Avatar-Platform

The avatar platform represents the graphical output of a conversational user interface. Commands delivered to the avatar are processed in different units. An overview of the avatar platform is given in Figure 3.

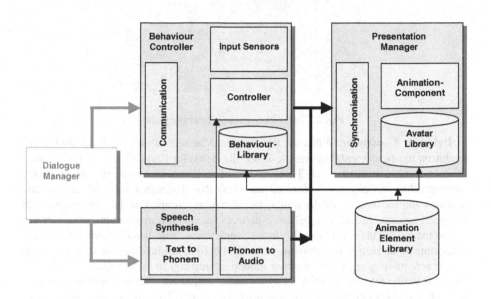

Fig. 3. Architecture of the Avatar Platform (with preceding Dialogue Manager)

This platform consists of the following components:

Presentation Manager: This module provides the functionality to present animated artificial characters, to perform facial animations, and to achieve lip sync. The facial structure is based on Morph Targets and efficiently realized as a Morph Node (Alexa et. al. 2000) [6]. Hereby, a wide range of facial expressions can be provided, while the parameterization of the face is kept simple and can be realized with just a few key values. Key-frames defining the state of the animated character may consist only of a small number of such values and playback is possible even over low-bandwidth networks and on small portable devices. Moreover, facial animations can easily be mapped to different geometries, thus further extending the possible choices for the user interface designer. In this way, photo-realistic avatars or comic-like characters can be displayed and animated. Figure 4 presents a more comic-like character model.

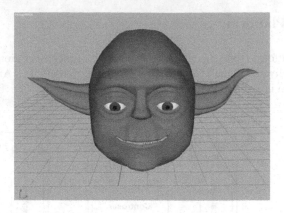

Fig. 4. Comic-like character (smiling yoda)

Behavior Controller: While the Presentation Manager allows for the control of the avatar on the fundamental geometric level, the Behavior Controller provides an interface on a more abstract level. Tasks and even motivations can be specified and the corresponding actions are performed automatically. Examples for such actions are gestures and movements of the avatar, but also more complex facial expressions with temporal aspects. In addition, behavior patterns for specific motivations or moods can be activated. This corresponds to a sometimes rule-based, sometimes non-deterministic activation of behavior elements. Possible applications for this are simple avatar actions (e.g. accidental looking around or smiling) to avoid repetitive behavior, which is easily detected as artificial by the human observer. One of our objectives is to make the avatar more natural and less artificial or stiff. Even if the underlying application layer does not invoke any action the avatar presents randomly generated behaviors like eye blinking or head movement. The different animation sequences representing an explicit gesture or an unconscious behavior are synchronized via a blackboard mechanism, which also controls the appearance of the emotional state of the avatar.

Speech Synthesis: An important requirement for the Avatar in order to achieve a realistic appearance is speech output with lip-sync. Since the dialogue with the user is not known in advance, prerecorded animation sequences with lip animation cannot serve as a solution. Instead, the real-time lip sync with the audio output generated by a speech synthesis module is developed. For this, the speech synthesis system is expected to generate phoneme information, which will be mapped to the appropriated viseme. Phonemes are communicated using the international standard SAMPA [7]. The mapping to a viseme or sequences of visemes is based on timing and frequency information available in SAMPA. Heuristics are used to generate nonverbal facial expressions from phoneme information. This concept offers several advantages:

Lip-sync is realized automatically assuming that speech synthesis works in real time. Interactive applications with speech generation during and based on the interaction are possible. This is in strong contrast to systems based on a set of pre-generated animations. A transparent system working with a speech synthesis for several languages is relatively easy to implement. New developments in the area of speech synthesis systems are easy to incorporate. Inclusion of new features of such systems appears to be a simple task. A general (system independent) problem is the fact that most commercial speech synthesis systems are not open. This means the intermediate phoneme level is not accessible from outside. In our implementation we use MBROLA [8], which is the result of an EU project and publicly available. We are also trying to emphasize the content of the speech with gestures and facial expressions. For this purpose we analyze the prosody of the text based on the generated phonemes. Depending on the emphasis in the spoken text the avatar performs supporting actions such as moving the eyebrows and the eyelids.

To give a better impression of the existing system some screenshots will be given. Figure 5 depicts a selection of frames of one animation sequence generated in real-time, showing the overlay of general facial expressions with the lip-sync information produced from a speech system. At the beginning the avatar is speaking an "o", then smiles, and at the end closes the eyes.

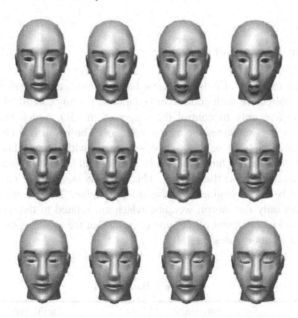

Fig. 5. Animation Sequence produced by the system

Figure 6 shows a screen shot of the running system.. One possibility is to type a sentence in the text field where pressing the speak button will cause the text to be spoken by the avatar with corresponding facial animations. In addition you can scale the avatar, change the position on the screen or initiate some hand movements.

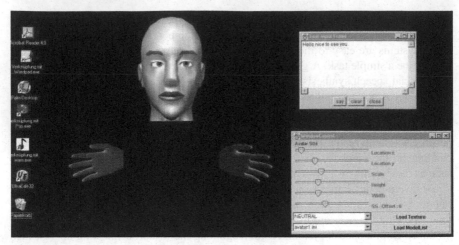

Fig. 6. Screenshot Avatar System

4 Separate 3D-Renderer

To improve the usability of existing avatar base systems components we developed a client server architecture with one server and arbitrary many Clients [9] [10]

The clients have only to control the output of the 3D model, that is a Java3D-Renderer. The server manages the avatar behavior. The result is a connection with a very small bandwidth because the control is managed with the weights of the different morph targets. The morph targets are only simple double values. Thus the control of the avatar is easily done via the internet. This was only possible through the separation of models and behavior engines and the morph engine. This means that the morph engine provides only the morph weights, which are related to the basic types. Basic types are defined independent of the type of being that the avatar is representing (e.g a woman, a man, a cat or a dog, etc.).

Table 1. Basic Types

mode	language	facial expression
normal	DGRS	left eyebrow
friendly	A	right eyebrow
angry	E	left eyelid
sad	I	right eyelid
	O	left ear
		right ear

In Table 1 the three main groups of morph targets are shown. The mode morph targets are the emotional behavior expression. The language morph targets are responsible for handling the avatar speech. The facial expression morph targets handle special expressions of the model face. The models can easily be exchanged at any time using a simple mouse click. The 3D-Renderer continues the animation at the same render position even when the model is changed. Additionally it is possible to control more than one model with the same behavior engine, see also [9] [10].

5 Work in Progress

Our work in progress is related to the steps three and four mentioned in the second chapter:
- Construct different renderers for different devices
- Optimize the renderers

For the existing 3D-Renderer (Java3D) some student projects are running to optimize the graphical output of the animation, i.e. the morph node. In Java3D a lot of graphical values are manipulated from the morph node. In our optimization only the animation relevant features are modified from the new morph node. Less varied values are not taken into consideration depending on the actual animation. These are for example: color, not moved vertices or nearly zero weight vector parts. Another approach is to use mesh reduction methods to adapt the complexity of the graphical output. Furthermore the different student groups have developed some methods for the performance measurement.

The students projects results will lead to an acceleration in the morphing process up to five times faster than before. A new Java3D-Class *FastMorph* was implemented to replace the existing morph class. The new class uses some precomputing, better initialization and modified method calls. Also only the changes in the weight vector and in other morph values like moving knots, color and normals are considered. One big problem is the overhead of the Java3D-Machine which is operating more graphical operations than the morph method on its own. To obtain a better acceleration other parts of the 3D-Renderering must be modified or another 3D-System should be used (for example OpenSG) [11].

For the new renderers some conceptual ideas to implement the morph process are topics of the ongoing development. They will be modeled on the principles of the 3D-Renderer which is mainly the morph process. The main idea is to replace the loading and morphing methods from Java3D with pseudo3D- and 2D-Renderer methods. Thus the animation uses the same dialogue generation and weight vectors but specialized morphing methods for pseudo3D and 2D images. At the moment are students working on an implementation of the 2D-Renderer, including a loader for 2D-Bitmaps and a morphing method for bitmaps.

6 Future Work

Our future work will consist of implementation of the pseudo3D, the 2D-Renderer and the Adaptation Engine and integrate all components to a full system for conversational user interfaces. Additionally there must be a variety of optimization methods to enable all renderers to be controlled from the Adaptation Engine. This optimization methods should be verified in different use cases. There should at least be efforts to port the renderers to existing hardware devices (PDAs, mobile phones) and make it easy to change the renderers on the same device. Nevertheless there must be a device and performance dependant integration of the speech output. After the integration of all this software components there should be tests in different use cases and scenarios to verify the advantages of the new graphical output facilities for avatars in the context of conversational user interfaces for all. One mobile device we are considering to run the system on, is the P800 from Sony-Ericsson which offers a Java virtual machine, more memory than normal mobile phones and a software development kit [12].

For a possible client-server architecture is to say that the aimed architecture makes it possible to use the conversational avatar in many different web contexts. The internet-usability is trending toward Browser-Plug-Ins. The client, which is in future a simple 3D model browser, is running on a conventional web browser. The models could be loaded and installed from an Avatar server via the Internet. The avatar control will still be running by the avatar server, which will continue the handling of the behavior engines.

7 Conclusion

We have presented the idea of a scalable avatar used for conversational user interfaces. This avatar will run on different systems and environments and will be adapted to the actual context of the user and performance conditions of the actual device. The final result will be a flexible system to build conversational user interfaces on many devices and thus a step towards user interfaces for all. The starting point of the main idea for a scalable avatar is an implementation of an avatar platform connected with a 3D-Rendering system.

The paper starts by giving an overview of this idea. This includes the development of new renderers and the integration via a Adaptation Engine to give the possibility of different graphical representations of the conversational avatar. Subsequently the existing system was described in detail, for example the used morph node, the animation principles and the separated 3D-Renderer. The ongoing work was then discussed in detail including optimizations of the Java3D morph node, first results of student work and conceptual ideas of the new avatar renderers.

The main findings of our work are:
1. We have an existing avatar system which can be extended by new renderers to achieve a usability on different devices and in different circumstances.

2. The existing system is prepared to exchange the 3D-Renderer by exchanging the loading and the morphing methods.
3. Some first steps have been taken to optimize the 3D-Output and to construct a 2D-Renderer using bitmaps.

The challenges for the future work are the development of the new renderers (pseudo-3D and 2D) including new morphing methods which should look pleasant and require less performance. Then all components must be integrated in one system, this includes the renderers and the Adaptation Engine. Another big challenge is the use of different devices to run the system on, especially on mobile phones.

Acknowledgements. This work was partially funded by the German "Bundesministerium für Bildung und Forschung, BMB+F through the Focus Project EMBASSI (BMB+F-No. FKZ 01 IL 904 U8) [http://www.embassi.de].

References

1. Interactions, volume IX.1, ACM 2002
2. P. Maes, Agents that Reduce Work and Information Overload. Comm. of the ACM, 37 (7). July 1994
3. Cassell, J., Sullivan, J., Prevost, S., Churchill, E. (ed.): *Embodied Conversational Agents*, MIT Press, Cambridge, MA 2000
4. Gerfelder, Müller, Spierling: „Novel User Interface Technologies and Conversational User Interfaces for Information Appliances", Extended Abstracts of ACM CHI2000, The Hague, Netherlands 2000
5. Ulrike Spierling: "Storytelling Metaphors for Human-Computer Interaction in Mixed Reality", Computer Graphic Topics 2/2002
6. Alexa, M., Behr, J., Müller, W. (2000). The Morph Node. Proc. Web3d/VRML 2000, Monterey, CA., pp. 29–34
7. SAMPA – Computer readable phonetic alphabet, http://www.phon.ucl.ac.uk/home/sampa/home.htm, 1995
8. The MBROLA Project – Towards a Freely Available Multilingual Synthesizer, http://tcts.fpms.ac.be/synthesis/mbrola.html, 1999
9. Rieger T. Braun N. Group Conversation within an Internet TV Community through a Lifelike Avatar. Proc. of Media Futures 2001, Florence, Italy
10. Rieger T. Braun N. Finke M. Community TV: An Approach to Interaction for Groups and Single Users on Internet Video. Proc. of WSES (MIV 2001), Qawra, Malta
11. OpenSG Forum http://www.opensg.org/, 2002
12. Sony-Ericsson, P800 Mobile Phone http://www.sonyericsson.com/, 2002

Evaluation and Validation of a Conversational Agent Embodied in a Bookstore

Giovanni Semeraro[1], Hans H.K. Andersen[2], Verner Andersen[2], Pasquale Lops[1], and Fabio Abbattista[1]

[1] Dipartimento di Informatica, Universitá di Bari, Italy
{semeraro, lops, fabio}@di.uniba.it
[2] Risoe National Laboratory, Denmark
{hans.andersen, verner.andersen}@risoe.dk

Abstract. This work presents an agent-based interface that is not merely reactive to some user request, but is proactive since it is capable of engaging in a goal-directed conversation with the user, e.g., by taking the initiative to recommend new products. The naturalness of interaction, especially for casual users, is enhanced by appropriate 2D facial models. The proactiveness of the agent is based on a recommendation engine that combines content-based retrieval, which exploits user profiles based on content features extracted from the dialogue and descriptions of items that users find relevant, with collaborative filtering, which clusters users according to their expressed taste to generate recommendations within these virtual communities. The proposed system has been evaluated and validated by using a top-down approach, focusing on the system/user interaction.

1 Introduction

In the era of Internet, huge amount of data are available to everybody, in every place and at any moment. Even though this is extremely useful and exciting, the ever-growing amount of information at disposal generates cognitive overload and even anxiety, especially in novice or occasional users. More specifically, in the field of e-commerce it is well known that the process of buying products and services often implies a high degree of complexity and uncertainty about the conditions of information seeking, items for sale, the purchase of wanted products and the actual navigation on a site. Some important problems concerning e-commerce in general and shopping at Internet bookstores in particular, are: Getting people started on the Web and making their first purchase; using traditional metaphors for shopping on web sites (users are so to speak forced to make their model of shopping fit into a web structure with which they are not familiar); getting people to submit personal information (for more information see [5,6]).

The common theme for the mentioned problems is uncertainty. Uncertainty about the new media, the new ways of shopping, adequate representation of products, trust in the e-commerce sites, the navigation of specific sites and the actual procedures for buying. It is very important to overcome these problems in order to facilitate the use

N. Carbonell, C. Stephanidis (Eds.): User Interfaces for All, LNCS 2615, pp. 360–371, 2003.
© Springer-Verlag Berlin Heidelberg 2003

and acceptance of e-commerce. The solution we proposed for the COGITO[1] project is based on "intelligent personalised agents" (chatterbots), which represent virtual assistants or advisors whose ability is modelled in order to support customers. There are many possible applications for such virtual assistants. They could instruct customers in the use of a Web site, point out new offers, help sift through products, and other support. The main problem of most of today's Web services is that they offer manifold navigation options and (usually simple) search functions, but leave it up to users to find their way through the many interface functions, understand them and interrelate them cognitively. Usually, users have to decide themselves which sequence of actions must be performed to solve a given task. Complex search queries, for example, must be constructed step by step. Beginners and occasional users are often daunted by the complexity of today's services and thus need "proactive" support or advice from the system in order to fully utilise the range of functions available. In order to verify the assumptions underlying the design decisions above, and to find out appropriate ways to adjust the system parameters, the technical development is accompanied and heavily influenced by in-depth evaluations of both the individual components as well as the system as a whole.

The remainder of the paper is organised as follows. Section 2 discusses the advantages coming from extracting dynamic profiles of the customers. Section 3 gives an overview of the whole COGITO architecture, while the retrieval process implemented is described in Section 4. Section 5 presents a thorough description of the empirical evaluation of the system. Finally, conclusions are drawn in Section 6.

2 Profile Extraction to Tailor Contents: Advantages

Personalization is very common in the area of e-commerce, where a user explicitly wants the site to store information on herself, such as her preferences. In fact, the more a system knows about users the better it can serve them effectively. But there are different styles, and even philosophies, to teach computers about user habits, interests and preferences.

User modelling simply means ascertaining a few bits of information about each user, processing that information quickly and providing the results to applications, all without intruding upon the user's consciousness. The final result is the construction of a user model or a user profile [9]. By user profile we mean all the information collected about a user that visits a web site, in order to take into account her needs, wishes and interests. A user profile, as intended within the COGITO project, is composed by two main frames - the frame of user data, which comprehends interaction data (number of searches or purchases within a category, number of connections, etc.) and the frame of user interests, which is a part of the profile built on the basis of supervised learning algorithms. The Profile Extractor [2,16] is the module responsible for the inference of user profiles. It is built upon an intelligent component, called Learning Server, developed in the context of a digital library service [15]. The preferences of the users automatically "learned" by the system, concern the ten main book categories the BOL (Bertelsmann Online virtual shop) product database is

---
[1] COGITO (IST-1999-13347) – 'eCommerce with Guiding Agents based on Personalised Interaction Tools' is an EU-funded project in the 5th Framework Programme.

subdivided into. User profiles are represented by XML files and are the key for personal recommendations because they enable the agent to customise its recommendations to the individual user. As pointed out in [18], the main advantages of using this approach in e-commerce are:

- making the site more attractive for users: A web site that takes into account user preferences is able to suggest products reflecting customer needs. It will probably turn a significant part of browsers into buyers;
- obtaining customer trust and confidence: Users will not be requested to explicitly insert information concerning their preferences and tastes, but they will be able to participate in the management and updating of their personal profile. This will result in an increase of their trust and confidence in a system able to automatically collect data about their preferences;
- improving customer loyalty: The effectiveness of a personalization system improves in the long run. Every time a customer interacts with the web site, the personalization mechanism collects new data about her preferences, so that a more and more satisfactory service can be offered. In this case, passing to the competition is often unfavourable for a customer. In fact, even if a competitor uses a personalization system, it has to learn a lot of information about the new customer to be able to offer the same satisfactory service.

3   An Overview of the COGITO Architecture

This section describes the COGITO architecture (Figure 1), identifying the role of the Profile Extractor module within the system. The general architecture is based on six macro modules: BOL Web-server, Connector, eBrain, Profile Extractor, Prompter and XML Content Manager (XML CM). The overall system architecture is centred around an existing chatterbot system, eBrain by Logica pdv, capable of engaging a conversation with users.

The integration with back-end systems is realized through the Connector that enables the system to access external services and knowledge sources. The XML CM provides a suite of web services to support the creation, management and distribution of XML documents and specific Document Type Definitions (DTDs) or Schemas.

In the COGITO architecture, the Profile Extractor module is the personalization component which dynamically discovers user preferences from data collected in the course of past dialogues with the chatterbot. By examining the dialogue histories, it extracts some characteristics that are useful for recognising the categories preferred by a buyer. Indeed, the module is capable of automatically assigning a customer with a subset of product categories (book categories).

Finally, the Prompter is an automatic query expansion system accessing the user profiles. Applying a rule interpreter, the prompter is able to use the structure of documents and, through comparisons with the profile terms, to expand the original query acquired via chatterbot.

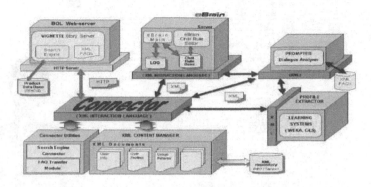

Fig. 1. The architecture of the COGITO system.

4   The Retrieval Process in COGITO

On the ground of the profile, the chatterbot offers a better support to customers during their interaction, providing personal recommendations and purchase incentives, or helping users in problematic situations during the search. This improves the usability of the BOL web site [1], as shown by the following scenarios of usage of the system.

Scenario 1: unknown user. A user is known by the COGITO system if she completes the BOL registration procedure. This step allows providing each customer with a personal identification number and is necessary to both recognise a user accessing the on-line media shop and collect data about her preferences for generating/updating her profile. In the first scenario, a dialogue (translated into English) between the chatterbot, named Susanna, and an unknown user asking the chatterbot for a book by author "King" is undertaken.

Susanna:	Good evening! My name is Susanna. What is your name?
User:	My name is Fabienne.
Susanna:	Nice to meet you, Fabienne. What can I do for you?
User:	I'm looking for a book.
Susanna:	Are you looking for a book by a specific author?
User:	Yes
Susanna:	What is the name of the author?
User:	King
Susanna:	I shall check whether we have a book by the author called King.

Susanna finds several books by the author "King" through a remote call (deep linking) to the search engine available on the BOL web site and displays them, as shown in Figure 2. It can be noticed that the books ranked first are by the author Stephen King. Books by other authors are found further down the list, which means that the user should scroll down a long list if she was not looking for a book by Stephen King. The customer who is not looking for a Stephen King book can now choose to either refine the search by using an advanced search function or continue to chat with Susanna about different fields of interest.

Fig. 2. Susanna offers a long list of books belonging to several categories by authors whose last name is "King".

Scenario 2: registered user. In the second scenario, the user has already been chatting with Susanna about some of her interests. Therefore a profile of this user is available to the system, which can exploit it to accomplish a more precise search in the product database. Let us suppose that the profile of such a user contains the category *Computer_und_Internet* with the highest degree of preference and the category *Kinderbücher* (children book) with a lower degree of preference, and that the submitted query is the same as the previous scenario.

Now, the first book displayed in the page of the search results is a book about Windows 2000 written by Robert King (Figure 3).

This result is due to the fact that the original query "King" has been automatically expanded by the system in "King" AND "Computer & Internet" (highlighted by the circle in Figure 3), since "Computer & Internet" is the category with the highest degree of interest in the profile of the user.

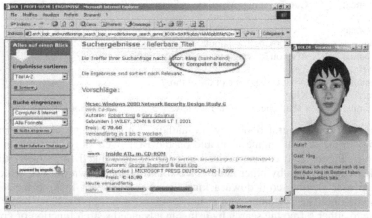

Fig. 3. List of books written by authors whose last name is "King" belonging to the book category "Computer & Internet".

These scenarios point out the dependence of the result set on the profile of the user that issued the query. In fact, when a user asks the chatterbot for a book by author "King", it dynamically builds an XML file containing the string "King" as the value of the proper tag – in this case <author> – and sends it to a module called Prompter [10], that performs the expansion of the original query by using the favourite book categories stored in the profile of the user. The query expansion process consists of an improvement of the criteria used for the specification of a query. This is usually achieved by modifying an already defined query by adding search terms taken from three different sources, that are a *product thesaurus, user profiles* and *usage patterns*. Products like books or other kinds of media are usually characterized by a textual description. The most relevant words contained in these descriptions are clustered according to their relations to the most frequently appearing ones, thus generating a *thesaurus* of terms. On the other hand, user profiles are accessed for identifying the book categories preferred by a user, which can be enclosed in a query for a more specific result identification. Concerning the Usage Patterns, the application of association rules to a specific user can lead to infer a possible interest of this user in a product or service [3]. In this way, the chatterbot can decide which dialogue context to use when the dialogue comes to a dead end, i.e. when the user does not want to neither take the initiative nor mention a specific topic of discourse. The information retrieved by the interface to the information sources (i.e. the expanded keywords, the preferred book category or the dialogue context coming out from an applied usage pattern) is used for the generation of a deep linking, which is directly forwarded to the chatterbot by the Prompter, responsible for determining a suitable query expansion method to be used, according to the information available in the input file. The decision process is thoroughly described in [11].

5   Empirical Evaluation

Our evaluation approach is inspired by numerous studies within the area of user modelling and user-adapted interaction (for an overview of these studies see Chin [12] and the empirical evaluation examples in Chin and Crosby [13]). Our experimental design is similar to that suggested by Litman and Pan [14], that is, the experiment is designed to test if a proactive agent supports users better than a non-proactive. In this way we have used a control group approach to our evaluation. Thus, in order to have a reference for evaluating the COGITO proactive agent, a baseline session was performed using the BOL site equipped with a non-proactive 'BOL state-of-the-art agent' for comparing the two agents. Our evaluation measures are described in the following sections.

The evaluation of the COGITO agent has been performed by letting the groups of test persons solve various tasks related to searching general information or specific products utilising the agent (for a description of the tasks-scenarios see [4]). The BOL agent had a level of chatting performance in line with existing agents of today and was integrated to the BOL site by having simple links to products being requested by the customer, i.e. this agent had no proactive features. The test persons recruited for the test sessions were grouped in four groups of eight persons each, two groups of novices and two groups of experienced users, in order to test the validity of the COGITO prototype for each of these types of end-users. These groups may be treated individually or – if preferred for improving statistical considerations – added two by two as groups of 16 persons for each agent to be compared. The test groups consisted of 19 students and 13 employed persons. The average age for all was 25,7. There was an equal distribution in gender. The criterion for being placed in a group of novices or experienced users was experience concerning use of computers, facilities on the Internet and using the net for buying purposes. Previous experience with agents on the Internet was not seen as an important criterion, and the background of the test persons showed that none of the novices had any experience with agents, whereas a few of the experienced users had worked with agents one or more times.

The evaluation is partly based on quantitative measures related to analysis of the conversation log, partly on eye-tracking specifying the time the user spent looking at the agent, the answers given by the agent, or the BOL site itself, and partly on qualitative measures based on fulfilment of detailed questionnaires. The test persons were requested to complete the questionnaire revealing their satisfaction with the system and the agent concerning various aspects as defined below.

5.1 Conversation Log Analysis

The analysis of the conversation log served the purpose of measuring the conversation performance in terms of number of correct text output, fallback sentences, and proactive sentences (see Figure 4). The measure "Correct text output" is based on manual analysis and interpretation of successful elements of the agent-user dialogue consisting of one user text input string, e.g. a request for information or a search query, and one agent output text string, e.g. delivering a correct answer and/or requesting further information from the user. The analysis related to the conversation log is based on 611 text strings created by the BOL agent and 368 text strings created by the COGITO agent. Using Chi-Square the COGITO agent shows significant better performance than the BOL agent with respect to the correct output category (61% vs. 47%; $p < 0,05$). It seems that the COGITO agent is better at recognising search terms; it has a better vocabulary and rule set than the BOL agent. Furthermore, the fact that the BOL agent is relatively passive and therefore does not in the same sense as the COGITO agent produce true proactive requests in response to user input adds further to the explanation. A proactive agent sentence is counted every time the agent successfully takes a word or a string of words and constructs a contextually meaningful response to user input. The BOL agent of course also asks questions, but they are more passive and general, and the agent does not utilise user input in stating further requests. These types of sentences we do not count as proactive. Examples of a proactive and a not proactive conversational sequence are given below, respectively:

A proactive:

| User: | Please tell me something about Microsoft Office? |
| Agent: | Which Office software do you most often use? |

and the not proactive:

| User: | What can I do online? |
| Agent: | How can I be of further assistance to you? |

In addition, we have also analysed the heterogeneousness of the conversations using two measures: the proportions of fallback sentences and the various sentence categories applied by the agents. We consider a large occurrence of fallback sentences as an expression of poor conversation performance. That is, there is a risk that the users will get frustrated if the agent "speaks" in phrases or clichés, which means that the users experience a rather stereotypical conversation. In this sense, both agents did not show optimal performance. A Chi-Square test showed that the BOL agent performed significantly better than the COGITO agent (22% vs. 27%; $p < 0,05$). However, the use of fallback phrases may be somewhat dubious, as a sentence like 'please, reformulate your input', which normally is a fallback sentence, may be seen as a correct input related to, e.g., a typing error by the user. In addition, the COGITO agent showed a larger variation in the conversation by using 9 different categories of fallback sentences, while the BOL agent only used 6 different categories. Another example of a fallback sentence is: "Interesting expression. Never heard it before. What do you really mean by that?".

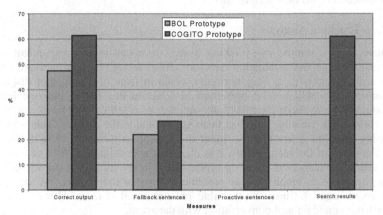

Fig. 4. The result of the analysis of the agent-user conversation log in terms of number of correct text output, fallback sentences, proactive sentences and % positive search results.

Moreover, we have also looked at the search results generated by the agent in prompting the BOL search machine. In this respect a successful query is counted every time the agent, on the basis of selected user input plus the added search terms created by the query expansion process, prompts the BOL search machine with queries that produce a correct list of search results in terms of relevance for a given user situation (task), no matter if the user recognises this. That is, we have repeated all the search queries listed in the conversation log using the BOL search machine and analysed the result in relation to the users tasks. The non-proactive BOL agent does not produce search queries. Instead, it operates with a concept of static "deep linking" based on general input from the user. However, most static deep links did not function because BOL changed its platform during the evaluation session.

Furthermore, we have analysed the average length of user queries. On an average, a user query contained 5,05 words when addressing the COGITO agent and 2,95 words when addressing the BOL agent. A T-test showed this variation significant ($p < 0,05$). In an analysis of queries posed by users at Excite, a major Internet search service, Jansen et al. [8] found that web queries are short. On an average, a query contained 2,21 words. Our users created queries that contained more than twice the number of words compared with the Excite users. Nevertheless, compared to studies of queries in traditional information retrieval systems like online databases (e.g.

DIALOG) and public access catalogues (e.g. library catalogues), the COGITO queries are relatively shorter. In traditional information retrieval systems the queries on an average varies from 7 to 15 words dependent on the users expertise varying from novices to very experienced (for more information on this topic see e.g. Fenichel [7] and Spink and Saracevic [17]). In fact, one of the main reasons for introducing intelligent agents on the web is exactly to overcome some of the obstacles of traditional information retrieval like e.g. the use of Boolean operators and at the same time to allow users in a natural way to type their queries in a conversational manner. With an average query length of 5,05 words, the proactive agent tended to perform better than the traditional web based search engines (like Excite) without demanding the users to use any Boolean operators, and as shown in Figure 4 with good performance in terms of search results.

5.2 Eye-Tracking Analysis

We have used a remote eye-tracking system to measure the respondent's visual behaviour during the evaluation session. This device is non-intrusive and the respondents can behave as they normally would in front of a computer display. The eye-tracking data will not be presented in detail in this paper, but one important conclusion that may be of interest to the suppliers of e-selling may be drawn. For both prototypes, much viewing time has been spent outside the display. This may not be surprising since the agent requires input in terms of written text using the keyboard. From the video of the respondents, it is clear that approximately 40% of the viewing time outside the display is spent on typing at the keyboard. So, if the supplier wants the user to spent as much time as possible looking at the display, the conversation might be arranged by use of selectable pre-structured phrases. However, this will diminish the aimed natural conversation with the agent.

5.3 Questionnaire Analysis

The members of the test groups indicated their impression and comparison of the two agents by filling out a detailed questionnaire concerning 7 measures: impression, command, effectiveness, navigability, learnability, aidability, and comprehension.

A few examples of the outcome concerning these criteria are presented below. The result of the 'Impression – users feelings or emotions' is presented in Figure 5 (for a full presentation of the evaluation see Andersen et al. [4]). The questions related to the impression of the agent are based on the agent being enjoyable or a bit awkward to use, and if the user would recommend use of the agent to colleagues. The groups of novices had rather negative feelings for both agents in this respect, probably because novices expect an agent - when being available - should act unimpeachably in all situations. The experienced users, however, are aware of the need of a period for maturing a new product, and in fact, the satisfaction among these users has increased from 44% for the state of the art agent to 61% for the COGITO agent as shown in Figure 5 concerning "Exp. 1" and "Exp. 2", respectively, summing the columns "Satisfied" and "Very Satisfied".

Another example is the comprehension shown in Figure 6. In this class, the questions were related to the user's personal feeling of understanding of the information given by the agent, the action of the agent, the interaction between the agent and the BOL site, and about how to operate the agent in relation to this site.

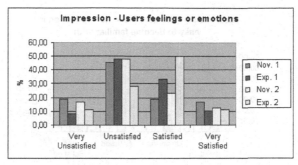

Fig. 5. User feelings or emotions. Numbers are shown in percentage of the total number of user ratings in each category.

Like for the 'impression', the satisfaction of the novices is less than the satisfaction of the experienced users. Both agents seem to appeal equally to the users in this respect as 44% of the novices feel satisfied or very satisfied with their understanding of the interaction for both agents, while the feeling of understanding is 72% for the experienced users.

However for the 'learnability' (see Figure 7), related to the information needed in beforehand in order to be able to act with the agent, as well as the acquaintance of the agent based on just short time of experience, the analysis indicated a significant increase in satisfaction for the novices having the satisfaction (satisfied and very satisfied) in using the agent increased from 37% for the state of the art agent to 55% for the COGITO agent. Once again the experienced users were even more satisfied, even though the satisfaction decreased from 77% to 70% going from the state of the art agent to the COGITO agent.

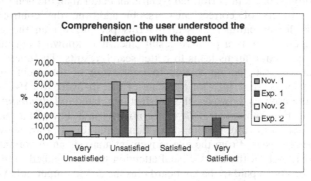

Fig. 6. How well did the users understand the interaction between the BOL site and the agent?

Due to the limited number of test persons (based on time and financial limitations), the results related to the questionnaire analysis are just indicative and not statistical significant. A Mann-Whitney test for 95% confidence indicated $p = 0,35$ for improved satisfaction among the experienced users for the *impression*, $p = 0,64$ for a difference in *comprehension* among experienced user, and $p = 0,37$ for improved *learnability* among the novices for the COGITO agent as compared with the BOL agent.

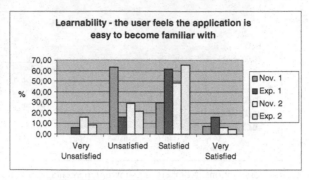

Fig. 7. Learnability of the prototypes.

6 Conclusions

The COGITO agent has been evaluated for two groups of test persons, novices and experienced users, to test if the agent is able to facilitate the interaction between the user and the BOL e-commerce site. The COGITO agent developed in the project has been compared with a BOL agent representing the state of the art of Internet agents of today. The conversation log analysis showed that the improved query facilities, based partly on the expanded search criteria (due to the improved thesaurus) and partly on the search criteria presented directly by the user related to the improved conversation, led to a relatively large number of positive search results. However, we were not able to compare the two agents on this measure. The log analysis also showed that the COGITO proactive agent performed significant better than the non-proactive agent in terms of numbers of correct answers. In addition, the control group used a significantly lower number of search terms per query than the group using the proactive agent. This is a positive result since it is known from other studies that entering more search terms leads to better search results. The questionnaire analysis showed that the satisfaction related to *impression* of the agent increased for the experienced users from 44% for the state of the art agent to 61% for the COGITO agent. For the novices, however, the satisfaction related to *learnability* increased from 37% to 55%. For both agents 44% of the novices said they had a good or very good comprehension of the user system interaction, while this measure showed 72% among the experienced users. From the eye-movement analysis an important result was that approximately half of the users' visual attention was not related to the display on the screen, but has been paid to the keyboard plus the agents' input field while typing.

References

1.   Abbattista, F., Degemmis, M., Licchelli, O., Lops, P., Semeraro, G., Zambetta, F.: Improving the Usability of an E-commerce Web Site through Personalization. In: F. Ricci, B. Smyth (eds.), Recommendation and Personalization in eCommerce, Proceedings of the Workshop on Recommendation and Personalization in eCommerce, 2nd International Conference on Adaptive Hypermedia and Adaptive Web Based Systems, Malaga, Spain (2002) 20–29

2. Abbattista, F., Fanizzi, N., Ferilli, S., Lops, P., Semeraro, G.: User Profiling in an Application of Electronic Commerce. In: Esposito, F. (ed.): AI*IA 2001: Advances in Artificial Intelligence, Lecture Notes in Artificial Intelligence, Vol. 2175. Springer: Berlin (2001) 87–98
3. Abbattista, F., Licchelli, O., Lops, P., Semeraro, G.: Usage Patterns Extractor. Deliverable 4.3, COGITO IST-1999-13347, University of Bari, IT (2001)
4. Andersen, V., Andersen, H.H.K.: Evaluation of the COGITO system. Deliverable 7.2, COGITO IST-1999-13347, Risoe National Laboratory, DK (2002)
5. Andersen, V., Andersen, H.H.K., Hansen C.B.: Establishing criteria for evaluating intelligent agents in E-commerce. In: Proceedings of the UM 2001 Workshop on Empirical Evaluations of Adaptive Systems (2001)
6. Andersen, V., Hansen, C.B., Andersen, H.H.K.: Evaluation of Agents and Study of End-user needs and behaviour for E-commerce, COGITO Focus group experiment, Risø-R-1264 (EN), CHMI-01-01, Risø National Laboratory, Roskilde, Denmark (2001)
7. Fenichel, C. H.: Online searching: Measures that discriminate among users with different types of experience. Journal of the American Society for Information Science, 32 (1981) 23–32
8. Jansen, B.J., Spink, A., Saracevic, T.: Real Life, Real Users, and Real Needs: A Study and Analysis of User Queries on the Web. Information Processing & Management, 36 (2000) 207–227
9. Kobsa, A.: User Modeling: Recent Work, Prospects and Hazards. In: Schneider-Hufschmidt, M., Kuehme T., Malinowski, U. (eds.): Adaptive User Interfaces: Principles and Practice. North-Holland, Amsterdam (1993) 111–128
10. L'Abbate, M., Thiel, U.: Helping Conversational Agents to Find Informative Responses: Query Expansion Methods for Chatterbots. In: Proceedings of the Autonomous Agents and Multi Agents System Conference July 2002, Bologna, Italy
11. L'Abbate, M., Thiel, U.: Intelligent Product Information Search in E-Commerce: Retrieval Strategies for Virtual Shop Assistants. In: Stanford-Smith, B., Chiozza, E. (eds.), E-work and E-Commerce - Novel solutions and practices for a global networked economy. Proceedings of the E-Work and E-Business Conference (e2001), IOS Press, Amsterdam (2001) 347–353
12. Chin, D.V.: Empirical Evaluation of User Models and User-Adapted Systems. User Modeling and User-Adapted Interaction, 11 (2001) 181–194
13. Chin, D.V., Crosby, M.: (Eds) Empirical Evaluation of User Models and User Modelling Systems. Special Issue of User Modeling and User-Adapted Interaction, 12 (2002)
14. Litman, D.J., Pan, S.: Designing and Evaluating and Adaptive Spoken Dialogue System. User Modeling and User-Adapted Interaction, 12 (2002), 111–137
15. Semeraro, G., Esposito, F., Fanizzi, N., Ferilli, S.: Interaction Profiling in Digital Libraries through Learning Tools. In: Borbinha, J., Baker, T. (eds.): Research and Advanced Technology for Digital Libraries, Lecture Notes in Computer Science, Vol. 1923, Springer: Berlin (2000) 229–238
16. Semeraro, G., Ferilli, S., Fanizzi, N., Abbattista, F.: Learning Interaction Models in a Digital Library Service. In: Bauer, M., Gmytrasiewicz, P.J., Vassileva, J. (eds.): User Modeling 2001, Lecture Notes in Artificial Intelligence, Vol. 2109. Springer: Berlin (2001) 44–53
17. Spink, A., Saracevic, T.: Interactive information retrieval: Sources and effectiveness of search terms during mediated online searching. Journal of the American Society for Information Science, 48 (1997) 741–761
18. Tasso, C., Omero, P.: Personalization of web content: e-commerce, i-access, e-government, Franco Angeli, Milano (2002) (in Italian)

Part V: Novel Interaction Paradigms –
Accessibility Issues

A Usability Evaluation of a Joystick-Operated Full-Screen Magnifier

Sri Hastuti Kurniawan, Alasdair King, David Gareth Evans, and Paul Blenkhorn

Department of Computation, UMIST
PO Box 88, Manchester, M60 1QD, United Kingdom
{s.kurniawan, a.king, g.evans, p.blenkhorn}@co.umist.ac.uk

Abstract. The paper reports on a usability evaluation of a full-screen magnifier. The evaluation was conducted with seven registered blind users in half-hour comprehension-based sessions using the 'thinking aloud protocol'. The goals of the study were to determine whether joystick control of a screen magnifier was useful. The users found joystick control intuitive and easy to use. The feature with the strongest support was automatically scrolling through the text; the most significant usability problem was over-sensitivity of the joystick in certain modes.

1 Introduction

Visually impaired people who have some functional vision often use a screen magnifier to operate a computer. A screen magnifier is an assistive software tool that displays a magnified portion of a computer's graphical output on a computer's display. There are a significant number of commercial products, for examples see [1]. They provide a number of features, one of the most prominent concerns the proportion of the computer display taken over by the magnified image. This may be: the complete screen, 'full-screen magnification'; a significant portion of the screen (often around half the screen), 'area magnification'; or the area under the mouse pointer, 'magnifying glass' [2]. Informal observation indicates that by far the most widely used mode is full-screen magnification and, consequently, this paper focuses exclusively on this type of magnification.

Whilst screen magnifiers are widely used, there seems to have been little significant evaluation of them from a usability perspective with their intended users, rather than simply gathering expert opinion (although there are a small number of exceptions, for example [3]). This lack of evaluation is perhaps unfortunate, especially when screen magnifiers are becoming increasingly feature laden, perhaps in an attempt by suppliers to gain a competitive advantage. The additional features may prove beneficial to more experienced users. However, the addition of more features may add complexity to the operation of the product, which may hamper novice users and those who will never become expert computer users. It seems appropriate, therefore, to investigate the usability of magnifiers with visually impaired users in order to determine which features are considered essential. The work

N. Carbonell, C. Stephanidis (Eds.): User Interfaces for All, LNCS 2615, pp. 375–386, 2003.

reported here goes some small way towards this goal by evaluating some of the more common features.

The function of a screen magnifier is to present an enlarged view of the user's area of interest. The magnifier determines the area of interest to be the current 'focus' [2], which is presented by the screen magnifier dependent on the current context of operations. The current context is determined from: the mouse pointer position; the cursor position (in for example a word processing application); and changes in operating system or application state resulting in, for example, a pop up window. As far as the user is concerned he/she operates the computer in the normal manner (using a mouse and the keyboard) and the current focus is presented in roughly the center of the screen. To a large extent, the user provides little explicit control of the operation of the magnifier. It is only when he/she needs to change some aspect of the magnifier's settings (for example, magnification level) that he/she issues direct commands, typically through the keyboard.

The authors propose that joystick, rather than standard mouse and keyboard control of screen magnifiers, may be of benefit for some users, especially non-expert computer users. There are a number of motivations for this:

- A joystick can be used as an absolute pointing device (i.e. the position of the joystick corresponds to the position of the mouse pointer – for further discussion see below). The hypothesis is that this should provide more intuitive control than a mouse, which has no spatial reference point. Work elsewhere has comparatively evaluated mouse and joysticks for authoring hypermedia-based user interfaces. The results are not clear, with some blind authors reporting that the mouse offers advantages (e.g. [4]) while in an academic discussion forum some researchers argued that theoretically a joystick is easier to use for a blind person (e.g. [5]).

- A joystick may be easier to control than a mouse for some users, especially older users who may have problems in grasping and manipulating a mouse.

- Modern joysticks (especially those that are designed for the control of computer games) typically have a large number of buttons and other controls. These can be assigned functions that are used to control the configuration of the magnifier (for example, setting magnification level) so that the user does not have to move back to the keyboard when he/she wants to change settings.

2   Goals of Study

This study described in this paper has three goals. The primary goal is to determine whether joystick control of a screen magnifier is easy to use by people with visual impairment. The other goals are to evaluate some features associated with joystick control of a magnifier (for example to evaluate different modes of operation – details are given later) and also to evaluate some of the common features provided by commercial magnifiers.

3 Screen Magnifiers and the Use of Joysticks

3.1 Common Features of Screen Magnifiers

As noted earlier, screen magnifiers provide a number of features for their users. In this section we describe some of the most common. The features that are included in this discussion are those that were evaluated in the user trials.

The user can control the degree of enlargement. Typically enlargement is given in integer multiples between 2 and 16 times, although some magnifiers permit enlargement of up to 32 times. Some magnifiers, including the magnifier used in this trial, allow independent control of magnification of the horizontal and vertical dimensions. When horizontal and vertical magnification levels differ, the enlarged image is distorted. However, it is thought that some users will benefit from this feature; typically the vertical magnification is set higher than the horizontal magnification for text processing activities in an attempt to trade-off readability of characters (i.e. by making the characters larger) against readability of words and sentences (by maximizing the amount of text that is visible on the screen).

The user has control over the colors. In the simplest systems (including the one used in this trial) the user is limited to the original presentation or an inversion of the colors. Typically, black text on a white background is color-inverted to give white text on a black background, which gives better contrast for some users (see Fig. 1). In other magnifiers the user can select the background and foreground colors from a more extensive set of color-schemes; yellow text on a blue background and amber text on a black background are widely used.

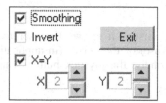

Fig. 1. An example of color inversion, the left part shows no inversion and the right is shown with color inversion.

Most commercial magnifiers (including the one used in this study) provide an option for smoothing the enlarged image. This feature is present because when the image is enlarged it can, for the reasons described in [2], appear 'blocky'. It is thought that 'blocky' text is difficult to read and thus magnifiers employ algorithms that 'smooth' the text. Fig. 2 shows enlarged text both with and without smoothing.

Finally, the screen magnifier used in this study provides a "panning window" – a feature that is found in few, if any, other magnifiers. The idea is that the user can display the full screen image (without enlargement) in which the enlarged portion of the image is represented as a highlighted block. The motivation for incorporating this feature was to allow the user to quickly obtain an idea of where the current magnified portion of the image fits into the whole image. In addition, when in this mode, the user can move the highlighted area (effectively the enlarged area) around the full screen and thus quickly change the area of the screen that is being magnified.

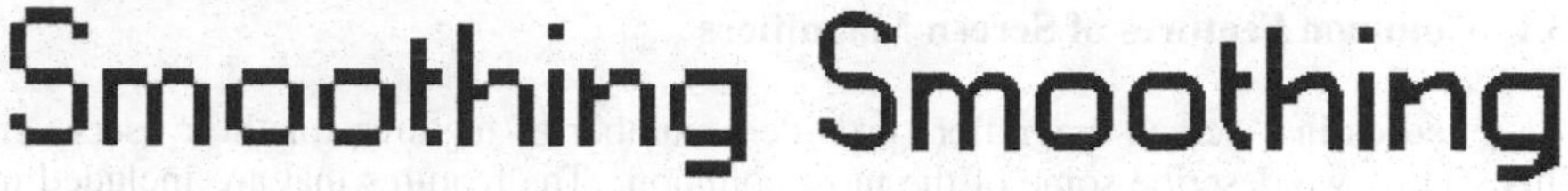

Smoothing Smoothing

Fig. 2. Text without (left) and with (right) smoothing

3.2 Magnifier Used in This Study

The magnifier used in this study, 'Magnus'[1], is a commercially-available screen magnifier developed by one of the authors. Magnus is intended to be competitive with commercial screen readers, but rather than be feature-laden, the designer has decided to reduce the number of basic features to those that are considered (but not yet evaluated as being) essential. The motivation for reducing the number of features is to try to produce a simple user interface.

Magnus provides screen enlargement from two to sixteen times magnification with independent control of horizontal and vertical enlargement. It provides simple color inversion (i.e. the color is simply inverted black becomes white etc.) rather than providing full user selection over colors. Smoothing can be turned off and on by the user and, as noted above, a panning window is provided.

3.3 Joystick Control

The joystick is used for two purposes. Firstly, it allows the user to control the position of the mouse pointer (in general use) or the cursor (in applications such as word processors and spreadsheets)[2]. Secondly, the joystick buttons can be used to control the operation of the magnifier.

3.4 Control of Cursor Position

Generally, the joystick controls the cursor position in an 'absolute positioning mode'. This means that the orientation of the joystick corresponds directly to the portion of the full image that is shown as the enlarged image on the screen. In this mode, to view the top left corner of the image, the user moves the joystick away and to the left and holds the joystick in this position, until he/she wishes to view a different part of the screen. In effect, each position of the joystick presents a different enlarged portion of the full, unmagnified display to the user. To explain this by analogy, one

---

[1] A screen magnifier called Magnus was developed in the mid 1990s by one of the authors and it is this program that is referred to in [1]. The 'Magnus' described in this paper is a completely separate development.
[2] In order to simplify the description we will refer to the control of the 'cursor position' to refer to the control of both mouse pointer and application cursor

could imagine the full computer image, prior to enlargement, being written on a piece of paper. Above the piece of paper is a camera, which is capable of viewing only a small portion of the paper and transmitting it to a computer monitor. In absolute positioning mode, the camera's position relative to the paper is controlled by a direct mechanical linkage between the joystick and the camera. In some respects this is similar to a pantograph[3].

Magnus also allows a user to control the cursor position using 'relative mode'. In this mode when the joystick is displaced from its center position, the magnifier moves the image in the selected direction. The image will continue to move whilst the joystick is displaced from its center. To modify the analogy given above, it is as if the direct mechanical linkage between the camera position and joystick position were broken and the camera position is controlled by motors that drive two rack and pinion gears with the camera mounted on a pair of orthogonal rods that connect to the gears. In this mode, there is no direct correspondence between the position of the joystick and the image on the screen. The motivation for including this mode was to provide a fine control mechanism to complement the coarser control of the absolute mode.

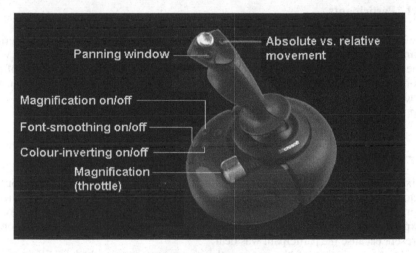

Fig. 3. The mapping of control buttons to magnifier features.

It should be noted that neither absolute positioning nor relative position modes are exactly the same as those in a mouse. One might view mouse control as being an absolute position device, but there is no fixed reference position (such as the center position on a joystick) and, of course, a user can pick up a mouse and move it without any change in cursor position. Another might view a mouse as a relative position device and, in this case there is a strong similarity, especially at the conceptual level. However, there is one slight difference, movement occurs when the mouse moves and stops when it is held still. The joystick's relative position mode causes cursor movement when the joystick is held still, movement stops only when the joystick is returned to its central position.

---

[3] A pantograph is "a jointed framework of rods based on the geometry of a parallelogram, for coping drawing, plans, etc. on the same, or a different scale"[5]

3.5 Using the Joystick to Control the Magnifier

The trials used a Microsoft ForceFeedback 2 joystick, because it is one of the most popular joysticks on the market [7] and because it offers a wide range of buttons that can be used to control magnification options. The mapping between features and buttons is shown in Fig 3. The 'fire' button, not shown in Fig 2, is mapped onto the left mouse button. Magnification is controlled by the throttle; the user moves the throttle away from him/herself to increase magnification and in the reverse direction to decrease magnification. The three buttons marked 'on/off' act as binary switches. The panning window is active only when the button is held down. The absolute vs. relative movement button is used to toggle between the two positioning modes.

4 Usability Evaluation

4.1 Participants

Seven registered blind users with some residual vision and some computer experience participated in the study. There were two females and five male participants with a mean age of 50.9 (Standard Deviation 17.80 years) and a mean of 9.2 years of prior computer experience. Six of the users had used a screen magnifier before, but none had used Magnus; four of the users had prior experience of using a joystick with applications. Table 1 summarizes the users and their experience.

4.2 Procedures

Six of the seven participants performed the test at a computer-training center for blind and visually impaired people in the North West of England, the seventh participant performed the tests in the authors' laboratory. In six of the test, only one experimenter and the participant were present. In the seventh test translator was present because the participant was deaf.

At the beginning of the session the participants were asked to fill in a short questionnaire to acquire demographic data and to record their past computer experience. The questionnaire, which was printed in Arial 24pt, also served to determine that the participants had some residual vision.

At the beginning of the session, the participants were informed that the purpose of the session was solely to test the usability of the joystick-operated magnifier. The participants were given a brief tutorial on the magnifier and the joystick interface and were then allowed to practice for 10 minutes with support given by the experimenter. The test subjects were then give four comprehension-based tasks to carry out (see later for a more detailed description). No time limit was set for the tasks during which the participants were encouraged to think aloud and comment (favorably and negatively) about features of the magnifier and could, if they desired, ask questions of the experimenter. The experimenter also asked questions of the participants in order to clarify the participants' comments and the experimenter's observations.

Table 1. The participants' demographic data and past experience.

Name	BC	TW	FW	DH	MA	BM	AK
Age	64	38	84	32	51	43	44
Gender	Male	Male	Male	Female	Female	Male	Male
Computer Experience (years)	1.5	17	20	4	1	10	11
Prior Magnifier Experience	Yes	Yes	Yes	Yes	No	Yes	Yes
Prior Joystick Experience	No	Yes	No	Yes	No	Yes	Yes

At the end of the session the participants were interviewed by the experimenter to ascertain whether there were any other usability issues that had not been mentioned in the session. The questions asked were as follows:

1. Did you find the joystick easy to use? Did it perform according to your expectations?
2. Did you find the magnifier program easy to use? Did it perform according to you expectations?
3. Do you think it will be easy for you to master this magnifier?
4. Are there any features that you would like to see added?
5. Are there any features that you would like to see removed?

Each session, from introductory questionnaire to post-trial interview lasted around half an hour. The experimenter's observations and the participants' comments were recorded in a real-time written report.

4.3 Stimulus

The tests were carried out using a laptop computer with a 1GHz Pentium processor, 512 MB memory, running Windows 2000 Professional and Microsoft Word XP. The screen was a 15" active matrix LCD display with resolution set 1280 x 1024 pixels and 32-bit color.

A Microsoft ForceFeedback 2 (USB) joystick was used. The force feedback element of the joystick was not enabled. This meant the joystick offered little resistance to movement and, once displaced from its central position it did not spring back into place. Magnus 1.0 was used as the screen magnifier.

The participants used the screen magnifier to answer comprehension-type questions from two set of documents (taken from http://www.aarp.org) presented in Microsoft Word. Each set of documents contained four articles, which were presented in two columns, with two articles in each column. Care was taken to ensure that the participants would not be able to answer any questions without reading the articles. Each article was roughly 150 words long and presented in 10pt Arial font, black text on a white background. The questions were read to the participants and the experimenter recorded the answers.

5 Results and Analysis

The results are taken from the experimenter's observations, the participants' comments recorded during the experiment and the participants' answers to the usability questions. In this paper the results are divided into: the set of features that the participants liked and the set of features that caused the participants problems.

Overall, most participants indicated that they felt that the screen magnifier with the joystick would be easy to use and master with some practice. They also stated that the screen magnifier matched their expectations (excluding some usability-related problems described below). It should be noted, however, that one user indicated that he would prefer to use the keyboard to control the magnifier instead of the joystick.

5.1 Favorably Received Features

Feature #1: Color Inversion. As noted earlier, Magnus allows the users to invert the presentation of the color (i.e. from black to white and vice versa – see Fig. 1). Six of the seven test subjects preferred to read the test documents with white text on a black background, the other participant read the documents with black text on a white background.

Feature #2: Scrolling. This feature was not originally planned but was a fortunate consequence of the implementation of the screen magnifier and the joystick used in the experiment. It manifests itself in the following way. Suppose a participant is reading a line of text and has selected relative mode (which, as noted earlier, was designed for fine control). As the participant reads the line of text he/she holds the joystick hard right to cause the text to scroll to the left. If the participant stops holding the joystick, it will remain in this position and the text continues to scroll. When the cursor reaches the end of the line, the user can press the down-arrow key, which moves the Word cursor, which is followed by the mouse pointer, which causes the screen magnifier to begin scrolling at the left hand side of the next line. Thus with the joystick held in one position and appropriate user intervention, the document is automatically scrolled through line by line. In addition, because in relative mode the distance from the joystick's central position is proportional to cursor speed, the participants found that they could control the speed of scrolling and match it to their own reading speed. However, because this feature was not planned, the participants found that very accurate positioning of the joystick was needed to match the scrolling speed to their reading speed (see usability-related problems below).

In summary, the participants found this feature useful but its implementation was not ideal. This feature will be incorporated into later trial versions of Magnus for further evaluation and will follow the suggestion of one of the participants in having the scroll speed set by the user.

Feature #3: Absolute Mode. The absolute positioning mode in which the position of the joystick corresponds directly to the location of the magnified area on the screen was found by the participants to be easier to understand and use than the relative mode. This may indicate that an absolute mode joystick-controlled screen magnifier may be more intuitive to use than one controlled by a mouse. Experiments that directly contrast mouse and joystick operation are required.

Feature #4: Smoothing. All seven participants reported favorably on smoothing, especially those that used high levels of magnification.

Feature #5: Control of Magnification Using the Joystick's Throttle Control. All seven participants reported favorably on this feature. The mapping between the throttle and the magnification level was easily understood by all.

Feature #6: Positioning Modes. As noted earlier, the relative mode was provided to give users fine control compared with the relatively coarse level of control provided by the absolute mode. However, the participants viewed positioning modes as different speeds (relative = slow, absolute = fast) rather than positioning modes as originally intended. They did, however, report favorably on the two modes, indicating that the relative mode was useful when precision was required and because it provided the (unintended) scrolling feature described earlier.

5.2 Usability-Related Problems

Problem #1: Over-Sensitivity and Lack of Precision of the Joystick. There were a number of problems reported with the joystick used in the experiment. The joystick was perceived as being over-sensitive and not sufficiently precise. This led to a number of issues. Firstly, it proved difficult for the participants to stop when they desired. This proved frustrating for the participants, especially as some were not familiar with the desktop and all were reading the documents for the first time. This problem caused all users to lose orientation. Secondly, participants found difficulty in maintaining their desired speed and maintaining their desired line. One elderly participant was concerned for other users of his age group, who may have trembling hands that may amplify this problem. The joystick also has a significant degree of inertia, this often caused participants to tilt the joystick further than they desired causing them to overshoot their desired location (in absolute positioning mode) or move too fast (in relative positioning mode).

The particular joystick used caused major problems for all users. It may be that this problem is unavoidable in using joysticks (for example [8] reports that joysticks are harder to control than mice) or it may be that the particular joystick chosen was inappropriate and that better joysticks exist. This issue will be investigated through further experiments. If the problem is endemic to joysticks, there may be software solutions that can be incorporated into the design of the magnifier. The participants recommend two solutions to the joystick problems: to use a less sensitive joystick (one with more resistance); or to provide the user with the means to limit movement to one direction only.

Problem #2: The Location of the Buttons. The participants commented unfavorably on the positioning of some of the buttons on the joystick used in the experiment. These were those toward the back of the joystick's base.   There were several problems. Firstly, the participants found them difficult to tell apart – all four buttons (see Fig. 3) are the same shape and color and, when in use, the stick obstructs the view of the buttons. In some cases, participants tried to locate the buttons by touch and in doing so altered the position of the throttle (causing the magnification level to change) or moved the stick. Some participants overcame these problems in time, but others experienced them throughout the experiment. Some participants suggested that using visual cues, such as shape and color, or altering the position of the buttons might lead to significant improvements.

Problem #3: Panning Window. As noted earlier, a 'panning window' in Magnus allows a user to determine where the enlarged image is relative to the overall unmagnified image and to quickly move to another part of the unmagnified image. The participants did not like the feature. One reason was due to the joystick's lack of precision. The participants found it difficult to accurately select the area that they wished to view. When the magnified image was presented, they discovered it was not the view that they wanted. This caused a loss of orientation and further use of the panning window, which was, of course, subject to similar problems. Another reason was that in order to view the panning window one of the joystick's buttons must be held down whilst the joystick is moved. The button is then released when the window has moved to the desired location in the unmagnified image. Most users found this difficult to do and suggested that the panning window should be toggled on and off using a button. So, rather than holding a button down when moving the joystick, they would depress and release the button to enter panning mode and depress and release it again to select the desired area. Finally, and perhaps most significantly, because the participants are visually impaired they cannot see the detail presented in the panning window and can only get an impression of the position of the magnifier window in the original image. This feature proved a little use.

Problem #4: Task-Specific Features. As noted earlier, the participants' task was to read text presented in two columns. Because the participants discovered the scrolling feature (described earlier), they expected to be able to scroll down a column (rather across both columns to the end of the line). One user overcame this problem by noting that if the down-arrow key was pressed when the scrolling reached the end of the left column, the 'scrolling window' would return to the start of the next line of text in the column. Another user abandoned the joystick altogether, and preferred to read the text by moving through it using the up- and down-arrow keys. Of course, scrolling was an accidental feature, but one that the participants found useful – further trials will be undertaken.

Problem #5: Presentation of Magnifier Information when Changing Magnification Level. Participants could change the magnification level by using the joystick's throttle. Whenever they did so, the screen magnifier's control window (as shown in the left of Fig. 1) appeared. This indicated the level of magnification that they had chosen, but the participants did not require this information, finding it easier to simply adjust the magnification until the level suited them. The appearance of the control window was an unwelcome distraction, particularly because the control window took the focus and moved the center of the magnified area away from the area that the participant wished to view. This caused participants to lose orientation.

Problem #6: Maximum Magnification Level. As noted earlier, the level of magnification was set by the throttle on the joystick. In the trials the maximum magnification level that could be set depended on how fast the throttle was moved; the faster the movement, the lower the maximum. This led to situations where the participants required a higher magnification level than it was possible to set. The relation between speed of throttle movement and number of magnification levels is a consequence of the implementation, rather than a deliberately designed feature.

6 Conclusions and Further Work

Despite problems with the particular joystick used in the experiment, the results of the experiment indicate that a joystick controlled screen magnifier is intuitive and easy to use. Further experiments in which a more suitable joystick is compared with mouse and keyboard control will be conducted. These experiments will also use a wider range of stimuli (including web pages and other application packages such as e-mail, spreadsheets and graphics); the present study is limited to reading text documents and the results may not be generalisable, especially to applications that require users to be aware of their layout (for example applications with buttons and toolbars) and when the user is creating, rather than reviewing information.

One significant issue is the set of positioning modes, from the experiment it seems that absolute and relative modes are both used, but the relationship between the modes is somewhat unclear.

Of the general features of magnifiers, smoothing and color inversion were appreciated by the users. The more esoteric 'panning window' was not liked.

Finally, the participants found the automatic scrolling through text to be useful (and would have perhaps found it more useful had it been aware of column breaks). We conclude that this is potentially a very useful feature.

The findings of the current study can also benefit a more general pool of computer users. Designers of navigation aids should acknowledge several points from this study. A joystick is mostly used for computer games and multimedia. However, this study suggested that a joystick is an intuitive navigation device. A wide avenue of possible further studies, such as investigating the use of a joystick to navigate around web pages or hierarchical diagrams, can result from this finding. Another more general implication of this study is that it is important to perform a usability evaluation of any product with representative users. If we would not have tested the application with registered blind users, perhaps many of the aforementioned problems and features would not have surfaced. Testing the product with representative pool of users had allowed us to get an insight of what users with low vision think about the usability of this product.

References

1. Becker, S., Battison, R., Boerjerson, K., Lundman, D.: CESAR Comparative Evaluation of Alternatives for Screen Reading, Closing the Gap: Computer Technology in Special Education and Rehabilitation, June-July 1997 [On-Line]. Available at: http://www.closingthegap.com/lib/pdf/1997/June-July97/becker.PM.pdf.
2. Baude, A., Blenkhorn, P., Evans, G: The Architecture of a Windows 9x Full Screen Magnifier, In Marinek, C., Bühler, C., Knops, H., Andrich, R. (Eds.): Assitive Technology – Added Value to the Quality of Life (AAATE 2001), IOS Press, Amsterdam, (2001) 113–118
3. Bornemann-Jeske, B.: Usability tests on computer access devices for the blind and visually impaired, In Kluas, J., Auff, E., Kremser, W., Zagler, W. L. (Eds.): Interdisciplinary Aspects on Computers Helping Peole with Special Needs, Proceeding of the 5th ICCHP '96, (Linz, Austria, July 1996), OCG Pres, 139–147
4. Petrie, H., Morley, S., McNally, P., O'Neill, A., Majoe, D.: Initial Design and Evaluation of an Interface to Hypermedia Systems for Blind Users. Proceedings of 8th ACM Conference on Hypertext and Hypermedia'97 (Southampton, UK, April 1997), ACM Press, 48–56.
5. Cunningham, S.: The Authoring and Application of Hypermedia-Based User Interfaces [On-Line]. Available at: http://mvc.man.ac.uk/SIMA/articles/ieewww.html.
6. The Chambers Dictionary, Chambers Harrap, Edinburgh, (1993)
7. PC World: Most Popular Top 25 Input Device Products, http://pcworld.procegrabber.com/home_mostpop.php/catzero=11/ut=c252679a21ee93.
8. Mithal, A. K., Douglas, S. A.: Differences in Movement Microstructure of the Mouse and the Finger-Controlled Isometric Joystick. Proceedings of ACM Conference on Human Factors in Computing Systems CHI'96 (Vancouver, Canada, April 1996), ACM Press, 300–307.

Finger Instead of Mouse: Touch Screens as a Means of Enhancing Universal Access

Andreas Holzinger

Institute for Medical Informatics, Statistics and Documentation (IMI)
Graz University Hospital
Engelgasse 13, A-8010 Graz, Austria
andreas.holzinger@uni-graz.at

Abstract. Touch-Screen Technology is the most natural of all input devices - even children can easily learn how to operate them. But this simple interaction proved also to be ideal for people who are not overly familiar with computers including elderly and/or disabled patients in a hospital. A pilot system of an interactive Patient Communications System (PACOSY) has been developed in a User Centered Design (UCD) process. Patients were enabled to retrieve and enter information interactively via various touch screen systems connected to the Hospital Intranet. This paper concentrates primarily on experimental experiences with touch technology and the technological requirements for a touch based Patient Information System (PATIS) serving as Point of Information (POI) for patients within a hospital or a future Point of Consultation (POC). People with low or no computer literacy found using touch screens easy and motivating. Together with a cheap, simple and user friendly interface design, such systems can enhance universal access within an information society for all.

"Each Pointing concept has its enthusiasts and detractors, motivated by commercial interests, by personal preference and increasingly by empirical evidence" (Ben Shneiderman, 1998, p.323 [1])."

1 Introduction

A pilot system of an interactive patient communications system (PACOSY) was developed at the Institute for Medical Informatics, Statistics and Documentation (IMI) using an User Centered Design (UCD) Process. The System was tested with and developed for elderly and partially impaired patients at the clinical department of Oncology at the Medical University Hospital in Graz (Test group). This 2.300 bed hospital is amongst the biggest in Europe and serves, together with 21 County hospitals, a population of more than 1,6 million people living in Styria (Austria). The aim of this paper is primarily to report experiences, with the focus on appropriate hardware, and secondarily to raise awareness and thereby stimulate extensive further research.

Experience with the focus on the User Centered Design (UCD) was presented at the 8th International Conference on Computers Helping People with Special Needs from 15-20 July 2002 at the University of Linz, Austria [2].

N. Carbonell, C. Stephanidis (Eds.): User Interfaces for All, LNCS 2615, pp. 387–397, 2003.

2 Aims and Goals: Simple, Cheap, Easy to Use

According to Stephanidis & Savidis (2001), [3] simple, cheap and easy to use solutions in information technology (IT) can be a step towards an information society where everyone can have access to relevant information, which is considered of paramount importance for its success [4]. The author is of the firm opinion that this project with patients in public hospitals is a start at achieving this ambitious objective.

The test group began with little to no computer literacy. According to McMillan (1996), [5] literacy is defined as the ability to process information using text. Thus, computer literacy may be defined as the ability to process information by using an information device. By using such systems this population can be made familiar with computers generally and the computer anxiety can be reduced [6]. It is interesting to note that, according to Robertson & Hix (2002), [7], most research on the use of computers by mentally (as apposed to physically) retarded people falls into two general categories:

- Computer science literature discusses advanced assistive technologies (e.g. speech synthesizers) but rarely addresses the usability of commonly available devices;
- Educational and psychological literature describes the use of computer technology in special educational settings, focusing on teaching techniques, but rarely addresses the usability of commonly available devices.

3 A Vision: Computers for Patient Education

Since almost every hospital bed has a television set, why not a computer?

According to Lewis (1999), [8], patient education has recently emerged as a component of health promotion and disease management programs in response to increased pressure to provide more relevant and concrete information at lower cost. Lewis (1999) further suggests that the use of information technology to increase patient knowledge and their involvement in health care decisions also leads to better health results and reports that several studies described that elderly patients, with very little prior computer experience, had reported satisfaction with computer based learning technologies and successfully acquired information about health and disease related self care (see also for example [9], [10], [11]).

According to Jones (2001), [12], particularly cancer patients tend to lack information regarding their illness and are often dissatisfied with the information and support they receive. In response, educators and health care professionals are developing better ways to inform patients and their families about their medical condition, possible treatment and self-care.

According to Ellis (1987), [13], or Bental et.al. (1999), [14] computers have been used generally in patient education for many years. Without being a replacement for personal contact with professionals, there is evidence that they complement this, providing the patient with easy access to both specialist and general health topics. Bental et al. (1999) discovered that patients, given a suitably designed interface, find accessing computer information acceptable and often less embarrassing than asking apparently trivial questions of health professionals. Direct access may not be neccessary, computers could be used to produce personalized leaflets and letters automatically, or dictate personalized spoken information over the telephone.

Adapting Information to Patients Needs

One potential advantage of computer based resources is the possibility of automatically adapting the material to the particular needs of individuals and organizations accessing the information. The material can be selected and presented according to rules supplied by the programmer. This *can* be as simple as inserting the patient's name to personalize the information. Bental et al. (1999) considers tailoring the content of the material or the way that the content is presented to fit the needs of the individual.

Electronic Questionnaires

It is obvious that paper usage can be reduced and information processing can be enhanced by using computer supported questionnaires (see for example [15]). These can either be on local POIs or more conveniently on mobile devices (e.g. a workpad solution).

4 POI, PATIS, and POC

Point of Information (POI)

In commerce, a multimedia kiosk is generally used as a Point Of Information (POI). If the kiosk includes a transaction component to buy goods and to pay for them by credit card it becomes a Point Of Purchase (POP) or a Point Of Sales (POS), similar to vending machines.

Patient Information System (PATIS)

PATISes are increasingly popular although, according to van't Riet, Berg, Hiddema and Sol (2001) [16], there are not many documented success stories: A core issue for such systems is their usability. This must include the extent to which the system takes the actual needs and capacities of the patients into account. Van't Ried et.al. recommends [17] for a review of PATIS.

Point of Consultancy (POC)

A point of consultancy could provide specific information on demand. The type and presentation manner of this information is a matter for further research.

5 The Patient Communication System PACOSY

A compulsory prerequisite of the design was to provide a stable system, which returned to a defined initial state on exit, however, no special precautions were taken to avoid deliberate vandalism.

At first the solution for a specific clinical task stood in the foreground: An interactive questionnaire, replacing the written questionnaire, is completed by the oncology patients immediately on arrival, and particularly asks about their state of mind. From the viewpoint of the departmental psychologist in charge the objective is a screening: on the basis of the responses he is able to build an opinion as to the necessity of immediate support etc. Comparisons between conventional usage of written and computerized questionnaires (e.g. from Peterson & Johannsson (1996), [18]) showed that computerized versions could be advantageous. An automatic alert is being considered, either over the network and/or in the form of a screen output and/or on the mobile phone of the psychologist in charge and will be implemented in a later version. Although anonymity is not considered advantageous, confidentiality is necessary to inspire trust. Special concern was given to navigation through the questionnaire (refer e.g. to Nielsen (1990), [19]) and the simplicity of the user interface.

A cheap, scalable, standard solution within the hospitals Internet with extensive use of the hospitals standard equipment (PCs, Microsoft-Windows, MS server) was aimed at. The same software supports touch screen and mouse alternatively. In the future this solution should be adaptable to other clinics with a minimum of expenditure and supplementary programming. The most important objective was maintainability of the content by clinic personnel (secretary etc.).

The system was constructed to act as a client server system defined by HTTP. The client connects, using a standard browser to a server within the Intranet via TCP/IP and requests the Webpage. This is sent in the form of an HTML page, which is correspondingly interpreted by the browser and displayed graphically [2].

6 The Finger as Natural Input

Since touch screens literally put the fingers in touch with what is on your computer screen, this technology is considered as the most natural of all input devices. The most obvious advantage of touch screens is that the input device is also the output device [20]. Being able to touch, feel and manipulate objects on a computer screen, in addition to seeing and hearing them, provides a sense of immersion [21].

Thus it is most commonly and effectively used for simple applications where any person can easily use without prior experience or instructions. Since touch screens do not need any added accessories such as keyboard and mouse, it also saves working space. On the other hand, they are not ideal for users who need to point accurately to a small area on the screen, for widespread searches or for handling significant amounts of data entry. Neither are they optimal for implementing complex tasks.

7 Experimental Setting and Methods Used

Twelve patients took part in specific experiments (also including the User Centered Design). The participants were tested individually. Each participant was first interviewed to gather demographic data; age, gender, preferred hand, visual and physical limitations, and computer literacy. All of them had absolutely no computing experience. Besides other inquiring techniques, video and audio recording was running and written notes were made (refer also to [2]).

8 Findings and Discussion

One of the main objectives of the first experiments was choosing the most appropriate hardware technology. At first we divided Touch Systems into two sections:
- Touch Screen Technology (resistive, capacitive, acoustic, infrared); and
- Casing types (kiosk, panel, webpad)

Almost all touch screen companies sell integrated systems as well as components to convert monitors into touch screens. The latter possibility was rejected. Each touch screen system includes three components that can be configured in various ways: 1. The sensor touch screen which serves as the user interface; 2. The controller, which processes the signals from the sensor screen and passes the event data to the computer; and 3. The driver software, which makes the touch screen compatible with the local operating system.

General Touch Advantages and Limitations

Although touch screens proved to be an intuitive interface, however it was recognized that they were unsuitable for entering large quantities of data.

Touch Screen Technology

There are several different types of technology employed by touch screens currently on the market: resistive, capacitive, surface acoustic wave and infrared light.
Only the first three types were examined and the following results obtained:
1. General
   The technical constraints that limit the design and deployment of these touch screens are very specific to each type. In general, these deal with factors such as the clarity of display, the specifics of interaction, and the maintenance of the touch screen equipment. Due to such constraints, touch screen deployment is limited to certain environments and specific tasks [22], [23]:

2. Resistive Touch Screens
   A mechanical pressure on this type of screen closes an electrical contact between two conductive layers. Since the pressure only sets up a connection between the two layers, the resistive touch screen can be activated by any solid object: a gloved finger, a pencil etc. This technology is used for Personal Digital Assistants (PDAs) e.g. the Psion and Palm. Advantages include no necessity of alignment (justifying), exact positioning and the possible use with gloves, i.e. in the medical field.

2. Capacitive Touch Screens

A pane of glass coated with ultra-thin metal lies over the actual screen of this type. From the corners of the display, a low voltage of alternating current, which creates a weak electrical field, is applied to the electrode grid of the conducting layer. When the user touches the screen they simulate a form of condenser electrode and "ground" the area (field). From the (low) electricity, which is diverted around the user's finger, the touch controller determines the respective coordinates of the contact point. Correspondingly, capacitive touch screens only respond to the touch with a conductive object (special metal pen, finger etc.). Advantages include higher resolution, higher light efficiency, not influenced by surrounding light; Disadvantages include the necessity of calibration and sensitivity to errors from exterior influences.

3. Acoustic Touch Screens: Surface Acoustic Wave (SAW) Technology

SAW-Technology is based on sound waves. The edges of the screen are equipped with ultra sound transmitters with reflectors at each opposite edge and a piezoelectric receiver in one corner. Ultra sound waves are continuously being sent across this reflector system. As long as this field is undisturbed the waves arrive without obstruction at the receiver. However, if the field is disturbed, through a finger, pen or similar, then the position of this object is determined from the missing wave course within this field.

The following table shows briefly the obtained results.

Table 1. Comparison of touch technology

	Touch Resolution	Luminance	Response time	Calibration
Resistive	high	< 160 cd/sqm	< 15 ms	once
Capacitive	high	200 cd/sqm	20 ms	regularly
Acoustic (SAW)	medium	> 250 cd/sqm	> 20 ms	once

Luminance

Luminance was the most critical parameter and finally the selection factor for the choice of touch screen. In principle it is the luminous intensity per unit area. The SI unit is candela per square meter (cd/sqm). The luminance can be measured by spectroradiometer. Typical Cathode Ray Tube (CRT) screens have a luminance of approximately 300 cd/sqm [22].

The resistive technology was not suitable due to the disadvantages: unfocused, low brightness - determined by the number of layers applied - and a less durable monitor.

Taking a normal LCD monitor with a brightness of 200 cd/m² and an LCD monitor with surface wave technology and 185 cd/sqm as the optimum parameters, it can be seen that a five-wire resistance touch screen, which proved to average less than 150 cd/sqm and a capacitive touch screen with more than 200 cd/m² were unsatisfactory.

Finally, the (SAW) technology proved to be the most usable for our purposes, due to its single glass panel and highest clarity. Its drawback was that it is relatively easily affected by contaminants on the screen, which absorb the waves and cause dead zones. Also it is not very flexible; in order for an acoustic wave to be sent, the screen must always be touched with a finger; something hard like a pen did not work.

Casing Types

Three types of casing types were examined: Kiosk systems, panels and webpads. Kiosk: An abundance of different Kiosk Systems were examined and tested, but proved to be unsuitable. Webpads: Currently available Webpads did not meet our specific demands. Future Webpads, if commercially available, could be advantageous but must be further tested.

Based on the results of our examinations we decided to rely on a Panel solution and excluded whole Kiosk Systems due to the fact that they are too heavy and unwieldy. The best experiences were made with Panel PC's which can be mechanically used in three different ways:

- mounted on a desk
- mounted on a wall (swivel arm) and
- used as a mobile panel

For bedside use we suggest a panel mounted on swivel arms. These are in use with television sets but not available to date with touch computers. The following table briefly shows the results of the examinations of the three types:

Table 2. The three categories of touch systems

		Weight	moveability	sturdiness	comment
Kiosk		> 100 kg	none	very high	robust, but not suitable for our specific task due to immobility and no adjustable viewing angle
Panel-PC		12 kg	good	medium	most suitable, chosen for further experiments
Webpad		< 1 kg	very good	low	could be suitable in the future, when better pads are available

Hand/Eye Coordination and Time for Pointing

The patients reported that they found the operation of our system easy. This was mainly due to the use of direct hand/eye co-ordination. Fitts' Law was taken into consideration during the design. According to Fitts (1954), [24], the average duration of responses is directly proportional to the minimum average amount of information per response. Also the time to move the hand into contact with a visually presented object (button) is a function of both the size of object and its distance from the hand. The time for pointing tp is a function of both the distance d of the reach and the width w of the target object. This relationship can be expressed in the following formula where a and b are empirical constants and vary depending the used device [25]:

$$tp = a + b * \log2 (2d/w)$$

The expression $\log2 (2d/w)$ is, according to Shneiderman (1998), [1] also called "index of difficulty". Understanding how manipulations of d and w affect the time tp is of considerable importance in developing efficient touch screen interfaces. Within certain parameters (including the dimensions of the screen) we had control over the size of target objects and the distance of the user from the screen (figure 1).

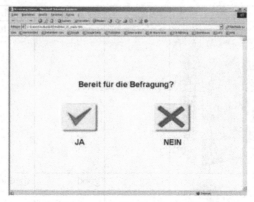

Fig. 1. An example for the used buttons

Measurements of time used for the selection of the touch bottoms showed similar results to the original experiments by Fitts (1954): We measured the time from the point where the participant's intention to touch the screen was recognizable to the actual triggering of the touch button. The results were as follows:

Minimum t = 2s
Maximum t = 10s
Average t = 3,3s

It was noticeable that run-aways to the above border were reduced with increasing examination time. The values oscillated more and more towards the average.

Viewing Angle

The Viewing Angle (refer to Schultz et.al. (1998), [26] for theoretical details) proved to be highly important and differences caused adaptations (i.e. we had to set the angle in dependence of the patient size), which were very disturbing during the experiment. In this case a Webpad could be a better solution.

9 Future Outlook

At the beginning the main concern was the thorough examination of useable touch screen technology and the comparison of different casing systems (Kiosk versus Panels).

The first stage was the implementation of a specific clinical task (questionnaire for screening) using an User Centered Design (UCD) involving patients and clinic personal. For further details refer to Holzinger (2002) [2].

At a further stage, the implementation of a generally usable Software/Hardware solution for patients on a variety of different terminals is planned. A possible application could run both in the Graz University Hospital and in all Styrian County Hospitals. Central research question could include:

- What demands on information do in-patients have?
- What demands on information do out-patients have?
- What must be considered in the information design?

It is possible to examine how different patient groups from different hospital departments (e.g. childrens department, eye-clinic, etc.) work with such systems and how these systems must be ideally designed (User Centered Design). As a benefit the departments gain a fully working global PACOSY with POIs in different locations and with bedside PACOSY.

The range of information intended for the patients could include:

- departmental information (about medical doctors, nurses, etc.)
- administrative information (insurance information, services, etc.)
- information about their illness (prevention, treatment and therapies)
- information about their surroundings (orientation, maps, views and floor plans).

The range of interaction for the patients could include:

- on-line questionnaires (e.g. screening, contentment, feedback, etc.)
- ordering menus (including diet consultancy)
- interactive medical and/or psychotherapeutic consultancy (in the sense of a on-line point of consultancy - POC)
- even surfing on the Internet could be possible on demand

Studies as to the kind of information relevant and helpful to patients, the type of interfaces which could be most beneficial and experiments with talking interfaces [27] would be interesting. Especially spoken language technology could be of real benefit to the targeted audience [28].

These aims are in close compliance with the research agenda of the European sixth framework program where the topic Human-Computer Interaction gains a steadily increasing importance [29] and these topics could be a focus within an future European Research Project.

10 Conclusion

Although the first sample population was small, the experiments showed results, which are in accordance with existing literature: Most of the patients reported that they "liked this kind of computer" and all found the touch interface simple to use. A Panel PC proved to be best suitable in connection with a simple interface design. The limits of such an approach are in speed and in the level of information, the depth of commands and arm fatigue. Thus, every interaction element must be carefully considered.

References

1. Shneiderman, B. *Designing the User Interface. Strategies for Effective Human-Computer Interaction.* Reading (MA): Addison Wesley (1998)
2. Holzinger, A., *User-Centered Interface Design for disabled and elderly people: First experiences with designing a patient communication system (PACOSY),* In: *Computers Helping People with Special Needs, 8th International Conference, ICCHP, Linz,* K. Miesenberger, J. Klaus, and W. Zagler (ed.), Berlin et al.: Springer (2002) 34–41
3. Stephanidis, C., Savidis, A. Universal Access in the Information Society: Methods, Tools and Interaction Technologies, *Universal Access in the Information Society,* 1 (1) (2001) 40–55
4. Emiliani, L.P., Stephanidis, C. From Adaptations to User Interfaces for All. 6th ERCIM Workshop "User Interfaces for All". Florence, Italy: (2000)
5. McMillan, S. Literacy and computer literacy: definitions and comparisons, *Computers & Education,* 27 (3–4) (1996) 161–170
6. King, J., Bond, T., Blandford, S. An investigation of computer anxiety by gender and grade, *Computers in Human Behavior,* 18 (1) (2002) 69–84
7. Robertson, G.L., Hix, D. Making Computer Accessible to Mentally Retarded Adults, *Communications of the ACM,* 45 2002) 171–183
8. Lewis, D. Computer-based approaches to patient education: a review of the literature, *Journal of the American Medical Informatics Association: JAMIA,* 6 (4) (1999) 272–282
9. Rippey, R.M., Bill, D., Abeles, M., Day, J., Downing, D.S., Pfeiffer, C.A., Thal, S.E., Wetstone, S.L. Computer-based patient education for older persons with osteoarthritis, *Arthritis and Rheumatism,* 30 (8) (1987) 932–935
10. Downing, D.S., Rippey, R., Peterson, M., Weinstein, A., Sheehan, T.J. Rheumatology education in an undergraduate program of physical therapy. A new outlook, *Physical Therapy,* 67 (9) (1987) 1393–1398
11. Bill-Harvey, D., Rippey, R., Abeles, M., Donald, M.J., Downing, D., Ingenito, F., Pfeiffer, C.A. Outcome of an osteoarthritis education program for low-literacy patients taught by indigenous instructors, *Patient Education and Counseling,* 13 (2) (1989) 133–142
12. Jones, J.M., Nyhof-Young, J., Friedman, A., Catton, P. More than just a pamphlet: development of an innovative computer-based education program for cancer patients, *Patient Education and Counseling,* 44 (3) (2001) 271–281
13. Ellis, L.B.M. Computer-based patient education, *Computers in Human Services,* 2 (3–4) (1987) 117–130
14. Bental, D.S., Cawsey, A., Jones, R. Patient Information Systems that tailor to the individual., *Patient Education and Counseling,* 36 1999) 171–180.

15. Hanna, A.W., Pynsent, P.B., Learmonth, D.J., Tubbs, O.N. A comparison of a new computer-based interview for knee disorders with conventional history taking, *The Knee,* 6 (4) (1999) 245–256
16. van't Riet, A., Berg, M., Hiddema, F., Sol, K. Meeting patients' needs with patient information systems: potential benefits of qualitative research methods, *International Journal of Medical Informatics,* 64 (1) (2001) 1–14
17. Brennan, P.F., Kuang, Y.S., Volrathongchai, K., *Patient-centered information systems: Patient Centered Systems,* In: *Yearbook of Medical Informatics 2000,* J.H.v. Bemmel and A.T. McCray (ed.), Stuttgart: Schattauer (2000) 79–86
18. Peterson, L., Johannsson, V. Computerized Testing in a Hospital Setting: Psychometric and Psychological Effects, *Computers in Human Behavior,* 12 (3) (1996) 339–350
19. Nielsen, J. *Usability Engineering.* New York: Academic Press (1993)
20. Greenstein, J.S., Arnaut, L.Y., *Input Devices,* In: *Handbook of Human-Computer Interaction,* M. Helander (ed.), Amsterdam: North Holland (1988) 495–519
21. Srinivasan, M.A., Basdogan, C. Haptics in virtual environments: taxonomy, research status, and challenges, *Computers & Graphics,* 21 (4) (1997) 393–404
22. Holzinger, A. *Multimedia Basics, Volume 1: Technology. Technological Fundamentals of multimedial Information Systems.* New Delhi: Laxmi Publications (2002)
23. Holzinger, A. *Basiswissen Multimedia. Band 1: Technologische Grundlagen multimedialer Informationssyteme. 2. Auflage.* Würzburg: Vogel (2002)
24. Fitts, P.M. The information capacity of the human motor system in controlling the amplitude of movement, *Journal of Experimental Psychology,* 47 1954) 381–391
25. MacKenzie, I.S. Fitts' law as a research and design tool in human-computer interaction, *Human-Computer Interactions,* 7 (1) (1992) 91–139
26. Schultz, K.L., Batten, D.M., Sluchak, T.J. Optimal viewing angle for touch-screen displays: Is there such a thing?, *International Journal of Industrial Ergonomics,* 22 (4–5) (1998) 343–350
27. Zajicek, M. Interface Support for Elderly People with Impaired Sight or Memory. 6th ERCIM Workshop "User Interfaces for All". Florence, Italy: (2000)
28. McTear, M.F. Spoken Dialogue Technology: Enabling the Conversational User Interface, *ACM Computing Surveys,* 34 (1) (2002) 90–169
29. Stephanidis, C. From User Interfaces for all to an Information Society for All: Recent achievements and future challenges. 6th ERCIM Workshop "User Interfaces for All". Florence, Italy: (2000)

A Multi-lingual Augmentative Communication System

Norman Alm[1], Mamoru Iwabuchi[1], Peter N. Andreasen[1], and Kenryu Nakamura[2]

[1]Division of Applied Computing, University of Dundee, Dundee, Scotland
[2]Department of Special Education, Kagawa University, Takamatsu, Japan

Abstract. A positive aspect of aiming for universal design is that solutions developed for people with particular needs can prove of benefit to all users. Such a case is described here. A prototype augmentative communication system has been developed which could give non-speaking people a multi-lingual capability. It is based on research into conversational modelling and utterance prediction, making use of prestored material. In fact, the system could also be used by people whose only communication disadvantage is not being able to speak a foreign language. A unique feature of the system is that both the non-speaking person and the communication partner will use this communicator in their dialogue. In comparison with a multi-lingual phrase book, the system helped the users to have more natural conversation, and to take more control of the interaction.

1 Introduction

The potential cross-fertilisation of ideas from work on systems for people with disabilities and the wider field of human-computer interaction has been pointed out by Newell, who notes that systems developed to help a minority of people who need help in ordinary situations may also be of use for everyone, when they find themselves in an unusual situation or environment [1,2]. In this study, a communication system for non-speaking people was devised in order to give them a multi-lingual capability. Given that communication is such an essential part of human existence, and with the difficulties that nonspeaking people experience, even with assistive systems, widening out their communicative potential is always a desirable goal. In this case, helping them to communicate across national barriers is an exciting prospect. Interestingly, it would be an example of the assisted communicator actually being at an advantage through needing to use a computer to communicate. Such a system has a wider application possibility as well. It could also be useful for people whose communication difficulty is simply that they do not speak another foreign language.

An increasing range of computer-assisted systems is available for supporting augmentative and alternative communication (AAC) [3,4,5]. It may be possible to implement a multi-lingual capability with many of these systems, to the extent that they are based on a finite number of prestored language units. This would be particularly true of systems, typically research prototypes thus far, which are based on the rapid navigation through prestored conversational material by means of conversation structure and utterance prediction [6].

Speech recognition and automatic translation systems have developed considerably in the last decade in particular. However both of these technologies fall short of

N. Carbonell, C. Stephanidis (Eds.): User Interfaces for All, LNCS 2615, pp. 398–408, 2003.

complete accuracy. The current situation is that until unrestricted speech recognition in noisy environments is a reality, automatic translation systems will need to rely on text which the user must somehow produce. Even if this is accomplished, however, available translation technology is still not accurate enough to be effective in a fast-paced interactive situation.

At present, various software packages for machine translation are available and are now widely used for the rough translation of text, with their effectiveness dependent on the subject matter [7,8]. The following examples of translation generated by typical systems illustrate the problem of translation inaccuracy. The first example shows some English text automatically translated into Spanish. The second example shows the same text automatically translated from English into Japanese. (SYSTRAN PROfessional and LogoVista E to J were used for the English-Spanish and English-Japanese translation, respectively.   SYSTRAN PROfessional is a trademark of SYSTRAN Software, Inc. LogoVista E to J is a trademark of LogoVista Co. Ltd.)

Original text :
Sorry, your wheelchair must be checked in. We will lend you one of ours.

Example 1
Spanish translation :   Apesadumbrado, su sillon de ruedas se debe llegar. Le prestaremos uno el nuestros.

which literally means :
Grieved, your armchair of wheels must arrive itself. We will lend one the ours.

Example 2
Japanese translation :
Sumimasen, anata no kuruma-isu wa touchaku o kiroku sare nakutewa naranai.
Wareware wa anata ni wareware no no 1-tsu o kasudearou.
which literally means :
Sorry, the arrival of your wheelchair must be recorded. We will lend one of ours to you.

The level of inaccuracy here is not unusual. Where the system is being used to translate a webpage, or a document, the user can either settle for a roughly accurate translation, or use what is produced as a first pass at the material, editing it into accurate form. In a spoken dialogue, however, the unedited version could cause confusion.

The additional problem for spoken dialogues is transforming spoken language into text. As noted, speech recognition technology has made considerable advances, but producing accurate text in any situation of the free-flowing speech of any speaker in a noisy environment is still beyond the capabilities of current systems.

It might seem that here an AAC user would have an advantage, in that they by necessity are first producing the text in order to communicate. However, the language of AAC users is often highly abbreviated and can contain numerous spelling or syntactic errors. This would further degrade the already less-than-perfect performance of an automatic translator. Even if these problems were overcome, a dialogue would be difficult to carry out effectively, since the production of text byan AAC user is a time-consuming process, despite the ongoing progress of AAC technology.

Conversation modelling has been proposed for AAC systems as a means to enhance communication rate. A number of prototypes have been developed to illustrate this approach. These have involved, for example, providing the user with predicted texts following the normal conversational sequence of : opening, smalltalk, discussion, wrapping-up, and closing [9,10,11,12,13]. Story telling with a large number of pre-stored utterances has made it possible for users to express their personalities and achieve more participation and control over conversations [14,15,16,17,18]. Focusing on transactional-type conversation is another recent approach, which is quite effective because of its provision of predictable communication patterns in everyday encounters [19,20,21,22,23,24,25].

These techniques, as well as offering the potential to increase the communication rate of AAC users, can be extended to provide them with a multi-lingual capability. With material translated beforehand, it would be possible to take into account language features such as idioms and slang, and also any cultural differences in language usage. A system such as this could just as easily be used by speaking people whose only communication disadvantage is not being able to speak another language.

2   Description of the Prototype

A system was developed to embody and test out these ideas in practice. The prototype contained 1000 phrases and also 1500 single words which were translated beforehand into several languages, taking full account of cultural as well as linguistic aspects of the utterances. The conversational material was arranged in accordance with anticipated frequency of use, conceptual grouping and conversation flow. The prototype contained a set of specific scenarios : 'at the airport', 'at a tourist information office', 'at a hotel', and 'at a hospital'. In addition it provided a symbol based communication facility for conveying simple messages by means of symbols. It also provided an on-screen keyboard.

The system was designed to be operated by two speakers who have different languages. When the user is composing an utterance, the interface is displayed for them in their own language. When the user chooses to have the utterance spoken by the system, the utterance is spoken in the other language and then all the labels on the screen interface are translated into that language, ready for the other participant to make use of them. In addition to being multi-lingual, the interface is a multimedia one, combining text with symbols and pictures. It was hoped that this pictorially enhanced interface would help users to recognize the pre-stored utterances quickly and also make the system more accessible for non-literate people.

When a user constructs text word by word, some text manipulation is often necessary before the meaning of the phrase is clear in another language. The prototype incorporates an automatic expression conversion function which corrects a certain amount of the word-by-word input grammatically in each of the languages which the system handles. The method by which this is done is a simple rule-based facility. This type of text manipulation would be beneficial particularly for the cross-language conversation between languages whose grammar is quite different, such as between European languages and Japanese. Although introducing such a facility will require individual adjustments to be made for particular languages, it was decided it was necessary for language pairs such as English-Japanese. The need for a facility such as this has been pointed out in a study involving picture-based sentences constructed by English and Japanese speakers [26].

The prototype was coded in Java, which allows it to run on any operating system without major change. This prototype is composed of two independent parts, the Java program and the data; hence the component layout and language information (including stored conversational materials) can be easily modified or added simply by editing the data part without any alteration to the program.

Although face-to-face conversation by means of the prototype will be the focus of this study, the system was intended for users to be able to communicate with others at a distance as well as face-to-face, using the same interface. The server and client modules of the system make it possible to communicate across the Internet.

3 Evaluation of the Prototype

The prototype was evaluated by comparing it to its nearest equivalent : a printed multi-lingual phrase book with a large number of phrases in the relevant languages, grouped by the setting in which they might be used. This book was used rather than a speech output computer-based system because the book offered a fuller range of phrases and thus would offer a more demanding test for the prototype.

3.1 Hypotheses

The following hypotheses were proposed :

Compared to using translated phrases in print :
1. Using the prototype would enable the participants to communicate more quickly
2. Using the prototype would help the participants to have a more natural and successful conversation

3.2 Method

This evaluation consisted of two phases, role plays and data analysis. In the first phase, twenty-four cross-language conversations were videotaped by four groups by using either the prototype or phrase book. Each group had three participants, English, Japanese, and Spanish native speakers, and these languages were ordered at random. There were six scenarios based on frequently occurring conversations at an airport check-in counter, and there were two roles in a conversation, the staff member and passenger, which were also performed in a random order.

In the second phase of the evaluation twenty native English speakers, who were different from the participants of the role plays, were asked to fill out a questionnaire after reading the translated transcriptions of the recorded conversations.

3.3 Role Plays

Scenarios. There were six scenarios as shown in Table 1. These six scenarios were allocated at random in the role plays.

Table 1. Scenarios of the role plays

Scenario	Content
1	Passenger to check in and confirm the boarding gate and departure time.
2	Passenger to check in as a disabled passenger.
3	Passenger to check in and ask how to transfer at the arrival airport.
4	Passenger to change the flight to an earlier one and check in.
5	Passenger to cancel the flight.
6	Passenger to correct the flight booked at the travel agency and check in.

Participants. Twelve people participated in the role plays. All were able to speak, but for the purposes of the evaluation, had to confine their communication to what they could communicate with the prototype or the phrasebook. Four were native English, four were native Japanese, and four were native Spanish speakers. Eight were male and four were female. Their ages varied as follows; one was in the 10 - 19 range, four were in the 20 - 29 range, five were in the 30 - 39 range, one was in the 40 - 49 range, and one was in the 50 - 59 range. Three of them had experience of checking in at an airport 6 - 9 times, and nine had experienced this more than 10 times.

Settings.   Each scenario had four conversations: two were carried out using the prototype and two using a phrase book. A mock passport, visa, and flight ticket, and luggage were provided for the passenger. The main task of the staff member was helping the passenger to accomplish his/her tasks in each scenario as described above. For example, when the passenger came to check in, the staff member was supposed to take the ticket, passport, and visa from the passenger, write out the boarding card (confirming if there were seats available on the computer screen), act out the checking-in of any luggage, and return all documents.

In the conversation with the prototype, a computer monitor and mouse were shared by the participants, and in the phrase book conversation, a phrase book was shared between them. The phrase book, which consists of a large set of phrases in five European languages and Japanese, is commercially available and one of the most common phrase books in the Japanese market (*Pocket Interpreter - 6-Language Conversation Book for Travellers.* Tokyo: Japan Travel Bureau, Inc. Publishing Division, 1997).

The technique for the multi-lingual communication was as follows. With the prototype, the speakers controlled the system in their own language and translation was done automatically into the other language. In the role plays, the participants interacted by means of text alone. Although the prototype has speech output, text only was used for these evaluations.   This was to ensure the fairest possible comparison between communication with the phrase book, which of course has no speech output. With the phrase book the participants found the phrase they wanted in their own language and then pointed out the linked phrase from the page in the partner's language.

Procedure. The background of this study was explained to the participants, and then an hour's preparation took place before the role plays, with each pair practising conversation by using the prototype and the phrase book. Each role play then had a rehearsal and a performance phase. The rehearsal was done in order for the participants to understand the tasks of each scenario. The performances were recorded on video.

Hypothesis 1. This hypothesis was tested by measuring the number of words produced per minute. The mean value was 9.64 words/min (SD = 5.00) for the prototype, and 7.97 words/min (SD = 5.73) for the phrase book. A two-way analysis of variance (method × scenario) showed no significant differences between the two methods or the six scenarios shown in Table 1 ($p > .05$ for both factors).

Hypothesis 2. Using the prototype would help the participants to have more natural and successful conversation.

Definition: Natural and successful conversation refers to conversation which has the following characteristics [27] :
1. a reasonable number of spoken words,
2. a speaker who is in a position of authority taking the initiative more often, i.e., initiates conversation and poses questions,
3. an agreement and understanding between the speakers,
4. the use of helpful social signs and polite phrases.

Number of words spoken. Although the cross-language conversations were carried out without speech in the evaluation, the phrases produced by the prototype played the same role as if spoken in ordinary single language conversation. Hence, the number of words in the text produced by the prototype and the number of words pointed out in the phrase book were the measure used. The mean value was 3.32 words/turn (SD = 1.11) for the prototype, and 1.98 words/turn (SD = 0.92) for the phrase book. A two-way analysis of variance (method × scenario) showed that the difference of conversational effect between the two methods was highly significant ($p < 0.01$ for the factor of method). By comparing the mean values, it was concluded that the number of words per turn will be greater when using the prototype than when using the phrase book. The difference among the six scenarios shown in Table 1, on the other hand, was not significant ($p > .05$ for the factor of scenario).

Conversational initiative. At the check-in counter, the staff member was assumed to be the one to take the initiative because they would be familiar with the procedures and aim to help the passengers through them. In the questionnaire, the respondents were asked to rate each conversation from 1 to 5 for the degree of conversation initiative taken by the staff member, comparing each case with the spoken single language conversation.

The mean score was 2.54 (SD = 0.91) for the prototype, and 2.35 (SD = 0.88) for the phrase book. A chi-squared test was applied to the analysis, where the first and last sets of two scores, the frequencies for scores of (1, 2) and (4, 5), were amalgamated for both methods in order to make all expected values exceeded 5 and retain uniformity of the analysis. The results indicated a statistically significant difference between the two methods (chi-square = 12.5, df = 2, p < .01). By taking into account the prototype's distribution which extends to larger scores, it was concluded that the prototype helped the staff member to take more conversational initiatives than did the phrase book.

Agreement and understanding. The mean score was 2.63 (SD = 0.70) for the prototype, and 2.63 (SD = 0.69) for the phrase book. A chi-squared test was applied in the same manner with amalgamation as performed for the data of conversation initiative. The results indicated no statistically significant difference between the two methods in terms of the degree of agreement and understanding (chi-square = 0.065, df = 2, p > .05).

Social routines. Social routines refer to feedback remarks, openers and closers which occur in everyday conversation such as "I see", "Hello", and "Goodbye" and also phrases of politeness such as "Please" and "Thank you".
The mean score was 2.45 (SD = 0.99) for the prototype, and 2.21 (SD = 1.04) for the phrase book. The results from a chi-squared test with data amalgamation showed that the difference between the two methods was highly significant (chi-square = 9.73, df = 2, p < .01). By taking into account the prototype's distribution which extends to larger scores, it was concluded that using the prototype helped the participants to have a conversation with more social routines.

Degree of success. In terms of the overall degree of success, the mean score was 2.75 (SD = 0.66) for the prototype, and 2.72 (SD = 0.63) for the phrase book. The results of a chi-squared test for this, with data amalgamation as above, indicated no statistically significant difference between the two methods (chi-square = 0.886, df = 2, p > .05).
In terms of the degree of success in sub-tasks, the mean score was 2.76 (SD = 0.67) for the prototype, and 2.54 (SD = 0.71) for the phrase book. The results from a chi-squared test with data amalgamation showed that the difference between the two methods was highly significant (chi-square = 10.5, df = 2, p < .01). By taking into account the prototype's distribution which extends to larger scores, it was concluded that using the prototype helped the participants to have a conversation with more degree of success in its sub-tasks.

4 Discussion

4.1 Communication Rate

In terms of the number of words conveyed per minute, it was concluded so far that there is no statistically significant difference between the two methods. This conclusion results primarily from the large deviation of the data. Is there any hidden substantial trend in this dispersed distribution ?

After an examination of the trends in the data, it was concluded that the involvement of people familiar with the prototype tended to raise the conversational efficiency of their groups overall, i.e., not only the conversations which they participated in, but also the conversations produced by the other members in the same group. The increased frequency of use for both communication methods suggested that the experienced person demonstrated what kind of words/phrases were available, and other group members learned it indirectly during the role plays. Another factor here is the importance of training in making use of a new communication system. It needs to be taken into account when evaluating any system such as this, that the system is a complex tool, whose usefulness will increase with training and familiarity.

4.2 Frequency of Use and Initiative

From the data it was concluded that the participants using the prototype used it to produce conversational contributions more frequently than the participants using the phrase book. This phenomenon was marked particularly for the staff member. This could be because there are few expressions for staff members in the phrase book, while on the other hand, about half the phrases on the prototype are for staff members. The lack of expressions for staff in the phrase book makes it difficult to have a balanced two-way conversation. This is one of the major weaknesses of existing commercial phrase books and portable electronic translators. Taking this into account, the result described that the staff members took more initiative with the prototype than with the phrase book, seems a natural outcome.

4.3 Agreement and Understanding and the Degree of Success

There was no statistically significant difference between the two methods in terms of the degree of agreement and understanding. The same result was obtained for the degree of success overall, although the prototype was better at accomplishing sub-tasks. However, it might have been an important factor that there was a rehearsal beforehand, and the participants already understood what the partner would do in the role plays. Further evaluation is needed concerning these points.

4.4 Social Routines

In conversations with strangers, such as those that occur at check-in counters, in hotels, and in restaurants, politeness is helpful in accomplishing the tasks pleasantly and efficiently [28]. With respect to this point, it was found that the prototype was superior to the phrase book. The prototype might be improved in the future by displaying automatically a card containing social routines, such as the "Chatting" card, when necessary since many social routines must be used with correct timing to be effective. In the evaluations, on the other hand, the participants had to choose the "Chatting" card manually.

5 Conclusions

Using the prototype helped the participants to produce a more natural and successful conversation, particularly due to the ability to take the initiative and increased use of social routines in a conversation. Although this first evaluation showed no significant difference between the two communication methods in terms of conversation efficiency, it was found that the participation of an experienced user of the communication method is an important factor in improving the efficiency. In addition to pointing out the value of training and familiarity in using a relatively complex system, this suggested a future improvement of the prototype might be an automatic display of suggested words/phrases according to the context, which would play a similar role as the developers did in this evaluation. In other words, users should be able to understand effortlessly what is available from the system. With respect to this, computer-based systems such as the prototype have the potential to be more effective than printed material because of the possibilities of dynamic display. Shared use of the same system by both speakers could help this strategy because the system could use a spoken utterance, which will be pre-stored in the system, to produce/predict a subsequent reply. It is worth considering that if future communication aids, regardless of their multi-lingual capability, for non-speaking people could in some way be used equally by both partners in a dialogue, this might add considerably to their effectiveness.

This prototype provides an example of the potential for a wider application of technology developed to assist people with disabilities. As well as providing an AAC user with a multi-lingual capability, the same system may be used to provide the same assistance to speaking people. It is an example of designing for people with special needs leading to solutions which could benefit everyone - truly universal design.

Acknowledgements. This work has benefited from the suggestions and comments of Dr Richard A. Brown at the Department of Mathematics, the University of Dundee, Scotland, in particular for the statistical treatment of the evaluation. This research project was supported by the grant from the New Energy and Industrial Technology Development Organization (NEDO), Japan, the British Council, and Access International Corporation, Japan.

References

1.   Newell, A. F.: Speech communication technology lessons from the disabled. Electronics and Power (1986) 661–664
2.   Newell, A. F.: Speech technology: Cross fertilization between research for the disabled and the non-disabled. *Proceedings of the First ISAAC Research Symposium in Augmentative and Alternative Communication* (1990) 131–134
3.   von Tetzchner, S., Jensen, M. (Ed.).: Augmentative and Alternative Communication : European Perspectives. Whurr Publishers Ltd, London (1996)
4.   Glennen, S.L., DeCoste D.C.: Handbook of Augmentative and Alternative Communication. Singular Publishing Group, Inc., San Diego (1997)

5. Beukelman, D. R., Mirenda, P.: Augmentative and Alternative Communication : Management of Severe Communication Disorders in Children and Adults. Second Edition. Paul H. Brookes Publishing Co., Baltimore (1998)
6. Alm, N., Arnott, J.L: Computer-assisted conversation for non-vocal people using pre-stored texts. IEEE Transactions on Systems, Man, and Cybernetics, Vol. 28 Part C No 3 (1998) 318–328
7. Whitelock, P., Kilby, K.: Linguistic and Computational Techniques in Machine Translation. UCL Press, London (1995)
8. Varile, G. B., Zampolli, A. (Ed.): Survey of the State of the Art In Human Language Technology. Cambridge University Press, Cambridge (1997)
9. Newell, A.F., Arnott, J.L., Alm, N.A.: The use of models of human conversation patterns within a prosthesis for non-speaking people. Bulletin of the Institute of Mathematics and Its Applications, 27 (12) (1991) 225–231
10. Todman, J., Elder, L., Alm, N., File, P.: Sequential dependencies in computer-aided conversation. Journal of Pragmatics21 (1994) 141–169
11. Todman, J., Alm, N., Elder, L.: Computer-aided conversation : a prototype system for non-speaking people with physical disabilities. Applied Psycholinguistics15 (1994) 45–73
12. Hickey, M., Alm, N.,Uytdenbroek, M.: Fuzzy information retrieval in an augmentative communication system. Proceedings of the 7th Biennial Conference of the International Society for Augmentative and Alternative Communication (1996) 483–484
13. Alm, N., Newell, A.F.: Lessons from applying conversation modeling to augmentative and alternative communication. Twelfth Annual Conference on Technology and Persons with Disabilities. Proceedings on disk. Rapidtext, Newport Beach, California (1997)
14. Schank, R.C.: Tell Me A Story: A New Look at Real and Artificial Intelligence. Macmillan Publishing Co., New York (1990).
15. Waller, A., Alm, N., Newell, A.F.: Aided communication using semantically linked text modules. Proceedings of the 13th Annual Conference of the Rehabilitation Engineers Society of North America (1990) 177–178
16. Waller, A., Broumley, L., Newell, A.F., Alm, N. : Predictive retrieval of conversational narratives in an augmentative communication system. Proceedings of the 14th Annual Conference of the Rehabilitation Engineers Society of North America (1991) 107–108
17. Waller, A.: Providing narratives in an augmentative communication system. Ph.D. Thesis, University of Dundee, Dundee, Scotland, U.K. (1992)
18. Alm, N., Waller, A., Arnott, J.L., Newell, A.F.: Improving assisted communication with narrative texts. Proceedings of ECART 2 – European Conference on the Advancement of Rehabilitation Technology (1993) Section 26.1 (3 pages)
19. Schank, R. and Abelson, R.: Scripts, Plans, Goals, and Understanding. Lawrence Erlbaum, New Jersey (1977)
20. Alm, N., Morrison, A., Arnott, J.L.: A communication system based on scripts, plans, and goals for enabling non-speaking people to conduct telephone conversations. Proceedings of IEEE Systems Man and Cybernetics Conference (1995) 2408–2412
21. van Geel, R., Neumann, H., Alm, N., Kamphuis, H.: Scaena : An advanced language device for interaction. Proceedings of the 7th Biennial Conference of the International Society for Augmentative and Alternative Communication (1996) 171–172
22. Vanderheyden, P., Demasco, P., McCoy, K., Pennington, C.: A preliminary study into schema-based access and organization of reusable text in AAC. Proceedings of the RESNA Conference (1996) 59–61
23. Carpenter, T., McCoy, K., Pennington, C.: Schema-based organization of reusable texts in AAC: User interface considerations. Proceedings of the RESNA Conference. (1997) 57–59
24. Dye, R., Alm, N., Arnott, J.L., Harper, G., Morrison, A.: A script-based AAC system for transactional interaction. Natural Language Engineering, 1 (1), (1997) 1–13

25. Harper, G., Dye, R., Alm, N., Arnott, J.L., Murray, I.R.: A script-based speech aid for non-speaking people. Proceedings of the Institute of Acoustics, Vol. 20 Part 6 (1998) 289–296
26. Nakamura, K., Newell, A.F., Alm, N. and Waller, A.: How do members of different language communities compose sentences with a picture-based communication system? – a cross-cultural study of picture-based sentences constructed by English and Japanese speakers. Augmentative and Alternative Communication **14** (2), (1998) 71–79
27. Cheepen, C. The Predictability of Informal Conversation. Pinter Publishers, London (1988)
28. Brown, P. , S. Levinson: Universals in language usage: politeness phenomena. In Goody, E. (ed.) Questions and Politeness: Strategies in Social Interaction. Cambridge University Press, London (1987) 256–289

E-cane with Situation Presumption for the Visually Impaired

Yoshihiro Yasumuro[1], Mikako Murakami[1], Masataka Imura[1],
Tomohiro Kuroda[2], Yoshitsugu Manabe[1], and Kunihiro Chihara[1]

[1] Graduate School of Information Science,
Nara Institute of Science and Technology,
8916-5, Takayama, Ikoma, Nara, 630-0101, Japan
{Yasumuro, mikako-m, imura, manabe, chihara}@is.aist-nara.ac.jp
http://chihara.aist-nara.ac.jp
[2] Department of Medical Informatics, Kyoto University Hospital,
54 Kawahara, Shogoin, Sakyo, Kyoto, 606-8607, Japan
Tomohiro.Kuroda@kuhp.kyoto-u.ac.jp

Abstract. The E-cane is an electronic aid equipment for the visually impaired to widely detect the obstacles that normal *white cane* cannot reach. We propose a situation presumption algorithm, "Wall/Floor-strategy" for the E-cane, which is capable of detecting the presuming the condition of spot where the blind user is stepping into. When some obstacles are recognised, E-cane informs the user about the types of the obstacles;the walls, gaps, stairs and so on by vibration and voice. This paper presents our proto-type implementation and some experimental results, that show the effectiveness of the proposed system.

1 Introduction

When the visually impaired people go out they usually need others' assistance or guide dogs, otherwise they use *the white canes* for their independent mobility. *The white cane* is widely prevailed and has a role to stand for the existence of the blind in public. However, the reach of the cane is so limited and some hazardous points such as drop-offs and downstairs are hardly judged even whether you can step forward or should keep off. Some electronic travel aids have been developed to extend the sensing reach and to supplement functions to avoid danger [1, 2]. Guiding to avoid the obstacles and navigating functionalities are also well developed, applying robotics autonomous techniques [3,4]. However, they do not really provide the information about the the surroundings including what kind of obstacles the blind user is facing at. Some traditional devices just convert the range range from the obstacles into a certain pattern of sound beacon [5,6]. However, this type of acoustic indication requires much attention to understand and interferes the other auditory information.

This paper presents a new framework to achieve the supplement function on the cane type electronic aid system based on a natural usage of *the white cane*, proposing a situation presumption algorithm to provide categorised simple information about the obstacles.

N. Carbonell, C. Stephanidis (Eds.): User Interfaces for All, LNCS 2615, pp. 409–421, 2003.

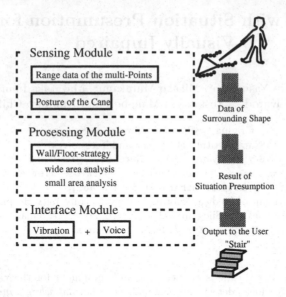

Fig. 1. Overview of the system: The system consists of 3 major modules

2   Proposed System

To inform the blind people about what kind of obstacles are ahead before he/she gets too close to them is very necessary and simple function, but existing electronic travel aids are not capable. Our approach is to extend the utility of the white cane, which the blind users are used to walk with them. Our attempt in this research is to achieve the capability of the cane to detect and categorise the distant hazardous conditions while swinging it in a usual way as ever.

We consider that the fundamental hazardous conditions for the blind pedestrians can be recognised by the surface shape of the surrounding objects. Assuming that the surrounding shape consists of pieces of surfaces, relative distance and the direction of the surface are the clues to presume the geometrical condition. For simplification, we roughly classify the surface conditions into 2 types; "wall" and "floor". The "wall" means the place you cannot step into and the "floor" stands for the flat plane where you can walk through. The "wall" includes the objects with the vertical surfaces such as poles, fences, parking cars, luggage on the floor and stairs, drop-offs, ditches and so on. Thus our approach is named "Wall/Floor-strategy." We apply range measurement using basic optical triangulation and utilising the way to swing the cane, scanning the ground ahead of the user can be done naturally. If multiple points range data can be acquired simultaneously, the system is able to monitor the surface information at each moment during the swing.

Proposed system consists of 3 major parts;sensing, processing and interface module(Fig. 1). Sensing module continuously gathers multiple range data of the ground from the cane and monitors the posture of the cane. Processing module performs "the Wall/Floor-strategy." to analyses the range and the direction of the surfaces of the ground and presumes the types of the geometry. Interface module informs the user of the existence of an obstacles with as clear patterns of vibrations associated with the obstacle types.

2.1   Sensing Module

To perform "Wall/Floor-strategy", the ground surface information is acquired by a triangulation of the points lit by the laser-pointers. The combination of multiple laser-pointers and a CCD camera as a 2D photo-array-sensor allows to measure multiple points simultaneously on each frame.

Range Sensing with Image Sensor. As shown in Fig. 2, let C-XYZ be as the camera coordinate, c-xy as the image-plane coordinate, f as the focal length of the camera, perspective projection is expressed by the equation (1). Let (α, β, γ) be as direction vector of a line though the point (X_0, Y_0, Z_0) is expressed by the equation (2).

$$X = \frac{x}{f}Z, \quad Y = \frac{y}{f}Z \tag{1}$$

$$\frac{X - X_0}{\alpha} = \frac{Y - Y_0}{\beta} = \frac{Z - Z_0}{\gamma} \tag{2}$$

The depth range Z is derived as equation (3) from (1), (2).

$$Z = \frac{b}{x - a} = \frac{d}{y - c} \tag{3}$$

$$(a, b, c, d : constants)$$

Moreover, the possible trajectory of luminous dot of the laser-pointer is expressed as a line segment on the image plane as equation (4).

$$k(x - x_0) = l(y - y_0) \tag{4}$$

$$(k, l : constants)$$

Settling the minimum and maximum measurement range and recording the known target positions of the luminous points, $(x_0, y_0), (x_1, y_1)$ on the image plane, the constants in equation (3), (4) are determined. Bresenham's algorithm [7] is employed to draw a line segment with proper width on the discrete image plane, by connecting the 2 points, (x_0, y_0) and (x_1, y_1). According to the equation (3), the luminous point on the line segments gives the actual distance of the pointed position on the ground. The luminous points of the each laser-pointer is mapped on the unique line on the image plane. The line segments are specified as many as the number of the laser-pointer and thus the simultaneous multiple points measurement is possible in one frame. Scanning along the limited number of lines to find the luminous points is far faster process comparing to stereo-vision approach [8].

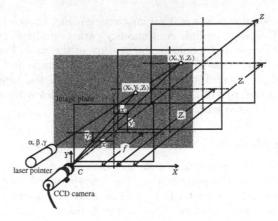

Fig. 2. Measurement principle is based on the fundamental triangulation: Using CCD camera and multiple laser beams, multiple triangulation on one frame is available

Extraction of the Illuminated Points. As depicted in Fig. 3, illuminated spots are captured by the CCD camera. The luminous spots show up on the line segment of equation (4) for each laser-pointer. The position of the luminous spot is detected as an intensity peak, searching along the line segment. The peak position on the camera coordinate gives the range and the relative position of the illuminated points from the camera by the equation (3).

Coordinate Transformation. The measured positions $[x_n, y_n, z_n]_c^T (n = 1, 2, 3)$ of the points on the ground expressed by the camera coordinate is transformed to the coordinate system based on the user's standpoint (Fig.4), $[X, Y, Z]_w^T$ by the equation (5). $T(\cdot)$ and $R(\cdot)$ express 3 dimensional parallel and rotational transformation respectively.

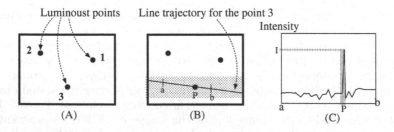

Fig. 3. Extraction of the luminous spots on the image: Captured luminous point on the image plane(A) is on its trajectory lines expressed eq.(4) as in (B). Along the line, the exact position can be extracted by scanning the intensity profile(C)

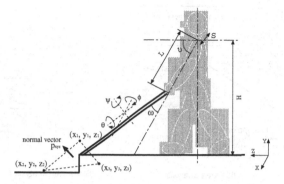

Fig. 4. Coordinate systems: Relative distance of the points on the ground from the cane and the posture of the cane are measured continuously. Relative geometry of the surfaces on the ground are expressed by the coordinate system fixed on the user

$$\begin{bmatrix} X \\ Y \\ Z \end{bmatrix}_w = T(S/2, H, 0)R(v, 0, 0)T(0, L, 0)R(\omega, 0, 0)R(\theta, \phi, \psi) \begin{bmatrix} x \\ y \\ z \end{bmatrix}_c \quad (5)$$

The gradient finder fixed on the handle of the cane monitors the posture of the cane expressed the angles, $\theta(roll), \phi(pitch), \psi(yaw)$. The height of the shoulder (H), width of the shoulders (S), arm length (L) and standard angle of the cane (ω) are initially calibrated for the user.

2.2   Processing Module

"The Wall/Floor-strategy" classifies the surface sets in a coarse-to-fine manner (Fig. 5). The process has 2 steps; wide area analysis and small area analysis. Comparing to the obstacles of a hollow shape and a downward surface, upward

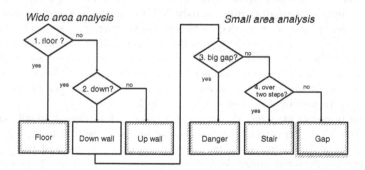

Fig. 5. Wall/Floor-strategy process flow: judgement is executed in a coarse-to-fine manner. If the surface goes up steeply, a "wall" is detected. If the surface goes down, detailed analysis is employed to judge whether a dangerous gap or a downstairs

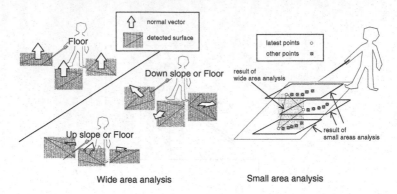

Fig. 6. Simultaneous multiple triangulation allows to monitor the surface direction(Wide area analysis). Multiple points sweep on the ground to scan the detailed changes in the sequence of the range and the surfaces while the user swings the cane(Small area analysis)

surfaces and protruding objects are easy to touch and find with the cane for the blind user. Therefore, when the downward geometrical features are detected, more detailed and precise investigation is necessary. Proposed strategy presumes following categories.

- Floor: flat plane, no obstacles, slight slope
- Upward: a wall or obstacles on the floor or upstairs
- Downward:
  - Stairway: more than 2 steps downstairs
  - Gap: a small drop-off
  - Danger: "Stop!"

In the wide area analysis of the "Wall/Floor-strategy", direction of the each surface piece is checked by monitoring the normal vector of a triangle formed by the points measured simultaneously. While the normal vectors are vertical enough the surfaces are regarded as "Floor." If the surface goes up too steeply, a "wall" is detected. If the surface goes down, the small area analysis is employed to judge whether a dangerous gap or a downstairs way to go shows up. Swinging the cane, illuminated points sweep over the ground. Using the sequence of the captured points, the depth between the gaps and the existence of the following stairway steps can be detected as depicted in Fig. 6.

Regarding each stroke of the swing as a term of detection, basically the result of the detection is transmitted when the swing direction is varied. The turning point of the swing is found by monitoring the time sequence of the yaw-angle, $\psi(t)$ from the gradient finder device. The angular acceleration of the cane swing is acquired as follows.

$$\psi'' = ((\psi(t+1) - \psi(t))) - (\psi(t) - \psi(t-1)) \tag{6}$$

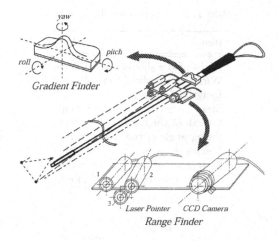

Fig. 7. Schematic overview of the sensing module: 3 laser-pointers, a CCD camera and gradient finder are fixed on the grip of the cane. The size of the module is 10cm x 10cm x 5cm

3   Implementation

We implemented a proto-type system to perform proposed method. More focusing on demonstrating the effectiveness of the "Wall/Floor-strategy" in realtime process, desk-top type PC is used for driving the system in this report. Main specification of the PC is as follows.

- CPU: Duron 800MHz
- Memory: 128 MB
- Video Capture Card: GV-VCP/PCI (I/O DATA)

3.1   Measurement Module

We use 3 laser-pointers (LD263-031:λ=635nm, 1mW by KANTUM elec.) and a miniaturised CCD camera(WAT-240R by WATEC) for range sensing. Image resolution is 320x240 pixels. The posture of the cane is measured by a gradient finder (INTERTRAX2 by INTER-SENSE). The error rate of the range sensor is no less than 1% for the 1m to 2m range measurement.

In order to sweep with the laser-pointers and to investigate geometry, measurement rate needs to be fast enough comparing to swinging and walking speed of the cane user. To ensure the practical performance speed we made a simulation under the condition shown in Table 1. Measurement target was settled to the downstairs which is the most complicated topology to be categorised in our system. We assume that the walking speed is proportional to the swing speed of the cane as one step is synchronised to one cycle of the swing. Varying the walking speed parameter, we made a simulation to detect the steps of the downstairs. Results from the simulation, the maximum walking speed not to miss the

Table 1. Parameters for the simulation

Item	Value
Hight of the shoulders	130 cm
Width of the shoulders	40 cm
Length of the arm	60 cm
Step	60 cm
Length of the cane	130 cm
Swing angle of the cane	24 deg
Measurement rate	30 Hz
Step of the stairs	28 cm
Gaps of the stairs	19 cm

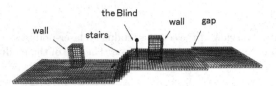

Fig. 8. Simulation course is prepared in the PC, where the subject walks around virtually. Swinging the cane controls the speed and the direction and the system output is transmitted to the subject by the vibration interface in the cane grip

steps of the stairway is 16.4 km/h. Considering that generally walking speed is up to 8 km/h, our system's performance is fast enough.

3.2   User Interface

As depicted in Fig. 9, E-cane has 3 vibrators driven by the micro-motors in the grip. The micro-motors are controlled by a PIC (Peripheral Interface Controller) and 4 patterns to activate the vibrator are assigned for the system outputs as follows;

- – vibrator a: "Wall"
- – vibrator b: "Stair"
- – vibrator c: "Bump"
- – vibrator a&b&c: "Danger"

We prepared 13 sighted subjects and 2 visually impaired subjects to test the readability of the user interface. Experimental setup is simulative walk-through course prepared in a computer as shown in Fig. 8. The E-cane is the controller and the feedback interface for the simulation. The speed and the direction of the swing reflects the speed and the direction to walk in the virtual course. Summing up the data of distance from the obstacles when the subjects notice the message from the system, the minimal distance was 100 cm. The transmission delay of

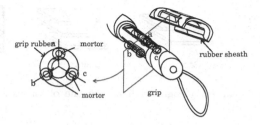

Fig. 9. Vibration interface: 3 vibration motors are equipped in the cane grip

the output message from the system with vibration interface sufficiently small. In Japan, for example, it is regulated that any obstacles should be more than 80 cm away from the textured paving blocks for the blind on the street. The correct ratio to read the output of the vibrator was 86 %. The most confused case was "Gap" and "Stair", because the system is designed to output "Gap" before "Stair" every time, according to the "Wall/Floor-strategy" process flow. In terms of calling of the user's attention, the system functions for the safety without any problems.

4   Presumption of the Real Obstacles

Using the proposed system, we performed the experiments in a real circumstance of our institute building. Fig. 11-13 show some examples of the cases in which approaching to a obstacle on the floor (Fig.11), a drop-off (Fig.12), a landing space and a downstairs (Fig.13). The result of the proposed method to presume the obstacle types are overlaid on each picture with the symbols shown in Fig.10.

In Fig.11 a side table is detected as a "wall" protruding from the floor. A hollow part on the floor is detected before the cane reach the edge of the dent(Fig.12). Reaching to the downstairs, the side wall and the balustrades are detected at first, then several steps are found and stairway is recognised (Fig.13). We assured that while the laser-pointers spots are sweeping over the flat floor, the system remains to recognise the expanse of the place to walk till surface conditions vary. Once the discontinuitiy of the piecewise surfaces' structure is detected, the system tells what kind of obstacle is there ahead of the cane.

5   Discussion

The fundamental performances of the proposed system is experimented in a actual day-to-day life circumstances. Presumption of the geometry type functions effectively to send the cautions to the visually impaired with limited number of categorised message patterns on the spot. One of the key technologies for the proposed system is the range sensing with a image sensor. The sampling rate and the precision are sufficient for the E-cane use, but sensitivity causes a problem in some cases. Fig. 14 shows the captured and processed image to extract the illuminated spots of the laser-pointers. Fig. 15 shows the failure case

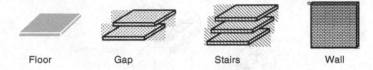

| Floor | Gap | Stairs | Wall |

Fig. 10. Objects to express recognised floor and the obstacles as the presumption results

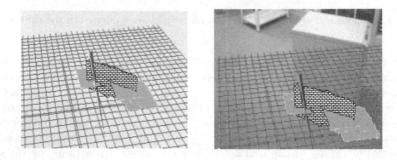

Fig. 11. Presumption Result: A small table is detected as a "Wall". The type and the position of the objects are expressed from the user' view (left) and overlaid with the background image (right)

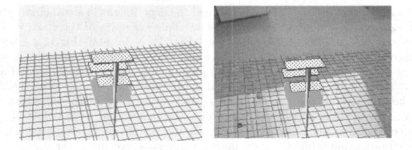

Fig. 12. Presumption Result: Downward "Gap" is detected before the cane has reached the edge

to capture the illuminated spots precisely. The distribution of the intensity in the captured image depends on the reflectance characteristics of the target materials and illumination conditions. Especially for the specular floors and direct sunlight cause difficult situation for sensing. To cope with the variety conditions mentioned above, complementary usage of different type of the sensors such as ultrasonic sensors can be considered. Our next step is to make the whole system as portable or wearable system and to try more various practical cases by the visually impaired subjects. Considering the specifications of the system used in this report, it is possible to down-size the system by replacing the PC with lap-top or other small-type processors.

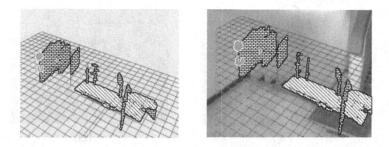

Fig. 13. Presumption Result in a stair way. Side wall and the balustrades are detected as "Wall" and downward stairs are detected as "Stair"

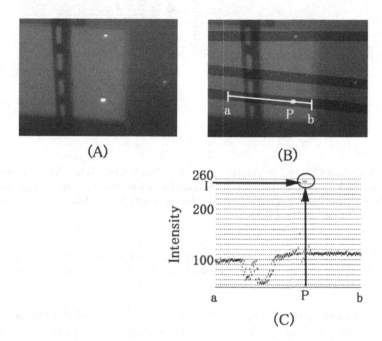

(A)   (B)

(C)

Fig. 14. Successfully Extracted Luminous Spots: (A) is a captured image which contains a pole, floor, and a wall. 3 dark thick lines in (B) are the trajectories on which the luminous points appear. Along the line a-b on (B), the distribution of the intensity is shown in (C). The luminous point is clearly found as a peak

6   Concluding Remarks

To aim the effective aid for the visually impaired people's independent mobility, we proposed E-cane which is capable to presume the obstacles' situation with extended reach of sensing range. Based on the idea of surface analysis of the sur-

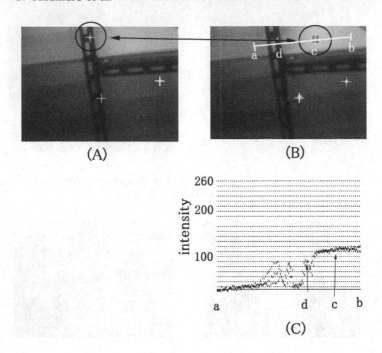

Fig. 15. Failure Case for Extraction of the Luminous Spots: The picture arrangement is as same as Fig. 14. Depending on the condition of the laser reflection on the surface of the object, clear peak is not obtained on the trajectory for the luminous point position, thus a measurement error occurs

roundings, "Wall/Floor-strategy" is implemented and our experimental results show the effectiveness to let the user know what kind of obstacle may be there before getting too close.

Acknowledgement. This research is partly supported by the Ministry of Education, Culture, Sports, Science and Technology of Japan, Grants-in-Aid for Scientific Research, (B-13558043), 2002.

References

1. Benjamin, J. M., Ali, N. A., and Schepis, A. F., 1973, "A Laser Cane for the Blind." Proceedings of the San Diego Biomedical Symposium, Vol. 12, pp. 53–57.
2. Y. Bellik, R. Farcy, "Comparison of Various Interface Modalities for a Locomotion Assistance Device", ICCHP 2002, 8th International Conference on Computers Helping People with Special Needs, University of Linz (Austria), 15–20 July, 2002.
3. Iwan Ulrich, Johann Borenstein, The GuideCane – Applying Mobile Robot Technologies to Assist the Visually Impaired: IEEE trans. on Systems, Man, and Cybernetics, part A:Systems and Humans, vol.31, No.2, pp. 131–136. (2001)

4. K. Goto, H. Matsubara, S. Myojo, A Guiding System for Persons Handicapped to Move: Proceedings vol.A of the third World Congress on Railway Research, pp.533–540, (1997).
5. A sonar Aid to Enhance Spatial Perception of the Blind: Engineering Design and Evaluation; Radio and Electronics Engineer, Vol.44, No.11, p. 605–627 (1974)
6. Wromald International Sensory Aids, 6140 Horseshie Bar Rd.,Loomis, CA 95659.
7. J.E. Bresenham, Algorithm for computer control of a digital plotter: IBM Systems Journal 4(No.1) p. 25–30 (1965)
8. N. Molton, S. Se, J.M.Brady, D. Lee, P. Probert, A Stereo vision-based aid for the visually impaired: Image and Vision Computing, Vol, 16 pp. 251–263. (1998).

Part VI: Mobile Computing – Design and Evaluation

Augmentative and Alternative Communication: The Future of Text on the Move

Anders Sewerin Johansen and John Paulin Hansen

The IT University of Copenhagen,
Glentevej 67
DK-2400 Copenhagen NV
Telephone: +45 38 16 88 88
Fascimile: +45 38 16 88 99
{dduck, paulin}@it-c.dk

Abstract. The current methods available for text entry on small mobile devices suffer from poor performance which presents a potential barrier to acceptance and growth. Our analysis of mobile text entry indicates that the likely solution lies in aggressive use of language technology which is beyond the capabilities of current mobile devices. We argue that research in augmentative and alternative communication is highly relevant to the mobile text entry problem and offers the opportunity to research solutions that will be possible on future generations of mobile devices. Fewer input buttons, Natural Language Prosessing (NLP) and multimodal inputs are techniques applied in our design.

1 Introduction – Mobile Texting

Mobile texting is a term for short text messages which are sent and received in a mobile setting, i.e. in situations where the user is not at the primary work setting (home or office) and may be engaging in another activity.

The most common example of mobile texting ("texting") is Short Message System (SMS). SMS is a part of the GSM standard for mobile phones and has gained popularity and users worldwide, especially in Scandinavia [1] where it is common to use SMS while on the bus, waiting in line and even while strolling or riding a bicycle. The use of SMS is strongly correlated with age (primary user group is the 15-24 age group), use of the Internet and an active lifestyle [1].

Mobile text messages are primarily of a social nature and are commonly used as an alternative to phone conversations rather than data entry or creation of actual documents. Topics are thus typically of a personal character, and the content is in general actual conversation or coordination of social activities.

In contrast to actual documents, presentation (paragraphs, text justification and the use of different fonts) is relatively unimportant. Correct spelling, punctuation and the use of capital letters have low priority, and the main focus is swift and precise communication.

Slang and abbreviations are very common among Scandinavian SMS users. A Danish study conducted in December 2001 recorded the 600 most commonly used slang words and abbreviations used in a group of 700 SMS users [29]. The most

N. Carbonell, C. Stephanidis (Eds.): User Interfaces for All, LNCS 2615, pp. 425–441, 2003.

common reason quoted for use of these shorthand notations is the low maximum length of SMS messages (<160 characters) and the performance characteristics of the input methods. Thus, the evolution of a domain specific language which parallels the evolution of codes and abbreviations used in Morse and among radio amateurs [13] in order to increase communication speed and lower costs.

1.1 On the Relevance of Mobile Texting

The low cost of an SMS message is often quoted as a major factor in the success of the system [2]. This is, in fact, not likely to be a contributing factor as the price of an actual SMS conversation, which usually spans several SMS exchanges, may exceed the price of a short voice call, and indeed in most countries it does.

The reason is more likely that text as a media complements speech in several areas. The most obvious of these are presented in Table 1.

Table 1. Qualitative and social differences between texting and voice conversation.

	Mobile texting	Voice call
Qualitative	Asynchronous/not interactive	Synchronous/interactive
	Unambiguous	Ambiguous
	Easy/cheap to archive	Hard/expensive to archive
	Easy to search/skim	Hard to search/skim
Social	Not impeded by noise	Demands quiet environment
	Discreet	May be overheard

It bears mentioning that many of these arguments are known from the use of email. On this basis, we believe that mobile texting is a distinct media for communication just like email and traditional physical letters rather than a substitute for voice calls.

In many situations, just one of the listed attributes may determine that texting is preferable to voice calls. A few examples from daily life is the asynchronous exchange of random thoughts ("Remember to pick up the kids after work"), unambiguous exchange of data (phone numbers, account numbers, addresses...) and the discreet exchange of personal messages while in a public setting ("I love you!").

1.2 The Mobile Input Problem

The three primary commercially successful text input methods are the standard SMS Multi Tap system, the pen based Graffiti used in the Palm Pilot PDA and the scaled-down QWERTY soft keyboard.

Multi Tap is the standard input system in the GSM mobile phone standard. It is described and evaluated in [3] and [4]. In brief, a Multi Tap user selects the desired letter from the International Telecommunication Union (ITU) standard phone keypad [14] by pressing the key marked with the letter one or more times. Selecting two letters residing on the same key (e.g. 'a' followed by 'b') requires the user to wait for a time-out (1.5 seconds on Nokia phones) or to use a "time-out kill" key.

Graffiti is the primary entry method for the Palm Pilot PDA. It is a simplified version of the roman capital letters, which reduces all English letters, signs and numbers to a single stroke. Graffiti and its immediate usability are examined in [5].

The QWERTY soft keyboard is available as an alternative input method in the Palm Pilot PDA. The features and performance of soft QWERTY is discussed in [6].

Unfortunately, all these input methods achieve rather low input performance, in the range of 8-30 words per minute (WPM), which is far below the rates commonly seen on the standard full-size QWERTY keyboard as shown in Table 2. Please note that expert QWERTY users are known to exceed the quoted speed by a comfortable margin, and that speech in ordinary conversation routinely reaches WPM rates in excess of 150 WPM. In other words, the numbers quoted here are indicative of the performance achievable on the above-mentioned input methods but not conclusive.

Table 2. Predicted and measured input speeds of common mobile and desktop text input methods

Input method	WPM predicted	WPM measured
Multi Tap	27.2 [4]	7.93 [3]
Graffiti	-	20 (estimate) [7]
Soft QWERTY w. stylus	8.9-30.1 [6]	-
QWERTY	-	64.9 [8]
Speech recognition	-	39 [9]

All these mobile text input methods are fairly easy to learn, Graffiti being probably the hardest with an estimated learning period of 5 minutes needed to achieve 97% accuracy [5].

All of them do, however, handle non-English localization in an unsatisfactory manner. As an example, QWERTY relegates the Danish letters 'æ', 'ø' and 'å' to the undesirable far right position (right hand little finger), and Multi Tap requires 8, 7 and 6 key presses respectively to enter these characters. As for Graffiti, entering several western European special characters and accents, including 'ø' and 'å', requires two strokes, whereas entering any English letter only requires one stroke.

In the case of QWERTY and Multi Tap, it is not possible to resolve these issues gracefully as it is impossible to place these letters in a manner that corresponds to their likelihood without changing the position of several other letters. In the specific case of Multi Tap, this would require diverging from the ITU standard telephone keypad. The localization issues in Graffiti could certainly be resolved and are likely a consequence of a less than careful implementation.

1.3 Full-Size Keyboards and QWERTY

The full-size QWERTY keyboard is the most common text input device. The primary characteristics of the QWERTY keyboard are:
- Direct selection of all characters.
- Can be operated with one or two hands and without visual attention (touch-typing).
- Performance exceeds 100 WPM with training.
- High performance (touch-typing) requires the full use of all 10 fingers.
- Shallow learning curve.

- Acceptable performance when used sub-optimally (hunt-and-peck estimated at ~23 WPM [27]).
- Well-known paradigm for text entry (one character at a time).
- Only two modes (shift) when entering ordinary text.
- Suitable for text entry, navigation and editing.
- Can be used by left-handed users.
- Just as easy (or hard) as handwriting for dyslexic users.
- Static layout.

When one considers the features listed, it is not surprising that the QWERTY has remained the standard text entry device despite competition from several alternative keyboard layouts – e.g. Dvorak [26] – which arguably are superior with regards to performance, learning curve and ergonomics. The QWERTY keyboard is flexible, efficient, easy to learn and forgiving for the novice user. If used with modern word processor software and spell-checkers, most errors are found and corrected at the earliest possible moment.

The primary limitations of the QWERTY keyboard are the limited mobile usability, the relatively high demands on motor performance for expert users and an upper limit on performance. However, in the most common scenario, namely text composition, an entry speed of 40-50 WPM is usually adequate, and this level of performance is in the reach of most users with a minimum of training.

When studied from an information theory-based point of view, as seen in [22], the QWERTY keyboard has far too many keys for the task at hand. The information content (entropy) of English text is approximately 1 bit per character. One selection on a QWERTY keyboard signals approximately 6.3 bits of information indicating that the QWERTY keyboard is inefficient by a factor of 6!

1.4 The Mobile Challenge

We, along with other researchers [2], believe that the performance limitations on the primary mobile text input methods are a barrier to the continuing use and proliferation of mobile texting beyond the largely young user group that is currently the primary SMS users. In usability studies it has often been found that difficult or slow operation limits the users inclination to activity [30]. If mobile texting can be made more efficient and/or easier to use, it is likely to increase the usage. The goal is to approach the performance (i.e. ~40 WPM for casual users) and relatively low cognitive load of the common QWERTY keyboard but in a mobile setting while still making mobile texting accessible to new and casual users.

2   Mobile Text Input: Theory, Technology, and Design Principles

Entering text messages can be viewed as a system consisting of a usage scenario, a user, a user interface for entering the text, a device hosting the interface and finally the actual text. In the following sections, we study these elements in order to identify the factors which are likely to be decisive in developing the replacement for current inadequate mobile text entry methods.

2.1 The Mobile Scenarios

As mentioned in the introduction, there is no one, single mobile usage scenario. The mobile text user desires the ability to communicate anywhere and anytime in the fashion of voice calls or ordinary conversation. Thus, the mobile scenarios span a wide range of physical limitations on motorical performance and the degree of attention available for the task.

We believe that these four scenarios are a fair representation of most mobile texting situations.

Table 3. Mobile texting scenarios.

Scenario	Posture	Physical freedom	Degree of attention	External interruptions
"Business class". Near-office conditions. Long journey by plane or train	Seated, table space available	Full mobility for both hands and arms. Device can be placed on table	Full	None or few
"Coach". Limited office conditions. Long journey by bus	Seated, no table available.	Limited mobility for both hands and arms with device in lap *or* full mobility for one hand and arm, other hand holding the device	Full	None or few
"Metro". Out of office conditions. Short journey by bus or subway or standing in line	Standing.	Full mobility for one hand and limited mobility for the arm, with the other arm and hand holding the device	Limited	Often. Noisy environment.
"Strolling". Full mobility in active environment. Walking down a busy street	Standing/ walking	Limited mobility for one hand and arm. Same hand holds and operates the device.	Very limited	Very frequent. Noisy environment

The mobile text user usually has the option to "upgrade" at will (or need) to a scenario that allows for a higher degree of motorical freedom and available attention, e.g. by sitting down on a public bench.

In order to support the most extreme scenario – "strolling" –, a user interface must perforce be very robust in the face of constant interruption and should preferably be usable in "eyes-free" mode, i.e. without demanding constant or frequent visual attention.

2.2 Factors in User Performance

When attempting to optimize or model user performance on some task, such as data entry, one common approach is to construct a model of the task and estimate user performance – either on the basis of a modeling framework such as GOMS, or by using rules for estimating motor and cognitive components of the task. For the latter purposes, the most commonly used rules are Fitts' law [16] which attempts to predict expert users' motor performance on target selection, and Hick-Hyman [17] [18], which attempts to predict the time used on visual scan in target identification.

The predictions obtained from Fitts' law are dependent on the relative size and relative placement of the targets and the likelihood of transitions between the targets.

Predictions using Hick-Hyman are dependent on log2 of the number of available alternatives. This seems rather optimistic as a log2 dependency on number of items indicates a very efficient search algorithm, i.e. binary search, which requires a sorted list of items to search in. This is supported by user comments recorded in post-interviews in the FOCL study [11]. These indicate that the actual strategy for visual search was a combination of gestalting the area surrounding the current center of interest – a 3x3 matrix of letters – and using a linear search (which is dependent on the number of items) as a backup strategy.

Be that as it may, none of these criticisms dispute that the visual search component is in some way dependent on the number of items. This is therefore likely to be an important factor in dynamic or semi-dynamic input systems.

All in all, the general conclusion is certainly that the optimal system presents as few targets as possible with a function as close to user expectations as possible, ideally placed as close as possible to the current area of interest and possibly sized according to likelihood.

2.3 Language, Text, and Language Technology

Text is highly redundant as can be seen from the fact that one usually achieves compression rates of 80-90% when compressing text with programs such as bzip and WinZip. Although we usually store text using 8 bits per character, experiments by Shannon [19] indicate that the entropy of English text is between 0.6 and 1.2 bits per character.

As mentioned in Section 1.4, this means that on average a very low input rate is required in order to compose text. This, however, is only possible if the device used for text entry is able to interpret this information correctly in effect inferring the other 7 bits from general knowledge of language and context using a *language model*.

Language models can be based on many different Natural Language Processing (NLP) algorithms with varying results in terms of performance, capabilities and resource consumption. A simple language model (frequency count) achieves an entropy of 4.03 bits per character [19]), and an advanced state-of-the-art model (maximum entropy) achieves 1.2 bits per character [20]. The traditional n-gram approach is relatively high performing at 1.5 bits per character [21]. David J. Ward tabulates the performance of most current approaches and discusses the construction of language models extensively in [22].

Most language models need to be primed in order to perform optimally. In the case of a 3-gram model, which predicts a word on basis of the two preceding words, it needs to be primed with two words in order to supply any predictions at all. In other words, most (possibly all) language models will supply unreliable predictions for the first few words or characters of input. As a consequence, when designing text input systems based on language models, one must allow for the possibility that the predictions are wrong!

One of the most common problems when using word-level language models is the dictionary problem: What happens when the user wants to enter a word which is not in the dictionary? It is possible to estimate the probability of an unknown word, but it is obviously impossible to predict the actual (unknown) word. It is not just impractical to add all known words to the dictionary (Websters Ninth New Collegiate Dictionary boasts almost 160.000 entries!) – it is virtually impossible as new words are constantly added to the vocabulary of all living languages.

As mentioned in the introduction, the Scandinavian SMS users do in fact use a very large number of slang words and abbreviations, many of which are local to the SMS domain. It is therefore to be expected that mobile texting is significantly more prone to the dictionary problem than the average newspaper article or novel. Likewise, users of an AAC-system may develop slang and abbreviations that are well understood by caretakers in a daily communication context but incomprehensible for outsiders.

2.4   The Mobile Text User Interface

Mobile devices are subject to several unique UI-related factors which make designing mobile solutions even more of a challenge than the more common desktop solutions. In [23] it is pointed out that mobile units are subject to extreme internationalization issues; a large proportion of new, novice or casual users; a lack of established metaphors and limited physical real estate for input, output and labeling of input devices. In Section 2.1 we discussed the usage scenarios which are rather more extreme than the usual office scenario.

The user population for mobile texting is to a large degree composed of new users, novices and casual users as indicated by the demographic breakdown of SMS usage patterns data in [10] and the simple fact that SMS is a very young media.

Research in UI design has led to the formulation of a series of general guidelines [25] [31]. The primary guidelines that apply to the mobile texting task are:

- Avoid a steep learning curve.
- Design the system in a fashion that enables the user to easily construct a mental model, preferably one that has similarities with comparable and well-known tasks in other domains.
- Give early, precise and clear feedback on operator errors.
- The system should be efficient for the task giving the user the satisfaction of a job well done with a suitable tool.
- Enable frequent users to use shortcuts.
- Allow for human diversity such as color blindness, left-handedness and mild dyslexia/illiteracy.
- Avoid the use of modes.

In the cases where technical or design limitations mandate that one or several guidelines are ignored, one should do so with the guidelines in mind and soften the blow (if possible). This can be done e.g. by documentation, on-line help and guides ("Wizards"). Not doing so presumes that the need of the users to use your device is so acute that they are willing to put up with bad design and a long and trying learning period. This is usually not the case when a simple and well-known and/or significantly easier alternative is available even if this alternative delivers lower performance.

That this is specifically not the case with regards to mobile texting is indicated by the results from a survey of SMS users, who have tried and later discarded the T9 text input system in favor of the less efficient but well-known Multi Tap system [24]. The mean number of tries before discarding the T9 system was only 3.6! T9 uses the ITU keypad as an ambiguous keyboard, thus only requiring the user to press a key once for each letter in the desired word. The ambiguous input is then compared to a built-in dictionary, and the user is required to acknowledge the systems' interpretation of the ambiguous input, and in some cases select from several alternative interpretations. An interactive demonstration of T9 is available at http://www.tegic.com.

The reported reasons for discarding the T9 system indicate that one or several of the guidelines were violated as they show a lack of understanding of the text entry paradigm used in T9 and/or general operator difficulties. The top 5 reasons cited are: 45% of the 102 respondents deem the system "difficult/complicated"; 36% complain that the system does not supply the desired words; 29% say they don't know how to use it; 18% say it is "too slow" and 13% say they are comfortable and/or familiar with the old system. Both model predictions [4] and empirical measurements [3] indicate that T9 is substantially more efficient than Multi Tap, and the process of adding new words to the dictionary is relatively simple. One must therefore assume that the disgruntled users were primarily influenced by design-related factors, or that the designers failed to anticipate the potential problems and supply sufficient documentation and/or design elements which compensated for the potential problems.

2.5 Current and Future Capabilities of Mobile Devices

The currently available mobile devices are clustered around three basic form factors, which offer differing levels of performance and richness of features as shown in Table 4.

In terms of performance and price, it is remarkable that each successively larger form factor offers an increase in available resources and price of approximately an order of magnitude maintaining a roughly equivalent price/performance ratio.

We can estimate the available resources in a given class of devices at a given point in the future with an acceptable margin of error by using Moore's "law". This rule-of-thumb says that the price/performance ratio for semiconductor-based devices doubles with a frequency of 18 months leading to an increase of two orders of magnitude over a period of approximately 10 years. In other words, we can expect the hand-held form factor to have the level of performance of a current (2002) notebook in approximately 10 years time (2012). The high-end notebook in 1992 did indeed sport a CPU speed of 16-32 MHz and 1-4 MB of RAM with the option of a few dozens of MB static storage, which is in the same order of magnitude as the current crop of mobile phones.

As new capabilities are added (eg. games, music playback), the input and output capabilities of the devices increase. A common feature in new models of both mobile phones and PDAs is selection devices such as scroll- and jogwheels suitable for e.g. choosing the next song to play from a selection of hundreds.

Table 4. Current classes of mobile devices and their available resources.

	Mobile phone	PDA	Laptop
Price	$10-$100	Hundreds of $	Thousands of $
Storage	<10 MB	Hundreds of MB	Tens of GB
CPU	<10 MHz	50-200MHz	~1GHz
Size	~3x10 cm	~6x10cm	~20x30cm
Input	Keys	Keys, touchscreen and pen	QWERTY + pointing device
Screen area	~10 cm2	Tens of cm2	Hundreds of cm2
Purpose	Communication	Organizer/data collection	Office tasks

2.6 Theory, Technology, and Design Principles – Discussion

It is indeed theoretically and technologically possible to devise an efficient input method for mobile texting as the required input bandwidth is low (~1 bit per character on average). This requires that the necessary resources for hosting an efficient language model are available. The resources needed for well-performing language models are already available on the smallest mobile devices (the phone form-factor) or will be soon.

The limiting factor is likely the quality of the design of the UI as results from investigations of current solutions indicate. This may in turn be dependant on factors that are related to the usage scenario and/or physical limitations of the device due to the form factor (which imposes limitations on the available input and output devices) rather than the available computing resources.

One obvious way of investigating the future UI for mobile text entry is experiments in the desktop segment as we can predict with reasonable confidence that a solution that demands the computational resources of a desktop is viable on even the smallest mobile device in only 10 years time.

3   Adaptive and Augmentative Communication – A Testing Ground for Future Mobile Text Input Solutions

In our research group, we mainly concentrate on developing new approaches to communications aids for severely physically disabled persons, i.e. augmentative and alternative communication (AAC). Our solutions are designed for use by people who suffer from amyotrophic lateral sclerosis (ALS), also known as Lou Gehrig's Disease. Our systems are built from off-the-shelf components, and one of our major sub-goals is to develop robust eye-tracking based AAC solutions. Our design motivation is detailed in [28].

This class of AAC solutions has several obvious parallels to mobile text input solutions, primarily:

• The need to do without QWERTY as an input device for text.
• Focus on producing conversation-like text.

- Focus on speed and accuracy rather than presentation.
- Focus on multimodal interaction in one unified interface.

The major difference is that we are not bound by the computational and (in some cases) physical limitations of current mobile devices (GSM mobile phones and first generation PDAs). This allows us to design solutions that use computational resources and storage 1-2 orders of magnitude beyond those available in the mobile setting.

Our initial goal was to re-think the usage- and user scenario (as reported in [28]) in the hope that this would lead to revolutionary rather than evolutionary advances. Our quantitative goal was to improve input speed by a factor of two from the 6-7 WPM found in contemporary AAC systems [15] to 10-15 WPM. At this point in time, we have developed a range of systems which incorporate language technology as a central design feature rather than as an enhancement of traditional operation. Our systems all share these features:

- Significantly fewer buttons/targets than QWERTY (4-10 buttons).
- Aggressive use of language technology.
- Multimodal input (mouse, keyboard, head/eye tracking).

3.1 Users and Usage Scenarios

Although there are many disabilities that lead to a need for an AAC solution, e.g. muscular dystrophy, strokes or spinal cord injuries, we focus our development on solutions suitable for ALS patients. ALS is a progressive neurodegenerative disease that attacks nerve cells in the brain and the spinal cord leading to progressive loss of motorical functions. The average life expectancy of an ALS patient from the date of diagnosis is approximately 2 years.

ALS is a suitable starting point for designing AAC systems as ALS patients progress through a series of stages (detailed in Table 5) which represent most other scenarios for AAC usage. The effect of designing for ALS patients is that the system is most likely usable by a wide range of other potential AAC users.

It is worth noticing that the physical limitations in the various stages of ALS are very similar to those imposed by the mobile scenarios shown in Table 3.

Table 5. Typical progression of ALS

	Symptoms	Input devices
1. stage	Fatigue is noticeable. Reduced mobility and strength in arms and hands. Often slurred speech	Keyboard with hand/arm rests and modified operation (sticky shift, no repeat)
2. stage	Fatigue is a factor. Unable to move arms due to lack of strength, but mobility is usually retained in one or both hands. Severely slurred speech, largely unintelligible to outsiders	Mouse, joystick, reduced keyboard (5-10 keys)
3. stage	Almost full lock-in. No speech function. Severely reduced mobility of all extremities	One or two switches, eye tracking
4. stage	Full lock-in	Eye tracking

For several reasons, AAC systems for ALS users must be designed with multimodal input and walk-up-and-use in mind:

- The user should be able to use the same system through all stages of the disease.
- Many ALS patients have little or no previous IT experience and are quite busy adapting to the severity of their situation.
- Several assistants who need to be able to help the user complete letters, edit text and use other functions in the program without having to learn an unfamiliar interaction method.
- Limited time and other resources among the specialist responsible for selecting, installing and configuring the system means that the duration and quality of user training is severely limited in many cases.
- The progression through the stages of ALS is gradual, and the fatigue factor often makes it necessary for the user to switch to a less efficient input method during the day.

As a final design constraint, it is vital to allow for the use of large fonts. Many common complications associated with ALS lead to reduced sight and altered color perception, and in many cases it is necessary to place the screen at a relatively large distance from the user in order to ensure accessibility for e.g. wheelchairs and assistants.

3.2 Traditional AAC Solutions for ALS Patients

The generic AAC solution for ALS patients is an on-screen keyboard which can be operated through the use of a pointing device (mouse, joystick, eye tracking...) or with the use of a single switch in "scanning" mode. When using scanning, a cursor moves automatically at a preset rate over the available targets, and a target is selected by the use of a switch which is wired to some motor function that the user is able to control reliably. Most on-screen keyboards integrate word completion or word prediction. It is usually possible to use the keyboard for text entry and navigation even when the program is configured for some other input modality.

Obviously scanning is slow which is the motivation to developing new and faster text entry modalities which are available to users who suffer from severe limitation on physical mobility as well as the implementation of a wide range of laborsaving functions in AAC systems

One alternative which, in theory, is promising is Morse code. Morse code is designed for efficient communication in a low bandwidth situation and assigns the shortest possible codes to the most frequent letters.

Unfortunately, Morse is a hard skill to learn, it is difficult to design software that gives meaningful visual feedback and it is no longer a common skill. Additionally, it is rather difficult for a computer to interpret single-switch Morse input reliably. One problem is determining the length of the dot ("dit") and dash ("dah") signals, and there is also a segmentation problem, i.e. determining where one letter ends, and the next letter starts. On the basis of the above-mentioned problems as well as measurements of input rates from actual users, a study that compared Morse input to mouthstick [12] eventually concluded that Morse is an unsuitable solution to the input problem, despite the potential for high performance.

3.3 Four AAC Solutions

As mentioned in Section 3, our quantitative goal was to achieve typing speeds in the 10-15 WPM range. At the earliest stage, we decided to base our system on the following design elements:

- The use of eye tracking as the primary input method. Eye tracking confirms to Fitts' law according to [33], and is the highest bandwidth input method available to all ALS patients.
- In order to use eye tracking based on off-the-shelf components and to increase robustness to environmental factors, such as ambient light, and increase the possibility of use in a mobile setting, we had a severe upper limit on the number of buttons/targets.
- The design should encourage the user to use the word prediction and completion function as this was the most likely way to increase typing speed.

A group of design students without initial knowledge of the AAC field were then given the task of suggesting suitable UI designs based on the available elements and limitations. Based on their suggestions, we decided to base our solution on a 4 by 3 grid of buttons (Fig. 1), two of which are used as a text editor window.

Our three experimental solutions are all based on this layout, and we intend to implement a fourth solution based on our current research prototype which we describe in the following sections.

The programs can be operated by mouse or eye tracker and uses a built-in dwell time activation function to select targets when in eye-tracker mode. As opposed to most commercial eye tracking solutions, there is no repeat on activation. If the user desires to activate the same button twice, she has to move the cursor away from the button to re-activate dwell activation. This feature helps to avoid stressing the user by eliminating the so-called "Midas Touch" problem: Everything you look at gets activated.

In addition to the point-based interface, the QWERTY keyboard is also available to assistants as a possible input device for text entry and editing.

(A1)	(B1)	C1	D1
A2	B2	C2	D2
A3	B3	C3	D3

Fig. 1. Our basic layout. An editor window occupies the positions A1 and B1

Our First Solution: Dynamic Soft-Keyboard with Letter Placement According to Likelihood. Our first solution consists of three modes:

1. The main letter entry mode, which features a dynamic 3 by 2 keyboard. It presents the currently most likely letters; buttons for backspace and space; and access to word prediction/completion mode and alphabetical letter entry mode.
2. Word prediction/completion mode which presents the current 8 most likely words in a 4 by 2 matrix and features access to alphabetical letter entry mode and the main letter entry mode.
3. Alphabetical letter entry mode which enables the user to select the desired letter in a two-stage process.

In the main letter entry mode, the most likely letters were placed according to the workings of the parafoveal vision, i.e. with the most probable suggestion in the center position (C2), and the suggestions placed according to probability in a clock-wise fashion around the center position (D2, D3, C3, B3 and B2). This was done on the assumption that users would quickly learn to anticipate the placement of the desired letter and then – in case the letter prediction did not supply this as the primary candidate – quickly be able to evaluate the other candidates with a minimum of eye movement. The A2 button displays up to 8 word completions/suggestions and selection switches to word prediction/completion mode. A space button was placed at position A3 and a backspace button at D1.

In the word prediction/completion mode, we arranged the word suggestions in keeping with the Western European tradition for visual search, i.e. with the suggestions occupying the positions A2..D2, A3..D3 with the most probable word at position A2, the second-most probable word at position B2, etc. After selection of a word, the program remains in word selection mode in order to encourage the user to use the suggestions for increased typing speed.

The alphabetical letter entry mode consisted of two sub-modes and required the user to first select a group of letters (e.g. "ABCDEFGH", "IJKLMNOP"...) and then the letter. We deliberately kept this entry mode as simple as possible as this was the backup strategy for new and/or confused users.

The system is conceptually similar to the proposed FOCL deriviate shown in fig. 10 in [11], in the sense that it supports two distinct strategies for letter entry: A primary strategy based on probability and a secondary based on the well-known paradigm of alphabetical search for the desired letter.

Our Second Solution – Incremental Refinement of the Original Solution. Based on user comments and observations from a usability test with 25 subjects of the first solution, we decided to implement a second iteration which features a minor and a major improvement.

The minor improvement was to change the layout of the word predictions in the word selection mode. Many users remarked that they felt the most intuitive search strategy was A2, A3, B2, B3, etc., i.e. placing the predictions in a left-to-right order based on their likelihood.

The major improvement was a re-working of the dynamic letter 3 by 2 keyboard. Many users remarked on the obvious problem that selecting the same button twice in a row was very time-consuming which was an obvious and frequent problem as the most probable letter always occupied the same position (D2). Furthermore several users felt that the placement of letters was arbitrary, i.e. the strategy of placing letters in accordance with their current likelihood was not in keeping with the users' expectations and led to time-consuming visual searches.

We therefore implemented a placement algorithm which assigns home positions to all letters as well as secondary and tertiary positions and so forth. The algorithm then attempts to place as many letters as possible in the most desirable positions while ensuring that the currently most likely letter is not placed on the position that was selected previously thus keeping the need to re-activate dwell time activation by leaving the button to a minimum, and at the same time attempting to keep the visual search component of operation to a minimum.

This solution is currently in external testing among ALS patients, and the initial response to the improvements has been favorable.

Our Third Solution – T9-like Ambiguous Keyboard. We also investigated another solution to the problem of unintuitive placement of letters – an ambiguous keyboard. This was partly motivated by the desire to offer the users a static placement of letters, which should eliminate the visual search component of operation and partly motivated by the reports of positive experiences with a highly ambiguous keyboard solution which featured a 6-button design, assigning only four buttons to letters [32].

The result was a major re-working of the main letter entry mode which was necessary in order to accommodate the dictionary-based entry method that is required by this type of ambiguous keyboard entry. We decided to split the letters in 6 groups by alphabetical order, i.e. "ABCDE", "FGHIJ", etc. We retained the placement and function of the word completion mode change button. The space button was replaced by a "end word + space" button, and the position previously used for access to alphabetical letter selection was used for a "end word + punctuation" button.

We added two modes: A mode for selecting the current word candidates and a mode for entering a word letter-by-letter in case the word the user was trying to enter was unknown to the system.

Initial internal testing in the research group gave positive feedback. The elimination of the visual search component of the letter entry task was felt to be a big improvement over the previous two systems, and the dictionary-based input paradigm was not seen as a barrier to productivity or initial acceptance.

A usability test with a group of 25 novice subjects was far less encouraging. Most subjects reported confusion with regards to the paradigm which was increased by the three different ways of entering a word (word completion and *two* ways to end a word) as well as the lack of an obvious way to check whether the intended button was indeed selected. This led to poor orientation in the current entry task (a word) which in turn made many subjects express concern about their ability to correct mistakes without deleting a partially written word and starting over.

Our tentative conclusion from this usability test is that most (but not all) of these problems can be handled by a re-design and minimal changes in functionality. Our main design error was probably that we had not devised a way of gently introducing the users to the unfamiliar text entry paradigm, which was compounded by the absence of a well-known backup strategy, i.e. alphabetical letter entry.

Although we did not get any comments on the size of the dictionary most of the other criticisms leveled at the T9 system in [24] were echoed by our subjects.

Our Fourth Solution – Maximally Ambiguous Keyboard. Inspired by Shannon [19], the report on highly ambiguous keyboards in [32] and the positive internal feedback on our first ambiguous keyboard solution, we decided to try to take the ambiguous keyboard entry method to the logical conclusion: A two-key keyboard.

This solution has many potential advantages, both from a theoretical and a practical point of view. Theoretically this would be the ultimate in key-based text input, as it would virtually eliminate all motor and visual search components of the text entry process when operated with two fingers which would then only have to leave the home keys in order to select alternative interpretations of the ambiguous input at the end of word entry. From our primarily practical point of view it would allow us to free sufficient buttons to integrate the word selection mode in the main letter entry mode, by making 5 buttons available for word suggestions, instead of the single button used to switch to word completion mode in our current systems.

We have implemented a mouse-operated prototype for initial internal testing, which uses left and right mouse button to signal letters 'a' to 'm' and 'n to 'z' respectively, and requires a point and click to select the intended word at word completion. Initial internal feedback is extremely encouraging, and as a consequence we intend to skip the planned second iteration of the original 6-key ambiguous keyboard solution, and instead design a 2-key ambiguous keyboard as our next experimental system.

3.4 Discussion of the Solutions

Iterative usability test using novice subjects has shown to be of great importance to our design process, as we, the members of the design team, are unable to estimate whether the systems satisfy the demands to walk-up-and-use usability. The comments from these novice subjects have turned out to be very useful as well as inspiring.

During the usability tests we have logged user performance. Individual performance has been in the range of 2.5 WPM and 6.8 WPM for the first 160 words. Our experience so far is that these performance figures from novice users are far from conclusive, as even simple UI design errors decrease user performance markedly. Thus, despite the fact that the 6-key ambiguous keyboard has been the worst performing solution so far, we have been able to gather sufficient relevant feedback from user comments that we feel confident as to which features should or should not be retained for the 2-key ambiguous keyboard.

3.5 Relevance to Mobile Text Entry and Mutimodal Interaction

While we obviously feel that AAC is interesting in and of itself, we also feel that the parallels to mobile text input methods are clear. We are trying to solve the same problem, i.e. how to input text in a low-input-bandwidth situation in an efficient and user-friendly manner. Therefore it is unsurprising that we have to deal with the same problems as the designers of mobile text input methods, and it is also indicative that there may be a large potential for knowledge transfer between these to research areas.

As a supporting argument, we submit that all of our AAC solutions described in previous sections are potential mobile text entry methods, since they – given the ability to host a sufficiently powerful language model – could easily be implemented under the physical limitations imposed by even the mobile phone class of mobile devices. As mentioned in Section 2.5, the required computational resources for even advanced language models are likely available in mobile phones within 10 years.

On this basis we believe that designing and evaluating AAC solutions for physically disabled people is a valid and useful method to gain insights in, and relevant feedback on the possible mobile text entry methods that can be hosted on future mobile devices with increased computational resources.

In a more general perspective, research within multimodal interaction suggests that movements of the hand, torso, head or eye may drive input pointers in future mobile and ubiquitous systems, if they possess tracking capabilities. Pointing may also be driven by movements of a handheld or head mounted information unit relatively to some fixed or tracked position in space. For instance, an information kiosk behind a shop window may be controlled by hand movements in front of the window; head tracking may drive pointing on head-up displays in vehicles and eye tracking may drive pointing in helmet mounted displays. In these cases, multimodal text entry seems to be a general design challenge, very similar to the challenges that we are confronted with in our AAC-system.

4 Conclusion

Linking the fields of AAC and mobile text input has the potential to benefit both research areas. Researchers in the mobile text input field gain awareness of a potential testing ground for the interfaces that are beyond the capabilities of the current crop of mobile devices. The AAC research area would obviously benefit from increased attention and awareness.

The potential gain for future users of mobile text input is also significant as a thorough evaluation of potential input methods in an AAC setting would likely identify and – if possible – help avoid potential design pitfalls when implementing new input solutions *before* they are implemented in mass-market products.

References

1   Smoreda, Z., Thomas, F. "Use of SMS in Europe", analysis of data from EURESCOM P903 study "Cross-cultural attitudes to ICT in everyday life" performed October to December 2000,
     http://www.eurescom.de/~ftproot/web-deliverables/public/P900-series/P903/sms_use/w1-sms.html, verified 17. April 2002
2   MacKenzie, S., Zhang, Shawn X., "An Empirical Investigation of the Novice Experience With Soft Keyboards" *Behaviour & Information Technology*, 20, 411–418
3   James, Christina L. ; Reischel, Kelly M. "Text Input for Mobile Devices: Comparing Model Prediction to Actual Performance", *SIGCHI'01 March 31-April 4, 2001*, pp. 365–371, Seattle, WA, USA
4   Silfverberg, Miika; MacKenzie, I. Scott ; Korhonen, Panu "Predicting Text Entry Speed on Mobile Phones", *Proceedings of the ACM Conference on Human Factors in Computing Systems – CHI 2000*, pp. 9–16, New York: ACM
5   MacKenzie, I. Scott ; Zhang, S. "The Immediate Usability of Graffiti" *Proceedings of Graphics Interface '97*, pp. 129–137, Toronto: Canadian Information Processing Society
6   Soukoreff, R. William; MacKenzie, Scott I. "Theoretical Upper and Lower Bounds on Typing Speed Using a Stylus and Soft Keyboard", *Behavior & Information Technology* 14, 1995, pp. 370–379
7   Zhai, Shumin ; Hunter, Michael ; Smith, Barton A. "The Metropolis Keyboard – An Exploration of Quantitative Techniques for Virtual Keyboard Design" *Proceedings of the ACM Symposium on User Interface Software and Technology (UIST 2000)*, November 5–8, 2000, pp. 119–128, San Diego, California
8   Matias, E.; MacKenzie, I. S., & Buxton, W. "Half-QWERTY: A one-handed keyboard facilitating skill transfer from QWERTY" *Proceedings of the ACM Conference on Human Factors in Computing Systems – INTERCHI '93*, pp. 88–94. New York: ACM
9   Jecker, Diane "Benchmark tests: Speech Recognition" *PC Magazine*, november 1999, http://www.zdnet.com/products/stories/reviews/0,4161,2385302,00.html verified 17. April 2002
10   A. T. Kearney/Judge Institute of Management "Mobinet Index # 4", February 2002, http://www.atkearney.com/pdf/eng/Mobinet_4_S.pdf verified 17. April 2002

11   Bellman, T.; MacKenzie, I. S. "A probabilistic character layout strategy for mobile text entry" *Proceedings of Graphics Interface '98*, pp. 168–176. Toronto: Canadian Information Processing Society

12   Levine, Simon P.; Gauger, John R. D ; Bowers, Lisa D. ; Kahn, Karen J. : "A comparison of Mouthstick and Morse Code Text Inputs", *Augmentative and Alternative Communication, 1(2)*, 1986, pp. 51–55, Decker Periodicals Inc., Hamilton, Ontario, Canada

13   Wikipedia in http://www.wikipedia.com/wiki/Morse+code, verified 17. April 2002

14   International Telecommunication Union recommendation E.161, available from http://www.itu.int

15   Lesher, G.W.; Moulton, B.J., ; Higginbotham, D.J.. "Techniques for augmenting scanning communication" *Augmentative and Alternative Communication*, 14, 1998, pp. 81–101, Decker Periodicals Inc., Hamilton, Ontario, Canada

16   Fitts, P. M. "The Information Capacity of the Human Motor System in Controlling the Amplitude of Movement" *Journal of Experimental Psychology 47*, 1954, pp. 381–391

17   Hick, W. E. "On the Rate of Gain of Information" *Quarterly Journal of Experimental Psychology*, 4, 1952, pp. 11–36

18   Hyman, R "Stimulus Information as a Determinant of Reaction Time" *Journal of Experimental Psychology*, 45, 1953, pp. 188–196

19   Shannon, C. E : "Prediction and Entropy of Printed English" *Bell Systems Technical Journal* 30, January 1951, pp. 50–64

20   Rosenfeld, R "A Maximum Entropy Approach to Adaptive Statistical Language Modelling" *Computer, Speech and Language*, 10, 1996, pp. 187–288

21   Tilbourg, H "An Introduction to Cryptology", 1988, Kluwer Academic Publishers

22   Ward, David J. "Adaptive Computer Interfaces", Ph.D.-thesis, Inference Group, Cavendish Laboratory, University of Cambridge, November 2001, http://www.inference.phy.cam.ac.uk/djw30/ verified 17. April 2002

23   Marcus, Aaron "Babyface Design for Mobile Devices and the Web" *Proceedings, Vol. 2, Human-Computer Interface Internat. (HCII) Conf.*, 5-10 Aug., 2001, pp. 514–518, New Orleans, LA, USA, Lawrence Erlbaum Associates, Mahwah, NJ USA

24   Gutowitz, Howard "Barriers to Adoption of Dictionary-Based Text-Entry Methods: A Field Study", submitted to CHI2002, September 2001 http://www.eatoni.com/research/field-study.pdf verified 17. April 2002

25   Schneiderman, Ben "Designing the User Interface: Strategies for Effective Human-Computer Interaction", 2. edition, 1992, Addison-Wesley Publishing Company

26   Dvorak, A.; Merrick, W. L. ; Ford, G. C. "Typewriting Behaviour", 1936, New York: American Book Company

27   Wiklund, M. E ; Dumas, J. S. ; Hoffman, L. R. "Optimizing a Portable Terminal Keyboard for Combined One-Handed and Two-Handed Use" *Proceedings of the Human Factors Society – 31ª annual Meeting* 1987, pp. 585–589, Santa Monica, CA: Human Factors Society

28   Hansen, Paulin J.; Witzner, Dan ; Johansen, Anders S. "Bringing Gaze-based Interaction Back to Basics" *Proceedings of Universal Access in Human-Computer Interaction (UAHCI 2001)*, New Orleans, Louisiana

29   User Evaluation dot Com, http://www.userevaluation.com/ verified 17. April 2002

30   Krug, Steve "Don't Make me Think", 2000, Que

31   Jordan, Patrick W. "An Introduction to Usability", 1999, Taylor & Francis, London

32   Kühn, Michael; Garbe, Jörn "Predictive and Highly Ambiguous Typing for a Severely Speech and Motion Impaired User" *Universal Access in Human-Computer Interaction. Proc. of UAHCI 2001*, New Orleans, August, 5–10. Mahwah (NJ): Lawrence Erlbaum Associates

33   Miniotas, Darius "Application of fitts' law to eye gaze interaction" *CHI 2000 Extended Abstracts*, pp. 339–340, 2000, New York, ACM

Sociability and Mobility Concepts for the Connected Home

Elmo Diederiks[1], Richard van de Sluis[1], and Ramon van de Ven[2]

[1] Philips Research Laboratories, Prof. Holstlaan 4, 5656 AA Eindhoven, The Netherlands
[2] Philips Design, PO Box 218, 5600 MV Eindhoven, The Netherlands
{elmo.diederiks, richard.van.de.sluis, ramon.van.de.ven}
@philips.com

Abstract. The functionality offered by interconnected devices in a networked home will be drastically increased by the possibilities of always-on broadband Internet. This broadband connection can enhance the communication among family members and friends. It can also make it easy to share content and activities such as watching a movie together or listen to the same music while having a videophone chat. While using all these functions people want to be able to move freely through their home. The advance of portable devices fulfils this need for mobility. These portable devices can be used either in isolation or in co-operation with the stationary devices in the house. Two novel interaction concepts are described that support sociability and mobility for people inhabiting the connected home.

1 Introduction

An increasing number of electronics products in the home are becoming both digital and networked. A networked home offers interesting new possibilities since networked interaction devices, such as screens, become universal access points to different types of content. This requires generic interaction mechanisms that support a consistent and coherent way of handling user activities across different types of devices. In our previous work we have been addressing this issue by investigating various ways to move user activities through the home, such as by using physical tokens or by means of voice control [1], [2]. While in this previous work the emphasis was on the possibilities of connected devices within the home, in our current research we focus on the opportunities of a broadband connection from the home to the outside world. This paper reports on the User Interaction part of the WWICE 2 project. This project is part of a large research program on Ambient Intelligence [3] and its goal is to explore how the advance of broadband always-on Internet will enlarge the possibilities of a networked home.

The research was started with an analysis of trends, both in technology and in society. Based on these trends, several application scenarios were developed. The scenarios were used to guide the development of architectural and interaction concepts. Figure 1 shows a few fragments that give an idea of the format of the application scenarios.

N. Carbonell, C. Stephanidis (Eds.): User Interfaces for All, LNCS 2615, pp. 442–457, 2003.
© Springer-Verlag Berlin Heidelberg 2003

... It is Friday night and Leon gets a video call from his friend Bob. They had arranged to go out to the local nightclub. They check things out on the web cam. The party looks like it is already in full swing so they agree to meet at the club in half an hour...

... Mum decides to set up a broadcast to the family and friends that cannot be there so that they can participate in Lara's birthday party. Mum sets up the video camera at the end of the living room with a good view of the table where they will serve the cake. She sets the camera to track Lara as it is her special day...

... Dad's presence triggers those items on the family pin-board that need his attention. The screen starts to show some pictures from his wife in Paris for all the family. It also pops up a special written message just for him...

Fig. 1. Some fragments of the application scenarios

1.1 Key Interaction Issues

The scenarios contain a large number of interesting applications and user interaction issues. In order to define a focus, two key interaction issues were selected that are considered to be essential elements for the connected home.

The first issue is related to computer-mediated social interaction between people. The ability to 'share and communicate' experiences is the essence of social life. Especially within groups of people, such as a family or a group of friends this is an essential need. Therefore, *supporting social groups in sharing and communication* was selected as a key issue for the connected home.

The second issue has to do with portable devices. People will own many portable devices that will be used on the move as well as in the home. On the move those portables are used in a 'stand-alone' mode whereas in the home it could be valuable to use a portable as an integral part of the networked home. This means that the main question is how we can *support portable devices* in such a way that these can be used in a stand-alone way but also in a seamless co-operation with the stationary devices in the home. In particular, portable pen-based screens can be powerful in this respect because of their versatility. Such a portable device cannot only be used to interact with content, but also as an advanced remote control and as a flexible content carrier. Therefore, pen- or touch-based portable screens were chosen as the primary means of interaction. The solutions developed to address the two key issues were targeted for this type of devices.

2 Supporting Social Groups

People have the intrinsic need to belong to one or more social groups such as a family, a group of friends, sports companions or colleagues. The different people in a social group often have things in common, for instance, they may have a similar background, have similar beliefs or have shared interests. Very often, the people in a social group share experiences with each other; in fact, they share parts of their life. Many people prefer to meet their beloved ones and friends in real life, but this is not always the easiest and most efficient way. The success of mobile telephony, e-mail and Internet-based photo sharing services have shown that there is a huge market for system-mediated social interaction that enables social groups to communicate and to share experiences in an efficient way.

Internet access and usage have been growing considerably over the last years. Additionally, the prospects for broadband Internet to the home have taken dramatic proportions. Broadband always-on Internet will increase the possibilities for communication and sharing. For instance, video communication will create news ways to communicate and interact with each other. It will also become easier to share self-created content such as photo albums or home videos with family members and friends.

2.1 Staying in Touch

Networking technologies have a huge impact on the current society and on the way that people live. Nowadays, many people do not want to be 'disconnected' anymore. They like to be able to explore the world from the home and, more importantly, they want to *stay in touch* with others. Also when they are on the move, people want to be in touch with their friends and family members. One of the side effects of this connectedness is that it starts to change the meaning of 'home'. In the past, our phone calls and messages were routed to our physical homes, whereas nowadays we have become used to the fact that we can access our messages such as e-mail and voice mail from all over the planet. This means that some aspects of the feeling of 'home' start to stretch out beyond the physical boundaries of the house.

In a similar way, teleworking allows us to do (part of) our work while being away from the office. More and more people choose to work from home since they want to shape their work patterns according to their own preferences. In analogy to the 'feeling of home', the notion of 'being at work' is also no longer restricted to the office environment. For most types of work, however, it is of crucial importance to stay in close touch with one's colleagues and to be able to share information with them.

2.2 Social Computing

To a large extent the Internet is already driven by the need to form communities, to share content and to communicate. Over the last couple of years, the Internet has grown from an information medium into a social environment. Due to this trend, on-line communities and system-mediated social interaction are hot topics in the world of Human-Computer Interaction. It is often argued that those 'social computing' applications should not only be optimised for usability but especially for sociability [4]. This basically means that system-mediated social environments should create a sense of being together for people that use a system to interact with each other from different physical places.

When people use a system to mediate social interaction, their goal is not to interact with the system. Their main goal is to interact with each other. Therefore, when designing social computing systems the ultimate goal should be to create a system that is as 'transparent' as possible and which eliminates the user's awareness of the mediation. This will allow the involved people to fully concentrate on each other so that they have a sense of 'being together', which is sometimes referred to as *social presence*. The main idea is that apart from inhabiting a physical space people start being virtually 'present' in a shared, artificial on-line space. This also implies that people want to be able to control their presence and representation in this virtual world. Furthermore, it is important to realise that people inhabit both an online space and the real world simultaneously. Therefore, the interrelationship between the virtual and the physical space needs to be taken into account [5].

Various research and development work has been done on applications that support social interaction in online spaces, for example *Babble* [6] and *ePlace* at IBM [7], or MIT's *Talking in Circles* [8] and *Chat Circles* [9]. Furthermore, on the Internet, chat applications exist that represent the users in a social setting, for example the *Habbo Hotel* [14] and *MSN communities* [15]. However, most of these applications are developed for a PC-based type of interaction. Our interest is in how family members or groups of friends or colleagues can share and communicate across space and time without being an experienced computer user. Different groups of people should be able to interact socially wherever they are, with any type of device, ranging from TV screens, web tablets and PDA's to PC's.

2.3 Places Enable Social Interaction

In the real world, particular locations facilitate people from a certain social group to meet each other and to engage in joint activities. The home, for instance, is a place where one expects to meet family members, whereas at the office one is more likely to meet one's colleagues. Besides those real-time 'affordances' of a physical place, a place also offers asynchronous possibilities for sharing and communication. For example, a pin-board or a written message left on the kitchen table can be forms of asynchronous communication. Moreover, locations enable content collections to be shared among a group of people. For instance, a family's book collection or CD collection can be placed in the living room so that each family member can easily access the collection that they share.

Network technologies enable social groups to meet each other and to share experiences at a given time while being present at different physical places. Furthermore, those technologies support asynchronous communication and sharing of content collections. The question is how these different possibilities can be represented to the user and how a user can interact with such a networked system. In some way the system should provide a clear, continuous context for meeting other people, exchanging content and sharing activities. Such a virtual, shared space should create an environment that frames the presence of people and provides mutual awareness. The persistent sense of location that people have in the real world should be exploited in an interaction concept to create this context. It should give people the awareness that this virtual space and its contents continues to be there, even if nobody is present in it [7].

3 Spaces

We developed a concept called *spaces*. A space can be considered as the *virtual* counterpart of a *physical* place. This implies that a space enables people from a certain social group to meet each other, to share activities and to share content. The idea is that a group of people should be able to create a space that is accessible for the whole group, independent of each one's physical location. For example, a *family space* would be accessible for all household members from all over the world, stretching the home beyond the physical boundaries of the house. In a similar way, a *work space* would be accessible from any location, facilitating working from home and co-operation between colleagues working at different locations. Ideally a person would have a space for each social group that he belongs to and every group should be able to create their own space easily. Besides those shared spaces, it would also be useful to have a *personal space* that is only accessible for the user himself. This personal space could contain personal content collections and support personal messaging and communication.

3.1 Contents of a Space

A space contains representations of respectively people, content, and activities. In order to emphasise the idea of being in a shared space, the view of a space is synchronised for all members. The main idea should be that '*what you see is what I see*'. This means that all people in a particular space have the same view on a space. All elements such as people, content and activity items have the same look and position in the space for all people that are present in a space. The only difference is that their own person icon (the user icon) is presented in a different way to clearly distinguish representation of the user from other people present in the space.

A space is only accessible for *people* that are members of a particular social group. For instance, the Friends Space is only accessible for a particular group of friends. People that are present in a space are represented by their person icons. In analogy with a physical place only the present people will be presented in a space. We can assume that people will know who is part of a particular social group so there is no direct need to represent absent members. Furthermore, representing only the present members makes it much easier to see who's present in a space in one glance. The icon for the user (the user icon) can be clearly distinguished from other people icons in the space (see Figure 2). The only person icon that a user can manipulate in a space is his user icon. It is impossible to manipulate other people icons.

People can put *content* items in a space, so that they can share this content within the group. These content items can be of any type, such as a TV program, a movie, a music track, a memo, a video card or a media album. The content is represented by icons that indicate the type of content. Furthermore, the size of the content icon reflects the frequency of use. If content is not used its icon decreases in size over time. Each time the content is activated the content icon increases in size. This allows the user to instantly recognise 'hot' content.

In a space, people can access and activate the available content, communicate with other present persons, and share content activities with them. All *activities* are indicated as combinations of people and content (see Figure 2). For example, two people icons in a bubble indicate that those people are having a dialogue using real-time video or voice communication. A bubble with multiple people icons and a content icon represents a shared activity, consisting of real-time video communication in combination with a synchronised experience of the content. All involved people arc able to control the content. For instance, if three people are watching a movie, each of them is able to pause, 'rewind' or fast-forward the movie and all three people will see the same, synchronised content presentation. In the user's view on a space, a visual distinction is made between activities in which the user is not involved and the activity in which the user is involved.

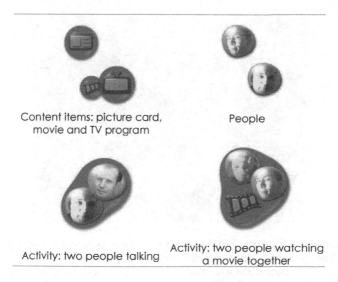

Content items: picture card,   People
movie and TV program

Activity: two people talking   Activity: two people watching a movie together

Fig. 2. Visualization of content, people and activities

3.2 Access to a Space

Each user has access to a particular set of spaces. For instance, a user can have access to his Personal Space, Family Space, Friends Space and his Work Space. As soon as the user is identified, his user icon appears on the top left of the screen and space icons appear that represent the spaces that are accessible for the user. This user identification is realised either by identifying oneself to the system by fingerprint or by the system recognising the user's face using computer vision.

The space icons appear in a so-called 'space bar'. On a screen, it is only possible to view one space at a time. The space bar allows the user to switch between spaces.

3.3 Synchronised View on a Space

To emphasise the sense of being present in a shared space, the view of a space is synchronised for all those present. All members see the same content, people and activity items at the same position. People can drag content icons as well as their own person icon (user icon) around within a space. This is visible in real-time to all other present members. It is not possible to move the person icon of another member.

There are two ways of manipulating icons in spaces:
- *Drag-and-drop*, for moving content icons and the user icon within a space, similar to moving a piece of paper on a table;
- *Pick-and-drop*, for copying content icons from one space to another, similar to picking up a piece of paper to bring it from one table to another. A long tap on the content icon with the pen 'picks up' the icon, next a long tap on the background of the space will 'drop' the icon.

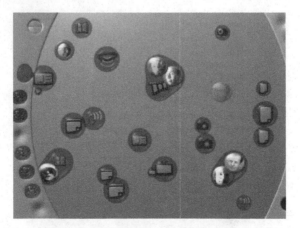

Fig. 3. Visualization of a space. The bar at the left contains icons representing the users' different spaces. The space itself shows different types of content, the people that are present, and their activities. The position and size of all items in a space is identical for all people viewing the space. If person A moves content in the space, it is visible in real-time for person B. A new content icon is big; content icons that are not often used gradually decrease in size

3.4 Activities in a Space

Activities can be starting by tapping on a content or person icon in the space. In the case of a content icon the content is activated, whereas in the case of a person icon a video communication activity is started with the person. On starting of an activity the user icon is moved towards the content or person icon by animation and a 'bubble' is drawn around them. It is also possible to join an ongoing activity by tapping on an existing 'activity bubble' or by moving one's user icon on top of a bubble. There is no confirmation required from the people that were already involved in the activity. In the real world people can also easily join a discussion or a TV-watching activity in a shared space, such as a living room. This can be achieved by simply moving close to the persons that are already involved in the activity. In real life, however, much contextual information about the state of the activity and the level of interaction is available. For instance, the person joining a TV-watching activity can see the other persons, their posture and facial expressions that indicate to what extent they are engaged in the TV program. This information can help to find the appropriate way to join the activity. A space, however, only shows an abstract representation of an activity. Since contextual information about the state of the social activity is missing, members of a space might develop space-specific social conventions. For instance, they might determine that it is appropriate to join activities in a quiet manner.

In a shared activity, the involved people have a synchronised experience of the content. For instance, in a shared music activity, all involved people hear the same content at the same time. Everyone involved can control the shared activity, such as, for instance, pausing a movie or selecting the next music track. The presentation settings, such as volume, can only be controlled locally by each participant. People can also create a picture card together or jointly make a drawing or letter on a piece of virtual paper. This collective input and control of shared activities might also give rise to social problems. In general, the expectation is that social groups will develop their own solutions and conventions for dealing with these social issues, based on the properties offered in a space.

Fig. 4. Two people watching a movie together in a shared activity

4 Supporting Portable Devices

More and more devices become both wireless and portable. As a result, people will be carrying around those devices and they will use them in different contexts and at various locations. Also in the home, portable devices will play an important role because people want to move around freely. Portable devices, such as pen-based tablets optimally fulfil this need for mobility (see Figure 5).

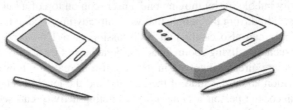

Fig. 5. Pen-based portable screens (palm and lap-size)

4.1 Portable Devices in the Home

Research has shown that people generally appreciate the moments that they are at home together with their family members [10]. Very often, however, it appears that all family members are doing 'their own thing'. This trend of individuality at home can be referred to as *parallel family play*. Probably the use of portable devices can support family members in their need to be together while also being involved in individual work or leisure activities using a portable device.

Another trend is that people want the home to be flexible and 'mobile'. In a similar way as people nowadays expect to be able to contact others wherever they are, in the near future they will expect to be able to access their collections at any time and from any place. Currently, content collections are often associated with the home environment. But this is mainly due to their physical restrictions. Ideally people would like to be able to access these collections at any time or place, so that they become part of their personal environment. A portable device could act as a permanent gateway to one's personal content collections. However, there might be a difference between the use of a portable in one's personal environment and using the same device in the home environment. In a personal environment the portable will operate in a stand-alone way, enabling the retrieval of content and providing the content experience, whereas in a (networked) home environment the portable could function as an advanced remote control which enables the retrieval of content and the control of the experience, while the content experience itself is provided by the stationary devices that are present in the environment.

With respect to portable devices, much work is done on the development of new interaction styles for those devices. For example, Microsoft Research has studied the use of sensing techniques for improving mobile interaction with a PDA [11]. Furthermore, Sony CSL has been working on easy ways to transfer files between portable screens [12]. However, little research has been done on the relation between a portable device and the stationary devices in a networked environment. Except for a docking station there are hardly any existing solutions for dynamically incorporating a portable device in the infrastructure available in a networked home.

4.2 Device Clusters

In previous research, we have introduced the idea that each room in the home operates as a coherent cluster of devices, allowing the user to interact with the 'room' as a whole instead of with all separate devices [1]. In such a 'device cluster', devices work seamlessly together in order to create the best user experience. This also allows a user to move an activity such as a videophone call or a movie to another room of the house, for instance, by saying: "send to kitchen".

Those device clusters can be static if all devices are stationary devices that remain at the same location. However, portable devices can be used in any room of the house and therefore this requires those device clusters to be dynamically created and adapted. In this way, a portable device can be used both in a stand-alone mode and in a 'co-operative mode' where it works together with the stationary devices in a particular room. It should be made easy for the user to let a portable device be dynamically added to or removed from an existing device cluster.

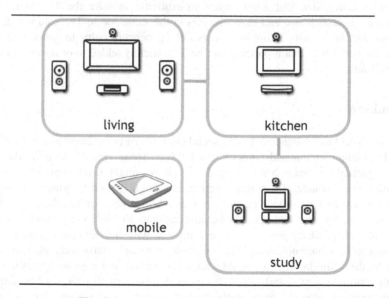

Fig. 6. A possible set of device clusters in the home

If a portable device is being added to a device cluster, it is possible to distribute an activity over various devices such that a portable device can be used to control activities that are presented on the stationary devices in a room. For instance, a music play list can be presented on and controlled from a portable screen, while the music is being played through the loudspeakers in the room. It is also possible that a *space* is presented on the portable screen, while the user is involved in activities in this space by means of the stationary equipment in the room (such as big screen, loudspeakers, camera) with the ability to control those activities from the portable.

Furthermore, a user may want to transfer the activity from the portable to the stationary device in the room or vice versa. If this transfer functionality could be made accessible easily, it would also allow a user to move an activity from one room to another room via a portable screen. For instance, one could transfer a movie from the TV in the living room to the portable screen, then go to the bedroom and transfer the movie from the portable to the bedroom TV. This gives the portable screen the function of an advanced follow-me token, one that even supports continuing the activity while being on the way to another room.

From a user interface point of view, the problem with these portable devices is that they are wireless. There are no longer cables running between the devices that help to indicate the relations between them. A conventional infrared remote control can be 'associated' with an output device by pointing the remote control to it. However, advanced remote controls, PDA's and web tablets use RF-based wireless communication, which means that they do not require 'line of sight' for communication. Technically these devices are able to control an output device in another room, while this might be unnecessary and confusing for the user. Therefore, a mechanism is required that allows users to explicitly indicate the desired relations between a wireless device and other devices in the same room. The solution that we introduce for this is called *'linking'*. This linking concept helps to support portable devices in such a way that a portable can be dynamically added to or removed from a device cluster.

5 Linking

In the real world the distance between social entities can be an important indicator for possible communication and co-operation between those entities. In a similar way, adding a portable screen to a stationary device cluster might also be based on physical proximity. For instance, if a portable screen is brought within viewing and listening distance of a stationary device cluster (such as a big screen, loudspeakers etc.) it can be indicated to the user that it might be advantageous to *'link'* the portable screen to the 'room'. This *linking* process can be compared with initiating and ending human communication. Communication between people normally starts and ends with greeting each other. Similarly, if a portable screen is moved into a room the room might 'see' the portable screen and 'greet' it. From the moment that the user holding the portable screen returns the greeting, the portable screen and the 'room' are on 'speaking terms'. Technically speaking, this means that the portable screen has been added to the device cluster. In user terms, we say that the portable screen has become *linked* to the room.

In more detail, the following happens when a portable screen is brought within viewing and listening distance of a stationary device cluster. A suggestion to link is presented on the portable screen. This *suggested link* is presented at the border of the screen in an unobtrusive way. The user carrying the portable screen can decide whether or not he wants to link the portable device to the room. The suggestion remains present as long as the portable device is in the proximity of the device cluster. The user can either ignore or confirm the suggestion to link. Once the portable device is 'linked' to another device or set of devices, it is considered to be part of that 'device cluster'. Graphical and auditory feedback on linking events is given on both the portable and on the stationary devices in the device cluster.

5.1 TapLink and ScreenLink

There are different ways of linking which yield different responses from the system. A so-called *TapLink* can be established by tapping on the (suggested) linking element that is presented on the portable screen. The idea of the TapLink is that the user complies with whatever is ongoing on the device cluster. For instance, a user can do a TapLink to continue with the existing big screen activity and control it from the portable screen. A user can also have the intention to link in order to continue a portable-screen activity on the device cluster. For instance, a user is watching a TV activity on the portable and wants to continue this on the big screen in a particular room. To accomplish this, a user can do a TapLink and subsequently drag the portable-screen activity to the linking bar. However, we also created an easier way of establishing a link and at the same time transferring the activity from portable to big screen, this is called *ScreenLink*. The user can perform a ScreenLink by moving the portable screen close to the big screen for one second. As a result the portable becomes linked to the device cluster and that the activity from the portable is moved to the device cluster. Any activity that was running on the big screen will be overruled.

In multi-user situations a TapLink is quite a concealed manner of linking, and therefore this should not instantly replace the big-screen activity. A ScreenLink, however, is quite explicit and other users in the room can easily interfere with this action.

5.2 Being Linked

While being linked the portable can be used to start, stop and control activities in the device cluster. Especially with regard to the Spaces concept it can be convenient to view or monitor a space on the portable while being involved in a (shared) activity on the big screen. By dragging a content icon from the space on the linking bar the portable can be used to start an activity in the 'room'. For instance, a user can start a movie that is presented on the big screen and loudspeakers in the room. Controlling the movie, such as pause, fast forward or adjusting the volume can then be done from the portable screen. Furthermore, when the portable is linked activities can be easily moved from the device cluster to the portable screen and vice versa.

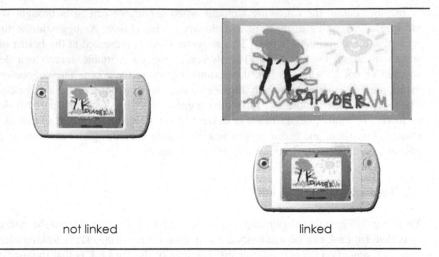

not linked   linked

Fig. 7. Making a drawing on the portable in unlinked mode (left) and in linked mode (right). When a portable device is linked to a device cluster, which contains the appropriate output devices, the controls are presented on the portable device. In the case of a drawing, the complete picture remains on the portable because the drawing itself functions as the main 'control'

5.3 TapUnlink, ScreenUnlink, and Implicit Unlink

To unlink a portable from a device cluster users have to execute actions that are similar to linking. However, it cannot be avoided that a user simply walks away with a portable that is linked. This results in implicitly unlinking the portable. Therefore, there are three ways of unlinking: a TapUnlink, a ScreenUnlink and an Implicit Unlink.

A *TapUnlink* is accomplished by tapping on the linking element on the portable screen. This results in an abrupt ending of the link, in the sense that whatever was presented on the wall-screen remains ongoing there and the user loses the possibility to control that activity via the portable. So a TapUnlink can be used to leave an activity behind.

The user can also have the intention to take the activity on the wall-screen along on the portable to continue it elsewhere, for example in the garden or in another room. An easy way to both unlink and move the activity from the room to the portable is done by means of a *ScreenUnlink*. In analogy to a ScreenLink, a ScreenUnlink can be realised by holding a linked portable close to the wall-screen.

It is also possible that the user simply walks away with a linked portable, which results in an *Implicit Unlink*. An Implicit Unlink behaves similarly to a ScreenUnlink in that any activity on the big screen is moved to the portable. Again, a TapUnlink is the most concealed manner of unlinking and therefore has minimal effect on whatever is ongoing on the big screen. ScreenUnlink and Implicit Unlink are the physically more explicit methods of Unlinking and allow intercession by possible other users that are present in the room.

6 Spaces and Linking Combined

The two concepts of spaces and linking are quite solid when considered separately. However, conflicts can arise when the two are integrated, especially with regards to the multi-user context and the social dynamics of the home.

The essence of *spaces* is that they can be used to connect people to each other in a virtual space independent of each person's physical place. The *linking* concept, however, enables users to connect devices in a physical place, independent of what they are doing in the virtual space. Since people simultaneously inhabit both a physical place and a virtual space, there is an intersection between the physical and the virtual environments. This gives rise to two types of multi-user conflicts.

The first problem is caused by the fact that in the real world it is easy to join an ongoing activity. So, if a person is involved in an activity on a device cluster controlled on a portable screen, a second person that is allowed to enter this physical place can easily join the activity. This joining means that the second person implicitly entered the space in which the activity is ongoing. However, since the system is not aware of this, the user will not be represented there. If, for example, the first person leaves the room with the portable screen (implicit unlink), the second user cannot continue the activity. If the second user is allowed to access this space, he can use another portable screen to link to the device cluster and continue the activity.

Another problem arises if in the above-mentioned situation the second user is not allowed to access the space. This implies that for this person it is useless to link his portable to the big screen. Therefore, the system might not provide a link suggestion. However, the second person can perform a ScreenLink and overrule whatever was ongoing on the device cluster.

As a consequence, it can be concluded that being linked implies having the same space on the portable as on the big screen.

7 Conclusions and Future Work

This paper has presented two interaction concepts for the connected home. First, it is assumed that broadband always-on Internet will enable new ways of sharing and communication for people. The concept of *spaces* supports this sociability for groups of people and offers new ways for people to stay in touch and to share experiences. It provides a way to monitor the events within a social group and to exchange information or content. Above all, it allows people to meet each other and to participate in shared activities. Those shared activities are synchronised and can be controlled by all people involved. A space can be compared to a shared physical space, such as a living room, a clubhouse or a café. Being present in such a space, means being easily accessible for others that have access to that particular shared space.

These spaces should be designed in such a way that they support social interaction. From architectural design, it is known that it is hardly possible to design *how* people will socially interact within real-life spaces. A similar conclusion can be drawn for the development of online spaces. In analogy with the design of buildings, the space should offer a variety of affordances that support and stimulate social interaction. Moreover the space should leave room for the development of new social conventions, and these conventions might be different for each group of people.

The second issue deals with the multitude of portable devices that people will own in the future. The *linking* concept enables users to dynamically incorporate a portable device into the stationary infrastructure of a room. As a result, the portable device can be used to control activities in the room and to transfer activities between the portable and the 'room'. Furthermore, using these transfer capabilities, the portable can act as a flexible content carrier that can be used to move an activity from one room in the home to another. More and more devices will become wireless and hopefully the interoperability between devices will improve. This means that mechanisms are needed that help people to explicitly indicate the desired relations between devices. The linking concept helps in making those associations between a wireless device and another device or set of devices easily.

The multi-user situation remains to be a complex issue. Do we want the future home to be aware of all persons in a room, and let the home determine which persons are involved in a particular activity? The question is whether a context-aware home will ever be able to do this. It would need to be able to sense where each person's attention is focused on. Besides this feasibility issue, such an approach might give rise to trust and privacy concerns.

The interaction concepts presented here have been realised in a fully working demonstrator. This will help to investigate the anticipated problems such as the multi-user problem as described in the previous section. One of the main purposes of the demonstrator will be to use it for evaluations by end-users in a realistic home setting. In this way, potential end-users will be able to judge whether and where the *spaces* add value in terms of sociability in sharing and communication. In a similar way, it will be validated how well the *linking* concept is understood by people and whether they see it as a means to improve their mobility and their freedom of control in the connected home.

Acknowledgements. We would like to render thanks to Koen Vrielink and Mark Verberkt for their contribution to the development of the presented concepts. Furthermore, we would like to thank Liesbeth Scholten, Paul Thursfield, Peter Penning from Philips Design for their input in the trends study, scenario work and graphics design.

References

1. Van de Sluis, R., Eggen, B., Jansen, J., Kohar, H.: User Interface for an In-Home Environment, In: M. Hirose (ed.), Human-Computer Interaction INTERACT '01, IOS Press (2001) 383–390
2. Diederiks E., Van de Sluis, R: "Bello", An Animated Character Facilitating Voice Control, In: M. Hirose (ed.), Human-Computer Interaction INTERACT '01, IOS Press, (2001) 686–687
3. Aarts, E., Harwig, R., Schuurmans, M.: Ambient Intelligence, in P.J. Denning (ed.), The Invisible Future: the Seamless Integration of Technology into Everyday Life, ACM Press (2001)
4. Preece, J., Designing usability, supporting sociability: Questions participants ask about online communities. In: M. Hirose (ed.), Human-Computer Interaction INTERACT '01, IOS Press, (2001) 3–12
5. Mynatt, E.D., Adler, A., Ito, M., O'Day, V.L.: Design for Network Communities. In: CHI '97 Conference Proceedings, ACM Press, (1997) 210–217
6. Erickson, T., Smith, D.N., Kellogg, W.A., Laff, M., Richards, J.T., Bradner, E.: Social Translucent Systems: Social Proxies, Persistent Conversation, and the Design of "Babble". In: CHI '99 Conference Proceedings, ACM Press, (1999) 72–79
7. Lee, A., Danis, C., Miller T., Jung, Y.: Fostering Social Interaction in Online Spaces. In: M. Hirose (ed.), Human-Computer Interaction INTERACT '01, IOS Press, (2001) 59–66
8. Rodenstein, R., Donath, J.S.: Talking in Circles: Designing A Spatially-Grounded Audioconferencing Environment. In: CHI 2000 Conference Proceedings, ACM Press, (2000) 81–88
9. Viegas, F.B., Donath, J.S.: Chat Circles. In: CHI '99 Conference Proceedings, ACM Press, (1999) 9–16
10. Eggen, B., Hollemans, G., Ter Horst, H., Meyer, A., Van de Sluis, R., Van Stuivenberg, L., Interaction Concepts for the Ambient Home, in: Proceedings of Oikos-2001, Methodologies on the Design of Household Technologies, Aarhus, Denmark (2001)
11. Hinckley, K., Pierce, J., Sonclair, M., Horvitz, E.: Sensing Techniques for Mobile Interaction. In: Proceedings of UIST 2000, ACM Press, (2000) 91–100
12. Rekimoto, J.: Pick-and-Drop: A Direct Manipulation Technique for Multiple Computer Environments. In: Proceedings of UIST'97, ACM Press, (1997) 31–39
13. Weiser, M.: The computer for the twenty-first century. In: Scientific American 265(3), (1991) 94–104
14. Habbo Hotel: http://www.habbohotel.com/ a 3D chat application on the Internet
15. MSN communities: http://communities.msn.com/ a service for online communities

Design Ideas for Everyday Mobile and Ubiquitous Computing Based on Qualitative User Data

Anu Kankainen and Antti Oulasvirta

Helsinki Institute for Information Technology
P.O. Box 9800,
02015 HUT, Finland
[anu.kankainen, antti.oulasvirta]@hiit.fi

Abstract. Academic research in mobile and ubiquitous computing has been mainly technology-driven. There is not enough understanding on what everyday needs are related to future mobile and ubiqitous computing. In this paper we will demonstrate that qualitative user data can be successfully utilized in designing for everyday activities of largely neglected user groups like the elderly. We will show how ethnographically based research can benefit the innovation of product concepts.

1 Introduction

Academic research in mobile and ubiquitous computing has been mainly technology-driven (for recent reviews, see [1], [6], [4]). One apparent drawback for such approaches is that the invented applications are restricted to use contexts and user groups that the inventors are most familiar with. Common examples include office and university environments, researchers and businessmen. Consequently, academic research groups seem to have no solid understanding on what everyday needs, expectations, or motivations are related to future technologies.

On the other hand, corporations have traditionally used market research methods, e.g. surveys, to investigate people's needs. Those methods have worked well in quantifying customers' preferences among existing solution options but they cannot really help in discovering needs that cannot be articulated [7], [9]. Consequently, more qualitative methods have recently been drawn from sociology and anthropology. These social research methods have provided rich information on people's behaviour, interactions, and environmental conditions. However, they tend to be more descriptive than prescriptive. That is, even the most detailed description of user behavior will not help product developers if it does not expose an opportunity for design.

Acknowledging these problems, there has been a growing interest in studying needs related to information technology [7], [9]. Discovering needs can be useful for entire business, providing value beyond the development of any single product. Following reasons can be provided in support for this argument:

- Human need lasts longer than any specific solution. Thinking of the company as a provider of solution might lead to continuously improving that solution and forgetting to create completely new offerings that satisfy the same need in different ways [9].

N. Carbonell, C. Stephanidis (Eds.): User Interfaces for All, LNCS 2615, pp. 458–464, 2003.

- Human needs are opportunities waiting to be exploited, not guesses at the future. Strategic product development does not have to depend only on predicting future because a crucial part of that future already exists in the form of human needs [9].
- Human needs provide a roadmap for development. A company may not have all those capabilities to satisfy needs but discovering them can help it to determine what corporate skills, strategic alliances, and core competences should be developed to grow its businesses [9].
- Empirical data wherefrom the needs are interpreted is valuable in all later stages of user-centered user interface design process [3], [2], [8], [12].

Our ambition is to demonstrate that qualitative user data can be successfully utilized in design for everyday activities of largely neglected user groups like the elderly. We will show how ethnographically based research can benefit the innovation of product concepts. In the remainder of this paper, we will present a three-staged study in user needs: In the first stage, we conducted user studies with five different user groups representing large demographical clusters. We focused on everyday activities occurring during moving through places that where occupied by other people and/or technological devices. In the second stage, we analyzed the data in order to elicit user needs underlying the behavior. Finally, we drew the two together by considering what kinds of services would be motivated and how they should be designed in order to be usable.

2 Understanding User Needs

2.1 User Research Participants

Altogether 25 people from five different user groups participated in our user research. The groups were defined in a workshop that was organised for our industrial partners. The selected user groups were the elderly, young singles, journalists, amateur actors, and middle-aged apartment house neighbours. We selected groups who knew each other well, because we were interested in socially dynamic situations.

2.2 User Research Methods

We started our research with focus groups. Before coming to a focus group session participants were asked to do a pre-assignment. They drew a map of their personal places and related activities (i.e., paying, memories, travelling, personal issues, common issues, safety, identification, free time, and goofing around). In the focus group sessions, activities and locations were then discussed and the participants were asked to tell concrete stories about them.

At the end of a focus group session, participants were given photodiaries and asked to photograph and write down events occurring while they were mobile. After two weeks participants were interviewed on the diaries.

From the diaries we selected activities that would be interesting to observe. Every participant was observed for one or two four-hour sessions. For example, we followed a middle-aged woman working in a community park and an elderly woman going swimming with her grandson.

2.3 Using Narratives for Prompting Design Ideas

The qualitative user data that was collected by using focus groups, diaries and observations was documented in the form of narratives. Narratives are recognized as good design tools because they are memorable and their informality is suitable for design-related knowledge that is often uncertain (Erickson, 1995).

Several afternoons were spent in reading and classifying the narratives in order to understand user needs. Sessions were guided by a researcher with a background in psychology. Needs were discussed in pairs and a common ground was established and documented. No particular need taxonomy was employed. Instead, needs and motivations driving the behavior described in a narrative were approached from a "common sense" point of view. After the classification of narratives several design idea generation sessions were held. The narratives including a recognized need were used as a basis for idea generation.

3 Results

We now present some of the most interesting results we gained from our study. In the following, a need is accompanied with a short description of a technological solution and preliminary discussion on user interface issues.

3.1 Mobile Shared Workspace

We noticed some problem solving situations in which participants had a need to be continuously aware of other people. For example, the theatre hobby group members had to decide on their new training schedule by selecting suitable dates from several choices given by their supervisors. Not all of the group members were present when the decision took place. It was therefore decided that those members who were present at that meeting, should inform those who were absent. The actors set up a call ring: Yasmine promised to call Effe, Effe should then call to Cira, etc. Mobile phones were mainly used. Of course, somebody had forgotten to call, and some of the actors did not come to the first training at all.

Our solution to this need was a shared mobile workspace, acting in a way similar to shared desktops but in mobile phones. Another example illustrating the need for mobile workspace came from our elderly users. Namely, a husband and a wife handled their daily shopping by writing shopping list before going to a shop. However, it often happened that when one of them had already gone to the shop the other wanted to add something onto the list. If they could have wrote the shopping items on a mobile workspace, the adding on the shopping list could have been possible afterwards.

From the user interface point of view, flexibility in information media should be strived after. Handwriting and drawing, audio clips, and pictures could be added in addition to keyboard typing.

3.2 Location-Based System Encouraging Spontaneous Meetings

Some of the users had a need to meet other group members when moving around the city. For example, some of the young people moved around in the city quite often, and they had some unexpected free time between the activities they were doing in the city (e.g. when waiting a train to come or when dropping by for a cup of coffee after shopping). In such situations company of friends would have been nice. Consequently, we propose a system that either presents the location of friends or automatically invites them to join the user when they were nearby. From the point of user interface, we believe that it would be important to make the requests for joining a friend uninterruptive for the current activity.

3.3 Location-Based Messaging

Some of the users had a need to gossip and to seek exceptions of everyday life. For example, the elderly users liked to comment on their everyday surroundings. They wished that others could see the same things as they did or the others would know if the place was good or bad regarding e.g. the service. Therefore, a system that could allow the users to attach comments with certain places could be a successful application among elderly. The young users who were moving a lot around the city could have found use for a system that informs them about local happenings while they pass by. The user interface should provide efficient means for selecting messages from the environment, for example by pointing the object of interest.

3.4 Route Guide

Some of the users had a need to know new routes. For example, an elderly user went to pick up flowers in an unfamiliar place by bus. She wanted to come back by walking but got lost. She could have had use for a system (see figure 1) that would have told her the walking route back home.

Another example illustrating the need related to digital route guide came from our group of journalists. They often got email invitations to events related to their work. The problem was always how to find the place of an event. If invitations would have included route instructions (see figure 2), the places would have been easier to find. In designing the user interface for route instructions, it should be kept in mind that most of the time these instructions should be useful when driving; hence, a map format could be more usable than list format.

3.5 Friendship Manager

Some of the participants demonstrated a need for keeping in contact with old friends. Especially, the middle-aged users had several friends that they needed to keep touch with, and they used several devices in order to do so. For example, a woman told us: "And then we have this common friend with Arja...a Greek Erasmus friend. I write text messages to her quite a lot because she does not have time to write personal messages since she is a student. Text messages were exchanged a couple of times per week and the connection remains. It is exciting that the contact needs to be maintained all the time."

Fig. 1. A handheld route guide that finds the best route by walking, bike, public transportation or car. The system recognizes the user's current location. The user needs to determine the destination and the form of moving.

Those participants who had several relationships to maintain could have use for a system helping in relationship management. The system could monitor how often the user is in contact with a specified group of friends. If it would seem that they do not do that often enough, the system could propose to send a message to a friend or friends who had been neglected. The user interface could provide statistics in a form of graphs to visualize how contacts have evolved. This would help in determining whether a friend should be added to the friendship manager.

4 Conclusions

Our results indicate that there are uncovered, everyday needs for mobile and ubiquitous services. The methods that we used in user research were suitable for exploring social and mobile everyday situations that provide new opportunities for

Fig. 2. An electronic invitation that is attached with route guide. The user can choose the form of moving, then the system suggests the best route to the place where the event will be held.

new technologies. Discovering needs was beneficial both for innovating new design ideas and understanding general requirements for user interfaces.

Our future work will concentrate on prototyping our design ideas. The design ideas work as hypothesis that we will test by conducting user evaluations in real life settings.

Acknowledgments. We would like to thank Tomi Kankainen, Esko Kurvinen, Sauli Tiitta for participating in conducting the user research. Many thank also to Matti Rantanen for commenting our paper, and other research group members for participating in idea generating. We also gratefully acknowledge support from our industrial partners: Almamedia, Elisa Communications, Nokia, SanomaWSOY and Sonera.

References

1. Abowd, G. D., Mynatt, E. D. (2000). Charting past, present and future research in ubiquitous computing. In ACM Transactions on Human-Computer Interaction, Vol 7, No. 1, 9–58.
2. Beyer, H., and Holtzblatt, K. (1998). Contextual Design. Defining Customer-Centered Systems. Morgan Kaufmann Publishers, Inc.
3. Carroll, J.M., Ed.(1995). Scenario-Based Design: Envisioning Work and Technology in System Development. John Wiley.
4. Chen, G., and Kotz. K. (2000). A survey of context-aware mobile computing research. Technical Report TR2000-381, Dept. of Computer Science, Dartmouth College.
5. Erickson, T. (1995). Notes on design practice: stories and prototypes as catalysts for communication. In J. Carroll (Ed.), Scenario-Based Design: Envisioning Work and Technology in System Development. New York: Wiley & Sons.
6. Huang, P. (2000). Promoting wearable computing: A survey and future agenda. In Proceedings of the International Conference on Information Society in The 21st Century: Emerging Technologies and New Challenges (IS2000).
7. Leyonard, D., and Rayport, J.F. (1997). Spark Innovation through Emphatic Design. Harward Business Review, November-December, 102 –113.
8. Norman, D. A., and S. Draper, Eds. (1986). User Centered System Design. Hillsdale, NJ: Lawrence Erlbaum Associates.
9. Patnaik, D., and Becker, R. (1999). Needfinding: The Why and How of Uncovering people's Needs. Design Management Journal, Spring 1999, 37–43.
10. Stanford, V. (2002). Using pervasive computing to deliver elder care. IEEE Pervasive Computing, 1 (1), 10–13.
11. Weiser, M. (1991). The Computer for the Twenty-First Century. Scientific American, September 1991, 94–104.
12. Winograd, T., and Flores, F. (1987). Understanding Computers and Cognition: A New Foundation for Design. Reading, MA: Addison-Wesley.

Providing Device Independence to Mobile Services

Stina Nylander and Markus Bylund

SICS, Lägerhyddsvägen 18, SE-752 37 Uppsala, SWEDEN
{stina.nylander, markus.bylund}@sics.se

Abstract. As electronic services are spreading in our society, they will need to be able to adapt to different users and different usage contexts. Different user interfaces will be needed for different devices and different contexts. We envision a way of developing services where the ability to adapt is included from the start. We use a set of *interaction acts* combined with customization information to create tailored user interfaces. A calendar service has been implemented with user interfaces for Java Swing, HTML and std I/O.

1   Introduction

Electronic services become more and more common in our society, and will continue to spread to new areas of our life. Soon we will be accustomed to use services in our everyday life ranging from very simple ones that for example let us control doors or lamps, to more complex ones providing teaching or entertainment.

Developing services in this context will create new requirements on service providers. Until now, the focus on service research and development has been access. When electronic services become more complex and a ubiquitous part of society, access will not be enough. Services must be capable of providing good user interaction with user interfaces that are tailored to the situation of use. This means adapting user interfaces to different devices, different contexts and different users.

In our vision, services are designed from the start to allow this. User interfaces should be created to be customizable for different kinds of use, different usage situations and different devices. The user interface of a certain application could e.g. be customized for a handheld device to be used during travel, or to be accessed from a speech user interface to accommodate users with repetitive strain injuries.

To realize this vision, we are experimenting with a set of *interaction acts* to describe the user-service interaction in a general way, without any device specific presentation information. The interaction acts are complemented with device and service specific presentation information. This way, no part of the work with development and maintenance will be done more than once, and the control of user interface presentations is kept with the service provider.

N. Carbonell, C. Stephanidis (Eds.): User Interfaces for All, LNCS 2615, pp. 465–473, 2003.

2   Background

In the last decade, the dominating ways to achieve services with user interfaces that are tailored to different usage situations have been to either implement a new version of the service for each device, or to find a common ground between devices and settle for a single minimal implementation for all of them. Neither of these solutions are satisfactory. Implementing a new version of a service for each device that will be used to access it, or each situation it will be used in, makes both development work and maintenance cumbersome. Different implementations will be made by different people at different times, which will make checks necessary to keep the user interface consistent over different platforms [2]. Using a basic ground between devices to make a service accessible from different devices makes it difficult to take advantage of device specific features like external buttons or scroll wheels. It also limits the user interface since it cannot exceed the capabilities of the thinnest client.

Model-based programming was another attempt to create services with user interfaces tailored to different devices, where the user interfaces were generated from a declarative model. This approach never caught on since the generated user interfaces were unpredictable and the models were difficult to work with [1, 5].

One way to make services accessible for people with special needs have been through assistive technology. Even if better design can improve the possibilities for users with special needs to use mainstream products, assistive technology will still be the best solution in many cases, and in some cases the only one [10]. However, assistive technology has some problems. It is often more expensive than mainstream products, and it seldom manages to keep up with new versions of applications [10]. In our vision, accessing services from assistive technology will be treated the same way as any other device. Thus, we hope to make it easier to connect assistive technology to electronic services.

3   Requirements and Limitations

To avoid multiplying development and maintenance work for services with different user interfaces, development methods need to be able to express service interactivity on a level of abstraction that is independent of device or situation, application, and type of user interface. They must not restrict services to certain types of interfaces, e.g. by excluding voice based user interfaces, or by relying on certain types of user-service interaction such as user-driven interaction. For example, HTML is device and application independent, but can only provide user-driven and page-based interaction. The abstract description of the user-service interaction must work on different platforms and different devices, and the abstract units of interaction must be useful for many different applications and different types of interaction.

It should be possible to develop a service for an open set of devices and user interfaces. Making a service available from a new device or a new user interface should not create a need to modify the existing application.

Development methods also need to give service providers all possibilities to control the presentation of services to end-users, the "look and feel" of the product

[3]. Branding and look and feel are commercially important, and a method that supports this is more attractive than others.

Our approach fulfills the above requirements by providing a description of the user-service interaction that is independent of type of application, type of device and type of user interface; allowing new interface types or devices to be added at any time without changing the service; and keeping the control of the presentation of the user interface with the service provider.

Although we are aiming for general solutions, which cover interaction with many sorts of applications via a large range of interface types, we realize that it might be difficult and in some cases not even desirable to develop services using interaction acts. Some services might be too complex, while others might be too device dependent to benefit from this approach (for example, a high-end multi-player game might not be interesting to play from other platforms than the one it was developed from). For the time being, we are therefore limiting our vision to a few interface types, (mainly windows-based GUIs, command-line interfaces, and speech interfaces), and more simple services (e.g. information services). Our long term-goal is, however, to achieve as wide and general solutions as possible.

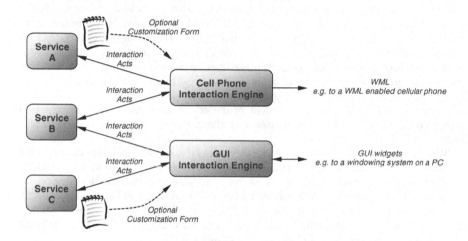

Fig. 1. A design overview of the system for device independent access to mobile services. A number of different services (A through C) executing on a server specify their interaction with interaction acts. Two different interaction engines generate user interfaces for two different types of devices based on the interaction acts of the services. Service A and C have tailored the generation of their interfaces by implementing customization forms. The cell phone interaction engine is running on a server, while the GUI interaction engine is running on the PC

4   Design

We propose a solution in which the user-service interaction is the level of abstraction. This interaction can be broken down to a small set of interaction acts, which in different combinations allow the user to accomplish different tasks. For example, the act of making a choice from a set of alternatives is the same independently of system and modality, while the means of presenting the alternatives and performing the choice may change, e.g. between a pull down menu, a menu in a speech user interface or physical buttons on an ATM machine. Using interaction acts, services can offer users all kinds of interaction without assuming how the final user interface will look, thus creating great flexibility. The interaction acts can at run-time be mapped to any kind of rendering technique to create a device and service specific user interface. A schematic picture of the system can be seen in figure 1.

Interaction Acts

An interaction act is an abstract unit of user-service interaction, which is stable over different types of user interfaces as well as different types of applications. No presentation information is included in the interaction act.

We have established a set of four basic interaction acts: `input`, `output`, `selection` and `modification`, where `input` is input to the system, `output` is output from the system that cannot accept user operations in return, `selection` is a choice between at least one alternative, and `modification` is an invitation to modify existing data (for example a calendar entry). These interaction acts can be grouped and groups can be nested to provide different interaction possibilities. All interaction acts or groups of interaction acts can be named. When running, services present hierarchically grouped sets of interaction acts from which user interfaces will be generated, and all actions performed by the users are sent back to the services encoded as interaction acts. The content of the set of interaction acts can be based either on user actions, (e.g. a response to a choice) or on system initiatives (e.g. a reminder).

With this approach, interactions of services can be generally specified once and for all. Since the user-service interaction is general, services never need to keep track of which device is currently used for access, and the same implementation can serve all devices. A service can be developed for an open set of devices and new interfaces can be added without changes in the service. This also allows for simple maintenance. With one single implementation of a service serving many different user interfaces, there will only be one version of the service to maintain.

Customization Forms

The general interaction descriptions can be complemented with optional customization forms that contain information about how the user interface should be rendered on a given device and user interface. Customization forms map single or groups of interaction acts to behavior. They can for example contain GUI widget templates for generation of dialog boxes based on selection interaction acts. They can also include media resources (such as images and sounds), or links to media resource databases. Mappings can be based on the type of interaction act, or on the type and the name of an interaction act in combination. As such, customization forms are both device and service specific. If customization forms are not provided, user interfaces can be rendered with default settings for look and feel. We have seen from earlier attempts that it is important that service providers can control the way services are presented to their end-users. The model-based systems for example, suffered from not being able to offer that, and many of the HTML plug-ins stem from the same need [3]. By providing detailed customization forms, application providers get full control of how every part of their user interfaces are generated for particular devices.

This approach will not only facilitate service development, it will also benefit the users. Users will get interfaces tailored to the devices that they use to access services. With interaction acts and customization forms combined it will be possible to use device specific features like scroll wheels and other external controls, designed to facilitate use in certain situations. It also ensures that user interfaces do not include components that the designated devices cannot handle, for example sound on a device without a speaker.

In a commercial setting, the customization form for a service is created by the service provider for the devices or user groups that the service targets. In those cases where the user-service interaction description is open, a customization form could be provided by other parties than the service provider.

5   Implementation

We have implemented the design described above. It is composed of two different parts: a device specific *interaction engine*, and an optional service specific *customization form* (see Figure 1). The user-service interaction is expressed in interaction acts, and interpreted by the interaction engine that renders the user interface. If an interaction customization form is provided the user interface is rendered according to that, otherwise default renderings are used. Additional modules for generating interaction acts, parsing interaction acts, and communication between interaction engines and services have been implemented.

To test the system, we have developed a simple calendar service.

Interaction Engine

Interaction engines are specific to both user interface type and device but independent of services. Their task is to interpret interaction acts presented by services and, using a customization form if there is one, generate a user interface of a certain type for a specific device. They are also responsible for interpreting user acts, which are encoded and returned to the service as interaction acts. Since an interaction engine is user interface and device specific, the interface that is generated is always adapted to the presentation and interaction capabilities of each device type. E.g. an interaction engine on a device with a monochrome display will not try to render a user interface with color-based presentations.

Interaction engines contain default renderings for the basic interaction acts to make sure that user interfaces can be generated even if customization forms are not present. In such cases, only the type of each interaction act is used to determine how it should be rendered.

Developers of interaction engines for new devices or user interface types need to implement the following functionality: parsing of interaction acts and encoding of user actions, creation of mappings between interaction acts and elements of the user interface, and, based on the above, generation of a user interface. In order to support the development of interaction engines, we have implemented a library of modules that the handle the parsing, encoding, and mapping functionality.

Some devices may have several interaction engines for different types of user interfaces. A personal computer might for example have an interaction engine for GUIs and another for web user interfaces. We have implemented interaction engines for Java Swing GUIs, HTML user interfaces, and std I/O based user interfaces.

Customization Forms

The customization forms are implemented as a structured set of mappings between templates of user interface components and interaction acts types and names of elements. The structure can also contain media resources. Customization forms allows the generation of different user interface components for the same type of interaction act, based on the symbolic name of the interaction act.

In our implementation, customization forms can be arranged in hierarchies, allowing one form to inherit mappings, resources, and links from another form. This allows for easy implementation of look and feel that is shared between several services.

Application

We have developed a calendar service to test the system. The calendar is written in java and supports the basic calendar operations: adding, editing and deleting events, browse calendar information, and presenting calendar information in different views (day, week, month). The calendar uses interaction acts to describe the user-service interaction, and thus, makes no assumptions about how the user interface will be presented. To complement the interaction acts, customization forms have been developed for Java Swing, std. I/O, and HTML.

Figure 2 shows screenshots of a day view of the Swing and the std I/O user interface of the calendar service.

6   Related Work

Adapting services and their user interfaces to capabilities and preferences of different users and devices is a research issue addressed in both the mobile and the universal access research communities.

The mobile community has mostly been concerned with device capabilities and technical problems, and has thus been more oriented towards solutions with a common ground for all devices, and questions of service discovery. The XWeb project has been inspired by the Web and Web browsers [6]. Data that is sent between services and user interfaces are encoded in a general way, and measures have been taken to provide full interactivity. Users can choose a client that interprets data and presents a user interface in a modality that they prefer. However, XWeb cannot take advantage of device specific features, and it does not provide means for service providers to control the presentation of the user interface. Both these features are provided by our approach.

Hodes et al. [4] describe a model-based approach that provides different user interfaces to choose from and complements these with a general interface description. If there is no user interface that suits the device, the general description is used to generate a user interface with the help of the user. This approach suffers from the same drawbacks that traditional model-based user interfaces do: generated user interfaces are unpredictable and the models are difficult to work with [1, 5]. They are also inflexible in that the hierarchy of the user interface is fixed with the model, which prevents generation of user interfaces that require other hierarchies (e.g. a GUI vs. a speech user interface). With our approach, the presentation and the structure of the user interface can be controlled with a customization form.

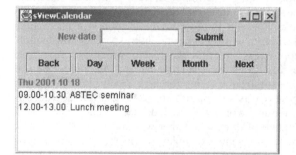 

Fig. 2. A Java Swing and a std I/O day view of the calendar

The mobile research community, with its focus on technical aspects, often has problems taking user needs into account. In contrast, the universal access community has primarily focused on how to adapt services to users' capabilities or preferences, both in terms of software and hardware aspects of user interfaces. Another issue in universal access research has been how to provide different user interfaces at the same time. For example, blind persons might be best served by a user interface tailored for blind people, but still need a GUI to be able to share their work with seeing co-workers [7].

The HOMER UIMS allows the parallel design of user interfaces for blind and seeing people using different structure and different metaphors for the different user interfaces when needed [7]. The authors argue that non-visual user interfaces should not be mere adaptations of graphical user interfaces, but need their own structure and their own tools. The concepts of Dual User Interfaces and virtual interaction objects are presented as a way to create a single user interface specification for both the visual and the non-visual user interface. There are strong similarities between the HOMER system and our approach, but the focus on blind users vs. seeing users in the HOMER project has strongly influenced the design of the language and the implementation. In contrast, our approach is developed to create user interfaces of many different types for different devices. This requires a more general design of the language and possibilities to handle a larger number of interface types than only visual and non-visual.

Unified User Interfaces (UUI) is a design and engineering framework composed by three parts: a method for design, a software architecture, and tools [9]. The goal of UUI is to provide user interfaces tailored to different user groups and situations of use in terms of users' physical capabilities, preferences and usage context. Our approach has a narrower scope, since we focus on adapting user interfaces to different device capabilities, which allows for greater flexibility. However, it could easily be seen as a tool that would fit in to the UUI framework, or alternatively, as a part of the software architecture suggested by Stephanidis and Savidis [8].

7   Conclusions

We have presented a vision for creating electronic services with user interfaces adapted to different user needs and different device capabilities. We are experimenting with a set of interaction acts to describe the user-service interaction, and then complement this description with device and user specific information. Although this is still work in progress, we find the results promising. We have implemented interaction engines for Java Swing, HTML and std I/O, and a calendar service as sample service with customization forms for Java Swing, HTML and std I/O. Even though the calendar service is very simple, it shows that the approach is working on an initial stage. Future work will include the implementation of interaction engines for a wider range of devices together with an assessment of how our approach scales in terms of creating more complex services and customization forms than described herein. The assessment will be used as input to an iterative redesign of our approach.

Acknowledgements. This work has been funded by the Swedish Agency for Innovation Systems (www.vinnova.se). Thanks to the members of the HUMLE laboratory at SICS, in particular Annika Waern, for thoughtful comments and inspiration.

References

1. Eisenstein, J. and Puerta, A., Adaption in Automated User-Interface Design. in *International Conference on Intelligent User Interfaces*, (2000).
2. Eisenstein, J., Vanderdonckt, J. and Puerta, A., Applying Model-Based Techniques to the Development of UIs for Mobile Computers. in *International Conference on Intelligent User Interfaces*, (2001).
3. Esler, M., Hightower, J., Anderson, T. and Borriello, G., Next Century Challenges: Data-Centric Networking for Invisible Computing. The Portolano Project at the University of Washington. in *The Fifth ACM International Conference on Mobile Computing and Networking, MobiCom 1999*, (1999).
4. Hodes, T.D., Katz, R., H., Servan-Schreiber, E. and Rowe, L., Composable Ad-hoc Mobile Services for Universal Interaction. in *MobiCom 1997*, (1997).

5. Myers, B.A., Hudson, S.E. and Pausch, R. Past, Present and Future of User Interface Software Tools. *ACM Transactions on Computer-Human Interaction*, *7* (1). 3–28.
6. Olsen, D.J., Jefferies, S., Nielsen, T., Moyes, W. and Fredrickson, P., Cross-modal Interaction using XWeb. in *UIST 2000*, (2000).
7. Savidis, A. and Stephanidis, C., Developing Dual User Interfaces for Integrating Blind and Sighted Users: the HOMER UIMS. in *Human Factors in Computing Systems*, (Denver, Colorado, 1995).
8. Savidis, A. and Stephanidis, C. The Unified User Interface Software Architecture. in Stephanidis, C. ed. *User Interfaces for All - Concepts, Methods, and Tools*, 2001, 389–415.
9. Stephanidis, C. The Concept of Unified User Interfaces. in Stephanidis, C. ed. *User Interfaces for All - Concepts, Methods, and Tools*, 2001, 371–388.
10. Vanderheiden, G.C. Universal Design and Assistive Technology in Communication and Information Technologies: Alternatives or Complements? *Assistive Technology*, *10* (1). 29–36.

User Interface Design for PDAs: Lessons and Experience with the WARD-IN-HAND Prototype

P. Karampelas[1], Demosthenes Akoumianakis[1], and Constantine Stephanidis[1,2]

[1] Institute of Computer Science, Foundation for Research and Technology-Hellas,
Science & Technology Park of Crete,
Heraklion, Crete, GR-71110, GREECE
Tel: +30-810-391741 - Fax: +30-810-391740
{ pkaramp, demosthe, cs }@ics.forth.gr
[2] Department of Computer Science, University of Crete

Abstract. This paper describes the process and outcomes of the evaluation of a user interface prototype running on a Personal Digital Assistant (PDA). The prototype was developed in the context of the IST-funded project WARD-IN-HAND and implements a PDA version of a ward information system. The evaluation, carried out by the IS4ALL project, was based on a usage scenario comprising mock-ups and textual descriptions of the typical tasks of the system. Although the evaluation revealed a range of usability issues to be addressed, in this paper we consider only those which feature prominent in the vast majority of PDA-based applications, such as adaptability, individualisation, user profiling, alternative dialogue styles, localisation, etc., and propose design solutions of general purpose, as a basis for improved design practice.

1 Introduction

Personal Digital Assistant (PDA) devices become increasingly popular for a wide variety of tasks, ranging from simple tasks such as storing information, i.e., phone numbers, documents, or maintaining to-do lists, to more advanced activities like searching databases (e.g., [1]) and web browsing (e.g., [2,3]). This tendency provides evidence that PDAs are not just about organizing personal data, but, more importantly for facilitating access to information. Text editors and pocket-sized database programs enable the user to take a wealth of information everywhere. More recently, there has been a strong demand for applications-oriented developments making use of PDAs. An example is in Health Telematics where PDAs are used to perform a broad range of professional activities, from accessing and ordering pharmaceuticals to data collection in clinical settings and workflow management.

In this paper, we are concerned with the usability of the user interfaces of mobile devices and in particular, user interfaces running on palmtop information appliances, such as PDAs. Our normative perspective is to investigate the application of popular HCI guidelines and heuristics in situations where palmtop devices are used to carry out domain-specific tasks, other than mere information handling. We approach this

N. Carbonell, C. Stephanidis (Eds.): User Interfaces for All, LNCS 2615, pp. 474–485, 2003.

target by considering a reference scenario from the domain of health telematics and making use of well-known user interface principles to gain insight to the design of the user experience with such devices. It is claimed that PDAs have their origin in information centric devices like desktop computers [20] and as a result their interfaces conform to models such as the Graphical User Interface (GUI). Thus, principles of GUI design could be used to inform user interface design for PDAs.

Our reference scenario is based on WARD-IN-HAND[1]. The WARD-IN-HAND system [4] aims to support the day-by-day activities of healthcare professional (i.e. doctors, nurses) within a hospital ward by providing a tool for workgroup collaboration and wireless access to the patient's clinical records. Such a system should respond accurately, reliably, effectively and efficiently under the challenging situation of a hospital ward, where the user should devote his attention to the patient and not on how the device is operated. The demands on mental workload should be minimal, while instant access and fast response times are required for robust system operation. Furthermore, special design constrains are imposed by specific properties of the target device. Limited screen resolution, absence of keyboard, pen-based manipulation of the widgets, point and click as primary interaction technique, are some of the design constrains that should be taken into account when designing user interfaces for PDAs.

The rest of the paper is structured as follows. The next section describes the evaluation procedure and the methods used. Then we present the results of the evaluation by means of discussing usability problems encountered and proposals for design improvements. The emphasis is not to exhaustively list all usability faults of the system, but rather to point out typical problems encountered with PDAs and corresponding design solutions of general applicability. Finally, the paper concludes with a list of general guidelines and recommendations for designing user interfaces for PDAs.

2 Usability Evaluation

Usability evaluation of WARD-IN-HAND was an activity planned and executed in the context of the IST-funded IS4ALL project[2]. IS4ALL is investigating several health telematics scenarios in an attempt to validate a universal access code of practice in health telematics [5]. One of the designated scenarios is focused on the WARD-IN-HAND early prototype. For the purposes of evaluation, the WARD-IN-HAND reference scenario comprised mock-ups and textual descriptions of the typical tasks and user experience with a high fidelity prototype of the system. The resulting scenario formed the basis for usability evaluation using a mix of heuristic techniques, which lead to further evolutions of WARD-IN-HAND incorporating some of the proposed recommendations.

In this section, we report the procedure, which was followed as well as the methods used to carry out the evaluation.

---

[1] http://www.wardinhand.org
[2] http://is4all.ics.forth.gr

2.1 Procedure

The evaluation case study was realised in the premises of Human Computer Interaction and Assistive Technology Laboratory of the Institute of Computer Science, Foundation of Research and Technology-Hellas, Crete, Greece. The evaluation procedure was initiated by a presentation of the prototype by the project coordinator of the WARD-IN-HAND consortium. The presentation provided a thorough review of all functions and computer-mediated tasks supported by the device. Following this presentation a tentative scenario was drafted and sent back to the WARD-IN-HAND project coordinator for comments. Following iterative exchanges, aspects of the scenario were refined and a final version was compiled for future reference. Subsequent phases in evaluation made use of this final version of the scenario. Finally, in terms of procedures used, it should be noted that experts taking part in the evaluation had not been previously exposed to the prototype, while the only reference materials at their disposal were the final version of the scenario and a WARD-IN-HAND conference paper [4], which outlined the aims and objectives of the system.

2.2 Methods

The evaluation methodology used was inspection-based, comprising the use of three different methods, which are briefly described below.

Cognitive walkthrough. A cognitive walkthrough [6, 7] involves the inspection of the effectiveness of the user interface by analysing how easily a user can learn to interact with the interface and how easily can comprehend the functionality of the interface. In our case, the materials inspected were paper screenshots as documented in the scenario. Two expert evaluators performed a thorough and detailed examination of how easily a user can learn to interact with the user interface, identifying at the same time potential problems of conception that the user may encounter. The profile of the target users, namely doctors and nurses, was analysed and useful conclusions were formulated regarding their potential attitude towards the system. It turned out that doctors and nurses usually exhibit high reluctance to divert from traditional techniques of completing tasks, low motivation to use sophisticated technology and devices, and low willingness to spend time for learning to interact with new devices.

Feature Inspection. This technique [7] involves the inspection of task related features of the user interface by examining its appropriateness for completing a task, the availability of required functions, the ability of being self explanatory and further usability aspects. A common task, for example, that the doctors using the device could accomplish is the review of blood pressure measurements. Features of the specific task e.g. how easily the user can access the respective screen, or how much memory load is required to comprehend the visual output of the screen, were examined and tentative suggestions and comments were produced.

One usability expert who focused on specific features of the user interface carried out feature inspection. The most important features analysed and proposed were the alternative navigation dialogues, the interaction alternatives, the consistent presentation of the interface elements, the self explanatory interface components, the accessibility of the user interface elements, and the adaptability of the user interface according to user requirements.

Heuristic Evaluation. Heuristic evaluation [8, 9] entails inspection of several characteristics of the user interface against a set of guidelines or general principles by examining the visibility of system status, the user control and freedom, the consistency of the system, the error prevention, and further usability aspects. In our case, three different usability experts examined individually the WARD-IN-HAND user interface prototype. The typical list of heuristics [9] was used to generate the systematic comments on the usability aspects of the user interface. As a result, a list of possible improvements regarding presentation of information, user guidance and navigation, design consistency and ease of data manipulation was produced.

3   Results

In this section we summarise the results of our usability evaluation and develop alternative design solutions, which could eliminate some of the problems encountered. Many of the proposed solutions are general enough to be applicable in other design cases involving the use of PDAs to carry out domain-specific activities.

3.1 Navigation Concepts and Styles

Navigation [10, 11] in user interface design is one of the key issues for the success and acceptability of the entire system. Robust, self-explanatory navigation aids the user to understand the structure of the application, to access faster the requested task, to use effectively and efficiently the application. Several guidelines have been developed concerning navigation in traditional GUI applications and websites. PDAs design constrains such as limited screen size, absence of keyboard etc, impose a very careful design of the navigation functions. A set of guidelines that the designer should bear in mind when designing the navigation style include: consistent presentation, use of alternative navigation tools (adaptability), retain major option accessibility, self-explanatory navigation.

Following the above guidelines, WARD-IN-HAND navigation, which is depicted in Figure 1 (left), could be revised as shown in the same figure (right).

The revised implementation combines a toolbar and a status bar in the upper part of the screen containing all the necessary navigation aids, like the Home icon which will always return the user to the main application screen (current screen), the Next and Back icons which will guide user in the other screens of application and the logout icon which will help users to quit the system immediately after completing a set of tasks.

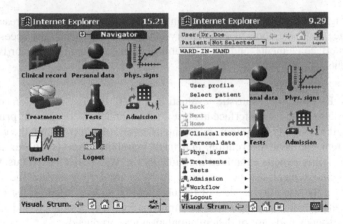

Fig. 1. Current (left) and alternative navigation implementation by menu dialogue prototype (right)

In addition, useful information is displayed on the left part of the bar, such as the name of the user logged in and the name of the patient whose electronic record is currently active. These features allow the user to carry out additional tasks, for example changing either his profile by tapping in his name or switching over into another's patient record by just tapping on the patient name and selecting from the combo box the name of the other patient. It must be noted that only the available options are enabled in the bar, while the unavailable options are visible for consistency purposes but greyed and inactive.

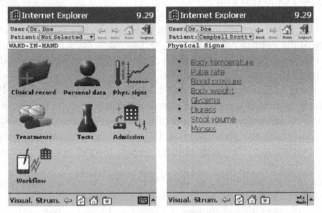

Fig. 2. Revised Navigation

A parallel navigation method is also implemented for providing users an alternative navigation style (see Figure 2). All navigation functions are available as nested menu options organised in logical groups. The unavailable options again are inactive and greyed.

3.2 On-Screen Keyboard

The absence of a real keyboard enforces the implementation of a virtual one in the available space. The virtual keyboard currently integrated in the WARD-IN-HAND application can be seen in Figure 3. This virtual keyboard, dubbed WTx, was developed by the Dept. of Information Sciences of the University of Genoa, Italy [18, 19], and acts as alternative to the standard QWERTY keyboard, and can be selected from the standard input panel of the PocketPC.

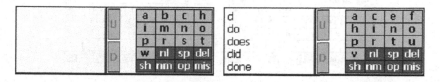

Fig. 3. WTx virtual keyboard

Users not familiar with the above virtual keyboard layout, may take some time to become accustomed to it. On the contrary the built in virtual keyboard of iPaq (Figure 4), implements the metaphor of the traditional 'QWERTY' keyboard, which is familiar to the user, since he/she uses it for all other applications. Therefore he/she could use it efficiently and effectively in any context. A more user-centered design approach could be to provide a virtual keyboard that is familiar to the user e.g. 'QWERTY' like keyboard, enhanced with context-sensitive capabilities. For example, if the context of use of this "smart" keyboard is the login screen, then an it could be presented as it is shown in Figure 4.

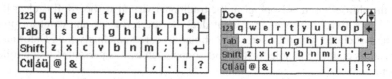

Fig. 4. Built-in virtual keyboard (left) and a smart context-sensitive keyboard used in the login screen (right)

The functionality of this keyboard is easily understood. The user types the first letter of the username and the sensitive list on the top displays the first username that starts with the character typed. By tapping the tick (✓) the user inserts the selected word in the login name field. Using up (▲) and down (▼) buttons placed right on the list, the user can view the previous and next words in the user list. In another context e.g. filling the name of a drug, the list should display only the affiliated names of the drugs. In case of free context of use where the user could type anything, the display list would contain all the available words in the vocabulary.

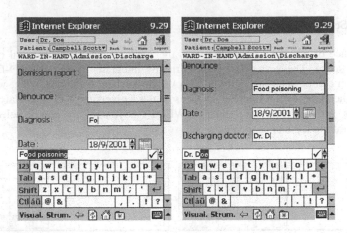

Fig. 5. Context-sensitive virtual keyboard in action

Figure 5 demonstrates how the context sensitive keyboard could behave in a complex data entry screen. In the left picture the user (doctor in this case) start filling in the diagnosis text entry field, using the context sensitive virtual keyboard. The keyboard binds its referenced vocabulary to the set of diagnosis keywords. By tapping the 'f' character the first entry related to diagnosis starting with 'f' is displayed on the attached panel of the virtual keyboard. By tapping the second character 'o' the relative word is displayed, in this case is 'Food poisoning'. If this is the right diagnosis the doctor has just to tap the tick (✓) button in the attached panel of the keyboard in order to accept the diagnosis. The aforementioned example provides evidence that the user completes the text entry task by tapping just three times on the virtual keyboard, instead of tapping fourteen times, which is the number of characters required to complete the phrase 'Food poisoning' in the traditional virtual keyboard. It is clear that the context sensitivity improves in a great deal user performance and comfort, provided that the associated with the context vocabulary is correspondingly rich. Dates and time field entries could be handled with another approach as it is presented in the following section.

The picture on the right in Figure 5 introduces a more advanced feature for the implementation of the context sensitive virtual keyboard. When the keyboard is ready to accept input for the 'Discharging doctor' field, adds automatically the job abbreviation 'Dr.' and then expects to enter the doctor's name. The associated with the entry field context is the list of doctors' names thus the user can select with minimal interaction the desired one. The field alternatively could be automatically filled in by the doctor's name currently logged in.

Additional intelligence could be incorporated in the context sensitive virtual keyboard, for instance when a field requires a person's name the first character could be capitalized automatically by the keyboard, without obliging the user to change to capital letters, tap the first letter, change to small letters and continue with writing the name. Utilising such quick and easy procedures in the framework of a portable device can dramatically increase the usability of the application and additionally of the device.

3.3 Data Entry

Due to constrains implied by the design of the PDA device several considerations should be taken into account during the design phase of an application. The absence of keyboard (as a physical input device) enforces the designers to attempt to reduce the necessity for data input. The main interaction method with the device is through point and click using the stylus. Alternative interaction method is by using the navigation buttons of the device which provide reduced functionality (four directions navigation). An approach to overcome these constrains entails a tolerable implementation of a virtual keyboard. Nevertheless it is not the cure for data entry. Hence the designers should design carefully the data entry dialogues, by reducing to the minimum the request for data entry.

Some general guidelines [12] could help towards this direction, namely the use of combo boxes with predefined values, the use of numerical input fields with default values and the provision of suitable functionality for the user to increase or decrease the value and additionally the use of a context sensitive virtual keyboard. However the implementation of such features should be supported by the operating system of the specific PDA device[3]. Examples of these input methods are provided in Figure 6.

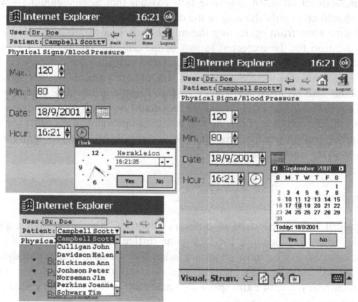

Fig. 6. Examples of input methods

---

[3] It should be also noted that not all PDA platforms currently support advanced features such as nested menu bars, popup windows, DHTML, applets, etc.). In the case of WARD-IN-HAND, the limitations of the version of Pocket Internet Explorer used at the time of developing the early prototype (used in the evaluation), made it impossible to adopt solutions such as those described above.

3.4 Colour Coding

Colour coding is a favourite usability issue since the introduction of coloured monitors in the early phases of graphic interaction. For that reason many guidelines and conclusions have been formulated to regulate the use of colours in computer based applications [13]. Some of the most important ones are: use colour sparingly, use colour consistently with user expectations, use colours that contrast well, don't use blue for text, don't use saturated colours, use colour redundantly, let users tailor colours. Standard conventions in real life such as red for stop, yellow for caution and green for go are also combinations that apply in the computer applications.

In a small device like PDA the colour coding could be used effectively in order to improve readability and categorisation of the information, since the available display space is less than in a conventional visual display terminal.

3.5 Date/Time Format

The use of a global date/time format from the default regional settings of the operating system is recommended. In date/time fields visual indications should show whether the user should enter only the date or the date and time. This will facilitate user's input and will save time from correcting the mistakes. It is also recommended to provide visual indication for the expected format of the date/time input. For instance, if the user is supposed to enter the time in hour and minute format the design should provide a visual indication that the expected input is hours and minutes but not seconds. Date fields should also be filled automatically, for example in our case study, when a test should be prescribed then the date of the test could be filled with the date of the next day, or of the current date if it is known that the implementation of this test would be immediate. A pop up window with the calendar should also be available for selecting dates close to the current date.

3.6 Localisation

If an application will be used in different countries, a priori design consideration should be taken into account for facing the difficulties that may brought about by alternate formatting. The most important issues that the user interface designer should bear in mind include [17]: use of regional settings for extracting format for date/time/currency, use of extra space allocated than in English, use standard graphics instead of text for task representation.

3.7 Help Functions

A help function is generally considered as necessary, especially for novice users [12]. Help functionality like the one provided by the device could be offered in the main menu as an option as it provided for the default applications (see Figure 7). The user consequently could use this help screen not only for acquiring information for the specific application functionality, but also to have an overview of the application's functionality at a glance. Browsing help screen the user can understand the full functionality of the application since the help taxonomy depicts the actual structure of the program and can explore and learn specific functions that he/she could possibly hesitate to explore otherwise.

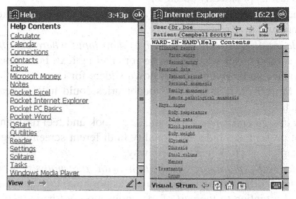

Fig. 7. System help vs. Application help

3.8 Use of Buttons

The general navigation method presented earlier should be adequate for interacting with the system. However advanced functionality requires additional manipulation, which could be accomplished by the use of buttons. The operating system implementation encourages the position of confirmation button in the Title bar of the application. The same approach should be adopted for the dialogues that require only affirmative response. For generic situations the use of buttons should follow the general guidelines [12, 14, 15, 16] for interactive windows graphical objects (widgets), namely frequently used options should be available as buttons, size buttons relative to each other, buttons should be grouped into panes, label buttons carefully, use industry/icon standards for labels, use greying out to show button's unavailability, place buttons in the centre of the screen or in the bottom right part of the screen for right handed users.

4 Discussion and General Recommendations

User interface design, in general, is based not only on the aesthetics and visualization of the information, but mainly on the logical flow of information and how the interface is satisfying the task specifications and user expectations. Several constrains though should be born in mind during the design which mainly are affected by the physical characteristics of the PDA. A list of the most important guidelines that the user interface designer should have in mind when designing for a PDA could be summarized as follows:

- *Keep user interaction minimal.* Provided that a PDA is not a traditional computer, but just a personal digital assistant the user would expect to complete the necessary task as fast as practically possible.
- *Minimize data entry.* The absence of a physical keyboard makes the data entry an awkward and time consuming task.
- *Provide intelligent (context sensitive) data input where possible.* Make extensive use of combo boxes where possible for entering text. For numerical values use default values and provide up and down sliders for correcting the exact value of an entry. Moreover, task-oriented vocabularies could help increase data entry completion times.
- *Retain design consistency.* Use the same look and feel throughout the application. Do not present and hide functionality in different screens. Use the same approach for completing a task in a uniform way.
- *Provide self-explanatory navigation with alternatives.* Make the navigation through the different screens as simple as possible. Provide visual clues to the user to direct attention to the part of the application he/she is interacting with. Disable the unavailable options without hiding them.
- *Use system format for date/time/currency fields.* In order to avoid user's confusion, use consistently the system format from the regional settings information to present information about date, time and currency.
- *Use standard graphics buttons instead of text buttons.* For international applications, it is recommended to use standard icons and graphics to avoid translation incompatibilities. The limited screen size can be a barrier to the appropriate translation of a text. By using a standard icon, there is no need for translating and localising the text of a button.
- *Provide help functionality.* Offer general hyperlink based help for explaining the functionality of the application.

Acknowledgements. The work reported in this paper has been carried out in the framework of the European Commission funded Thematic Network (Working Group) "Information Society for All" - IS4ALL (IST-1999-14101) and the IST-1999-10479 - WARD-IN-HAND project ("Mobile Workflow Support and InformAtion distribution in hospitals via voice-opeRateD, wIreless-Networked HANDheld PCs").
The IS4ALL Consortium comprises one co-ordinating partner, the Institute of Computer Science, Foundation for Research and Technology – Hellas (ICS-FORTH), and the following member organisations: Microsoft Healthcare Users Group Europe, European Health Telematics Association, Consiglio Nazionale delle Ricerche - Istituto di Ricerca sulle Onde Elettromagnetiche, Forschungszentrum Informationstechnik GmbH, Institut National de Recherche en Informatique et Automatique - Laboratoire lorrain de recherche en informatique et ses applications and Fraunhofer-Gesellschaft zur Foerderung der angewandten Forschung e.V. - Institut fur Arbeitswirtschaft und Organisation. Several other co-operating organisations participate as subcontractors.

The WARD-IN-HAND Consortium comprises of the following partners: British Maritime Technology Ltd., Universita degli Studi di Genova, Relational Technology S.A., Staedtische Kliniken Offenbach, Universita degli Studi di Genova and Corporacio Sanitaria Clinic.

The authors would also like to explicitly acknowledge the co-operation with Salvatore Virtuoso (TXT e-Solutions Spa, Italy) Project Manager of WARD-IN-HAND.

References

1. Dunlop, M. D., Davidson, N.: Visual information seeking on palmtop devices, Proceedings of HCI2000, Vol. 2 (2000) 19–20
2. Buchanan, G., Jones, M.: Search interfaces for handheld Web browsers, 9th World Wide Web Conference, (2000) 86–87
3. Buyukkokten, o., Molina, H. G., Paepcke, A., Winograd, T.: Power Browser: Efficient Web Browsing for PDAs, Proc. of the Conf. on Human Factors in Computing Systems (2000)
4. M.Ancona, E.Coscia, G.Dodero, M.Earney, V.Gianuzzi, F.Minuto, S.Virtuoso – Proc. TEHRE 2001 m-Health Conference, 1st Annual Conference on Mobile & Wireless Healthcare Applications, London, UK (2001)
5. Stephanidis, C., Akoumianakis, D.: Towards a design code of practice for universal access in Health Telematics, Universal Access in the Information Society, 1 (3), (2002) 223–226
6. Wharton, C., Rieman, J., Lewis, C and Polson, P.: The cognitive walkthrough method: A practitioner's guide. In Nielsen, J., and Mack, R. (Eds.) Usability inspection methods. NY: Wiley (1994)
7. Jordan, Patrick: An Introduction to Usability, Taylor & Francis, London. (1998) 79–80
8. Nielsen, J.: Usability Engineering, San Diego, Academic Press (1993)
9. Nielsen, J.: Heuristic Evaluation, In Nielsen, J., and Mack, R. (Eds.) Usability inspection methods. NY: Wiley (1994)
10. Weinschenk, S., Jamar, P., Yeo, S. C.: GUI Design Essentials for Windows'95, Windows 3.1, World Wide Web, NY: Wiley (1997)
11. Raskin, J.: The Humane Interface: New Directions for Designing Interactive Systems, Berkeley, Addison-Wesley (2000)
12. Johnson, J.: GUI Bloopers: Don'ts and Do's for Software Developers and Web Designers. San Francisco, Morgan Kaufmann (2000)
13. Najjar, L.: Using color effectively (or peacocks can't fly) (IBM TR52.0018), IBM (1990)
14. Najjar, L.: Multimedia user interface design guidelines (IBM TR52.0046), IBM (1992)
15. Weinschenk, S., Yeo, S.: Guidelines for enterprise-wide GUI design, NY: Wiley (1995)
16. Hix, D., Hartson, H.R.: Developing User Interfaces: Ensuring usability through product and process, NY, Wiley (1993)
17. Kano, N. Developing International Software for Windows 95 and Windows NT, Redmond: Microsoft Press (1995)
18. M. Ancona Locati, A. Romagnoli: Context and location aware textual data input, ACM SAC 2001 Symposium on Applied Computing Las Vegas (2001)
19. M. Ancona, D. Comes: WordTree A pen based editor of short texts, IGS'99 Proc. (1999)
20. Weiss S.: Handheld usability, NY: Wiley (2002)

Evaluating User Interfaces with Metaphors
of Human Thinking

Kasper Hornbæk[1] and Erik Frøkjær[2,*]

[1] Natural Sciences ITC Competence Centre, University of Copenhagen,
Universitetsparken 5, DK-2100 Copenhagen,
KHornbaek@nik.ku.dk
[2] Department of Computing, University of Copenhagen,
Universitetsparken 1, DK-2100 Copenhagen
erikf@diku.dk

Abstract. Inspection techniques are a useful tool for identifying potential usability problems and for integrating at an early stage evaluation with design processes. Most inspection techniques, however, do not consider users' thinking and may only be used for a limited range of devices and use contexts. We present an inspection technique based on five metaphors of essential aspects of human thinking. The aspects considered are habit; the stream of thought; awareness and associations; the relation between utterances and thought; and knowing. The proposed inspection technique makes users' thinking the centre of evaluation and is readily applicable to new devices and non-traditional use contexts. Initial experience with the technique suggests that it is usable in discussing and evaluating user interfaces.

1 Introduction

This paper presents an inspection technique for evaluating user interfaces. The technique is based on five metaphors of human thinking. The technique aims at helping evaluators consider users' thinking when evaluating user interfaces.

Inspection techniques for evaluating user interfaces aim at uncovering potential usability problems by having evaluators inspect the user interface with a set of guidelines or questions [29]. Inspection techniques seem to be a useful supplement to empirical techniques for identifying potential usability problems and for integrating at an early stage evaluation with design processes. Inspection techniques include heuristic evaluation [30], where inspection is guided by heuristics such as "Be consistent" or "Prevent errors" [30], p. 249; and cognitive walkthrough [21,42], where evaluators ask questions related to how users perceive the user interface and plan actions.

To us, existing inspection techniques have two shortcomings. The first is that most inspection techniques do not explicitly consider users' thinking. Guidelines, for example, often do not mention users' thinking or relate to psychological principles. The first 37 guidelines in the collection by Smith & Mosier [39] refer to users' thinking or psychological principles in only 10 cases: however, this is done in superficial phrases

---

* The authors contributed equally to the paper.

N. Carbonell, C. Stephanidis (Eds.): User Interfaces for All, LNCS 2615, pp. 486–507, 2003.

such as "Most users will forget to do it" or "People cannot be relied upon to pay careful attention to such details" [39], p. 34. Heuristic evaluation, as in [30], mentions only the user explicitly in two heuristics, and the heuristic "minimize users' memory load" is the only heuristic that comes close to considering users' thinking. One exception to our point, it may be argued, is cognitive walkthrough, which was developed with a basis in psychological theories of exploratory learning [21]. However, even for this inspection technique refinement has led to less emphasis on the psychological basis. In [42], the original list of nine questions (some with sub-questions) was reduced to four by some of the inventors of cognitive walkthrough. And recently, in the so-called stream-lined cognitive walkthrough [41], only two questions are asked with no reference to psychological theory: "Will the user know what to do at this step?" and "If the user does the right thing, will they know that they did the right thing, and are making progress towards their goal?", [41] p. 355. So existing inspection techniques consider users' thinking only vaguely, thus ignoring potential important insight in how thinking shapes interaction.

A second shortcoming of inspection techniques is that many of the guidelines or questions used are useful only for a particular device/interaction style (e.g. Windows Icons Menus Pointers-interfaces) or context of use (e.g. computing in front of the desktop). Again take Smith & Mosier [39] as an example: their guidelines discuss the use of "reverse video", "the ENTER key" and "Teletype displays"—all of these obviously is linked to a certain device/interaction style. A related concern was recently stressed by Preece et al. who in a discussion of heuristic evaluation writes:

"However, some of these core heuristics are too general for evaluating new products coming onto the market and there is a strong need for heuristics that are more closely tailored to specific products.", [35], p. 409

It is not clear, therefore, that mainstream inspection techniques can be successfully used to inspect emerging technologies, such as mobile devices or context aware systems. Pinelle and Gutwin [32] found too little focus on the work context in inspection techniques used on groupware and have tried to extend cognitive walkthrough to include such a focus. This is just one example of the limited transferability of inspection techniques to other use contexts.

As a solution to these problems, and as an effective inspection technique in its own right, we propose an inspection technique based on Metaphors Of Thinking—the MOT-technique. We use the term thinking broadly to denote mental activity as this takes place for a person as part of his or her activities. The MOT-technique is inspired by William James's and Peter Naur's descriptions of human thinking [19,23-26]. Similar descriptions along with many brilliant design discussions have lately been introduced to HCI in Jef Raskin's book *The Humane Interface* [36]. Naur's and Raskin's work are complementary to most psychology used in HCI, but is supported by extensive evidence from classic introspective psychology [19], and from experimental psychology and neurology [1,2]. Several of the aspects of human thinking described in this work are of critical importance to successful human-computer interaction: (1) the role of habit in most of our thought activity and behaviour—physical habits, automaticity, all linguistic activity, habits of reasoning; (2) the human experience of a stream of thought—the continuity of our thinking, the richness and wholeness of a person's mental objects, the dynamics of thought; (3) our awareness—shaped through a focus of attention, the fringes of mental objects, association, and reasoning; (4) the incompleteness of utterances in relation to the thinking underlying them and the ephemeral nature of those utterances; and (5) knowing—human knowing is always under construction and incomplete.

We base the MOT-technique on these five aspects that combined and separately catch important properties of thinking shared by humans. Each aspect of thinking is described also by a metaphor. The metaphor is meant to help the evaluator in understanding and focusing on the aspect considered; it is *not* intended as an interface metaphor. The number of metaphors is not important; nor is our choice of metaphors meant to catch all aspects of human thinking. Still we hope to show that the metaphors are valuable in evaluating user interfaces.

We have chosen to present these aspects of human thinking by quotations from James [19] and Naur [25-27]. Naur has studied the 1377 pages of James's book *The Principles of Psychology* and through quotations, summaries and extended discussions illuminated James's work and to us made it more accessible. For readers who might not be aware of the continued importance of James's classical work in psychology, and who therefore might feel uncomfortable with our paper's building so directly on sources published more than hundred years ago, we quote the renowned cognitive psychologist Bernard Baars who in 1997 writes:

'Remarkably, the best source on the psychology of consciousness is still William James's elegant 'Principles of Psychology', first published in 1890. [...] James' thoughts must be understood in historical context, but the phenomena he describes so well have not changed one bit.' [2], p. 35

Table 1 summarizes the metaphors, indicate the implications for user interfaces, and give examples of key questions that the metaphors raise. The following five sections (section 2 to section 6) describe in detail each metaphor. In section 0 we discuss how to conduct an inspection using the MOT-technique, and section 8 discuss the potential and problems of the MOT-technique.

2   Support of Existing Habits and, When Necessary, Development of New Ones

Fundamental for effective use of interfaces is that users can use existing habits, such as common association of a word to an object or using certain key combinations for inserting text. Similarly, the user should be able to develop effective work habits with the interface: it should be possible to predict layout and functioning of the interface, accelerators should be provided, it should be easy to accomplish frequent work tasks, etc.

Habit as a Landscape Eroded by Water

Every person's habit formation is like a landscape eroded by water. By this metaphor we mean to indicate how a person's formation of habits leads to more efficient actions and less conscious effort, like a landscape through erosion adapts for a more efficient and smooth flow of water. Creeks and rivers will, depending on changes in water flow, find new ways or become arid and sand up, in the same way as a person's habits will adjust to new circumstances and, if unpracticed, vanish.

Table 1. Summary of the MOT-technique. The five metaphors, their implications for user interfaces, and examples of questions to be raised

Metaphor of human thinking	Implications for user interfaces	Key questions/Examples
Habit formation is like a landscape eroded by water.	Support of existing habits and, when necessary, development of new ones.	Are existing habits supported? Can effective new habits be developed? Is the interface predictable?
Thinking as a stream of thought.	Users' thinking should be supported by recognizability, stability and continuity.	Do the system make visible and easily accessible the important task objects and actions? Do the user interface make the system transparent or is attention drawn to non-task related information? Does the system help users to resume interrupted tasks? Is the appearance and content of the system similar to the situation when it was last used?
Awareness as a jumping octopus.	Support users' associations with effective means of focusing within a stable context.	Do users associate interface elements with the actions and objects they represent? Can words in the interface be expected to create useful associations for the user? Is the graphical layout and organization helping the user to group tasks?
Utterances as splashes over water.	Support changing and incomplete utterances.	Are alternative ways of expressing the same information available? Are system interpretations of user input made clear? Do the system make a wider interpretation of user input than the user intends or is aware of?
Knowing as a site of buildings.	Users should not have to rely on complete or accurate knowledge—design for incompleteness.	Can the system be used without knowing every detail of it? Do more complex tasks build on the knowledge users have acquired from simpler tasks? Are feedback given to ensure correct interpretations?

According to James the most important general property of the thinking and behavior of people is that each person is a bundle of habits. Building on James, Naur writes [27]:

'All our grasping of things around us that we see, hear, feel, that which we call perception, is entirely a question of the habits each of us has trained. In addition our locomotion, the way we move our arms and legs while moving around, is almost entirely habitual. In addition, our talking with each other, the way we grasp what others say to us and the way we move our tongue, lips, and other organs of speech while talking, all this has been trained as habits. All education is a matter of training habits.

Any part of a human organism may be involved in a habit. In a certain sense every habit involves the entire person.'

Key Questions

The key questions for already established habits are whether they are transferable to the user interface in question. Can often-used shortcuts or common associations between command names and functions known from other applications be used? Are actions that are executed almost automatically by many users supported, e.g. pressing return after entering a query word? On the other hand, be cautious in the use of modes as they may hinder transfer of habits.

A key question for users is whether the user interface allows for habit formation of often-used actions. Can the central user tasks be effectively done in the user interface? To allow users develop new habits, the interface should be predictable and responsive. When an interface is predictable, information and controls (e.g. menus), appear in the same place every time the program is used. Such predictability allows users to begin moving the mouse towards a menu item or a button even before they have oriented themselves in the interface. Responsiveness in this context means that the interface should allow the user to begin typing commands or pressing buttons immediately, for example even when parts of a web-page is still loading. Similarly, the user should be allowed to type ahead in menus or forms.

Examples

There is an abundance of examples of user interfaces that violate human habits. One example is adaptive menus, used for example in Microsoft Office 2000, see Fig. 1. Adaptive menus change the layout of the menu according to how often menu items are used, for example by removing or changing the position of items seldomly used. However, adaptive menus make it impossible to form habits in the selection of menu items [36], since their position may be different from when they were previously selected. A study by Somberg [40] showed the efficiency of constant position placement of menu items compared to menus that change based on use frequency. Somberg, however, did not explicitly link habit formation to the usefulness of constant placement of menu items. Note that the common practice of adding a fixed number of, say, recently used files or fonts to the bottom or top of a menu does not interfere with habit formation and may decrease time taken to select a menu item [37].

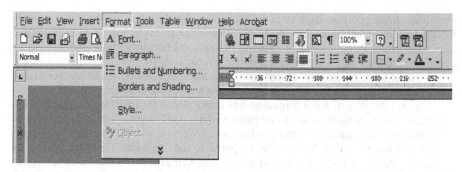

Fig. 1. Adaptive menus in Microsoft Word. Some menu items in the Format menu have been hidden based on the frequency with which they have been used. This, however, prevents the user from forming habits

The discussion of consistency in user interfaces may be illuminated in terms of habit. In a classic paper on consistency [13], Grudin argues that focusing on consistency per se leads to a lack of focus on users and their tasks. In several examples he shows how consistency can be interpreted in different ways and how different aspects of usability contradict each other in what some call consistent designs. From our point of view, Grudin's critique of the notion of consistency concerns the role of habit in the interface. With a focus on habits, the aim of consistency is to allow the habits that users develop to be transferred within or between systems they use. In addition, a system should also allow effective habits to be established in the first place, especially for often-used functions. Consistency between systems is not critical if interface elements or functions are not a habitual part of the users' repertoire of actions. Habitual association of words, however, might be useful for grouping or naming interface elements.

The central design issue with respect to consistency, and thus habit formation, is whether to utilize existing habits in the design of the system or create new ones. Grudin's [13] discussion of choosing effective keyboard layouts (e.g. QWERTY or DVORAK) is an example where it is essential for users to establish effective new habits, rather than transferring real-world habits (such as associating letters in alphabetical order) to the interface. One reason why consistency is a problematic notion is that it obscures long-term usability—especially the efficiency gained by supporting inattentive, i.e. habitual, use.

Perhaps designers in HCI more often should aim for establishing new, effective habits. Even the most radical changes of interfaces may be mastered if the interface is used often. An analogue of this is shown in Stratton's experiments with glasses that turned his visual field upside down [12]. When wearing the glasses constantly, in less than 7 days he had become habituated to viewing the world upside down and could walk, write, etc.

An example of a user interface that exploits that habit formation is not always wanted, is found in the evaluation version of the compression utility WinZip, see Fig. 2. When WinZip is run, an initial screen with five buttons is shown. Three buttons allow the user to get access to license information, to a screen for registration, and to information about how to order. The last two buttons are of interest here. One button quits the utility; another lets the user proceed to the main screen of WinZip. To prevent users from going straight to the main screen, the designers of WinZip randomly interchange the position of the two buttons when the utility is run. This prevents the user from establishing a habit of clicking the proceed button without noticing the license and ordering information on the initial screen.

As pointed out by Raskin, many error messages will not be noted by the user if they often or always appear when something potentially harmful are initiated:

'The inevitability of habit formation has implications for interface design. For example, many of us have used computer systems that, before they will perform an irreversible act, such as deleting a file, ask, 'Are you sure?' You then must type, say, a *Y* for yes or an *N* for no in response to the question. This idea is that, by making you confirm your decision, the system will give you a chance to correct an otherwise irrecoverable error. This idea is widely accepted. For example, Smith and Duell (1992), addressing a nursing environment, say, 'If you inadvertently delete part of the permanent record (which is hard to do because the computer always asks if you're sure)...' (p. 86). Unfortunately, Smith and Duell are unrealistic in their assessment: you can readily make an incidental deletion even when this kind of confirmation is required. Because errors are relatively rare, you will usually type *Y* after giving any command that requires confirmation. Due to the continual repetition of the action, typing *Y* after deleting soon becomes habitual. Instead of being a separate mental operation, typing the *Y* becomes part of the delete-file action; that is, you do not pause, check your intentions, and then type the *Y*. The computer system's query, intended to serve as a safety measure is rendered useless by habituation; it serves only to complicate the normal file-deletion process. The key idea is that *any confirmation step that elicits a fixed response soon becomes useless*. Designers who use such confirmations and administrators who think that the confirmations confer protection are unaware of the powerful habit-forming property of the cognitive unconscious.' [36], p. 22

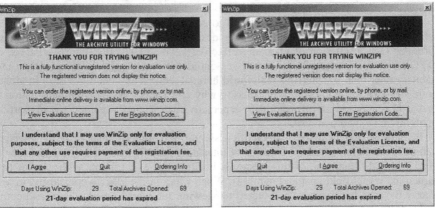

Fig. 2. Two versions of the initial screen in Winzip, which shows how the position of the 'I Agree' button change, so as to ensure that users pay a minimum amount of attention to the information on the screen

3   Users' Thinking Should be Supported by Recognizability, Stability, and Continuity

Mental activity is most effective when not interrupted and may be concentrated and flowing when the activity is challenging, yet well known. Mental activity is constantly changing as a result of inner and outer factors, for example physiological, psychological, and social—and of situation-specific factors: what has happened for the person up to now and what is the expectations for the near future. Thus mental activity is a very complex unity. A user interface should complement this changing complexity with recognizability, stability and continuity.

Thinking as a Stream of Thought

The metaphor of human thinking as a stream of thought is the result of James's own choice. He says [19], vol. I p. 239:

'Consciousness, then, does not appear to itself chopped up in bits. Such words as 'chain' or 'train' do not describe it fitly as it presents itself in the first instance. It is nothing jointed; it flows. A 'river' or a 'stream' are the metaphors by which it is most naturally described. In talking of it hereafter, let us call it the stream of thought, of consciousness, or of subjective life.'

Naur summarizes James's description of human thinking as a stream of thought in this way [26], p. 85:

'In William James's Principles of Psychology the stream of thought denotes something happening in all of our wake moments, to wit our experience of thinking and feeling. The stream of thought is known to every one of us through introspection, that is through our turning the attention inward, towards the way we experience our thoughts and feelings. What we may register through introspection is merely a picture of rough outlines. The stream of thought changes incessantly and has a vast number of details, most of which are present only vaguely, far more than may be seized by introspection.

The stream of thought happens independently of our desire. We may, when we so wish, more or less successfully think of something definite, but we cannot make the stream of thought cease, as experienced by every person suffering from insomnia.

The stream of thought may be described as something that flows, an incessantly changing, complicated mixture of something that may be denoted explicitly as images, sounds and bodily impressions, with additional vague moods and feelings. As stressed by James we do not in the stream of thought experience sharply delimited parts or elements of any kind. At each moment our thought is occupied by something that is complicated, but that is experienced as a whole. These wholes James calls thought objects [Our remark: also called 'mental objects']. Within each thought object one may distinguish between something more at the center, that which is the subject of our attention, and something that forms a fringe. [...] [E]very thought object embraces feelings, including those of the personal well-being, moods and bodily presence.

In its continued changing the stream of thought alternates between substantive states of relative repose and transitive states of rapid change. During the transitive states the changes of the thought objects happen so rapidly that they cannot be seized by introspection.

In the experience of the stream of thought the present moment has a duration of a few seconds. As one thought object fades away by being replaced by another one, it is retained in the fringe of the coming one. Every sudden impression is always experienced as a whole with what was there immediately before it happened.'

Key Questions

User interfaces should respect these traits of mental activity. The objects and actions that the user focus on when doing tasks should be clearly visible in the user interface. Users' thinking about their tasks is centred on a few task objects. Does the application make these task objects visible and easily accessible? Is the user interface of the application transparent, meaning that it does not demand attention on non-task related objects and actions? Recognizability of objects is a key priority; as is the relevance of user interface objects and actions to the users' tasks.

The description of the stream of thought makes it clear that interruptions, breaks, and pauses are characteristic of human mental activity. Another key question is how well the application supports the interruption and resumption of work. Most work done with computers is interrupted or discontinued for seconds, hours, or months. Does the application help users come back to their tasks, keeping available the situation from before the interruption or discontinuation? Does the user interface help the user establish part of the stream of thought experienced when the work was interrupted? Are the appearance and content similar to the previous occasion on which the program was used? Can the user resume interrupted or old work easily? Does the user have direct access to previously used files and directories?

Another key question concerns the changing of thought and the influence of an application on changes in our thoughts. Error messages, e-mail notifications or information on windows updates are likely to change users' stream of thought. Such messages should be used sparingly. System initiated dialogs are in principle harmful, when not about critical failures, and should be kept at a minimum. Often used functions should be easily locatable and have default values, so as to disturb the users' stream of thought as little as possible.

Another way of supporting the users' changing stream of thought is to provide stability and predictability in the interface. Key questions are whether changes in the interface are kept to a minimum and whether actions have stable and predictable results.

Examples

One example of poor support for the resuming of an interrupted task is found in the application SPSS (see www.spss.com), intended for statistical analyses. In SPSS, it is possible to specify certain statistical analyses with syntax. Such analyses are always run on a data file. However, SPSS does not recreate or save information about which data file a syntax file is associated with. So, when one loads a syntax file and tries to run it, error messages occur, and one has to figure out which file, possibly out of a number of files, you have made the syntax file for. A better solution would be to automatically run the syntax file on the data file it was created with or last executed.

A simple, yet effective, attempt to recreate part of the richness of the stream of thought when users return to resume interrupted work, is Raskin's design of the Canon Cat [36]. When the Canon Cat is started, the display immediately shows up as it was before work was suspended. Not only does this allow the user to start thinking about the task at hand while the system is booting. It also provides help in remembering and recreating the stream of thought as it was when work was interrupted.

The fragility of the stream of thought is not well protected in many user interfaces. E-mail notifications, instant messengers, news on demand, automatic spelling and grammar corrections are useful at times, but may also disrupt concentrated work. Research on instant messengers, for example, has documented the harmful effects of interruptions on task completion time [8]. As a personal note, one of the authors of this paper has recently removed all notifications of arriving e-mails from his computer. Even the .5 cm $\times$.5 cm icon in the lower right corner of the screen that show the arrival of new e-mail could create an intense feeling of urge to check the e-mail—which would initially be in the fringe of the current object of attention, but eventually would lead the author to start of the e-mail program. This seemed especially to happen when that author was struggling with a difficult task. In general, we find that most user interfaces fail to support shifting between what we experience as two phases of work: concentrated working, where interruptions and distractions are detrimental, and explorative working, where a free flow of associations, inspirations, breaks, and even interruptions can be useful.

An example of the dynamics of thinking that is closely related to the stream of thought is found in information retrieval studies concerning changes in relevance judgments of documents. One study [9] showed that the order in which subjects viewed document descriptions influenced the subjects' perception of the relevance of those descriptions. While this effect in part may be due to the categorical rating scales used, a psychological explanation is also possible. When looking at document descriptions, the themes of the previous descriptions will be in the fringe of the subject's mental object. Those fringes will influence the perception of the task and the judgment of the current document description. Thus, different orderings of documents will give different relevance judgments; significant differences in relevance judgments were found even between random orderings of the documents to be judged. Thus, relevance judgments seem to be dynamic in a sense closely related to the metaphor of the stream of thought.

An often-added interface feature that helps coming back to an interrupted task is a list of recently used files (see Fig. 3), even though such file names are often heavily truncated. Such information often makes sense to users. A similar idea is to save the entire layout of an application, so that the application will look similar next time it is run.

The recognizability of central objects and actions in the users' task are recommended in many methods and tools for systems development. One example is Ben Shneiderman's Object-Action Interface Model, [38] p. 61, which suggests that objects and actions from the task domain should form the basis of the objects and actions in the interface. Such recommendations are coherent with the description of thinking as a stream of thought in which objects that the user is acquainted with are anchored.

4   Support Users' Associations with Effective Means of Focusing within a Stable Context

Awareness as a Jumping Octopus

'The mental activity is like a jumping octopus in a pile of rags', says Naur [25] and continues to illustrate the dynamics of thinking:

'This metaphor is meant to indicate the way in which the state of consciousness at any moment has a field of central awareness, that part of the rag pile in which the body of the octopus is located. The arms of the octopus stretch out into other parts of the rag pile, those parts presenting themselves vaguely, as the fringes of the central field. [...] The jumping about of the octopus indicates how the state of consciousness changes from one moment to the next.'

The rags of the pile may through focusing come to the field of central awareness. Here associations play a central role. On this Naur [26], p. 11, summarizes from James:

'One object of thought is replaced habitually by the next. We say then that the two thoughts are associated or that the next thought appears through its association to the first one. [...] [W]hat enters into the association of thoughts is not elementary 'ideas', but complicated *thought objects* which are experienced as wholes but each of which includes more central parts and a *fringe* of vague connections and *feelings*.'

Associations may happen by contiguity and by similarity. Association by contiguity is essentially a matter of habit formation. James [19], vol. I, p. 561 says:

'[...] objects once experienced together tend to become associated in the imagination, so that when any one of them is thought of, the others are likely to be thought of also, in the same order of sequence or coexistence as before. [...] it expresses merely a phenomenon of mental habit, the most natural way of accounting for it is to conceive it as a result of the laws of habit in the nervous system.'

Fig. 3. Support for resuming work. This screen-shot shows the list of recently used files in Adobe Acrobat reader. This way it is efficient for users to come back to recently used files

Association by similarity is:

'[...] association between thought objects that have become connected in the thought merely by having the same abstract property in common, in other words by being similar in some respect.' [26], p. 12

Association by similarity plays an important role in reasoning. Reasoning is concerned with solving problems, or answering questions, related to situations involving certain known things, having certain known properties, in which the person cannot reach the solution or the answer by direct association from the known properties. James explains how successful reasoning builds upon the person's noticing and attending to certain definite properties of the situation at hand, to wit such properties that point to a way of reaching the goal by direct association. James makes clear how reasoning in this sense is a decisive factor in human inventiveness and discovery, including that of scholars and scientists, see [27].

Key Questions

One key question concerns which associations users create in response to user interface objects. Such associations can happen by physical proximity, habitually associations of words, relation to central task objects, etc. Do users associate interface elements with the actions and objects they represent? Can words and labels in the interface be expected to create useful associations for the user? Are contiguity and similarity used in the graphical layout to help the user to group and understand tasks?

User interfaces should help users keep focus and should respect associations that make users wanting to switch between different parts of the interface. Key questions are: Does the user interface force the user into a specific order of tasks? Are modal dialog boxes used more than necessary? Can the user switch flexibly between different parts of the interface?

In general, our thinking when using computers has a main focus and an associated host of feelings, vague connections, associations, etc. The main focus will often correspond to part of the user interface. User interfaces should respect this. Do not expect the user to focus only on specific parts of the user interface. For example, when users go back and forth between web-pages in order to correct information, they are not likely to notice that information is deleted or changed.

Examples

Modal dialog boxes prevent the user from switching to potentially relevant information—in Microsoft Word, for example, it is not possible to switch back to the document to look for a good file name once the 'save as ...' dialog has began.

The metaphor of the octopus can be illuminated by recent studies of awareness, e.g. [11,14]. Common to these studies is an aspiration to design for peripheral awareness, to design also for the fringes of the octopus so to speak. As an example consider Grudin's study of how multiple monitors are used [14]. Grudin found that among 18 users who used multiple monitors simultaneously, the multiple monitors were not used as additional space, but to partition the information used. Users would for example delegate secondary tasks such as debugging windows in a programming environment to the second monitor, and some users would have e-mail, news alerts, and instant messengers on the secondary monitor. Grudin's study is coherent with and supportive of the metaphor of awareness in two important ways. First, users employ the degree of attention they give information to dived their work between monitors. Less important information is in the periphery of the eye and thereby to some extent in the fringes of the current mental object. This may reflect how users introspectively realize that some information sources may in subtle ways distract us, but that they may be useful for creating fringes. Second, Grudin's work and other recent papers on awareness show opportunities for designing for peripheral attention, and even for in-attentive use of computers. It is evident from the metaphor of the octopus that the fringes of mental objects form a large part of our thinking—and this should be taken into account when designing.

The characteristics of awareness and the association of objects thought of with other objects are not unfamiliar descriptions of human thought in HCI. Already Van-nevar Bush in his vision of the Memex [4] exemplify this:

'When data of any sort are placed in storage, they are filed alphabetically or nu-merically, and information is found (when it is) by tracing it down from subclass to subclass. It can be in only one place, unless duplicates are used; one has to have rules as to which path will locate it, and the rules are cumbersome. Having found one item, moreover, one has to emerge from the system and re-enter on a new path.

The human mind does not work that way. It operates by association. With one item in its grasp, it snaps instantly to the next that is suggested by the association of thoughts, in accordance with some intricate web of trails carried by the cells of the brain. It has other characteristics, of course; trails that are not frequently fol-lowed are prone to fade, items are not fully permanent, memory is transitory. Yet the speed of action, the intricacy of trails, the detail of mental pictures, is awe-inspiring beyond all else in nature. Man cannot hope fully to duplicate this mental process artificially, but he certainly ought to be able to learn from it.'

However, as pointed out by Wendy Hall at the Hypertext'01 Conference, links that take the user to web pages associated with the link description are fairly uncommon at the web [15]. In hypertext research, such links are called associative or referential links [7], as opposed to for example navigational or organizational links. According to Hall, less than 1% of links on the World Wide Web are associative: the rest are pre-dominantly navigational links. On one side this suggests that Bush's warning has been taken seriously—human awareness and association are not directly modelled on the WWW. On the other side, we feel that the lack of associative links might suggest that designers have paid too little attention to awareness, associations, and how to craft links that use this fundamental trait of human thinking.

As an example of a notion in HCI that may become clearer from the metaphor of the octopus, we would like to briefly discuss information scent. Information scent re-fers to:

'... the (imperfect) perception of the value, cost, or access path of information sources obtained from proximal cues, such as bibliographic citations, WWW links, or icons representing the sources' [33]

In HCI this notion has recently received much attention in relation to web design [5]. From our perspective, information scent is the ability of proximal cues to create in the mind of the user associations related to the content looked for. The degree to which WWW links or icons have 'information scent' is only a matter of the associations they create for individual users. In some studies of information scent, e.g. [34], an information scent score is developed. Subjects are given the top levels of a hierarchical link structure and the information scent score is the proportion of subjects who correctly identify that a certain link contains the answer to some task. Thus, subjects assess the links from the associations created in relation to the task. The second aspect of the definition of information scent—the cost of accessing information sources—is related to habit. We most often follow our habits in traversing information structures rather than pondering the cost of certain ways of navigation. Information scent may in this way be easily understood through the metaphors of awareness and habit.

The terminology used in a computer application is sometimes technical and obscure; for some users such terminology will if they read it fail to create useful associations.

5   Support Changing and Incomplete Utterances

Human utterances are often vaguely related to the intentions behind the utterances. In addition, humans use a variety of ways for expressing similar intentions. Applications should be designed so as to respect this changing and incomplete character of all utterances, whether they are mouse movement, voice input, typing, gestures or other means of input. Special care should be taken when applications use utterances to infer the insights and feelings behind them.

Utterances as Splashes over Water

'A person's utterances relate to the person's insights as the splashes over the waves to the rolling sea below', says Naur [25] and continues:

'This metaphor is meant to indicate the ephemeral character of our verbal utterances, their being formed, not as a copy of insight already in verbal form, but as a result of an activity of formulation taking place at the moment of utterance.'

The metaphor also emphasizes how utterances are vague and incomplete expressions of the complexity of a person's current mental object, in the same way as the splashes tell little about the sea below.

Key Questions

Applications should accommodate the variety and flexibility in which humans express themselves. For example, are different ways of expressing the same information (such as centimeters, inches, points, etc. as input for length) available? If file names, logins, naming, short-cuts, or other user utterances are part of the user interface, users should be supported in recalling which utterance they last used. If a fixed format or content of an utterance for some reason is needed, the application should help the user as far as possible. For example, if calendar dates should be input in a special format, that format should be exemplified and fields coded to suggest the order in which to input days and months, and the number of digits required when entering a year.

Another key question concerns how the application interprets users' utterances. What inferences about user intention and insight are drawn, and how do these affect the interaction? Does the application make a wider interpretation of user input than warranted? Are interpretations made clear and are they easily understandable? Is feedback given about what the system is doing as a result of a user utterance? The last point is especially important for utterances that require interpretation on the part of the system.

Examples

One implication of the metaphor of utterances as splashes over the water is that we must expect users to describe the same objects and functions incompletely and in a variety of ways. Furnas et al. [10] investigated the diversity in words used for describing commands and everyday objects. On the average, two participants described the same command or object by the same term with less than 20% probability. The most popular name was chosen only in 15-35% of the cases. Furnas et al.'s suggestion for relieving this problem is called the unlimited alias approach. Instead of using a fixed set of words for commands and functions, the unlimited alias approach lets users enter any term they want. If the term is not in the range of terms initially suggested by the designer of the system—which the data of Furnas et al. and the metaphor suggest it often will not be—the system may interactively suggest appropriate commands or object names. This approach is coherent with the metaphor and uses interactivity to clarify the intentions of the user. On the other hand, the approach partly goes against the metaphor of habit formation.

We believe that the relation between queries made on the WWW and what users are looking for may be made easier understandable by use of the metaphor. Queries on the WWW are on the average 2.2 words long [20]. However, such short queries cannot possibly reflect all aspects of the pages users are looking for, nor can they reflect the myriads of interests, questions, etc. that may suddenly become the locus of attention when triggered by otherwise irrelevant web pages. In information retrieval, the difficulty in interpreting the intention (or information need) behind the queries has long been recognized as problematic, as have the difficulty of expressing one's information need in the first place [3]. Harter [16] has gone so far as to suggest that the information need is indeed our full mental constitution—which is impossible to express in a few words or queries. This is in accordance with the metaphor of utterances as splashes over the water and respects the complexity of mental objects, as described by the stream of thought and the octopus metaphors.

There are numerous examples of user interfaces that do not respect the metaphor of utterances. Many of these involve systems that try to predict, given a few utterances, the needs and wishes of the user—something that is unlikely to succeed given the ephemeral and incomplete nature of utterances. One example is the attempt of the Office Assistant in Microsoft Word to infer which kind of document the user is writing given one or two words from that document. Another is the annoyance of screen savers or sleep modes of laptops, if they are initiated by interpreting the lack of user input as a lack of user work with the application.

If the application interprets users' utterances, then it should make the interpretation clear. This helps the user understand subsequent output. One simple example of this is the use of feedback when searching at Google, see Fig. 4. When the users' input is interpreted, and in this case partly ignored, an explanation is given.

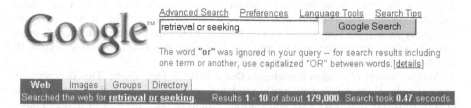

Fig. 4. Example of feedback when interpreting user input. When using the term 'or' in a search, the Google website (www.google.com) will give an explanation of the interpretation made of that term

6 Users Should Not Have to Rely on Complete or Accurate Knowledge-Design for Incompleteness

Human knowing, for example of tasks and user interfaces, is constantly changing. In addition, much of what we know is incomplete, inconsistent, and even seriously flawed. Applications should respect these traits of human knowing and take them into account as far as possible. Conversely, users should not have to rely on complete or accurate knowledge about applications.

Human Knowing as a Site of Buildings

Human knowing is like a site of buildings in an incomplete state of construction, developed through maintenance and rebuilding. In Naur's [25] formulation:
    'A person's insight is like a site of buildings in incomplete state of construction. This metaphor is meant to indicate the mixture of order and inconsistency characterizing any person's insight. These insights group themselves in many ways, the groups being mutually dependent by many degrees, some closely, some slightly. As an incomplete building may be employed as shelter, so the insights had by a person in any particular field may be useful even if restricted in scope. And as the unfinished buildings of a site may conform to no plan, so a person may go through life having incoherent insights.'

Key Questions

One key questions concerns whether both novices and experts can work effectively with the application, given that their knowing about the application and task domain may be very different. This concerns also to what degree applications support users in developing an understanding of that application. In general, users can only be expected to develop knowing about an application to at most the level that will enable them to complete the task. Users will therefore have insecure and shaky knowledge about a range of applications.

Other key questions are the following. Can users start using the application immediately or is it required that the user pay attention to technical or configuration details? Can the application be used without knowing every detail of it? Can simple tasks be completed in a simple way? Do more complex tasks build on the knowledge users may have from simple tasks? The last two questions concern whether all users can effectively accomplish simple tasks and whether effective habits (see section 0) may be developed.

Another aspect of human knowing is that it is often incomplete. This is especially true of applications that are seldomly used, and of knowing about the internal workings of hardware and software. Applications should respect this trait of human knowing. Key questions concerning this aspect are as follows. Are the users supported in remembering and understanding information and relations in the application? Is feedback given to ensure correct interpretations? Are error situations handled in a graceful way that supports the users' possibly limited understanding of the error?

Examples

Similar to the advice of designing for incomplete knowing is the HCI maxim "support recognition over recall" [38]. One example of this principle in use is given in Fig. 5.

Examples where the metaphor of a person's knowing is not respected are easy to find. Systems that require a full understanding of the system before they may be used are cases in point. An example is described in Chen & Dhar's study [6] of an online library catalogue. They observe how 30 subjects take wrong actions in using the system, how they use wrong query terms, and how they use a sub-optimal procedure for accomplishing tasks. The faulty actions arise from the subjects' misconceptions about the topic they are searching for, about the way the online catalogue works, and about the nature of the classification system used. Each subject displayed at least one misconception. First of all this shows that even for a common task like searching a library system, the subjects' knowing about the program was incomplete. Second, Chen &

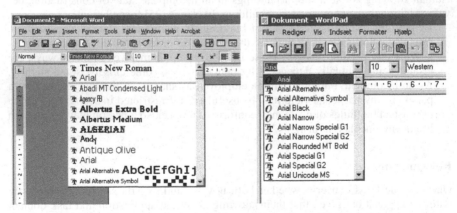

Fig. 5. Two ways of specifying fonts. The left screen shot shows Word, which succeeds in supporting an incomplete knowing of the appearance of various fonts. The right screen shot shows WordPad, which requires the user to know the appearance of fonts or to try them out

Dhar's results show that the design of the online catalogue violated the metaphor of the site of buildings in several ways. As one example, the system only recognizes official Library of Congress subject headings, which in essence requires the subjects to have a complete and precise understanding of how their problem relate to the official terms. The lack of support for cross-referencing and inferring correct headings worsens this.

Another example of ignorance of the idea of the developing and incomplete nature of human knowing, is the use of technical information in a number of applications that are to be used by users who do not know the technical details of how a program works. A number of applications seriously flawed in this way is shown on http://www.iarchitect.com/, Fig. 6 shows one example accompanied by the following explanation:

> "*Microsoft Word 6.0* when asked to open a document from an unknown version of *Word* displays the above message. *Word*'s conversion utility seems to be asking, "I think it's a Word '97 document, but it might be one of these other types. What do you think?" **How the #$%@& would I know!** This is the result of a confirmation-happy programmer. The conversion utility knows exactly what type of file it is (the raw file contains two explicit references to the type of file), yet the program wants the *user* to confirm the program's ability to read these references. The user, on the other hand, unless he or she created the file, has absolutely no knowledge of the file type. By needlessly asking the user, the program needlessly creates uncertainty and an opportunity for the user to cause an error."

Mental models have been extensively discussed in HCI. Consider as an example Norman's [31] description of the use of calculators. He argues that the use of calculators is characterized by users' incomplete understanding of the calculators, by the instability of the understanding, by superstitions about how calculators work, and by the lack of boundaries in the users' understanding of one calculator and another. These empirical observations by Norman are coherent with the ideas expressed by the metaphor of knowing. In summary, the library catalogue and the use of calculators show that users solve the actual tasks despite inconsistencies and incompleteness of their knowing. Conversely, systems that require a precise and complete understanding are often awkward to use.

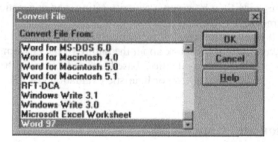

Fig. 6. Dialog asking the user to specify the program a document was created with. One problem with this dialog is that it assumes that user's technical knowledge is complete and that users actually know with which system the file was created

504   K. Hornbæk and E. Frøkjær

7   How to Do a Metaphor-Based Evaluation

The basic procedure when using the metaphors for evaluating user interfaces is to inspect the interface, noting when it supports or violates the aspects of human thinking captured in the metaphors and the key questions. This enables the evaluators to identify potential usability problems.

More concretely, one way to do an evaluation after having read section 2 to 6 about metaphors of human thinking is to follow the steps below.

1. Familiarize yourself with the application.
2. Find three tasks that users typically would do with the application. These tasks may be thought up, may be based on observations of users, or may be based on scenarios used in systems development.
3. Try to do the tasks with the application. Identify major problems found in this way. Use the key questions and the metaphors to find usability problems.
4. Do the tasks again. This time, take the perspective of each of the metaphors at a time and work through the tasks. Use the key questions and the metaphors to find usability problems.
5. If more time is left, find some more tasks. See if new problems arise in step 3 and 4 for those tasks. Iterate step 3 and 4 until each new task reveals few new problems or until no time is left.

The above procedure is normally carried out by one evaluator. Several studies have documented that different evaluators find different problems [18,28]. Therefore, it may be useful to combine lists of problems with those found by other evaluators who have also inspected the application using the metaphors. The evaluations must be carried out individually before results are discussed and combined.

The duration of an evaluation based on the metaphors will normally be between one and two hours.

The evaluation will result in a list of usability problems, each described with reference to the application and to the metaphor that was used to uncover the problem. The usability problems may then be given a severity rating, and suggestions may be made as to how to correct the problem.

We consider it likely that different evaluation methods will find different usability problems and give different feedback about the nature of the problems. Evaluators are well advised to combine the evaluation based on metaphors with other evaluation methods, such as think aloud [17,22] or heuristic evaluation [28,29].

8   Discussion and Conclusion

This proposal of a new inspection technique must be critically evaluated from at least the following points of view:

1. Can the MOT-technique be used effectively and efficiently in revealing important usability problems of new designs? And if so—what kind of training is necessary for the evaluators? In different stages of system development, how should the evaluation process be organized? Does the technique work better if adjusted or

supplemented for specific contexts of usage, e.g. types of devices, interaction styles, or types of users?

2. Do the evaluators consider the study and training of the MOT-technique to be relevant, easy and interesting? Are the five metaphors well chosen, individually and combined?

3. After acquisition, how do the evaluators and system developers use the technique in their design work—is the MOT-technique convenient and adequate and how is it combined with other design and evaluation techniques?

We are far from being able to answer these questions. Many empirical studies involving other researchers, system developers, and users of IT-based devices need to be completed. However, a few initial answers can be reported.

Ad 1: In a major HCI evaluation experiment, designed as project work for 87 computing science bachelor students, a medium complex web application was investigated for usability problems using the MOT-technique and the heuristic evaluation technique [28]. The effectiveness of the two techniques showed similar results and to our surprise the students spent a little less time to do the evaluation with the MOT-technique than with heuristic evaluation.

In an advanced course on HCI for computing science master students, all 17 students chose in their final project to use the metaphors of the MOT-technique in their discussions of selected HCI phenomena described in the scientific literature. Their projects covered a wide range of issues such as new interaction devices, Computer Supported Cooperative Work, information visualization, heuristic evaluation, cognitive walkthrough, GOMS, and WIMP interfaces. The projects showed that the students were able to make original and comprehensive use of the metaphors.

Ad 2: The master students mentioned above found the study of the metaphors of the MOT-technique very interesting, but not easy. James's ideas about thinking, especially thinking as a stream of thought and thought objects, did call for a demanding and radical new thinking of ideas that the students had developed over many years, e.g. about consciousness/sub-consciousness, cognitive/mental models, and conceptualization. During the course, the master students seemed to find the five metaphors of the MOT-technique well chosen and useful in the discussions of psychological aspects of HCI phenomena. Only the jumping octopus metaphor of awareness did cause some 3-4 students a little trouble, especially before it was used concretely in discussions. These students found the picture of the jumping octopus in a pile of rags to be too unrealistic as a "serious" vehicle of expression.

Ad 3: We have not yet carried out any studies that tell us about the usability of the MOT-technique in industry. In the near future we hope to be able to do experiments with system developers and HCI experts. Compared to students, experiments with developers and HCI experts will raise new kinds of challenges, e.g. that we have to "detrain" old habits and ways of thinking before the new ideas in the MOT-technique can be trained. Instead of teaching the metaphors as an inspection technique, it might be more effective to teach developers and HCI experts the metaphors of human thinking as a possible new design vehicle. Afterwards, it can be studied if and how the metaphors are used in design and evaluation activities.

A related question is whether usability problems uncovered by use of the MOT-technique will support system developers better in how to re-design compared to other inspection techniques.

Acknowledgements. We wish to thank Peter Naur for his ongoing sharing of ideas leading us to this paper and his permission to quote extensively from his writings.

References

1. Baars, B. J.: A Cognitive Theory of Consciousness. Cambridge University Press, Cambridge (1988)
2. Baars, B. J.: In the Theater of Consciousness. Oxford University Press, New York (1997)
3. Bates, M.: The Design of Browsing and Berrypicking Techniques for the on-Line Search Interface. Online Review. 13 5 (1989) 407–431
4. Bush, V.: As We May Think. The Atlantic Monthly. July (1945)
5. Card, S., Pirolli, P., Van Der Wege, M., Morrison, J. B., Reeder, R. W., Schradley, P. K., & Boshart, J.: Information Scent as a Driver of Web Behavior Graphs: Results of a Protocol Analysis Method for Web Usability. In: Proceedings of CHI 2001 (2001) 498–505
6. Chen, H. & Dhar, V.: User Misconceptions of Information Retrieval Systems. International Journal of Man-Machine Studies. 32 (1990) 673–692
7. Conklin, J.: Hypertext: An Introduction and Survey. IEEE Computer. Sep (1987) 17–41
8. Cutrell, E., Czerwinski, M., & Horvitz, E.: Notification, Disruption, and Memory: Effects of Messaging Interruptions on Memory and Performance. In: Proc. of Interact 2001 (2001)
9. Eisenberg, M. & Barry, C.: Order Effects: A Study of the Possible Influence of Presentation Order on User Judgments of Document Relevance. Journal of the American Society for Information Science. 39 5 (1988) 293–300
10. Furnas, G. W., Landauer, T. K., Gomez, L. M., & Dumais, S. T.: The Vocabulary Problem in Human-System Communication. Communications of the ACM. 30 11 (1987) 964–971
11. Greenberg, S. & Rouding, M.: The Notification Collage: Posting Information to Public and Personal Displays. In: Proceedings of CHI 2001 ACM Press (2001) 514–521
12. Gregory, R. L.: Eye and Brain. Princeton University Press, Princeton, NJ (1997)
13. Grudin, J.: The Case Against User Interface Consistency. CACM. 32 10 (1989) 1164–1173
14. Grudin, J.: Partitioning digital worlds: focal and peripheral awareness in multiple monitor use. In: Proceedings of CHI 2001 (2001) 458–465
15. Hall, W.: Mostly Linkless. In: Proceedings of Hypertext'01 ACM Press (2001) 3
16. Harter, S. P.: Psychological Relevance and Information Science. Journal of the American Society for Information Science. 43 (1992) 602–615
17. Helms Jørgensen, A.: Thinking-Aloud in User Interface Design: a Method Promoting Cognitive Ergonomics. Ergonomics. 33 4 (1990) 501–507
18. Hertzum, M. & Jacobsen, N. E.: The Evaluator Effect: A Chilling Fact About Usability Evaluation Methods. Int. Journal of Human-Computer Interaction. 13 (2001) 421–443
19. James, W.: Principles of Psychology. Henry Holt & Co. (1890)
20. Jansen, B. J., Spink, A., Bateman, J., & Saracevic, T.: Real Life Information Retrieval: A Study of User Queries on the Web. SIGIR Forum. 32 1 (1998) 5–17
21. Lewis, C., Polson, P., Wharton, C., & Rieman, J.: Testing a Walkthrough Methodology for Theory-Based Design of Walk-Up-and-Use Interfaces. In: Proc. of CHI'90 (1990) 235–242
22. Molich, R.: Brugervenlige edb-systemer (in Danish). Teknisk Forlag (1994)

23. Naur P.: Human knowing, language, and discrete structures. (1988) In: Computing: A Human Activity, ACM Press/Addison Wesley (1992)
24. Naur, P.: Knowing and the Mystique of Logic and Rules. Kluwer Academic Publishers, Dordrecht, The Netherlands (1995)
25. Naur, P.: CHI and Human Thinking. In: Proceedings of NordiCHI 2000 (2000)
26. Naur, P.: Anti-philosophical Dictionary. naur.com Publishing (2001)
27. Naur, P.: Psykologi i videnskabelig rekonstruktion (Eng. Psychology in Scientific-Scholarly Reconstruction) (2001)
28. Nielsen, J.: Usability Engineering. Academic Press, San Diego CA (1993)
29. Nielsen, J. & Mack, R. L.: Usability Inspection Methods. Wiley and Sons Inc. (1994)
30. Nielsen, J. & Molich, R.: Heuristic evaluation of user interfaces. In: Proc. of CHI'90 (1990) 249–256
31. Norman D.: Some Observations on Mental Models. In: Gentner, D. & Stevens, A.L. (Eds.), Mental Models, Erlbaum, Hillsdale NJ (1983), 7–14.
32. Pinelle, D. & Gutwin, C.: Groupware walkthrough: adding context to groupware usability evaluation . In: Proceedings of CHI 2002 (2002) 455–462.
33. Pirolli, P. & Card, S.: Information Foraging. Psychological Review. 106 4 (1999) 643–675.
34. Pirolli, P., Card, S., & Van Der Wege, M.: The Effect of Information Scent on Searching Information Visualizations of Large Tree Structures. In: Proc. of AVI'2000 (2000) 161–172
35. Preece, J., Rogers, Y., & Sharp, H.: Interaction Design. John Wiley & Sons (2002)
36. Raskin, J.: The Humane Interface: New Directions for Designing Interactive Systems. Addison-Wesley, Reading MA (2000)
37. Sears, A. & Shneiderman, B.: Split Menus: Effectively Using Selection Frequency to Organize Menus. ACM Transactions on Computer-Human Interaction. 1 1 (1994) 27–51
38. Shneiderman, B.: Designing the User Interface. Addison-Wesley, Reading, MA (1998)
39. Smith, S. L. & Mosier, J. N.: Guidelines for designing user interfaces for software. ESD-TR-86-278 (1986) The MITRE Corporation
40. Somberg, B. L.: A Comparison of Rule-Based and Positionally Constant Arrangements of Computer Menu Items. In: Proceedings of CHI+GI'87 (1987) 255–260
41. Spencer, R.: The Streamlined Cognitive Walkthrough Method, Working Around Social Constraints Encountered in a Software Development Company. In: Proceedings of CHI'2000 (2000) 353–359
42. Wharton C. et al.: The cognitive walkthrough method: a practitioner's guide. In: Nielsen, J. & Mack, R. Usability Inspection Methods, John Wiley & Sons, New York NY (1994), 105–140

Evaluating Sonified Rapid Serial Visual Presentation: An Immersive Reading Experience on a Mobile Device

Mikael Goldstein[1], Gustav Öquist[2], and Staffan Björk[3]

[1] Ericsson Research, Usability & Interaction Lab,
Torshamnsgatan 23, 164 80 Kista, Sweden
mikael.goldstein@era.ericsson.se
[2] Uppsala University, Department of Linguistics,
PO Box 527, 751 20 Uppsala, Sweden
gustav@stp.ling.uu.se
[3] Interactive Institute, PLAY Studio,
PO Box 620, 405 30 Göteborg, Sweden
staffan.bjork@interactiveinstitute.se

Abstract. Can the addition of sound enhance the reading experience on small screens when using Rapid Serial Visual Presentation (RSVP) for dynamic text presentation? In this paper we introduce Sonified RSVP and report findings from a usability evaluation where the experience of reading texts enhanced with nomic auditory icons was evaluated. At a comfortable pace 12 subjects read long Swedish texts of equal difficulty with and without the addition of sound on a handheld device. Reading speed (M≈217 wpm) and comprehension (M≈58% correct) did not differ significantly between the two conditions. The evaluation revealed a rather high task load for both conditions but no significant differences. However, the subjective rating of Immersion was rated significantly higher for the Sonified condition. Causes, implications and directions for further work are discussed based on these findings.

1   Introduction

With the advent of the mobile Internet and the ensuing increase in information resources available to mobile devices, such as Personal Digital Assistants (PDAs) and cellular phones, mobile users will eventually have access to the same amount of information as the stationary users. The fact that the mobile devices are much smaller does however constrain the usefulness of this advancement. The limited input capabilities make them primarily suitable for information retrieval, but the limited screen space currently constitutes a bottleneck for such appliances [9]. Since it is the customer's demand for small devices that sets these constraints they are likely to remain in the future as well. This notion, combined with the fact that readability has long been considered important as even small improvements can ease reading for large groups of people [19], has made the issues concerning the reading experience on small screens progressively more important for mobile usability.

N. Carbonell, C. Stephanidis (Eds.): User Interfaces for All, LNCS 2615, pp. 508–523, 2003.

Reading from small screens differs in many ways from reading both on paper and on large screens. The average reading speed on paper for English text is around 300 words per minute (wpm) [25], whereas early research on screen reading has revealed that reading speed decreases by 20-30% when reading on large screens [27]. As screen resolution has improved and people have gotten more used to them, readability on large screens has become more or less equal to paper [30]. The evolution in readability on small screens is however not likely to follow the same pattern. Screen resolution will surely improve and thus improve legibility, but decreased readability will most likely remain intrinsic to limited screen space [8].

The quandary with the size-readability trade-off does however presuppose that the text is presented in the traditional page format with a spatial layout. One approach to overcome the size constraints may be to design interfaces that utilize the possibilities offered by mobile devices to trade space for time [5]. Rapid Serial Visual Presentation (RSVP) and Leading are the two major techniques that have been proposed for dynamic text presentation [27]. Leading, or the Times Square Format, scrolls the text on one line horizontally across the screen whereas RSVP presents the text as chunks of words or characters in rapid succession at a single visual location (Fig. 1). Both formats offer a way of reading texts on a very limited screen space [27, 28]. Comparisons between the formats have so far been inconclusive [20, 23], but at normal reading speeds RSVP appears to be more efficient. From a physiological perspective RSVP also seems more *natural* to use, the reason for this is that the text moves successively rather than continuously [43].

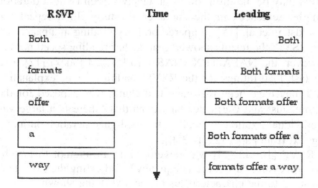

Fig. 1. Snapshots over time of text presentation via RSVP (left) compared to Leading (right)

Since dynamic presentation of text offers a potential improvement in readability on small screens it is important to explore its possibilities. In this paper we focus on the possible enhancement of the RSVP format by adding sounds to the text. First, a background to previous work on RSVP is presented together with motivation for the development of Sonified RSVP. This is followed by a description of a prototype for Sonified RSVP called Bailando. The design of the usability evaluation is then presented along with the experimental results. A discussion based on the findings together with possible implications for future work concludes the paper.

510   M. Goldstein, G. Öquist, and S. Björk

2   RSVP

RSVP originated as a tool for studying reading behavior [10, 13, 35] but has lately received more attention as a presentation technique with a promise of optimizing reading efficiency, especially when screen space is limited [15, 21, 36, 44]. The reason for the interest is that the reading process works a little different when RSVP is used and that it requires much smaller screen space than traditional text presentation. Reading a text with a spatial layout, like this page, consists of three distinct visual tasks: processing information in fixed gazes or *fixations*, performing *saccadic* eye movements to move between fixations, and moving to the next line using *return sweeps*. Whereas the saccadic eye movements and return sweeps are performed very quickly (~40 ms and ~55 ms respectively), fixations take longer time (~230 ms for fast readers and ~330 ms for average readers) [37]. RSVP displays the text as small chunks successively within a small area, which is assumed to minimize the need for saccadic eye movements and return sweeps [35, 38]. Moreover, RSVP is thought to increase reading speed since the format prevents re-reading of adjacent text segments. More important for mobile usability is however that RSVP reduces the need for physical interaction, in the form of paging or scrolling, when reading from small screens [43].

Juola et al. [20] found text comprehension between RSVP and traditional presentation techniques equal whereas Masson [26] found that comprehension of RSVP presented text was poorer than for page-presented text. A possible explanation for the different results may be the insertion of an empty screen (with a duration of 200-300 ms) between the sentences in the Juola et al. study. In a repeated-measurement evaluation, Goldstein et al. [15] compared ordinary reading in a paper book to reading on a PDA via RSVP; the results showed that neither reading speed nor comprehension differed. However, the NASA-TLX (NASA Task Load Index) [17] revealed significantly higher task load ratings for the RSVP conditions. One explanation to the high cognitive load may have been that each text chunk was exposed for the same fixed duration of time. Just and Carpenter has found that "there is a large variation in the duration of individual fixations as well as the total gaze duration on individual words" when reading text from paper [22, p. 330].

Adaptive RSVP [16, 43, 44] was developed as an attempt to match the reader's cognitive text processing pace more adequately by adjusting the exposure time of each chunk with respect to the characteristics of the text being shown. In an evaluation of adaptive RSVP, where all conditions were performed on a PDA, Öquist and Goldstein [44] found that adaptation could indeed decrease task load for most factors. The evaluation also showed that RSVP might increase reading speed compared to traditional text presentation on mobile devices. In an experiment with a similar approach, Castelhano and Muter [6] found that the introduction of punctuation pauses, interruption pauses and pauses at clause boundaries made the RSVP format significantly more liked. Although these evaluations are not fully comparable they all seem to indicate that the RSVP format has some potential but also some flaws that yet remains to be resolved. Nevertheless, dynamic presentation formats like RSVP also have some additional advantages over traditional text presentation that can be used to enhance the reading experience.

3   Sonified RSVP

One of the less explored properties of the RSVP format is its capability to present other media simultaneously with exact timing in respect to the text being read. The advantage of adding sound to visual text presentation, compared to using a text-to-speech engine generating audio output, is mainly retrieval speed. Listening to a text read aloud in English is comfortable at a rate of around 150 wpm [42], whereas silent self-paced reading is roughly twice as fast as that [25]. Adding sound to a text or a picture is generally considered not to impose any harmful effects. When watching a movie, sound is even considered to be a mandatory attribute and movies with sound are generally more popular than those without. Does the same line of reasoning apply for adding sound to the text being read?

3.1   Multimodal Aspects

According to Paivio's dual coding theory [33], information is processed through two generally independent channels. One channel processes verbal information (oral or written) while the other channel processes non-verbal communication (e.g. illustrations, pictures, melodies, or ambient sounds). Paivio stated "Human cognition is unique in that it has become specialized for dealing simultaneously with language and with nonverbal objects and events" [34, p. 53]. The use of both channels simultaneously to convey information is called referential processing and has been shown to have an additive effect on recall [34]. Students instructed with redundant multimedia generally performed better when the multimedia supports referential processing [31]. However, adding a redundant modality does not always show the expected beneficial effects. In fact, the addition of an exact audio replica to visually presented text instructions generated negative effects on learning due to excessive working memory load. Kalyuga [24] found that concurrent duplication (auditory explanation appearing simultaneously with the same visually presented text) of information using the different modes of presentation increased the risk of overloading working memory, resulting in a negative effect on learning. Based on these findings, Sonified RSVP [14, 16] has been introduced as a way of augmenting the visual communication channel of RSVP with non-verbal sounds.

3.2   Sounds Suitable for Sonified RSVP

Auditory icons is one form of non-verbal sounds that has been introduced as a way of creating intuitive links to objects or actions occurring within a interface by linking these to natural sounds. Gaver [11] identified three different types of auditory icons: Symbolic, metaphorical and nomic. Symbolic icons are based on social conventions, e.g., using applause for approval, while metaphorical icons use similarities to convey meaning. Nomic auditory icons are straight depictions of the information to be conveyed, e.g. using the sound of a paper being crumbled and being thrown into a trashcan when a file is dragged to the trashcan icon on the desktop.

An alternative to using auditory icons are Earcons, structured sounds introduced by Brewster et al. [3] as a substitute for graphical icons when navigating a hierarchy of nodes in a Graphical User Interface (GUI). Earcons are abstract, synthetic tones constructed from motives using timbre, register, intensity, pitch and rhythm [4]. Although limitations have been identified with all methods of using sound (Learning time for earcons and scalability for auditory icons) [18], nomic auditory icons had several attributes making them feasible for Sonified RSVP.

Nomic auditory icons can be directly linked to the content of the text in a one-to-one fashion and they require little or no training to recognize. Norman [32] stresses the importance of developing a conceptual model that the user understands, and with the one-to-one mapping offered by nomic auditory icons this is easily achieved. Finally, the auditory content of nomic auditory icons can be designed to augment the RSVP reading experience in a fashion similar to that of using sound effect when watching a sound movie and they can be synchronized to appear simultaneously with the RSVP text presentation at any selected reading speed.

3.3   Sonification of a Paper-Based Book

The idea of adding sound to text is not new but has until recently usually taken the form of adding simple sounds to images in children's books. The Listen Reader is a more serious attempt by Back et al. [1] to augment a book with sound. In a museum setting, a children's book was enhanced with ambient sound linked to different pages by electric field sensing, tactile interaction from the reader's hands were detected and used to trigger the sounds. The Listen Reader used a paper-based book in order not to lose the affordances of a real book; the resulting device became a quite large installation where the synchronization between the sounds and the text passage read was put in the user's control. Although many affordances of a real book were kept in the Listen Reader, one important property was lost due to its size: the ability to read a book wherever you want. The authors considered handheld devices to be too intrusive and attention demanding to use and stated that "…thus immersive reading is difficult if not impossible." to accomplish [1, p. 24].

4   BAILANDO: A Mobile Reader with Sonified RSVP

Bailando is a prototype incorporating Sonified RSVP capabilities that has been developed at Ericsson Research's Usability & Interaction Lab in Kista, Sweden [16, 39, 43, 44]. The prototype runs on a Compaq iPAQ 3630 Pocket PC, a small PDA with a touch sensitive high-resolution color display. The primary motivation for using a PDA compared to using a smaller handheld device, e.g. a cellular phone, was that it had the sound and memory capabilities necessary for developing and evaluating Sonified RSVP. Although the iPAQ actually offers far more screen space than is needed for the RSVP format it still shares many properties of smaller handheld devices and the size and weight of the device is similar to a pocket book of approximately 250 pages.

Since a lot of screen space was available all the application controls were implemented in the GUI (Fig. 2). This also makes the Bailando software easier to run on other PDAs, since button assignments differ between devices. The GUI contains flow control buttons to start, pause and to resume text presentation. The text presentation can also be paused and resumed by touching anywhere on the text presentation area of the screen. The user can move backwards in the presentation (<<) if he feels he missed or misunderstood some text and can skip text (>>) if browsing. Reading speed is decreased (-) or increased (+) with the speed control buttons in steps of 10 wpm.

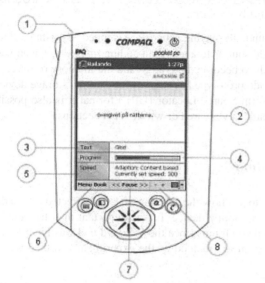

1. Earphone jack
2. Text window
3. Text title
4. Progress bar
5. Speed settings
6. Application menus
7. Flow control buttons
8. Speed control buttons

Fig. 2. The Bailando prototype running in reading mode on a Compaq iPAQ 3630 Pocket PC

In order to support memory of spatial location while reading there is a progress bar that shows the amount of remaining text. Previous studies have shown that the user preference for RSVP increase with the inclusion of a completion meter [36]. The text presentation window has a width of 25 characters and the text was presented left justified in a 10-pt. sans-serif typeface. While presenting text the Bailando prototype tries to fit as many words as possible in each text window. The exposure time for each window was calculated using a content adaptive [16, 43, 44] formula (Eq. 1):

$$time_l = (nwrd+nchr)/(davg*wpm/60) . \tag{1}$$

The formula uses the number of words (nwrd) and the number of characters (nchr) as a basis for the results. Both arguments are added and divided by the product of the average word length including delimiters (davg) and the currently set speed in words per minute (wpm) divided by 60. The result is a variable exposure time (time$_l$) depending on the content the current text chunk. A delay of 250 ms was added at sentence boundaries and an extra blank window was shown for 250 ms when the end of a sentence completely filled the text presentation window.

The Bailando prototype supports Sonified RSVP by using tags in the XML (eXtensible Markup Language) document format. When a <SOUND...> tag is found in the text chunk to be displayed, the appropriate audio file linked to it is played. Thus, exact synchronization between text and sound is easily attainable and works at any user-selected reading speed:

```
At a high speed a car speeded down the street, as
<SOUND SRC="HONK.WAV"> it honked it's horn all </SOUND>
the children fled to the curb.
```

When a </SOUND> tag is found, all playing sounds are stopped. By using a markup language it is not harder to add sounds to a text than adding images to a web page. Since the file size of sounds tends to become quite large and the memory resources of PDAs tend to be small the Bailando prototype has support for external storage devices. By employing the standard Uniform Source Locator (URL) format it is also possible to retrieve sounds from other locations via wired or wireless connections.

5   The Usability Evaluation

The aim with the evaluation was to see how the addition of sound affected the reading experience when using RSVP on a mobile device. It was important that the same device and software was used for all conditions since the look and feel was likely to bias the assessment. First we will present the method of the experiment and then we will present the findings.

5.1   Method

Sonified RSVP was benchmarked against Unsonified RSVP in a usability evaluation. The following null hypotheses were set for reading with and without sound:

- No difference in Reading speed
- No difference in Comprehension
- No difference in Task load
- No difference in Attitude

The hypotheses were tested in the SPSS V10.0 software using the repeated-measurement General Linear Model (GLM). The significance level was set to 5% and the level of multiple comparisons was Bonferroni adjusted.

Design. A repeated-measurement within-subject design was adopted where each subject participated in both a Sonified and an Unsonified RSVP condition. Two different texts were used and each could either appear as Sonified or Unsonified according to a balanced design, thus creating four different presentation order combinations. All subjects were randomly assigned to one of the four presentation orders in groups of three.

Subjects. Twelve computer literate students varying in age between 20-33 years (M=26 years) from the Department of Computer Science at the University of Stockholm were enrolled with the following selection criteria: Swedish as a native language, experience of using a PDA and a keen interest in reading fiction. Ten were males and two were females, all read an average of one 'paper' book of fiction/month, or more. Two had a slight hearing impairment in one ear and five wore glasses during the experiment. Seven had experience of listening to audio books during childhood; one had also listened to audio books as an adult. None had any prior knowledge of the RSVP paradigm and all but one was familiar with reading longer texts from a large screen.

Apparatus. All texts were presented on a Compaq iPAQ 3630 running the Bailando prototype in content adaptive RSVP mode. In the Sonified condition, earphones were plugged to the audio output of the PDA.

Texts. Two Swedish texts with similar length and readability rating were chosen (Table 1), "Behind rose-red laces" (Text A) and "Markurells in Wadköping" (Text B). The readability ratings were measured with LIX [2], a readability rating developed for Swedish texts comparable to the Flesh index for English texts [40]. One additional text, "The red room" (Text T), was used as a training text.

Table 1. Text material used in the experiment

Text	Title (in Swedish)	Author, chapter	Words	LIX	Sounds
A	Bakom rosenröda snören	Johan Wahlborg, chapter 1	4040	40	20
B	Markurells i Wadköping	Hjalmar Bergman, chapter 1	3733	39	24
T	Röda rummet	August Strindberg, chapter 1	1702	48	14

Sounds. For the Sonified conditions a number of different nomic auditory icons (14 to 24 sounds) of varying duration were added to the texts (Table 1). Each nomic auditory icon fitted a certain passage in each text (blowing wind, siren, restaurant background sound, birds twittering, church bells ringing, etc.). The duration of the nomic auditory icons were tailored to fit a lowest reading speed of 100 wpm and a highest reading speed of 600 wpm; each subject selected a volume level they felt comfortable with.

Instructions. Each subject was given the following instruction on paper: You will be presented with a new way of reading text on a small PDA screen. When adjusting the reading pace, try to set a pace that is as *comfortable* as possible according to your preferences. You will be given a multiple-choice comprehension, a workload and an attitude inventory after each read text.

Setting. The experiment took place in a dedicated usability lab outfitted with audio and video-recording facilities (Fig. 3, next page). While reading the subject was seated in a comfortable chair in a room separated from the experimenter by a one-way mirror. Before the experiment started each subject had some time to get acquainted with the facilities in order to create a relaxed, and consequently controlled, setting.

Fig. 3. Interior of the usability lab with the observation room (left) and the test room (right)

Training. Each subject participated in two training sessions where they read the same training text twice (Text T, Table 1), first without and then with sound. The reason for reading the same text twice was to give each subject an early success experience and making them more willing to experiment with the user interface. The experimenter first set the reading speed to a low value (app. 100-wpm) and encouraged the subject to read at this pace. Then the reading pace was set to a much higher value (app. 300-wpm) and the subject was encouraged to lower the reading pace until reaching a *comfortable* reading pace. All subjects were instructed that they could alter the reading pace at their own will whenever desired. After the completion of the training sessions, a comprehension inventory of 10 multiple-choice questions with three alternatives was administered. Then each subject had a 20-minute break before the first experimental condition started.

Procedure. Each subject was exposed to one of the texts (Text A or B in Table 1) presented as either Unsonified or Sonified, the subject selected the initial reading speed. After having read the first text, the subject answered a set of inventories. If the first text was read in Unsonified mode, the second text was read in Sonified mode, and vice versa. The same set of inventories was administered after the second text.

Inventories. After each experimental condition three inventories were administered. The first inventory was a comprehension test made up of 10 multiple-choice questions with four-alternatives. The second inventory was the NASA-TLX Task Load Index [17] designed to check Mental, Physical, and Temporal demands, as well as Performance, Effort and Frustration levels. This measure of workload was chosen since the results would then be comparable to previous evaluations where the measure was rewardingly used [15, 44]. Finally, an attitude inventory was administered. It contained seven questions regarding the reading: Experience, Excitement, Comfort, Stimulation, Immersion, Understanding and Speed, using a 10-graded (1 to 10) discrete ordinal scale with two verbal bi-polar anchor points. The questions were formulated in the following form: "How did you perceive the Experience while reading?" (Irritating-Fantastic).

5.2   Results

All subjects completed the experiment and there were few problems with understanding what to do or how to do it. The presentation of the results is divided into four sections: Reading speed, Comprehension, Task load and Attitude. Under each section the null hypotheses regarding no difference is tested.

Reading Speed. Reading speed was calculated as words read per minute based on the *total* time it took for the subjects to read a text including all kind of interruptions like pauses, regressions, speed changes etc. The null hypothesis regarding no difference in mean reading speed between Unsonified (M=215 wpm) and Sonified RSVP (M=218 wpm) was kept. The number of speed changes amounted to an average of 2 per read text.

Comprehension. Comprehension was computed as percent correctly answered multiple-choice questions out of 10. The null hypothesis regarding no difference in mean comprehension between Unsonified (M=57.5 %) and Sonified (M=59.2 %) RSVP was kept.

Task Load. Task load ratings were calculated as percent of millimeters to the left of the tick mark on a 120-mm scale. The null hypothesis regarding no difference in workload between Unsonified and Sonified RSVP was kept since none of the factors turned out to be significant. The Performance ratings reflected the objective metrics of reading speed and comprehension (Fig. 4).

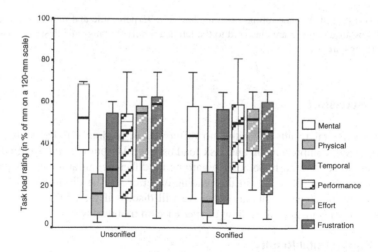

Fig. 4. Box plot of NASA-TLX Task Load Index ratings with median, 25-, 75-percentile and min/max values represented. Unsonified ratings are clustered to the left and the Sonified ratings are clustered to the right, lower ratings are better

Attitude. Attitude ratings were calculated as mean average rating on the 10-point scale. The null hypothesis regarding no difference in attitude between Unsonified and Sonified RSVP was partly rejected since the rating of perceived Immersion showed significance in favor of Sonified RSVP ($F[1, 11]=11.88$, $p=0.005$). Perceived reading speed and comprehension reflected the objective metrics of reading speed and comprehension (Fig. 5).

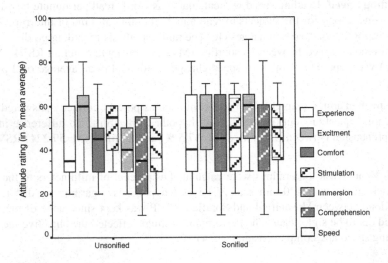

Fig. 5. Box plot of Attitude ratings with median, 25-, 75-percentile and min/max values represented. Unsonified ratings are clustered to the left and Sonified ratings are clustered to the right, higher ratings are better

6   Discussion

The experimental results indicated no difference in reading efficiency in terms of reading speed, comprehension and task load between Unsonified and Sonified RSVP. However, since the null hypothesis regarding no difference in attitude was partly rejected there was a difference in the reading experience. The discussion will first be based on the obtained results and then we will discuss if the addition of sound is a plausible enhancement of the reading experience on mobile devices.

6.1   Experimental Results

That the addition of non-verbal sound to RSVP in the form of nomic auditory icons did not cause any difference in reading efficiency seems to support the dual coding theory [33]. In any case, the addition of nomic auditory icons did not seem to affect reading efficiency in any negative way.

Reading Speed. The obtained reading speed was close to what Rahman and Muter found [36], but considerably slower than what Goldstein et al. [15] reported. The difference amounted to around 100 wpm (217 vs. 320 wpm). The difference may be attributable to priming; the subjects were instructed to optimize for speed in the Goldstein et al. experiment and to select a comfortable reading speed in this experiment. Further, the Bailando prototype gave the user control over the presentation, which has been shown to yield lower reading speed [7, 29]. The average reading speed on paper for an adult Swedish reader is around 240 wpm [2] and in this light the lower reading speed is not discouraging, as the motivation for the prototype was to facilitate comfortable and user-controlled reading on small displays rather than improving reading speed in general.

Comprehension. Given the simultaneous information conveyance of Sonified RSVP, referential processing [34] implies that comprehension would be greater for the condition adding the non-verbal channel using the aural medium. This was not the case in the experiment and a probable cause might be that the questions that made up the comprehension questionnaire did not relate directly to the sounds, as sound was used to enhance the emotional or social setting rather than act as an informative voice-over.

Task Load. Surprisingly, the NASA-TLX ratings remained high comparable to the Goldstein et al. [15] experiment even though reading speed was substantially lower due to the fact that the subjects were instructed to optimize for comfortable reading. This may imply that the size of the assumed trade-off between reading speed and cognitive task load is negligible for the RSVP format, quite contrary to the size of the well-established speed-accuracy trade-off [41]. An increase in task load is probably inherent to the RSVP format, but more elaborate adaptation models [43] and interaction techniques [45] may decrease task load even further. An increase in task load may even be acceptable if it is compensated with an increase in reading efficiency, especially in the mobile context where time often equals money [44].

Attitude. The only significant difference in the attitude inventory was the rating of Immersion, where Sonified RSVP was rated higher. Although one should always be cautious when relying on subjective measures, this finding seems to suggest that an immersive reading experience is possible to achieve on a handheld device and not impossible as claimed by Back et al. [1]. However, it seems a little surprising that there existed no positive co-dependence between Immersion and the ratings of Stimulation, Excitement and Experience. If Immersion increased significantly these ratings were somehow expected to increase in a similar fashion as well. Therefore, adding nomic auditory icons to text using the RSVP format does not seem to enhance the reading experience in a clear-cut fashion. Since the only significant difference in this evaluation was subjective, it would have been interesting to have more qualitative results to base the discussion on, e.g. user comments, but unfortunately such were not collected in this evaluation.

6.2   Can Sound Enhance the Reading Experience on Mobile Devices?

Although individual and cultural differences in the assessment of what is beneficial for the reading experience are likely to be large, and the experiment conducted here is quite small and limited to RSVP, the answer to the question seems to be yes. It is promising that even simple sonification with nomic auditory icons increased the feeling of immersion while reading using RSVP on a handheld device. The lack of co-dependence with the ratings of Stimulation, Excitement and Experience may be an artifact from the experimental design: the selection of sounds to match the text, the choice of text and target user group, and how the questionnaire was written. However, one can identify at least one other reason for the outcome: the difference between what we chose to call *realistic* and *dramatic* soundscapes.

A realistic soundscape enhances the reading experience by adding information that brings more detail to the description of the physical environment, e.g. playing the sound of a seagull when events in the text take place at a harbor. By giving more detail to the place described in the text, one can assume that users have a greater possibility to feel immersed in the story. In contrast, a dramatic soundscape increases the reading experience by providing additional information about characters internal emotions and reactions or by creating dramatic tension. Gaver [12] mentions the music played in the motion picture Jaws, before the first witnessed shark attack, as an example of such emotion provoking sound.

Thus, adding a dramatic soundscape to a text can evoke emotional responses such as excitement from readers without trying to place the reader within the story. The soundscape used in the experiment was realistic, primarily motivated by the fact that a compelling dramatic soundscape would require a professional sound producer, but also since a simple realistic soundscape was considered less likely to confuse the users conceptual model [32]. Although a dramatic soundscape is usually created by playing continuous music with durations longer than that of certain typical transient nomic auditory icons, one can imagine a dramatic soundscape created only by using auditory icons. One hypothesis is that a dramatic soundscape used for Sonified RSVP would yield higher ratings of Stimulation, Excitement and Experience as well.

Gaver [12] claimed that memory limitations is one reason why sounds are not generally used in interfaces on a larger scale, but adding elaborate soundscapes to texts presented on mobile devices is, at least from a technical perspective, likely to be a viable enterprise quite soon. Earphones are already widely used as accessories to cellular phones (as hands-free attachments) and most mobile devices will eventually have the required capabilities for high-quality sound playback. By defining a standardized markup language for sonification of RSVP it may be possible for publishers of e-books to add sound to texts of various genres. Real-time streaming of sounds over wireless networks may further reduce the size of a reader and cut costs.

On the other hand, although it may be a technically feasible to create applications that use Sonified RSVP, the question remains if this is something that the users want. We believe that, at the end of the day, it is up to the users to decide which presentation formats they want to use and which enhancements they deem appealing. RSVP has been found to have potential for improving readability on small screens, but if it is the most appropriate presentation format to use remains to be answered. Although the addition of nomic auditory icons did not enhance the reading experience in a clear-cut fashion in this experiment, we have at least shown that Sonified RSVP can increase the feeling of immersion while reading on a mobile device. Based on the findings from this evaluation, we think that further exploration of sound-enhanced text presentation formats may bring forward novel and interesting applications that a wide range of users would find useful and benefit of.

7   Conclusions

We have shown that the addition of sound to text displayed using the RSVP format can improve some aspects of the reading experience on a small screen. More specifically we found that the rating of perceived Immersion was significantly higher when nomic auditory icons were played simultaneously with the text presentation. The addition of a more elaborate soundtrack to strengthen the dramatic presence of the text has been suggested as a possibility to further enhance the reading experience on small screens. The most important finding in this evaluation is however that it actually is possible to create a more immersive reading experience on a small screen by adding sound to the text presentation.

8   Further Work

Bailando is the first prototype for reading with Sonified RSVP. Currently the sound playback capabilities are quite limited and several improvements can be made that may improve the user experience, e.g. the ability to play several sounds simultaneously, to fade in and out, and to repeat sounds perpetually. A follow-up experiment using a dramatic soundscape instead of a realistic one could determine if the findings from the current experiment depend on the design of the soundscape or other factors. It would also be interesting to see if other dynamic text presentation formats could benefit from the addition of sound in a similar way that RSVP did, and last but not least, it would be interesting to collect more qualitative data on how users experience the addition of sound while reading on a small screen.

Acknowledgements. The authors would like to thank Master's Thesis student Mandana Bayat-M for implementing the nomic soundscapes and conducting the experiment. We would also like to thank Peter Ljungstrand at the Interactive Institute for rewarding discussions around the concept of Sonified RSVP.

References

1.   Back, M., Cohen, J., Gold, R., Harrison, S. and Minneman, S. (2001). Listen reader: an electronically augmented paper-based book. *Proceedings of the SIG-CHI on Human Factors in Computing Systems 2001*, 23–29, Seattle, WA, USA, ACM Press.
2.   Björnsson, C.H. (1968). *Läsbarhet*, Stockholm, Liber (in Swedish).

3. Brewster, S., Raty V.P., and Kortekangas, A. (1996). Earcons as a method of providing navigational cues in a menu hierarchy. *Proceeding of Human-Computer Interaction'96* by M.A. Sasse, R.J. Cunningham and R.L. Winder (Eds.), People and Computers.
4. Brewster, S. (1998). Using non speech sounds to provide navigation cues. *ACM Transactions on Computer Human Interaction,* 5(3), 224–259.
5. Bruijn, O. and Spence, R. (2000). Rapid Serial Visual Presentation: A space-time trade-off in information presentation. *In Proceedings of Advanced Visual Interfaces,* AVI'2000.
6. Castelhano, M.S. and Muter, P. (2001). Optimizing the reading of electronic text using rapid serial visual presentation. *Behaviour & Information Technology,* 20(4), 237–247.
7. Chen, H.C. and Chan, K.T. (1990). Reading computer-displayed moving text with and without self-control over the display rate. *Behaviour & Information Technology,* 9, 467–477.
8. Duchnicky, R.L. and Kolers, P.A. (1983). Readability of text scrolled on visual display terminals as a function of window size. *Human Factors,* 25, 683–692.
9. Ericsson, T., Chincholle, D. and Goldstein, M. (2001). Both the device and the service influence WAP usability, *IHM-HCI2001,* Volume II, Usability in Practice by J. Vander-donckt, A. Blandford and A. Derycke (Eds.), Short paper, 10–14 September, Lille, France, 79–85.
10. Forster, K.I. (1970). Visual perception of rapidly presented word sequences of varying complexity. *Percep. Psychophys. 8,* 215–221.
11. Gaver, W. (1986). Auditory icons: Using sound in computer interfaces. *Human-Computer Interaction,* 2, 167–177, Lawrence Erlbaum Associates, Inc.
12. Gaver, W. (1998). Auditory interfaces. In *Handbook of Human-Computer Interaction,* 2nd ed., 1003–1041.
13. Gilbert, L.C. (1959). Speed of processing verbal stimuli and its relation to reading. *J Educ Psychol,* 58, 8–14.
14. Goldstein, M., Anneroth, M., Sicheritz, K. and Lundberg, T. (2000). Enhancing the reading experience: Sonified on-line reading from a small PDA screen using RSVP. *Fourth Swedish Symposium on Multimodal Communication,* SsoMC.
15. Goldstein, M., Sicheritz, K. and Anneroth, M. (2001). Reading from a small display using the RSVP technique. *Nordic Radio Symposium,* NRS01.
16. Goldstein, M., Öquist, G., Bayat-M, M., Ljungstrand, P. and Björk, S. (2001). Enhancing the reading experience: Using adaptive and sonified RSVP for reading on small displays. *Proceedings of Workshop on Mobile Devices* at IHM-HCI 2001, Lille, September 10–14.
17. Hart, S.G. and Staveland, L.E. (1988). Development of NASA-TLX (Task Load Index): Results of empirical and theoretical research. *Human Mental Workload,* by P.A. Hancock and N. Meshkati (Eds.). Elsevier Science Publishers, B.V. North-Holland.
18. Hearst, M.A. (1997). Dissonance on audio interfaces. *IEEE Expert,* 12, 5, 10–16, IEEE Computer Press.
19. Huey, E.B. (1968). *The Psychology and Pedagogy of Reading.* Massachusetts: MIT Press. (Originally published 1908).
20. Joula, J.F., Ward, N.J. and MacNamara, T. (1982). Visual search and reading of rapid serial presentations of letter strings, words and text. *J. Exper. Psychol.: General,* 111, 208–227.
21. Juola, J.F., Tiritoglu, A., and Pleunis, J. (1995). Reading text presented on a small display. *Applied Ergonomics,* 26, 227–229.
22. Just, M. A., and Carpenter, P. A. (1980). A theory of reading: From eye fixations to comprehension. *Psychological Review,* 87(4), 329–354.
23. Kang, T.J., and Muter, P. (1989). Reading Dynamically Displayed Text. *Behaviour & Information Technology,* 8(1), 33–42.

24. Kalyuga, S. (2000). When using sound with a text or picture is not beneficial for learning. *Australian Journal of Educational Technology,* 16(2), 161–172.
25. Kump, P. (1999). *Break-trough rapid reading.* New Jersey: Prentice-Hall Press.
26. Masson, M.E.J. (1983). Conceptual processing of text during skimming and rapid sequential reading. *Memory & Cognition,* 11(3), 262–274.
27. Mills, C.B. and Weldon, L.J. (1987). Reading text from computer screens. *ACM Computing Surveys,* 19(4), ACM Press.
28. Muter, P. (1996). Interface Design and Optimization of Reading of Continuous Text. In *Cognitive aspects of electronic text processing.* H. van Oostendorp and S. de Mul (Eds.). Norwood, N.J.:Ablex.
29. Muter, P., Kruk, R. S., Buttigieg, M. A., and Kang, T. J. (1988). Reader controlled computerized presentation of text. *Human Factors,* 30, 473–486.
30. Muter, P. and Maurutto, P. (1991). Reading and skimming from computer screens and books: The paperless office revisited? *Behavior & Information Technology,* 10, 257–266.
31. Najjar, L.J. (1996). Multimedia information and learning. *Journal of Educational Multimedia and Hypermedia,* 5, 129–150.
32. Norman, D.A. (1988). *The Psychology of Everyday Things.* Doubleday, NY, USA.
33. Paivio, A. (1971). *Imagery and Verbal Processes.* New York: Holt, Rinehart & Winston, Inc.
34. Paivio, A. (1986). *Mental Representations.* New York: Oxford University Press.
35. Potter, M.C. (1984). Rapid Serial Visual Presentation (RSVP): A method for studying language processing. In *New Methods in Reading Comprehension Research.* Kieras, D.E. and Just, M.A. (Eds.). Hillsdale, N.J.:Erlbaum.
36. Rahman, T. and Muter, P. (1999). Designing an interface to optimize reading with small display windows. *Human Factors,* 1(1), 106–117, Human Factors and Ergonomics Society.
37. Robeck, M.C. and Wallace, R.R. (1990). *The Psychology of Reading: An Interdisciplinary Approach,* Lawrence Erlbaum Associates, Hillsdale, New Jersey, 2nd edition.
38. Rubin, G. S. and K. Turano. (1992). Reading without saccadic eye movements. *Vision Research,* 32(5), 895–902.
39. The Bailando prototype web page. A tool for research on small screen readability, available at: http://stp.ling.uu.se/~gustav/bailando/ (June 2002).
40. Tekfi, C. (1987). Readability formulas: An overview. *Journal of Documentation,* 43(3), 261–273.
41. Wickens, C. D. (1992). *Engineering psychology and human performance,* 2nd edition, Chapter 8, HarperCollins Publishers Inc., New York.
42. Williams, J. R. (1998). Guidelines for the use of multimedia in instruction. *Proceedings of the Human Factors and Ergonomics Society 42nd Annual Meeting,* 1447–1451.
43. Öquist, G. (2001). *Adaptive Rapid Serial Visual Presentation.* Master's Thesis, Department of Linguistics, Uppsala University, Sweden.
44. Öquist, G. and Goldstein, M. (2002). Towards an improved readability on mobile devices: Evaluating Adaptive Rapid Serial Visual Presentation. *Proceedings of Mobile HCI'2002,* 19–20 September 2002, Pisa, Italy, Springer Verlag.
45. Öquist, G., Björk, S. and Goldstein, M. (2002). Utilizing gaze detection to simulate the affordances of paper in the Rapid Serial Visual Presentation format. *Proceedings of Mobile HCI'2002,* 19–20 September 2002, Pisa, Italy, Springer Verlag.

Universal Remote Console – Prototyping for the Alternate Interface Access Standard

Gottfried Zimmermann, Gregg Vanderheiden, and Al Gilman

Trace R&D Center, University of Wisconsin-Madison,
5901 Research Park Blvd., Madison, WI, 53719, USA
{zimmer,gv}@trace.wisc.edu, asgilman@iamdigex.net

Abstract. A Universal Remote Console is a device that can be used to operate any compatible services or devices. The Universal Remote Console (URC) renders a user interface for the target service or device in a way that accommodates the user's needs and preferences. The V2 technical committee of the InterNational Committee for Information Technology Standards (INCITS) is currently developing a standard for "Alternative User Interface Access" that includes URCs. This paper describes preliminary design aspects of the standard under development, in particular an XML-based language that is used to communicate an abstract user interface definition for the target service or device to a URC. Prototypical implementations for URCs developed at the Trace Center serve as the basis for experimental research for the standard under development, and will be demonstrated at the workshop.

1 Introduction

Today the majority of network-based services and electronic devices such as home security systems, thermostats, copy machines, or public kiosks are operable only through the one built-in user interface (UI). This may change in the near future, as wireless technologies are already invading our environments at home, at work, in public places, and on the move. By employing network based technologies, people could, in the future, remotely control connected services and electronic devices from anywhere, using a wide variety of remote console devices, such as cell phones, PDAs, car radios, wrist watches, and wearable and other computers. To do this however, a means must be found to accommodate the diverse user interface needs of access devices today and tomorrow, without having to implement a separate UI for each of them. For example, a wrist watch cannot accommodate the same graphically rich UI as a desktop computer, and a UI written for a handheld computer will be different from an audio based UI of a car radio.

In a similar manner, people with different types of disabilities find it difficult or impossible to directly use electronic devices and services because the device's/service's user interface cannot accommodate the special needs of certain user groups (such as users with visual, hearing, or mobility impairments). People with

N. Carbonell, C. Stephanidis (Eds.): User Interfaces for All, LNCS 2615, pp. 524–531, 2003.
© Springer-Verlag Berlin Heidelberg 2003

disabilities therefore have to rely on service and device implementations that are specifically designed for them (or implementations whose user interfaces have been re-implemented for special needs). However, relying on special implementations rather than being able to use standard services and devices has several disadvantages. First, special implementations of services and devices may not be available at all, or may not be provided in the same variety as their mainstream counterparts. This means, that people with disabilities often do not have the same range of choices, and often must put up with services and devices implementing older technologies. Second, it is expensive for those who have special needs because special service implementations are only used by a small fraction of the population, and special devices are produced in small numbers. Third, this approach does not work for services and devices to be used in public places (e.g. ATMs, and information kiosks), as it is not reasonable to provide a multitude of alternate implementations, each offering the same service but tailored for a different user group.

1.1 V2 Universal Remote Console Specification

For many services and devices this could be made possible through the development of a standard for allowing a separate device to be used as an alternative UI (an alternate 'console'). People could then use their personal choice of devices appropriate to their preferences or abilities to control the various services and devices in their environments at home, at work and in communities.

In order to define a standard for flexible and replaceable user interfaces for electronic services and devices, INCITS has established a technical committee called V2 (http://www.ncits.org/tc_home/v2.htm). Members of this committee include representatives from user groups, industry, government, and academia. V2 is currently working on a "Universal Remote Console" (URC) specification as part of a to-be-developed "Alternative User Interface Access" standard. The scope of the URC specification covers the full range of requirements and technologies needed to discover services and devices (targets), to provide secure ways of communication, and to allow the user to explore a target's functions and control it from any "personal" device. This paper focuses on UI related issues of the specification.

The URC approach is simple though powerful: A person carries their own "personal" device which can act as a remote console to other services and devices (targets). This personal (URC) device is tailored to their specific needs. It may employ graphical user interfaces, voice interfaces, braille-based interfaces, switch-based input methods, etc., or any combination of these. Common examples of the remote console would be a mobile device like a PDA or cell phone, a home or office computer, or ultimately an inconspicuous wearable computer. For people with disabilities, though, it could also be a special adaptive device such as a note-taker (a pioneering form of PDA) or laptop with a Braille display.

This personal remote console is a "universal" remote console, because it lets the user control any target that supports the standard, from the thermostat at home to the public kiosk in the town hall. The target transmits an abstract (modality-independent) user interface to the URC which provides the particular input and output mechanisms appropriate for its user. Target UIs on URC devices may be presented in a variety of modalities, including visual, audio, and tactile, and any combination of these. Input from the user may be accepted via keyboard, mouse, stylus, speech recognition, braille keys, switches, etc.

Under this URC approach, the target manufacturer is not responsible for devising different UIs for many types of access devices and users. Instead, the target manufacturer need only supply the "user interface needs" of their product in the standard form. The user brings their own appropriate UI binding with them.

2   Related Work

The idea of "abstract UI descriptions" goes back to the concept of model-based User Interface Management Systems (UIMS, e.g. [1, 2]) which emphasize the separation between application logic, dialog control, and presentation component according to the Seeheim model [3]. Myers [4] uses the notion of interactors to provide a high-level interface for user input in a graphical user environment.

Former work of Trace in the area of universal remote controllers include input emulation efforts [5], and the development of the infrared-based Universal Remote Console Communication (URCC) Protocol [6].

The Total Access System uses a personal information appliance (called "accessor") to provide alternative ways of performing keyboard, mouse and/or monitor functions on a computer system [7].

UIML aims to provide a target platform independent XML-based user interface description language that can be automatically rendered on a diversity of user interface platforms [8]. Cross-platform vocabularies for UIML have yet to be defined. However, work in this area seems to be in progress for UIML2.

The Pittsburgh Pebbles PDA Project [9] introduces the "Personal Universal Controller" (PUC), which resembles the "Universal Remote Console" in many aspects, in particular the notion of state variables and commands describing an abstract user interface that can be downloaded from a device or service.

XWeb [10] aims to support an abstract notion of interaction that is independent of a particular set of interactive techniques, by harnessing existing Web technologies.

XForms (http://www.w3.org/MarkUp/Forms/) defines a set of abstract controls for UIs. However, these controls are designed to be embedded in a host container (e.g. an HTML document), which may or may not be accessible. Depending on the technology a particular XForms implementation is built upon, it may or may not support two-way synchronization of state information between server and client, which would be needed for implementing highly interactive UIs on remote consoles.

Sun's Jini technology transmits UI code from a target device to a remote control [11]. However, this technology requires that the target provide different UI implementations for different classes of remote console devices.

3 URC Design Concepts

A key part of the Universal Remote Console (URC) scenario is the definition of a language to convey a UI description from a service or device (target) to the URC. This language, with the code name "Alternate Abstract Interface Markup Language" (AAIML), must be sufficiently abstract (in terms of modality independence), so that a particular URC device can render the provided UI in its own way, taking advantage of the specific interaction techniques the URC device is capable of. The URC specification is still under development, with the current working draft employing basic components such as the ones depicted in fig. 1.

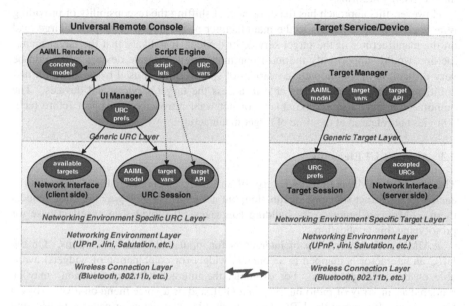

Fig. 1. Basic components of the URC specification under development, shown in a layered presentation. The arrows indicate usage dependencies (arrows originate from the calling component and point to the called component)

3.1 Abstract UI Description Language

By rendering the abstract UI description, the URC translates the elements of an abstract UI into the concrete UI elements available on its specific platform. For example, a PDA could render the UI description by using GUI elements (visual) for output, and pointing with a stylus, as well as hand writing recognition for input; a car radio would render the same UI description auditorially with sound and synthetic speech for output, and speech recognition for input; and a braille note-taker would use its braille output and input capabilities in order to render the very same UI description tactily. However, all URC devices would allow access to all functions of the target, each in a peculiar way.

3.2 Why the URC Needs an Abstract UI Description Language

One might argue that we could accommodate the same variety of remote UIs without an abstract UI language, solely by providing separate UI implementations for each remote console device. And that this approach would yield better UIs, by taking advantage of the very specific implementation techniques available on the specific remote console platforms.

However, this approach has the drawback of shifting the responsibility of providing remote console-specific UIs to the manufacturer of the target. This puts a large load on the manufacturer of the target service or device. It is likely that the target manufacturer would support only the most common remote console devices. It would be very difficult to accommodate the variety of special devices used by people with disabilities and they would not be able to access the target services and devices. The manufacturer may also not be able to or not want retroactively support future technologies not released at the time of target manufacture.

3.3 Abstract UI Elements

The goal of AAIML is to provide a set of abstract UI elements (called "interactors"), each with a distinct semantic or function, but not restricting the way the URC renders them. XML is a language for building languages. It provides an excellent base for prototyping this application.

AAIML defines a variety of interactors for input and output operations. On the URC an interactor is mapped to a concrete widget (or combination of widgets) available on the URC platform. For example, the interactor "string-selection" may be rendered as an array of radio buttons on a GUI, and as a voice menu on a voice-based UI platform. It is up to the URC device to decide what mapping patterns to use, and the target does not have to have any knowledge about it.

3.4 Layered Help Texts and Feature Classes

AAIML allows for help texts being attached to the entire UI (for describing general concepts related to the target, its controls and the information it presents), to groups of interactors (for an explanation of concepts specific to the group, and/or help on using the group), to interactors, and to options that are contained in interactors such as string-selection. For each of these instances the help text may be layered to start with a short help first, and at the user's request provide more in-depth explanations.

In order to allow for the generation of simplified UI on a URC device, individual interactors are assigned to the different feature classes. The class of "basic" interactors consists of controls that cover the simpler functions of the target; "general" interactors include commonly used UI elements; and "full" refers to the complete UI.

4 Prototypical Implementations

The Trace Center is supporting the development of the URC specification by hosting a URC prototyping project. This project aims to pursue experimental research by implementing an array of URC scenarios, varying both the remote console device and the target. Prototypes take advantage of powerful existing technologies, like Bluetooth, 802.11b, Universal Plug and Plug (UPnP), and Jini/Java.

Goals of the prototyping project include the support for the V2 committee by:

- Writing code and building physical prototypes necessary to explore the proposed ideas for the standard.
- Identifying potential problems in the emerging standard, and proposing solutions to the V2 technical committee.
- Soliciting early user feedback on real-life implementations.
- Providing proof-of-concept implementations for the standard.

4.1 Prototypes Developed and in Development

As outlined before, the URC specification should not depend on any specific platform for implementation, whether it is the URC, networking environment, or target platform. Therefore the prototyping project at Trace strives to develop as many implementations as possible, varying all three dimensions of the solution space: URC device type, networking environment technology, and target.

All prototypes are implemented mainly in Java, and take advantage of third-party tools for middleware and wireless communication implementations. For demonstrational targets we use a TV simulation and video player running on a PC, as well as a small fan, and a desk lamp. A gateway to a real VCR is currently in development.

At present, 5 different URC implementations have been developed, and 2 additional ones are in development:

- A Swing URC running on a Linux based Compaq iPAQ, showing a graphical rendition of the target's UI (see fig. 2).
- A Windows CE based BrailleNote providing braille based access to a target.
- A "talking" iPAQ implementation with large-scaled text output and a speech synthesizer, which can be used by persons with visual impairments.
- An alternative and augmentative communication (AAC) device (Pathfinder from Prentke Romich) for user input, optionally involving head tracking or scanning.
- A Swing based graphical URC that runs as an applet in any Web browser, connecting to a "configurable target" applet (for demonstrational purposes only).

The following prototypical implementations are in development:

- A graphical URC running on a PocketPC based iPAQ.
- A simple "open text" URC, which will allow a user to type or speak any text in order to control a target. For example, "Tune to the Weather Channel" would

switch to the appropriate channel on the remotely controlled TV. A verbal feed-back on status changes of the target will be provided to the user.

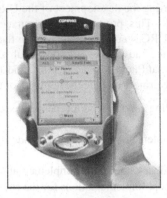

Fig. 2. A prototypical URC implementation on a Linux based iPAQ handheld computer, re-motely controlling a TV, a small fan, a desk lamp, and a video player

5 Future Work

The V2 technical committee is currently exploring options to harmonize AIAP-URC with W3C's XForms technology for next-generation Web forms. The underlying technologies of networked devices and Web services are merging already. In the future, users of V2 compliant URC devices should expect using the same access mechanisms for electronic devices and Web services.

At present, user interfaces as provided by AAIML rely on text-only elements and their ability to be represented in any modality. However, the ability to provide richer user interfaces by adding presentation-specific elements such as icons, and sounds, is also being explored. The challenge is to prevent use of these features in a way that would render the UI inaccessible to others.

Another area of exploration deals with modality specific presentation streams. For some applications, there is a need for providing modality-specific information streams from the target to the URC, and vice versa. For example, a user might want to initiate a link into a performance of a violin concerto and use the URC to then listen to it. V2 will address the need for the delivery of modality specific information, but at the same time make sure that access to modality specific content does not compromise accessi-bility to devices and services in general.

Another area V2 is working on is the specification of discovery mechanisms for target services and devices, including the kind of information from targets that is needed by the URC and the user prior to actually controlling the target.

In order to vet the evolving standard and technologies used to implement the standard, more prototypical systems need to be built. This should ideally involve manufacturers of targets and Assistive Technology devices.

6 Conclusions

The emerging V2 standard addresses the alternate interface connection needs of people with and without disabilities. The URC specification will enable people using their personal URC device to control electronic devices and Web based services in their environment. The standards work is continuing.

Acknowledgments. This work was partly funded by the National Institute on Disability and Rehabilitation Research (NIDRR), US Department of Education under grants H133E980008, & H133E990006; and the National Science Foundation (NSF) via the Partnership for Advanced Computational Infrastructure (PACI). Opinions expressed are those of the authors and not the funding agencies or V2.

References

1. Hayes, P. J.; Szekely, P. A.; Lerner, R. A. (1985). Design alternatives for user interface management systems based on experience with COUSIN. Proceedings of the CHI '85 conference on Human factors in computing systems, April 1985.
2. Savidis, A.; Stephanidis, C. (1995). Developing dual user interfaces for integrating blind and sighted users: the HOMER UIMS. Conference proceedings on Human factors in computing systems, May 1995.
3. Pfaff, G.E., (1985). User Interface Management Systems. Springer-Verlag, Berlin, 1985.
4. Myers, B.A. (1990). A new model for handling input. ACM Transactions on Information Systems (TOIS), July 1990, Volume 8, Issue 3.
5. Vanderheiden, G. (1981). Practical Applications of Microcomputers to Aid the Handicapped. *Computer*, IEEE Computer Society, January.
6. Vanderheiden, G. C. (1998). Universal remote console communication protocol (URCC). Proceedings of the 1998 TIDE Conference, Helsinki, Finland: Stakes.
7. Scott, N.G., & Gingras, I. (2001). The Total Access System. CHI 2001 Extended Abstracts, pp. 13–14.
8. Abrams, M., Phanouriou, C., Batongbacal, A.L., Williams, S., & Shuster, J.E. (1999). UIML: An Appliance-Independent XML User Interface Language. WWW8 conference, May 1999, Toronto, Canada.
9. Nichols, J.; Myers, B.A.; Higgins, M.; Hughes, J.; Harris, T.K.; Rosenfeld, R.; Pignol, M. (2002). Generating Remote Control Interfaces for Complex Appliances. CHI Letters: ACM Symposium on User Interface Software and Technology, UIST'02, 27–30 Oct. 2002, Paris, France. http://www-2.cs.cmu.edu/~pebbles/papers/PebblesPUCuist.pdf.
10. Olsen Jr., D.R., et al. (2000). Cross-modal Interaction Using XWeb. Proceedings UIST'00, 2000, San Diego, CA, pp. 191–200. Retrieved 21 June, 2002, from the WWW: http://icie.cs.byu.edu/ICE/LabPapers/CrossModalXwebInteraction.pdf.
11. Beard, M., & Korn, P. (2001). What I Need is What I Get: Downloadable User Interfaces via Jini and Java. CHI 2001 Extended Abstracts, pp. 15–16.

Author Index

Lecture Notes in Computer Science

For information about Vols. 1–2523

please contact your bookseller or Springer-Verlag

Vol. 2560: S. Goronzy, Robust Adaptation to Non-Native Accents in Automatic Speech Recognition. Proceedings, 2002. XI, 144 pages. 2002. (Subseries LNAI).

Vol. 2561: H.C.M. de Swart (Ed.), Relational Methods in Computer Science. Proceedings, 2001. X, 315 pages. 2002.

Vol. 2562: V. Dahl, P. Wadler (Eds.), Practical Aspects of Declarative Languages. Proceedings, 2003. X, 315 pages. 2002.

Vol. 2566: T.Æ. Mogensen, D.A. Schmidt, I.H. Sudborough (Eds.), The Essence of Computation. XIV, 473 pages. 2002.

Vol. 2567: Y.G. Desmedt (Ed.), Public Key Cryptography – PKC 2003. Proceedings, 2003. XI, 365 pages. 2002.

Vol. 2568: M. Hagiya, A. Ohuchi (Eds.), DNA Computing. Proceedings, 2002. XI, 338 pages. 2003.

Vol. 2569: D. Gollmann, G. Karjoth, M. Waidner (Eds.), Computer Security – ESORICS 2002. Proceedings, 2002. XIII, 648 pages. 2002. (Subseries LNAI).

Vol. 2570: M. Jünger, G. Reinelt, G. Rinaldi (Eds.), Combinatorial Optimization – Eureka, You Shrink!. Proceedings, 2001. X, 209 pages. 2003.

Vol. 2571: S.K. Das, S. Bhattacharya (Eds.), Distributed Computing. Proceedings, 2002. XIV, 354 pages. 2002.

Vol. 2572: D. Calvanese, M. Lenzerini, R. Motwani (Eds.), Database Theory – ICDT 2003. Proceedings, 2003. XI, 455 pages. 2002.

Vol. 2574: M.-S. Chen, P.K. Chrysanthis, M. Sloman, A. Zaslavsky (Eds.), Mobile Data Management. Proceedings, 2003. XII, 414 pages. 2003.

Vol. 2575: L.D. Zuck, P.C. Attie, A. Cortesi, S. Mukhopadhyay (Eds.), Verification, Model Checking, and Abstract Interpretation. Proceedings, 2003. XI, 325 pages. 2003.

Vol. 2576: S. Cimato, C. Galdi, G. Persiano (Eds.), Security in Communication Networks. Proceedings, 2002. IX, 365 pages. 2003.

Vol. 2578: F.A.P. Petitcolas (Ed.), Information Hiding. Proceedings, 2002. IX, 427 pages. 2003.

Vol. 2580: H. Erdogmus, T. Weng (Eds.), COTS-Based Software Systems. Proceedings, 2003. XVIII, 261 pages. 2003.

Vol. 2581: J.S. Sichman, F. Bousquet, P. Davidsson (Eds.), Multi-Agent-Based Simulation II. Proceedings, 2002. X, 195 pages. 2003. (Subseries LNAI).

Vol. 2583: S. Matwin, C. Sammut (Eds.), Inductive Logic Programming. Proceedings, 2002. X, 351 pages. 2003. (Subseries LNAI).

Vol. 2585: F. Giunchiglia, J. Odell, G. Weiß (Eds.), Agent-Oriented Software Engineering III. Proceedings, 2002. X, 229 pages. 2003.

Vol. 2586: M. Klusch, S. Bergamaschi, P. Edwards, P. Petta (Eds.), Intelligent Information Agents. VI, 275 pages. 2003. (Subseries LNAI).

Vol. 2587: P.J. Lee, C.H. Lim (Eds.), Information Security and Cryptology – ICISC 2002. Proceedings, 2002. XI, 536 pages. 2003.

Vol. 2588: A. Gelbukh (Ed.), Computational Linguistics and Intelligent Text Processing. Proceedings, 2003. XV, 648 pages. 2003.

Vol. 2589: E. Börger, A. Gargantini, E. Riccobene (Eds.), Abstract State Machines 2003. Proceedings, 2003. XI, 427 pages. 2003.

Vol. 2590: S. Bressan, A.B. Chaudhri, M.L. Lee, J.X. Yu, Z. Lacroix (Eds.), Efficiency and Effectiveness of XML Tools and Techniques and Data Integration over the Web. Proceedings, 2002. X, 259 pages. 2003.

Vol. 2591: M. Aksit, M. Mezini, R. Unland (Eds.), Objects, Components, Architectures, Services, and Applications for a Networked World. Proceedings, 2002. XI, 431 pages. 2003.

Vol. 2592: R. Kowalczyk, J.P. Müller, H. Tianfield, R. Unland (Eds.), Agent Technologies, Infrastructures, Tools, and Applications for E-Services. Proceedings, 2002. XVII, 371 pages. 2003. (Subseries LNAI).

Vol. 2593: A.B. Chaudhri, M. Jeckle, E. Rahm, R. Unland (Eds.), Web, Web-Services, and Database Systems. Proceedings, 2002. XI, 311 pages. 2003.

Vol. 2594: A. Asperti, B. Buchberger, J.H. Davenport (Eds.), Mathematical Knowledge Management. Proceedings, 2003. X, 225 pages. 2003.

Vol. 2595: K. Nyberg, H. Heys (Eds.), Selected Areas in Cryptography. Proceedings, 2002. XI, 405 pages. 2003.

Vol. 2597: G. Păun, G. Rozenberg, A. Salomaa, C. Zandron (Eds.), Membrane Computing. Proceedings, 2002. VIII, 423 pages. 2003.

Vol. 2598: R. Klein, H.-W. Six, L. Wegner (Eds.), Computer Science in Perspective. X, 357 pages. 2003.

Vol. 2600: S. Mendelson, A.J. Smola, Advanced Lectures on Machine Learning. Proceedings, 2002. IX, 259 pages. 2003. (Subseries LNAI).

Vol. 2601: M. Ajmone Marsan, G. Corazza, M. Listanti, A. Roveri (Eds.) Quality of Service in Multiservice IP Networks. Proceedings, 2003. XV, 759 pages. 2003.

Vol. 2602: C. Priami (Ed.), Computational Methods in Systems Biology. Proceedings, 2003. IX, 214 pages. 2003.

Vol. 2604: N. Guelfi, E. Astesiano, G. Reggio (Eds.), Scientific Engineering for Distributed Java Applications. Proceedings, 2002. X, 205 pages. 2003.

Vol. 2606: A.M. Tyrrell, P.C. Haddow, J. Torresen (Eds.), Evolvable Systems: From Biology to Hardware. Proceedings, 2003. XIV, 468 pages. 2003.

Vol. 2607: H. Alt, M. Habib (Eds.), STACS 2003. Proceedings, 2003. XVII, 700 pages. 2003.

Vol. 2609: M. Okada, B. Pierce, A. Scedrov, H. Tokuda, A. Yonezawa (Eds.), Software Security – Theories and Systems. Proceedings, 2002. XI, 471 pages. 2003.

Vol. 2612: M. Joye (Ed.), Topics in Cryptology – CT-RSA 2003. Proceedings, 2003. XI, 417 pages. 2003.

Vol. 2614: R. Laddaga, P. Robertson, H. Shrobe (Eds.), Self-Adaptive Software: Applications. Proceedings, 2001. VIII, 291 pages. 2003.

Vol. 2615: N. Carbonell, C. Stephanidis (Eds.), Universal Access. Proceedings, 2002. XIV, 534 pages. 2003.

Printed in the United States
By Bookmasters